PHILIP'S

KU-779-598

STREET ATLAS

Oxfordshire

First published in 1994 by

Philip's, a division of
Octopus Publishing Group Ltd
2-4 Heron Quays, London E14 4JP

Third colour edition 2005
First impression 2005

ISBN-10   0-540-08767-X (pocket)
ISBN-13   978-0-540-08767-9 (pocket)
OXFCA

© Philip's 2005

Ordnance Survey®

This product includes mapping data licensed from
Ordnance Survey® with the permission of the
Controller of Her Majesty's Stationery Office.
© Crown copyright 2005. All rights reserved.
Licence number 100011710.

Printed by Toppan, China

Contents

III **Key to map symbols**

IV **Key to map pages**

VI **Route planning**

VIII **Administrative and Postcode boundaries**

1 **Street maps** at 2⅔ inches to 1 mile

261 **Street map of Oxford city centre**
at 5⅓ inches to 1 mile

262 **Index** of towns and villages

264 **Index** of streets, hospitals, industrial estates, railway
stations, schools, shopping centres, universities
and places of interest

Digital Data

The exceptionally high-quality mapping found in this atlas is available as digital data in TIFF
format, which is easily convertible to other bitmapped (raster) image formats.

The index is also available in digital form as a standard database table. It contains all the details
found in the printed index together with the National Grid reference for the map square in which
each entry is named.

For further information and to discuss your requirements, please contact Philip's on
020 7644 6932 or james.mann@philips-maps.co.uk

Motorway with junction number		◆	**Ambulance station**
Primary route – dual/single carriageway		◆	**Coastguard station**
A road – dual/single carriageway		◆	**Fire station**
B road – dual/single carriageway		◆	**Police station**
Minor road – dual/single carriageway		✚	**Accident and Emergency entrance to hospital**
Other minor road – dual/single carriageway		H	**Hospital**
Road under construction		✛	**Place of worship**
Tunnel, covered road		ℹ	**Information Centre** (open all year)
Rural track, private road or narrow road in urban area		🛒	**Shopping Centre**
Gate or obstruction to traffic (restrictions may not apply at all times or to all vehicles)		P P&R	**Parking, Park and Ride**
Path, bridleway, byway open to all traffic, road used as a public path		PO	**Post Office**
		Ⅹ 🚐	**Camping site, caravan site**
Pedestrianised area		▶ ⊠	**Golf course, picnic site**
DY7 **Postcode boundaries**		Prim Sch	**Important buildings, schools, colleges, universities and hospitals**
County and unitary authority boundaries			**Built up area**
Railway, tunnel, railway under construction			**Woods**
Tramway, tramway under construction		River Medway	**Water name**
Miniature railway			**River, weir, stream**
⇄ Walsall **Railway station**			**Canal, lock, tunnel**
🚂 **Private railway station**			**Water**
South Shields **Metro station**			**Tidal water**
🚋 🚋 **Tram stop, tram stop under construction**		Church	**Non-Roman antiquity**
Bus, coach station		ROMAN FORT	**Roman antiquity**

Acad	**Academy**	Inst	**Institute**	Recn Gd **Recreation**
Allot Gdns	**Allotments**	Ct	**Law Court**	**Ground**
Cemy	**Cemetery**	L Ctr	**Leisure Centre**	Resr **Reservoir**
C Ctr	**Civic Centre**	LC	**Level Crossing**	Ret Pk **Retail Park**
CH	**Club House**	Liby	**Library**	Sch **School**
Coll	**College**	Mkt	**Market**	Sh Ctr **Shopping Centre**
Crem	**Crematorium**	Meml	**Memorial**	TH **Town Hall/House**
Ent	**Enterprise**	Mon	**Monument**	Trad Est **Trading Estate**
Ex H	**Exhibition Hall**	Mus	**Museum**	Univ **University**
Ind Est	**Industrial Estate**	Obsy	**Observatory**	W Twr **Water Tower**
IRB Sta	**Inshore Rescue Boat Station**	Pal	**Royal Palace**	Wks **Works**
		PH	**Public House**	YH **Youth Hostel**

87 **Adjoining page indicators and overlap bands**
237 The colour of the arrow and the band indicates the scale of the adjoining or overlapping page (see scales below)

Enlarged mapping only

Railway or bus station building

Place of interest

Parkland

■ The small numbers around the edges of the maps identify the 1 kilometre National Grid lines
■ The dark grey border on the inside edge of some pages indicates that the mapping does not continue onto the adjacent page

| The scale of the maps on the pages numbered in blue is 4.2 cm to 1 km • 2⅔ inches to 1 mile • 1: 23810 | 0   ¼   ½   ¾   1 mile |
| | 0   250m   500m   750m   1 kilometre |

| The scale of the maps on pages numbered in red is 8.4 cm to 1 km • 5⅓ inches to 1 mile • 1: 11900 | 0   220 yards   440 yards   660 yards   ½ mile |
| | 0   125m   250m   375m   ½ kilometre |

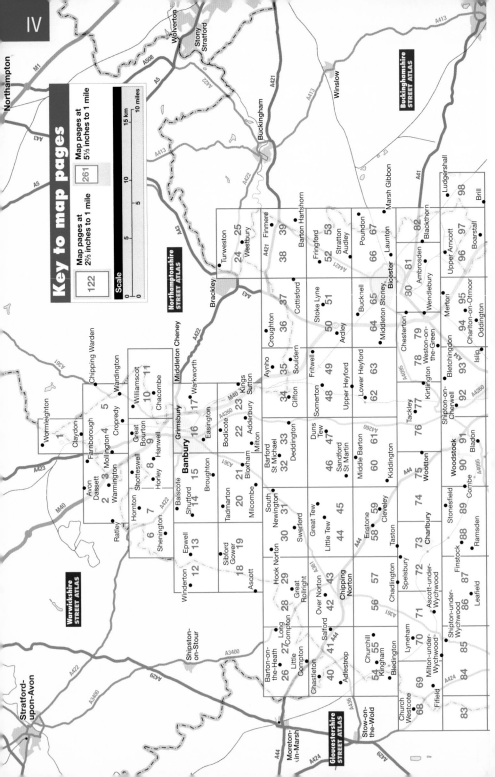

IV

Key to map pages

Map pages at
2⅓ inches to 1 mile

122

Map pages at
5⅓ inches to 1 mile

261

Scale

0	5	10	15 km
0	5	10 miles	

Northamptonshire STREET ATLAS

Buckinghamshire STREET ATLAS

Warwickshire STREET ATLAS

Gloucestershire STREET ATLAS

Aylesbury
A4010
A4129
Haddenham
A418
A4129
Princes Risborough
M40

A4155
A4130
Twyford
A4
Henley-on-Thames
Wargrave
Sonning
Caversham
Reading
A329
A33

130
Thame
A418
148 149
Toversey
Henton
168 169
Chinnor
Kingston Blount
188 189
Bledlow Ridge
Beacon's Bottom
Stokenchurch
226
Fawley
Lower Assendon
244
254 255
Shiplake
260
A4155

128 129
Long Crendon
A329
146 147
Shabbington
Tiddington
A40
166 167
Tetsworth
Sydenham
186 187
Aston Rowant
Lewknor
Watlington
206 207
Greenfield
224 225
Middle Assendon
Nettlebed
243
Stoke Row
242
252 253
Sonning Common
258 259
Tokers Green

106 107
Freeland
120 121
Eynsham
Cassington
138 139
Cumnor
Sutton
Stanton Harcourt
Northmoor
156 157
Appleton
Longworth
176 177
Kingston Bagpuize
Garford
196 197
East Hanney
Grove
214 215
Wantage
Ardington
232 233

A4010
Beckley
110 111
Noke
124 125
Stanton St John
Marston
142 143
Horspath
Garsington
161
Sandford-on-Thames
181
Radley
201
Sutton Courtenay
Culham
219
Aston Upthorpe
237

M40
Horton-cum-Studley
112
126 127
Worminghall
Holton
144 145
Wheatley
Cuddesdon
164 165
Great Haseley
Stoke Talmage
184 185
Chalgrove
Brightwell Baldwin
204 205
Benson
Ewelme
222 223
Crowmarsh Gifford
Nuffield
240 241
Woodcote
250 251
Whitchurch Hill
256 257
Pangbourne
A340

Kidlington
108 109
Yarnton
122 123
Wolvercote
Botley
North Hinksey
140 141
Kennington
160
162 163
Little Milton
Stadhampton
182 183
Berinsfield
Dorchester
202 203
Long Wittenham
Brightwell-cum-Sotwell
220 221
Wallingford
Cholsey
238 239
Moulsford
South Stoke
248 249
Goring
Aldworth
247

Oxford
261
A4144
A34

102 103
Minster Lovell
Crawley
116 117
Curbridge
Brize Norton
134 135
Aston
Bampton
Black Bourton
Cote
154 155
Hinton Waldrist
Buckland
174 175
Charney Bassett
194 195
Stanford in the Vale
Denchworth
212 213
Sparsholt
Childrey
230 231
Letcombe Bassett
246

100 101
Burford
114 115
Shilton
Alvescot
Filkins
Langford
132 133
Carterton
152 153
Littleworth
Clanfield
Kelmscott
172 173
Faringdon
Great Coxwell
192 193
Longcot
Baulking
210 211
Uffington
Woolstone
228 229
Ashbury
245
Baydon

99
Great Barrington
Westwell
113
Eastleach Martin
131
Southrop
150 151
Lechlade-on-Thames
170 171
Buscot
Watchfield
190 191
Highworth
Shrivenham
208 209
Bourton
Bishopstone
227

Taynton
104 105
North Leigh
Witney
118 119
South Leigh
Ducklington
136 137
Standlake

A40
A361
A415
A420
A417
A420
A361
A419
A346

Swindon
A4185
A338
A4074
A417
A4130
A329
A4074

Berkshire STREET ATLAS
Wiltshire & Swindon STREET ATLAS

M4

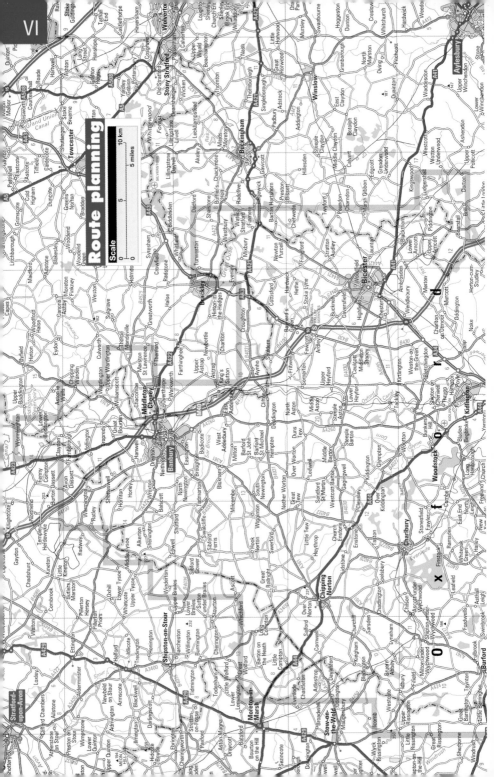

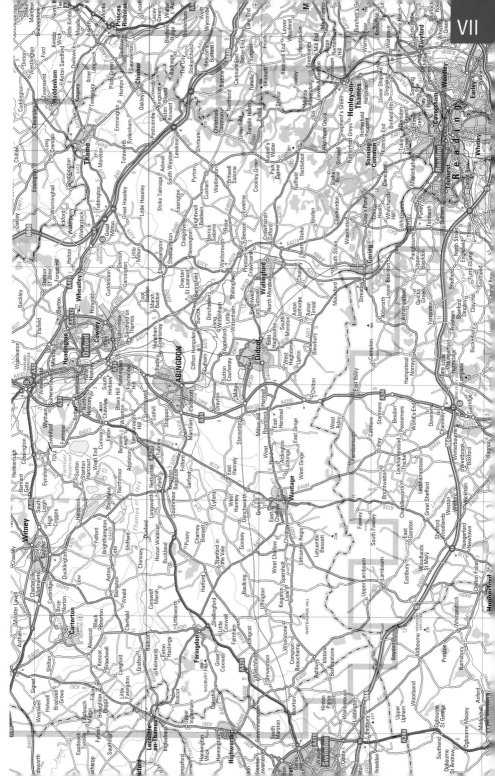

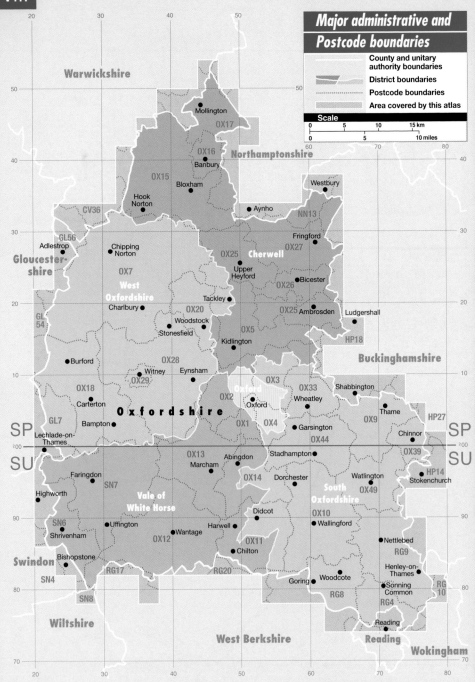

Major administrative and Postcode boundaries

County and unitary authority boundaries
District boundaries
Postcode boundaries
Area covered by this atlas

Scale
0   5   10   15 km
0   5   10 miles

Warwickshire

Mollington

OX17

OX16
Banbury

Northamptonshire

OX15
Bloxham

Westbury

Hook Norton

CV36

Aynho

NN13

GL56
Adlestrop

Gloucester-shire

Chipping Norton

OX7

Fringford

OX25   Cherwell   OX27

Upper Heyford

West Oxfordshire

Charlbury

OX20
Woodstock

OX26   Bicester

Tackley

GL 54

Stonesfield

OX25   Ambrosden   Ludgershall

Kidlington

OX5

Burford

OX28

HP18

Buckinghamshire

Witney
OX29

Eynsham

OX18

Carterton

OX2   OX3   OX33
Oxford   Wheatley   Shabbington

Oxford

Thame

OX9

HP27

GL7

Bampton

OX1   OX4   Garsington

Chinnor

Oxfordshire

SP

SU

Lechlade-on-Thames

OX44

OX39

Faringdon

SN7

OX13
Marcham

Stadhampton

HP14
Stokenchurch

Highworth

Abingdon

OX14   Dorchester

Watlington

South Oxfordshire

OX49

Vale of White Horse

SN6
Shrivenham

Uffington

Didcot

OX10

Wallingford

Bishopstone

SN4

RG17

OX12

Wantage

Harwell

OX11
Chilton

Nettlebed

RG9

Henley-on-Thames

Sonning Common

RG4

Swindon

RG20

Goring   Woodcote

RG8

RG 10

SN8

Reading

Wiltshire

West Berkshire

Reading

Wokingham

Marcham

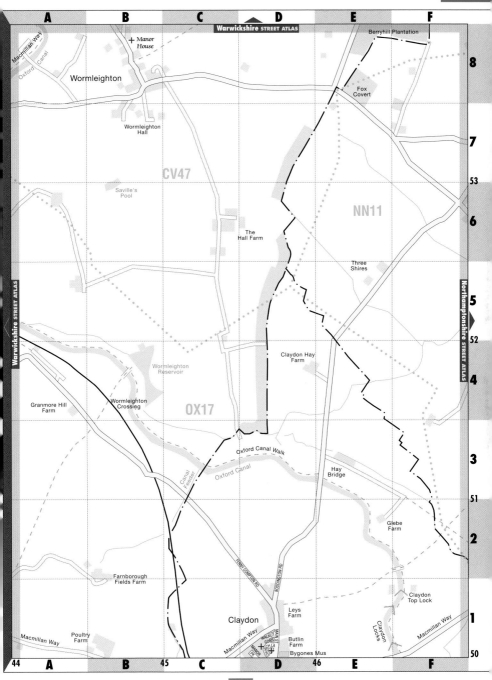

Warwickshire STREET ATLAS

Berryhill Plantation

Macmillan Way

Oxford Canal

Manor House

Wormleighton

Wormleighton Hall

Fox Covert

CV47

NN11

Saville's Pool

The Hall Farm

Three Shires

53

6

52

5

Claydon Hay Farm

Wormleighton Reservoir

Wormleighton Crossing

OX17

4

Granmore Hill Farm

Canal Feeder

Oxford Canal Walk

Oxford Canal

Hay Bridge

3

51

Glebe Farm

2

Farnborough Fields Farm

Claydon Top Lock

Claydon Locks

Macmillan Way

1

Claydon

Leys Farm

Macmillan Way

Poultry Farm

Macmillan Way

WALNUT
CONS ST
SCH LA
MANOR

Butlin Farm

Bygones Mus

FENNY COMPTON RD

OLD WLSMCOOTE RD

MAIN ST

44 A   B   45   C   D   46   E   F   50

Northamptonshire STREET ATLAS

Warwickshire STREET ATLAS

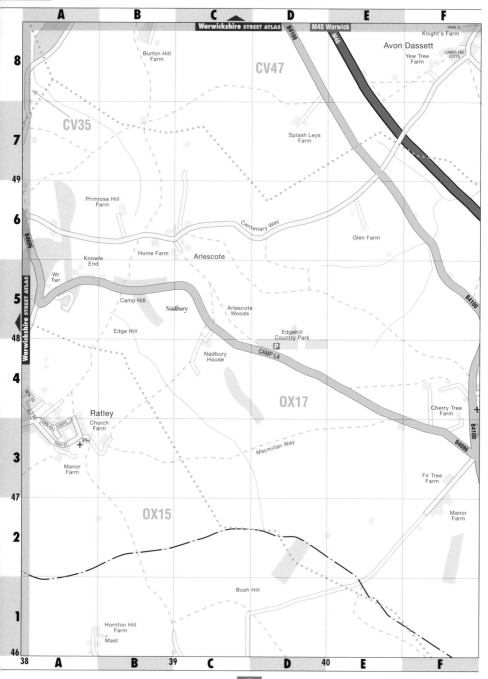

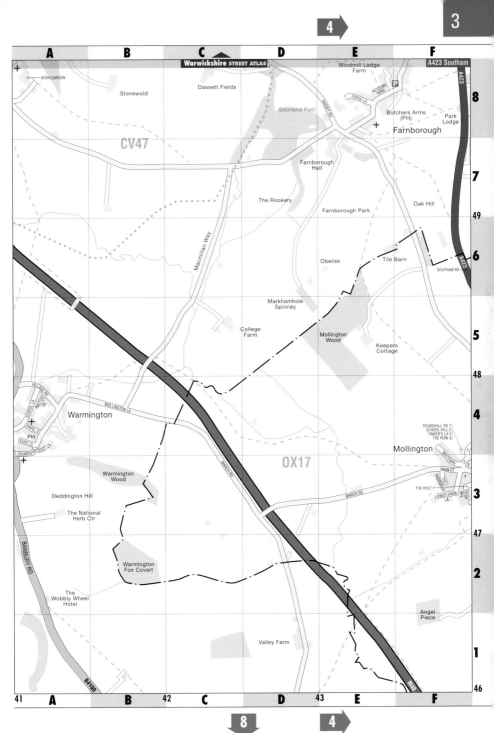

4

3 1

3 9

A B C D E F

8

Farnborough Hill Farm

Macmillan Way

Claydon Crossing

Manor Farm

MANOR PK

BIGNOLDS CL

Filter Bed

Claydon Locks

Macmillan Way

7

Farnborough Hill

Firs Farm

Lawn Hill

49

Clattercote

Oxford Canal Walk

Oxford Canal

Towing Path

6

Oathill Farm

Clattercote Reservoir

5

Cropredy Lawn

OX17

Lambert's Barn

48

Beecham's Cottages

4

Mollington

SOUTHAM RD

ROUNDHILL RD

CHURCH ST

MAIN ST

THE HOLLOWAY

CHURCH LA

ORCHARD RISE

IVY LA

CHESTNUT RD

Manor Farm

Mill Farm

CLAYDON RD

3

OXHEY HILL

47

Cropredy Hill

Oxhay Farm

Cemy

CREAMPOT CRES

CHAPEL ROW 1
NEW PL 2
VICARAGE FLATS 3

KYE RD

NEWS LA

CREAMPOT LA

CREAMPOT CL

ORCHARD VIEW

RED LION ST

CHURCH ST

2

Cropredy

PH

CUP AND SAUCER

CHERRY FIELDS

PLANTATION

STATION RD

Oxford Canal

River Cherwell

1

Manorfields Farm

A423

Cropredy CE Prim Sch

46

44 A B 45 C D 46 E F

Thickthorn Farm

A423

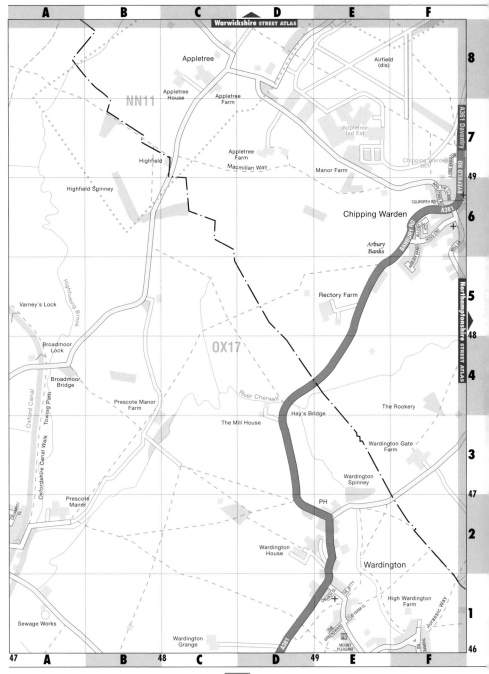

Appletree

Airfield
(dis)

NN11

Appletree
House

Appletree
Farm

Appletree
Ind Est

Chipping Warden
Sch

A361 Daventry

Highfield

Appletree
Farm

Macmillan Way

Manor Farm

THE CLOSE

APPLETREE RD

BYFIELD RD

49

Highfield Spinney

CULWORTH RD

Chipping Warden

A361

6

Highfield Brook

Arbury
Banks

BANBURY RD

ALLENS ORCH

ARBURY BANKS

HOGG END

MILL LA

Northamptonshire STREET ATLAS

Varney's Lock

Rectory Farm

5

48

OX17

Broadmoor
Lock

4

Oxford Canal

Towing Path

Oxfordshire Canal Walk

Broadmoor
Bridge

Prescote Manor
Farm

River Cherwell

The Mill House

Hay's Bridge

The Rookery

Wardington Gate
Farm

3

47

CHERWELL CL

Prescote
Manor

Wardington
Spinney

PH

Wardington
House

Wardington

2

CHURCH CL

THE JETTY

High Wardington
Farm

Jurassic Way

Sewage Works

Wardington
Grange

A361

THE GREENSWARD

PO

STUB FARM CL

THORPE RD

MOUNT
PLEASANT

1

46

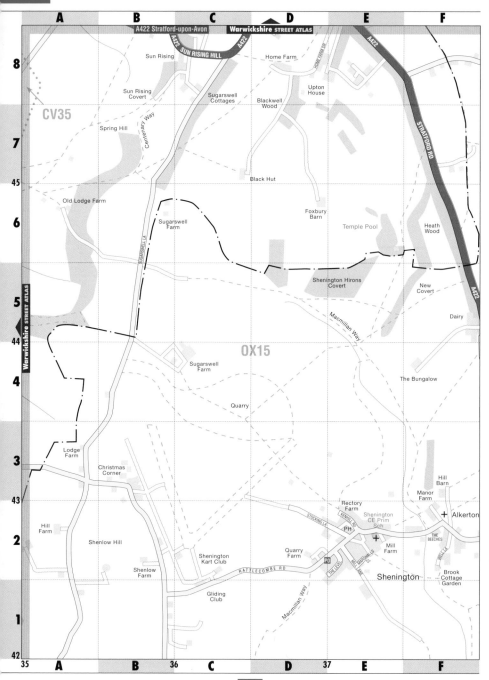

CV35

Sun Rising

SUN RISING HILL

Home Farm

HOME FARM DR

Upton House

Sun Rising Covert

Sugarswell Cottages

Blackwell Wood

Spring Hill

Centenary Way

STRATFORD RD

Old Lodge Farm

Black Hut

Foxbury Barn

Sugarswell Farm

Temple Pool

Heath Wood

SUGARSWELL LA

Shenington Hirons Covert

New Covert

A422

Warwickshire STREET ATLAS

Dairy

Macmillan Way

OX15

Sugarswell Farm

The Bungalow

Quarry

Lodge Farm

Christmas Corner

Hill Barn

Manor Farm

Rectory Farm

Shenington CE Prim Sch

Alkerton

THE BEECHES

Hill Farm

Shenlow Hill

STOCKING LA

KENHILL RD

PH

PO

Mill Farm

Quarry Farm

WELL LA

Shenington Kart Club

Shenlow Farm

RATTLECOMBE RD

MARSHALLS CL

MILL LANE

THE LEYS

Shenington

Brook Cottage Garden

Gliding Club

Macmillan Way

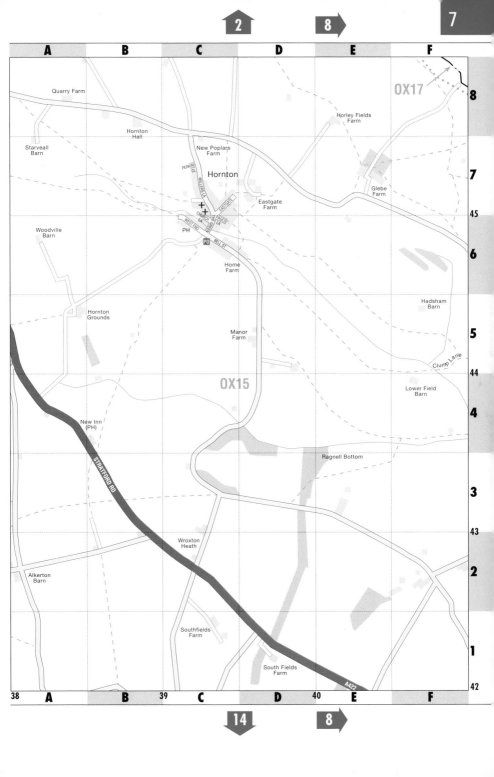

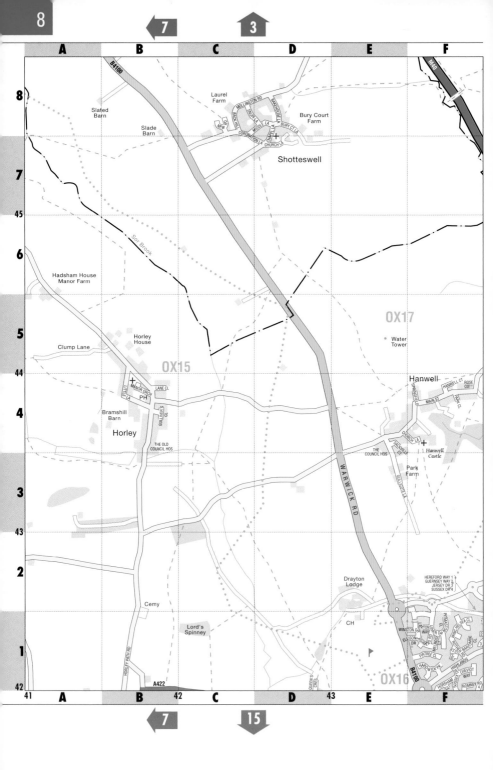

8

7

45

6

5

44

4

3

43

2

1

42

A B C D E F

41   42   43

Slated
Barn

Slade
Barn

Laurel
Farm

MOLLINGTON RD

BACK LA

SHOP LA

MIDDLE LA

LIMES LA

BURY CT LA

THE NEW

CORONATION LA

CHURCH LA

Bury Court
Farm

Shotteswell

Sor Brook

OX17

Hadsham House
Manor Farm

Water
Tower

Horley
House

Hanwell

HANWELL CT

ROSE
COTT

Clump Lane

OX15

SPRINGFIELD

MAIN ST

PARK CL

MANOR ORCH

LANE CL

LITTLE
LA

PH

BRAILEY'S
CL

Bramshill
Barn

Horley

THE OLD
COUNCIL HOS

CHURCH LA

CRESSWELL

Hanwell
Castle

THE
COUNCIL HOS

GULLICOTE LA

Park
Farm

WARWICK RD

Cemy

Lord's
Spinney

HORLEY PATH RD

A422

Drayton
Lodge

CH

QUEEN'S CRES

HEREFORD WAY 1
GUERNSEY WAY 2
JERSEY DR 3
SUSSEX DR 4

PYTHALL RD

WINSTON DR

ELLISON

FIRTREE CL

WICK YK

HORSHAM RD

ROMNEY RD

CHEVIOT

OX16

B4100

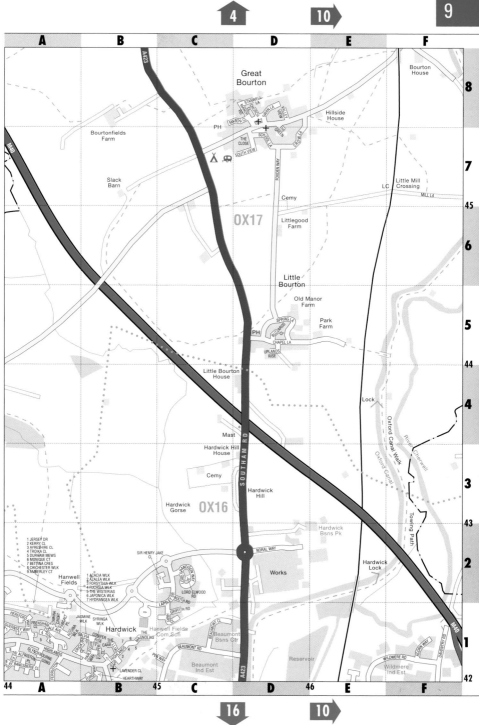

A B C D E F

8

Great
Bourton

Bourton
House

Hillside
House

PH

STANWELL LA

MAIN LA

VALLEY

MANOR CL

CROW LA

SCHOOL LA

SOUTH VIEW

THE
CLOSE

GREEN LA

FOXON WAY

Bourtonfields
Farm

7

Slack
Barn

Little Mill
Crossing

LC

MILL LA

45

OX17

Cemy

Littlegood
Farm

6

Little
Bourton

Old Manor
Farm

Park
Farm

5

PH

SPRING LA

SUZANNE
CL

CHAPEL LA

UPLANDS
RISE

Lock

44

Little Bourton
House

Oxford Canal Walk

Oxford Canal

River Cherwell

4

Mast

Hardwick Hill
House

Cemy

SOUTHAM RD

Hardwick
Hill

3

Hardwick
Gorse

OX16

43

Hardwick
Bsns Pk

1 JERSEY DR
2 KERRY CL
3 AYRSHIRE CL
4 TROIKA CL
5 DURHAM MEWS
6 MONIQUE CT
7 BETTINA CRES
8 CHICHESTER WLK
9 AMBERLEY CT

SIR HENRY JAKE
CL

NORAL WAY

Works

Hardwick
Lock

Towing Path

2

Hanwell
Fields

1 ACACIA WLK
2 AZALEA WLK
3 FORSYTHIA WLK
4 FUCHSIA WLK
5 THE WISTERIAS
6 JAPONICA WLK
7 HYDRANGEA WLK

SANDICAR WAY

LORD ELWOOD
RD

IS BOOTH RD

LAPSLEY DR

GRIFFITH RD

HEREFORD

FRENSHAM
CL

HIGHLANDS

GUERNSEY WAY

GLYNDEBOURNE
GDNS

ALFRISTON CL

BARNESMERE CL

FERGUSON
DR

JASMINE
WLK

SYRINGA
WLK

CONIFER

THE LILACS

JUNIPER

DALE AVE

RISE

CRICKET RD

SALVIA

THE
MAGNOLIAS

CAMEL

PEN WAY

FORD

LAVENDER CL

HEARTHWAY

Hardwick

Hanwell Fields
Com Sch

BEAUMONT CL

Beaumont
Bsns Ctr

BEAUMONT RD

Beaumont
Ind Est

Reservoir

WILDMERE RD

ACORN WAY

DAVENTRY RD

Wildmere
Ind Est

1

A423

M40

A423

| | A | B | C | D | E | F |

8

Lower Lodge

Mount Pleasant

Bennetts Farm

Trent Farm

Barn Farm

Upper Wardington

THE COUNCIL HOUSES

Williamscot

Williamscot House

Village Spinney

Weir

Oxford Canal

Oxford Canal Wlk

7

45

Peewit Farm

Dawkins's Barn

River Cherwell

6

Bell Land

Jurassic Way

Williamscot Hill Farm

A361

WARDINGTON RD

5

Redlunch Barn

Marsh Barn Farm

Coton Farm

Bridge Lake Fisheries

WILLIAMSCOT HILL

Works

44

OX17

The Priory

SILVER ST

POPLARS RD

Chacombe

Chacombe CE Prim Sch

CHURCH LA

PH

THORPE RD

BENNETTS CL

4

BANBURY RD

THORNHILL

MIDDLETON RD

CH

BANBURY RD

Chacombe House

3

43

Castle Farm

2

Jurassic Way

Seale's Farm

Yew Tree Cottage

B4525

BANBURY LA

CHENEY GDNS

CHACOMBE RD

STANWELL LEA

OX16

Huscote Farm

STANWELL LEA T

STANWELL DR

MICHAELMAS CL

1

Windmill Farm

CHENEY CT

GLOVERS LA

RECTORY LA

42

A361

M40

B4525

| 47 | A | B | 48 | C | D | 49 | E | F |

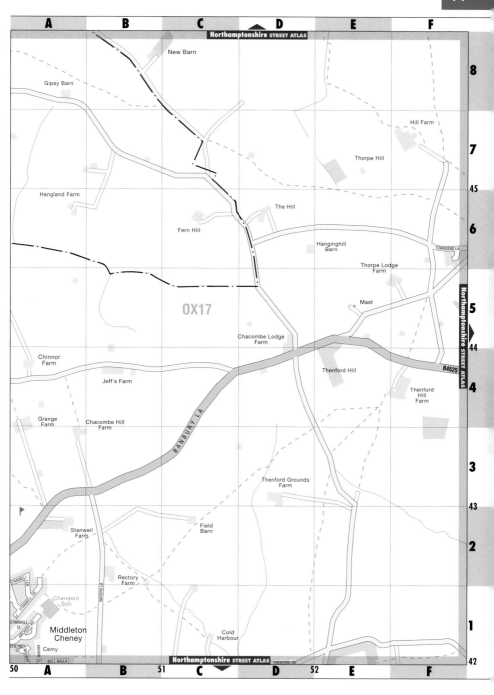

New Barn

Gipsy Barn

Hill Farm

Thorpe Hill

Hangland Farm

The Hill

Fern Hill

Hanginghill Barn

Thorpe Lodge Farm

TOWNSEND LA

OX17

Mast

Chacombe Lodge Farm

Thenford Hill

B4525

Chinnor Farm

Jeff's Farm

Thenford Hill Farm

Grange Farm

Chacombe Hill Farm

BANBURY LA

Thenford Grounds Farm

Stanwell Farm

Field Barn

STANWELL LA

WATERS LA

Rectory Farm

CHEYNEY CT

Chenderit Sch

STANWELL CL

ARBURY RD

Middleton Cheney

Cemy

BULL BAULK

Cold Harbour

THENFORD RD

45

7

8

44

5

4

3

43

2

1

42

50 51 52

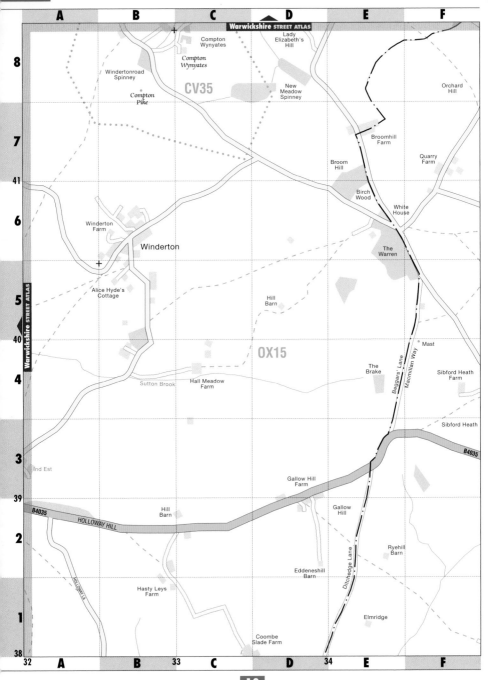

A **B** **C** **D** **E** **F**

8

Compton Wynyates
Lady Elizabeth's Hill

Compton Wynyates

Wintertonroad Spinney

Orchard Hill

CV35

New Meadow Spinney

Compton Pike

7

Broomhill Farm

Quarry Farm

41

Broom Hill

Birch Wood

White House

6

Winderton Farm

The Warren

Winderton

Alice Hyde's Cottage

5

Hill Barn

Mast

40

OX15

Sibford Heath Farm

The Brake

4

Beggars' Lane

Macmillan Way

Sutton Brook

Hall Meadow Farm

Sibford Heath

3

B4035

Ind Est

Gallow Hill Farm

39

B4035

Hill Barn

HOLLOWAY HILL

Gallow Hill

2

Ryehill Barn

Ditchedge Lane

Eddeneshill Barn

Hasty Leys Farm

1

Elmridge

Coombe Slade Farm

38

32 **A** **B** **33** **C** **D** **34** **E** **F**

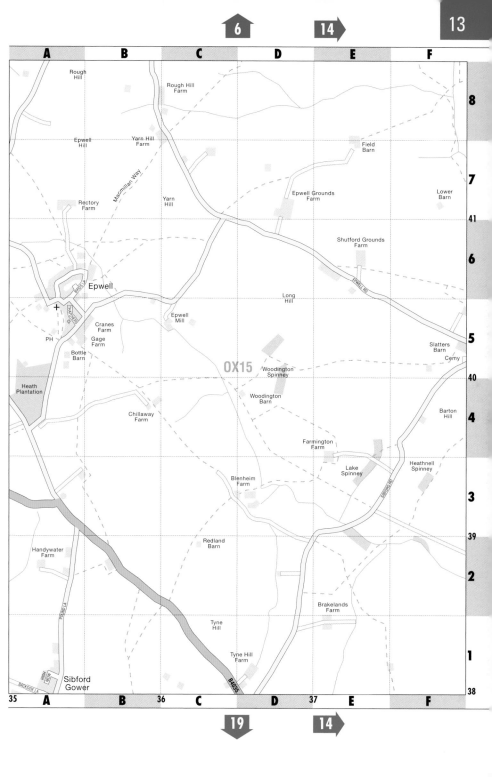

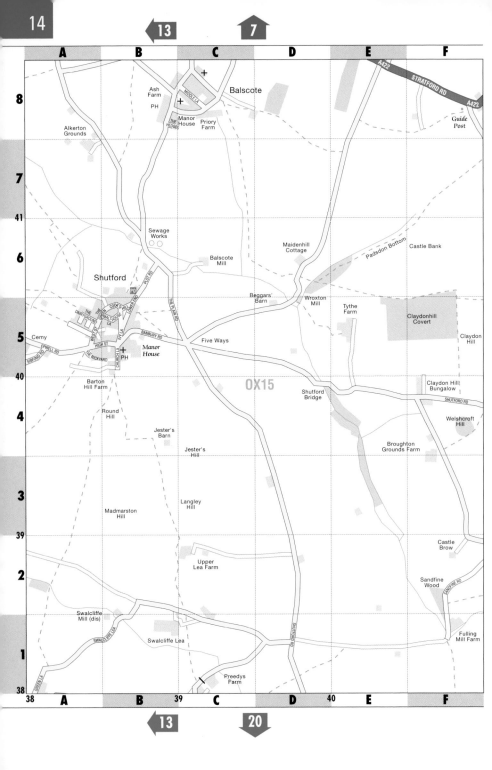

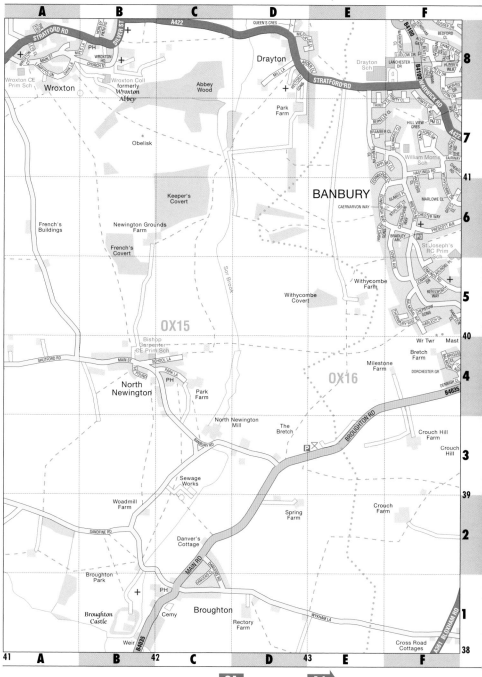

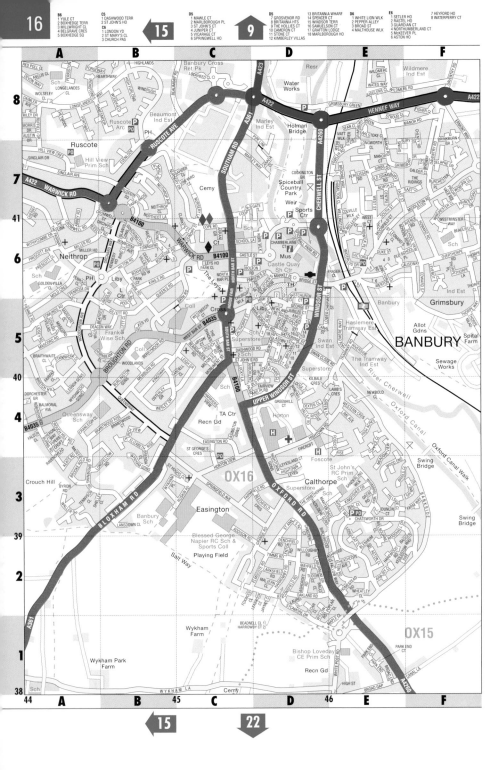

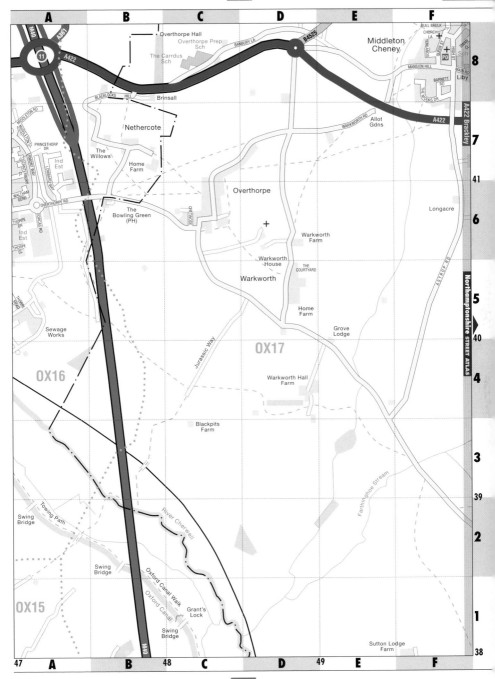

12

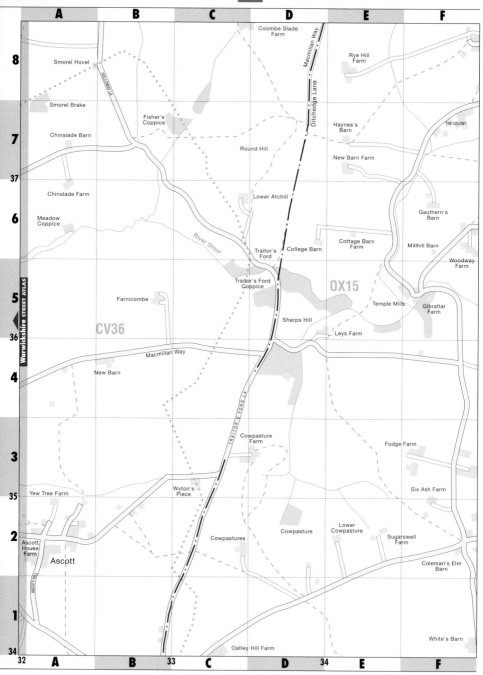

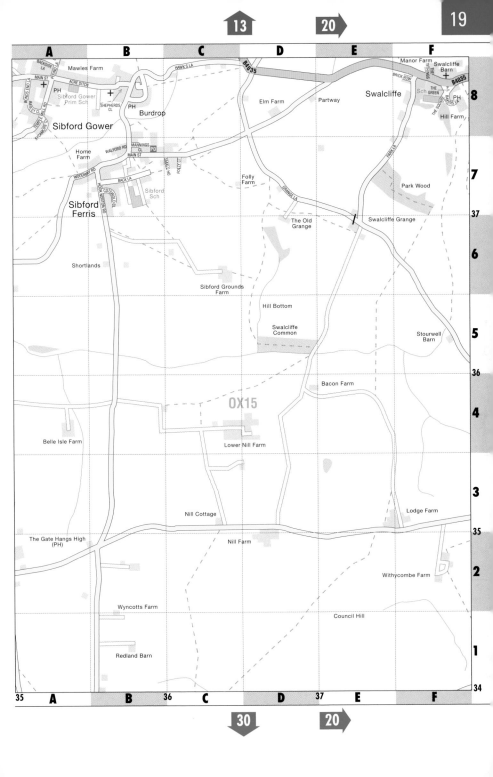

19
14

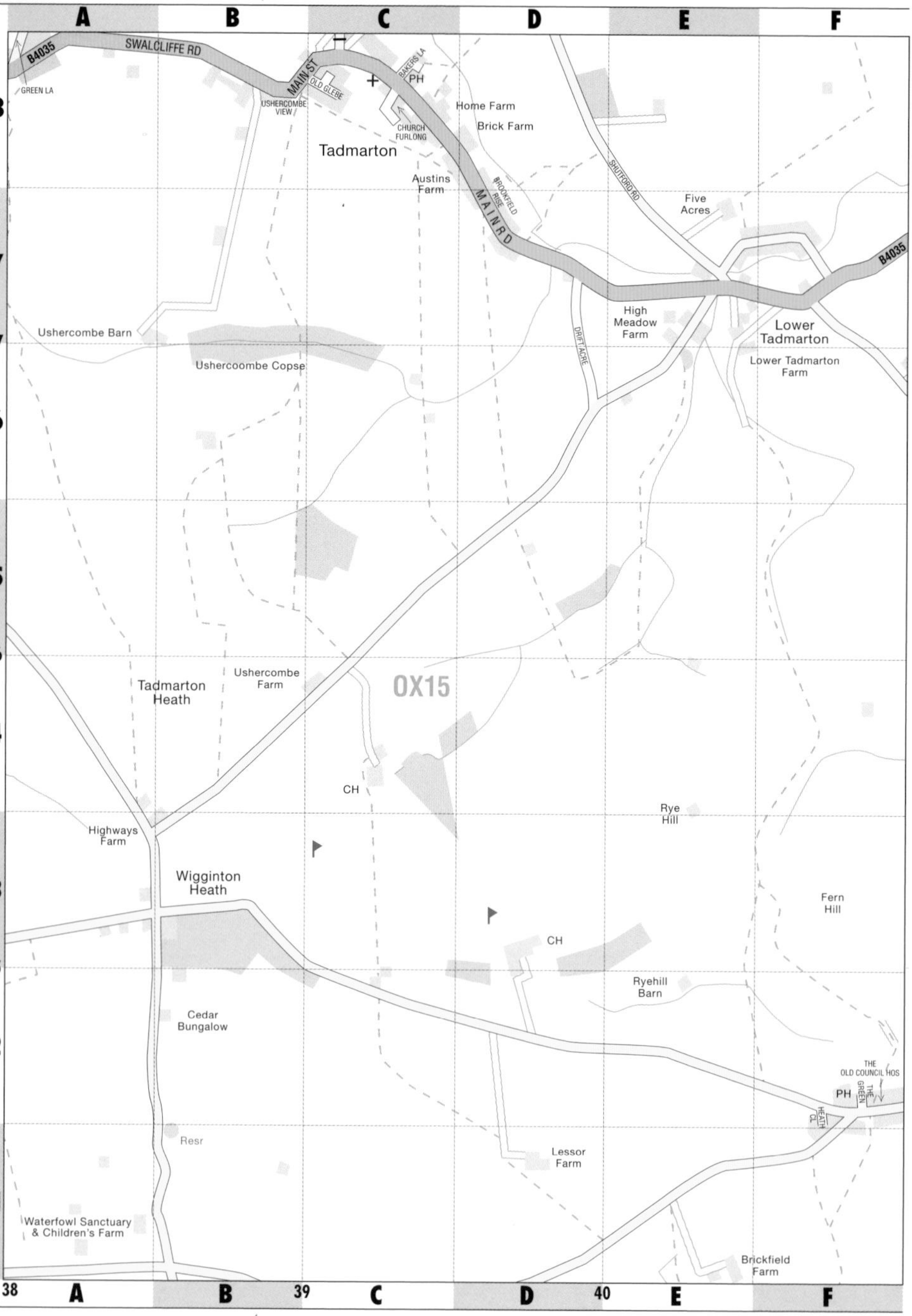

B4035

SWALCLIFFE RD

GREEN LA

MAIN ST

USHERCOMBE VIEW

OLD GLEBE

GLEBE LA

PH

Home Farm

Brick Farm

Tadmarton

Austins Farm

CHURCH FURLONG

MAIN RD

BROOKFIELD

Five Acres

SHUTFORD RD

B4035

Ushercombe Barn

Ushercoombe Copse

DRY LANE

High Meadow Farm

Lower Tadmarton

Lower Tadmarton Farm

Tadmarton Heath

Ushercombe Farm

OX15

CH

Rye Hill

Highways Farm

Wigginton Heath

CH

Fern Hill

Ryehill Barn

Cedar Bungalow

THE OLD COUNCIL HOS

THE GREEN

PH

HEATH LA

Resr

Lessor Farm

Waterfowl Sanctuary & Children's Farm

Brickfield Farm

38 A B 39 C D 40 E F

34 1 2 35 3 4 36 5 6 37 7 8

A B C D E F

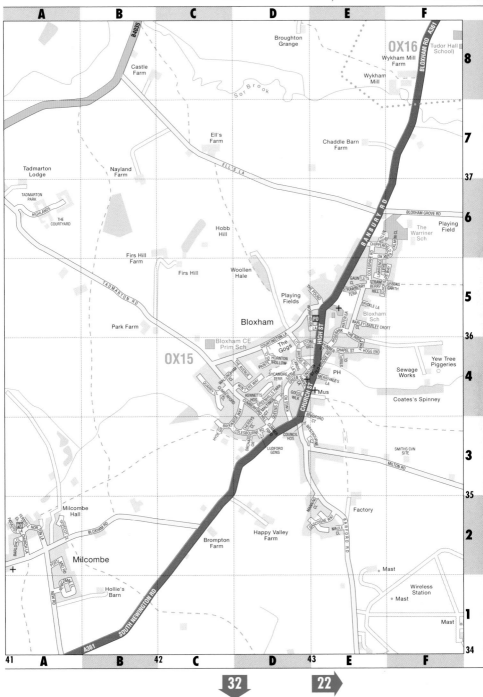

8

7

37

6

5

36

4

3

35

2

1

34

A   B   C   D   E   F

Broughton Grange

B4035

OX16

Tudor Hall School

Wykham Mill Farm

BLOXHAM RD   A361

Castle Farm

Sor Brook

Wykham Mill

Ell's Farm

Chaddle Barn Farm

Tadmarton Lodge

Nayland Farm

ELL'S LA

TADMARTON PARK

HIGHLANDS

THE COURTYARD

Hobb Hill

Bloxham Grove Rd

BLOXHAM GROVE RD

The Warriner Sch

Playing Field

BANBURY RD

Firs Hill Farm

Woollen Hale

Playing Fields

BUTLER CL

CHIPPERFIELD PL   PALLOWN CL

COLEGRAVE RD

LAWRENCE CL

DM CROFT

Firs Hill

THE POUND

NORTHUMBRIA

GAUNTLETS CL

STRAWBERRY TERR

STRAW BERRY CL

HILL CL

GREENS GARTH

TADMARTON RD

Park Farm

Bloxham

OX15

Bloxham CE Prim Sch

COURTINGTON LA

The Gogs

PO

HIGH ST

BRIDGE HILL

BRINKLE LA

Bloxham Sch

BARLEY CL   BARLEY CROFT

THE RIDGE

HOGG END

STONE HILL

CHAPEL ST

WATER LA

Yew Tree Piggeries

THE AVENUE

HORNTON HOLLOW

PAINTE

SYCAMORE TERR

WILL STES WAY

GREEN LA

STEPLE CL

PH

Mus

Sewage Works

Coates's Spinney

QUARRY CL

KENNETTS HOS

CUMBERFORD

MARTENS PARK

PRESTWELL CL

GREENS CL

BRETCH HILL

GOOSE WLK

MERRIVALE'S LA

CHURCH ST

BRADFORD CT

WYTHECROME CL

SMITHS CVN SITE

MILTON RD

HYDE GR

ORCHARD CL

COLESBOURNE RD

LUDFORD GDNS

COUNCIL HOS

BARFORD RD

Milcombe Hall

BLOXHAM RD

Brompton Farm

Happy Valley Farm

Factory

MANSEL CL

LASCOGNE WAY

MAULE CL

Mast

PRIMROSE LA

HOR LA

CHAPEL LA

BROAD MARSH

Milcombe

POST LA

BAKERS LA

MILCOMBE RD

NEW INN RD

Hollie's Barn

SOUTH NEWINGTON RD

A361

41   A   42   B   C   D   43   E   F

32   22

21
16

	A	B	C	D	E	F

8

Wykham Park

Tudor Hall Sch

OX16

Cemy

PADDOCK FARM LA

THE RYDES

College Farm House

CLOSE LA

HIGH ST

CHAPEL LA

WATERCRESS

WEEPING CROSS

A4260

MALTHOUSE LA

PH

EAST ST

EASTERN TERR

WALTON

OXFORD RD

PH

DEERS CL

ROOKERY

WISE CL

SICKLEIGH RD

Bodicote

Bodicote Park

DILLON CT

FRI

ANS RD

PO

WISE CL

MOLYNEUX

BLACKW

DEER'S FARM

WARDS CL

SEFTON PL

AUSTIN RD

HOBBS CL

7

Bodicote Mill House

Cotefield House

37

Old Barn Farm

Upper Grove Mill

Lower Grove Mill

6

BLOXHAM GROVE RD

Bloxham Grove

Sor Brook

Windmill

5

Wayhouse Farm

OX15

36

4

3

Brickhouse Farm

LE HALL PL

MANOR RD

CROSS HILL RD

NEW RD

PO

ADDERBURY PARK

DOG CL

ROUND C

Manor Farm

West Adderbury

HORN HILL RD

PARTRIDGE CT

Recn Gd

CHAPEL LA

PH

Milton

OX17

TANNERS CL

THE LEYS

35

Church Farm

LITTLE GROUND

MILTON RD

ST MARY'S RD

ADDERBURY HILL RD

OXFORD RD

NORRIS CL

2

Wyatt's Barn

1

Airfield (disused)

Wireless Station

A4260

OXFORD RD

34

Mast

Mast

44	A	B	45	C	D	46	E	F

21
33

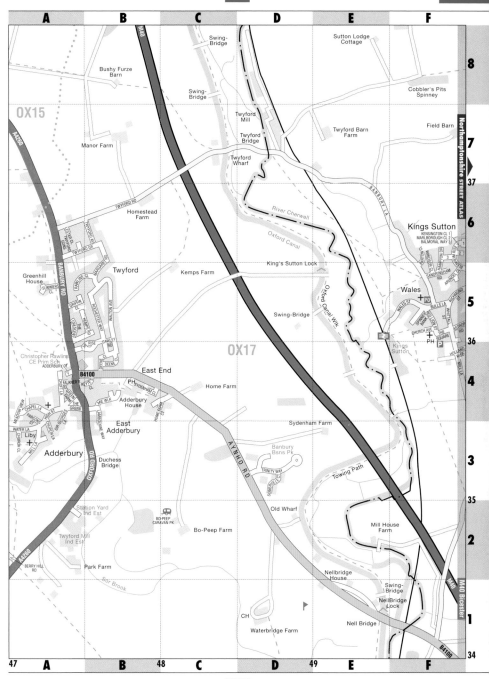

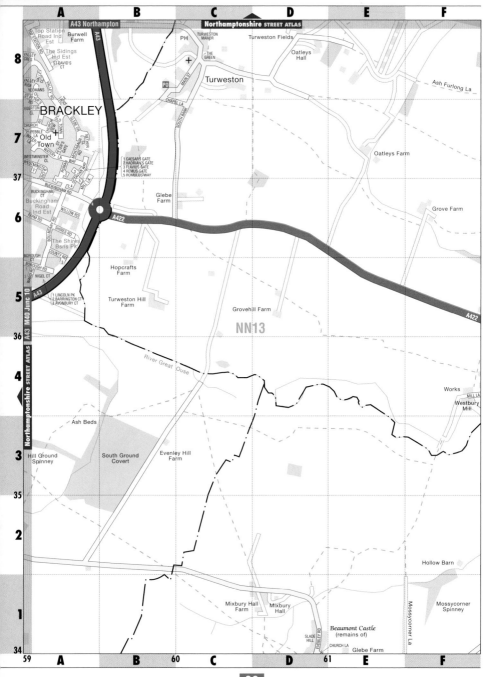

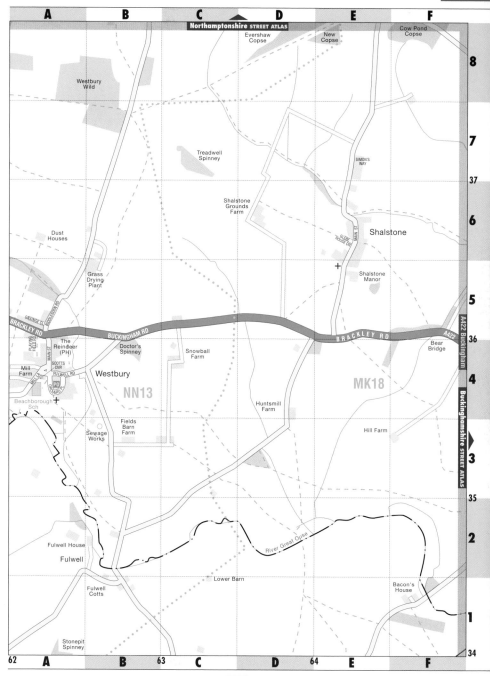

Evershaw Copse

New Copse

Cow Pond Copse

Westbury Wild

Treadwell Spinney

SIMON'S WAY

Shalstone

Dust Houses

Shalstone Grounds Farm

GLEBE HOUSE DRI

MAIN ST

Grass Drying Plant

Shalstone Manor

BRACKLEY RD

BUCKINGHAM RD

BRACKLEY RD

A422

A422 Buckingham

The Reindeer (PH)

Doctor's Spinney

Snowball Farm

Bear Bridge

Buckinghamshire STREET ATLAS

PLAYING

MAIN ST

MILL LA

SCOTTS CNR

FULWELL RD

Mill Farm

Westbury

NN13

MK18

Beachborough Sch

Huntsmill Farm

Fields Barn Farm

Hill Farm

Sewage Works

Fulwell House

River Great Ouse

Fulwell

Lower Barn

Bacon's House

Fulwell Cotts

Stonepit Spinney

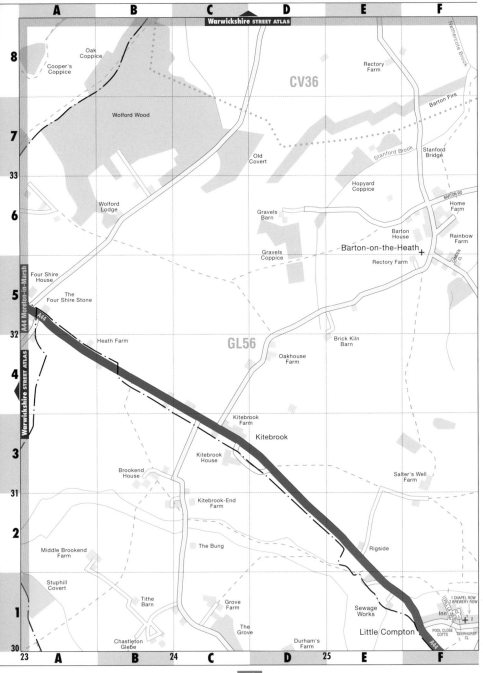

A **B** **C** **D** **E** **F**

8

Oak
Coppice

Cooper's
Coppice

Rectory
Farm

CV36

Barton Firs

Wolford Wood

7

Stanford Brook

Old
Covert

Stanford
Bridge

33

BARTON RD

Hopyard
Coppice

Home
Farm

Wolford
Lodge

6

Gravels
Barn

Barton
House

Rainbow
Farm

Gravels
Coppice

Barton-on-the-Heath

Rectory Farm

CAMDEN CL

Four Shire
House

A44 Moreton-in-Marsh

5

The
Four Shire Stone

Brick Kiln
Barn

32

Heath Farm

GL56

Oakhouse
Farm

A44

Warwickshire STREET ATLAS

4

Kitebrook
Farm

Kitebrook

3

Kitebrook
House

Brookend
House

Salter's Well
Farm

31

Kitebrook-End
Farm

2

Middle Brookend
Farm

The Bung

Rigside

Stuphill
Covert

1 CHAPEL ROW
2 BREWERY ROW

1

Tithe
Barn

Grove
Farm

Sewage
Works

Inn

POOL CLOSE
COTTS

DEERHURST
CL

The
Grove

Little Compton

Chastleton
Glebe

Durham's
Farm

A44

30

28

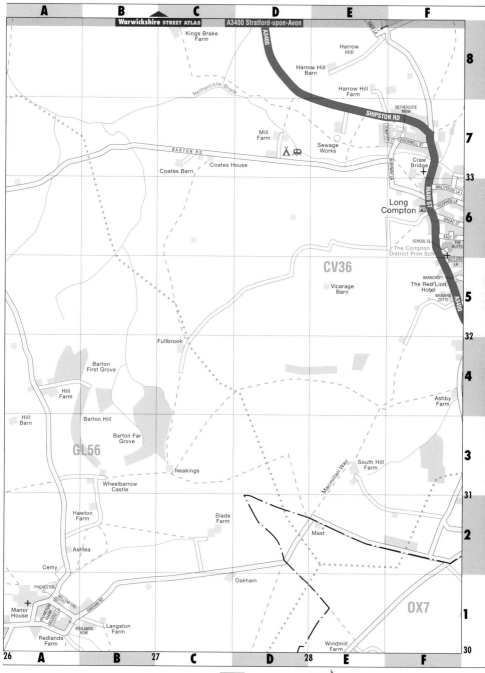

Warwickshire STREET ATLAS

A3400 Stratford-upon-Avon

A **B** **C** **D** **E** **F**

Kings Brake Farm

Nethercote Brook

Harrow Hill

Harrow Hill Barn

Harrow Hill Farm

NETHERCOTE MDW

SHIPSTON RD

BARTON RD

Mill Farm

Sewage Works

Coates Barn

Coates House

CROCKWELL ST

Craw Bridge

BURWAY LA

MALTHOUSE LA

Long Compton

PO

VICARAGE LA

BROAD ST

EAST ST

MAIN ST

SCHOOL CL

THE BUTTS

The Compton District Prim Sch

BUTLERS LA

CV36

Vicarage Barn

BARNCROFT

The Red Lion Hotel

WEAVERS COTTS

A3400

Fullbrook

Barton First Grove

Hill Farm

Hill Barn

Barton Hill

Barton Far Grove

Ashby Farm

GL56

Neakings

Wheelbarrow Castle

South Hill Farm

Macmillan Way

Hawton Farm

Slade Farm

Mast

Ashlea

Cemy

Oakham

PINCHESTER CL

MILLOW END

OAKHAM RD

Manor House

RIVINGTON CLOSE

DRIVERS LA

REDLANDS ROW

Langston Farm

Redlands Farm

Windmill Farm

OX7

8 **7** **33** **6** **5** **32** **4** **3** **31** **2** **1** **30**

41 28

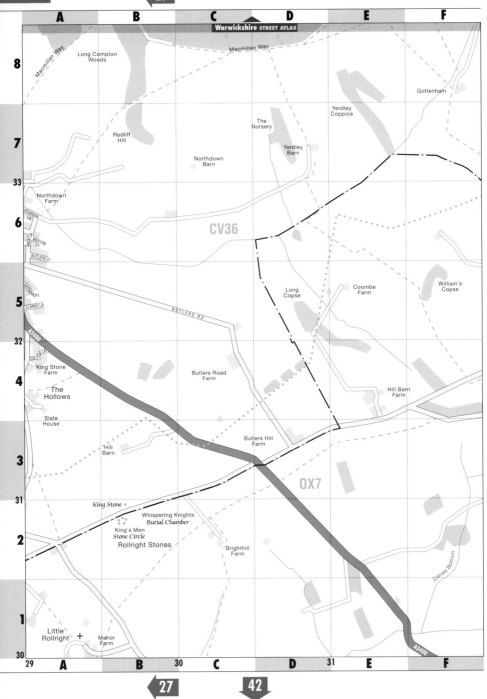

8

Macmillan Way

Long Compton Woods

Macmillan Way

Gottenham

Yerdley Coppice

7

Redliff Hill

The Nursery

Yerdley Barn

Northdown Barn

33

Northdown Farm

CV36

6

VICARAGE LA

WESTON CT

BUTLERS CL

Long Copse

Coombe Farm

William's Copse

5

CARSCROFT

CLARKS LA

BUTLERS RD

32

A3400

COLC... LA

4

King Stone Farm

The Hollows

Butlers Road Farm

Hill Barn Farm

Slate House

3

Hill Barn

Butlers Hill Farm

31

King Stone

OX7

Whispering Knights Burial Chamber

King's Men Stone Circle

2

Rollright Stones

Brighthill Farm

Danes Bottom

1

Little Rollright

Mahor Farm

A3400

30

29   A   30   B   C   D   31   E   F

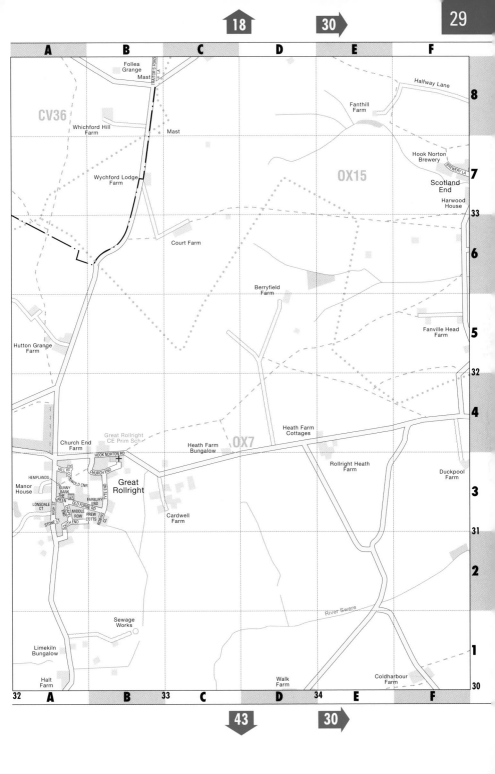

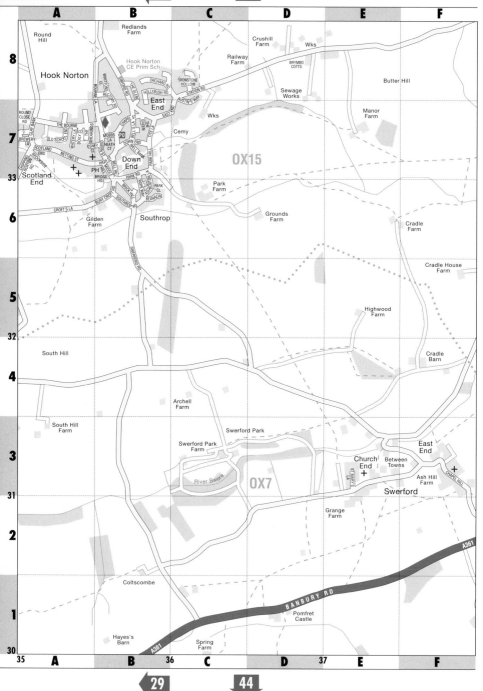

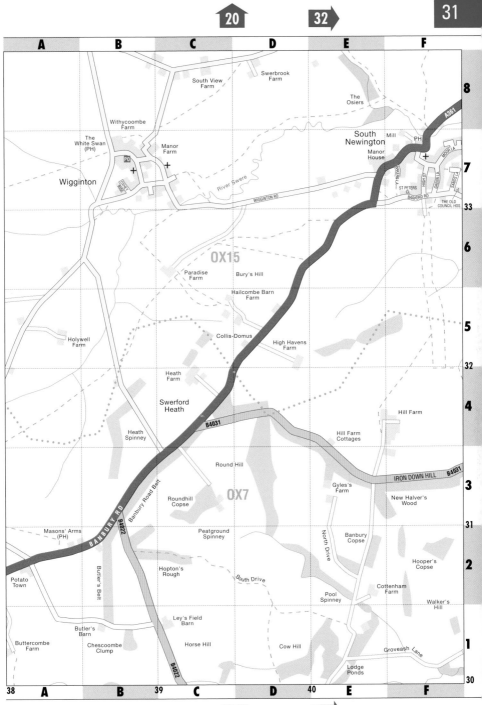

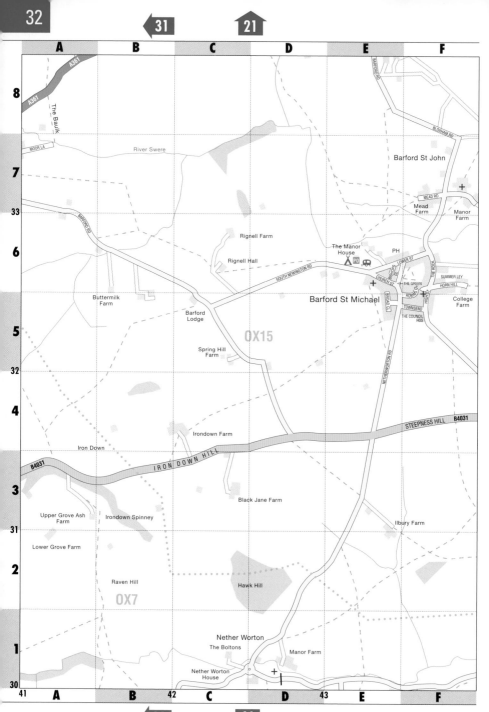

31
21
31
46

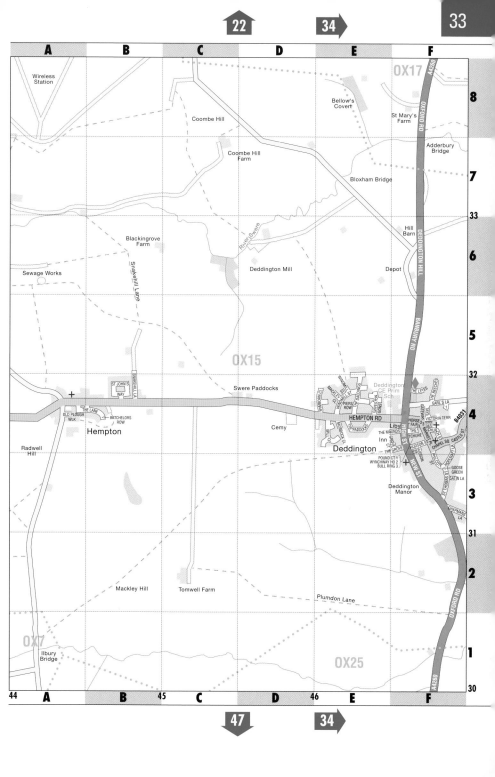

33
23

A **B** **C** **D** **E** **F**

8

River Swere

Adderbury Grounds
Farm

Sor Brook

Nellbridge
Farm

Aynho
Junction

Paper Mill
Cottages

OX17

7

Hazelhedge
Farm

Wilson's
Gorse

Aynho
Fishing
Venue

33

6

Field
Barn

Oxford Canal Walk

Oxford Canal

Hazel
Hedge

Aynho
Wharf

5

TITHE LA

River Cherwell

Great Western
Arms
(PH)

B4031 STATION RD

Towing Path

32

Duke of Cumberlands
Head
(PH)

COUNTY VIEW

THE
CHESTNUTS

County
Bridge

4

EARL S ST

CASTLE ST

B4031

CLIFTON RD

PEPPER ALLEY

WALNUT CL

OX15

Home
Farm

Manor
Farm

Clifton

Deddington Castle
Earthworks

Wharf
Farm

3

OX27

The
Fishers

31

CHAPMANS LA

Sewage
Works

2

Leadenporch
Farm

1

Bowman's
Bridge

OX25

Chisnell
Farm

Danehill
Covert

30

47 **A** **B** 48 **C** **D** 49 **E** **F**

B4100

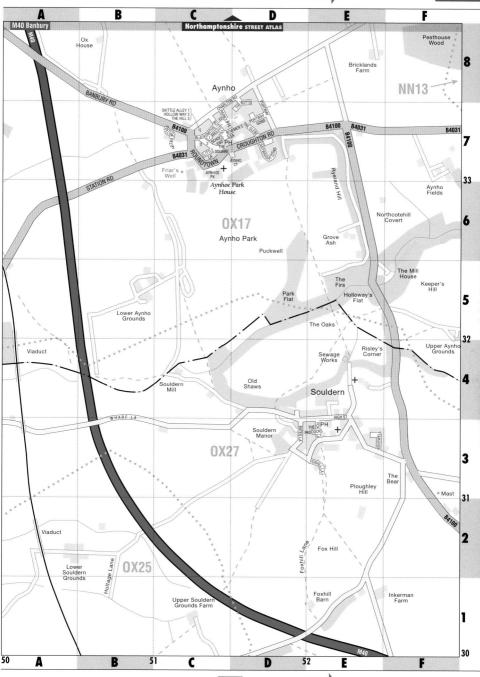

Northamptonshire STREET ATLAS

M40 Banbury

Ox House

Aynho

Bricklands Farm

Pesthouse Wood

NN13

BANBURY RD

SKITTLE ALLEY 1
HOLLOW WAY 2
THE HILL 3

B4100

B4031

STATION RD

ROUNDTOWN

CHARLTON RD

THE BUTTS

PORTWAY

BLACKSMITHS

SCHOOL

CHAPEL END

BOWMEN'S LEA

THE GLEBE

CATHENS

PH

CROUGHTON RD

LITTLE LA

THE SQUARE

AYNHO CT

B4100

B4031

B4031

Friar's Well

AYNHOE PK

Aynhoe Park House

Ryeland Hill

Aynho Fields

33

OX17

Aynho Park

Puckwell

Grove Ash

Northcotehill Covert

6

The Mill House

Keeper's Hill

Park Flat

The Firs

Holloway's Flat

5

Lower Aynho Grounds

The Oaks

32

Viaduct

Sewage Works

Risley's Corner

Upper Aynho Grounds

Souldern Mill

Old Shaws

Souldern

4

WHARF LA

Souldern Manor

THE PADDOCKS

PH

HIGH ST

RAIN ST

TWYFORD RD

OX27

FOXHILL LA

The Bear

3

Ploughley Hill

Mast

31

Viaduct

Foxhill Lane

Fox Hill

2

Lower Souldern Grounds

Holtage Lane

OX25

Upper Souldern Grounds Farm

Foxhill Barn

Inkerman Farm

1

M40

30

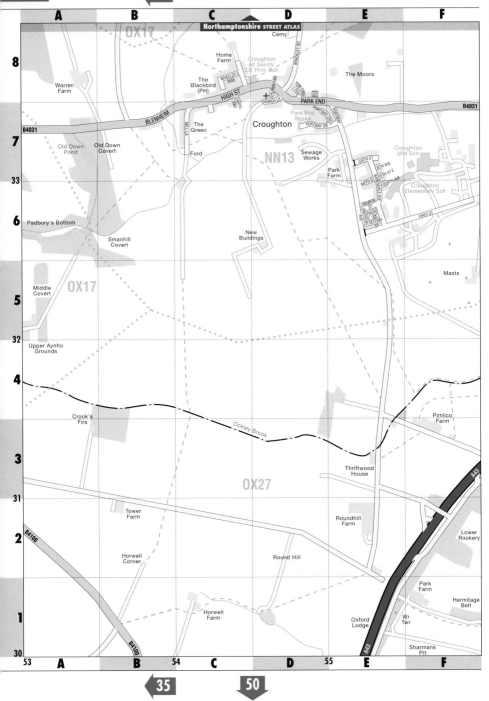

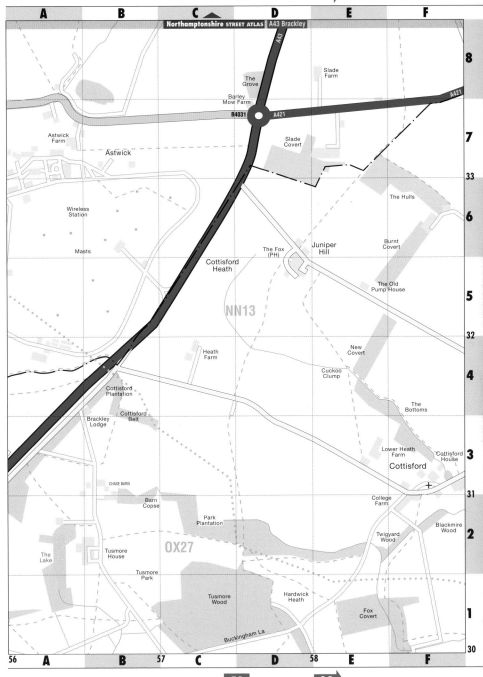

Northamptonshire STREET ATLAS A43 Brackley

A43
A421
B4031 A421

The Grove
Barley
Mow Farm
Slade
Farm

Astwick
Farm
Astwick

Slade
Covert

The Hulls

Wireless
Station

Burnt
Covert

Masts

The Fox
(PH)
Juniper
Hill

Cottisford
Heath

The Old
Pump House

NN13

New
Covert

Heath
Farm

Cuckoo
Clump

Cottisford
Plantation

The
Bottoms

Cottisford
Belt

Brackley
Lodge

Lower Heath
Farm
Cottisford
House

Cottisford

CHASE BARN

College
Farm

Barn
Copse

Blackmire
Wood

Park
Plantation

Twigyard
Wood

OX27

The
Lake

Tusmore
House

Tusmore
Park

Tusmore
Wood

Hardwick
Heath

Fox
Covert

Buckingham La

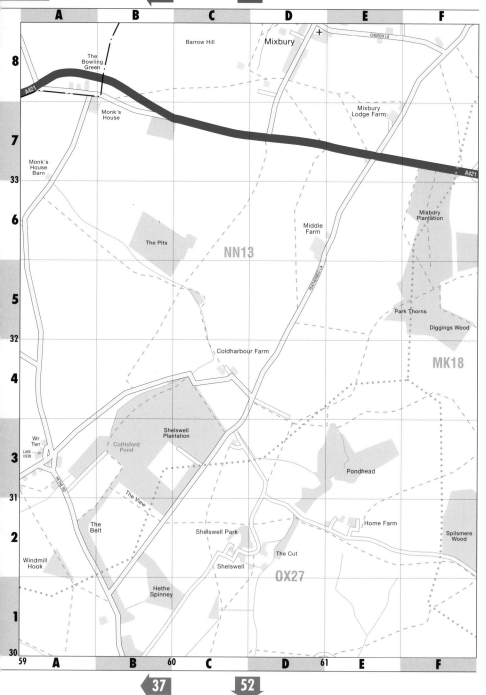

A   B   C   D   E   F

8

The Bowling Green

Barrow Hill

Mixbury

CHURCH LA

A421

Monk's House

Mixbury Lodge Farm

7

Monk's House Barn

33

6

The Pits

NN13

Middle Farm

Mixbury Plantation

FEATHERBED LA

5

Park Thorns

32

Diggings Wood

Coldharbour Farm

MK18

4

Wr Twr

LAKE VIEW

Shelswell Plantation

Cottisford Pond

Pondhead

3

HETH RD

31

The View

The Belt

Home Farm

2

Shelswell Park

The Cut

Spilsmere Wood

Windmill Hook

Shelswell

OX27

Hethe Spinney

1

30

59   A   60   B   C   61   D   E   F

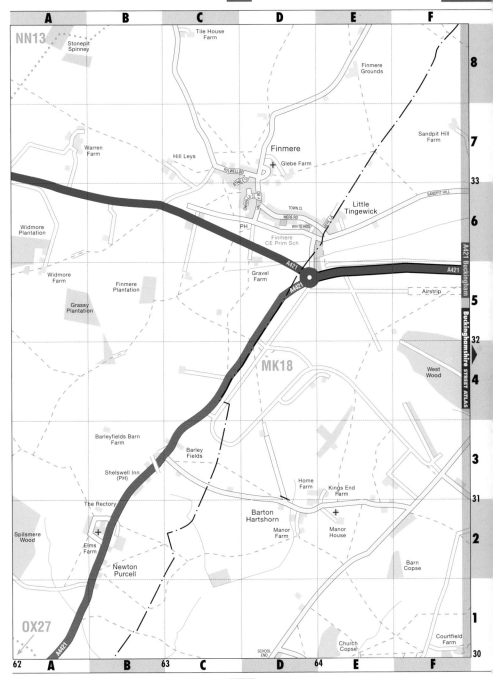

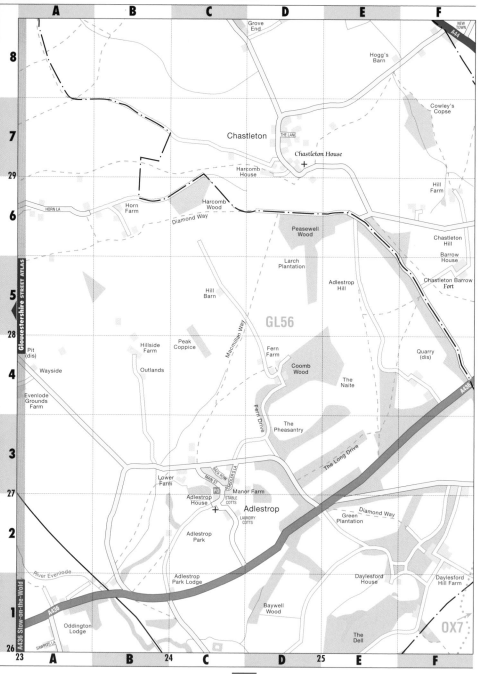

A B C D E F

8

7

29

6

5

28

4

3

27

2

1

26

23 24 25

A B C D E F

Gloucestershire STREET ATLAS

A436 Stow-on-the-Wold

NEW TOWN
A44

Grove End

Hogg's Barn

Cowley's Copse

Chastleton

THE LANE

Chastleton House

Hill Farm

Harcomb House

Horn La

Horn Farm

Harcomb Wood

Diamond Way

Chastleton Hill

Barrow House

Chastleton Barrow Fort

Peasewell Wood

Larch Plantation

Adlestrop Hill

Hill Barn

GL56

Pit (dis)

Hillside Farm

Peak Coppice

Macmillan Way

Fern Farm

Coomb Wood

Quarry (dis)

A436

Wayside

Outlands

The Naite

Evenlode Grounds Farm

Fern Drive

The Pheasantry

The Long Drive

Lower Farm

BACK ROW

MAIN ST

ORCHARD LA

Manor Farm

Green Plantation

Diamond Way

Adlestrop House

PO

STABLE COTTS

Adlestrop

LAUNDRY COTTS

Adlestrop Park

River Evenlode

A436

Adlestrop Park Lodge

Baywell Wood

Daylesford House

Daylesford Hill Farm

OX7

Oddington Lodge

SAWPITS LA

The Dell

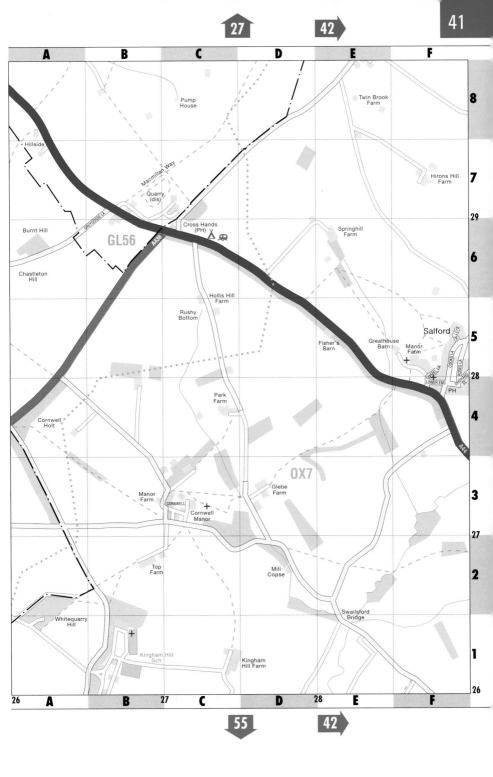

A B C D E F

8

Manor Farm

Choicehill Farm

Little Meadows

A3400

7

29

B4026

6

Rectory Farm

Over Norton House

Witts Farm

Over Norton Park

THE PENN

PENFIELD

Home Farm

Firs Farm

Over Norton

MAIN ST

RIDING HILL

OVER NORTON RD

QUARRY HILL

CHOICEHILL RD

5

GOLDEN LA

NEW HOUSE YD

THE GREEN

Larches Farm

CLEEVES CNR

BLUE ROW

28

THE CLOSE

OX7

The Cleeves

4

A44

Salford Mill

WILCOX RD

NICKEL VILLAS

CLEEVES AVE

FOLLAND

Chipping Norton

ACKERMAN RD

CROMWELL PK

BANBURY RD

A361

3

Bridge Field

WHITEHOUSE LA 1
VICTORIA PL 2
GODDARDS LA 3
MIDDLE ROW 4
KING'S HEAD MEWS 5
HILL LAWN CT 6
WITHERS CT 7
COWGATE TERR 8
MARKET PL 9

MARL BOROUGH RD

SUMMERTON

ROCK HILL

ROCKHILL FARM CT

Holy Trinity RC Sch

LONDON RD A44

BANBURY ROAD CROSSING

B4026

Elmsfield Farm Ind Est

CHURCH LA

CHURCH ST

Libv

H

PORTLAND PL

DICKENSON CT

SHEPPEY

BRASSEY CL

Monks Dene Bsns Ctr

Worcester Road Ind Est

Cemy

NEW ST A44

Mus

PO

P

ROWELL

ALBION PL

27

Nuholme

WORCESTER RD

Primsdown Ind Est

SPRING ST

WARDS RD

LODGE TERR

Wr Twr

Tank Farm

2

Cornwell Hill Farm

Chipping Norton Common

Station Yard Ind Est

LEWIS RD

WEBB CRES

DIEHARD WAY

WILLIAM

P

GLOVERS

DR

SPRING

HITCHMAN

P

A361

CHIPPING NORTON

1 ALFRED TERRS
2 JOHNSTON'S WAY
3 NORTON GREEN CT
4 VERNON HO
5 BRAGENOSE VILLAS

Sewage Works

WARPING HOUSE COTTS

THE MILL

BLISS MILL

THE LEYS

Chipping Norton Sch

1

Meads Farm

Westend Farm

PARADISE TERR

LORDS PIECE RD

TILSLEY RD

ALEXANDRA

St Mary's CE Prim Sch

1 BRASSEY HO
2 WILKINS HO
3 BLISS HO

HAILEY CRES

COTSWOLD CRESCENT BGLWS

Chipping Norton Sch

COTSWOLD TERR

Allot Gdns

BURFORD RD

A361

B4026

26

Westfield Farm

CHURCHILL RD

CORNISH LA

B4450

A B C D E F

29 **30** **31**

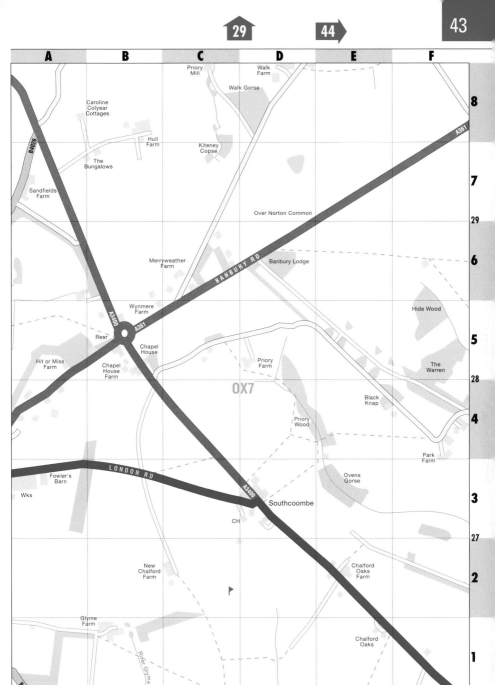

A   B   C   D   E   F

8

Priory
Mill

Walk
Farm

Walk Gorse

Caroline
Colyear
Cottages

Hull
Farm

Kiteney
Copse

A361

The
Bungalows

7

Sandfields
Farm

Over Norton Common

29

6

Merryweather
Farm

Banbury Lodge

BANBURY RD

Hide Wood

Wynmere
Farm

A3400

A361

Resr

5

Chapel
House

Priory
Farm

The
Warren

28

Hit or Miss
Farm

Chapel
House
Farm

OX7

Black
Knap

Priory
Wood

4

Park
Farm

LONDON RD

Fowler's
Barn

Ovens
Gorse

A3400

Southcoombe

3

Wks

CH

27

New
Chalford
Farm

Chalford
Oaks
Farm

2

Glyme
Farm

River Glyme

Chalford
Oaks

1

B4026

A44

26

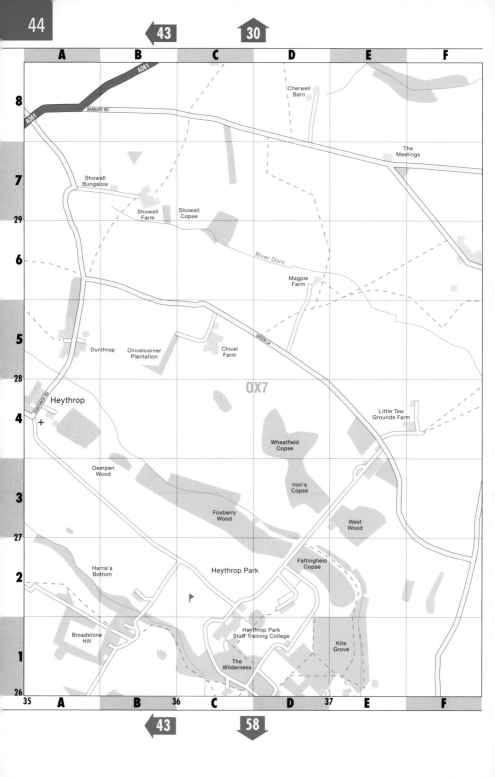

A B C D E F

A361

BANBURY RD

A361

Cherwell
Barn

The
Meetings

8

7

29

Showell
Bungalow

Showell
Farm

Showell
Copse

River Dorn

6

Magpie
Farm

5

28

Dunthrop

Chivelcorner
Plantation

Chivel
Farm

GREEN LA

OX7

Little Tew
Grounds Farm

Heythrop

4

DUNTHROP RD

Deerpen
Wood

Wheatfield
Copse

Iron's
Copse

West
Wood

3

27

Foxberry
Wood

Harris's
Bottom

Heythrop Park

Fattingfield
Copse

2

Broadstone
Hill

Heythrop Park
Staff Training College

Kite
Grove

1

The
Wilderness

26

35 A B 36 C D 37 E F

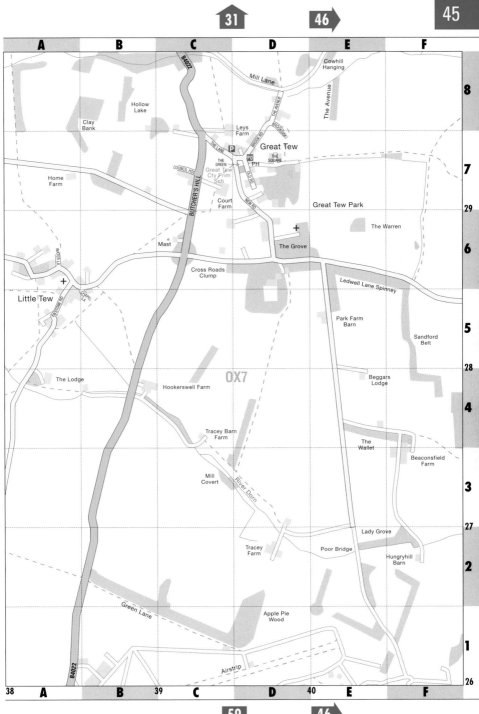

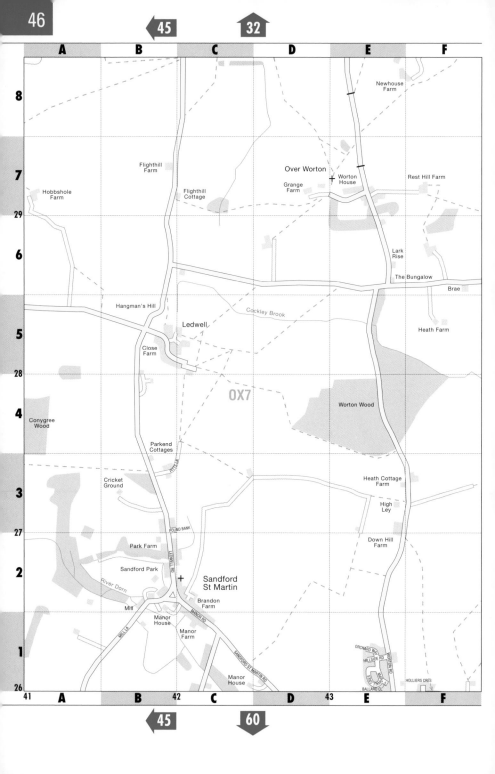

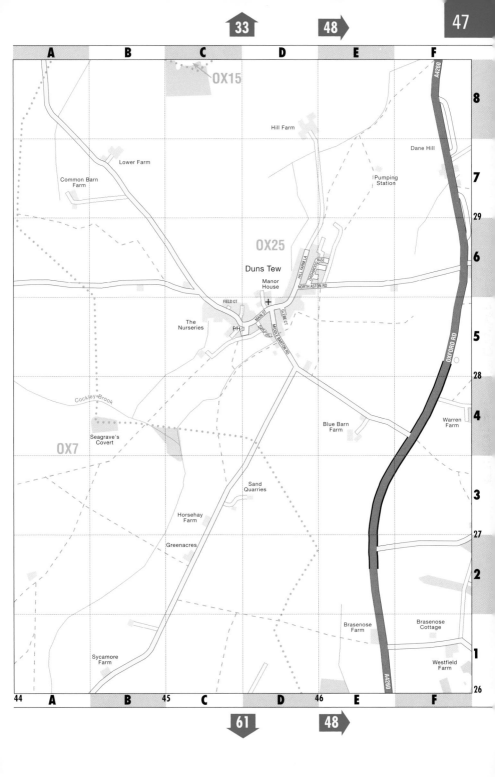

47
34

A **B** **C** **D** **E** **F**

8

Coldharbour Farm

Somerton Lock

Dane Hill Farm

Ram Spinney

Manor House Farm

7

Mill Cottage

Millhouse

Rectory Farm

29

The Green

SOMERTON RD

PO

THE HALL CL

North Aston Hall

North Aston Farm

North Aston

WHARF LA

WATER ST

CHURCH ST

HIGH ST

ANSLEY RD

6

Somerton

The Folly

Jersey Manor Farm

Towing Path

5

River Cherwell

Oxford Canal Walk

Oxford Canal

Hendon Farm

28

MIDDLE ASTON LA

OX25

Warren Copse

Warren Lodge

Grange Farm

LC

Somerton Crossing

4

3

Pig Unit

Middle Aston

27

Middle Aston House

Heyford Common Lock

2

Lakeside Farm

Hatch End Ind Est

The Brambles

1

SHEPHERDS HILL

TENBAY

WATER LA

GRANGE LA

Dr Radcliffe's CE Prim Sch

FIR LA

NORTH SIDE

COW LA

Allen's Lock

ALLEN'S LA

RISING HILL

OLD RECTORY 1 NEW COLLEGE SO 2

MILL LA

HIGH ST

SOMERTON RD

PH

26

47
62

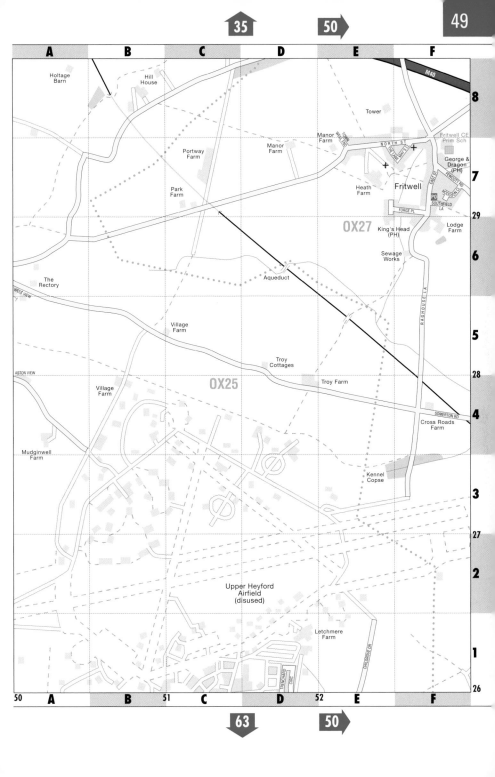

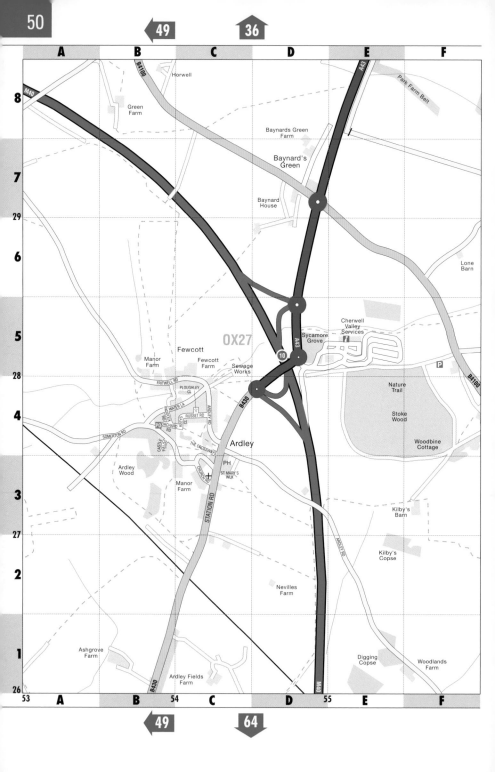

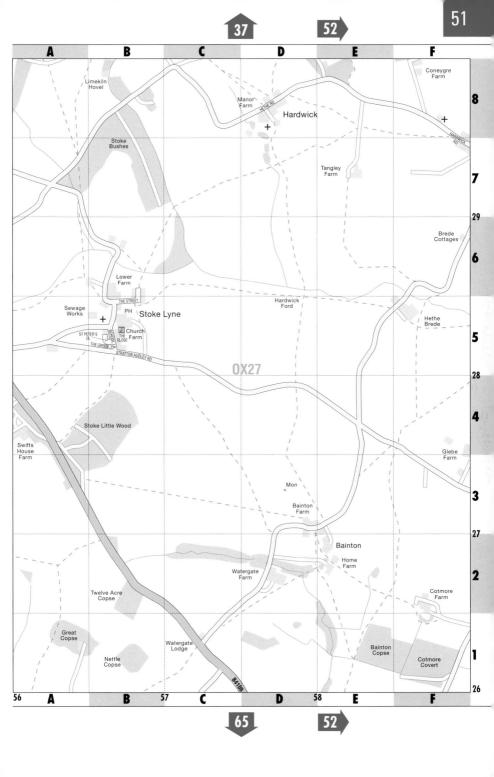

	A	B	C	D	E	F

8

Hethe Lodge

Warins Barn

Willaston Farm

Hethe

PH

MAIN ST

7

Sewage Wks

Montague Farm

Willaston Spinney

Fringford Manor

Poplar Spinney

Newton Morrell

HARDWICK RD

Green Farm

Fringford Bridge

Padbury Brook

MANOR YD

Manor Farm

Hopyard Spinney

BARNTON RD

29

LITTLE PADDOCK

LAURENS

CHURCH

ST MICHAEL'S CL

BU PLACE

Sewage Wks

6

Green Farm

THE GREEN

MAIN ST

Hall Farm

Fringford CE Prim Sch

Fringford Mill

THE LAURELS

Fringford

Mill Race

Hollow Barn

MILL CRES

Butchers Arms (PH)

STRATTON AUDLEY RD

5

Fringfordhill Covert

28

OX27

Fringford Hill

Ivy Cottage

4

The Stable Cottage

Home Farm

Glebe Farm

Stratton Audley Park

Park Cottages

3

Waterloo Farm

27

Crow Barn

Cotmore House

2

Stratton Audley

The Willows Farm

WILLOWS GATE

GLEN D

CHAPEL LN

MAIN ST

Elm Farm

MILL RD

1

WESTON RD

BICESTER RD

STOCK LANE

CAVERSFIELD

STRATTON AUDLEY MANOR

PO

PH

Manor Farm

26

Hall Farm

LAUNTON RD

A4421

| 59 | A | 60 | C | D | 61 | E | F |

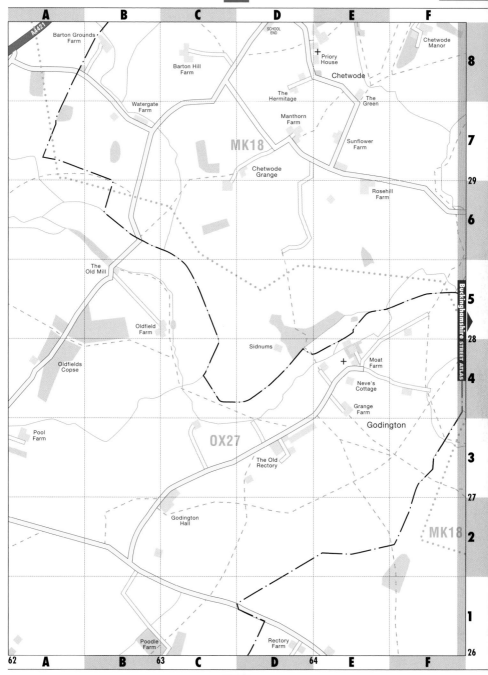

39

A B C D E F

A421

Barton Grounds
Farm

Chetwode
Manor

8

Barton Hill
Farm

Priory
House

Chetwode

Watergate
Farm

The
Hermitage

The
Green

MK18

Manthorn
Farm

7

Sunflower
Farm

Chetwode
Grange

29

Rosehill
Farm

6

The
Old Mill

Buckinghamshire STREET ATLAS

5

Oldfield
Farm

Sidnums

28

Oldfields
Copse

Moat
Farm

4

Neve's
Cottage

Pool
Farm

Grange
Farm

Godington

OX27

3

The Old
Rectory

27

Godington
Hall

MK18

2

1

Poodle
Farm

Rectory
Farm

26

62 A B 63 C D 64 E F

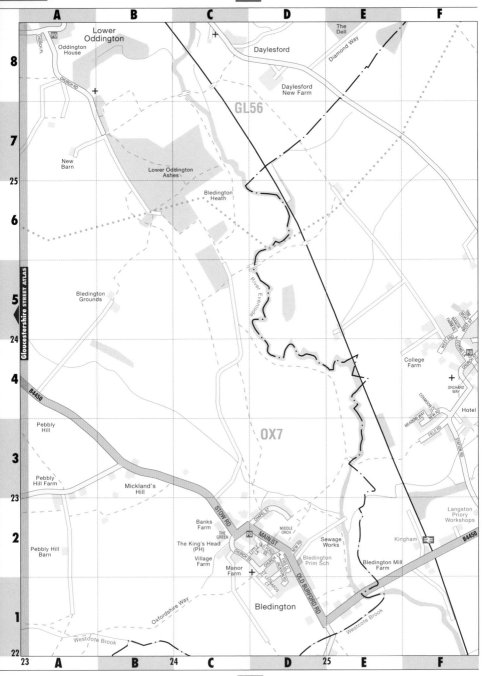

A   B   C   D   E   F

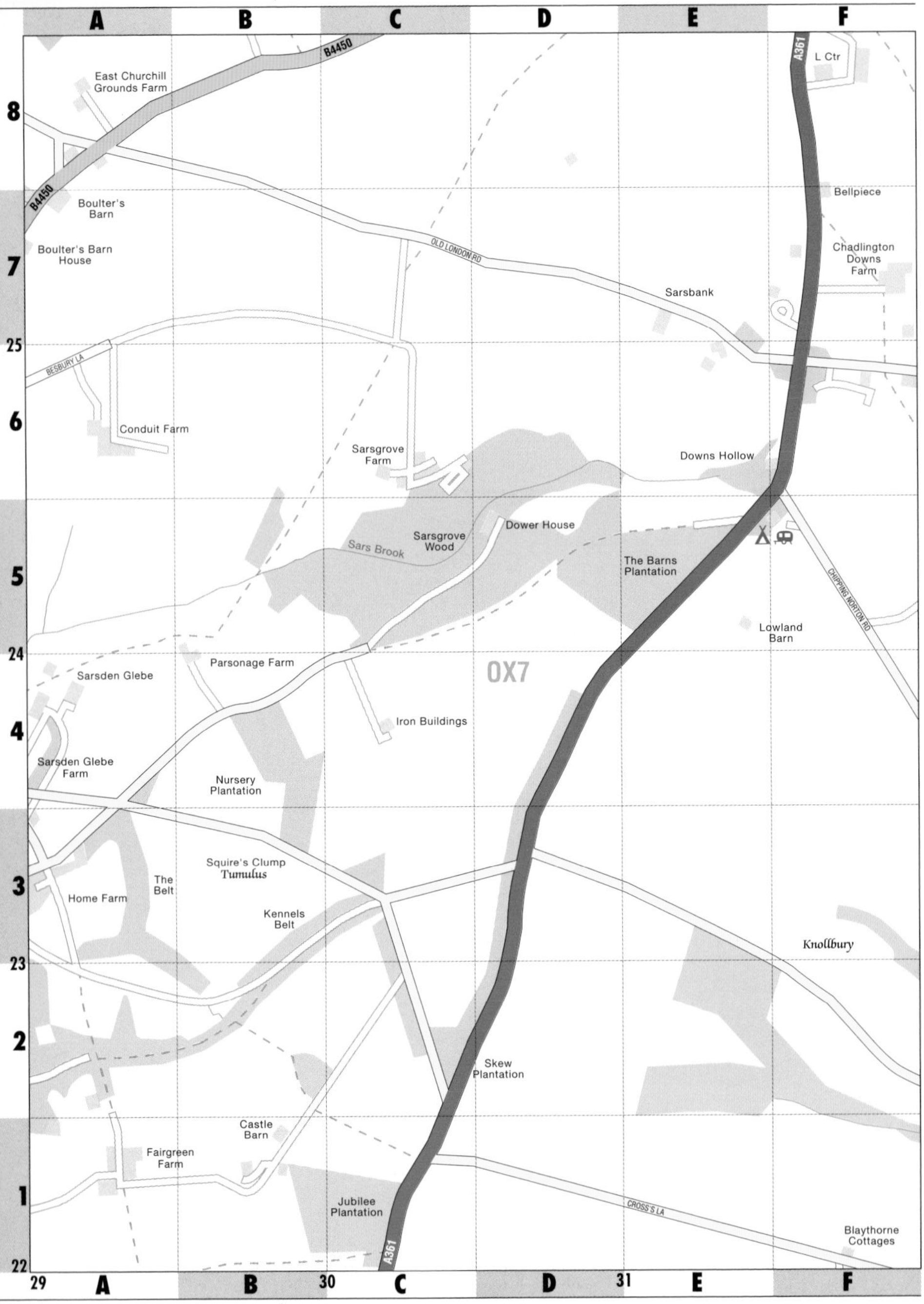

8

B4450

East Churchill
Grounds Farm

L Ctr

A361

7

B4450

Boulter's
Barn

Boulter's Barn
House

OLD LONDON RD

Sarsbank

Bellpiece

Chadlington
Downs
Farm

25

BEGBURY LA

6

Conduit Farm

Sarsgrove
Farm

Downs Hollow

5

Sars Brook

Sarsgrove
Wood

Dower House

The Barns
Plantation

Lowland
Barn

CHIPPING NORTON RD

24

Sarsden Glebe

Parsonage Farm

OX7

4

Sarsden Glebe
Farm

Iron Buildings

Nursery
Plantation

3

Home Farm

The
Belt

Squire's Clump
Tumulus

Kennels
Belt

Knollbury

23

2

Skew
Plantation

1

Castle
Barn

Fairgreen
Farm

Jubilee
Plantation

A361

CROSS'S LA

Blaythorne
Cottages

22

29   A   B   30   C   D   31   E   F

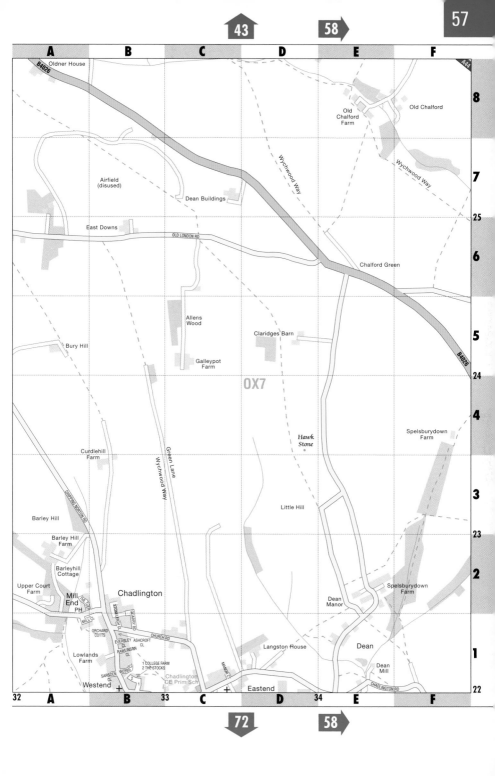

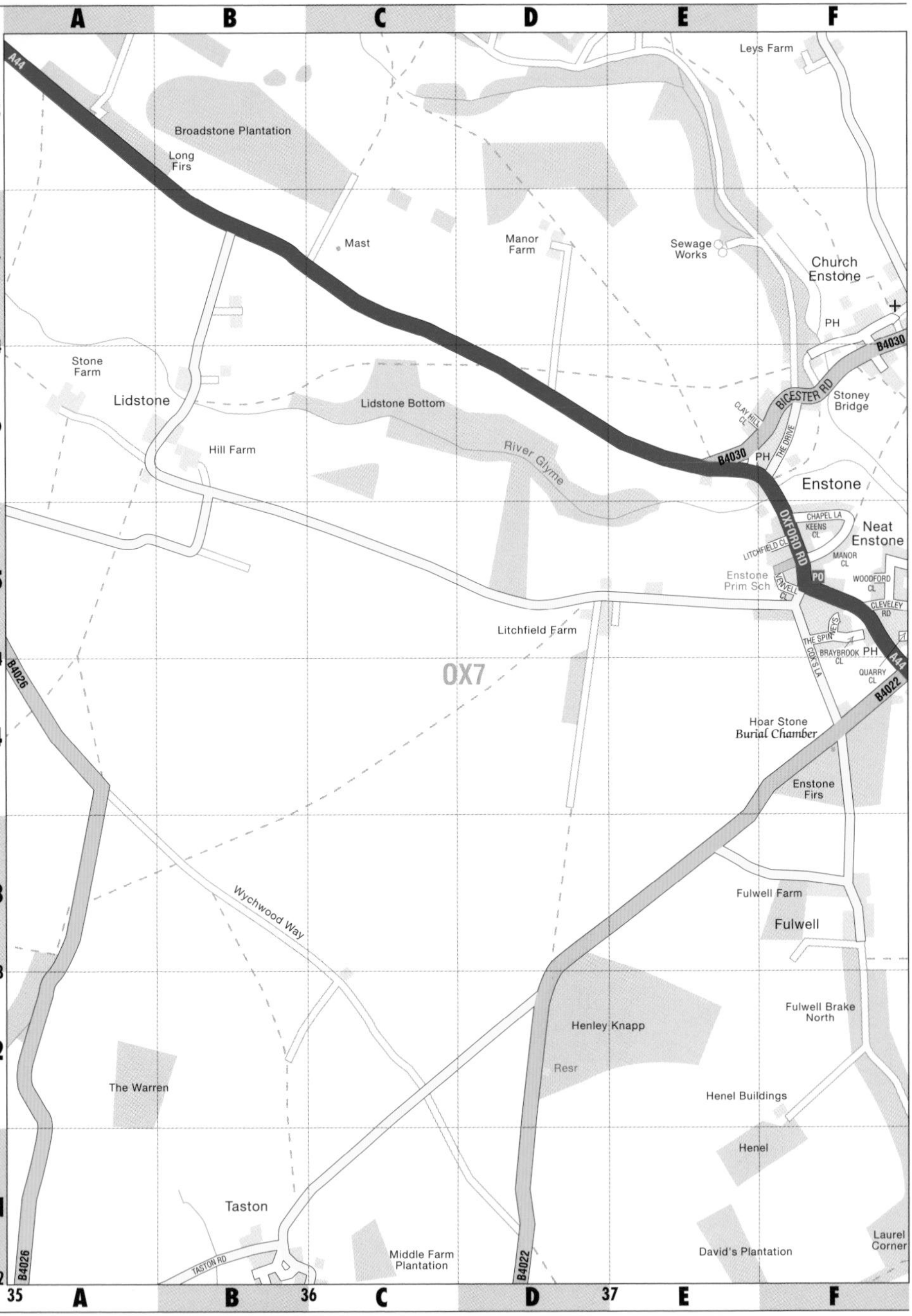

A B C D E F

8
Leys Farm
Broadstone Plantation
Long Firs
24
Mast
Manor Farm
Sewage Works
Church Enstone
PH
B4030
7
Stone Farm
Lidstone
Lidstone Bottom
River Glyme
Stoney Bridge
CLAY HILL CL
BICESTER RD
THE RYPE
6
Hill Farm
B4030
PH
Enstone
KEENS CL
CHAPEL LA
OXFORD RD
Neat Enstone
MANOR CL
LITCHFIELD CL
Enstone Prim Sch
YOXELL
PO
WOODFORD CL
CLEVELEY RD
5
Litchfield Farm
THE SPINE
BRAYBROOK
COCK LA
PH
QUARRY CL
A44
24
B4026
OX7
Hoar Stone
Burial Chamber
B4022
4
Enstone Firs
Wychwood Way
Fulwell Farm
Fulwell
3
23
Fulwell Brake North
Henley Knapp
Resr
2
The Warren
Henel Buildings
Henel
Taston
1
Laurel Corner
B4026
David's Plantation
PASTON RD
Middle Farm Plantation
B4022
22
35 A B 36 C D 37 E F

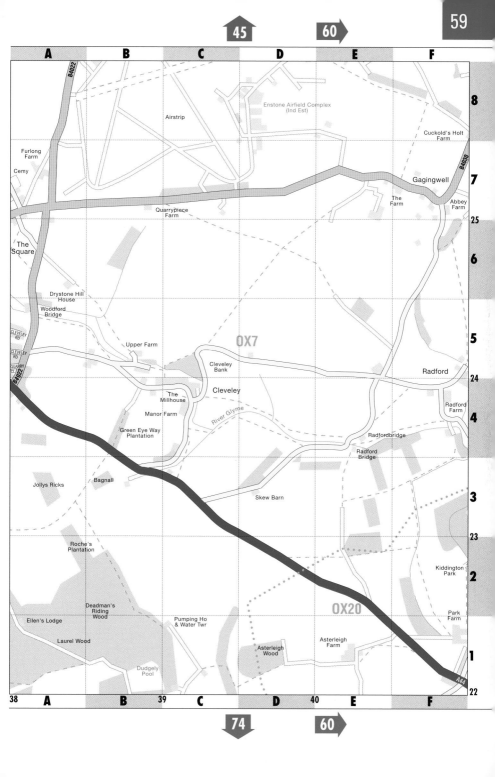

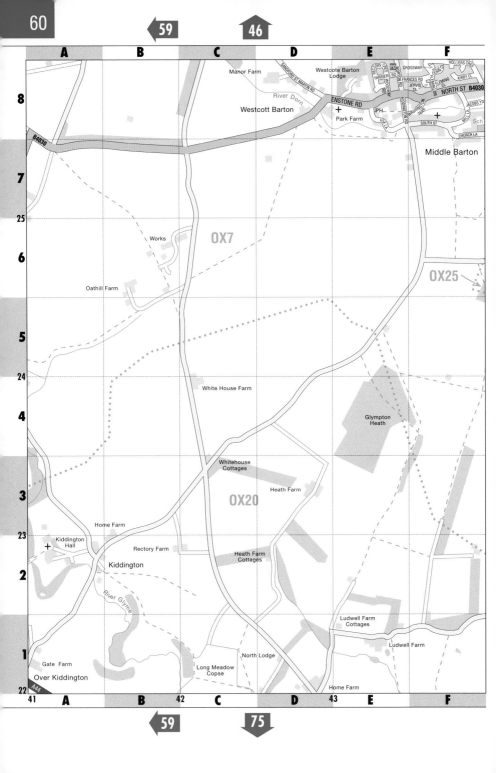

59
46

A **B** **C** **D** **E** **F**

8

Manor Farm

River Dorn

Westcote Barton
Lodge

HOLLIERS CRS

PRIORY CL
RECTORY
FARRERS RD FRANCES RD
CL MOWBRAY
RD

CROSSWAY

FLEMING
PL

KIRBY CL

JERVIS
PL
CL

ENSTONE RD

NORTH ST B4030

JACOBS YD

Westcott Barton

B4030

WASHINGTON

KIDDINGTON RD

TOLL

+

Park Farm

PH

SOUTH ST

CHURCHILL DR

MILL ST

Sch

CHURCH LA

Middle Barton

7

OX7

25

Works

6

OX25

Oathill Farm

5

24

White House Farm

4

Glympton
Heath

Whitehouse
Cottages

3

Heath Farm

OX20

Home Farm

23

Kiddington
Hall

+

Rectory Farm

Heath Farm
Cottages

2

Kiddington

River Glyme

Ludwell Farm
Cottages

Ludwell Farm

1

Gate Farm

North Lodge

Over Kiddington

Long Meadow
Copse

Home Farm

22

A84

41 **A** **B** **42** **C** **D** **43** **E** **F**

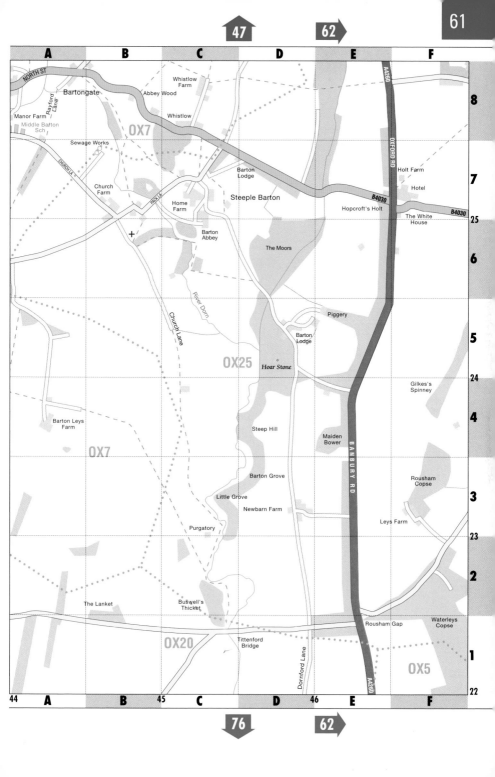

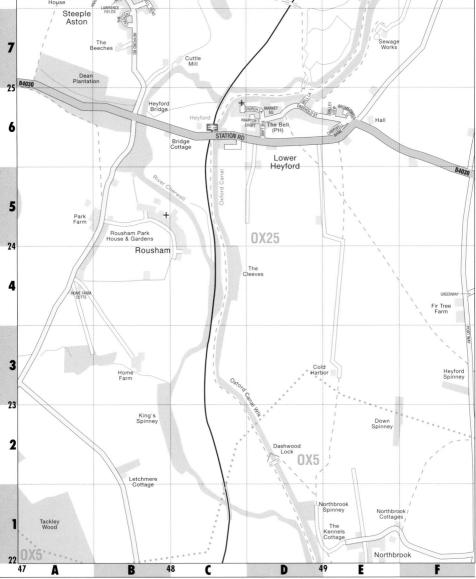

Hill Ho.
The Red Lion (PH)
Seven Springs House
Steeple Aston
The Beeches
Dean Plantation
B4030
Cuttle Mill
Cow Lane

Upper Heyford
ALLENS LA
HIGH ST
THE GREEN
CAMP RD
SOMERTON RD
ORCHARD
Sewage Works

Heyford Bridge
Heyford
Bridge Cottage
STATION RD
CHURCH LA
MARKET SQ
KNAPTON'S CROFT
THE LANE
The Bell (PH)
FREEHOLD ST
MILL LA
VALLEY VIEW
BROMESWELL
CHERWELL BANK
Hall
B4030
Lower Heyford

Park Farm
Rousham Park House & Gardens
Rousham
River Cherwell
Oxford Canal
OX25

Home Farm Cotts
Home Farm
The Cleeves
GREENWAY
Fir Tree Farm
PORT WAY
Heyford Spinney

King's Spinney
Oxford Canal Wlk
Cold Harbor
Down Spinney
23

Letchmere Cottage
Dashwood Lock
OX5
Northbrook Spinney
Northbrook Cottages

Tackley Wood
OX5
The Kennels Cottage
Northbrook

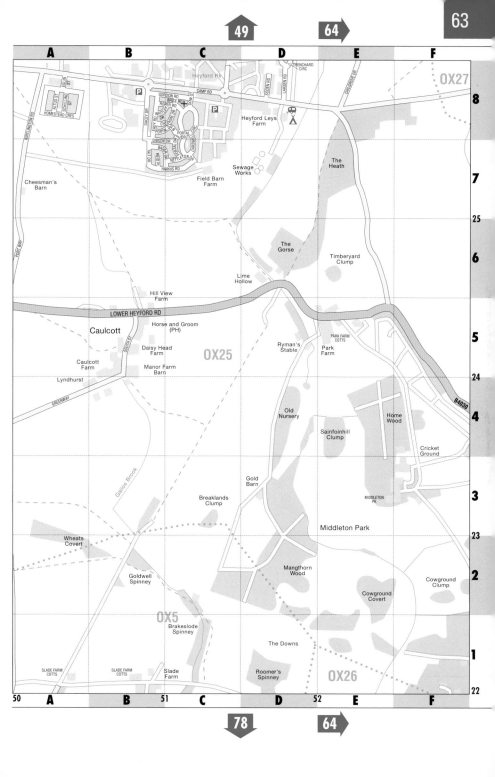

| | A | B | C | D | E | F |

8

OX27

Homelands
Farm

Home
Farm

PH

7

25

Birch
Spinney

Manor
Farm

Trow
Pool

Trowpool La

Swallowfield
Farm

Grunthill
Copse

6

Trowpool
Spinney

Wr
Twr

Crowmarsh
Farm

Gagle Brook

5

Manor Farm
Cottages

Dewars
Farm

24

OX25

Burntclose
Copse

Bucknell Lodge

4

HEYFORD RD

Sewage
Works

Jersey Arms
(PH)

BULLMARSH

BICESTER RD

Linkslade

Rectory
Farm House

Middleton
Stoney

Lovelynch
House

3 +

23

OX26

B4030

The
Belt

Big Covert

2

Bignell Park

Chesterton Fields
Farm

Bignell Park
Farm

1

Old
Covert

Bignell
House

Swiss
Cottage

A4095

A4095

22

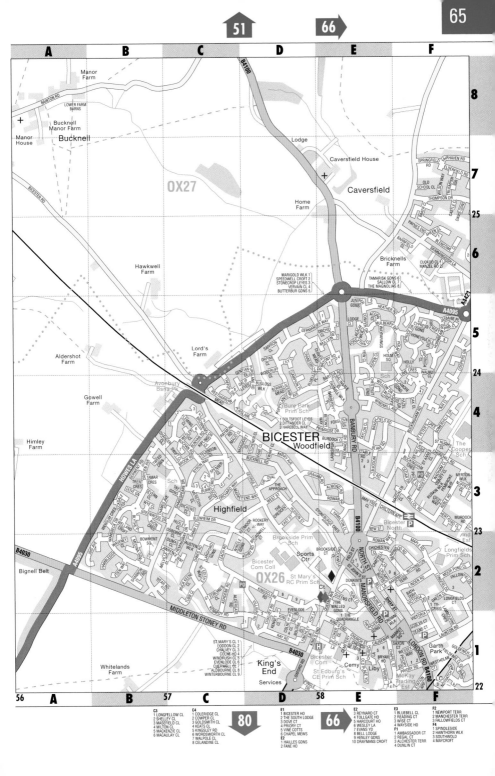

A B C D E F

8
7
25
6
5
24
4
3
23
2
1
22

OX27

Manor Farm

LOWER FARM BARNS
Bucknell Manor Farm
Manor House
Bucknell
BICESTER RD

Lodge

Caversfield House

Home Farm

Caversfield

SPRINGFIELD RD
WARHAVEN RD
ELLNERFIELD RD
OLD SCHOOL
WILSON WAY
THOMPSON DR

PAYNES END

Bricknells Farm

CUCKOO CL 1
MANZEL RD 2

TAMARISK GDNS 6
SALLOW CL 7
THE MAGNOLIAS 8.

MARIGOLD WLK 1
SPEEDWELL CROFT 2
STONECROP LEYES 3
VERVAIN CL 4
BUTTERBUR GDNS 5.

A4421
A4095

Hawkwell Farm

Lord's Farm

Avonbury Bsns Pk

Aldershot Farm

Gowell Farm

Himley Farm

Bure Park Prim Sch

1 COLTSFOOT LEYES
2 DITTANDER CL
3 HAREBELL WAY

BICESTER
Woodfield

BANBURY RD

HOWES LA

Sch

Highfield

The Oval

THE APPROACH

The Green

Brookside Prim Sch

Sports Ctr

Bicester Com Coll

OX26

St Mary's RC Prim Sch

NORTH ST
MANDSFIELD RD

Bicester North

Longfields Prim Sch

B4100

B4030

A4095

Bignell Belt

MIDDLETON STONEY RD

Whitelands Farm

ST MARY'S CL 1
LODDON CL 2
CHALVEY CL 3
COLNE HO 4
WINDRUSH CL 5
EVENLODE CL 6
CHERWELL CL 7
ALDBOURNE CL 8
WINTERBOURNE CL 9.

King's End

Bicester Com

St Edburg's CE Prim Sch

Cemy

Liby

Garth Park

LONDON RD
B4100

McKay Trading Est

Services

C3
1 LONGFELLOW CL
2 SHELLEY CL
3 MASEFIELD CL
4 MILTON CL
5 MACKENZIE CL
6 MACAULAY CL

C4
1 COLERIDGE CL
2 COWPER CL
3 GOLDSMITH CL
4 KEATS CL
5 KINGSLEY RD
6 WORDSWORTH CL
7 WALPOLE CL
8 CELANDINE CL

E1
1 BICESTER HO
2 THE SOUTH LODGE
3 DOVE CT
4 PRIORY CT
5 VINE COTTS
6 CHAPEL MEWS
E2
1 HAILLES GDNS
2 FANE HO

E2
3 REYNARD CT
4 TOLLGATE HO
5 HARCOURT HO
6 WESLEY LA
7 EVANS YD
8 BELL LODGE
9 HENLEY GDNS
10 DRAYMANS CROFT

E3
1 BLUEBELL CT
2 READING CT
3 WISE CT
4 WAYSIDE HO
F1
1 AMBASSADOR CT
2 REGAL CT
3 ALCHESTER RD
4 DUNLIN CT

F2
1 NEWPORT TERR
2 MANCHESTER TERR
3 FALLOWFIELDS CT
F4
1 SPINDLESIDE
2 HAWTHORN WLK
3 SOUTHWOLD
4 MAYCROFT

A B C D E F

8

Dymock's Farm

Fringford Lodge

Hall

The Kennels

West Farm

Sewage Works

Brashfield House

FAIRHAVEN RD

CHERWOOD HOUSE COTTS

Quarry

BICESTER RD

THE BRAMBLES

LAUNTON RD

7

OX27

25

A4421

6

1 GRIFFITHS GDNS
2 MANZEL RD
3 SKIMMINGDISH LA

Airfield

Field Barn

A4421

5

COOPERS GN

WARWICK CT 1
GAYDON WLK 2
HERALD WAY 3
SHACKLETON CL 4
LYSANDER CL 5

24

Bardwell Sch

SKIMMINGDISH LA

Glory Farm Prim Sch

4

The Cooper Sch

BICESTER

OX26

LC

3

1 SPITFIRE CL
2 STERLING CL
3 BEAUFORT CL
4 MERTON WLK

Folly Cottage

STATION RD

23

Launton Bsns Ctr

GRANVILLE WAY

LC

Manor Farm

Launton CE Prim Sch

Grange Farm

GRANGE MEWS

BLENHEIM DR

2

Ind Est

CHARBRIDGE LA

BICESTER RD

THE CLOSE

SHERWOOD RD

SYCAMORE RD

ANGLE AVE

LANES END

SHARPES COTTS

Tubb's Crossing

CHARBRIDGE WAY

FOREST CL

THE POPLARS

PH

A4421

Launton

1 MERGANSER DR
2 HERON CT
3 FALCON MEAD
4 SANDPIPER CL
5 THE BUNTINGS
6 GREBE RD
7 GOLDFINCH CL

1

CHAFFINCH RD

GARMAN DR

HERALD DR

WEST LEA

CHESTNUT CL

WEST RD

BLACKTHORN RD

22

59 A B 60 C D 61 E F

53

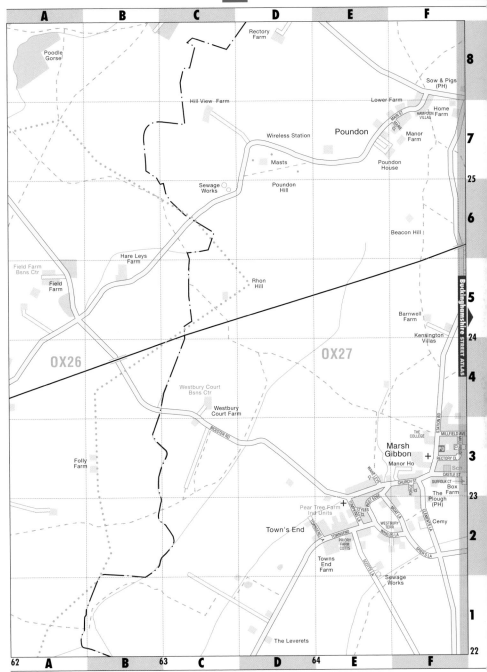

Poodle Gorse

Rectory Farm

Sow & Pigs (PH)

Hill View Farm

Lower Farm

Home Farm

HAMPDEN VILLAS

MAIN ST

Wireless Station

Poundon

Manor Farm

Masts

Poundon House

Sewage Works

Poundon Hill

Beacon Hill

Hare Leys Farm

Rhon Hill

Field Farm Bsns Ctr

Field Farm

Barnwell Farm

Kensington Villas

OX26

OX27

Westbury Court Bsns Ctr

Westbury Court Farm

BICESTER RD

STATION RD

THE COLLEGE

MILLFIELD AVE

Marsh Gibbon

Manor Ho

RECTORY CL

Sch

CASTLE ST

SUFFOLK CT

Folly Farm

Box Farm

WARE LEYS CL

CHURCH ST

The Plough (PH)

Pear Tree Farm Ind Units

Cemy

TUCKING CL

STYLES CL

WEST EDGE

MARSH LA

CLEMENTS LA

WESTBURY TERR

Town's End

PRIORY FARM COTTS

MYDHLES LA

TOWNSEND LA

Priory Farm Cotts

Towns End Farm

SCOTTS LA

SPIRES LA

Sewage Works

The Leverets

GL54

OX7

A424 Stow-on-the-Wold (A429)

Gloucestershire STREET ATLAS

Booth's Barn

Westcote Brook

Gawcombe

Oxfordshire Way

Diamond Way

Diamond Way

Wyck Beacon Farm

Gawcombe Woods

Wyck Beacon

Hawkwell

Court Hayes Farm

Church Westcote

THE CONVENT

BURTONS BANK

New Inn (PH)

Nether Westcote

Far Hill Coppice

DE HAVILLAND RD

Far Hill Barn

Bunting's Hill Copse

Little Glebe Farm

Upper Rissington

SNIPE RD

SANDY LA

Brookfield

Peak's Coppice

Ansell's Hill Coppice

Westcote Hill

Idbury

A424

Collier's Hill Barn

SANDY LANE CT

SOUTH GATE CT

GL54

Upper Rissington Sens Pk

Workham Farm

Workham Bottom

Little Rissington Airfield (disused)

Limekiln Plantation

Ram Plantation

Warren Farm

20 A B 21 C D 22 E F

8 21 7 6 20 5 4 3 19 2 18 1

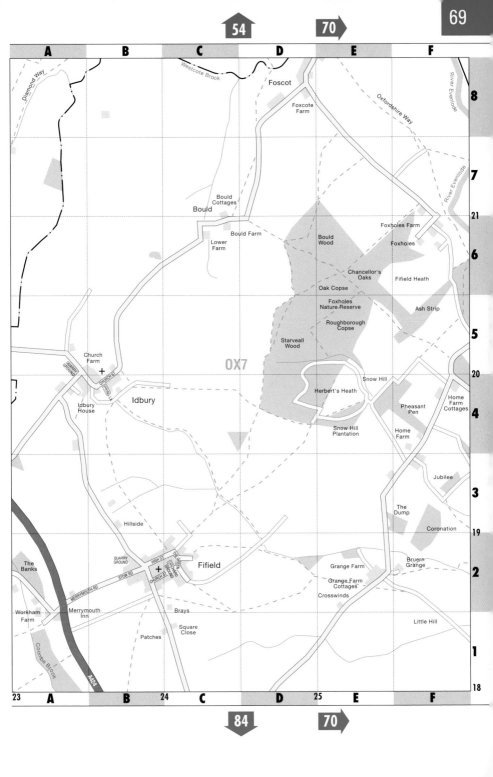

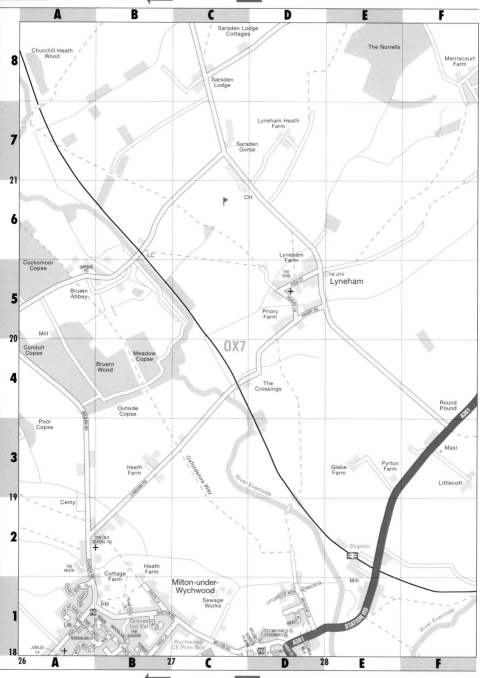

A **B** **C** **D** **E** **F**

8

Churchill Heath Wood

Sarsden Lodge Cottages

The Norrells

Merriscourt Farm

7

Sarsden Lodge

Lyneham Heath Farm

21

Sarsden Gorse

CH

6

Lyneham Farm

LC

Cocksmoor Copse

GARAGE YD

THE ROW

HIGH ST

THE LEYS

Lyneham

5

Bruern Abbey

PRIORY LA

Priory Farm

PRIORY RD

Mill

20

Conduit Copse

Meadow Copse

OX7

4

Bruern Wood

The Crossings

Round Pound

A361

Outside Copse

3

Pool Copse

Heath Farm

Oxfordshire Way

River Evenlode

Glebe Farm

Pyrton Farm

Mast

Littlecott

BRUERN RD

LYNEHAM RD

19

Cemy

2

THE OLD SCHOOL HO

Shipton

Mill

River Evenlode

THE HEATH

CHURCH RD

Cottage Farm

Heath Farm

Milton-under-Wychwood

GREEN LA

SHIPTON RD

Sewage Works

PEAR TREE

REYNOLDS CL

STATION RD

1

PH

PO

Lib

JUBILEE LA

WYCH WOOD

Groves Ind Est

THE SQUARE

GREENLANDS

FROG LA

Wychwood CE Prim Sch

MILTON RD

LITTLEBROOK MDW

1ST MICHAELS CL 2 COOMBES CL

WILLOW

PO

2

MEAD CL

MEADOW LT

HIGH ST

A361

18

26 A 27 B C 28 D E F

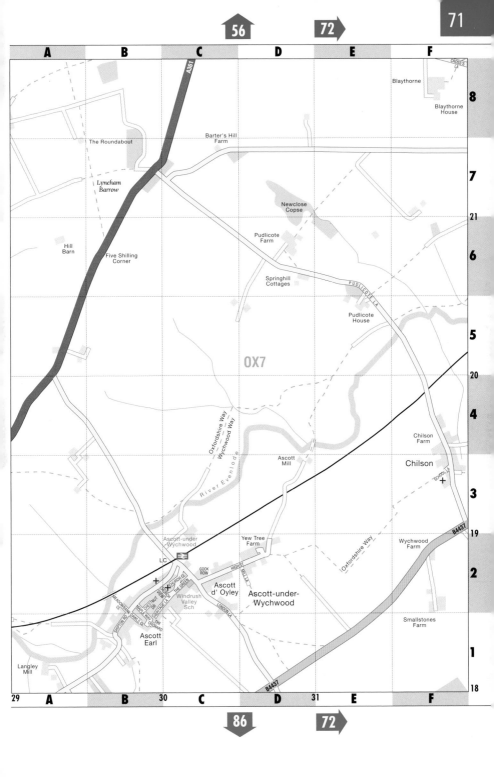

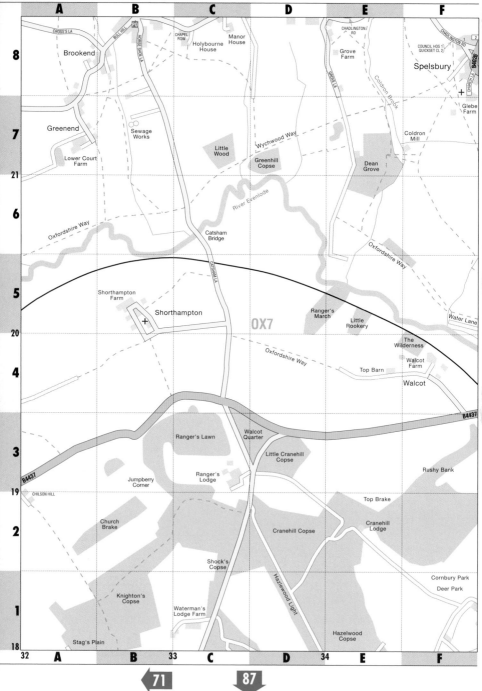

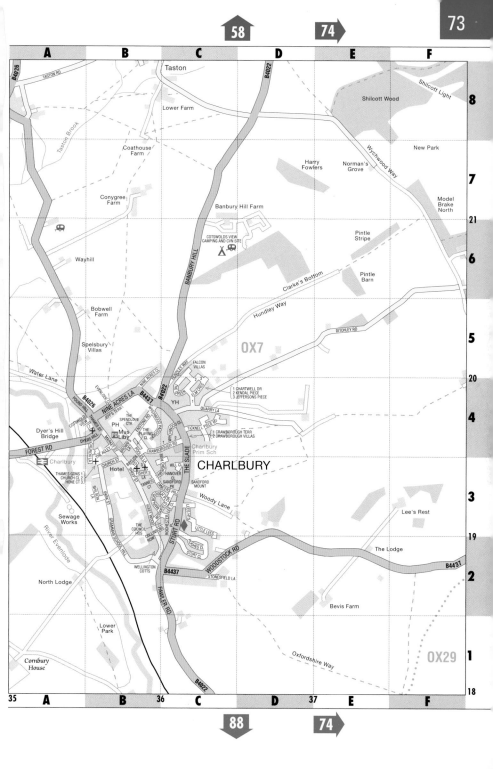

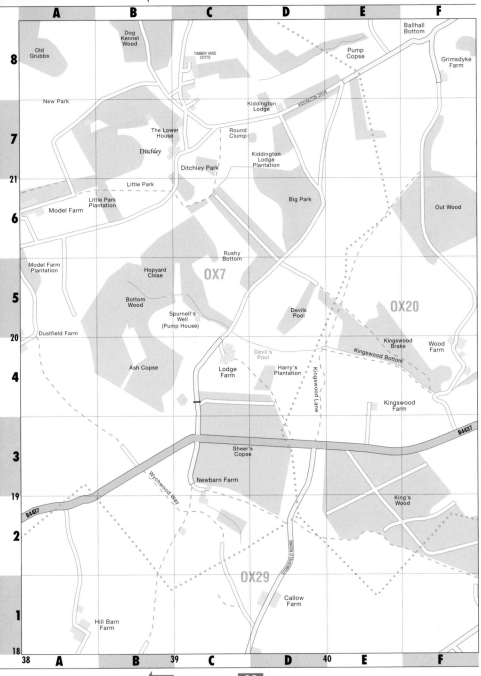

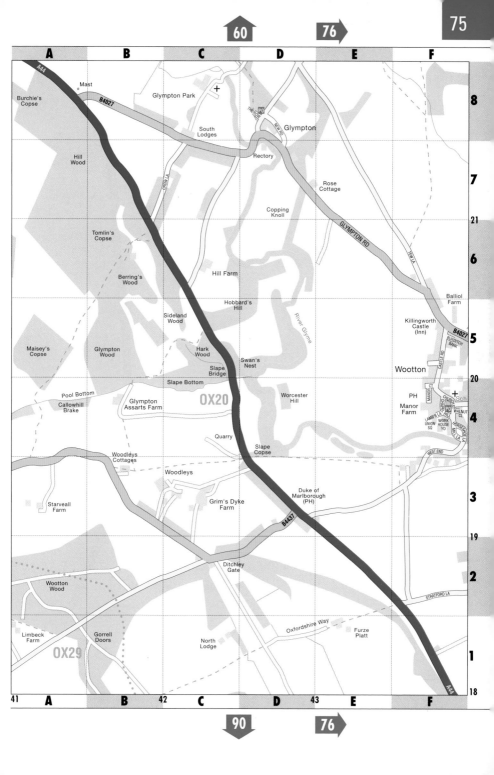

75
61

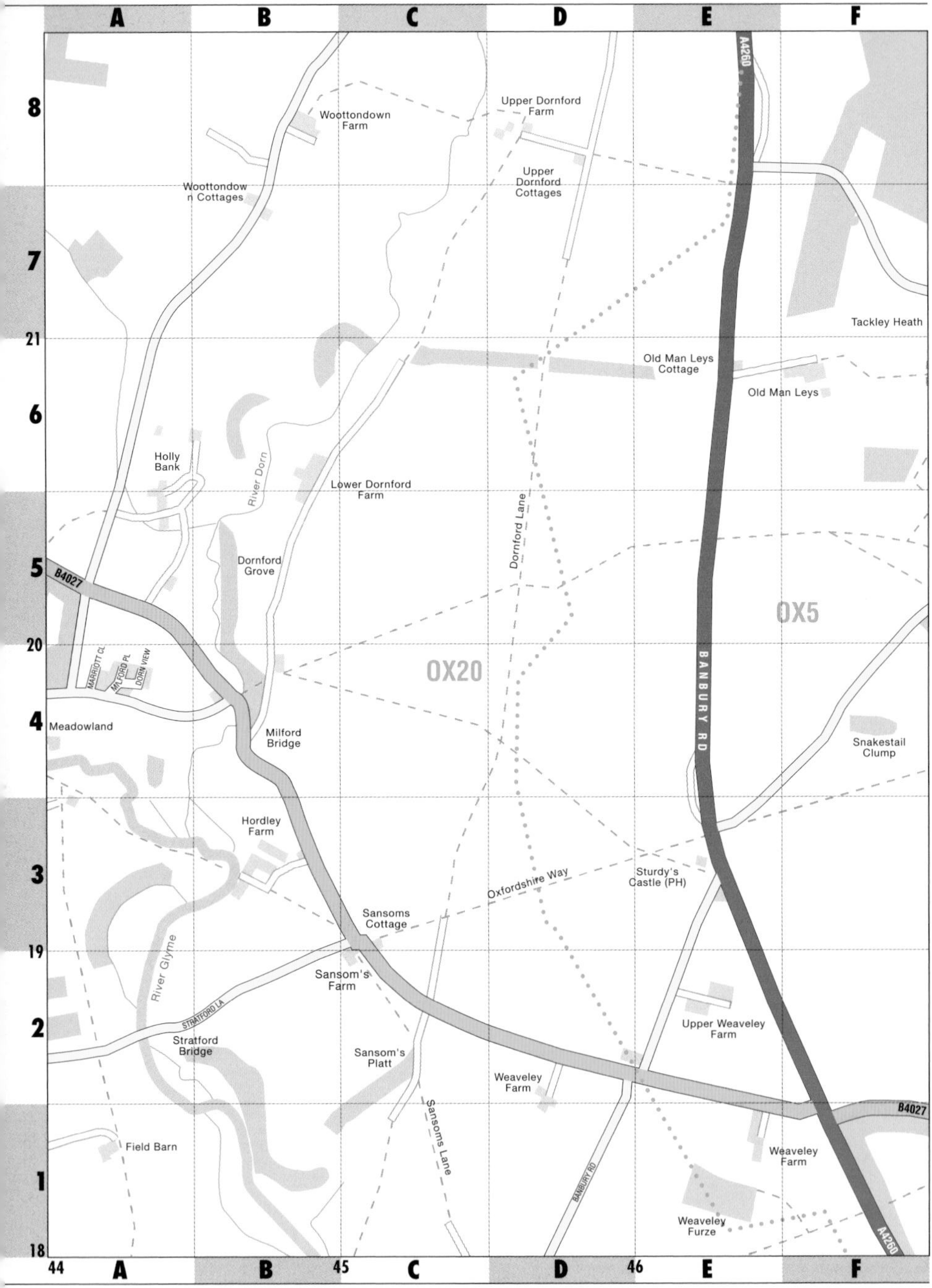

A **B** **C** **D** **E** **F**

8

Woottondown Farm

Upper Dornford Farm

Woottondown Cottages

Upper Dornford Cottages

7

Tackley Heath

21

Old Man Leys Cottage

Old Man Leys

6

Holly Bank

River Dorn

Lower Dornford Farm

5

B4027

Dornford Grove

Dornford Lane

OX5

20

MARRIOTT CL

ORCHARD PL

DORN VIEW

OX20

4

Meadowland

Milford Bridge

Snakestail Clump

Hordley Farm

3

Oxfordshire Way

Sturdy's Castle (PH)

Sansoms Cottage

19

River Glyme

STRATFORD LA

Sansom's Farm

2

Stratford Bridge

Sansom's Platt

Upper Weaveley Farm

Weaveley Farm

Field Barn

Sansoms Lane

BANBURY RD

B4027

1

Weaveley Farm

Weaveley Furze

A4260

18

44 **A** **B** 45 **C** **D** 46 **E** **F**

A4260

BANBURY RD

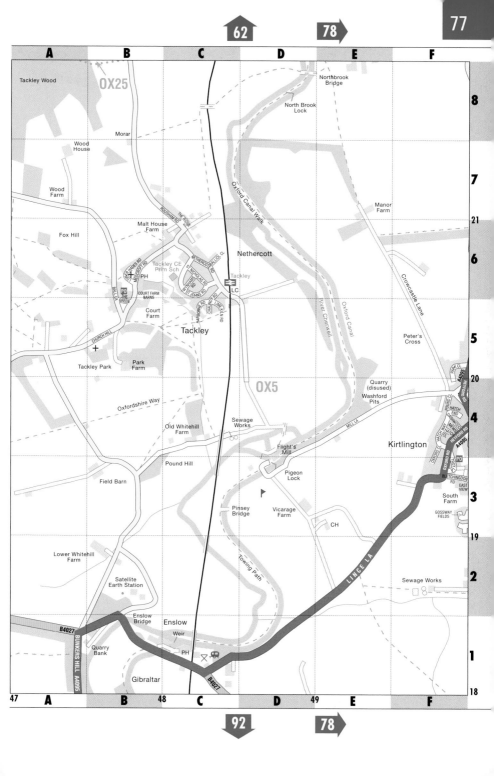

77
63

A **B** **C** **D** **E** **F**

8

Middleton Park

OX25

Hoarstone Spinney

Gallas Brook

Greatfield Spinney

Stud Farm

OX26

7

Cranmoor Plantation

PORT WAY

The Grove

21

Weston Bsns Pk

The Bushes

6

Werghill Copse

Gallos Brook

HEYFORD RD

Polo Ground

Park Farm

Gallosbrook Plantation

Kemsley Barn

LANDSCAPE CL

Mill Mound

5

1 AKEMAN CL
2 FOXTOWNS GN

Kirtlington Park

Home Farm

A4095

20

PH

THE CHESTNUTS

Cockshot Copse

OX5

Stonepit Hills

4

Kirtlington CE Prim Sch

Kirtlington Park

SOUTH GN

Long Plantation

OX25

Manor House Farm

CHURCH LA

SOUTHEND COTTS

Oxfordshire Way

3

Walkers Farm Buildings

BLETCHINGDON RD

Stonehouse Farm

GOSSWAY FIELDS

19

Kirtlington Park

Cordle Bushes

2

Winterlake

Cordle Door

Brookside Farm

Newbridge Farm

SPRINGHILL HILL

1

Ash Wood

Bletchingdon Park

TOLLBROOK CNR

CHURCH LA

Staplehurst Farm

18

50 **A** **B** 51 **C** **D** 52 **E** **F**

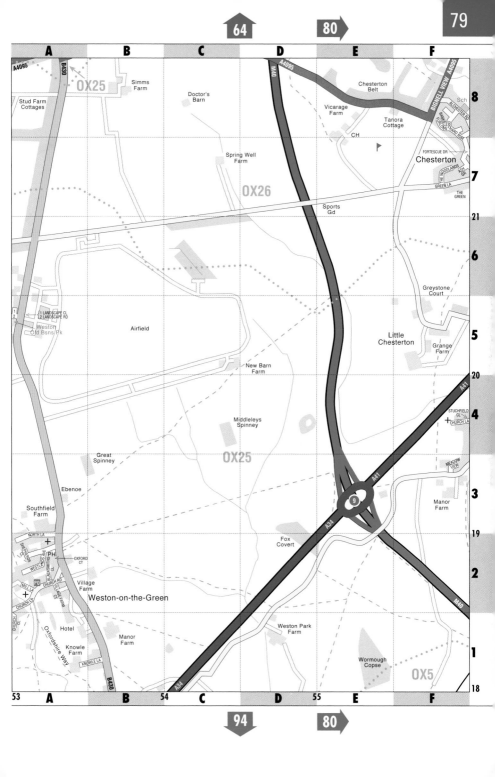

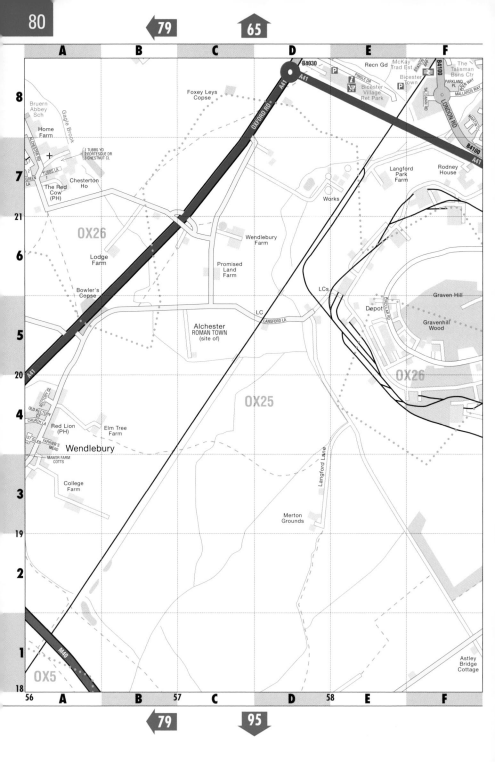

A B C D E F

8

7

21

6

5

20

4

3

19

2

1

18

56 A B 57 C D 58 E F

B4030

Recn Gd

McKay
Trad Est

The
Talisman
Bsns Ctr

PINGLE DR

Bicester
Village
Ret Park

Bicester
Town

PARKLAND
PL

MALLARDS WAY

B4100

LONDON RD

A41

B4100

A41

Foxey Leys
Copse

OXFORD RD

A41

Langford
Park
Farm

Rodney
House

Bruern
Abbey
Sch

Home
Farm

Gagle Brook

1 TUBBS YD
2 FORTESCUE DR
3 CHESTNUT CL

Works

GREEN
LA

Chesterton
Ho

TUBBS LA

The Red
Cow
(PH)

ALCHESTER RD

OX26

Lodge
Farm

Wendlebury
Farm

Promised
Land
Farm

LCs

Graven Hill

Bowler's
Copse

LC

Depot

Gravenhill
Wood

Alchester
ROMAN TOWN
(site of)

LANGFORD LA.

FIRCLE RD

OX26

A41

Red Lion
(PH)

OLD RECTORY
CT

RECTORY CL

CHURCH LA

ST GILES
CL

FARRIER'S
CL

Elm Tree
Farm

OX25

FARRIER'S
MEAD

Wendlebury

MANOR FARM
COTTS

College
Farm

Langford Lane

Merton
Grounds

M40

OX5

Astley
Bridge
Cottage

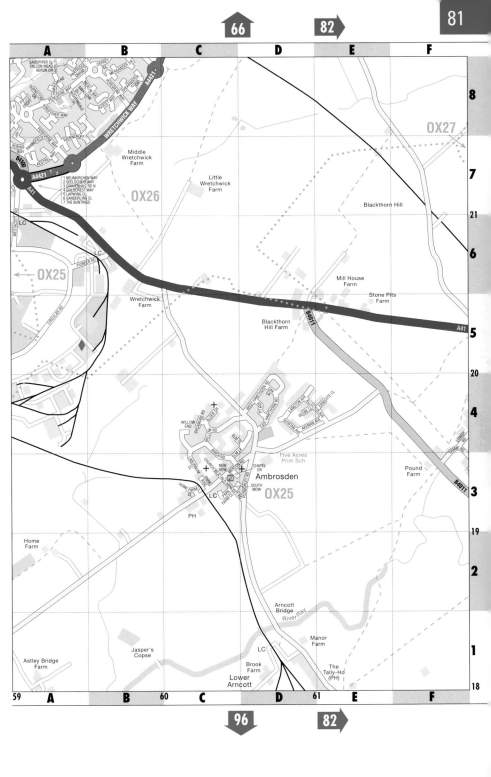

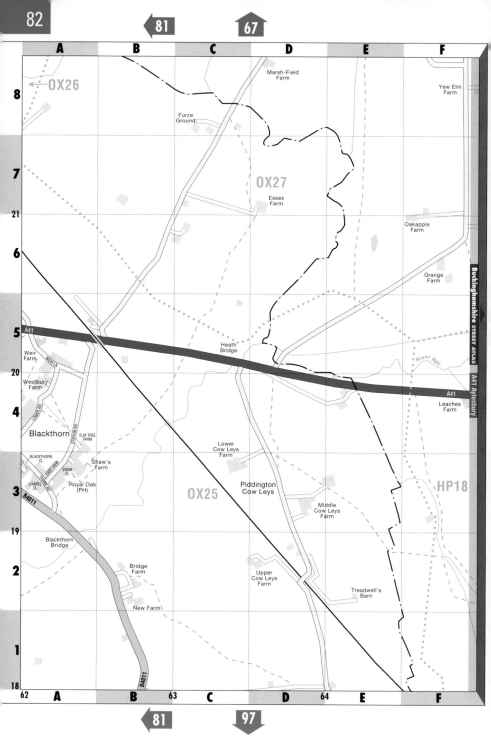

Buckinghamshire STREET ATLAS

OX26

Marsh-Field
Farm

Furze
Ground

Yew Elm
Farm

OX27

Essex
Farm

Oakapple
Farm

Grange
Farm

A41

Weir
Farm

Heath
Bridge

River Ray

Westbury
Farm

A41

Leaches
Farm

Blackthorn

ELM TREE
FARM

Lower
Cow Leys
Farm

HP18

BLACKTHORN
CL

Shaw's
Farm

SWAN
CL

Piddington
Cow Leys

CHAPEL
CL

Royal Oak
(PH)

OX25

Middle
Cow Leys
Farm

B4011

Blackthorn
Bridge

Bridge
Farm

Upper
Cow Leys
Farm

Treadwell's
Barn

New Farm

B4011

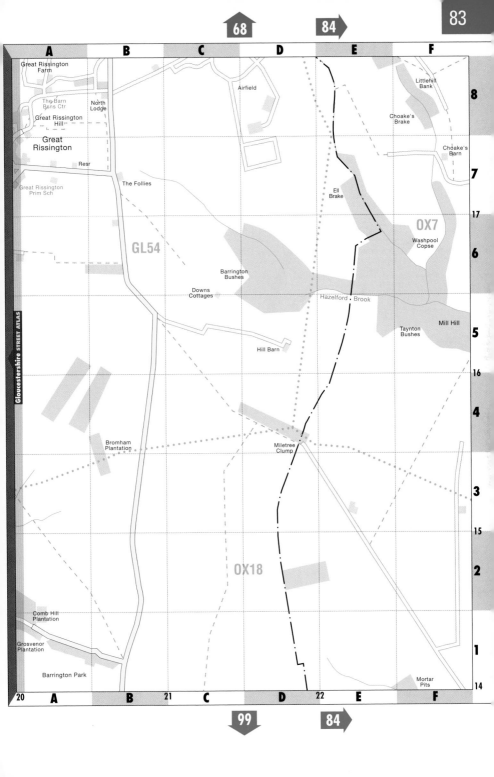

83
69

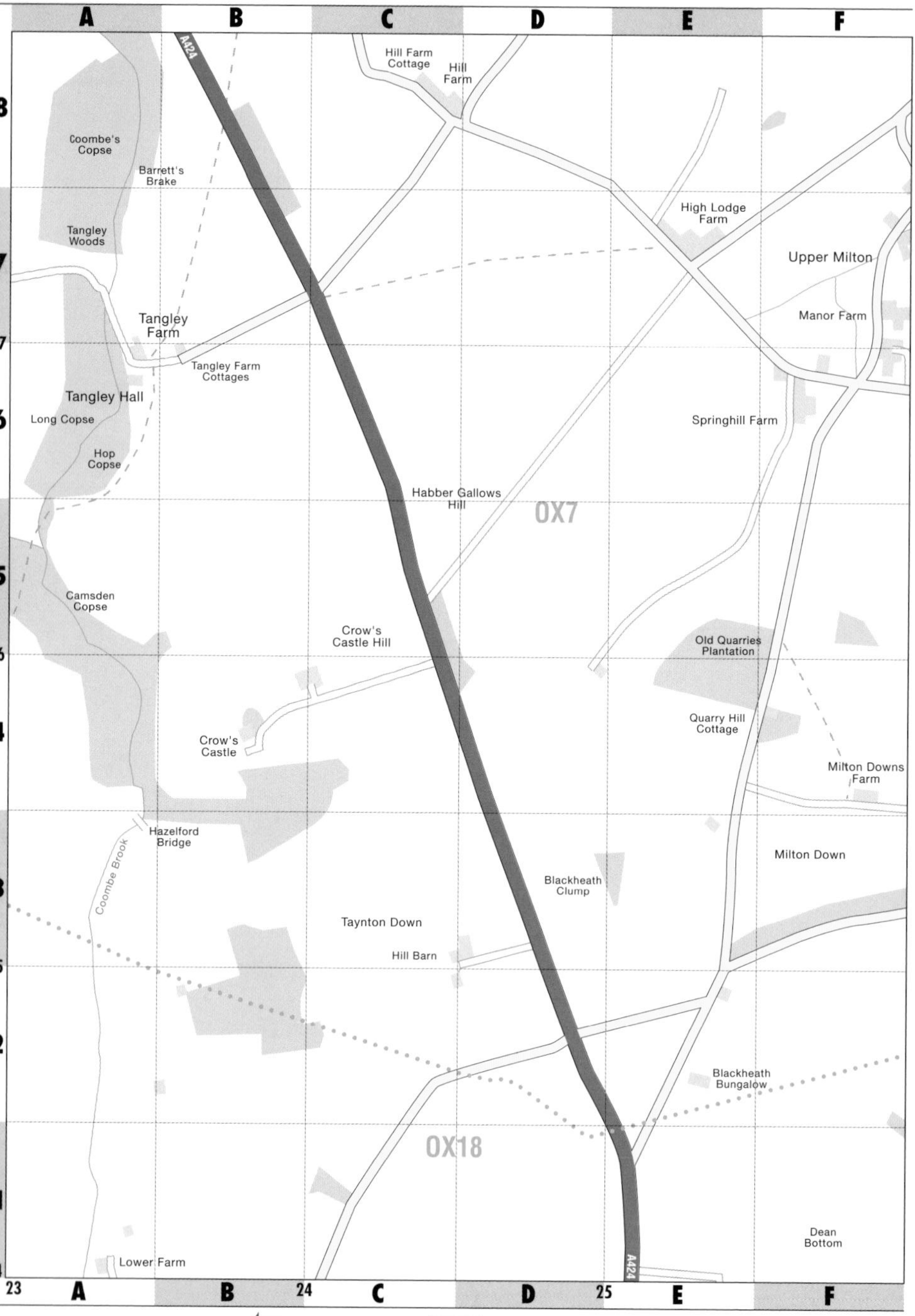

A   B   C   D   E   F

8

Coombe's
Copse

Barrett's
Brake

Tangley
Woods

Hill Farm
Cottage

Hill
Farm

High Lodge
Farm

Upper Milton

7

A424

Tangley
Farm

Manor Farm

17

Tangley Farm
Cottages

Tangley Hall

Long Copse

Springhill Farm

6

Hop
Copse

Habber Gallows
Hill

OX7

5

Camsden
Copse

Crow's
Castle Hill

Old Quarries
Plantation

16

Quarry Hill
Cottage

4

Crow's
Castle

Milton Downs
Farm

Hazelford
Bridge

Milton Down

3

Coombe Brook

Blackheath
Clump

Taynton Down

15

Hill Barn

2

Blackheath
Bungalow

OX18

1

Dean
Bottom

14

Lower Farm

A424

23   A   B   24   C   D   25   E   F

83
100

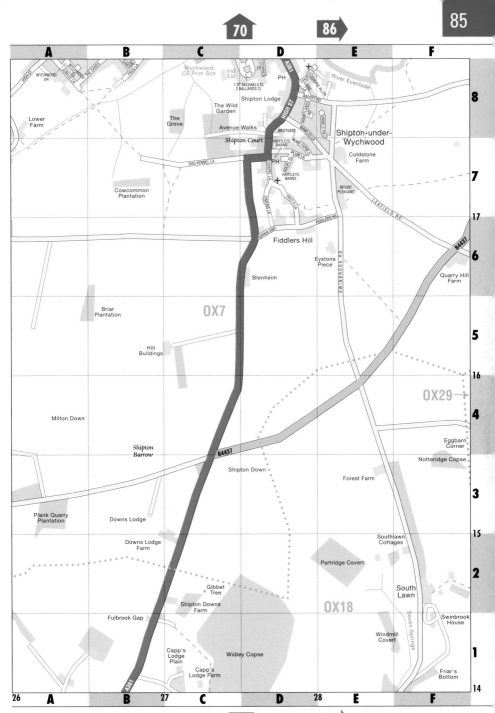

A B C D E F

High St
Wychwood Dr
The Sands
Sands Cl
Jubilee Cl
1 St Michaels Cl
2 Ballards Cl

Wychwood CE Prim Sch

Ind Est

River Evenlode

8

Lower Farm

The Grove

The Wild Garden

Shipton Lodge

PH

Church Rd
Manor La
Ascott Rd
Court Lands
Mawles Ct

Shipton-under-Wychwood

Avenue Walks

Westgate

Shipton Court

Hartleys Barns

Home Farm Cl

High St

Plum La

Coldstone Farm

Dog Kennel La

Chapel La

PH

Hartleys Barns

7

Cowcommon Plantation

Sandys La

Trots La

Mount Pleasant

Leafield Rd

17

Fiddlers Hill

Upper End

Fiddlers Hill

Eystons Piece

Swinbrook Rd

6

Blenheim

B4437

Quarry Hill Farm

OX7

Briar Plantation

5

Hill Buildings

16

Milton Down

OX29 →

4

Shipton Barrow

B4437

Eggbarn Corner

Shipton Down

Notteridge Copse

3

Plank Quarry Plantation

Downs Lodge

Forest Farm

Downs Lodge Farm

Southlawn Cottages

15

Partridge Covert

2

Gibbet Tree

OX18

South Lawn

Shipton Downs Farm

Fulbrook Gap

Windmill Covert

Seven Springs

Swinbrook House

1

Capp's Lodge Plain

Widley Copse

Capp's Lodge Farm

A361

Friar's Bottom

14

26 A B 27 C D 28 E F

85
71

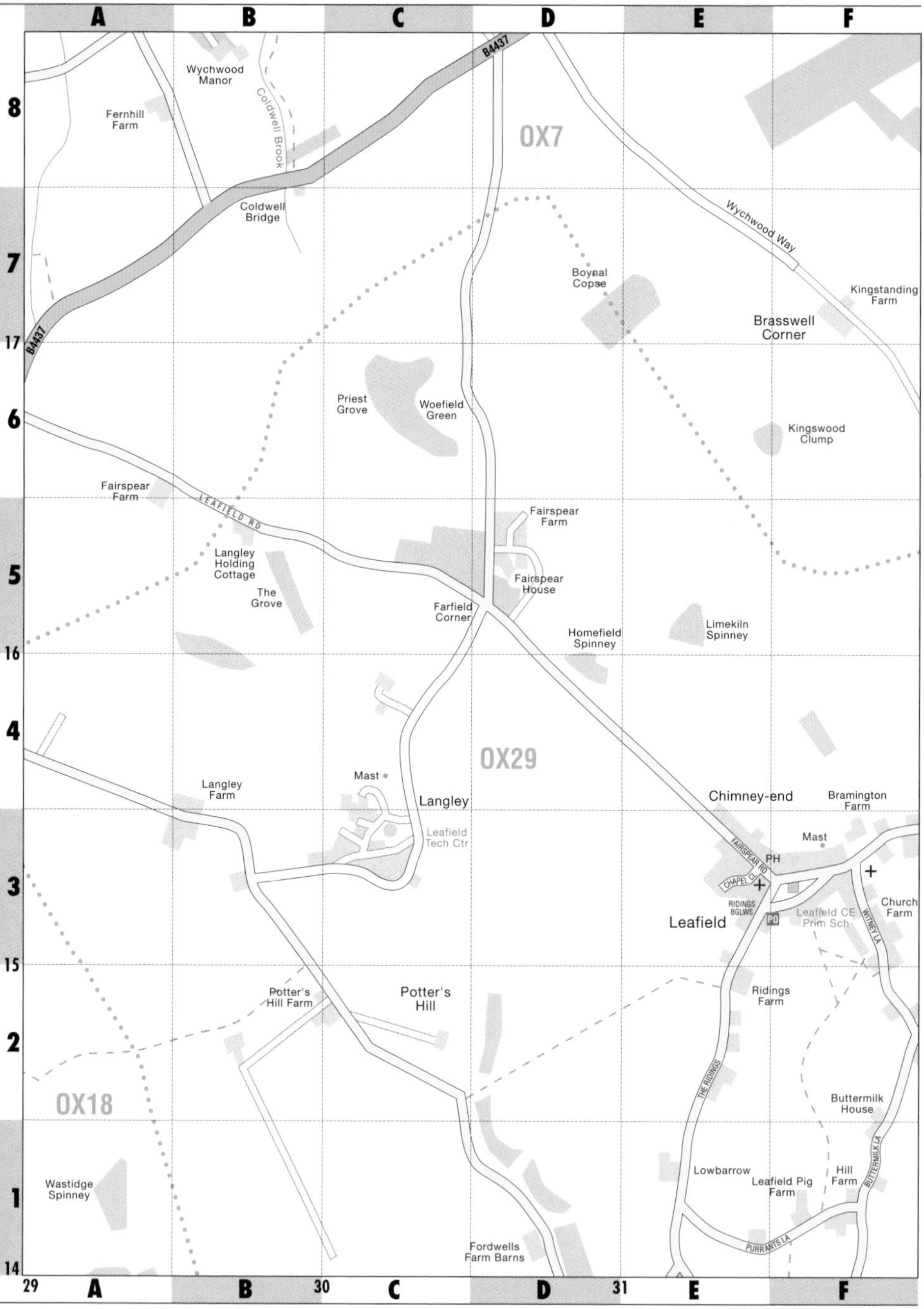

A B C D E F

8

Wychwood Manor

Fernhill Farm

Coldwell Brook

B4437

OX7

7

Coldwell Bridge

Boyeal Copse

Wychwood Way

Kingstanding Farm

17

B4437

Brasswell Corner

6

Priest Grove

Woefield Green

Kingswood Clump

Fairspear Farm

LEAFIELD RD

Fairspear Farm

5

Langley Holding Cottage

The Grove

Fairspear House

Farfield Corner

Homefield Spinney

Limekiln Spinney

16

4

Langley Farm

Mast

Langley

OX29

Chimney-end

Bramington Farm

Mast

Leafield Tech Ctr

FAIRSPEAR RD

PH

CHAPEL RD

Church Farm

3

RIDINGS BGLWS

Leafield CE Prim Sch

WITNEY LA

Leafield

15

Potter's Hill Farm

Potter's Hill

Ridings Farm

2

THE RIDINGS

Buttermilk House

OX18

PLANTATION LA

1

Wastidge Spinney

Lowbarrow

Leafield Pig Farm

Hill Farm

14

Fordwells Farm Barns

PURBRITS LA

29 A B 30 C D 31 E F

85
102

72
88

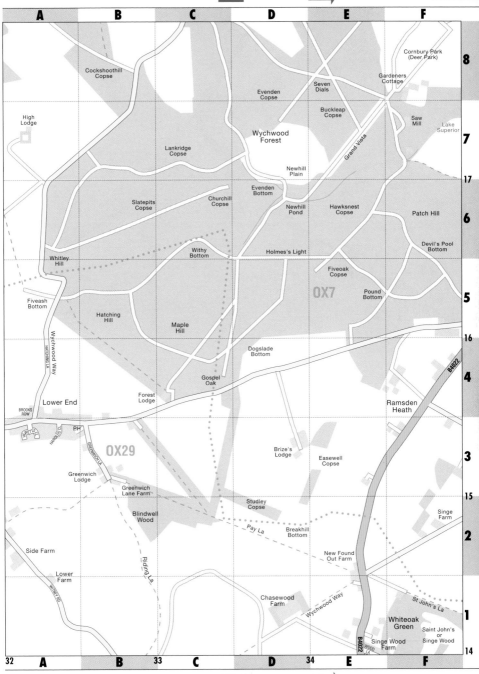

103
88

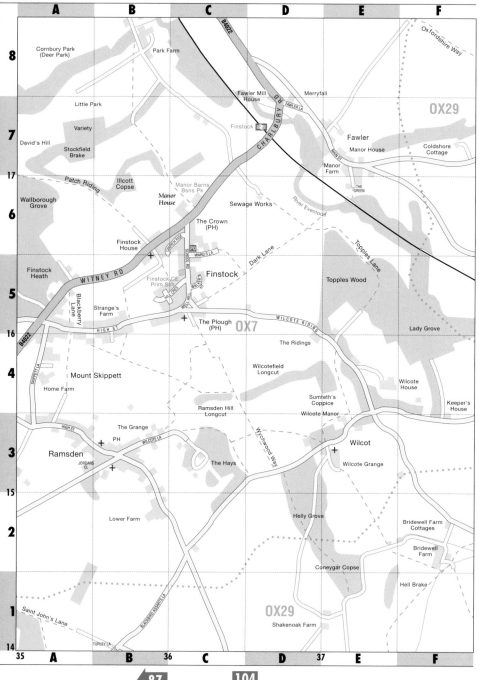

A B C D E F

8 Cornbury Park (Deer Park)
Park Farm
B4022
Oxfordshire Way
OX29

7 Little Park
Variety
David's Hill
Stockfield Brake
Fawler Mill House
Merryfall
Finstock
CHARLBURY RD
FAWLER LA
Fawler
Manor House
Coldshore Cottage
MAIN ST

17 Patch Riding
Illcott Copse
Manor Barns Bsns Pk
Manor Farm
THE GREEN

6 Wallborough Grove
Manor House
Sewage Works
River Evenlode
The Crown (PH)

5 Finstock Heath
Finstock House
CHURCH RISE
PO
WARD'S LA
Dark Lane
Topples Lane
Topples Wood
Finstock CE Prim Sch
Finstock
WITNEY RD
Blackberry Lane
Strange's Farm

16 HIGH ST
The Plough (PH)
OX7
WILCOTE RIDING
Lady Grove

4 Mount Skippett
Home Farm
SKIPPETT LA
B4022
The Ridings
Wilcotefield Longcut
Wilcote House
Keeper's House

3 Ramsden
HIGH ST
The Grange
PH
WILCOTE LA
Ramsden Hill Longcut
The Hays
Sumteth's Coppice
Wilcote Manor
Wychwood Way
Wilcot
Wilcote Grange
JORDANS CL

15 Lower Farm
Holly Grove
Bridewell Farm Cottages
Bridewell Farm

2 Coneygar Copse
Hell Brake

1 Saint John's Lane
BLACKBIRD ASSARTS LA
OX29
Shakenoak Farm

14 TURLEY LA
35 A B 36 C D 37 E F

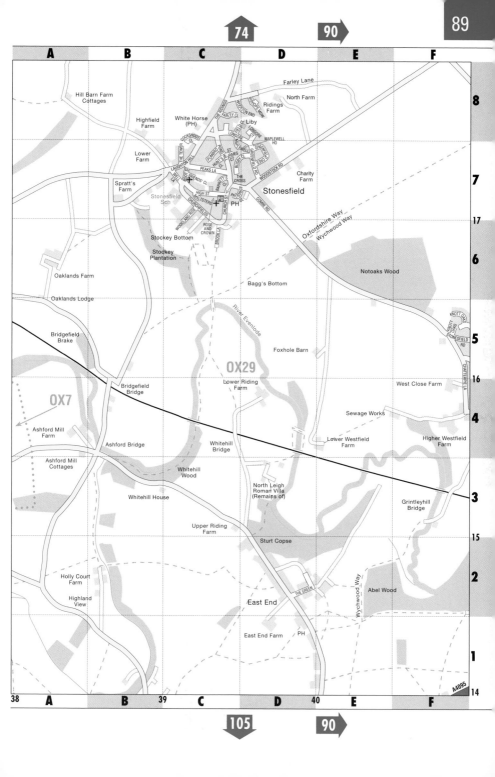

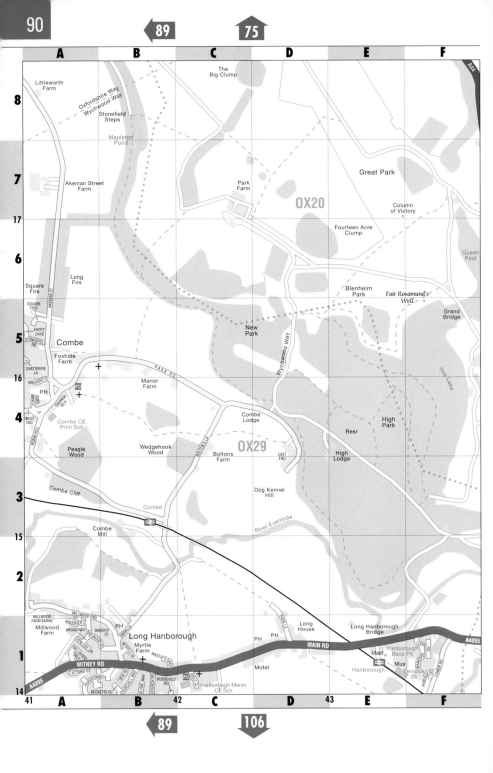

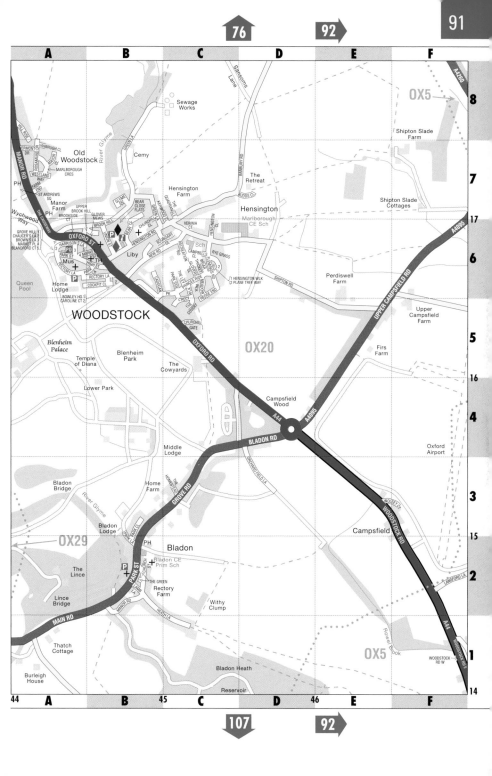

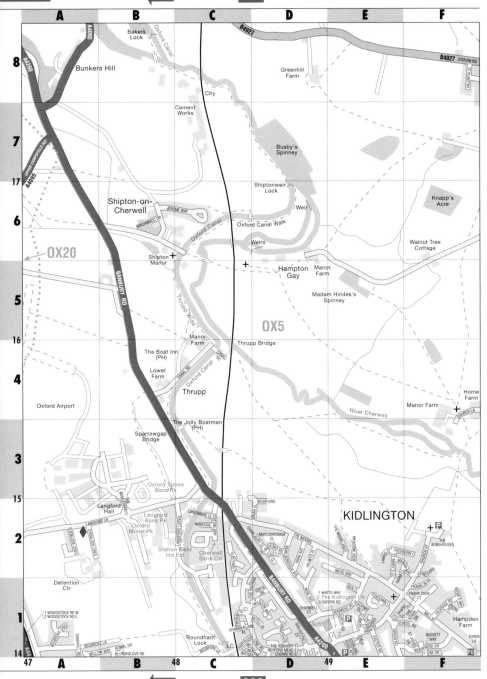

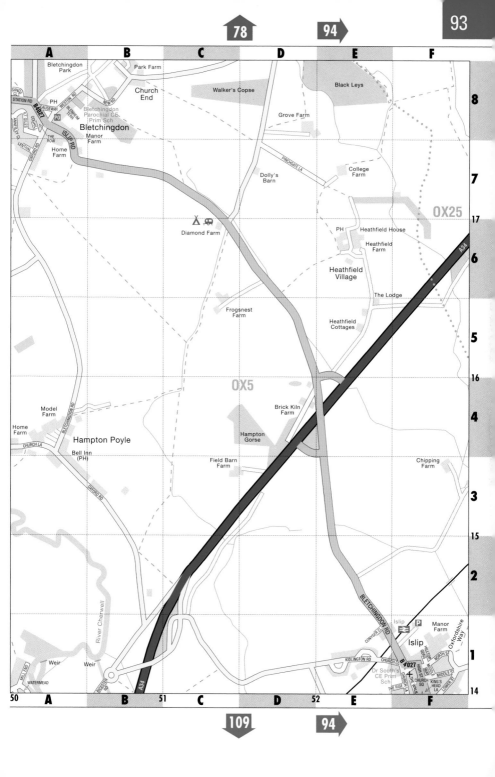

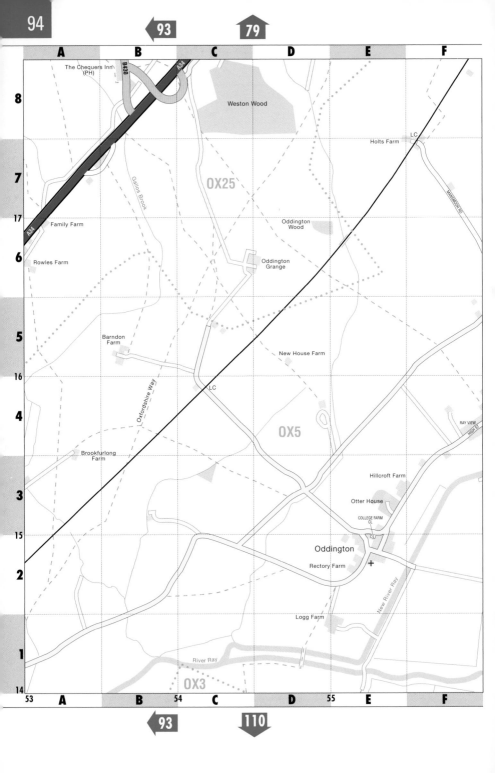

93
79

A B C D E F

8

7

17

6

5

16

4

3

15

2

1

14

The Chequers Inn
(PH)

B430

A34

Weston Wood

LC

Holts Farm

MARSGFORD RD

Gallos Brook

OX25

A34

Family Farm

Oddington
Wood

Rowles Farm

Oddington
Grange

Barndon
Farm

Oxfordshire Way

New House Farm

LC

OX5

RAY VIEW

HIGH ST

Brookfurlong
Farm

Hillcroft Farm

Otter House

COLLEGE FARM
CL

Oddington

Rectory Farm

New River Ray

Logg Farm

River Ray

OX3

53 A B 54 C D 55 E F

93
110

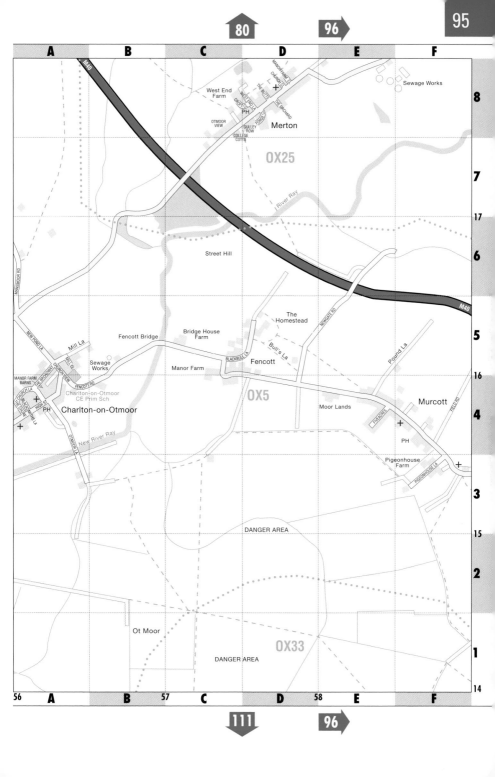

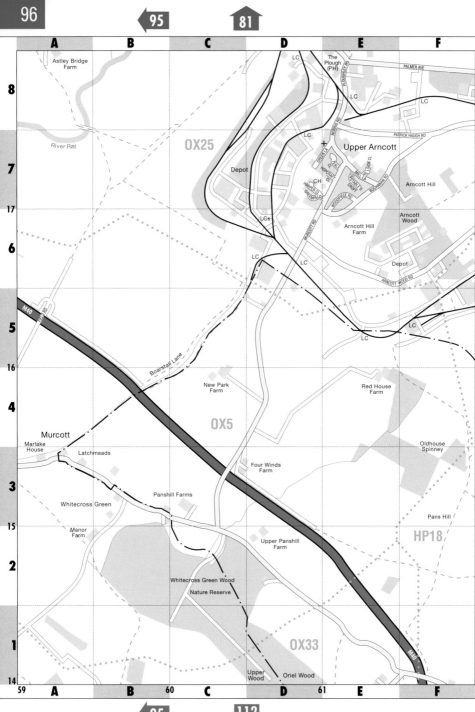

Astley Bridge Farm

River Ray

OX25

The Plough (PH)

PALMER AVE

LC

LC

LC

LC

PATRICK HAUGH RD

Upper Arncott

Depot

Arncott Hill

CH

Arncott Wood

Arncott Hill Farm

LCs

Depot

LC

LC

ARNCOTT WOOD RD

LC

LC

Boarstall Lane

New Park Farm

Red House Farm

M40

OX5

Murcott

Marlake House

Latchmeads

Oldhouse Spinney

Four Winds Farm

Whitecross Green

Panshill Farms

Pans Hill

Manor Farm

Upper Panshill Farm

HP18

Whitecross Green Wood

Nature Reserve

Upper Wood

Oriel Wood

OX33

M40

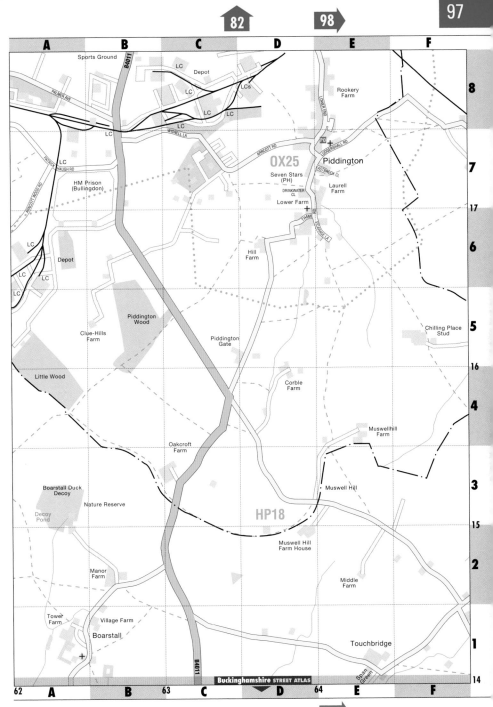

A **B** **C** **D** **E** **F**

Sports Ground

B4011

PALMER AVE

LC
Depot
LC
LCs
LC
LC
LC
LC

WIDNELL LA

ARNCOTT RD

OX25

Rookery
Farm

LOWER END

Piddington

LUCKERSHALL RD

EASTBROOK CL

Seven Stars
(PH)

Laurell
Farm

DRINKWATER
CL
Lower Farm

THAME RD

PATRICK HAUGH RD

LC

HM Prison
(Bullingdon)

ARNCOTT WOOD RD

8

7

17

6

Hill
Farm

TICKELL'S LA

LC

Depot

LC
LC
LC

Piddington
Wood

Clue-Hills
Farm

Piddington
Gate

Corble
Farm

Chilling Place
Stud

5

16

4

Little Wood

Oakcroft
Farm

Muswellhill
Farm

Boarstall Duck
Decoy

Nature Reserve

Decoy
Pond

Muswell Hill

HP18

Muswell Hill
Farm House

3

15

2

Manor
Farm

Middle
Farm

Tower
Farm

Village Farm

Boarstall

B4011

Span Green

Touchbridge

1

14

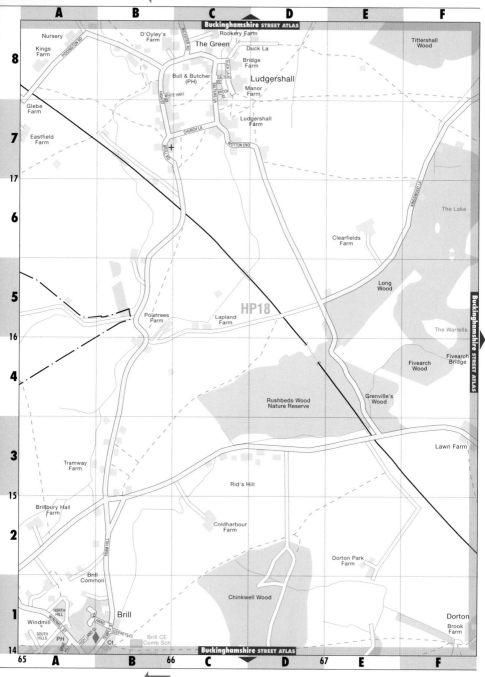

Nursery

D'Oyley's Farm

Rookery Farm

Tittershall Wood

Kings Farm

The Green

Duck La

PIDDINGTON RD

BICESTER RD

Bridge Farm

Ludgershall

Glebe Farm

Bull & Butcher (PH)

DUCK LA

GALTERS

Manor Farm

WHITE HART

HIGH ST CL

GALTERS LA

BROOK CL

Eastfield Farm

Ludgershall Farm

CHURCH LA

Ludgershall Farm

BRILL RD

POTTON END

KINGSWOOD LA

The Lake

Clearfields Farm

Long Wood

HP18

Poletrees Farm

Lapland Farm

The Warrells

Fivearch Wood

Fivearch Bridge

Rushbeds Wood Nature Reserve

Grenville's Wood

Tramway Farm

Lawn Farm

Rid's Hill

Brillbury Hall Farm

TRAM HILL

Coldharbour Farm

Dorton Park Farm

Brill Common

Chinkwell Wood

Dorton

NORTH HILL

THE LAWNS

Brill

WINDMILL ST

Windmill

GODFREY'S CL

Brook Farm

PH

SOUTH HILLS

BRILL HILL

HIGH LAND

Ct

Brill CE Comb Sch

65   66   67

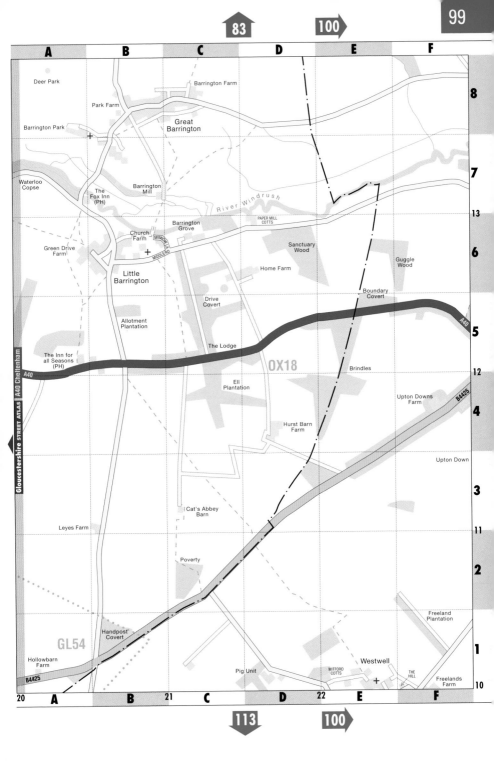

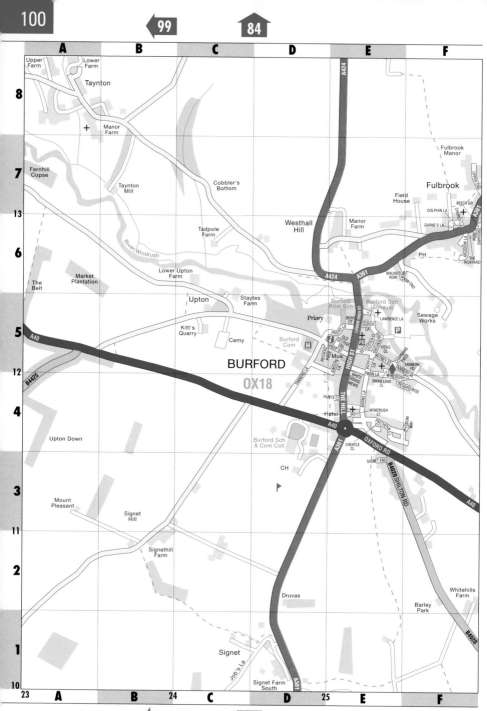

BURFORD

OX18

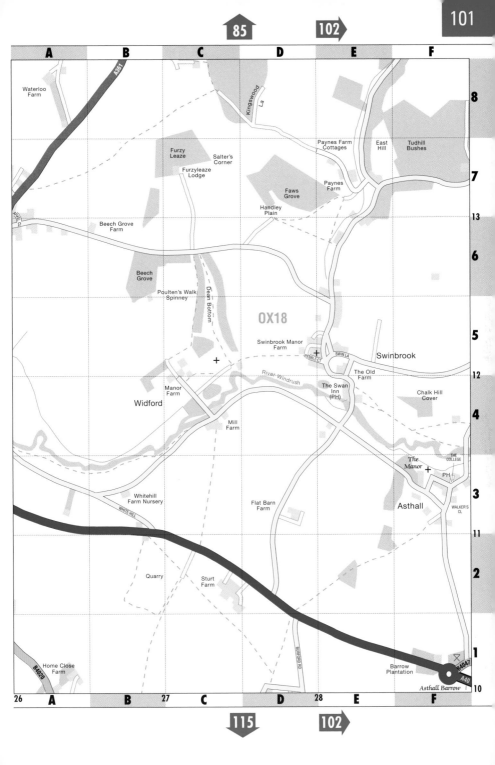

85 102

A B C D E F

8

Waterloo
Farm

Kingswood La

Furzy
Leaze

Salter's
Corner

Furzyleaze
Lodge

Paynes Farm
Cottages

East
Hill

Tudhill
Bushes

7

Faws
Grove

Paynes
Farm

Beech Grove
Farm

Handley
Plain

13

6

Beech
Grove

Poulten's Walk
Spinney

Dean Bottom

OX18

Swinbrook Manor
Farm

PEBBLE CT

SWIN LA

Swinbrook

5

River Windrush

The Old
Farm

12

Manor
Farm

Widford

The Swan
Inn
(PH)

Chalk Hill
Cover

4

Mill
Farm

THE
COLLEGE

The
Manor

PH

Whitehill
Farm Nursery

WHITE HILL

Flat Barn
Farm

Asthall

WALKER'S
CL

3

11

Quarry

Sturt
Farm

2

BURFORD RD

Home Close
Farm

B4020

A40

B4047

Barrow
Plantation

Asthall Barrow

1

10

26 A B 27 C D 28 E F

115 102

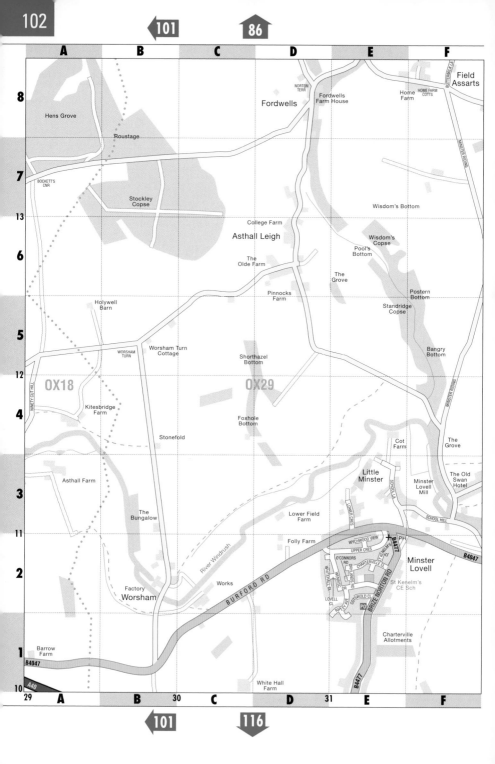

101
86

A B C D E F

8

Hens Grove

Roustage

Fordwells

NORTON TERR

Fordwells Farm House

Home Farm

HOME FARM COTTS

Field Assarts

BUTTERMILK LA

7

BOCKETT'S CNR

Stockley Copse

MINSTER RIDING

13

College Farm

Asthall Leigh

Wisdom's Bottom

Wisdom's Copse

6

The Olde Farm

Pinnocks Farm

The Grove

Pool's Bottom

Postern Bottom

Standridge Copse

Holywell Barn

5

WORSHAM TURN

Worsham Turn Cottage

Shorthazel Bottom

Bangry Bottom

12

OX18

NINETY CUT HILL

OX29

MINSTER RIDING

4

Kitesbridge Farm

Stonefold

Foxhole Bottom

Cot Farm

The Grove

Asthall Farm

3

Little Minster

SCHOOL LA

Minster Lovell Mill

The Old Swan Hotel

SCHOOL HILL

The Bungalow

11

LOWER B CRES

Lower Field Farm

Folly Farm

WYCHWOOD VIEW

UPPER CRES

PH

B4477

Minster Lovell

B4047

2

CHARTERVILLE CL

FERNDALE

BRIZE NORTON RD

St Keeelm's CE Sch

Factory

Worsham

Works

BURFORD RD

D'CONNORS RD

WHITHALL DR

RD

COTSWOLD CL

LOVELL CL

RIPLEY CRES

PO

1

Barrow Farm

B4047

B4477

Charterville Allotments

10

A40

White Hall Farm

29 A B 30 C D 31 E F

River Windrush

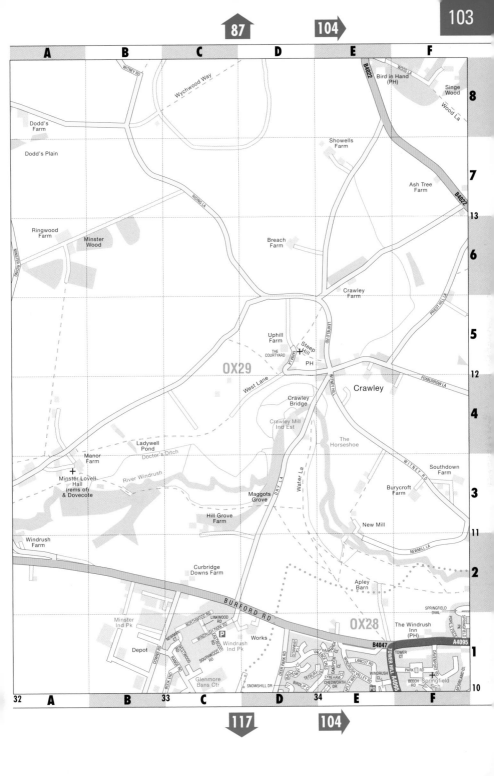

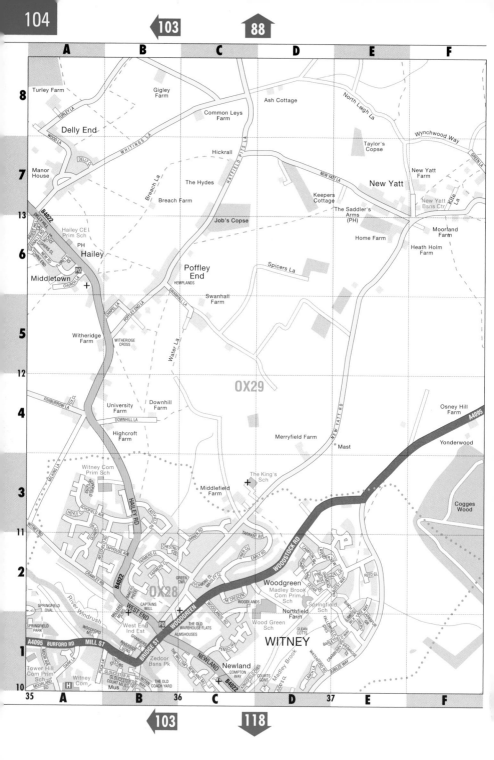

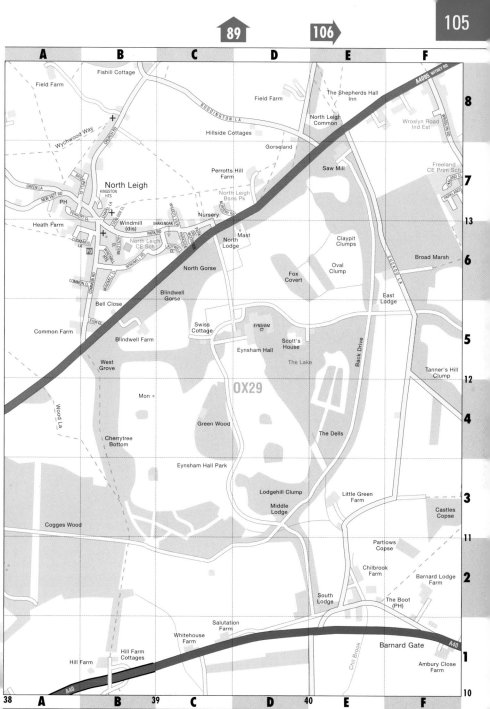

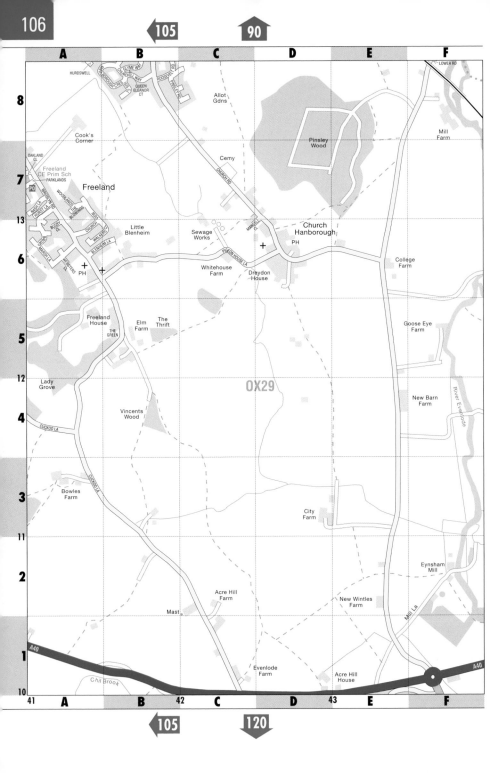

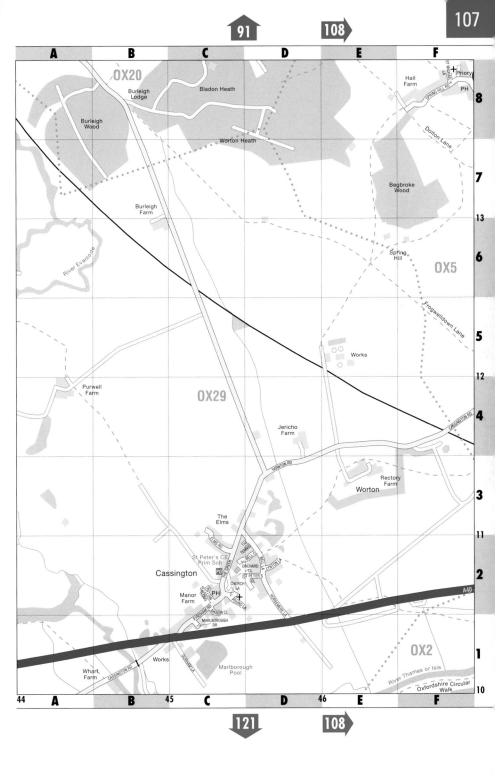

OX20

Burleigh Lodge

Bladon Heath

Hall Farm

Priory PH

Burleigh Wood

Worton Heath

Dolton Lane

8

Begbroke Wood

7

Burleigh Farm

13

Spring Hill

OX5

River Evenlode

6

Frogwelldown Lane

5

Works

Purwell Farm

12

OX29

CASSINGTON RD

4

Jericho Farm

YARNTON RD

Rectory Farm

Worton

3

The Elms

11

St Peter's CE Prim Sch

TENNIS

BELL CL

BELL LA

LYNTON LA

PO

ORCHARD CL

Cassington

ST PETER'S CL

THE GREEN

A40

2

Manor Farm

PH

CHURCH LA

NORSEMAN LA

EYNSHAM RD

MANOR CL

POUND LA

MARLBOROUGH DR

OX2

River Thames or Isis

Wharf Farm

CASSINGTON RD

Works

DURHAM LA

Marlborough Pool

Oxfordshire Circular Walk

1

10

44

45

46

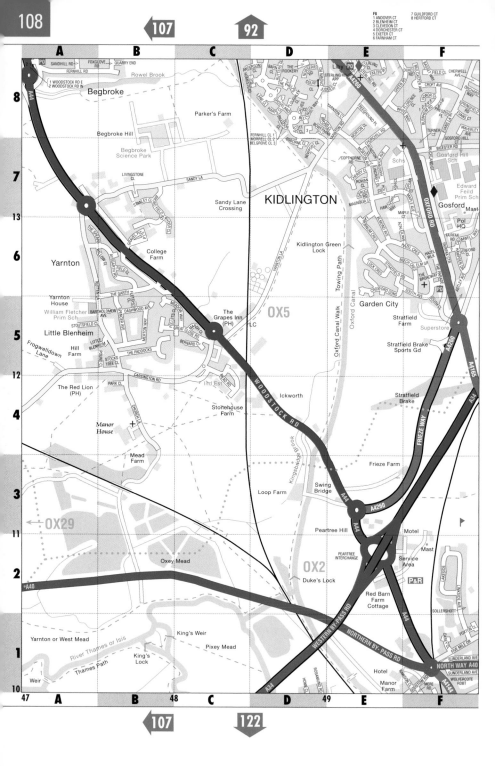

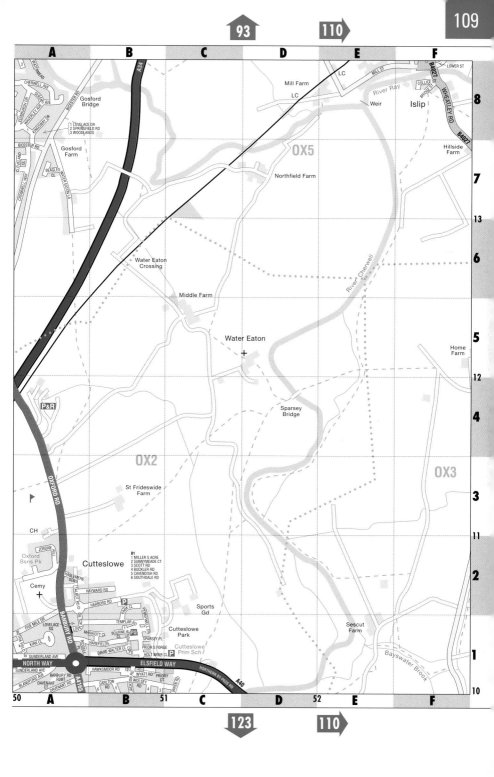

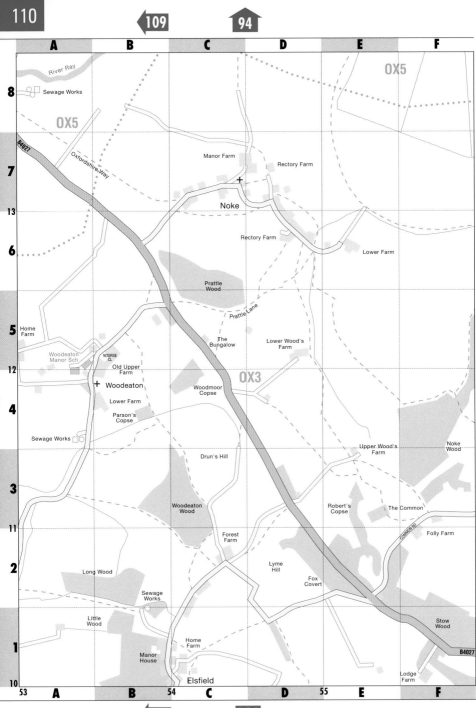

River Ray

Sewage Works

OX5

OX5

B4027

Oxfordshire Way

Manor Farm

Rectory Farm

Noke

Rectory Farm

Lower Farm

Prattle Wood

Prattle Lane

Home Farm

The Bungalow

Lower Wood's Farm

Woodeaton Manor Sch

NOURSE CL

Old Upper Farm

Woodeaton

OX3

Woodmoor Copse

Lower Farm

Parson's Copse

Sewage Works

Drun's Hill

Upper Wood's Farm

Noke Wood

Woodeaton Wood

Robert's Copse

The Common

COMMON RD

Forest Farm

Folly Farm

Long Wood

Lyme Hill

Fox Covert

Sewage Works

Little Wood

Home Farm

Stow Wood

Manor House

B4027

Elsfield

Lodge Farm

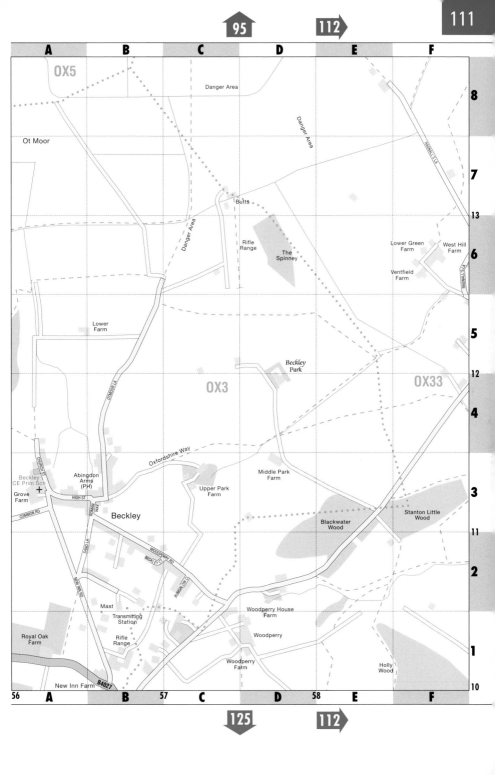

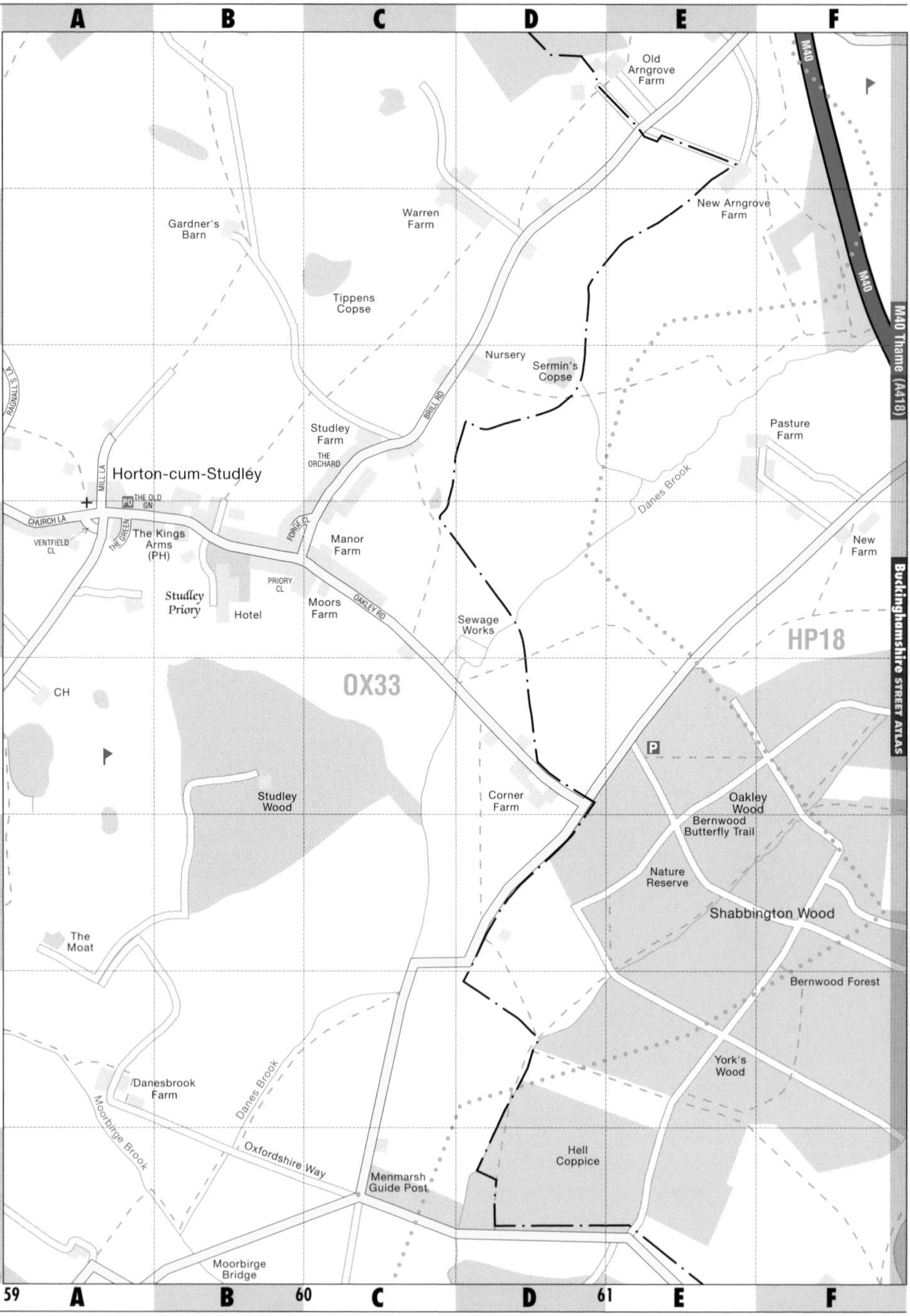
A
B
C
D
E
F
8
7
13
6
5
12
4
3
11
2
1
10
59
60
61
Old Arngrove Farm
New Arngrove Farm
Warren Farm
Gardner's Barn
Tippens Copse
Nursery
Sermin's Copse
M40
M40 Thame (A418)
RAGNALL'S LA
Studley Farm
THE ORCHARD
BRILL RD
Horton-cum-Studley
MILL LA
PO
THE OLD GN
CHURCH LA
VENTFIELD CL
THE GREEN
The Kings Arms (PH)
FORGE CL
Manor Farm
Pasture Farm
Danes Brook
New Farm
Studley Priory
Hotel
PRIORY CL
Moors Farm
OAKLEY RD
Sewage Works
HP18
Buckinghamshire STREET ATLAS
CH
OX33
P
Studley Wood
Corner Farm
Oakley Wood
Bernwood Butterfly Trail
Nature Reserve
Shabbington Wood
The Moat
Bernwood Forest
York's Wood
Danesbrook Farm
Danes Brook
Moorbirge Brook
Oxfordshire Way
Hell Coppice
Menmarsh Guide Post
Moorbirge Bridge

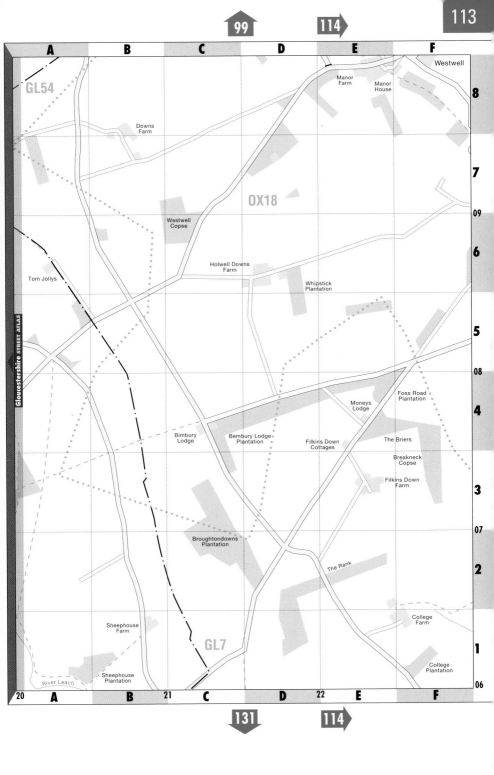

Westwell

GL54

Manor
Farm

Manor
House

8

Downs
Farm

7

OX18

09

Westwell
Copse

6

Holwell Downs
Farm

Whipstick
Plantation

Tom Jollys

5

08

Foss Road
Plantation

Moneys
Lodge

4

Bimbury
Lodge

Bembury Lodge
Plantation

Filkins Down
Cottages

The Briers

Breakneck
Copse

Filkins Down
Farm

3

07

Broughtondowns
Plantation

The Rank

2

College
Farm

Sheephouse
Farm

College
Plantation

GL7

1

River Leach

Sheephouse
Plantation

06

Gloucestershire STREET ATLAS

20 A   B   21   C   D   22   E   F

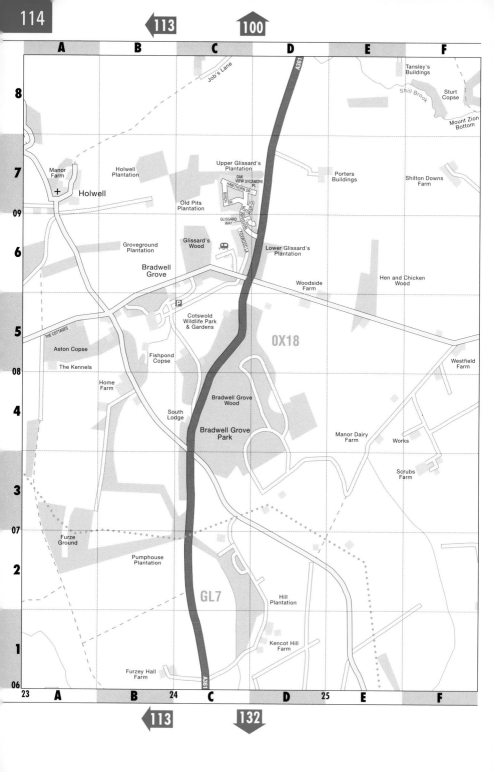

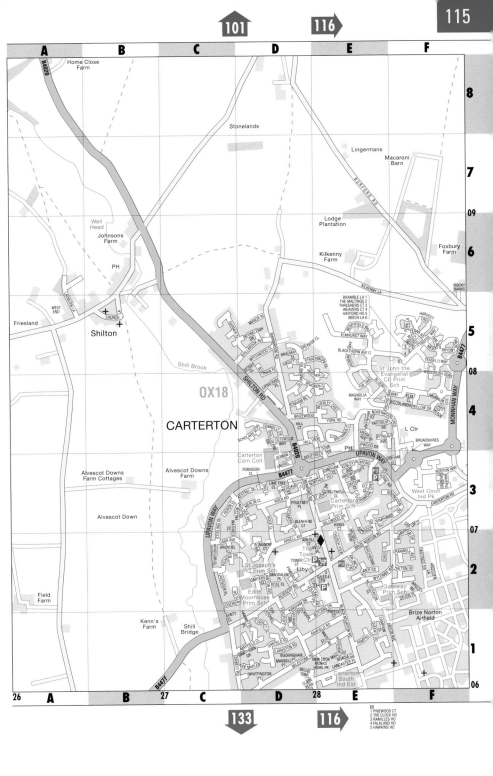

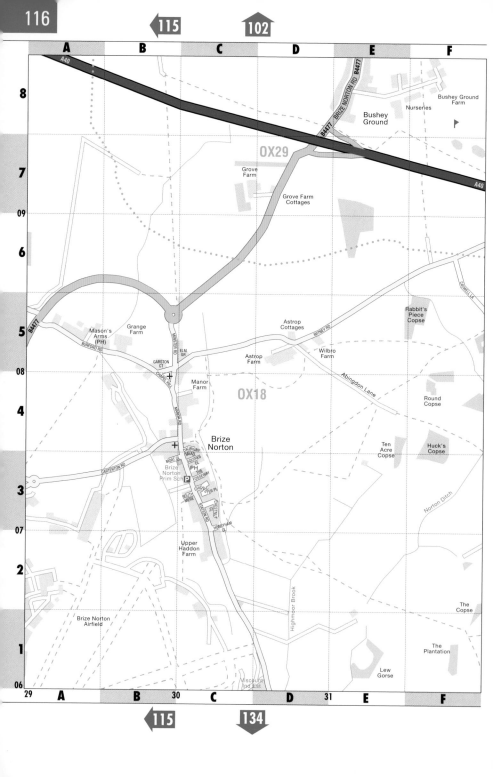

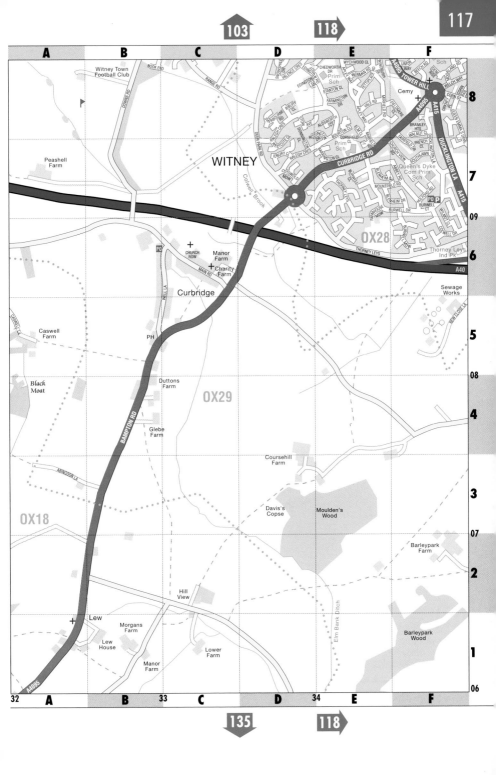

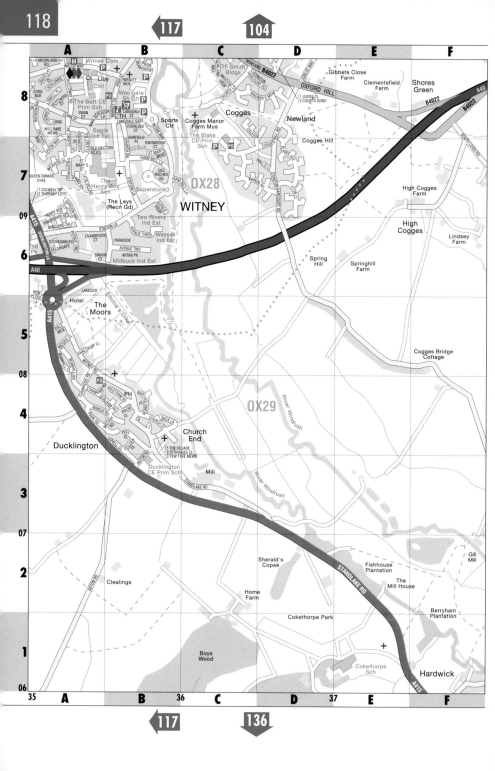

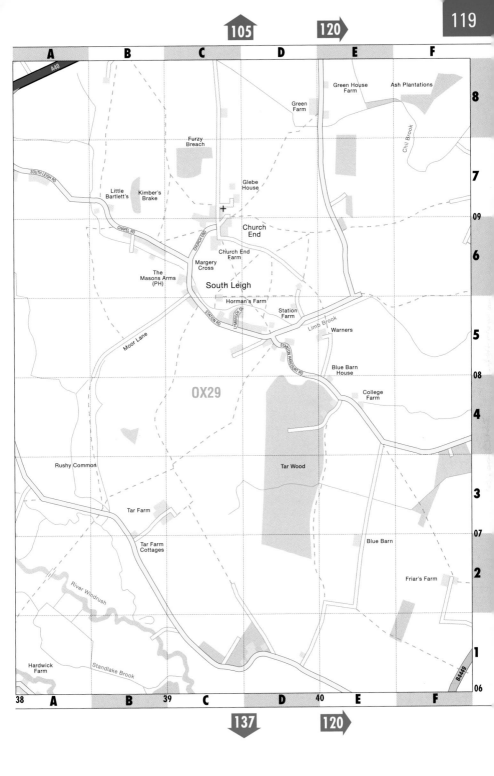

A40
SOUTH LEIGH RD
CHAPEL RD
CHURCH END
STATION RD
LYMBROOK LA
STATION HARCOURT RD

8
7
09
6
5
08
4
3
07
2
1
06

A B C D E F

Green House Farm
Ash Plantations
Green Farm
Chil Brook
Furzy Breach
Glebe House
Little Bartlett's
Kimber's Brake
Church End
Church End Farm
Margery Cross
The Masons Arms (PH)
South Leigh
Horman's Farm
Station Farm
Limb Brook
Warners
Moor Lane
Blue Barn House
OX29
College Farm
Rushy Common
Tar Wood
Tar Farm
Tar Farm Cottages
Blue Barn
River Windrush
Friar's Farm
Hardwick Farm
Standlake Brook
B4449

38 A B 39 C D 40 E F

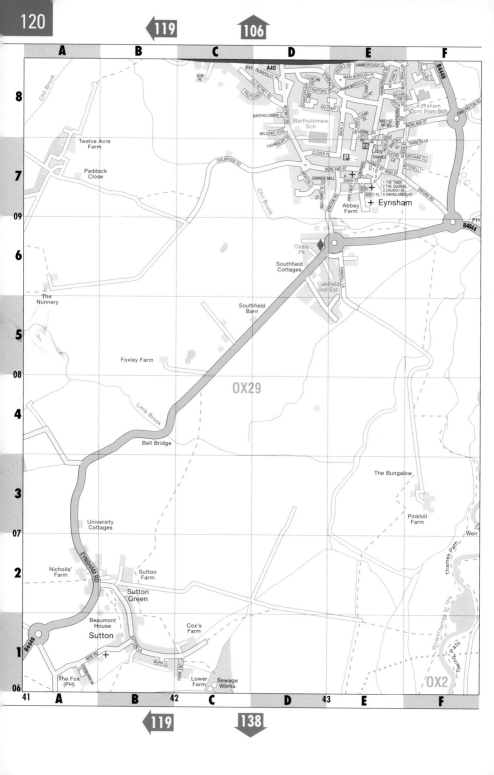

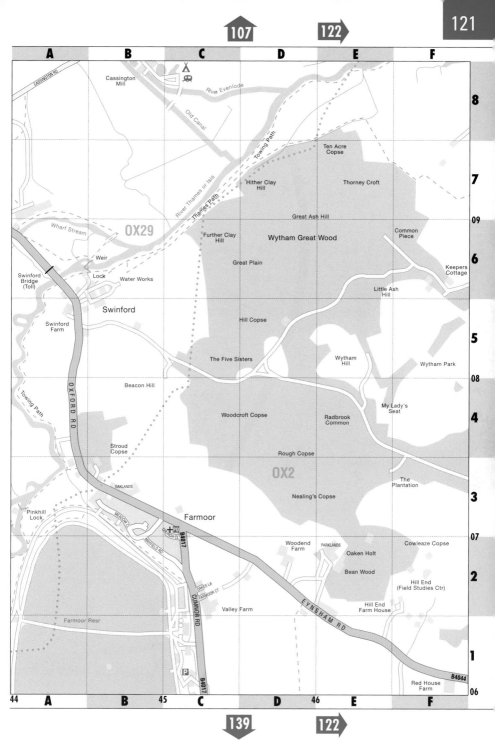

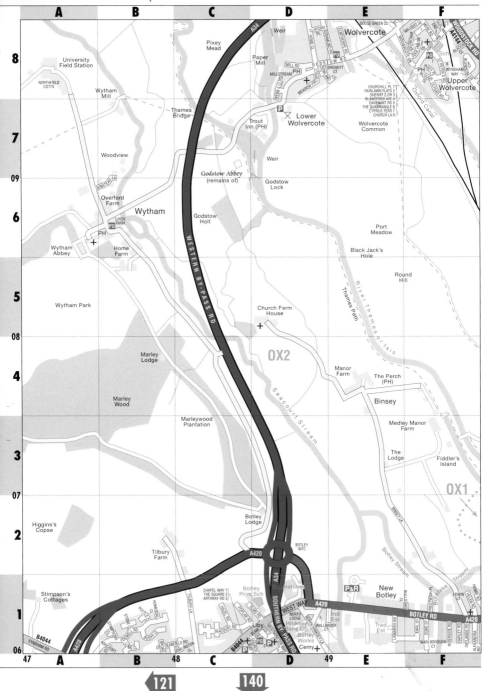

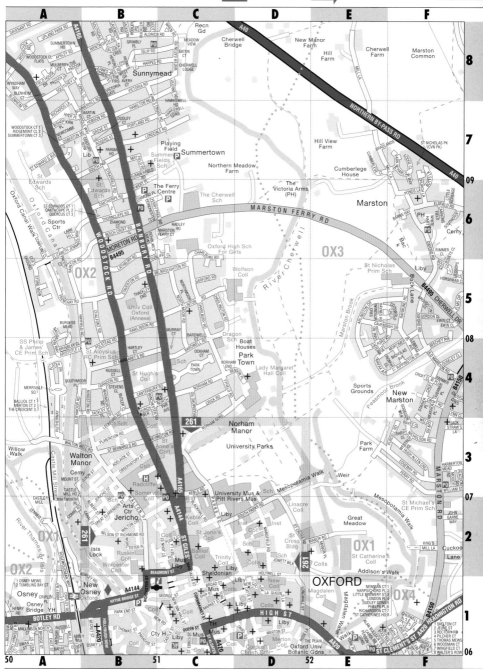

For full street detail of the highlighted area see page 261.

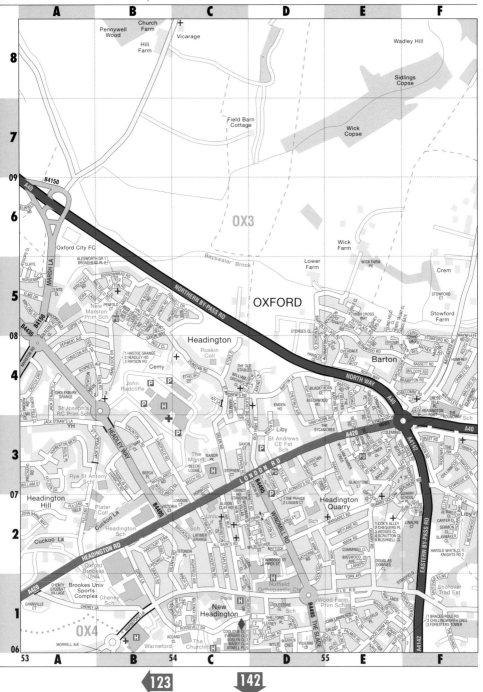

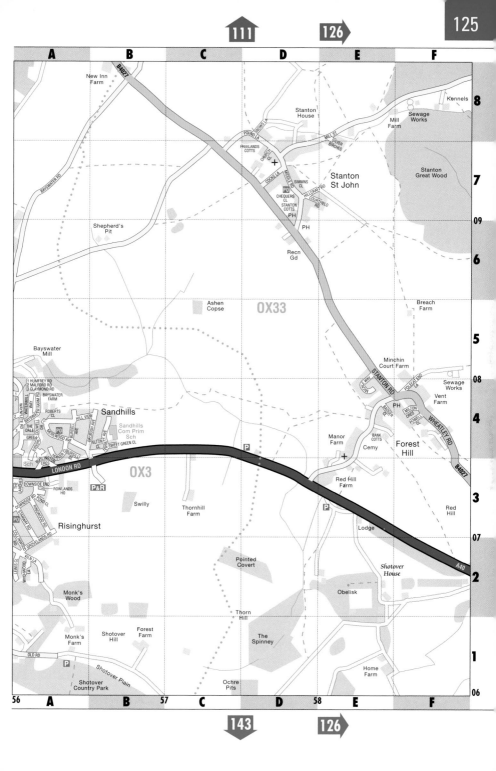

125
112

	A	B	C	D	E	F

8

Wood Farm

HP18

Clearsale

Hursthill

Waterperry Common

7

Commonleys Farm

Bernwood Forest

09

Waterperry Wood

Park Farm

Park Farm House

6

Polecat End

Drunkard's Corner

Oxfordshire Way

Parson's Farm

Marsh Copse

5

Polecat End Hollows

Ledall Cottage

08

Holton Wood

OX33

4

Buryhook Barn

Holton Brook

3

Warren Farm

Pond Farm

Keeper's Cottage

Warren Wood

Old Park Farm

07

Lyehill Quarries (dis)

BURYHOOK CNR

Cottage Copse

2

Warwick Close Farm

The Rectory

Holton Place

Wheatley Park Sch

Rech Gd

Liby

Sports Ctr

Holton

BARNS CL

John Watson Sch

1

Wheatley

Church Farm

Wheatley Campus (Brookes Univ)

Garden Copse

06

WESTFIELD RD

LONDON RD

A40

COLLEGE CL

| 59 | A | | B | 60 | C | | D | 61 | E | | F |

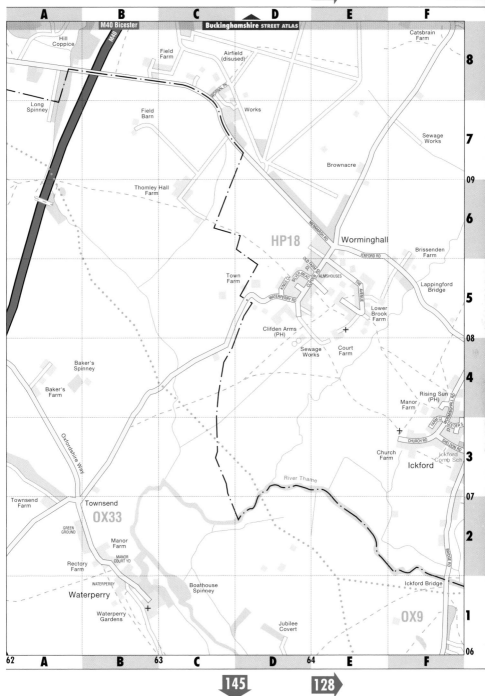

Hill Coppice

Field Farm

Airfield (disused)

Catsbrain Farm

8

Long Spinney

Field Barn

Works

Sewage Works

7

09

Thomley Hall Farm

Brownacre

HP18

Worminghall

6

Town Farm

OLD TOWN CL

SILVER MEADOW CL

ALMSHOUSES

KING'S CL

WATERPERRY RD

THE AVENUE

ICKFORD RD

Brissenden Farm

Lappingford Bridge

5

08

Clifden Arms (PH)

Sewage Works

Court Farm

Lower Brook Farm

Baker's Spinney

Baker's Farm

Rising Sun (PH)

Manor Farm

FARM CL

WORMINGHALL RD

ELDER S

4

Oxfordshire Way

CHURCH RD

SHELDON RD

Church Farm

Ickford Comb Sch

Ickford

3

River Thame

07

Townsend Farm

Townsend

OX33

GREEN GROUND

Manor Farm

MANOR COURT YD

BRIDGE RD

Ickford Bridge

2

Rectory Farm

WATERPERRY

Boathouse Spinney

Waterperry

Waterperry Gardens

Jubilee Covert

OX9

1

06

127

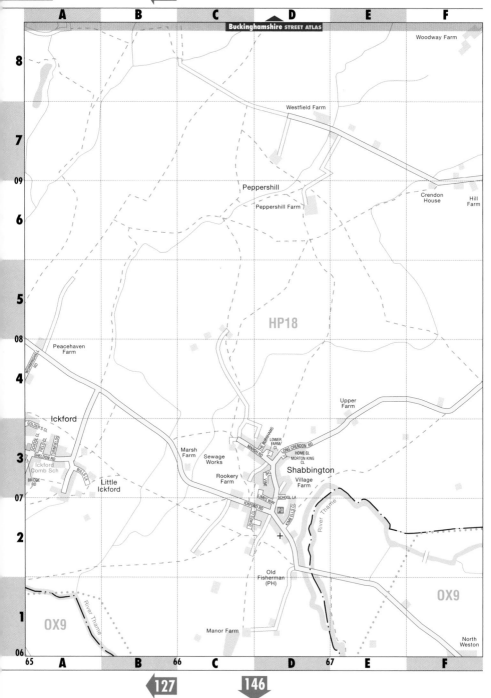

Woodway Farm

Westfield Farm

Peppershill

Peppershill Farm

Crendon House

Hill Farm

HP18

Peacehaven Farm

Upper Farm

Ickford

Marsh Farm

Sewage Works

Lower Farm Cl

Long Crendon Rd

Home Cl

Morton King Cl

Shabbington

Rookery Farm

Village Farm

Little Ickford

Ickford Comb Sch

School La

Ickford Rd

Old Fisherman (PH)

River Thame

OX9

OX9

River Thame

Manor Farm

North Weston

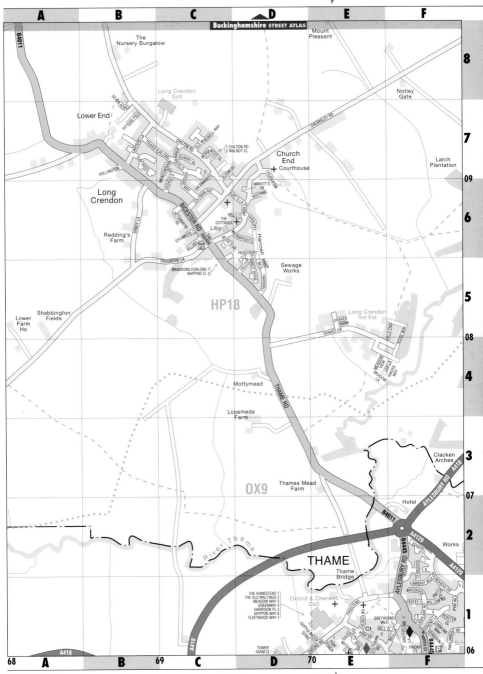

Buckinghamshire STREET ATLAS

The Nursery Bungalow

Long Crendon Sch

Lower End

Notley Gate

Mount Pleasant

CHEARSLEY RD

Larch Plantation

Church End
Courthouse

1 CHILTON RD
2 WALNUT CL

ARNOTT'S YD
WAPPING

Long Crendon

Redding's Farm

BICESTER RD

Liby
THE COTTAGES

Harroell

FROGMORE LA

BRADDONS FURLONG 1
NAPPINS CL 2

PEASCROFT

Sewage Works

HP18

Lower Farm Ho

Shabbington Fields

Long Crendon Ind Est

DRAKES FARM

DRAKES DR

Mottymead

THAME RD

Lopemede Farm

Clacken Arches

OX9

Thames Mead Farm

Hotel

B4011

AYLESBURY RD

A4129

B4445

Works

River Thame

THAME

Thame Bridge

AYLESBURY RD

A4129

THE HOMESTEAD 1
THE OLD MALTINGS 2
MEADOW WAY 3
GREENWAY 4
HARRISON PL 5
SKIPPON WAY 6
FLEETWOOD WAY 7

Oxford & Cherwell Coll

Greyhound WLK

BELL LA

TOWER FARM CL

A418

8
7
09
6
5
08
4
3
07
2
1

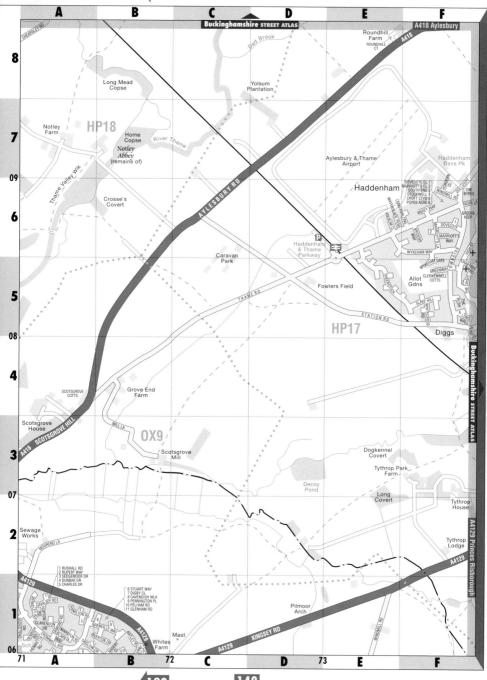

129

Buckinghamshire STREET ATLAS

A418 Aylesbury

A B C D E F

8

7

6

5

4

3

2

1

Cheansley Rd

Roundhill Farm
ROUNDHILL CT

A418

Buckinghamshire STREET ATLAS

Dad Brook

Yolsum Plantation

Long Mead Copse

HP18

Notley Farm

Home Copse
Notley Abbey (remains of)

River Thame

Thame Valley Wlk

Crosse's Covert

AYLESBURY RD

Aylesbury & Thame Airport

Haddenham Bsns Pk

DOVECOTE CL 1
MARRIOTT'S CL 2
SOUTH END 3
STOCKWELL 4
CROFT CTYD 5
POPES ACRE 6

WINDMILL RD

DOVECOTE

THE BYRES

TACKS LN

GREENS KEEP

Haddenham

09

Caravan Park

Haddenham & Thame Parkway

MARRIOTT'S WAY

WYKEHAM WAY

WATERSIDE

LONG ENDING

STANDALL'S

ASLET WAY

VON SEAT CL

DOVECOTE WAY

THAME RD

Fowlers Field

STATION RD

WYNDHAM GATE

GREENWAY

CLERKENWELL COTTS

SHEEPSTOR

SLADE HILL

WHITEFORDS

Allot Gdns

HP17

Diggs

CRABTREE RD

THE RYE

SNAKE LN

WELL LN

08

Scotsgrove Cotts

SCOTSGROVE HILL

Grove End Farm

MILL LA

OX9

Scotsgrove House

A418

Scotsgrove Mill

Dogkennel Covert

Tythrop Park Farm

Long Covert

Decoy Pond

Tythrop House

A4129 Princes Risborough

07

Sewage Works

MORENO LA

Tythrop Lodge

1 RUSHALL RD
2 RUPERT WAY
3 SEDGEMOOR DR
4 DUNBAR DR
5 CHARLES DR

6 STUART WAY
7 DIGBY CL
8 CAVENDISH WLK
9 PENNINGTON PL
10 PELHAM RD
11 GLENHAM RD

A4129

HAMILTON RD

CAVENDISH RD

CHALFONTS

SCHOOL

CLARENDON DR

GRENVILLE WAY

ANTLEY WAY

OVERTON DR

A4129

Mast

Whites Farm

A4129

KINGSEY RD

Pilmoor Arch

RD TYTHROP

06

71 A B 72 C D 73 E F

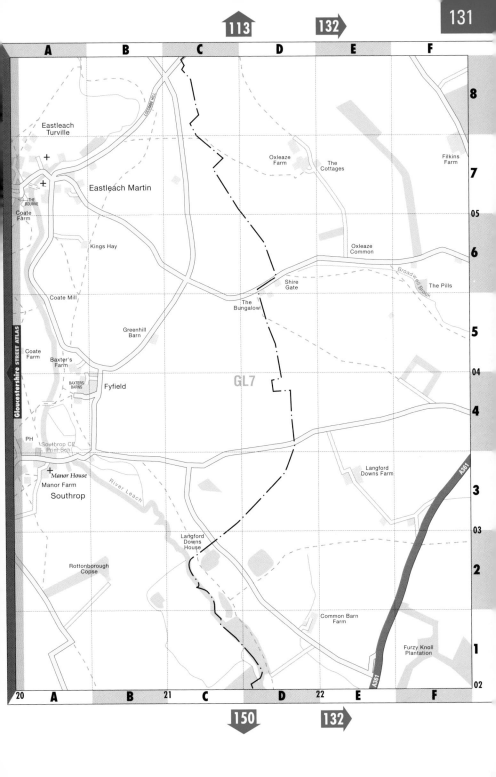

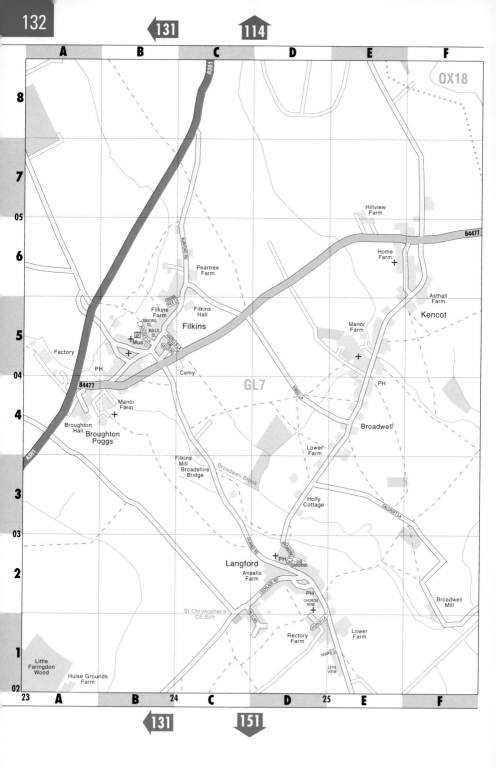

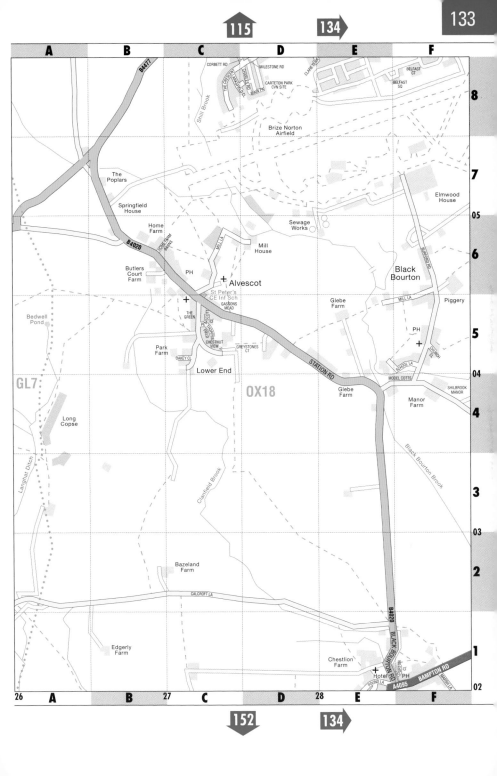

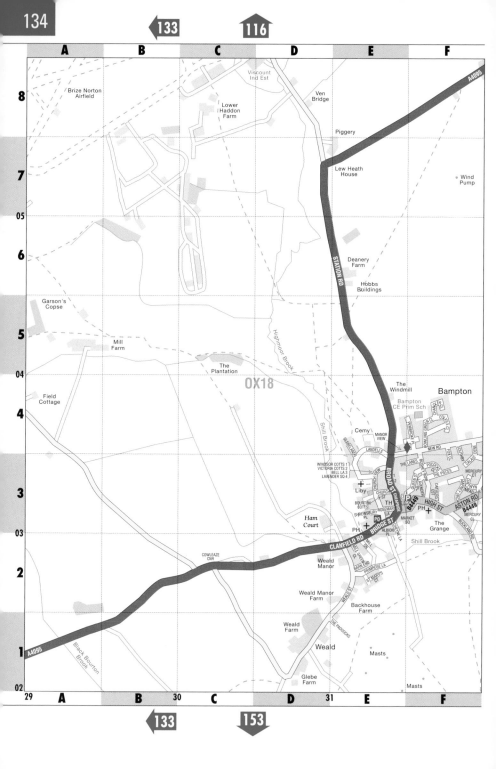

A B C D E F

8
7
05
6
05
5
04
4
3
03
2
03
1
02

Brize Norton
Airfield

Viscount
Ind Est

Lower
Haddon
Farm

Ven
Bridge

Piggery

Lew Heath
House

Wind
Pump

STATION RD

Deanery
Farm

Hobbs
Buildings

Garson's
Copse

Mill
Farm

The
Plantation

Highmoor Brook

OX18

The
Windmill

Bampton

Bampton
CE Prim Sch

Field
Cottage

Shill Brook

Cemy

MANOR
VIEW

Liby

WINDSOR COTTS 1
VICTORIA COTTS 2
BELL LA 3
LAVENDER SQ 4

THE LANES

LANDELLS

BROAD ST

HIGH ST

ASTON RD

B4449

B4449

The
Grange

MERCURY

Ham
Court

BOURTON
COTTS

SHREWSBURY
PL

TH

PH

MARKET
SQ

The
Pieces

POCOCK

NEW RD

PH

CLANFIELD RD

BRIDGE ST

Shill Brook

COWLEAZE
CNR

Weald
Manor

ALBION
PL

PRIMROSE LA

ST MARY'S
CT

BARN END

THE GREEN

Weald Manor
Farm

Backhouse
Farm

THE PADDOCKS

Weald
Farm

Weald

Masts

A4095

Black Bourton
Brook

Glebe
Farm

Masts

A4095

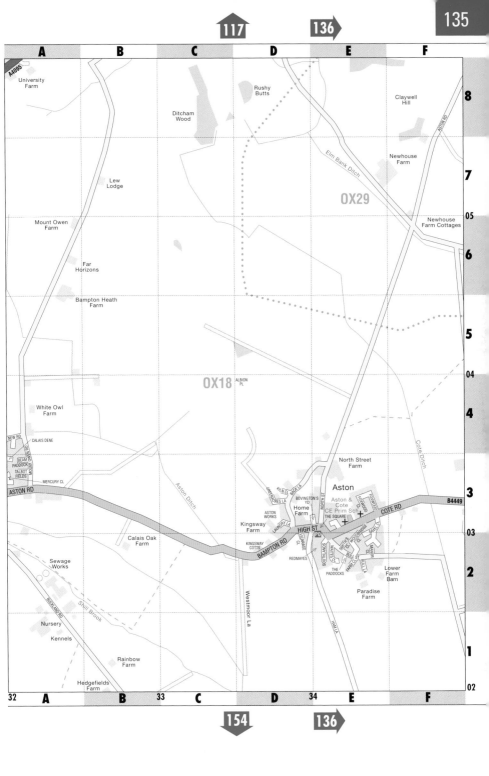

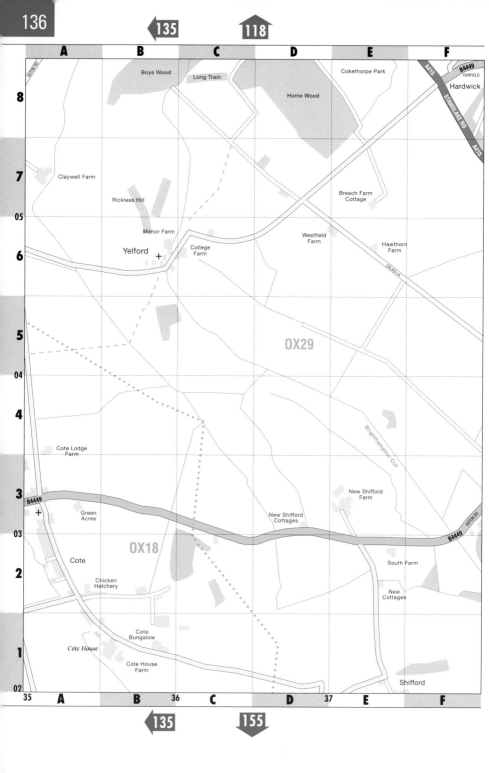

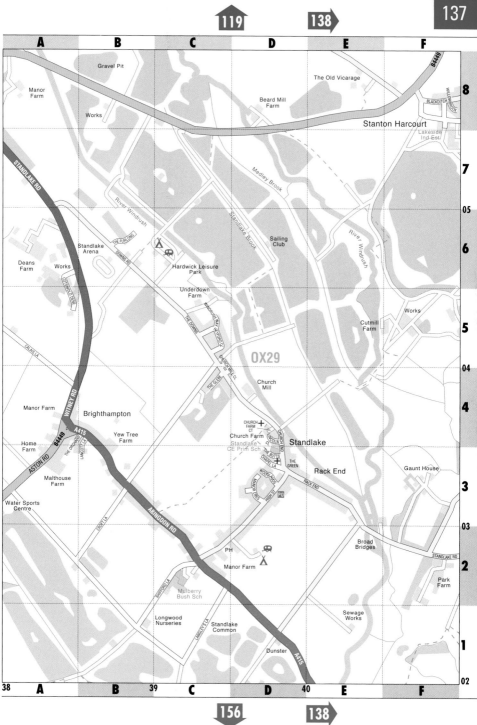

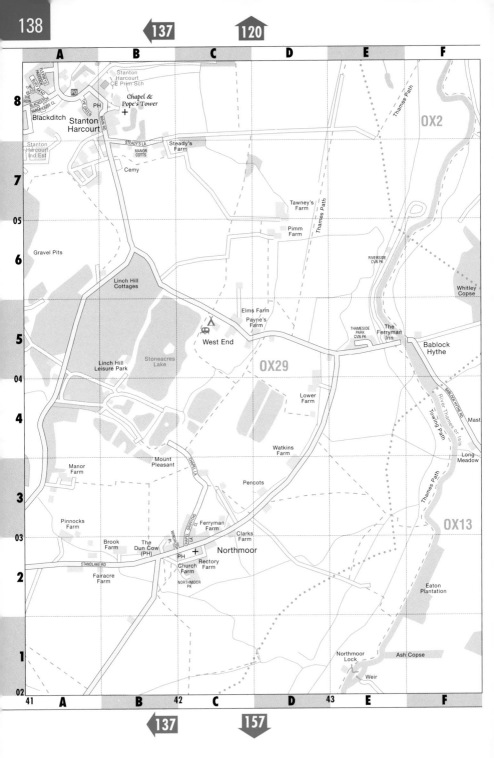

A **B** **C** **D** **E** **F**

OX2

Stanton Harcourt CE Prim Sch

THE QUEENS HARROLS CL

PO

THE ROW

BLACKDITCH HAMMHOUSE CL

PH

8

Chapel & Pope's Tower

Blackditch

Stanton Harcourt

MAIN RD

THE GREEN

Stanton Harcourt Ind. Est

STEADY'S LA

MANOR COTTS

Steady's Farm

7

Cemy

05

Tawney's Farm

Thames Path

Pimm Farm

Gravel Pits

6

RIVERSIDE CVN PK

Linch Hill Cottages

Whitley Copse

Elms Farm

Payne's Farm

THAMESIDE PARK CVN PK

The Ferryman Inn

5

West End

OX29

Bablock Hythe

Linch Hill Leisure Park

Stoneacres Lake

BABLOCK HYTHE RD

River Thames of Isis

04

Lower Farm

Towing Path

Mast

4

Watkins Farm

Long Meadow

Manor Farm

Mount Pleasant

CHAPEL LA

CROFT LA

Pencots

Thames Path

OX13

3

Pinnocks Farm

Ferryman Farm

Clarks Farm

Brook Farm

The Dun Cow (PH)

WINDMILL

PH

Rectory Farm

Northmoor

03

STANDLAKE RD

Church Farm

2

Fairacre Farm

NORTHMOOR PK

Eaton Plantation

Northmoor Lock

Ash Copse

1

Weir

02

41 **A** **B** 42 **C** **D** 43 **E** **F**

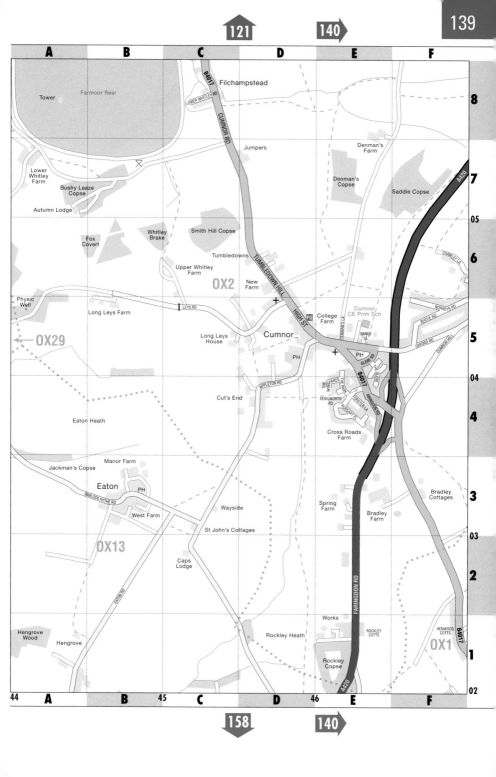

A **B** **C** **D** **E** **F**

TUDOR CT

EYNSHAM RD

B4044

B4044

FIELD HD

New Botley

FERRY HINKSEY RD

COACH MEAD

Kings Meadow

Bulls Wood

North Hinksey Village

Dean Court

Botley

MAPLE CL

LARCH CL

CHESTNUT RD

CHERRY TREE CT

CEDAR RD

BEECH RD

Hid's Copse

ARNOLD'S WAY

SYCAMORE RD

LIME RD

Raleigh Park

The Fold

Conduit House

Hinksey Stream

Long Copse

Cumnor Hill

OX2

Matthew Arnold Sch

Dene House

Westminster Inst of Ed (Harcourt Hill Campus)

Harcourt Hill

Chawley

Hurst Hill

Playing Field

5

04

Powder Hill Copse

Hen Wood

Chiswell Farm

4

Youlbury Wood

Whitebarn

Chiswell House (Priory)

Birch Copse

CHISWELL LA

3

03

Youlbury Pond

Mast

Pickett's Heath Farm

OX1

Chiswell Farm Cottages

Henwood Farm

Upper Youlbury Heath

West Gardens

2

WHITE BARN LA

Yatscombe Copse

HENWOOD DR

Wootton Close

Jarn Mound

Boars Hill

Oxford Preservation Trust

1

Henwood

Mayo's Farm

Old Boars Hill

JARN WAY

Foxcombe Hall

02

White Hill Farm

ORCHARD LA

OLD BOARS HILL

WOODLAND WLK

47 **A** **48** **B** **C** **48** **D** **49** **E** **F**

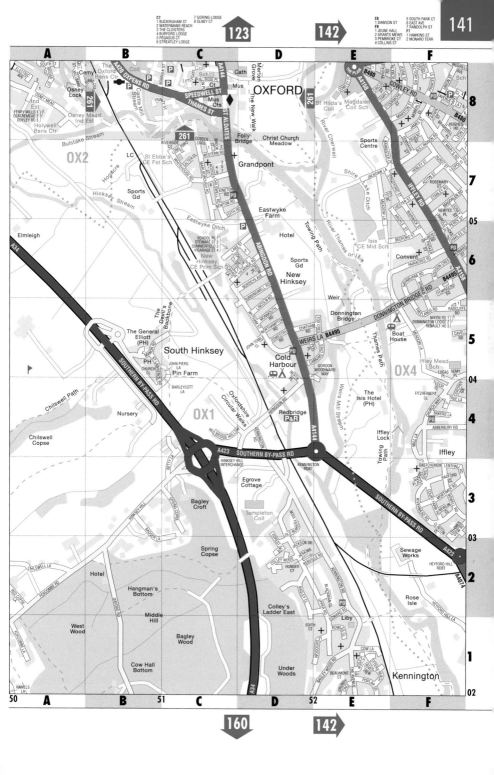

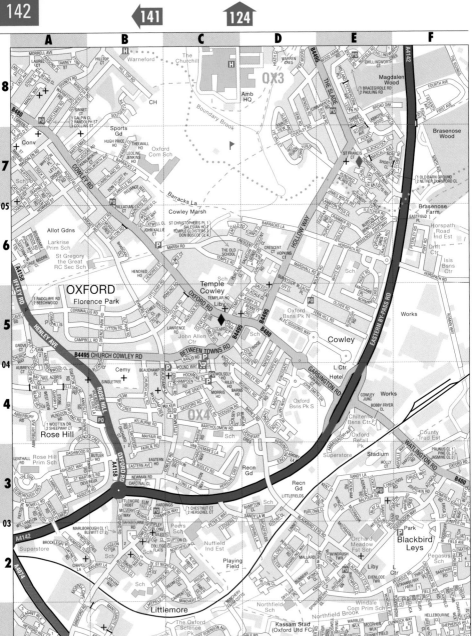

OX3

Warneford
The Churchill
OX3
Amb HQ
Boundary Brook
Magdalen Wood
1 BRACEGIRDLE RD
2 PAULING RD
Brasenose Wood

THE SLADE

Sports Gd
Oxford Com Sch
Brasenose Farm
1 OLD BARN GROUND
2 NETHER DURNFORD CT

Allot Gdns
Larkrise Prim Sch
Cowley Marsh
Barracks La
Horspath Road Ind Est
Isis Bsns Ctr

St Gregory the Great RC Sec Sch
1 ST CHRISTOPHER'S PL 1
SALESIAN HO 2
TEMPLE CLOISTERS 3
DON BOSCOE CT 4
The Old School
Crescent
Hopkins CH

OXFORD
Florence Park
Temple Cowley
Templar Ho
Liby
Oxford Bsns Pk N
Works

Lawrence Ctr
John Allen Ctr
Cowley
Works

B4495 CHURCH COWLEY RD
BETWEEN TOWNS RD
GARSINGTON RD
L Ctr
Hotel
Cowley Bsns Pk S
Cowley Junc
Bobby Fryer Cl
Chilterns Bsns Ctr
Oxford Retail Pk
Superstore
Stadium
County Trad Est

Rose Hill
Rose Hill Prim Sch
OX4
Recn Gd
Blackbird Leys
Park
Pegasus Sch

Superstore
Littlemore
Pedrs Sch
Nuffield Ind Est
Playing Field
Recn Gd
Littlefields
Orchard Meadow Fst Sch
Windrush Twr
Liby
Ctr

St Nicholas
The Oxford Science Pk
Northfield Sch
Windale Com Prim Sch

Littlemore
Littlemore Brook
Northfield Brook
Kassam Stad
(Oxford Utd FC)
Sewage Works

B3
1 CRANSTON CT
2 ROSE CT
3 HILLSBOROUGH CL

C4
1 LEWIN CL
2 THE SQUARE
3 UPPER BARR
4 COMPASS CL
5 Templars Sq

E1
1 NUTHATCH CL
2 VERBENA WAY
3 BROOKLINE WLK
4 CLEAVERS SQ
5 SAXIFRAGE SQ
6 BERGAMONT PL
7 FOXGLOVE CL
8 CRANESBILL WAY

F2
1 BUTTERWORT PL
2 REST HARROW
3 PERIWINKLE PL
4 STARWORT PATH
5 TIMOTHY WAY

E2
1 WHITETHORN WAY
2 NORTHBROOK HO
3 WINDALE HO

F1
1 FORGET-ME-NOT WAY
2 PEARTREE CL
3 FIRS MDW
4 BLUEBELL CT
5 COLTSFOOT SQ
6 CELANDINE PL
7 SAGE WLK
8 POCHARD PL
9 CORIANDER WAY

10 BUTTERCUP SQ
11 BLACKSMITHS MDW
12 MARIGOLD CL
13 WOODPECKER GN
14 NORMAN SMITH RD
15 SWALLOW CL
16 JACK ARGENT CL
17 MOLE PL
18 CAMPION CL
19 SWIFT CL

20 PRIMROSE PL
21 JANE SEAMAN CT

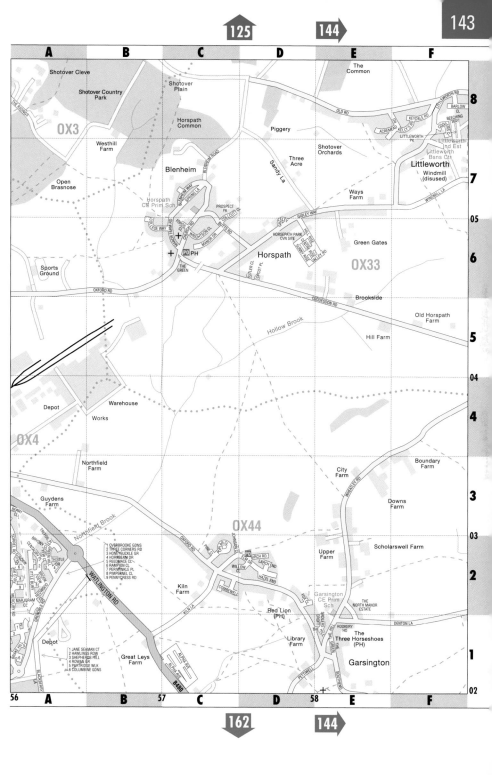

A   B   C   D   E   F

Shotover Cleve

The Common

Shotover Country Park

Shotover Plain

LITTLEWORTH RD

BARLOW CL

BEECHING WAY

OX3

THE BLOORS

OLD RD

ACREMEAD

KEYDALE RD

KELLY'S RD

Horspath Common

Westhill Farm

Piggery

Shotover Orchards

LITTLEWORTH PK

Littleworth Bsns Ctr

Littleworth Ind Est

Littleworth

Blenheim

Sandy La

Three Acre

WINDMILL LA

Windmill (disused)

Open Brasnose

BLENHEIM WAY

SPRING LA

Horspath CE Prim Sch

PROSPECT PK

Ways Farm

8

7

05

COLLEGE WAY

OLD RD

CHURCH RD

FORD LA

WRIGHTSON CL

OXCUT CL

BUTTS RD

MANOR DR

KELLY RD

GIDLEY WAY

Horspath

Green Gates

OX33

6

Sports Ground

+

+

PO PH

THE GREEN

OXFORD RD

BUTLER CL

DENTON CL

Horspath Park Cvn Site

VALLEY RD

CUDDESDON RD

Brookside

Old Horspath Farm

Hollow Brook

Hill Farm

5

04

Depot

Warehouse

Works

OX4

Northfield Farm

City Farm

Boundary Farm

Guydens Farm

WHEATLEY RD

Downs Farm

3

03

Northfield Brook

BERRY

TREFOIL LN

BRYONY

CENTAURY

THISTLE DR

LITTLE BURY

OXFORD RD

OX44

Scholarswell Farm

Upper Farm

2

WATLINGTON RD

7 OVERBROOKE GDNS
2 THREE CORNERS RD
3 HONEYSUCKLE GR
4 HORNBEAM DR
5 REEDMACE CL
6 RAMPION CL
7 PERIWINKLE PL
8 PIMPERNEL CL
9 PENNYCRESS RD

JOHNSON LA

PINES

WILLOW CL

BIRCH RD

LARCH END

HAZEL END

COMBEWELL

Kiln Farm

Garsington CE Prim Sch

THE NORTH MANOR ESTATE

DENTON LA

MERCURY RD

MARJORAM CL

Depot

1 JANE SEAMAN CT
2 HAWLINGS ROW
3 SHEPHERDS HILL
4 ROWAN GR
5 PARTRIDGE WLK
6 COLUMBINE GDNS

KILN LA

ALDER

Red Lion (PH)

Library Farm

FOXY

SOUTHEND

ROOKERY HO

The Three Horseshoes (PH)

1

Great Leys Farm

ALPHA RD

B480

PETTIWELL

THE GREEN

Garsington

02

56   A   57   B   C   58   D   E   F

8

Wheatley

WESTFIELD RD
KENT LA
BLENHEIM LA
LITTLEWORTH LA
BARLOW CL
Wheatley
CE Prim Sch
MORLAND RD
GARDINER
ST MARY'S
CHURCH RD
HIGH ST
P Liby
PO
CROWN SQ
COLLEGE CL
Wheatley Campus
(Brookes Univ)
FAIRFAX GATE
BISCOE CT
A40
Holton Mill
House

LITTLEWORTH
PK
HOWE CL
KELHAM HALL DR
BEECH RD
CROWN RD
FARM CLOSE
SIMON'S CL
HATHAWAYS
WINDMILL LA
LADDER HILL
CULLUM
RD
WINDOWS
CT
THE AVENUE
LONDON RD
ELTON CRES
ROMAN RD
Wheatley
Bridge
Sewage
Works
PH Hotel
A40
A418
ASHHURST
CT
M40

05

Coombe House

OX33

6

Castle Hill
Farm

Castle Hill

New Barn

Coombe Wood

Cuddesdon Brook

5

CUDDESDON RD

River Thame

STADHAMPTON RD

04

The
Farmhouse

Slay Barn

Sluice

4

Sunset
Lodge
PARKSIDE
BISHOP'S WOOD

3

Ripon
Coll
Dovehouse
Farm

OX44

Cuddesdon

03

VINE
COTTS
THE
GREEN
PH
FIELD & CL
HIGH ST
THE LANE
CHURCH CL

Upper
Farm
BROOKSIDE

DENTON HILL

2

Cuddesdon Mill
(dis)

Mill House

Denton
House

Castle Farm

College
Farm

Denton

DENTON LA

Lower Farm

1

02

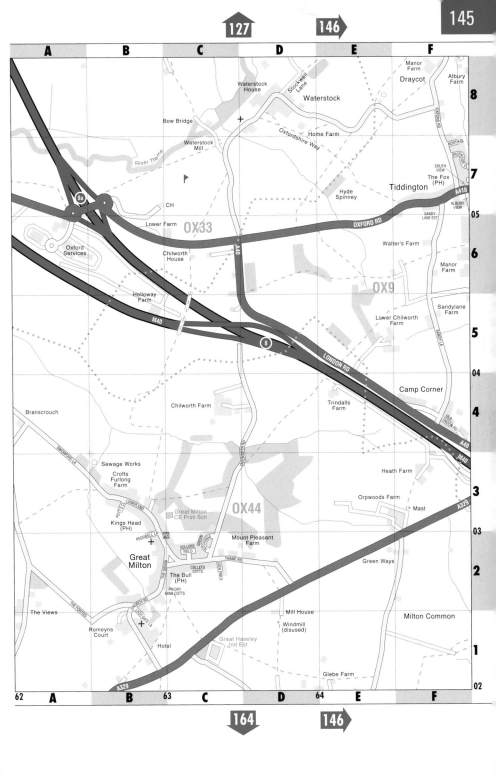

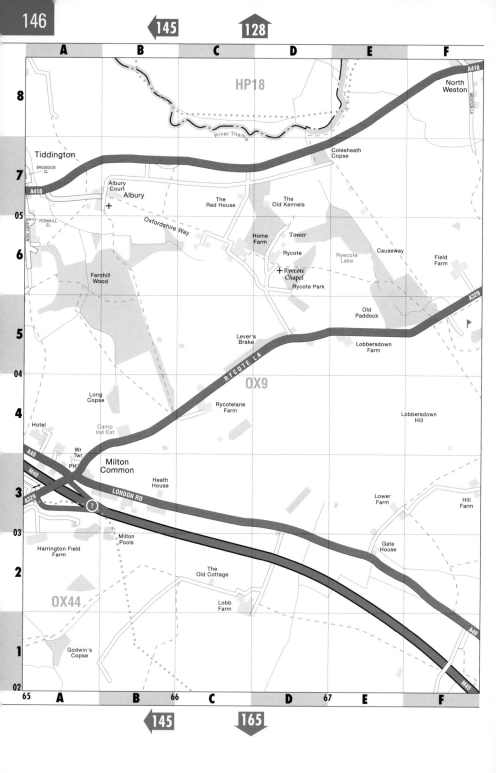

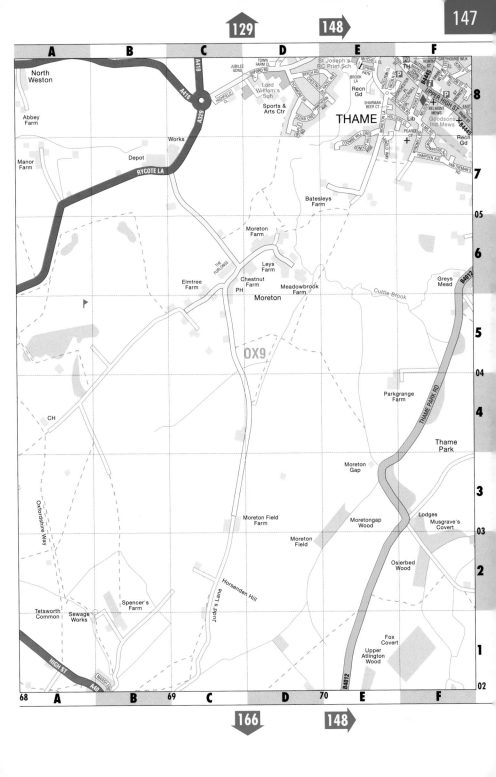

147
130

New Barn Farm
Whites Farm
Sewage Works

Lower Green Farm

Towersey Rd
Cotmore Wells
Westfield Farm
Quash Farm
Church Farm
Manor

THAME

Cotmore Wells Farm

Manor Farm

Towersey
Upper Green Farm

Deans Farm
PH

1 GARDEN CITY
2 WALKERS DR
3 LASSY DR
4 PEARCE WAY

Works
Home Farm

Works

Nursery

Blackditch Farm

The Copperlites

CHINNOR RD

Cuttle Brook

OX9

Sydenham Hurst

Westbrook Farm

Square Covert

Thame Park

The Belt

Waterlands Farm

New Park

Brooklands

Hollier's Covert

Sea Pond Wood

Sydenham Grange Farm

Stocken Corner Covert

OX39

The Inn at Emmington (PH)

Manor Farm

THAME RD

Park View

147
167

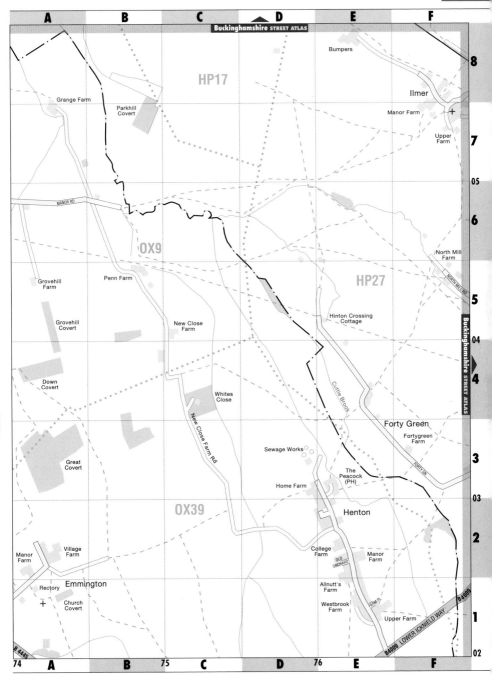

HP17

Bumpers

Ilmer

Grange Farm

Parkhill
Covert

Manor Farm

Upper
Farm

8

7

05

MANOR RD

OX9

6

Grovehill
Farm

Penn Farm

HP27

North Mill
Farm

Grovehill
Covert

New Close
Farm

Hinton Crossing
Cottage

5

04

Down
Covert

Whites
Close

4

Cuttle Brook

Forty Green

Fortygreen
Farm

Great
Covert

Sewage Works

The
Peacock
(PH)

3

03

New Close Farm Rd

OX39

Home Farm

Henton

2

Manor
Farm

Village
Farm

College
Farm

Manor
Farm

OLD
ORCHARD

Rectory

Emmington

Allnutt's
Farm

Westbrook
Farm

Upper Farm

1

Church
Covert

B 4445

74

75

76

02

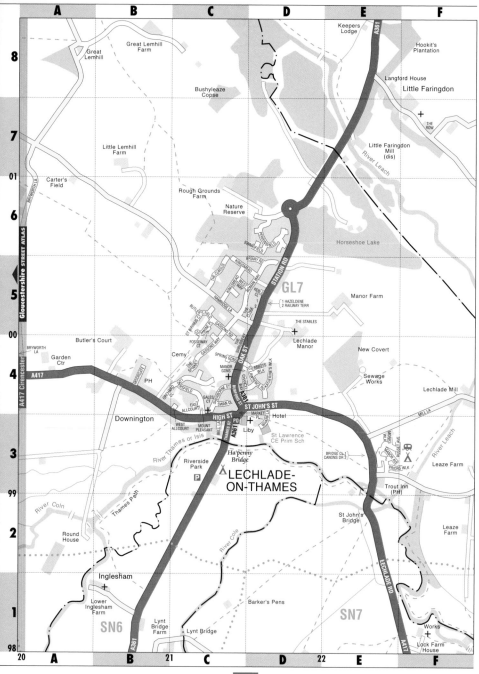

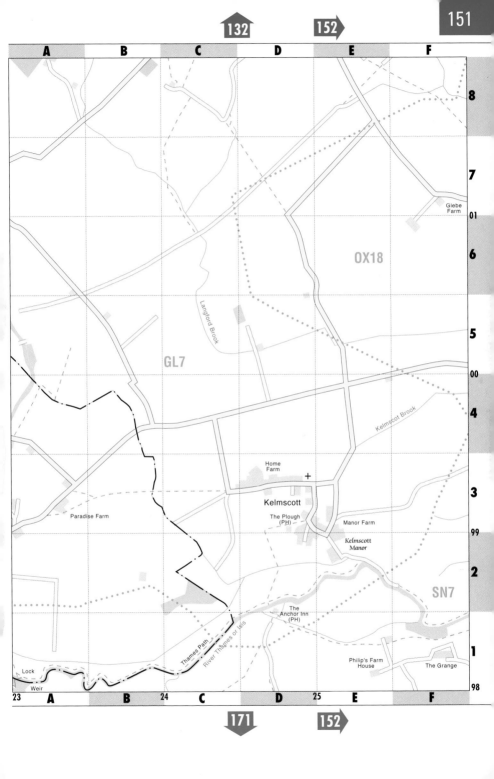

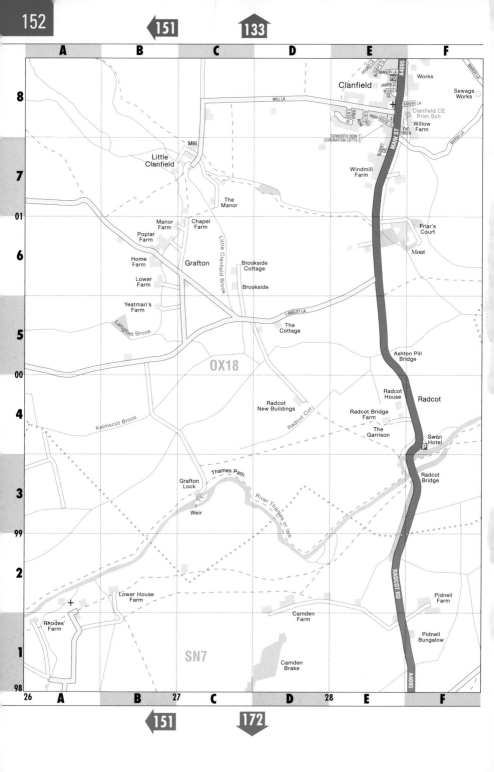

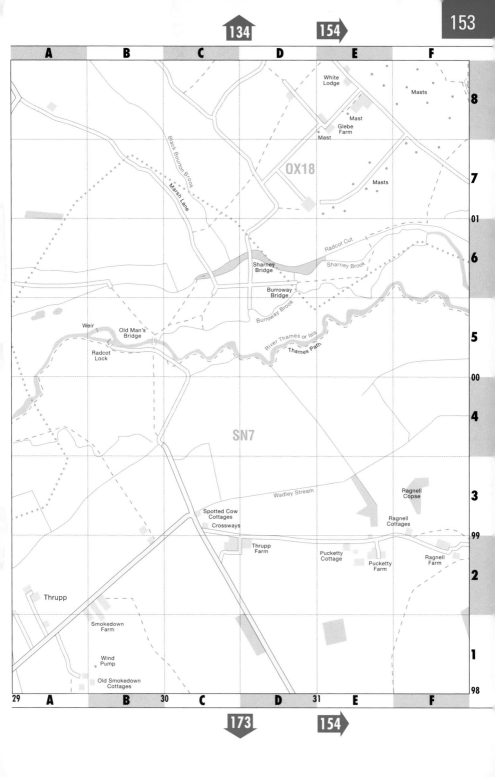

A B C D E F

8

White Lodge

Masts

Mast

Glebe Farm

Mast

OX18

7

Masts

01

Black Bourton Brook

Marsh Lane

Radcot Cut

6

Sharney Bridge

Sharney Brook

Burroway Bridge

Weir

Old Man's Bridge

Burroway Brook

River Thames or Isis

5

Radcot Lock

Thames Path

00

4

SN7

Wadley Stream

3

Ragnell Copse

Spotted Cow Cottages

Crossways

Ragnell Cottages

99

Thrupp Farm

Pucketty Cottage

Pucketty Farm

Ragnell Farm

2

Thrupp

Smokedown Farm

Wind Pump

1

Old Smokedown Cottages

98

29 A B 30 C D 31 E F

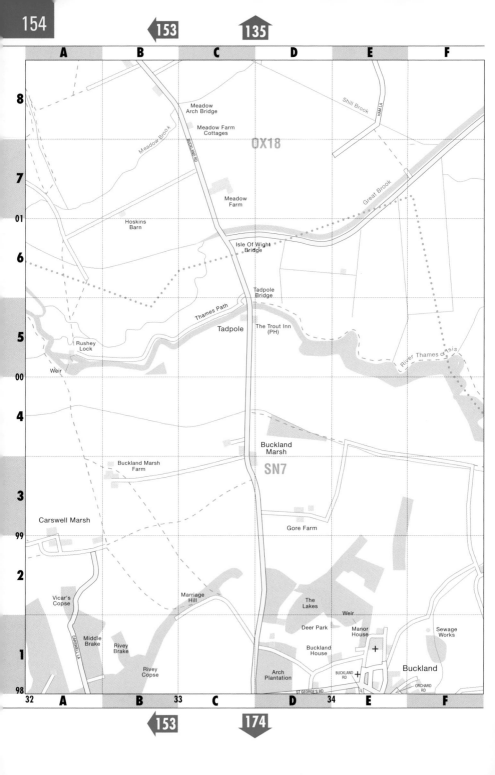

153
135

8

Meadow
Arch Bridge

Meadow Farm
Cottages

OX18

7

Meadow
Farm

01

Hoskins
Barn

Isle Of Wight
Bridge

6

Tadpole
Bridge

Thames Path

Tadpole

The Trout Inn
(PH)

5

Rushey
Lock

Weir

River Thames oasis

00

4

Buckland
Marsh

Buckland Marsh
Farm

SN7

3

Carswell Marsh

Gore Farm

99

2

Vicar's
Copse

Marriage
Hill

The
Lakes

Weir

Middle
Brake

Rivey
Brake

Deer Park

Manor
House

Sewage
Works

1

Rivey
Copse

Buckland
House

BUCKLAND
RD

Buckland

ORCHARD
RD

Arch
Plantation

ST GEORGE'S RD

98

Meadow Brook

BUCKLAND RD

Shill Brook

Great Brook

CASSELL LA

32   A   B   33   C   D   34   E   F

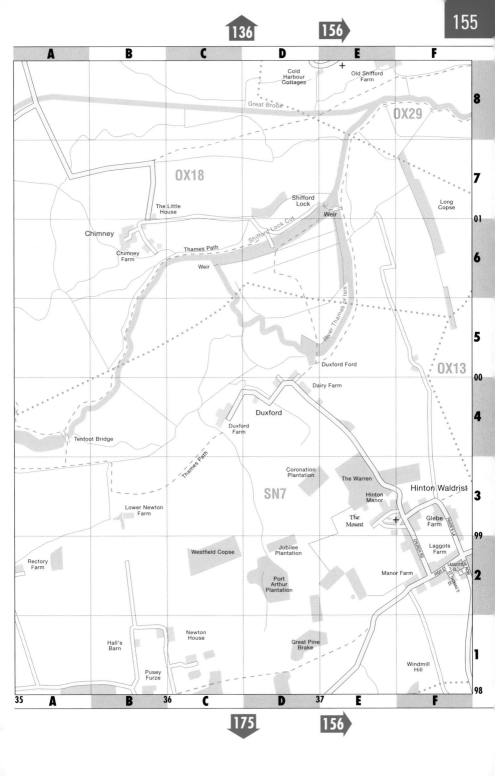

A   B   C   D   E   F

Cold
Harbour
Cottages
Old Shifford
Farm

8

Great Brook

OX29

7

OX18

The Little
House

Shifford
Lock

Long
Copse

Weir

01

Chimney

Shifford Lock Cut

Chimney
Farm

Thames Path

6

Weir

River Thames or Isis

5

Duxford Ford

OX13

00

Dairy Farm

4

Duxford

Duxford
Farm

Tenfoot Bridge

Thames Path

Coronation
Plantation

The Warren

Hinton Waldrist

3

SN7

Hinton
Manor

Lower Newton
Farm

The
Mount

Glebe
Farm

99

Rectory
Farm

Westfield Copse

Jubilee
Plantation

Laggots
Farm

CHURCH RD

THORPE'S LA

LAGGOTS RD

HIGH ST

ST THOMAS'S CL

Manor Farm

2

Port
Arthur
Plantation

Hall's
Barn

Newton
House

Great Pine
Brake

Windmill
Hill

1

Pusey
Furze

98

35   A   B   36   C   D   37   E   F

155
137

A B C D E F

8

7

6

5

4

3

2

1

01

00

99

98

OX18

OX29

OX13

SN7

Bankfield Lodge
Bankside
Langley's La
Standlake Common
Newbridge Mill
A415
River Windrush
Newbridge
MORETON LA
Rose Revived (Inn)
The May Bush (PH)
New Bridge
Thames Side Farm
River Thames or Isis
Thames Path
Newbridge Farm
Harrowdown Hill
Marsh La
Kingston Brake
Brake Cottage
Kingston Hill Farm
Common La
Kingston Hill
Church Copse
Windmill Cottage
Glebe Cottage
Longworth Prim Sch
Longworth
Tuck's La
Draycott Moor Farm
COLLEGE SQ
CHURCH LA
PH
THE SQUARE
BOWBANK
BOWBANK CL
SUDBURY LA
Sudbury Farm
Northfield Farm
Longworth Manor
RODNEY PL
OWL LA
Marten's Hall Farm
HINTON RD
FACTORY LA
APPLETON RD
St Mary's Cottage
Farmlands
MARTENS LAKE
GREEN LA
New Barn Farm
HARRIS LA
Kingston Bagpuize
DRAYCOTT RD
A420
THE WARREN
Ashen Copse
PINE BROOK RD
Glen Farm
Southmoor
LARCH CL
SANDY AVE
NORWOOD CL
John Blandy Prim Sch
FIR TREE CL
PH
OXFORD RD
WORCESTER PL
PADDOCK
BEECHES LA
GREENHEART WAY
FARINGDON RD
BELLAMY CL
NORWOOD AVE
A415
A420
THE PADDOCK

38 39 40

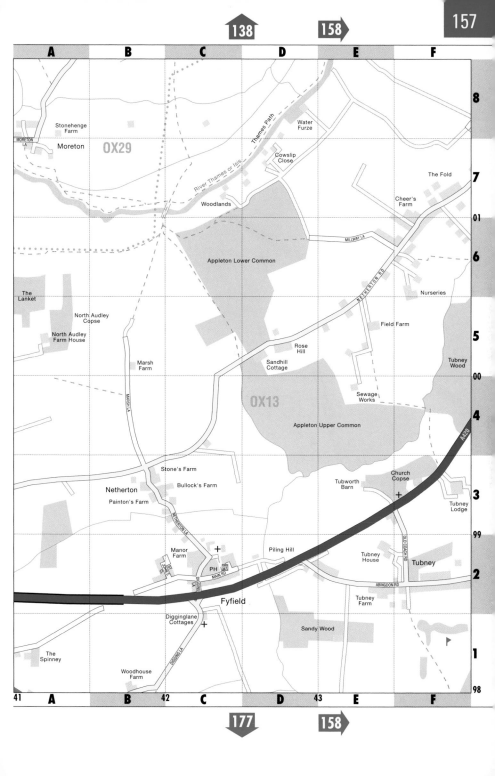

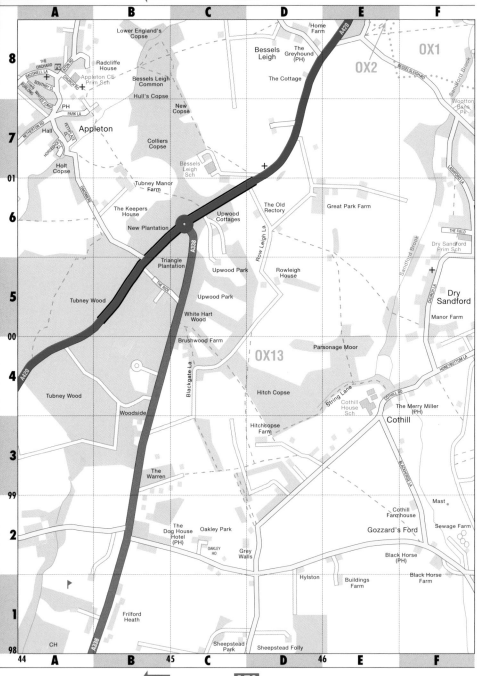

OX1

OX2

Home Farm

Bessels Leigh

The Greyhound (PH)

Lower England's Copse

Radcliffe House

Appleton CE Prim Sch

Bessels Leigh Common

Hull's Copse

The Cottage

Bessels Leigh Sch

A420

BESSELS LEIGH RD

Wootton Bassett Pk

Sandford Brook

THE ORCHARD

BAGGWELL LA

SOUTHBY LT

WHITES CLOSE

EATON RD

CHURCH RD

PH

PARK LA

New Copse

Colliers Copse

Hall

PETTIPLACE

HORSESHOE CL

NETHERTON RD

Appleton

Holt Copse

Tubney Manor Farm

DASHWERE

The Keepers House

Upwood Cottages

The Old Rectory

Great Park Farm

Row Leigh La

THE FIELD

Dry Sandford Prim Sch

New Plantation

Triangle Plantation

THE RIDE

Upwood Park

Rowleigh House

Sandford Brook

CHURCH LA

Dry Sandford

Manor Farm

Tubney Wood

Upwood Park

White Hart Wood

OX13

Parsonage Moor

HONEYBOTTOM LA

A420

Brushwood Farm

Blackgate La

Tubney Wood

Woodside

Hitch Copse

String Lane

Cothill House Sch

COTHILL RD

The Merry Miller (PH)

Cothill

Hitchcopse Farm

BLACKDELL LA

The Warren

The Dog House Hotel (PH)

Oakley Park

OAKLEY HO

Grey Walls

Cothill Farmhouse

Mast

Gozzard's Ford

Sewage Farm

Black Horse (PH)

Hylston

Buildings Farm

Black Horse Farm

Frilford Heath

CH

A338

Sheepstead Park

Sheepstead Folly

44   45   46

8 01 7 6 5 00 4 3 99 2 1 98

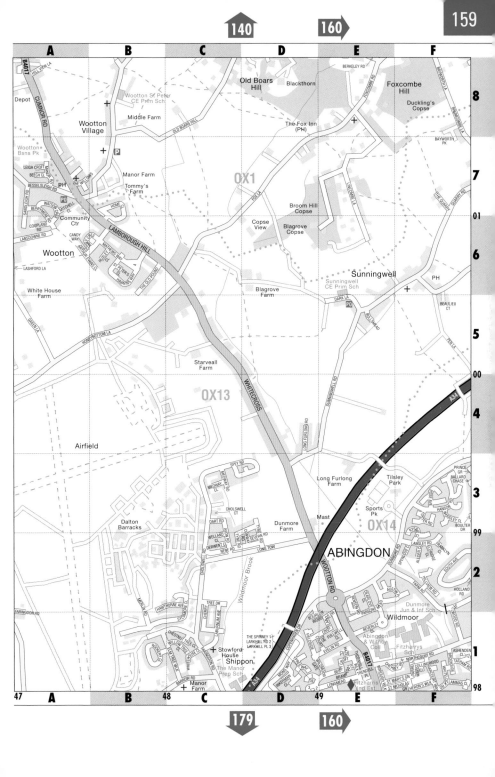

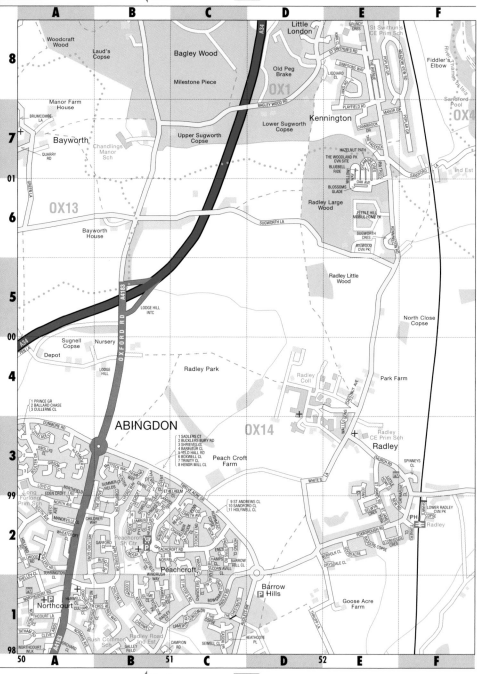

8

7

01

6

5

00

4

3

99

2

1

98

Woodcraft Wood

Laud's Copse

Bagley Wood

Milestone Piece

Little London

St Swithin's CE Prim Sch

GRUNDY CRES

ST SWITHIN'S RD

SIMPSONS WAY

Old Peg Brake

OX1

Fiddler's Elbow

Sandford Pool

OX4

Manor Farm House

BRUMCOMBE LA

Bayworth

QUARRY RD

GREEN LA

Chandlings Manor Sch

Upper Sugworth Copse

Lower Sugworth Copse

Kennington

LIDGARD CL

PLAYFIELD RD

MANOR GR

POPLAR GR

CRANBROOK DR

THE PADDOCK

Ind Est

OX13

Bayworth House

SUGWORTH LA

HAZELNUT PATH

THE WOODLAND PK CVN SITE

BLUEBELL RIDE

OAK AVE

WILLOW WAY

SYCAMORE CRES

BLOSSOMS GLADE

Radley Large Wood

PEEBLE HILL MOBILE HOME PK

SUGWORTH CRES

BIGWOOD CVN PK

KENNINGTON RD

Radley Little Wood

North Close Copse

A34

PERRIN WAY

A4183

LODGE HILL INTC

OXFORD RD

Sugnell Copse

Nursery

Depot

LODGE HILL

Radley Park

Radley Coll

CHESTNUT AVE

Park Farm

ABINGDON

1 PRINCE GR
2 BALLARD CHASE
3 CULLERNE CL

OX14

1 SADLERS CT
2 BUCKLERS BURY RD
3 SHRIEVES CL
4 BARBLEUR CL
5 YELD HALL RD
6 BOXWELL CL
7 TRINITY CL
8 HENOR MILL CL

Peach Croft Farm

Radley CE Prim Sch

Radley

CHURCH RD

SPINNEYS CL

DUNMORE RD

LOVE AGE CL

KNOLLYS

GIBSON

ALEXANDER CL

MATTOCK WAY

SUMMERFIELDS

CARBEL CL

WELLE ACRE DR

ETHELHELM CL

WHITE LA

Long Furlong Prim Sch

EDEN CROFT

NORTH AVE

SOUTHLAKE

NORTHFIELD

MANDEVILLE CL

CHILDREY WAY

WHEATCROFT

WELLESLEY

LUMBERD RD

ELIZABETH AVE

9 ST ANDREWS CL
10 SANDFORD CL
11 HOLYWELL CL

ST AMES CRES

ST AMES CT

STONEHOUSE CRES

LOWER RADLEY CVN PK

Radley

SELLWOOD RD

PEACHCROFT RD

GARFORD CL

PYKES CL

STOCKEY END

FOXBOROUGH RD

PH

Radley

NORFOLK CL

COPSE ACRE

DRYSDALE CL

SHELLEY LA

HARWELL CL

CULHAM

GLYME

Peachcroft Sch Ctr

NORRIS

WINDRUSH WAY

ACORN AVLL

Barrow Hill CL

CHAMPS CL

ENEV

ST PETERS RD

BOWGRAVE

BARROW HILL CL

Barrow Hills

Goose Acre Farm

Northcourt

THCOURT LA

TATHAM

CLEVE

ORCHARD

A4183

Rush Common Sch

Radley Road Ind Est

GALLEY FIELD

CAMPION

SEWELL CL

THE COPSE

HEATHCOTE PL

50   A   B   51   C   D   52   E   F

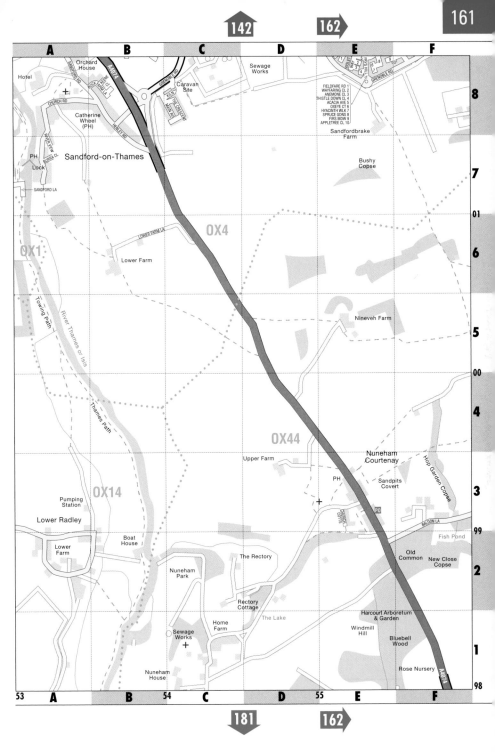

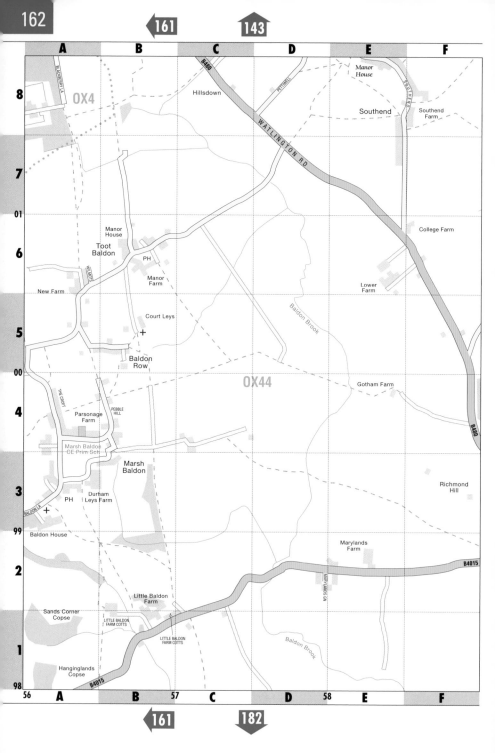

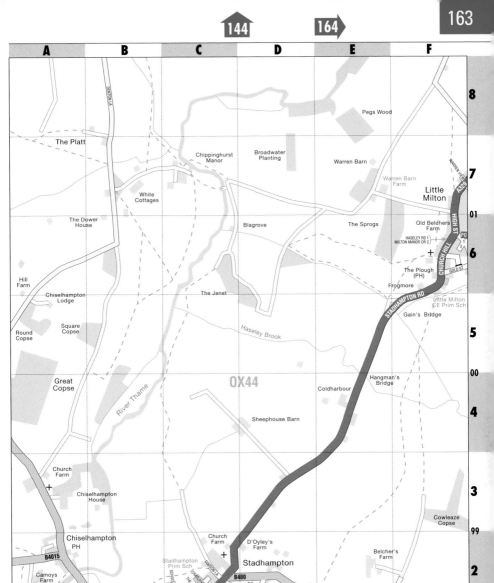

A   B   C   D   E   F

8

The Platt

Chippinghurst Manor

Broadwater Planting

Pegs Wood

Warren Barn

7

Warren Barn Farm

Little Milton

White Cottages

The Dower House

Blagrove

The Sprogs

Old Beldhers Farm

01

HASELEY RD 1
MILTON MANOR DR 2

6

PO

Hill Farm

Chiselhampton Lodge

The Jenet

The Plough (PH)

Frogmore

GOLD ST

Little Milton CE Prim Sch

Square Copse

Round Copse

Haseley Brook

STADHAMPTON RD

Gain's Bridge

5

Great Copse

OX44

Hangman's Bridge

00

River Thame

Coldharbour

4

Sheephouse Barn

Church Farm

Chiselhampton House

3

Cowleaze Copse

99

Chiselhampton PH

Church Farm

D'Oyley's Farm

Belcher's Farm

B4015

Stadhampton Prim Sch

Church Farm

Stadhampton

2

Camoys Farm

Camoys Court

SCHOOL LA
THE LAINES
BROADHAMPTON CL

B480

THE GREEN

Manor Farm

Moat

Ascott Park

B480

NEWINGTON RD

PO
REAR LA

PH

NEWELL'S CL

Brookhampton

Newell's Farm

Ascott

Ascott Farm

1

WARREN HILL

Fish Ponds

98

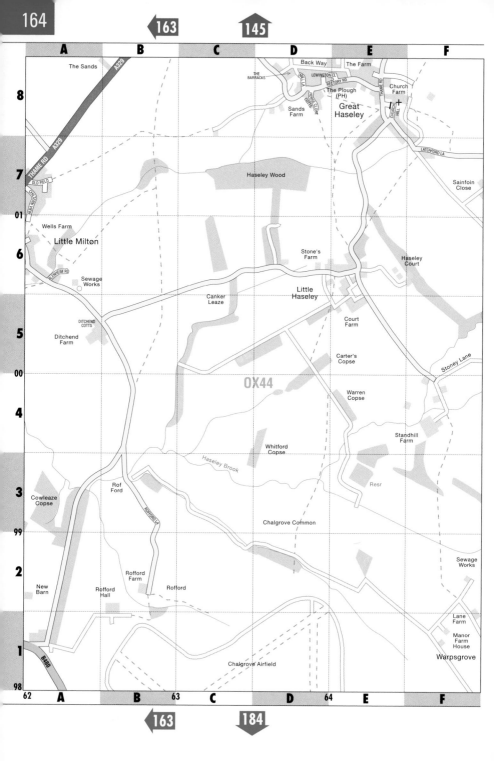

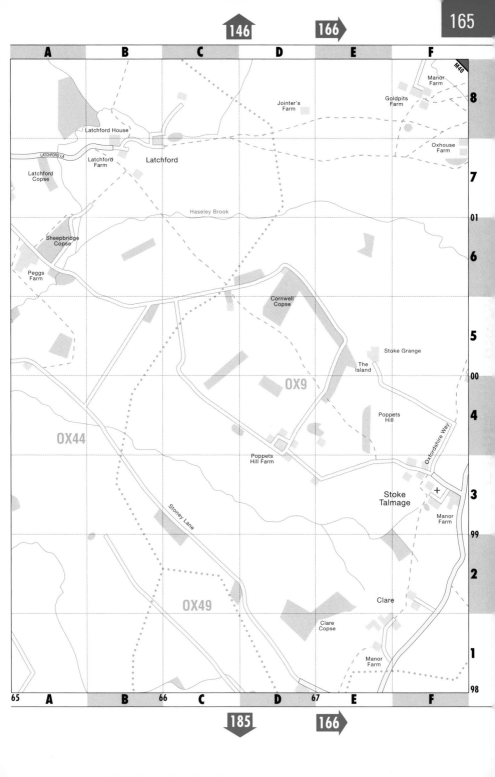

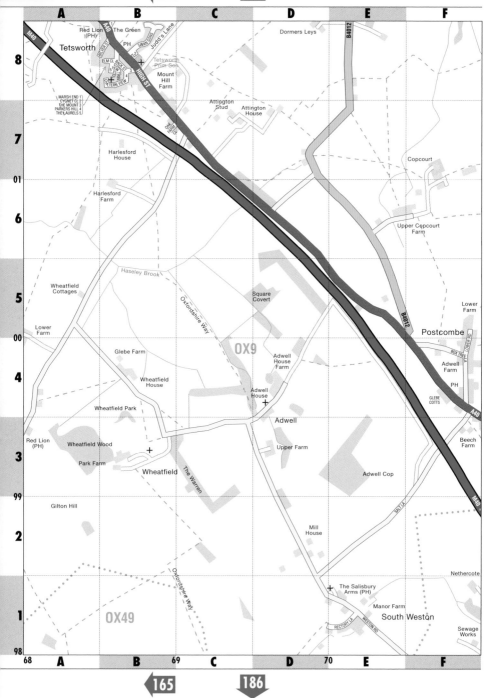

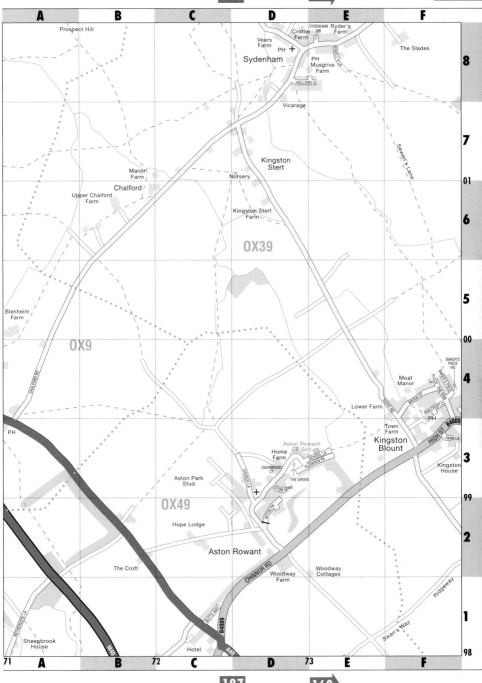

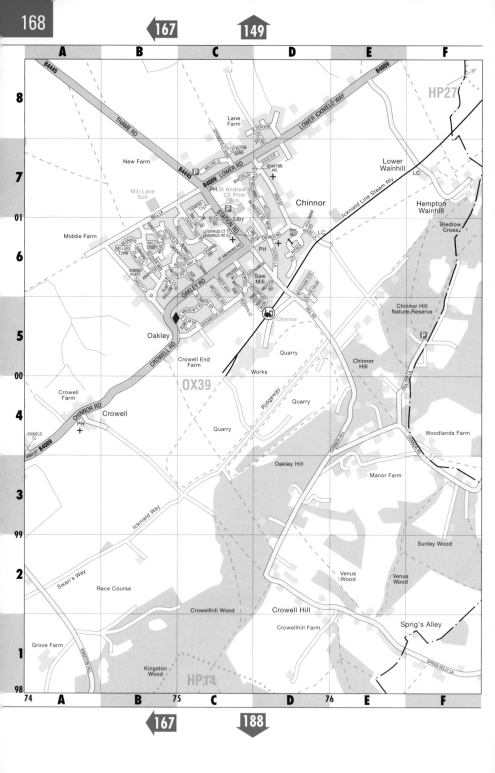

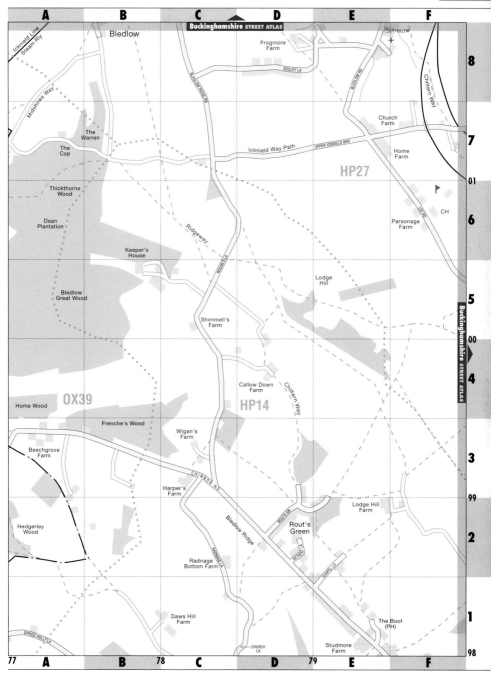

Bledlow

Frogmore Farm

TROUT HULLOW

ODDLEY LA

BLEDLOW RIDGE RD

BLEDLOW RD

Chiltern Way

Icknield Line Steam Rly

Midshires Way

The Warren

The Cop

Church Farm

Home Farm

Icknield Way Path

UPPER ICKNIELD WAY

HP27

01

Thickthorne Wood

Dean Plantation

Ridgeway

Parsonage Farm

CH

LEE RD

6

Keeper's House

WIGAN'S LA

Lodge Hill

Bledlow Great Wood

5

Shimmell's Farm

00

OX39

Callow Down Farm

Chiltern Way

4

Home Wood

HP14

Frenche's Wood

Wigan's Farm

3

Beechgrove Farm

CHINNOR RD

Harper's Farm

99

Lodge Hill Farm

Hedgerley Wood

Bledlow Ridge

ROUTS GRN

Rout's Green

2

RADNAGE LA

RED LA

Radnage Bottom Farm

CHAPEL LA

1

Daws Hill Farm

The Boot (PH)

Studmore Farm

SPRIGS HOLLY LA

CHURCH LA

98

77   A   B   78   C   D   79   E   F

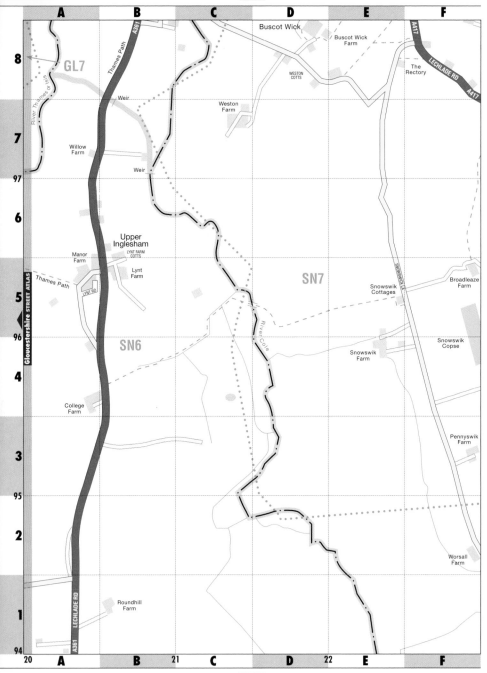

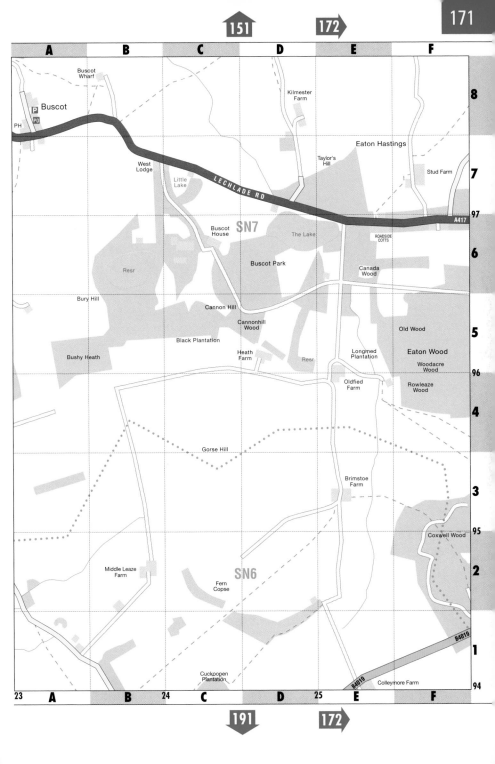

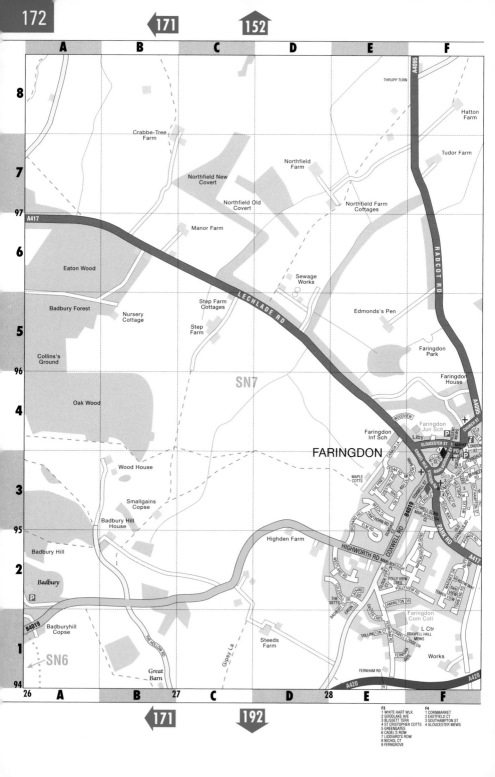

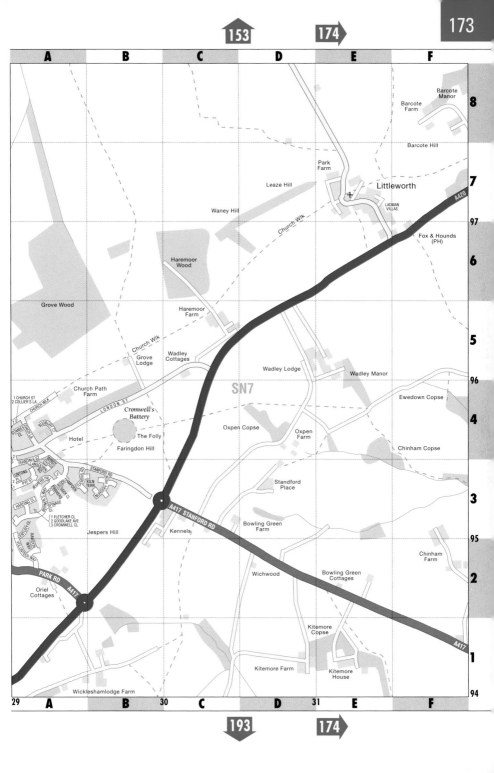

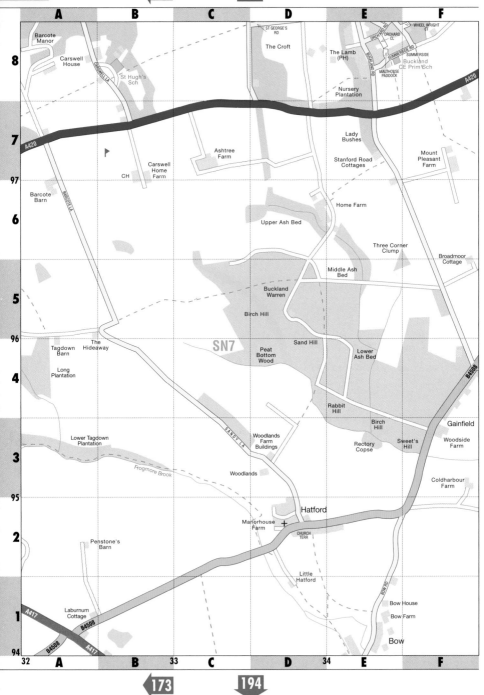

173
154

8
7
97
6
5
96
4
3
95
2
1
94

A   B   C   D   E   F

Barcote Manor
Carswell House
CASSWELL LA
St Hugh's Sch
CH
Carswell Home Farm
A420
Barcote Barn
BARCOTE LA

ST GEORGE'S RD
The Croft
The Lamb (PH)
Nursery Plantation
BIRCH RD
ORCHARD CL
BECKLAND RD
SUMMERSIDE RD
WHEEL WRIGHT CT
SUMMERSIDE
MALTHOUSE PADDOCK
Buckland CE Prim Sch
A420

Ashtree Farm
Lady Bushes
Stanford Road Cottages
Mount Pleasant Farm

Home Farm
Upper Ash Bed
Three Corner Clump
Broadmoor Cottage
Middle Ash Bed

Buckland Warren
Birch Hill
Sand Hill
Lower Ash Bed

SN7
Tagdown Barn
The Hideaway
Long Plantation
Peat Bottom Wood

Rabbit Hill
Birch Hill
Gainfield
B4508
Lower Tagdown Plantation
SANDY LA
Woodlands Farm Buildings
Rectory Copse
Sweet's Hill
Woodside Farm

Frogmore Brook
Woodlands
Coldharbour Farm

Hatford
Manorhouse Farm
CHURCH TERR

Penstone's Barn
Little Hatford
BOW RD
Bow House
Bow Farm

A417
B4508
Laburnum Cottage
B4508
A417
Bow

32   A   B   33   C   D   34   E   F

173
194

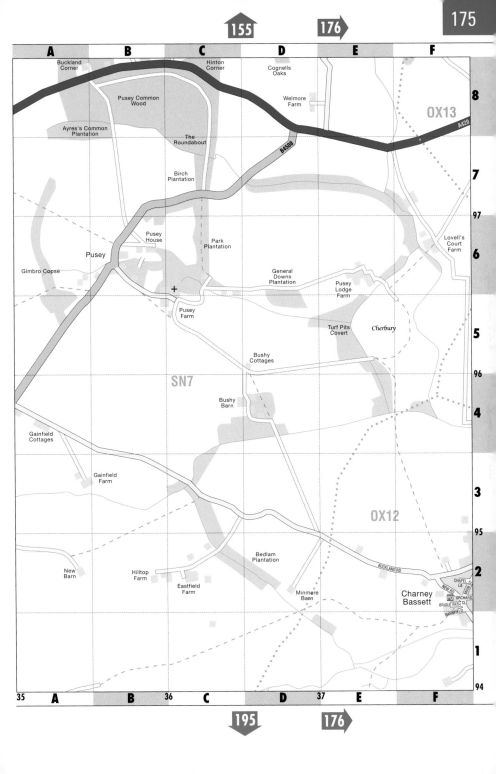

A B C D E F

8

Buckland Corner

Hinton Corner

Cognells Oaks

Pusey Common Wood

Welmore Farm

OX13

A420

Ayres's Common Plantation

The Roundabout

B4508

7

Birch Plantation

97

Pusey House

Park Plantation

Lovell's Court Farm

6

Pusey

Gimbro Copse

General Downs Plantation

Pusey Lodge Farm

Pusey Farm

Turf Pits Covert

Cherbury

5

Bushy Cottages

96

SN7

Bushy Barn

4

Gainfield Cottages

Gainfield Farm

3

OX12

95

New Barn

Bedlam Plantation

Hilltop Farm

BUCKLAND RD

2

Eastfield Farm

Minmere Barn

Charney Bassett

CHAPEL LA

NEW RD

MAIN ST

PO ORCHARD

BRIDLE PATH CL

BARNFIELD

1

94

175
156

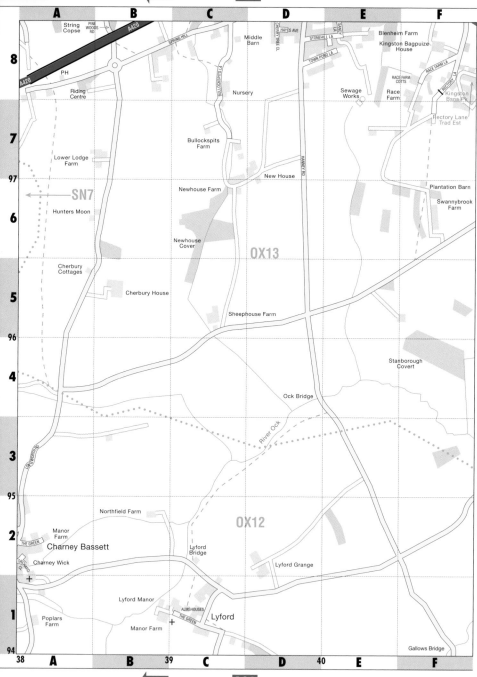

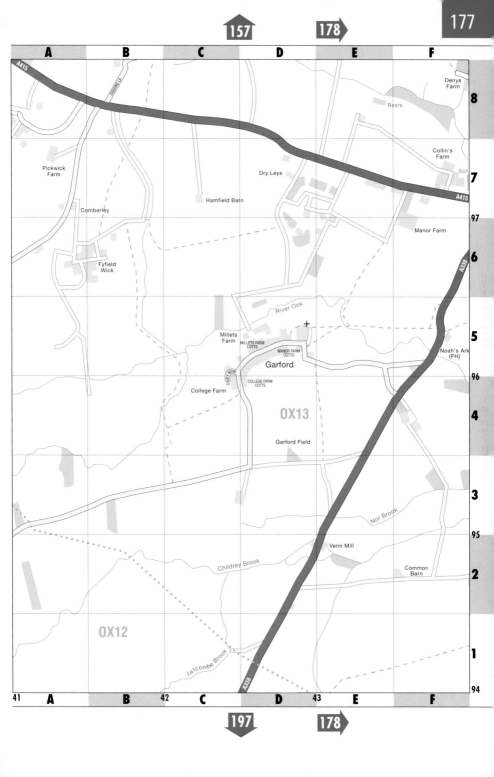

A B C D E F

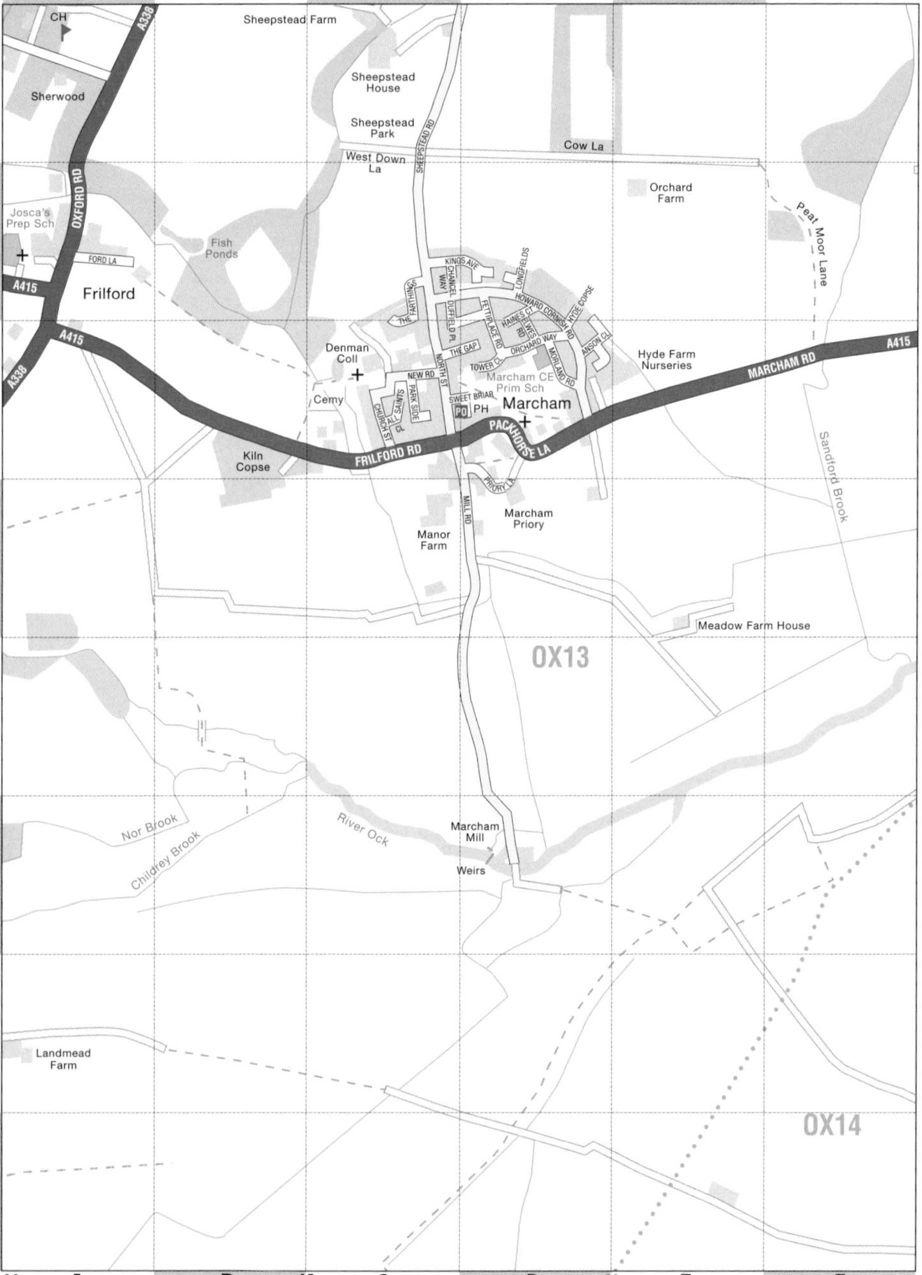

8

CH

Sherwood

Sheepstead Farm

Sheepstead House

Sheepstead Park

West Down La

Cow La

7

Josca's Prep Sch

OXFORD RD

FORD LA

A415

Frilford

Fish Ponds

Orchard Farm

Peat Moor Lane

97

A415

A338

6

Denman Coll

Cemy

KINGS AVE

CHANCEL WAY

THE

LONGFIELDS

HOWARD CORNISH RD

WHYTE COPSE

HALL

LUFFIELD PL

THE GAP

LITTLE ACE

ORCHARD WAY

HAINES WAY

NAPER CLS

NEW RD

TOWER CL

PARK RD

CHURCH ST

SWEET BRIAR

MARLBO RD

SHEEPSTEAD RD

Marcham CE Prim Sch

PO PH

Marcham

PACKHORSE LA

PRIORY LA

Hyde Farm Nurseries

MARCHAM RD

A415

Kiln Copse

FRILFORD RD

MILL RD

Manor Farm

Marcham Priory

Sandford Brook

5

OX13

96

Meadow Farm House

4

Nor Brook

Childrey Brook

River Ock

Marcham Mill

Weirs

3

95

2

Landmead Farm

OX14

1

94

44 A 45 B C 45 D 46 E F

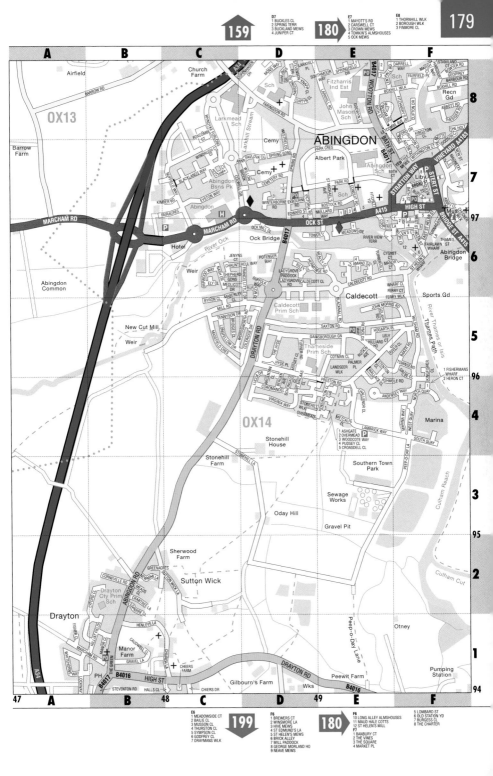

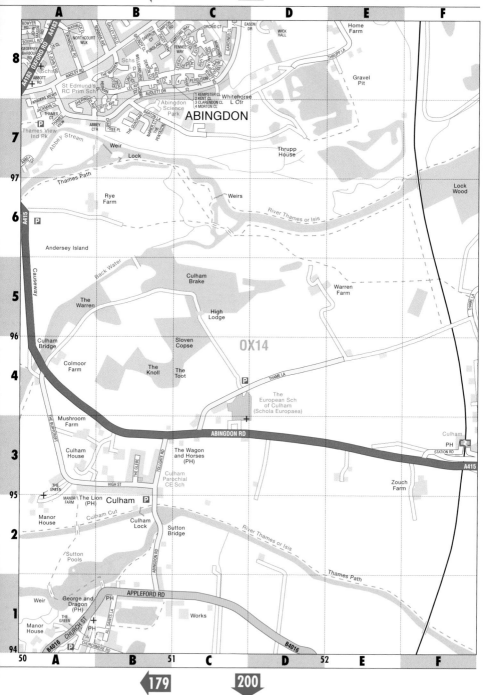

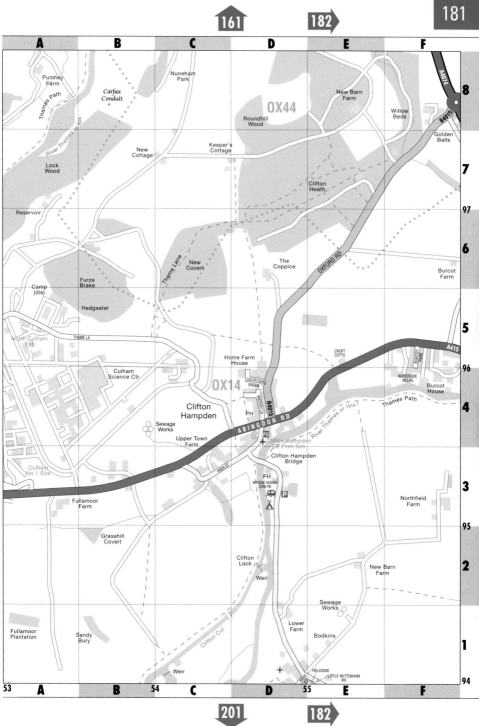

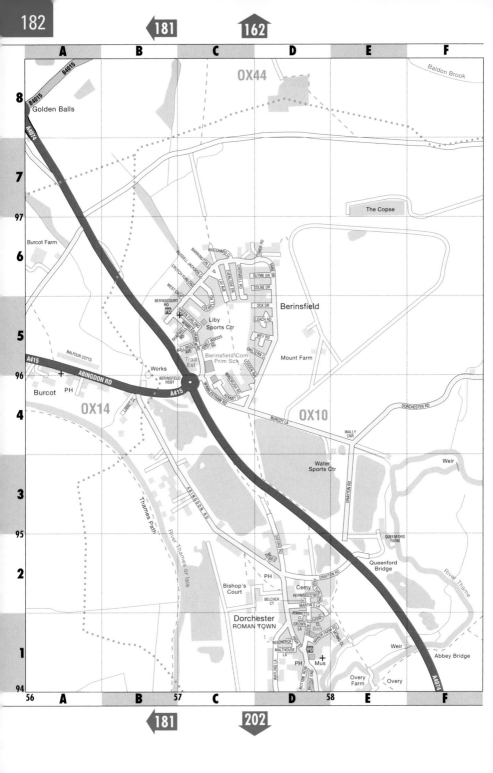

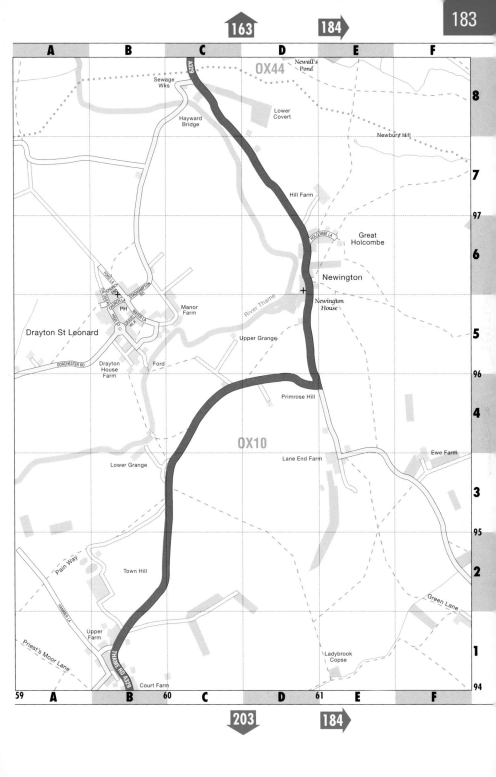

OX44

Newall's
Pond

Sewage
Wks

Lower
Covert

Hayward
Bridge

Newbury Hill

Hill Farm

Great
Holcombe

HOLCOMBE LA

Newington

FORD LA CHURCH

STADHAMPTON RD

Manor
Farm

River Thame

Newington
House

Drayton St Leonard

DOVE LA

RIDGE WK

Upper Grange

DORCHESTER RD

Drayton
House
Farm

Ford

Primrose Hill

OX10

Lower Grange

Lane End Farm

Ewe Farm

Pain Way

Town Hill

HAMMETT LA

Green Lane

Priest's Moor Lane

Upper
Farm

Ladybrook
Copse

THAME RD A329

Court Farm

8 7 97 6 5 96 4 3 95 2 1 94

A B C D E F

59   60   61

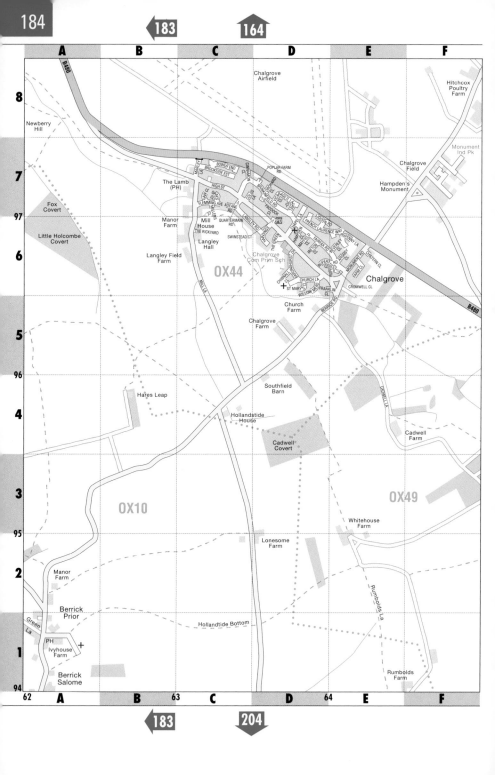

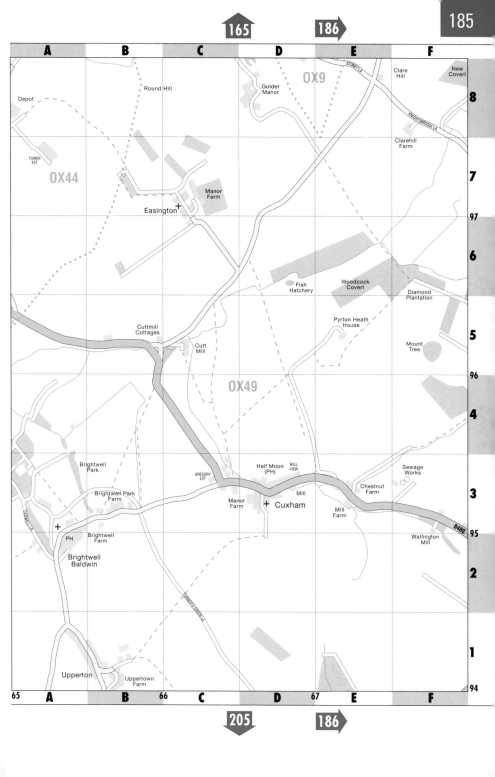

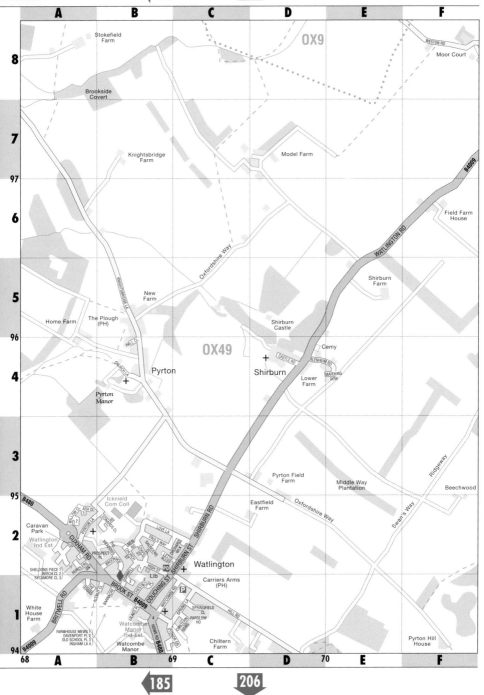

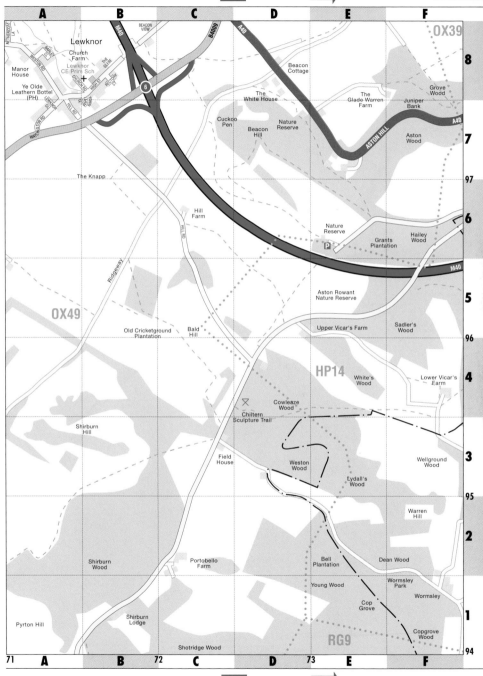

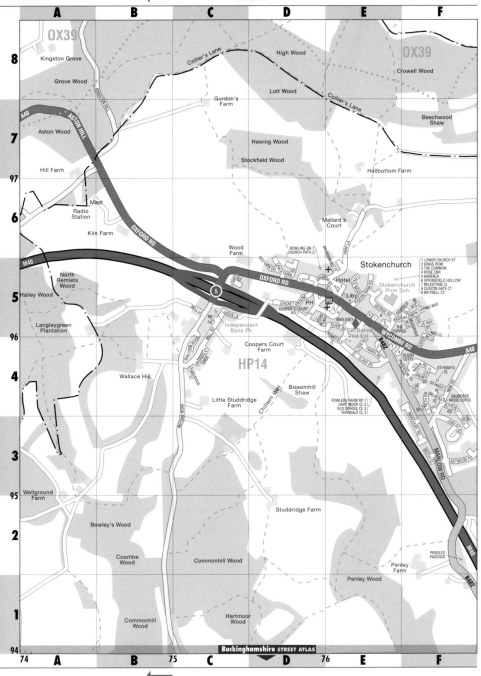

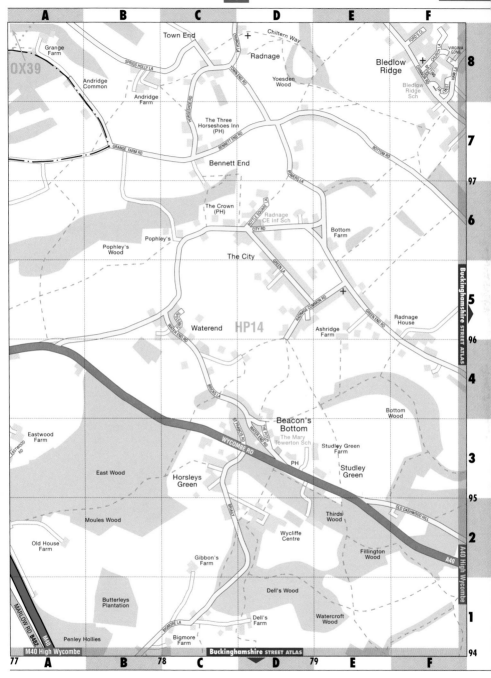

OX39

Grange
Farm

Andridge
Common

Sprigs Holly La

Andridge
Farm

Town End

Chiltern Way

Radnage

Yoesden
Wood

Bledlow
Ridge

Bledlow
Ridge
Sch

VIRGINIA
GDNS

The Three
Horseshoes Inn
(PH)

Bennett End

Grange Farm Rd

Bennett End Rd

Bottom Rd

Bowers La

97

The Crown
(PH)

Pophley's

Pophley's
Wood

Radnage
CE Inf Sch

Bottle Square La

City Rd

Bottom
Farm

6

The City

Green La

Waterend

HP14

Radnage Common Rd

Green End Rd

Ashridge
Farm

Radnage
House

96

Water End Rd

Brick's La

Beacon's
Bottom

Bottom
Wood

4

Eastwood
Farm

Eastwood Rd

Wycombe Rd

St Francis Rd

The Pitch

The Mary
Towerton Sch

PH

Studley Green
Farm

Studley
Green

3

East Wood

Horsleys
Green

Old Dashwood Hill

95

Moules Wood

Bix La

Wycliffe
Centre

Thirds
Wood

Fillington
Wood

A40 High Wycombe

2

Old House
Farm

Gibbon's
Farm

Dell's Wood

Watercroft
Wood

Butterleys
Plantation

Bigmore La

Dell's
Farm

Marlow Rd B482

M40

M40 High Wycombe

Penley Hollies

Bigmore
Farm

Buckinghamshire STREET ATLAS

Buckinghamshire STREET ATLAS

77

78

79

94

1

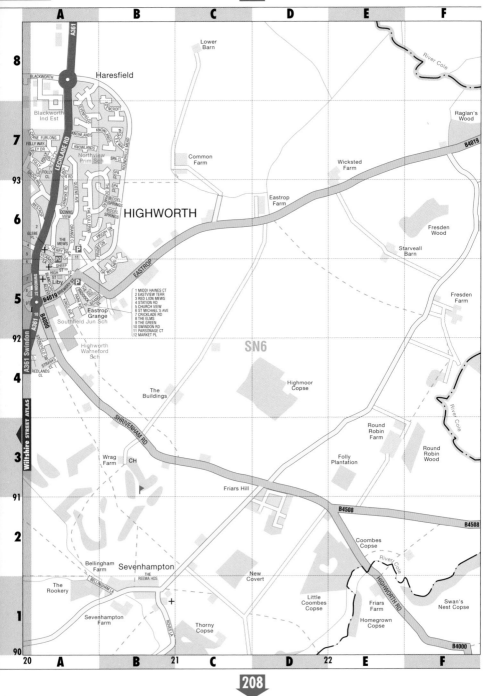

Index for grid references:

1 MIDDI HAINES CT
2 EASTVIEW TERR
3 RED LION MEWS
4 STATION RD
5 CHURCH VIEW
6 ST MICHAEL S AVE
7 CRICKLADE RD
8 THE ELMS
9 THE GREEN
10 SWINDON RD
11 PARSONAGE CT
12 MARKET PL

Wiltshire Street Atlas

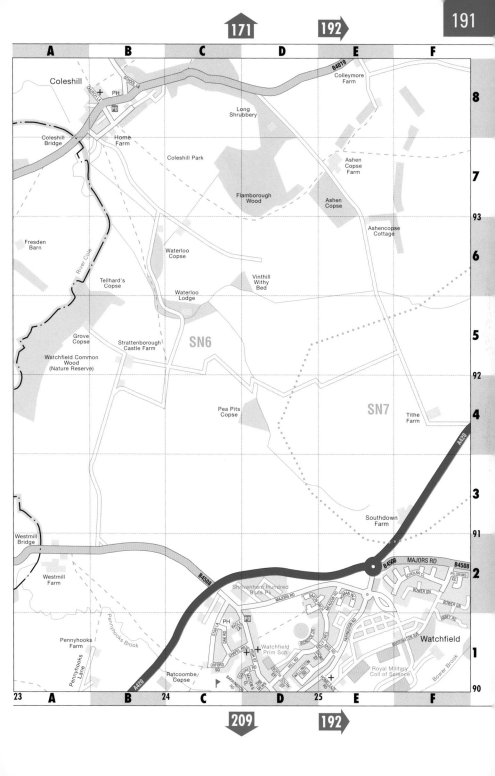

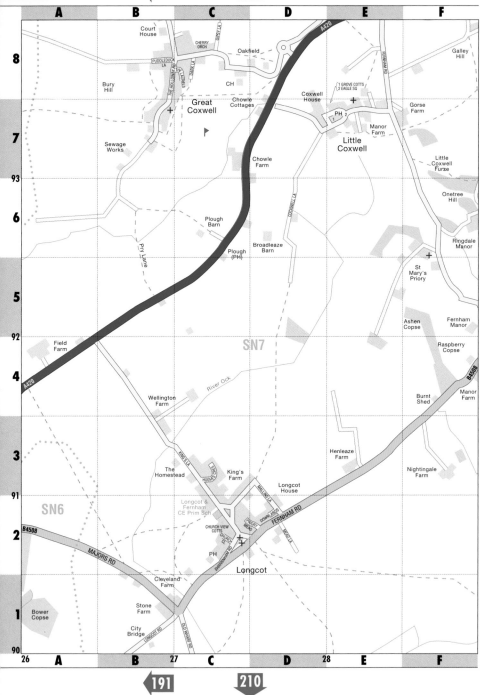

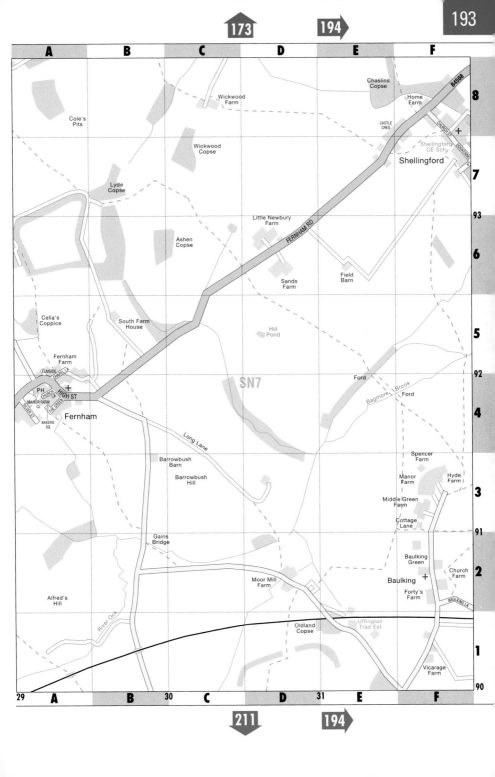

A B C D E F

8

Chaslins
Copse

Home
Farm

B4508

Cole's
Pits

Wickwood
Farm

CASTLE
CRES

CHURCH ST

DOWSELL

Shellingford
CE Sch

Wickwood
Copse

Shellingford

7

93

Lyde
Copse

Little Newbury
Farm

FERNHAM RD

6

Ashen
Copse

Sands
Farm

Field
Barn

Celia's
Coppice

South Farm
House

Hill
Pond

5

92

SN7

Ford

Bagmore Brook

Ford

Fernham
Farm

ELMSIDE
CHAPEL LA

PH

HIGH ST

MANOR FARM
CL

CHURCH
LA

THE GREEN

4

SILVER ST

BAKERS
SQ

Fernham

Long Lane

Spencer
Farm

Barrowbush
Barn

Barrowbush
Hill

Manor
Farm

Hyde
Farm

Middle Green
Farm

3

Cottage
Lane

Gains
Bridge

91

Baulking
Green

Alfred's
Hill

Moor Mill
Farm

Baulking

Church
Farm

2

Forty's
Farm

River Ock

Oldland
Copse

Uffington
Trad Est

BAULKING LA

1

Vicarage
Farm

29 A 30 B C 31 D E F 90

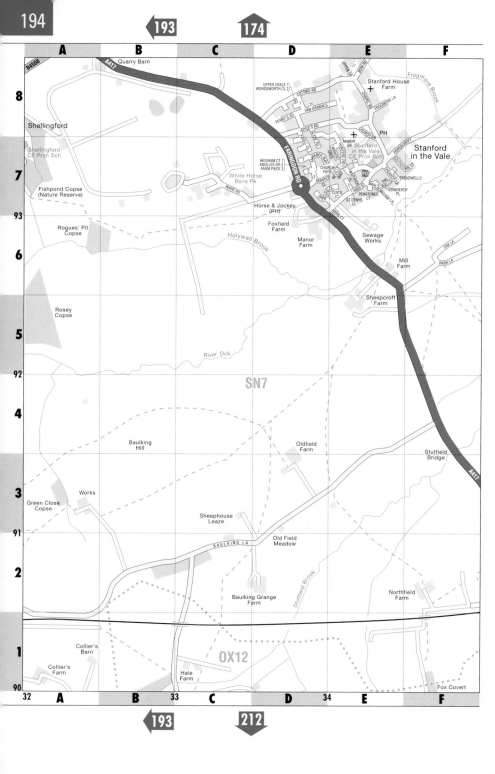

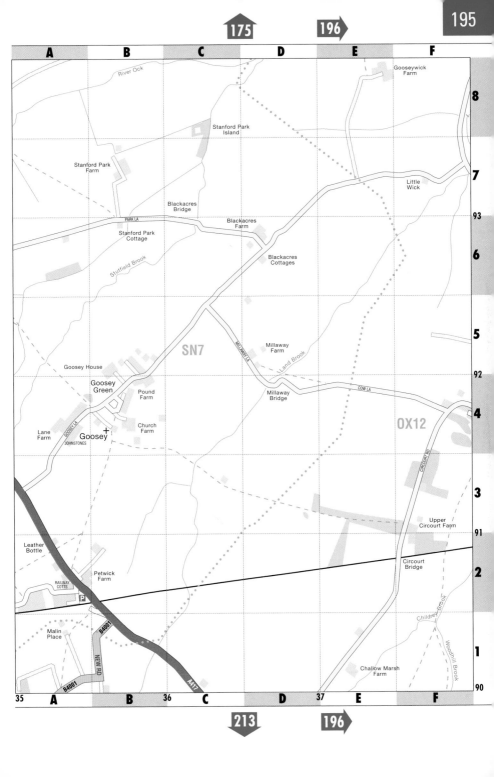

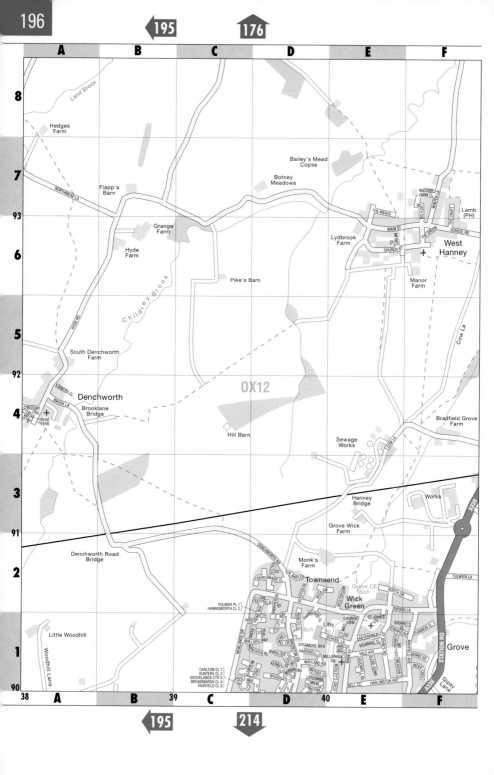

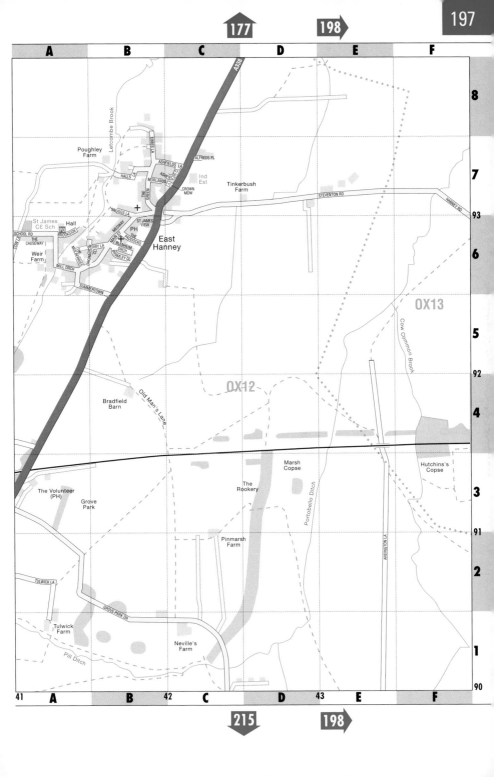

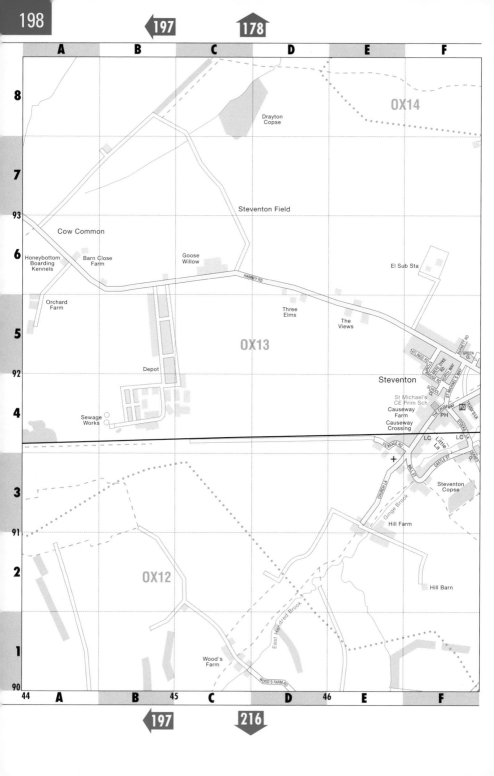

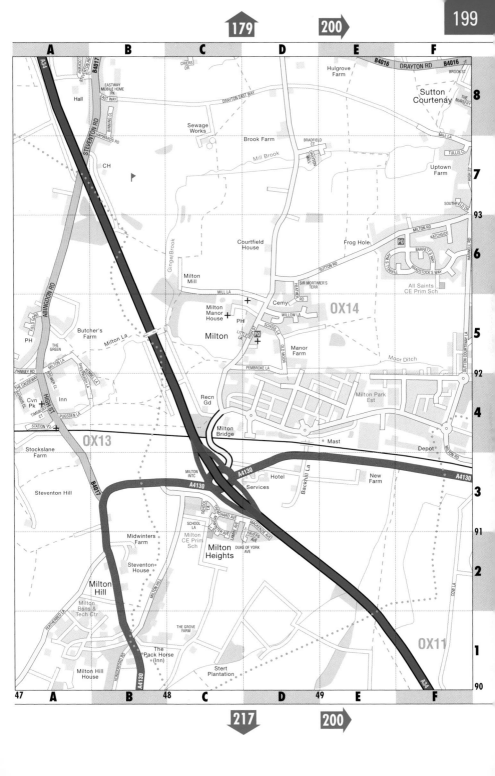

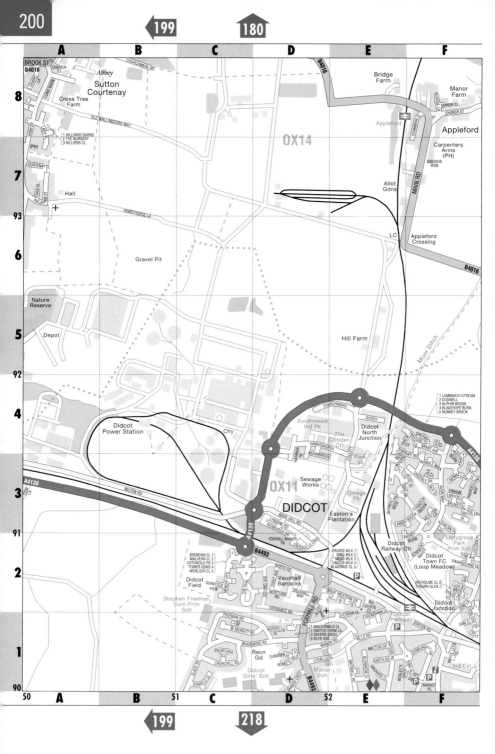

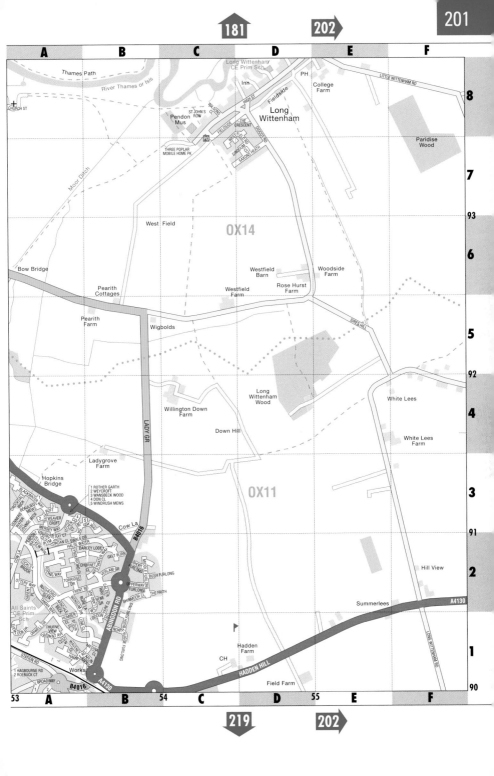

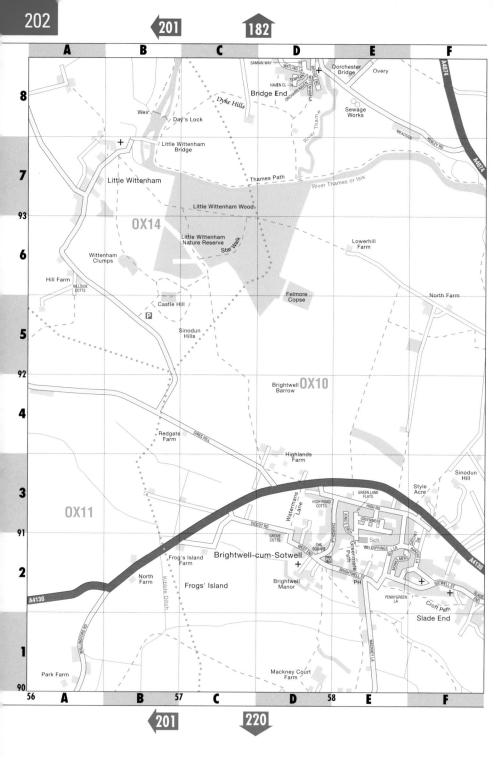

201
182

A　B　C　D　E　F

8

SAMIAN WAY
WATLING LA
HAVEN CL
ORCHARD MEADOW
TEMPEST
Bridge End
Dorchester Bridge
Overy
Weir
Dyke Hills
River Thame
Sewage Works
Day's Lock
MEADSIDE
HENLEY RD
A4074

Little Wittenham Bridge

7
Little Wittenham
Thames Path
River Thames or Isis

93
OX14
Little Wittenham Wood
Little Wittenham Nature Reserve
Star Walk
Lowerhill Farm

6
Wittenham Clumps
Hill Farm
HILLSIDE COTTS
Castle Hill
Felmore Copse
North Farm

P

5
Sinodun Hills

92
Brightwell Barrow
OX10

4
Redgate Farm
SIRES HILL
Highlands Farm
Sinodun Hill

3
OX11
Watermans Lane
HIGH ROAD COTTS
GREEN LANE FLATS
HIGH RD
Style Acre
DIDCOT RD
CHURCH LA
KING'S CL
GREENMERE
Sch
DIDCOT RD
A4130

91
GROVE COTTS
WEST END
THE SQUARE
Greenmere Path
WELLSPRINGS
BELL LA
MONKS MEAD

2
North Farm
Frog's Island Farm
Frogs' Island
Brightwell-cum-Sotwell
Brightwell Manor
BRIGHTWELL ST
PH
SOTWELL ST
PENNYGREEN LA
Croft Path

A4130
WALLINGFORD RD
Kibble Ditch
MACKNEY LA
Slade End

1

90
Park Farm
Mackney Court Farm

56　A　B　57　C　D　58　E　F

201
220

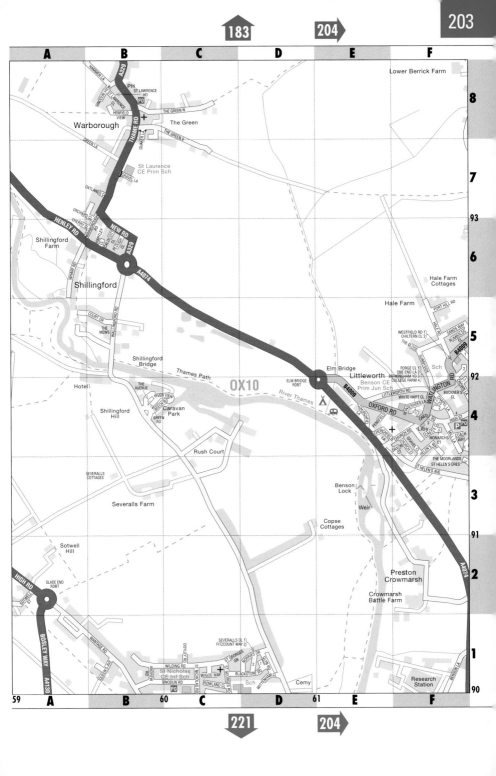

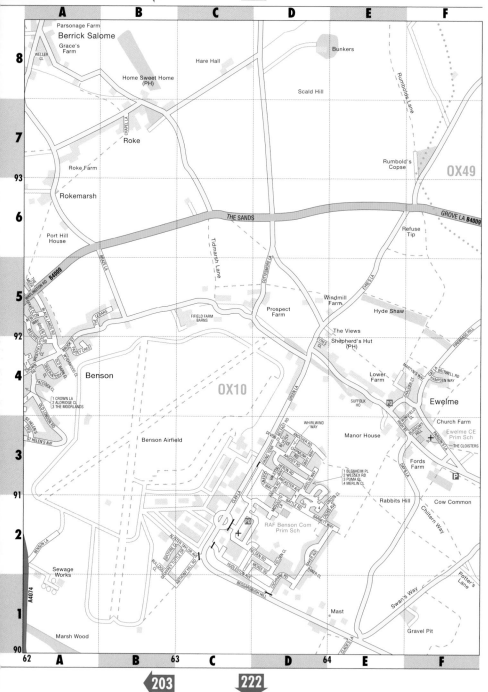

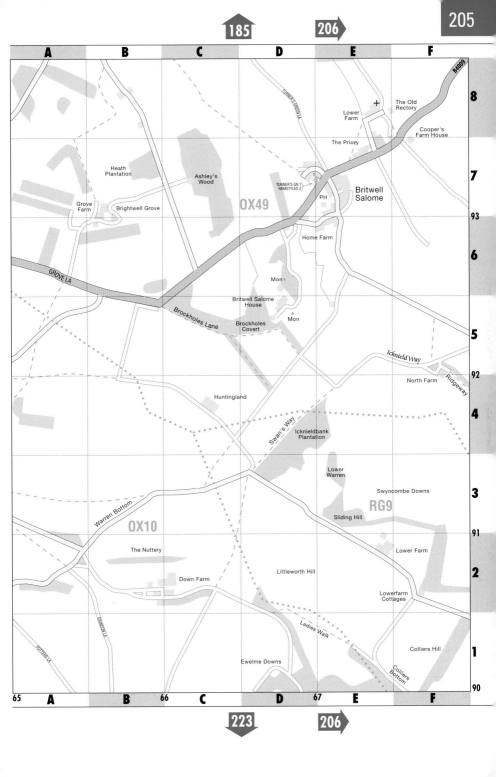

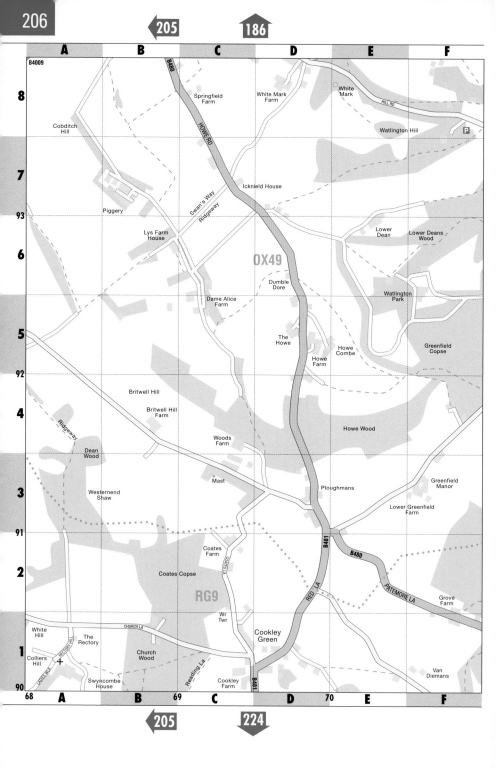

205
186
205
224

B4009

A B C D E F

8

Cobditch
Hill

Springfield
Farm

White Mark
Farm

White
Mark

Watlington Hill

HILL RD

P

7

HOME RD

Icknield House

93

Piggery

Swan's Way
Ridgeway

Lys Farm
House

Lower
Dean

Lower Deans
Wood

6

OX49

Dumble
Dore

Watlington
Park

Dame Alice
Farm

5

The
Howe

Howe
Combe

Greenfield
Copse

92

Howe
Farm

Britwell Hill

4

Britwell Hill
Farm

Ridgeway

Woods
Farm

Howe Wood

Dean
Wood

3

Westernend
Shaw

Mast

Ploughmans

Greenfield
Manor

91

Lower Greenfield
Farm

Coates
Farm

B481

B480

2

Coates Copse

COATES LA

RED LA

PATEMORE LA

Grove
Farm

RG9

Wr
Twr

Cookley
Green

1

White
Hill

The
Rectory

CHURCH LA

Church
Wood

Reading La

Van
Diemans

Colliers
Hill

LADIES WK

RECTORY HILL

Swyncombe
House

Cookley
Farm

B481

90

68 A B 69 C D 70 E F

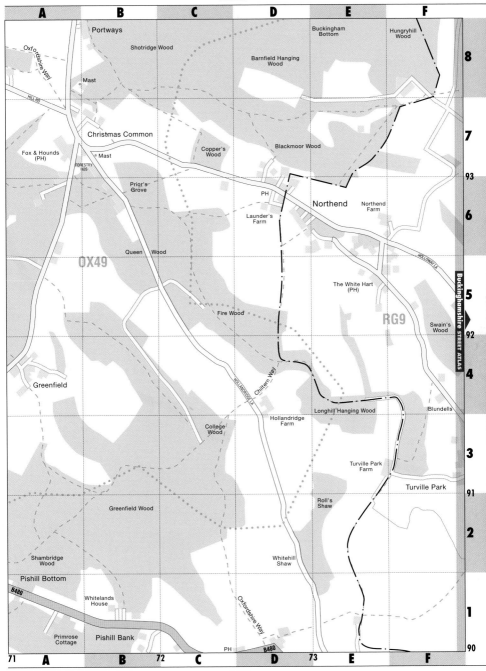

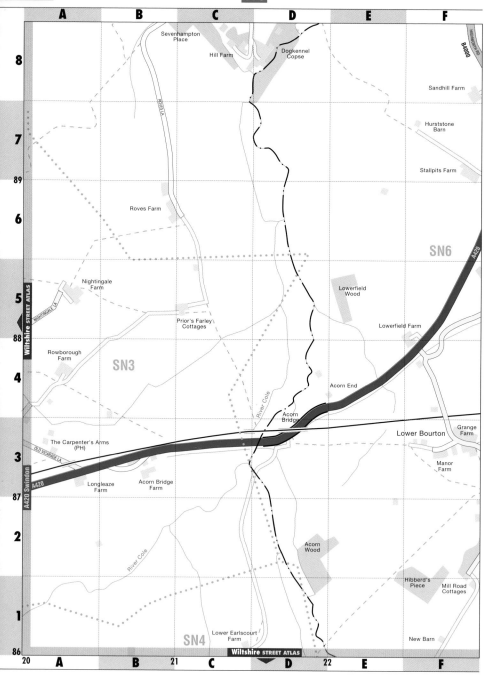

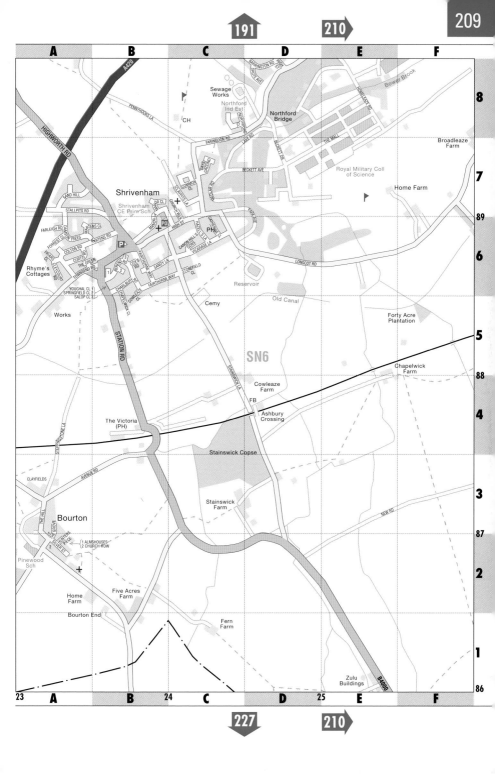

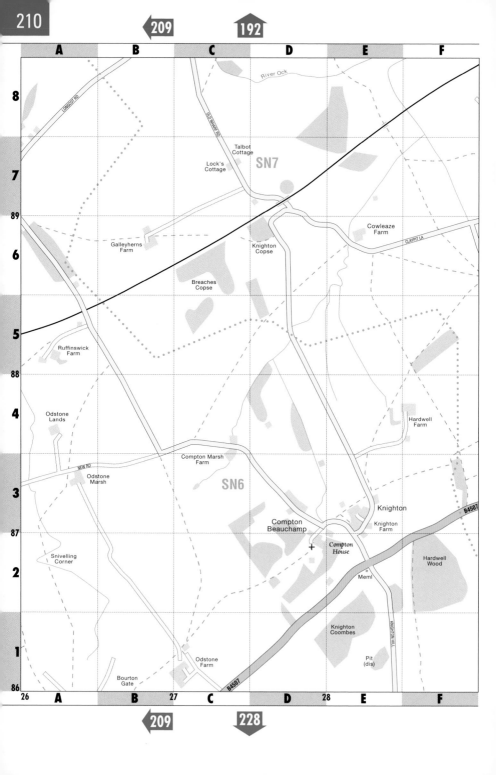

209
192

A B C D E F

8

7

89

6

5

88

4

3

87

2

1

86

River Ock

LONGCOT RD

OLD WHARF RD

Talbot Cottage

Lock's Cottage

SN7

Galleyherns Farm

Knighton Copse

Breaches Copse

Cowleaze Farm

CLAYPIT LA.

Ruffinswick Farm

Odstone Lands

Hardwell Farm

NEW RD

Odstone Marsh

Compton Marsh Farm

SN6

Snivelling Corner

Compton Beauchamp

Knighton

Knighton Farm

B4507

Compton House

Meml

Hardwell Wood

Odstone Farm

Bourton Gate

B4507

Knighton Coombes

KNIGHTON HILL

Pit (dis)

26 A B 27 C D 28 E F

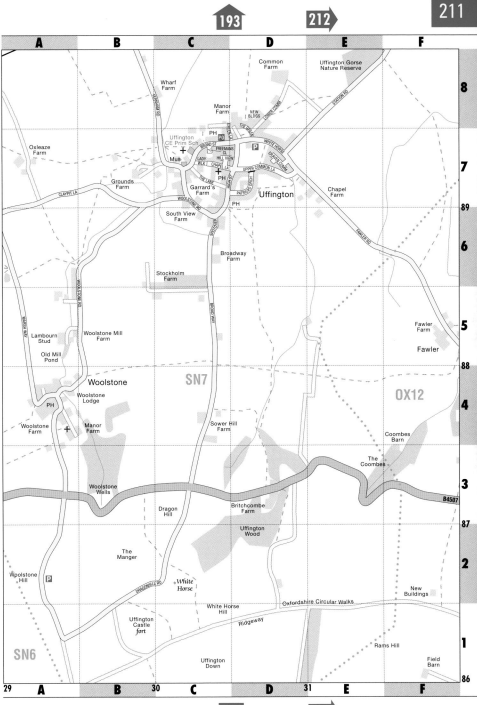

193
212

A **B** **C** **D** **E** **F**

Common Farm

Uffington Gorse Nature Reserve

8

Wharf Farm

Manor Farm

NEW BLDGS

STATION RD

Oxleaze Farm

Uffington CE Prim Sch

PH

PO

THE GREEN

WHITE HORSE

7

Mus

FREEMANS CL

HILL VIEW

CHAPEL LA

CHAPEL LANE

LADY WLK

UPPER COMMON LA

Grounds Farm

CLAYPIT LA

THE LANE

Garrard's Farm

HIGH ST

PATRICK'S ORCH

PH

Uffington

Chapel Farm

89

WOOLSTONE RD

South View Farm

SCHOOL RD

PH

6

Broadway Farm

FAWLER RD

Stockholm Farm

BROAD WAY

5

WOOLSTONE RD

Fawler Farm

MARSH WAY

Woolstone Mill Farm

Lambourn Stud

Fawler

Old Mill Pond

88

SN7

Woolstone

OX12

Woolstone Lodge

4

PH

Sower Hill Farm

Woolstone Farm

Manor Farm

Coombes Barn

The Coombes

Woolstone Wells

3

B4507

Dragon Hill

Britchcombe Farm

87

Uffington Wood

The Manger

2

Woolstone Hill

P

White Horse

New Buildings

White Horse Hill

Oxfordshire Circular Walks

Uffington Castle fort

Ridgeway

Rams Hill

1

SN6

Uffington Down

Field Barn

86

29 **A** **B** 30 **C** **D** 31 **E** **F**

229
212

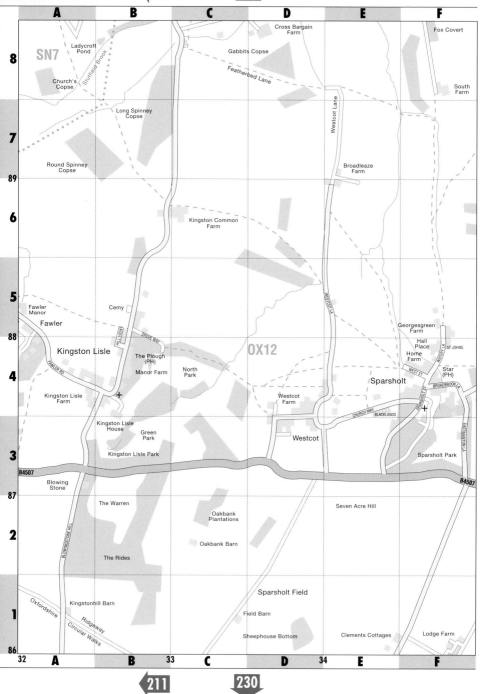

195
214
231
214

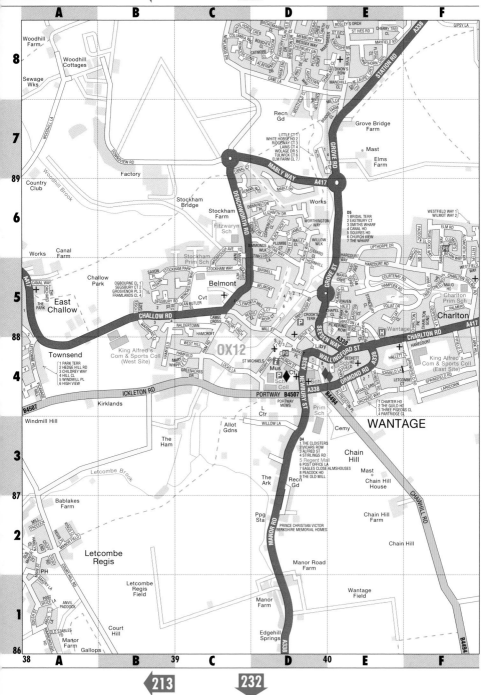

A | B | C | D | E | F

8

Woodhill Farm

Woodhill Cottages

Sewage Wks

LITTLE CT 1
WHITE HORSE HO 2
RIDGEWAY CT 3
LAINS CT 4
WOLAGE DR 5
TULWICK CT 6
ELM FARM CL 7

7

Grove Bridge Farm

Mast

Elms Farm

89

Country Club

Factory

Stockham Bridge

Woodhill Brook

DOWNSVIEW RD

CANAL CT

ROMAN RD

MABLY WAY

A417

GROVE RD

STATION RD

A338

GIPSY LA

MAYFIELD AVE

CHERRY TREE

ST IVES RD

6

Works

Stockham Farm

Fitzwaryn Sch

Stockham Prim Sch

Worthington Way

Works

D5
1 BRIDAL TERR
2 EASTBURY CT
3 SMITHS WHARF
4 CANAL HO
5 SQUIRES HO
6 CHURCH VIEW
7 THE WHARF

WESTFIELD WAY 1
WILMOT WAY 2

Works

Canal Farm

Challow Park

OGBOURNE CL 1
SEGSBURY CT 2
GROSVENOR PL 3
FRAMLANDS CL 4

Belmont

Charlton Prim Sch

Charlton

5

East Challow

The Park

Challow Park

SAXON

Cvt

DEAN BUTLER

CHALLOW RD

Wantage

CHARLTON RD

A417

88

Townsend

1 PARK TERR
2 HEDGE HILL RD
3 CHILDREY WAY
4 HILL CL
5 WINDMILL PL
6 HIGH VIEW

King Alfred's Com & Sports Coll (West Site)

NALDERTOWN

HAMCROFT

WEST HILL

OX12

ST MICHAELS

Liby

SEESEN WAY

WALLINGFORD ST

ORMOND RD

A338

Wantage

King Alfred's Com & Sports Coll (East Site)

H

HARCOURT

4

ICKLETON RD

Kirklands

HAMFIELD

WHIPPLE

GREENACHES

LOCKS LA

MARSH

PORTWAY B4507

Mus

Art Coll

NEWBURY ST

A338

ORCHARD WAY

B494

1 CHARTER HO
2 THE GUILD HO
3 THREE PIGEONS CL
4 PARTRIDGE CL

3

Windmill Hill

The Ham

Allot Gdns

The Ark

WILLOW LA

Recn Gd

D4
1 THE CLOISTERS
2 VICARS ROW
3 ALFRED ST
4 STIRLINGS RD
5 REGENT MALL
6 POST OFFICE LA
7 EAGLES CLOSE ALMSHOUSES
8 PEACOCK HO
9 THE OLD MILL

Chain Hill

Mast

Chain Hill House

WANTAGE

Cemy

Prim Sch

87

Bablakes Farm

Letcombe Brook

Chain Hill Farm

Chain Hill

2

Letcombe Regis

Letcombe Regis Field

MANOR RD

Ppg Sta

PRINCE CHRISTIAN VICTOR BERKSHIRE MEMORIAL HOMES

Manor Road Farm

Chain Hill

CHAINHILL RD

1

PH

POST OFFICE LA

ANVIL PADDOCK

Court Hill

Manor Farm

Edgehill Springs

A338

Wantage Field

B494

86

Manor Farm

Gallops

38 | A | B | 39 | C | D | 40 | E | F

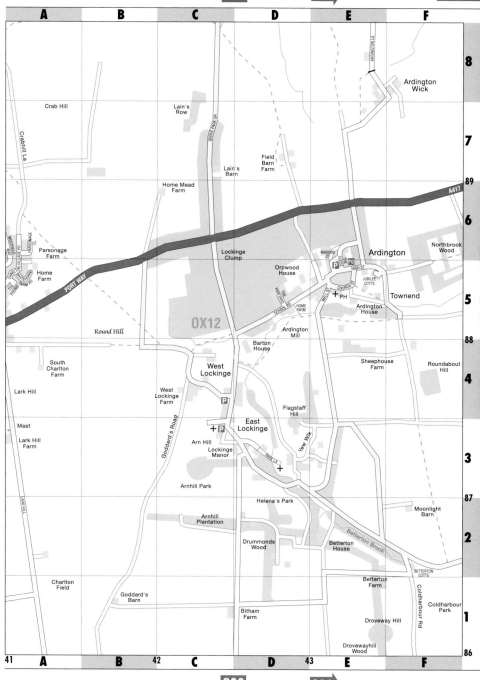

215 198

8

Quab Hill

Quab Hill
Farm

East Hendred Brook

Ludbridge Mill
(disused)

Greensands

New Barn

7

Lud Bridge

A417

The Hare
Inn

READING RD

Sheephouse
Barn

East
Hendred

89

A417

THE GREENWAY

MILL LA

BACKSIDE

ALLIN ST

COULINGS CL

WHITE RD

SMITHS

ORCHARD CL

HOME FARM LA

WOOD'S FARM RD

FIELD RD

ORCHARD LA

MILL LA

Recreation
Ground

CHAPEL SQ

Chapel

CAT ST

Eyston Arms
(PH)

6

THE MILLHAM

MANOR LA

The Mill

West Hendred

The Hendreds
CE Sch

FORD LA

CAT ST

Hendred
House

Lydebank
Plantation

Lookinge Brook

Hall

SPINNEY

CHURCH ST

St Amand's
RC Prim Sch

DEN S

HORN LA

MOUNT
PLEASANT
COTTS

THE LYNCH

The Moors

Cow Road

Ginge Brook

Red Barn

5

Hill Farm

NEWBURY RD

Goldbury
Hill

Park Hill

GOLDBURY
COTTS

88

Park Hill
Row

Icknield

OX12

Pump
House

4

Black Mills
Row

Aldfield
Common

Shadwell's Row

3

Parsonage
Barn

87

Lower Farm

West
Ginge

Ellaway's
Barn

STILEWAY ROAD

2

Ginge
House

East
Ginge

Deer Park

TWENTIETH ST

OX11

1

Upper Farm

Ginge
Manor

Downs
Cottage

Meashill
Plantation

White Way

86

44 **A** 45 **C** 46 **E**

215 234

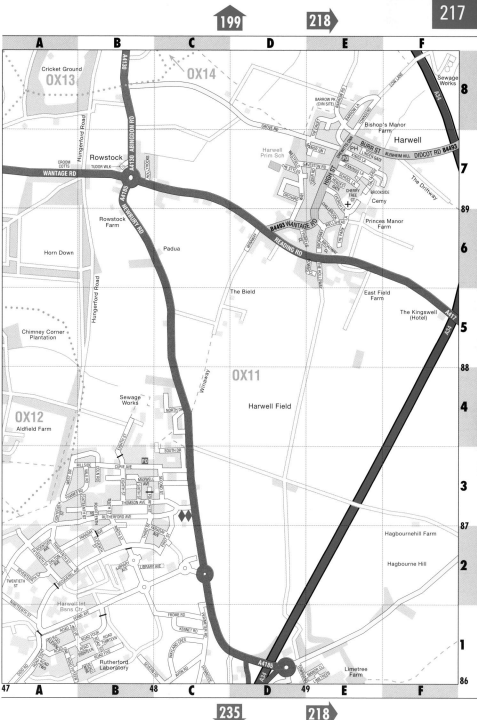

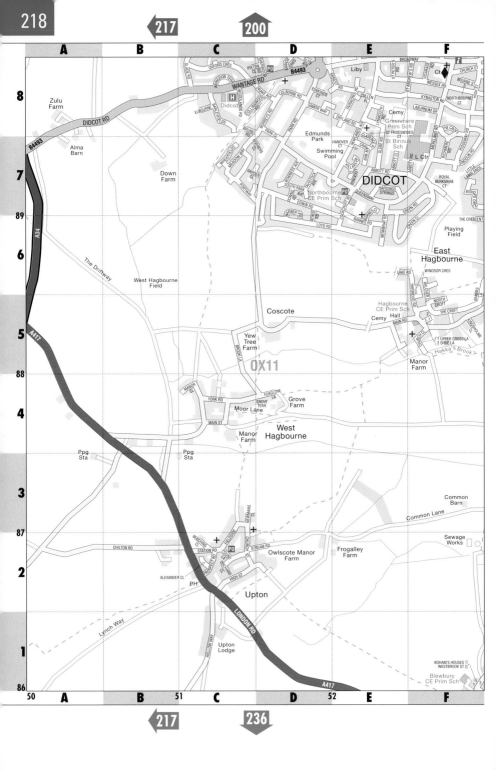

217
200

A   **B**   **C**   **D**   **E**   **F**

8

Zulu
Farm

Oxford Cres

Wantage Rd

B4493

Liby

Broadway

Church St

Bourne St

Northbourne Ct

DIDCOT RD

Didcot

H

Didcot

Edmunds
Park

Swimming
Pool

Greenmere
Prim Sch

St Frideswides
Ct

St Birinus
Sch

Cemy

L Ctr

7

B4493

Alma
Barn

Down
Farm

DIDCOT

Northbourne
CE Prim Sch

Royal
Berkshire
Ct

89

A34

The Crescent

Playing
Field

6

The Driftway

West Hagbourne
Field

East
Hagbourne

Lake Rd

Windsor Cres

Hagbourne
CE Prim Sch

Coscote

Cemy

Hall

North
Croft

The Croft

5

A417

Yew
Tree
Farm

1 Upper Cross La
2 Shoe La

Hakka's Brook

Manor
Farm

88

OX11

4

Manor
Cl

York Rd

Moor Lane

Main St

Foxglove
La

Grove
Terr

Grove
Farm

West
Hagbourne

Manor
Farm

3

Ppg
Sta

Ppg
Sta

Common
Barn

Common Lane

Sewage
Works

87

Chilton Rd

Beechlea

Station Rd

PO

Eelocote

Church

Stream Rd

Owlscote Manor
Farm

Frogalley
Farm

2

Alexander Cl

PH

High St

Upton

Lynch Way

1

Upton
Lodge

Boham's Houses 1
Westbrook St 2

Blewbury
CE Prim Sch

86

London Rd

A417

50   **A**   **B**   **51**   **C**   **D**   **52**   **E**   **F**

217
236

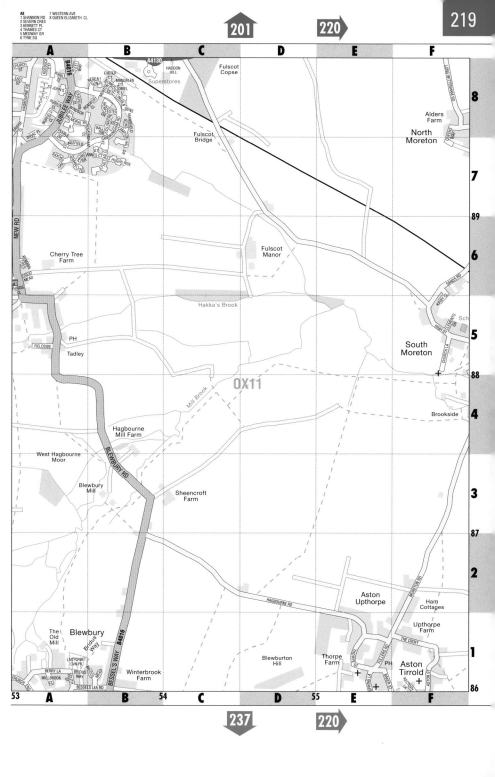

219
202

Mackney

MACKNEY LA

Sherwood
Farm

Kibble Ditch

North
Moreton

The Bear
(PH)

L.S.M. RD

WALLINGFORD RD

LONG WITTENHAM RD

HIGH ST

BEAR LA

DUNSOMER HILL

Landing Strip

Mill Brook

Glebe
Cottage

Hithercroft
Farm

The Crown
(PH)

South
Moreton

OX11

HITHERCROFT RD

DIDCOT LA

OLD MILL LA

MILL LA

ANSDORE LA

MORETON RD

Cholsey Hill

OX10

Hillgreen
Farm

Poultry
Farm

The Manor

Sewage
Works

Manor
Farm

Cholsey and Wallingford Rly

The
Lees

CHURCH RD

GOLDFINCH LA

Red Lion
(PH)

Cholsey
Prim Sch

WALLINGFORD RD

CROSS RD

CHEQUERS
PL.

THE
POUND

Caravan
Park

THE
FORTY

ILGES LA

POUND LA

Lees
Cottages

MANEY RD

West
End

CHOLSEY

COLLEGE
CL.

BEEHIVE
CL.

ST. GEORGE'S

CRESCENT

BUCKTHORN

WEST END

CHEVESIDE

BROOKSIDE

DAIRY LA

FORD CL.

KENTWOOD
RD

WESTFIELD
RD

PAPIST WAY

Pancroft
Farm

The
Elms

Cholsey

THE
ROWANS

219
238

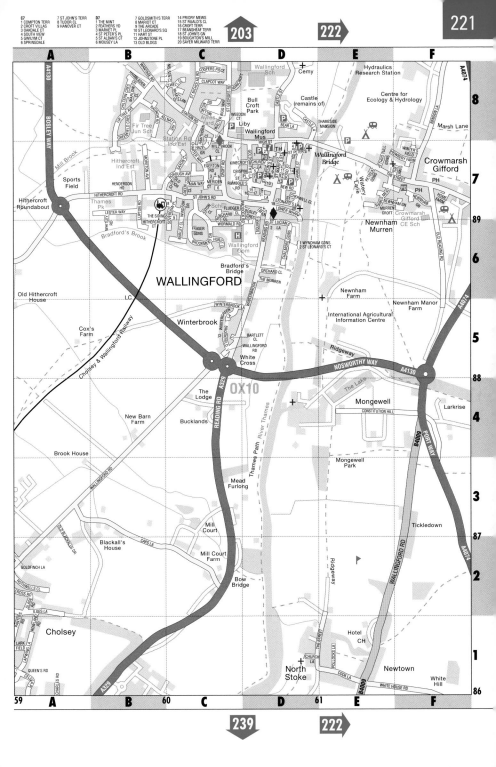

	A	B	C	D	E	F

8

Marsh Wood

CLACK'S LA

Gould's Grove Farm

Troy Cottage

Clack's Farm

MARSH LA

Shepherds Cottage

7

Coldharbour Farm

Public Refuse Tip

LANE END

THE STREET

MEADOW LA

89

A4130

CROWMARSH HILL

Oakley Wood

Hillview

A4130

6

PARK WAY

ROBERT SPARROW GDNS

Oakley Wood Farm

Western View

5

Lonesome Farm

Swan's Way

Turners Court Farm

NUFFIELD LA

COX'S LA

Blenheim Farm

Whitley House

OAKLEY CT

88

OX10

4

Cart Gap

Ridgeway

Sheepcot Farm

Oaken Copse

3

Woodhouse Farm

Batchelor's Hill

FOREST ROW

Wicks Hill

Wicks Wood

87

2

A4074

Drunken Bottom

Pigtrough Bottom

Black Barn Farm

Poors Shaw

Poors Farm

1

PORT WAY

Coblers Hill

Hailey Compton

A4074

86

| 62 | A | | B | 63 | C | | D | 64 | E | | F |

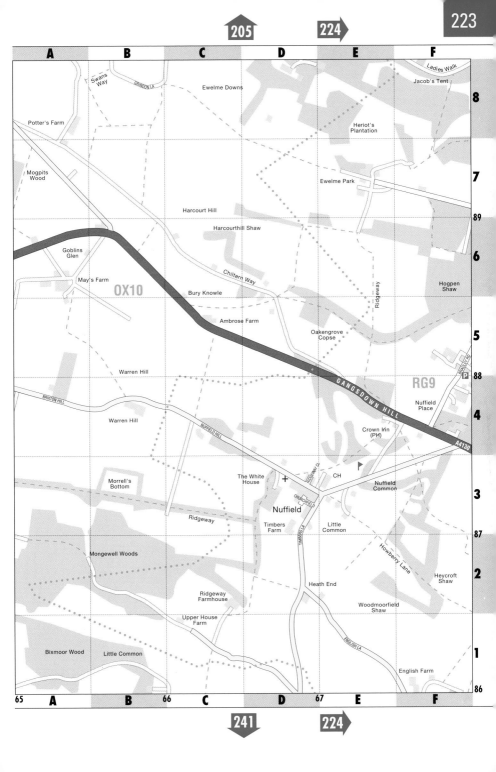

223
206

A **B** **C** **D** **E** **F**

B461

8

Chiltern Way

Russell's
Water

Law La

Haycroft Wood

Devil's Hill

Straights
Plantation

Reading La

Redpitts La

7

Redpitts
Farm

89

Priors Wood

Parkcorner
Farm

Park Corner

THE COUNCIL
HOS

Chears
Farm

Chiltern Way

6

Darkwood Farm

Westwood Manor
Farm

Chiltern Way

Hazel Wood

DIGBERRY LA

Shepherds
Barn

Berrick Trench

BRADLEY RD

5

RG9

Huntercombe Place
(HM Young Offender
Institution)

88

Huntercombe End
Farm

Soundess
Farm

HUNTERCOMBE END LA

4

Park Wood

Copse Wood

Huntercombe End

A4130

Priest Hill
Farm

Windmill Hill

Bushes La

3

Groveridge
Wood

PRIEST LA

Priest's
Hill

Nettlebed
Common

87

PORT HILL

WATLINGTON ST

CROCKER
END

HAYDEN LA

Hayden Farm

2

Manor Farm

Nettlebed
Com Sch

Old
Kiln

The
Cat

Catslip

The Bothy

Nettlebed

Joyce
Grove

Tylers

Hospice

Sewage
Wks

1

Black Wood

B461

Lowercommon
Wood

A4130

Top
Copse

86

A 68 **B** 69 **C** **D** 70 **E** **F**

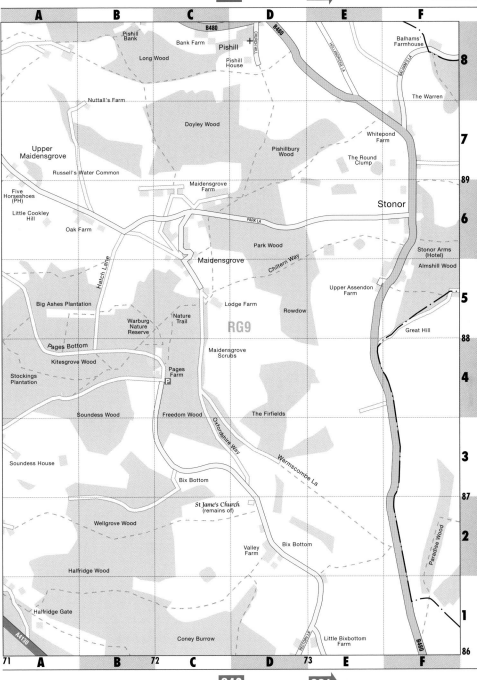

Southend
Farm

Southend

Drovers

Binfield Bottom

Balham's Wood

Great Wood

Chiltern Way

Stonor House

Old Luxters
Farm Brewery

Kimble Farm

Kildridge Wood

DUDLEY LA

Gussetts
Wood

Jubilee Plantation

Stonor Park
(Deer Park)

Henleyhill Wood

Woodcocks
Bill

Coxlease

Upper Woodend
Farm

Coxlease
Farm

RG9

Bosmore
Farm

Hanging
Wood

Lower Woodend
Farm

Jubilee
Plantation

Roundhouse
Farm

Highfield
Plantation

The Walnut Tree
(PH)

Great Wood

Great Wood Ho

Jackson's Farm

Fawley
Green

Fawley Green
Farm

Red Hill

Fawley Bottom

Fawley Bottom
Farm House

Fawley

Kitchener's
Firs

Pallbach Hill

FAWLEY BOTTOM LA

Eversdown

Benhams

OX11

Brackenhill
Stud Farm

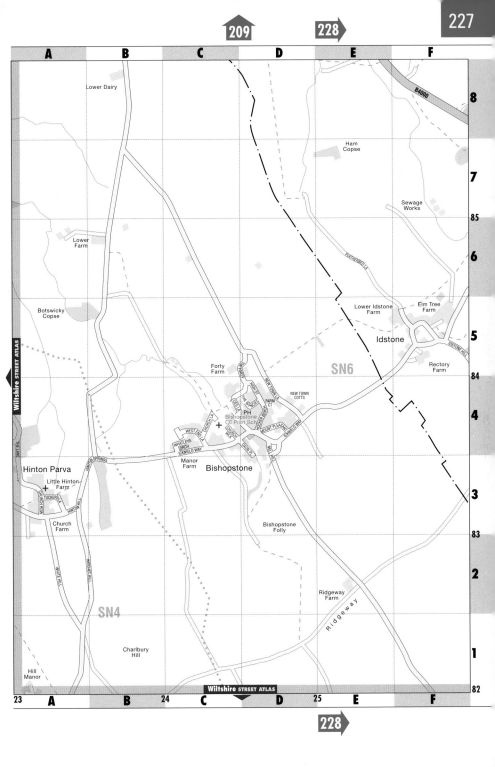

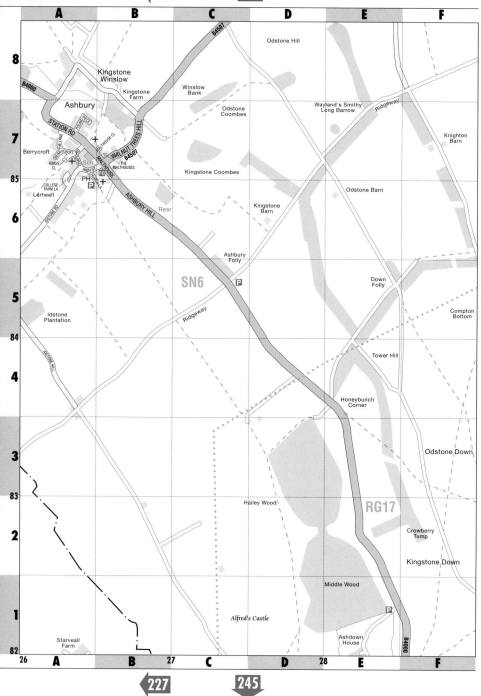

227
210

	A	B	C	D	E	F

B4507

8

Odstone Hill

Kingstone
Winslow

B4000

Winslow
Bank

Kingstone
Farm

Ashbury

Wayland's Smithy
Long Barrow

Ridgeway

Odstone
Coombes

7

STATION RD

Knighton
Barn

Berrycroft

BERRYCROFT RD

WALNUT TREES HILL

Sch

KINGS
CL

HIGH ST

THE
MALTHOUSES

B4507

Kingstone Coombes

85

COLLEGE
FARM LA

PH

Odstone Barn

Lertwell

ASHBURY HILL

Kingstone
Barn

6

Resr

IDSTONE RD

Ashbury
Folly

Down
Folly

5

SN6

Compton
Bottom

Idstone
Plantation

Ridgeway

84

IDSTONE HILL

Tower Hill

4

Honeybunch
Corner

Odstone Down

3

Hailey Wood

RG17

Crowberry
Tump

2

Kingstone Down

Middle Wood

1

Alfred's Castle

B4000

Starveall
Farm

Ashdown
House

82

26	A		B	27	C		D	28	E		F

227
245

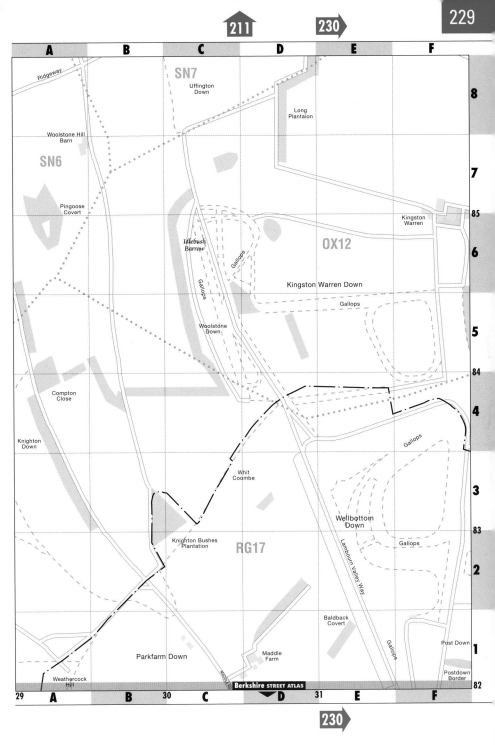

Ridgeway

SN7

Uffington
Down

Long
Plantaion

Woolstone Hill
Barn

SN6

Pingoose
Covert

Idlebush
Barrow

Kingston
Warren

OX12

Gallops

Kingston Warren Down

Gallops

Woolstone
Down

Compton
Close

Knighton
Down

Whit
Coombe

Gallops

Wellbottom
Down

Knighton Bushes
Plantation

RG17

Gallops

Lambourn Valley Way

Baldback
Covert

Post Down

Gallops

Parkfarm Down

Maddle
Farm

Postdown
Border

Weathercock
Hill

MADDLE RD

Berkshire STREET ATLAS

29 A   B   30 C   D   31 E   F

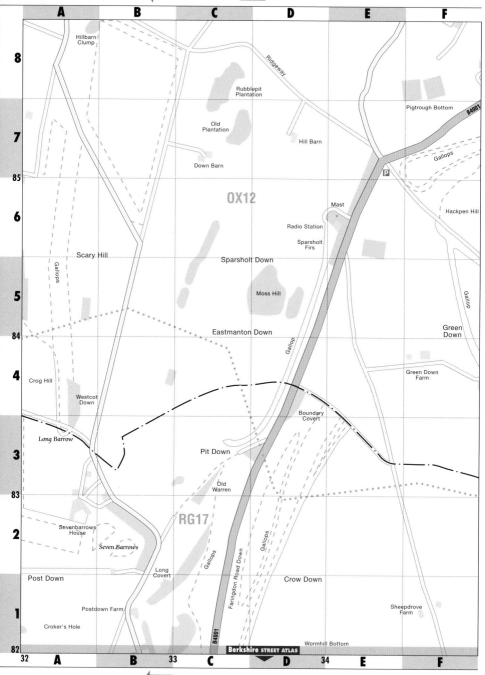

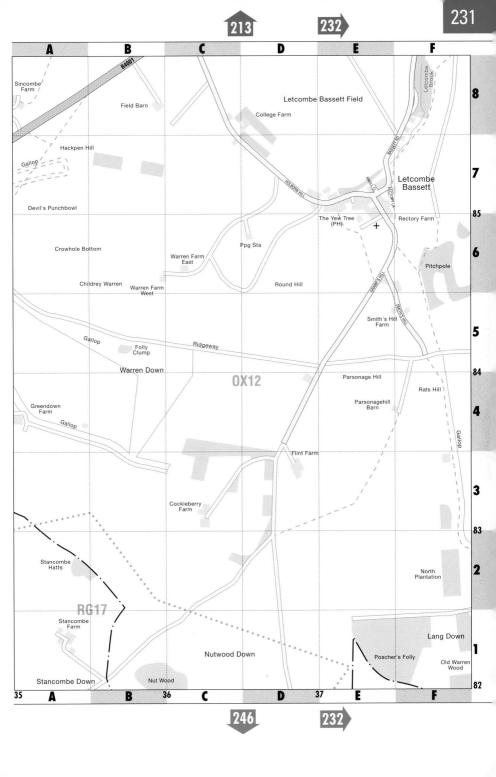

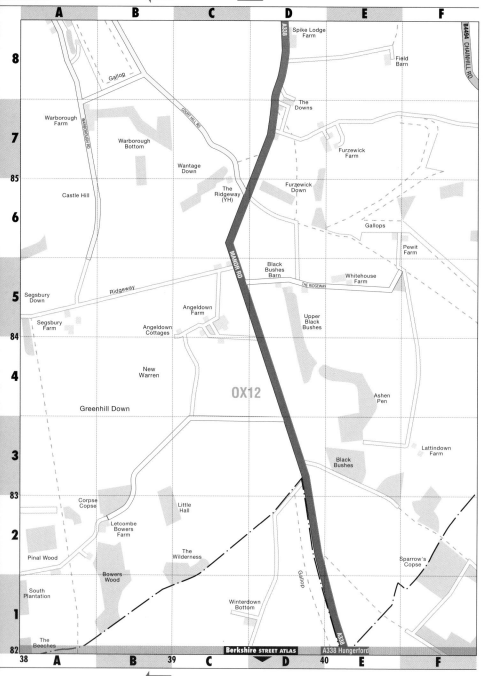

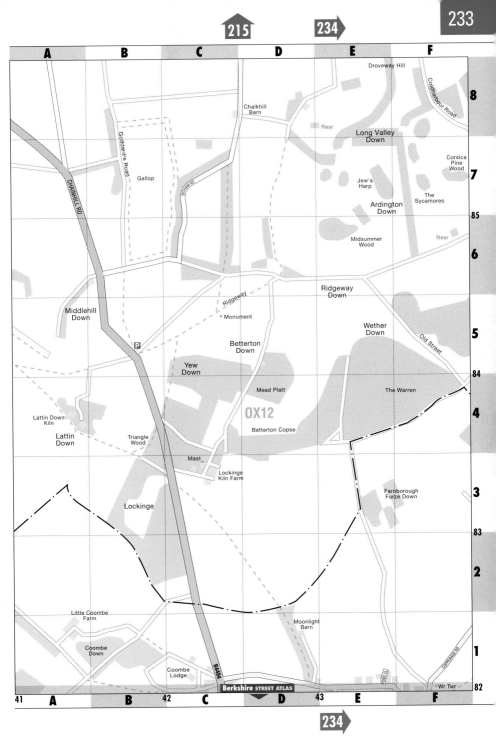

8

85

7

6

5

84

4

3

83

2

1

82

Droveway Hill

Coldharbour Road

Chalkhill
Barn

Resr

Long Valley
Down

Corsica
Pine
Wood

Goddard's Road

Gallop

BITHAM RD

CHAINHILL RD

Jew's
Harp

The
Sycamores

Ardington
Down

Midsummer
Wood

Resr

Ridgeway
Down

Ridgeway

Middlehill
Down

Monument

Wether
Down

Old Street

P

Betterton
Down

Yew
Down

The Warren

Mead Platt

OX12

Lattin Down
Kiln

Betterton Copse

Lattin
Down

Triangle
Wood

Mast

Lockinge
Kiln Farm

Farnborough
Furze Down

Lockinge

Little Coombe
Farm

Moonlight
Barn

COPPERAGE RD

Coombe
Down

Coombe
Lodge

B4494

POND CL

Wr Twr

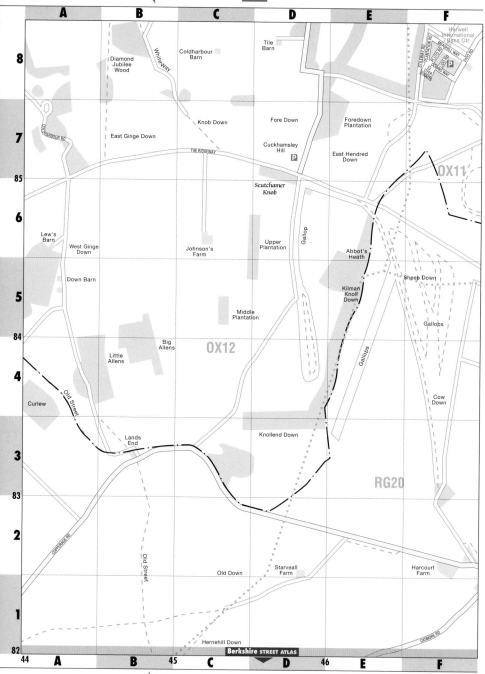

A B C D E F

8 Diamond
Jubilee
Wood

WhiteWay

Coldharbour
Barn

Tile
Barn

STILLWAY RD
PLANTATION RD
MERSHILL RD
AUTOR RD
DOWNS WAY
STRAITS

7 COLD HARBOUR RD

East Ginge Down

Knob Down

Fore Down

Foredown
Plantation

Cuckhamsley
Hill

East Hendred
Down

OX11

THE RIDGEWAY

85

Scutchamer
Knob

6 Lew's
Barn

West Ginge
Down

Johnson's
Farm

Upper
Plantation

Gallop

Abbot's
Heath

Down Barn

Sheep Down

Kilman
Knoll
Down

5 Middle
Plantation

Gallops

84 Big
Allens

OX12

Gallops

Little
Allens

4 Curlew

Old Street

Cow
Down

Lands
End

Knollend Down

3 RG20

83 COPPRAGE RD

2 Old Street

Starveall
Farm

Harcourt
Farm

Old Down

1 CATMORE RD

82 Hernehill Down

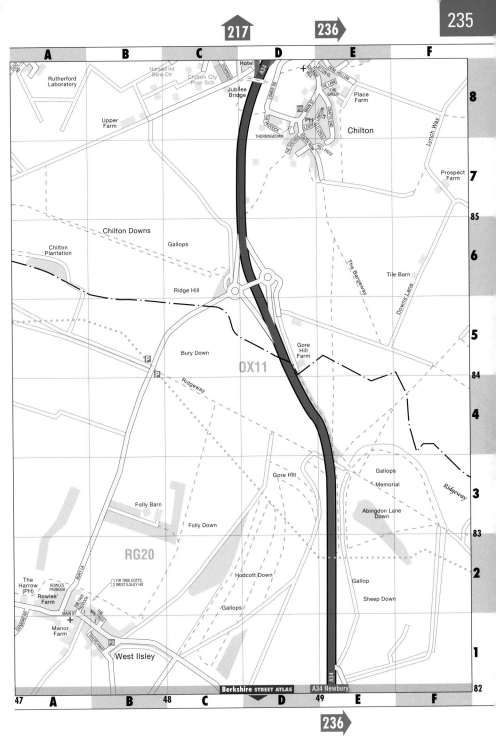

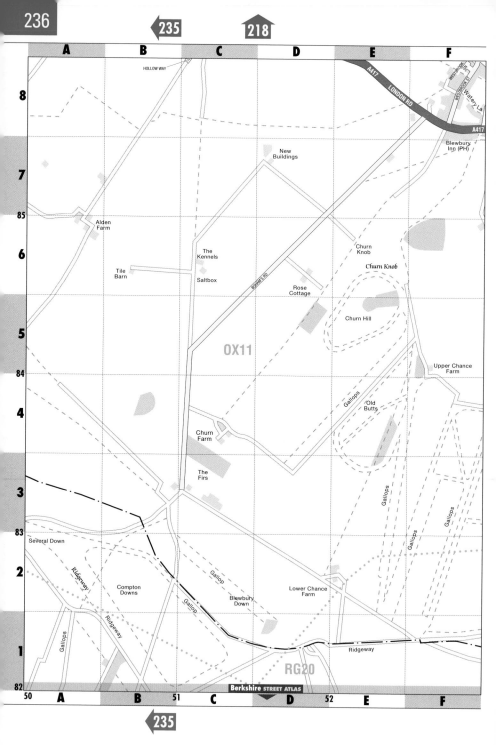

HOLLOW WAY

A417 LONDON RD

WEST BROOK ST

Watery La

A417

Blewbury Inn (PH)

New Buildings

Churn Knob

Alden Farm

The Kennels

Churn Knob

Tile Barn

Saltbox

Rose Cottage

Churn Hill

OX11

Upper Chance Farm

Gallops

Old Butts

Churn Farm

The Firs

Gallops

Gallops

Gallops

Several Down

Ridgeway

Gallop

Lower Chance Farm

Compton Downs

Gallop

Blewbury Down

Ridgeway

Gallops

Ridgeway

Ridgeway

RG20

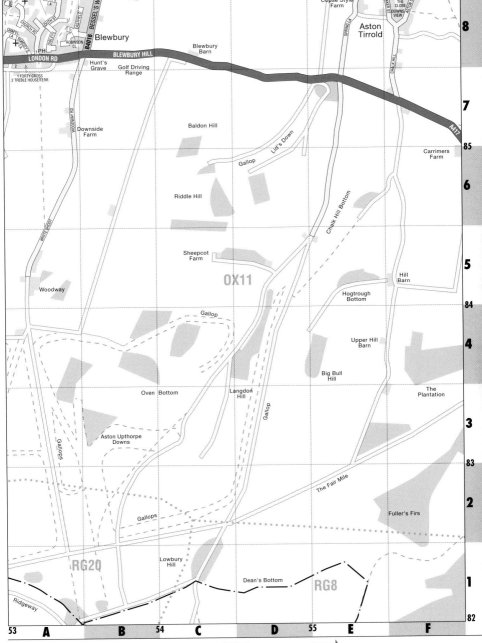

A **B** **C** **D** **E** **F**

Church End | WATT'S LA
CHURCH END
SOUTH ST
EASTFIELD
BESSEL'S WAY
B4016

Copse Style Farm

RECTORY LA

THE CLOSE
DOWNS VIEW

Chapel LA
BUSSEY'S
PH
LONDON RD
2
1 FORTY CROSS
2 TREBLE HOUSE TERR

Blewbury

Aston Tirrold

SPRING LA
CHALK HILL

8

Hunt's Grave
BLEWBURY HILL
Golf Driving Range

Blewbury Barn

M11

7

WOODWAY RD

Downside Farm

Baldon Hill

Lid's Down

Gallop

Carrimers Farm

85

6

WHITE SHOOT

Riddle Hill

Chalk Hill Bottom

Sheepcot Farm

OX11

Hill Barn

5

Woodway

Hogtrough Bottom

84

Gallop

Upper Hill Barn

4

Oven Bottom

Langdon Hill

Gallop

Big Bull Hill

The Plantation

3

Gallops

Aston Upthorpe Downs

83

The Fair Mile

2

Gallops

Fuller's Firs

RG20

Lowbury Hill

Dean's Bottom

RG8

1

Ridgeway

82

53 **A** **B** 54 **C** **D** 55 **E** **F**

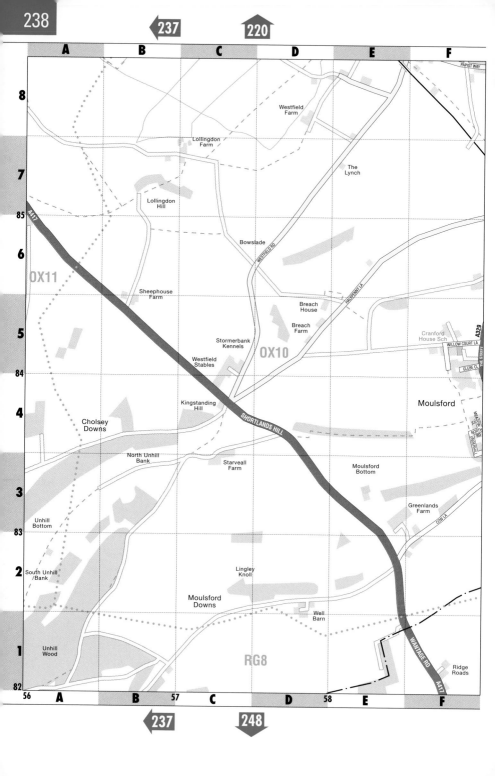

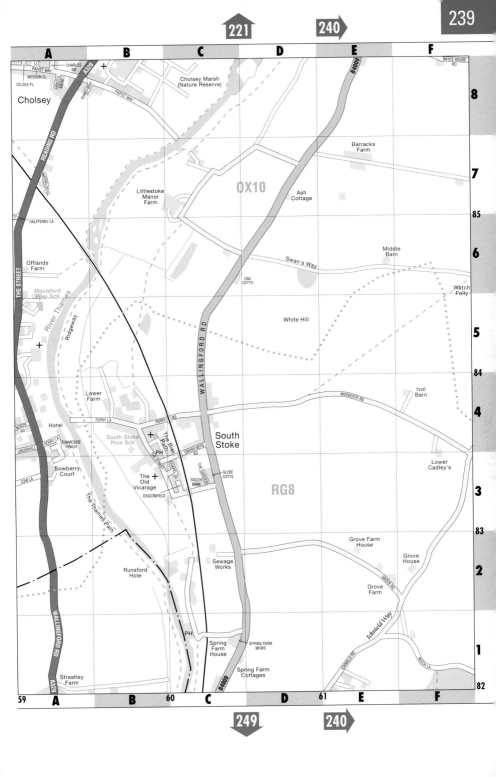

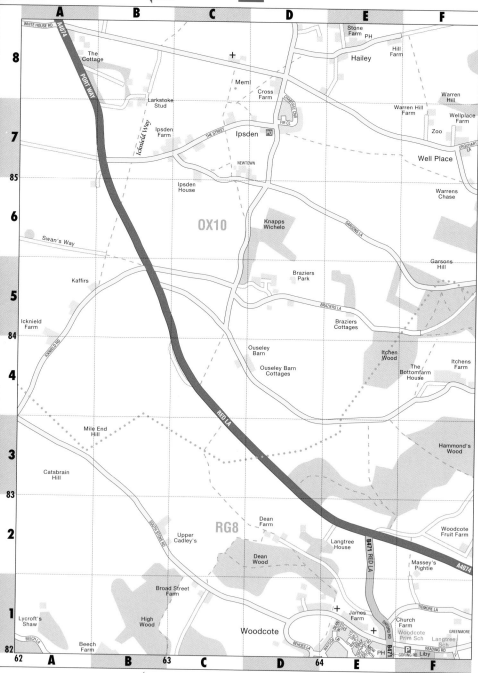

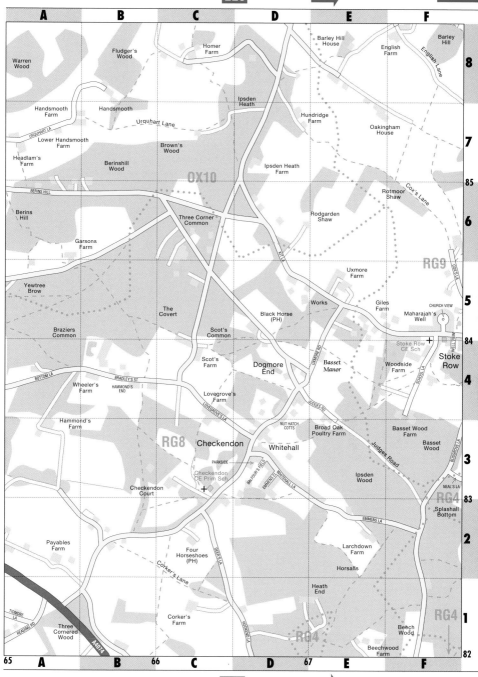

223
242

A **B** **C** **D** **E** **F**

Warren Wood

Fludger's Wood

Homer Farm

Barley Hill House

English Farm

Barley Hill

English Lane

8

Handsmooth Farm

Handsmooth

Urquhart Lane

Ipsden Heath

Hundridge Farm

Oakingham House

7

URQUHART LA

Lower Handsmooth Farm

Brown's Wood

Ipsden Heath Farm

Rotmoor Shaw

Cox's Lane

85

Headlam's Farm

Berinshill Wood

OX10

Rodgarden Shaw

BERINS HILL

Berins Hill

Three Corner Common

RG9

6

Garsons Farm

COX'S LA

Yewtree Brow

The Covert

Uxmore Farm

5

Black Horse (PH)

Works

Giles Farm

CHURCH VIEW

Braziers Common

Scot's Common

Maharajah's Well

Stoke Row CE Sch

WELL LANE

84

Scot's Farm

Dogmore End

Basset Manor

Woodside Farm

Stoke Row

BOTTOM LA

BRADLEY'S ST

Wheeler's Farm

HAMMOND'S END

Lovegrove's Farm

LOVEGROVE'S LA

UXMORE RD

JUDGES RD

SCHOOL LA

4

Hammond's Farm

RG8

Checkendon

Whitehall

NUT HATCH COTTS

Broad Oak Poultry Farm

Judges Road

Basset Wood Farm

Basset Wood

BUSGROVE LA

3

PARKSIDE

Checkendon CE Prim Sch

BALFOUR'S FIELD

EMDENS CL

WHITEHALL LA

Ipsden Wood

NEAL'S LA

RG4

Checkendon Court

RG8

Splashall Bottom

83

EMMENS LA

Payables Farm

Four Horseshoes (PH)

Corker's Lane

BEREC'S LA

Larchdown Farm

Horsalls

2

TITMORE LA

READING RD

Corker's Farm

HOOKEND LA

Heath End

RG4

Beech Wood

RG4

1

Three Cornered Wood

A4074

Beechwood Farm

82

65 **A** **B** **66** **C** **D** **67** **E** **F**

251
242

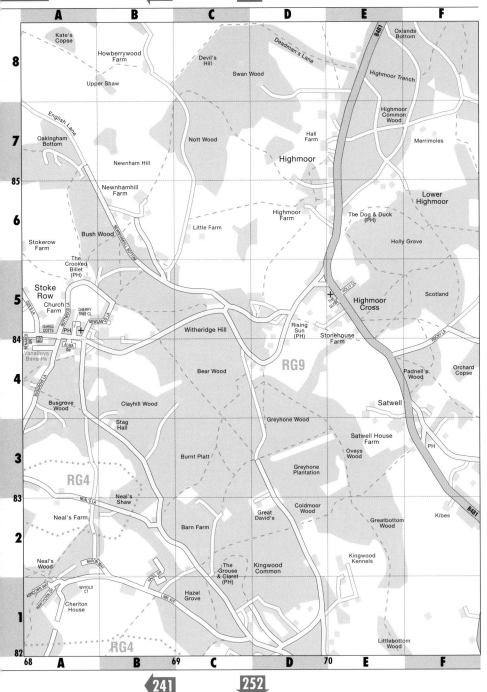

241
224

A   B   C   D   E   F

8

Kate's Copse

Howberrywood Farm

Devil's Hill

Deadman's Lane

Swan Wood

B481

Oxlands Bottom

Highmoor Trench

Upper Shaw

7

English Lane

Oakingham Bottom

Nott Wood

Hall Farm

Highmoor

Highmoor Common Wood

Merrimoles

Newnham Hill

85

Newnhamhill Farm

Lower Highmoor

6

Stokerow Farm

Bush Wood

Little Farm

Highmoor Farm

The Dog & Duck (PH)

Holly Grove

The Crooked Billet (PH)

5

Stoke Row

Church Farm

CHERRY TREE CL

NEWLAN'S LA

THE GLEBE

HOLLY CR

Highmoor Cross

Scotland

ISHREE COTTS

PH

Witheridge Hill

Rising Sun (PH)

Stonehouse Farm

84

BENHANS DR

PO

ALMA GN

Vanalloys Bsns Pk

RG9

Padnell's Wood

Orchard Copse

4

Busgrove Wood

Bear Wood

Satwell

Clayhill Wood

Stag Hall

Greyhone Wood

Satwell House Farm

PH

3

RG4

Burnt Platt

Greyhone Plantation

Oveys Wood

83

NEAL'S LA

Neal's Shaw

Coldmoor Wood

Great David's

Greatbottom Wood

Kibes

B481

Neal's Farm

2

Neal's Wood

BARON WAY

Barn Farm

Kingwood Kennels

WYFOLD CT

HAZEL DR

The Grouse & Claret (PH)

Kingwood Common

ASHDOWN WAY

NORTHCOT DR

1

Cheriton House

LIME AVE

Hazel Grove

Littlebottom Wood

82

RG4

68   A   B   69   C   D   E   70   F

241
252

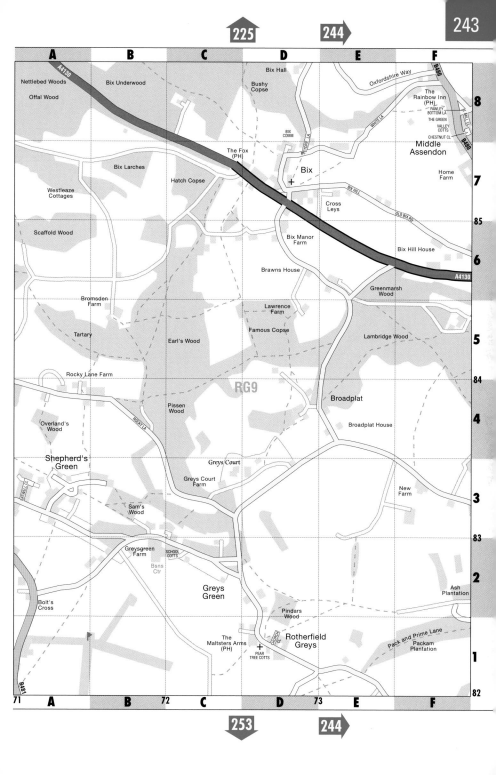

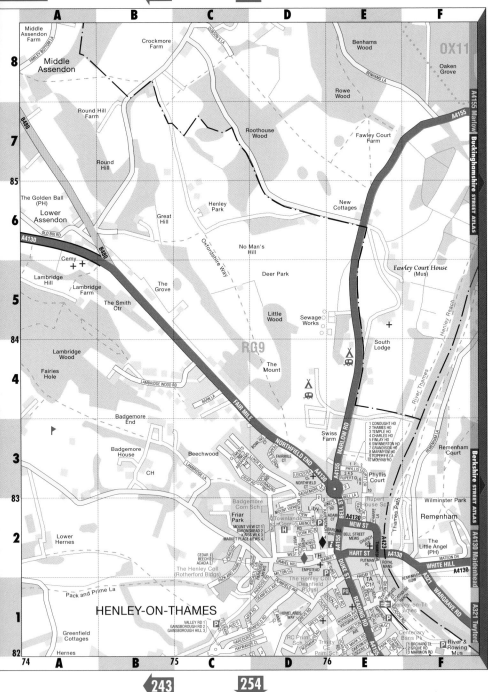

243
226
243
254

A B C D E F

8

7

85

6

5

84

4

3

83

2

1

82

74 A 75 B C 76 D E F

Middle
Assendon
Farm

Middle
Assendon

Crockmore
Farm

Benhams
Wood

OX11

Oaken
Grove

Round Hill
Farm

Roothouse
Wood

Rowe
Wood

Fawley Court
Farm

A4155

A4155 Marlow

Buckinghamshire STREET ATLAS

The Golden Ball
(PH)

Lower
Assendon

Round
Hill

Great
Hill

Henley
Park

New
Cottages

A4130
OLD BIX RD

B480

B480

Cemy

Lambridge
Hill

Lambridge
Farm

The Smith
Ctr

The
Grove

No Man's
Hill

Deer Park

Fawley Court House
(Mus)

Henley Reach

Lambridge
Wood

RG9

Little
Wood

Sewage
Works

South
Lodge

River Thames

Fairies
Hole

LAMBRIDGE WOOD RD

BARN LA

The
Mount

FAIR MILE

Badgemore
End

Badgemore
House

CH

Beechwood

FAIRMILE
CT

Swiss
Farm

MARLOW RD

NORTHFIELD END

Remenham
Court

Lower
Hernes

LAMBRIDGE LA

Friar
Park

Badgemore
Com Sch

Northfield
CT

Badgemore
RD

A4155

A4130

1 CONOUGHT HO
2 THAMES HO
3 TEMPLE HO
4 CHARLES HO
5 FINLAY HO
6 SWINNERTON HO
7 GRANDISON HO
8 MARMYON HO
9 RUPERT-E CA
10 MOLYNS HO

PHYLLIS
COURT

Phyllis
Court

Wilminster Park

Remenham

Berkshire STREET ATLAS

CEDAR 1
BEECH 2
ACACIA 3

MOUNT VIEW CT 1
BARONSMEAD 2
KINGS WLK 3
MARKET PLACE MEWS 4

Townlands

Liby

KINGS
RD

ADAM
CT

BELL ST

BELL LA

Rupert
House Sch

Thames Path

Remenham

The
Little Angel
(PH)

A4130 Maidenhead

The Henley Coll
(Rotherford Bldgs)

WEST ST

NEW ST

CLARENCE
RD

BELL STREET
MEWS

HART ST

CHURCH

THAMESIDE

MATSON DR

A321

A4130

WARGRAVE RD

A321 Twyford

HENLEY-ON-THAMES

Pack and Prime La

GRAVEL HILL

MILTON CL

The Henley Coll
(Deanfield
Bldgs)

EMPSTEAD
CT

MARKET
PL

DUKE ST

KINGS
RD

PUTMAN
CL

Royal
MANS

RC Prim
Sch

Trinity
C of E
Prim Sch

Greenfield
Cottages

Hernes

VALLEY RD 1
GAINSBOROUGH RD 2
GAINSBOROUGH HILL 3

HARCOURT CL

HAYWARDS CL

DEANFIELD AVE

DEANFIELD RD

HOMELANDS
WAY

GREYS HILL

GREYS RD

VICTORIA
RD

NORMAN
AVE

LUPTON CL

FRIDAY ST

READING RD

A4155

TA
Ctr

Henley-on-Th
Thames

Centenary
Bsns Pk

1 ORCHARD CL
2 GROVE RD
3 MARMION RD

River &
Rowing
Mus

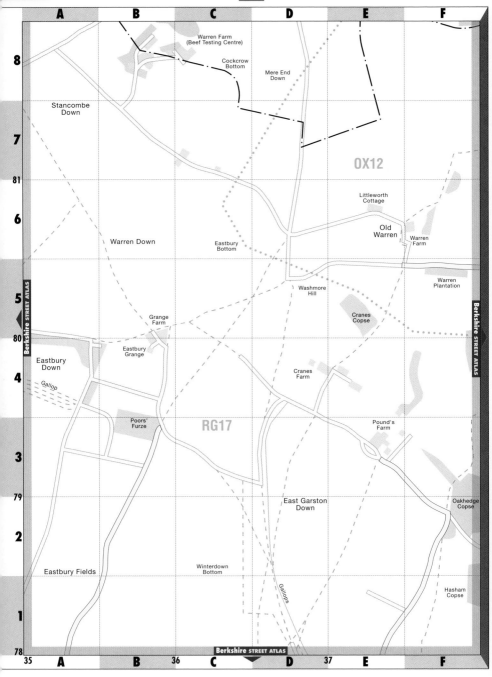

Warren Farm
(Beef Testing Centre)

Cockcrow
Bottom

Mere End
Down

OX12

Stancombe
Down

Littleworth
Cottage

Old
Warren

Warren
Farm

Warren Down

Eastbury
Bottom

Warren
Plantation

Washmore
Hill

Grange
Farm

Cranes
Copse

Eastbury
Grange

Eastbury
Down

Cranes
Farm

Gallop

Pound's
Farm

Poors'
Furze

RG17

East Garston
Down

Oakhedge
Copse

Eastbury Fields

Winterdown
Bottom

Gallops

Hasham
Copse

35   A   B   36   C   D   37   E   F

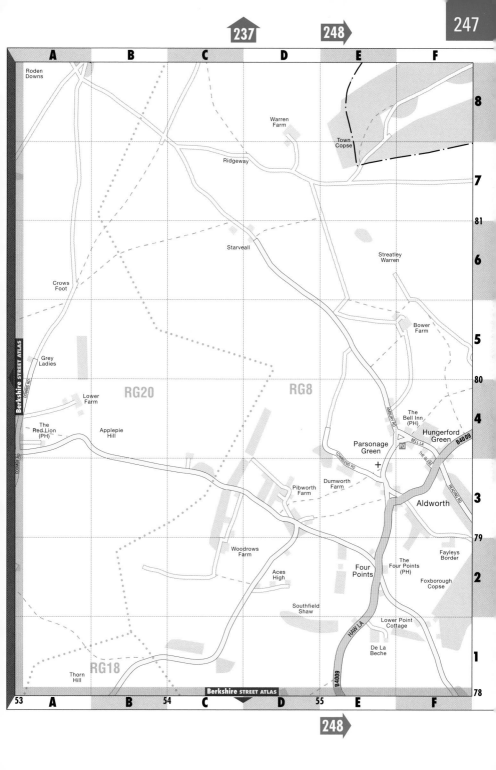

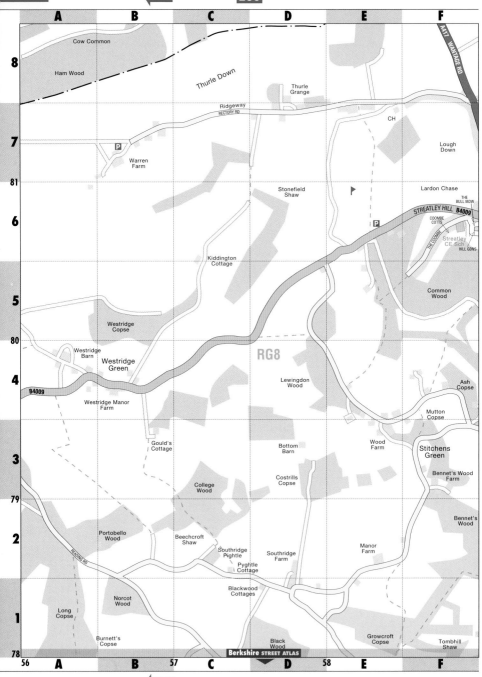

247
238

A417 WANTAGE RD

Cow Common

Ham Wood

Thurle Down

Thurle
Grange

Ridgeway
RECTORY RD

CH

Lough
Down

P

Warren
Farm

Stonefield
Shaw

Lardon Chase

THE
BULL MDW

STREATLEY HILL **B4009**

COOMBE
COTTS

THE COOMBE

Streatley
CE Sch

HILL GDNS

Kiddington
Cottage

Common
Wood

Westridge
Copse

RG8

Westridge
Barn

Westridge
Green

Lewingdon
Wood

Ash
Copse

B4009

Mutton
Copse

Westridge Manor
Farm

Gould's
Cottage

Bottom
Barn

Wood
Farm

Stitchens
Green

College
Wood

Costrills
Copse

Bennet's Wood
Farm

READING RD

Portobello
Wood

Beechcroft
Shaw

Southridge
Pightle

Southridge
Farm

Manor
Farm

Bennet's
Wood

Pyghtle
Cottage

Blackwood
Cottages

Norcot
Wood

Long
Copse

Black
Wood

Growcroft
Copse

Tombhill
Shaw

Burnett's
Copse

Berkshire STREET ATLAS

56   57   58

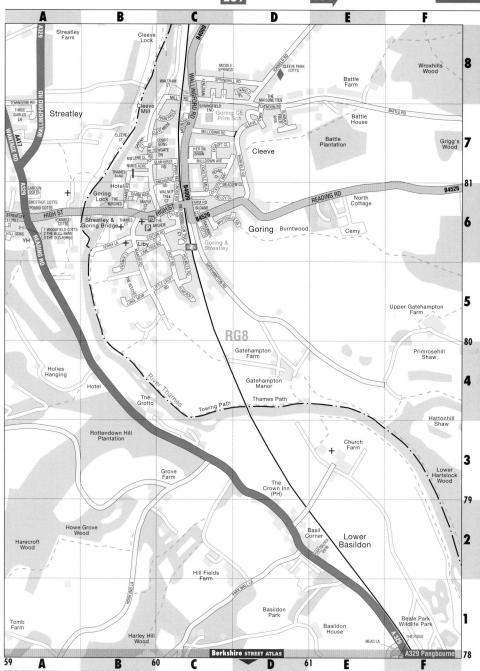

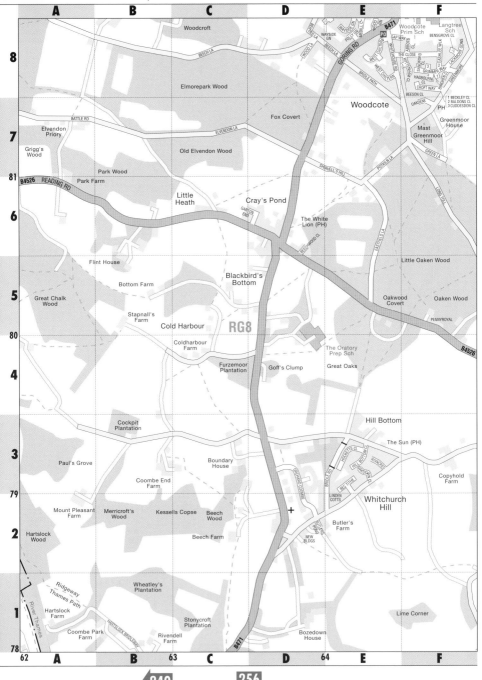

A **B** **C** **D** **E** **F**

8

7

81

6

5

80

4

3

79

2

1

78

62 **A** **B** 63 **C** **D** 64 **E** **F**

Woodcroft

BEECH LA

Elmorepark Wood

Fox Covert

WAYSIDE GN

B471

Woodcote Prim Sch

Langtree Sch

BENSGROVE CL

GAP WAY

THE CLOSE

GORING RD

Woodcote

Greenmoor House

1 BECKLEY CL
2 BALDONS CL
3 CUDDESDON CL

PH

BATTLE RD

Elvendon Priory

ELVENDON LA

Old Elvendon Wood

SHIRVELL'S HILL

Mast Greenmoor Hill

POTKIN LA

GREEN LA

LONG TOLL

Grigg's Wood

B4526

READING RD

Park Wood

Park Farm

Little Heath

Cray's Pond

GARTON END

The White Lion (PH)

BEECHWOOD CL

EASTFIELD LA

Little Oaken Wood

Flint House

Bottom Farm

Blackbird's Bottom

Great Chalk Wood

Oakwood Covert

Oaken Wood

PENNYROYAL

Stapnall's Farm

Cold Harbour

RG8

B4526

Coldharbour Farm

The Oratory Prep Sch

Furzemoor Plantation

Goff's Clump

Great Oaks

Cockpit Plantation

Hill Bottom

The Sun (PH)

Paul's Grove

Boundary House

HOCKETT'S CL

THE BOTTOM

HYACRES

BRIDLE RD

Copyhold Farm

Coombe End Farm

Whitchurch Hill

Mount Pleasant Farm

Merricroft's Wood

Kessells Copse

Beech Wood

LINDEN COTTS

Butler's Farm

Hartslock Wood

Beech Farm

NEW BLDGS

Ridgeway Thames Path

River Thames

Wheatley's Plantation

HARTSLOCK BRIDLEWAY

Lime Corner

Hartslock Farm

Coombe Park Farm

Stonycroft Plantation

Rivendell Farm

B471

Bozedown House

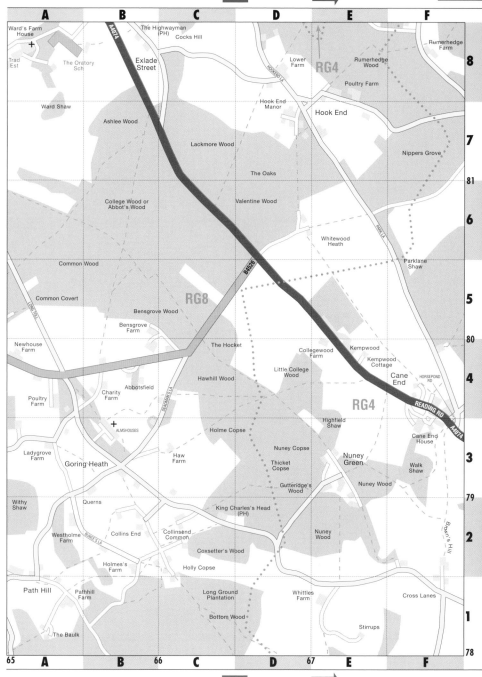

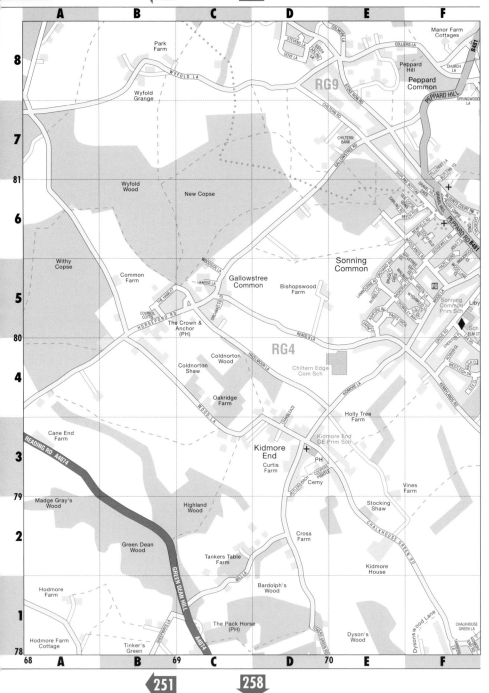

A   **B**   **C**   **D**   **E**   **F**

Manor Farm Cottages

STEVENS LA

COLMORE LA

COLLIERS LA

Peppard Hill

CHURCH LA

B481

8

Park Farm

DOVE LA

WRFOLD LA

RG9

Peppard Common

PEPPARD HILL

Wyfold Grange

CHILTERN RD

STOKE ROW RD

SPRINGWOOD LA

CHELTENHAM LA

BUTLERS YD

7

CHILTERN BANK

GALLOWSTREE RD

GRAVEL HILL

GRAVEL HILL

PEPPARD RD B481

81

Wyfold Wood

New Copse

SCHOOL BOTTOM DRIVE

CARLING RD

OLD COPSE

BEECH RD

BLOUNT COURT RD

6

Withy Copse

WOODSIDE LA

NEWFIELD RD

HAZEL GROVE

Sonning Common

LAMBOURNE RD

ORCHARD RD

WALNUT GRES

BALTIC RD

WYCHWOOD

GALLOWSTREE RD

5

Common Farm

HEARNS LA

THE HAMLET

DRMGMGFIELD

Gallowstree Common

Bishopswood Farm

Sonning Common Prim Sch

Liby

COUNCIL COTTS

HORSEPOND RD

Sch

ELM CT

80

The Crown & Anchor (PH)

READE'S LA

RG4

HAZELMOOR LA

CHERRY CL

WESTLEIGH DR

KENNYLANDS RD

4

Coldnorton Shaw

Coldnorton Wood

Chiltern Edge Com Sch

KIDMORE LA

WOOD LA

CHAIN LANE

Holly Tree Farm

Oakridge Farm

3

Cane End Farm

Kidmore End

Kidmore End CE Prim Sch

Vines Farm

READING RD A4074

Curtis Farm

BUTLERS FINCH

COOPERS PIGHTLE

PH

Cemy

Stocking Shaw

79

Madge Gray's Wood

Highland Wood

CHALKHOUSE GREEN RD

2

Green Dean Wood

Cross Farm

Kidmore House

GREEN DEAN HILL

Tankers Table Farm

Bardolph's Wood

Dyson's Wood Lane

CHALKHOUSE GREEN LA

1

Hodmore Farm

MILL LA

The Pack Horse (PH)

LONGS GREEN RD

Dyson's Wood

Hodmore Farm Cottage

SHEPHERDS LA

Tinker's Green

A4074

78

68   **A**   **B**   69   **C**   **D**   70   **E**   **F**

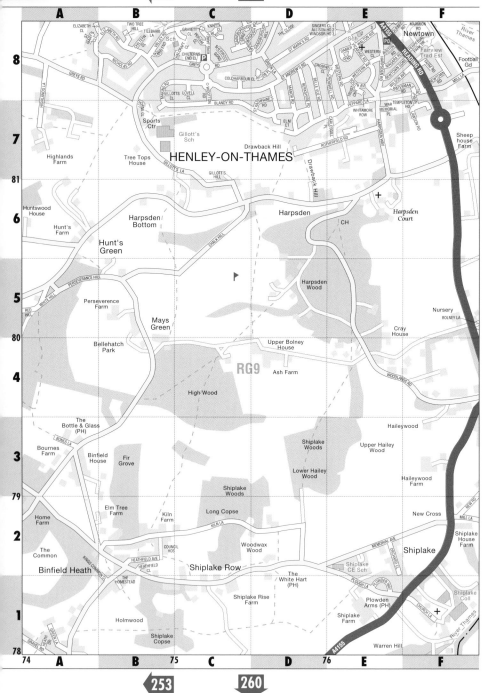

HENLEY-ON-THAMES

Newtown

River Thames

Fairview Trad Est

Football Gd

Sheep house Farm

Highlands Farm

Huntswood House

Hunt's Farm

Tree Tops House

Harpsden Bottom

Harpsden

Harpsden Court

Hunt's Green

Harpsden Wood

Nursery

Perseverance Farm

Mays Green

Cray House

Bellehatch Park

Upper Bolney House

RG9

Ash Farm

High Wood

Haileywood

The Bottle & Glass (PH)

Bournes Farm

Shiplake Woods

Upper Hailey Wood

Binfield House

Fir Grove

Lower Hailey Wood

Haileywood Farm

Shiplake Woods

Elm Tree Farm

Long Copse

New Cross

Kiln Farm

Shiplake House Farm

Home Farm

Woodwax Wood

Shiplake

The Common

Binfield Heath

Shiplake Row

Shiplake CE Sch

The White Hart (PH)

Shiplake Coll

Holmwood

Shiplake Rise Farm

Plowden Arms (PH)

Shiplake Farm

River Thames

Shiplake Copse

Warren Hill

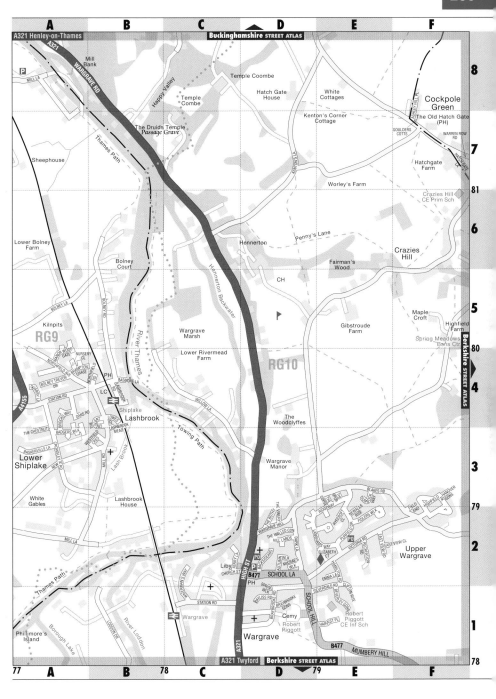

A | B | C | D | E | F

8
7
81
6
5
80
4
3
79
2
1
78

Mill
Bank

WARGRAVE RD

A321

P

MILL LA

Happy Valley

Temple
Combe

Temple Coombe

Hatch Gate
House

White
Cottages

Kenton's Corner
Cottage

Cockpole
Green

The Old Hatch Gate
(PH)

GOULDERS
COTTS

WARREN ROW
RD

HATCHGATE

The Druids Temple
Passage Grave

Thames Path

Sheephouse

Hatchgate
Farm

Worley's Farm

Crazies Hill
CE Prim Sch

Lower Bolney
Farm

Bolney
Court

Penny's Lane

Hennerton

CH

Crazies
Hill

Fairman's
Wood

Maple
Croft

Highfield
Farm

Spring Meadows
Bsns Ctr

BOLNEY LA

RG9

ROLNEY RD

River Thames

Hennerton Backwater

Wargrave
Marsh

Lower Rivermead
Farm

Gibstroude
Farm

RG10

Kilpits

NURSERY
CL

NOR WOOD
GATE

MOORFIELD CL

BRAMPTON
CHASE

MOORELLS

PH

BASMORE LA

Shiplake

LC

Lashbrook

BOLNEY TREVOR
DR

STATION RD

OAKS RD

A4155

HENLEY CL

BRICKS WAY

BADGERS WLK

WESTFIELD
RD

WILLOW LA

The
Woodclyffes

Towing Path

THE CHESTNUTS

BASKERVILLE LA

PARSLEY RD

Lower
Shiplake

SHIPLAKE
MEAD

Lash Brook

MILL RD

Wargrave
Manor

BLAKES RD

RIDGEWAY

WARGRAVE HILL

THE WALLED GDN

HILL LANDS

DARK LA

FIELD
END

HANDOVER
RIDING

HIGHFIELD

White
Gables

Lashbrook
House

MILL LA

Thames Path

Liby

FERRY LA

HIGH ST

B477

PO

PH

SCHOOL LA

SPRING
WLK

BROADMOOR
RD

MORRIS
WLK

BRAYBROOKE
GDNS

ELIZABETH
CT

WAY

VICTORIA RD

EMMA LA

SILVERDALE RD

EAST VIEW CL

EAST VIEW RD

CLIFTON RISE

Upper
Wargrave

PUDDING LA

RECREATION RD

STATION RD

Wargrave

River Loddon

Borough Lake

Phillimore's
Island

SCHOOL HILL

Cemy

Robert
Riggott

HAIRST PL

Robert
Piggott
CE Inf Sch

B477

MUMBERY HILL

Wargrave

A321

77 | A | B | 78 | C | D | 79 | E | F | 78

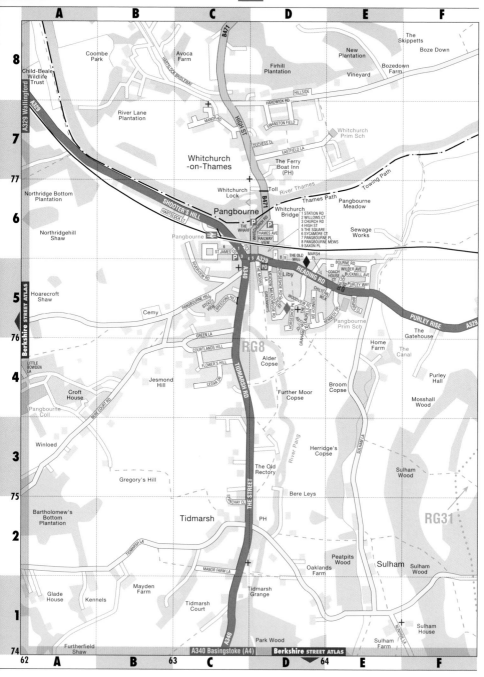

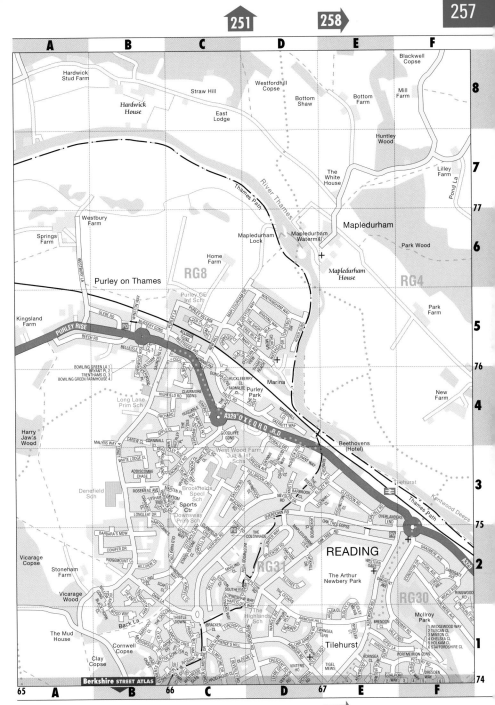

Blackwell
Copse

Hardwick
Stud Farm

Straw Hill

Westfordhill
Copse

Bottom
Shaw

Bottom
Farm

Mill
Farm

8

Hardwick
House

East
Lodge

Huntley
Wood

River Thames

Thames Path

The
White
House

Lilley
Farm

Pond La

7

77

Westbury
Farm

Mapledurham
Lock

Mapledurham
Watermill

Mapledurham

Park Wood

6

Springs
Farm

Home
Farm

RG8

Mapledurham
House

RG4

Purley on Thames

Purley CE
Inf Sch

Park
Farm

Kingsland
Farm

PURLEY RISE

GLEBE RD

BEECH RD

NURSERY GDNS

WINTON WAY

Purley GE
Inf Sch

5

BOWLING GREEN LA 1
BRYANT PL 2
TRENTHAMS CL 3
BOWLING GREEN FARMHOUSE 4

BELLEISLE RISE

Marina

76

New
Farm

4

Harry
Jaw's
Wood

CAREW CL
CORNWALL

MALYNS WAY

WHITE LODGE

ADDISCOMBE
CHASE

A329 OXFORD RD

West Wood Farm
Jun & Inf
Schs

GOODLIFFE
GDNS

Beethovens
(Hotel)

Tilehurst

Thames Path

Kentwood Deeps

3

Denefield
Sch

ROSEMEAD AVE

LONGLEAT DR

Brookfields
Specl
Sch

Sports
Ctr

Downsway
Prim Sch

OVERDOWN RD

OAK TREE COPSE

OVERLANDERS
END

75

Vicarage
Copse

Stoneham
Farm

Vicarage
Wood

BARBARA'S MDW

CONIFER DR

RIDGEMOUNT CL

HILLVIEW LA

THE
COLONNADE

RG31

READING

The Arthur
Newbery Park

RG30

GRASMERE AVE

A329

2

The Mud
House

Cornwell
Copse

Back La

THISTLE
DOWN

The
Highlands
Sch

Tilehurst

McIlroy
Park

1 WEDGEWOOD WAY
2 TUSCAN CL
3 MINTON CL
4 CHELSEA CL
5 HOLKAM CL
6 STAFFORDSHIRE CL

1

Clay
Copse

PIERCE'S HILL

PORTMEIRION GDNS

POTTERY RD

74

65

A

Berkshire STREET ATLAS

B

66

C

D

67

E

F

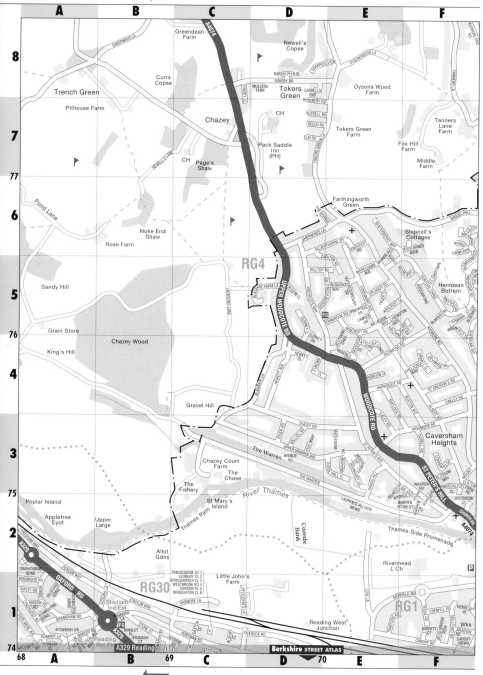

A   **B**   **C**   **D**   **E**   **F**

8

Greendean Farm

Newell's Copse

Trench Green

BARDOLPH'S CL

Currs Copse

ROKEBY DR

Dysons Wood Farm

Pithouse Farm

MULLENS TERR

Tokers Green

GASKELLS END

Tanners Lane Farm

Chazey

CH

ROSEBERY RD

RUSSELL RD

Tokers Green Farm

BEECH RD

Fox Hill Farm

7

CH

ELM RD

Pack Saddle Inn (PH)

Page's Shaw

Middle Farm

NEWELL'S LANE

77

Pond Lane

Farthingworth Green

6

Noke End Shaw

SHEPHERDS LA

Shipnell's Cottages

Rose Farm

SILVERTHORNE DR

MIDSUMMER MDW

Hemdean Bottom

RG4

CARLTON RD

HILLTOP RD

5

Sandy Hill

GROVE FARM LA

UPPER WOODCOTE RD

Grain Store

76

Chazey Wood

King's Hill

4

HEWETT CL

Gravel Hill

BLACKWATER LA

HEWETT RD

WOODCOTE RD

HARROGATE RD

St ANDREW'S RD

OAKLEY RD

Caversham Heights

3

CHAZEY RD

The Warren

UPPER WARREN AVE

Chazey Court Farm

AVENUE RD

The Chase

THE WARREN

St PETER'S AVE

St PETER'S HILL

75

The Fishery

River Thames

St Mary's Island

Poplar Island

Thames Path Rd

Coombe Bank

LAURENCE ALLISON MEWS

WARREN HOUSE CT

Thames Side Promenade

Appletree Eyot

Upper Large

WOODROW CT

2

A329

Allot Gdns

CHURCHILL

A4074

CRANBOURNE GDNS

PANGBOURNE ST 1

Little John's Farm

Rivermead L Ctr

RIPLEY RD

LEDBURY CL 2

OXFORD RD

BRIDGEWATER CL 3

WESTBROOK RD 4

GORDON PL 5

BROUGHTON CL 6

RICHFIELD AVE

KINSON RD

RG30

WIGMORE LA

RG1

1

Stadium Ind Est

STADIUM WAY

BRAMSHAW RD

STONE ST

PORTMAN RD

Reading West Junction

MOWBRAY DR

WINSLET

BRANAGH CT

CARDIFF RD

A329

LOVEROCK RD

74

A329 Reading

Berkshire STREET ATLAS

68   **A**   **B**   **69**   **C**   **D**   **70**   **E**   **F**

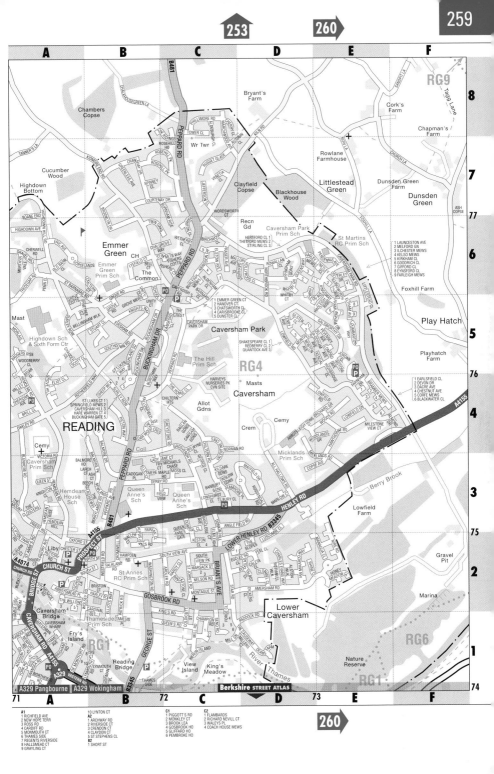

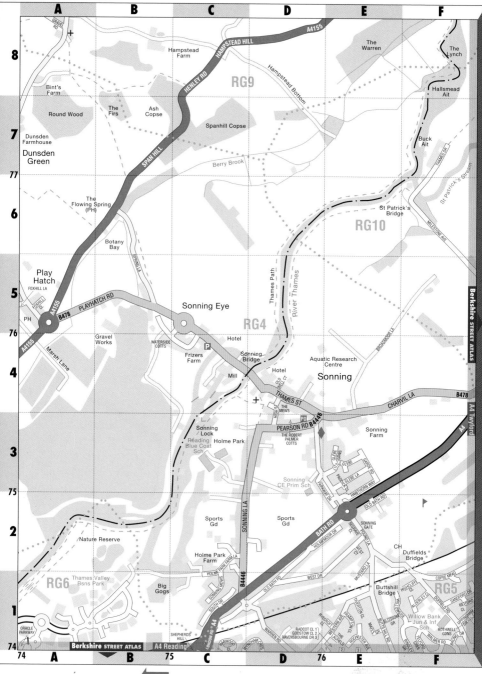

A   B   C   D   E   F

8

A4155

Hampstead Hill

Hampstead
Farm

HENLEY RD

RG9

The
Warren

The
Lynch

Hampstead Bottom

Bint's
Farm

Hallsmead
Ait

7

Round Wood

The
Firs

Ash
Copse

Spanhill Copse

Buck
Ait

Dunsden
Farmhouse

Dunsden
Green

SPAN HILL

Berry Brook

St Patrick's Stream

77

The
Flowing Spring
(PH)

St Patrick's
Bridge

RG10

MILESTONE AVE

6

Botany
Bay

SPRING LA

THAMES DR

Play
Hatch

FOXHILL LA

PLAYHATCH RD

Sonning Eye

Thames Path

River Thames

RG4

Berkshire STREET ATLAS

5

A4155

B478

Gravel
Works

WATERSIDE
COTTS

P

Hotel

Sonning
Bridge

Aquatic Research
Centre

76

PH

A4155

Marsh Lane

Frizers
Farm

Mill

Hotel

Sonning

CHARVIL LA

B478

A4 Twyford

4

Sonning
Lock

Reading
Blue Coat
Sch

Holme Park

THAMES ST

THE
MEWS

PEARSON RD

THE ROBERT
PALMER
COTTS

Sonning
Farm

B4446

A4

3

Sonning
CE Prim Sch

GLEBE LA

HART'S THORN WAY

75

Sports
Gd

Sports
Gd

SONNING LA

HOLMACOTT DR

Sonning
Gate

CH

Duffields
Bridge

2

Nature Reserve

Holme Park
Farm

HOLME PARK FARM LA

HOLME
MEWS

SOUTH DR

BATH RD

OLD BATH RD

WEST DR

Buttshill
Bridge

COPSE MEAD

RG5

RETFORD

1

ORACLE
PARKWAY

RG6

Thames Valley
Bsns Park

Big
Gogs

SHEPHERDS
HILL

B4446

MAINOAK LA

THE A4

RADCOT CL 1
GODSTOW CL 2
RAVENSBOURNE DR 3

Willow Bank
Jun & Inf
Sch

ROTHWELL
GDNS

PALMER RD

74

74   A   B   75   C   D   76   E   F

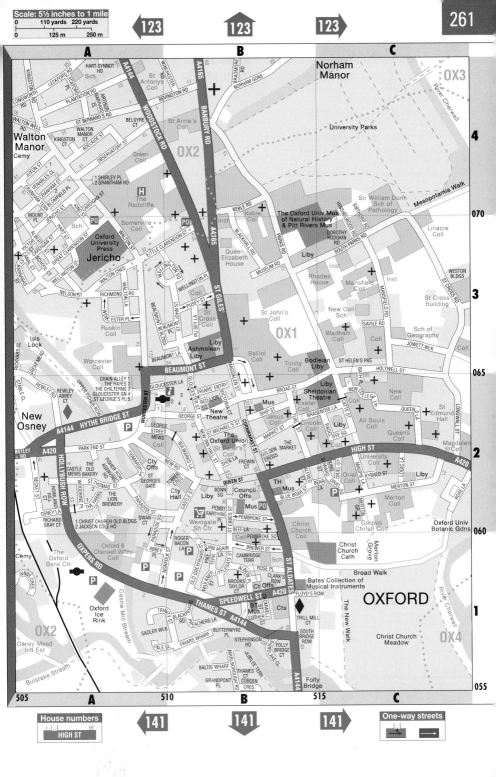

Index

Place name May be abbreviated on the map

Location number Present when a number indicates the place's position in a crowded area of mapping

Locality, town or village Shown when more than one place has the same name

Postcode district District for the indexed place

Page and grid square Page number and grid reference for the standard mapping

Church Rd **6** Beckenham BR2.........**53** C6

Public and commercial buildings are highlighted in magenta   Places of interest are highlighted in blue with a star★

Abbreviations used in the index

Acad	**Academy**	Comm	**Common**	Gd	**Ground**	L	**Leisure**	Prom	**Prom**

Acad **Academy** · App **Approach** · Arc **Arcade** · Ave **Avenue** · Bglw **Bungalow** · Bldg **Building** · Bsns, Bus **Business** · Bvd **Boulevard** · Cath **Cathedral** · Cir **Circus** · Cl **Close** · Cnr **Corner** · Coll **College** · Com **Community**

Comm **Common** · Cott **Cottage** · Cres **Crescent** · Cswy **Causeway** · Ct **Court** · Ctr **Centre** · Ctry **Country** · Cty **County** · Dr **Drive** · Dro **Drove** · Ed **Education** · Emb **Embankment** · Est **Estate** · Ex **Exhibition**

Gd **Ground** · Gdn **Garden** · Gn **Green** · Gr **Grove** · H **Hall** · Ho **House** · Hospl **Hospital** · HQ **Headquarters** · Hts **Heights** · Ind **Industrial** · Inst **Institute** · Int **International** · Intc **Interchange** · Junc **Junction**

L **Leisure** · La **Lane** · Liby **Library** · Mdw **Meadow** · Meml **Memorial** · Mkt **Market** · Mus **Museum** · Orch **Orchard** · Pal **Palace** · Par **Parade** · Pas **Passage** · Pk **Park** · Pl **Place** · Prec **Precinct**

Prom **Prom** · Rd **Road** · Recn **Recreation** · Ret **Retail** · Sh **Shopping** · Sq **Square** · St **Street** · Sta **Station** · Terr **Terrace** · TH **Town Hall** · Univ **University** · Wk, Wlk **Walk** · Wr **Water** · Yd **Yard**

Index of localities, towns and villages

A

Abingdon..........179 E7
Adderbury..........23 A3
Adlestrop..........40 D2
Adwell..........166 D3
Albury..........146 B7
Aldworth..........247 F3
Alkerton..........6 F2
Alvescot..........133 C6
Ambrosden..........81 D3
Appleford..........200 F8
Appleton..........158 A7
Appletree..........5 C8
Ardington..........215 E6
Ardington Wick..........215 F8
Ardley..........50 C4
Arlescote..........2 C6
Ascot
 Hook Norton..........18 A2
 Stadhampton..........163 E1
Ascott d'Oyley..........71 C2
Ascott Earl..........71 B1
Ascott-under-
 Wychwood..........71 D2
Ashbury..........228 A7
Asthall..........101 F3
Asthall Leigh..........102 D6
Aston..........135 E3
Aston Rowant..........167 C2
Aston Tirrold..........237 E8
Aston Upthorpe..........219 E2
Astwick..........37 B7
Avon Dassett..........2 F8
Aynho..........35 C8

B

Bablock Hythe..........138 F5
Bainton..........51 E2
Baldon Row..........162 B5
Balscote..........14 C8
Bampton..........134 F4
Banbury..........16 F5
Barford St John..........32 F7
Barford St Michael..........32 E5
Barnard Gate..........105 F1
Barrow Hills..........160 D1
Barton..........124 E4
Bartongate..........61 A8
Barton Hartshorn..........39 D2
Barton-on-the-Heath..........26 E6
Baulking..........193 F2
Baydon..........245 E1
Baynard's Green..........50 D7
Bayworth..........160 A7
Beacon's Bottom..........189 D3

Beckley..........111 B3
Begbroke..........108 B8
Belmont..........214 C5
Bennett End..........189 C7
Benson..........204 A4
Berinsfield..........182 D5
Berrick Prior..........184 A2
Berrick Salome..........184 A1
Bessels Leigh..........158 D8
Bicester..........65 D4
Binfield Heath..........254 A2
Binsey..........122 E4
Bishopstone..........227 C3
Bix..........243 D7
Blackbird Leys..........142 F2
Blackbird's Bottom..........250 D5
Black Bourton..........133 F6
Blackditch..........138 A8
Blackthorn..........82 A4
Bladon..........91 C2
Bledington..........54 D1
Bledlow..........169 B8
Bledlow Ridge..........189 E8
Blenheim..........143 C7
Bletchingdon..........93 B8
Blewbury..........237 B8
Bloxham..........21 D5
Boars Hill..........140 D1
Boarstall..........97 B1
Bodicote..........22 D8
Botley..........140 D8
Bould..........69 C7
Bourton..........209 A3
Bow..........174 E1
Brackley..........24 A7
Bradwell Grove..........114 B6
Brasswell Corner..........86 F7
Bridge End..........202 D8
Brighthampton..........137 B4
Brightwell Baldwin..........185 A2
Brightwell-cum-
 Sotwell..........202 C2
Brill..........98 B1
Britwell Salome..........205 E7
Brize Norton..........116 C4
Broadplat..........243 E4
Broadwell..........132 E4
Brookend..........72 A8
Brookhampton..........163 C1
Broughton..........15 C1
Broughton Poggs..........132 B4
Buckland..........154 F1
Buckland Marsh..........154 D4
Bucknell..........65 A7
Bunkers Hill..........92 A8
Burcot..........182 A4
Burdrop..........19 B8
Burford..........100 D5
Buscot..........171 A8

Buscot Wick..........170 D8
Bushey Ground..........116 E8

C

Caldecott..........179 E6
Calthorpe..........16 D3
Camp Corner..........145 F4
Campsfield..........91 E3
Cane End..........251 F4
Carswell Marsh..........154 A3
Carterton..........115 C4
Cassington..........107 C2
Caulcott..........63 B5
Caversfield..........65 E7
Caversham..........259 D4
Caversham Heights..........258 F3
Caversham Park..........259 C5
Chacombe..........10 F4
Chadlington..........57 B2
Chalford..........167 B6
Chalgrove..........184 E6
Chalkhouse Green..........253 A1
Charlbury..........73 C3
Charlton..........214 F5
Charlton-on-Otmoor..........95 A4
Charney Bassett..........176 A2
Chastleton..........40 C7
Chawley..........140 A6
Chazey Heath..........258 C7
Checkendon..........241 C3
Chesterton..........79 F7
Chetwode..........53 E8
Childrey..........213 C4
Chilson..........71 F3
Chilton..........235 E8
Chimney..........155 B6
Chimney-end..........86 E4
Chinnor..........168 D7
Chipping Norton..........42 F2
Chipping Warden..........5 E6
Chiselhampton..........163 A2
Cholsey..........221 A1
Christmas Common..........207 B7
Church End
 Bletchingdon..........93 B8
 Ducklington..........118 C4
 Long Crendon..........129 D7
 South Leigh..........119 D6
 Swerford..........30 E3
Church Enstone..........58 F7
Church Hanborough..........106 D6
Churchill..........55 E5
Church Westcote..........68 D6
Clanfield..........152 E8
Clare..........165 E2
Clattercote..........4 D7
Claydon..........1 D1

Cleeve..........249 D7
Cleveley..........59 C4
Clifton..........34 E4
Clifton Hampden..........181 C4
Cockpole Green..........255 F8
Cogges..........118 C8
Cold Harbour
 Oxford..........141 D5
 Woodcote..........250 C5
Coleshill..........191 A8
Combe..........90 A5
Common Beauchamp..........210 D3
Cookley Green..........206 D1
Cornwell..........41 C3
Coscote..........218 D5
Cote..........136 A2
Cothill..........158 E3
Cottisford..........37 F3
Cowley..........142 E5
Coxlease..........226 A5
Crawley..........103 E4
Cray's Pond..........250 D6
Crazies Hill..........255 F6
Cropredy..........4 E2
Croughton..........36 D7
Crowell..........168 B4
Crowell Hill..........168 D2
Crowmarsh Gifford..........221 F7
Crowsley..........253 C4
Cuddesdon..........144 B3
Culham..........180 B2
Cumnor..........139 D5
Cumnor Hill..........140 C7
Curbridge..........117 C6
Cutteslowe..........109 B2
Cuxham..........185 D3

D

Daylesford..........54 D8
Dean..........57 E1
Dean Court..........140 B8
Deddington..........33 E4
Delly End..........104 A8
Denchworth..........196 A4
Denton..........144 A1
Didcot..........200 D3
Diggs..........130 F5
Dogmore End..........241 D4
Dorchester..........182 C1
Dorton..........98 F1
Down End..........30 B7
Downington..........170 C6
Draycot..........145 F8
Drayton
 Abingdon..........179 A1
 Banbury..........15 D8
Drayton St Leonard..........183 A5

Dry Sandford..........158 F5
Ducklington..........118 A4
Dunsden Green..........259 F7
Duns Tew..........47 D6
Duxford..........155 D4

E

Easington
 Banbury..........16 C3
 Chalgrove..........185 C7
East Adderbury..........23 B3
East Challow..........214 A5
Eastend..........57 D1
East End
 Adderbury..........23 B4
 Hook Norton..........30 B7
 Swerford..........30 F3
East Ginge..........216 B2
East Hagbourne..........218 F6
East Hanney..........197 B6
East Hendred..........216 E7
Eastleach Martin..........131 B7
Eastleach Turville..........131 A8
East Lockinge..........215 D3
Eaton..........139 B3
Eaton Hastings..........171 E7
Eaton Wood..........171 F5
Elsfield..........110 C1
Emmer Green..........259 B6
Emmington..........149 A1
Enslow..........77 C1
Enstone..........58 F6
Epwell..........13 B6
Ewelme..........204 F4
Exlade Street..........251 B8
Eynsham..........120 C1

F

Faringdon..........172 E3
Farmoor..........121 C3
Farnborough..........3 F8
Fawler
 Finstock..........88 E7
 Uffington..........211 F5
Fawley..........226 D2
Fawley Bottom..........226 B2
Fawley Green..........226 D2
Fencott..........95 D5
Fernham..........193 A4
Fewcott..........50 C5
Field Assarts..........102 F8
Fifield..........69 C2
Filchampstead..........139 C8
Filkins..........132 C5
Finmere..........39 D7

Finstock 88 C5
Florence Park 142 B5
Fordwells 102 D8
Forest Hill 125 F4
Forty Green 149 F3
Foscot 69 D8
Four Points 247 E2
Foxcombe Hill 159 F8
Freeland 106 A7
Frilford 178 A7
Fringford 52 D6
Fritwell 49 F7
Frogs' Island 202 C2
Fulbrook 100 F7
Fulwell
  Enstone 58 F3
  Westbury 25 A2
Fyfield
  Kingston Bagpuize 157 C2
  Lechlade-on-Thames 131 B4

G
Gagingwell 59 F7
Gainfield 174 F3
Gallowstree Common 252 C5
Garden City 108 E5
Garford 177 D5
Garsington 143 E1
Gawcombe 68 C7
Gibralter 77 B1
Glympton 75 D8
Godington 53 E3
Golden Balls 182 A8
Goosey 195 B4
Goosey Green 195 B4
Goring 249 D6
Goring Heath 251 A3
Gosford 108 F7
Gozzard's Ford 158 E2
Grafton 152 C6
Grandpont 141 D7
Great Barrington 99 C8
Great Bourton 9 D8
Great Coxwell 192 C7
Great Halcombe 183 E6
Great Haseley 164 E8
Great Milton 145 B2
Great Rissington 83 A7
Great Tew 45 D7
Greenend 72 A7
Greenfield 207 A4
Greys Green 243 C2
Grimsbury 16 F5
Grove 196 F1

H
Haddenham 130 E6
Hailey
  Wallingford 240 E8
  Witney 104 A6
Hampton Gay 92 D5
Hampton Poyle 93 B4
Hanwell 8 F4
Harcourt Hill 140 E6
Hardwick
  Banbury 9 B1
  Stoke Lyne 51 D8
  Witney 118 F1
Haresfield 190 B8
Harpsden 254 D6
Harpsden Bottom 254 B6
Harwell 217 F7
Hatford 174 D4
Hawkwell 68 C6
Headington 124 C4
Headington Hill 124 A2
Headington Quarry 124 E2
Heathfield Village 93 E6
Hempton 33 B4
Hempton Wainhill 168 F7
Henley-on-Thames 244 B1
Hensington 91 D7
Henton 149 E2
Henwood 140 A1
Hethe 52 A8
Heythrop 44 A4
High Cogges 118 F6
Highfield 65 C3
Highmoor 242 D7
Highmoor Cross 242 E5
Highworth 190 B6
Hill Bottom 250 E3
Hinton Parva 227 A3
Hinton Waldrist 155 F3
Holton 126 C2
Holwell 114 A7
Hook End 251 E7
Hook Norton 30 A8
Horley 8 B4
Hornton 7 C7
Horsleys Green 189 C3
Horspath 143 D6
Horton-cum-Studley 112 A6
Hungerford Green 247 F4
Huntercombe End 224 B4
Hunt's Green 254 B6

I
Ickford 128 A3
Idbury 69 B4
Idstone 227 F5

Iffley 141 F4
Ilmer 149 F8
Inglesham 150 B1
Ipsden 240 C7
Islip 109 F8

J
Jericho 261 A3
Juniper Hill 37 D6

K
Kelmscott 151 D3
Kencot 132 F5
Kennington 160 E7
Kiddington 60 B2
Kidlington 108 D7
Kidmore End 252 D3
Kingham 55 A4
King's End 65 D1
Kings Sutton 23 F6
Kingston Bagpuize 156 E2
Kingston Blount 167 D7
Kingstone Winslow 228 B8
Kingston Lisle 212 A4
Kingston Stert 167 D7
Kirtlington 77 F4
Kitebrook 26 D3
Knighton 210 E3

L
Langford 132 C2
Langley 86 C4
Lashbrook 255 B4
Latchford 165 B7
Launton 66 D1
Leafield 86 E3
Lechlade-on-Thames 150 D3
Ledwell 46 C5
Letcombe Bassett 231 F7
Letcombe Regis 214 B2
Lew 117 B1
Lewknor 187 B8
Lidstone 58 B6
Little Barrington 99 B6
Little Blenheim 108 A5
Little Bourton 9 D5
Little Clanfield 152 B7
Little Compton 26 E1
Little Coxwell 192 E7
Little Faringdon 150 F8
Little Haseley 164 D6
Little Heath 250 C6
Little Ickford 128 B3
Little London 160 D8
Little Milton 164 A8
Little Minster 102 E3
Littlemore 142 C1
Little Rollright 28 A1
Littlestead Green 259 E7
Little Tew 45 A5
Little Tingewick 39 E6
Little Wittenham 202 B7
Littleworth
  Faringdon 173 E7
  Wheatley 143 F7
Long Compton 27 F6
Longcot 192 C2
Long Crendon 129 B6
Long Hanborough 90 B1
Long Wittenham 201 D8
Longworth 156 C3
Lower Arncott 81 C1
Lower Basildon 249 E2
Lower Bourton 208 F3
Lower Caversham 259 D1
Lower End
  Alvescot 133 C5
  Leafield 87 A4
  Long Crendon 129 B7
Lower Heyford 62 D6
Lower Highmoor 242 F6
Lower Odington 54 B8
Lower Radley 161 A3
Lower Shiplake 255 A3
Lower Tadmarton 20 F7
Lower Wainhill 168 E7
Lower Wolvercote 122 D7
Ludgershall 98 D8
Lyford 176 C1
Lyneham 70 E5

M
Mackney 220 D8
Maidensgrove 225 C5
Mapledurham 257 E6
Marcham 178 D6
Marsh Baldon 162 B3
Marsh Gibbon 67 F3
Marston 123 E6
Mays Green 254 B5
Merton 95 D8
Middle Assendon 243 F7
Middle Aston 48 B3
Middle Barton 60 F7
Middleton Cheney 11 A1
Middleton Stoney 64 B3
Middletown 104 A6
Milcombe 21 B2
Mill End 57 A2

Milton
  Banbury 22 C3
  Didcot 199 C5
Milton Common 146 B3
Milton Heights 199 C2
Milton Hill 199 B2
Milton-under-
  Wychwood 70 C1
Minster Lovell 102 F2
Mixbury 38 D8
Mollington 4 B4
Mongewell 221 E4
Moreton
  Appleton 157 A7
  Thame 147 D5
Moulsford 238 F4
Murcott 95 F4

N
Neat Enstone 58 F5
Neithrop 16 A6
Nethercote 17 B7
Nethercott 77 D6
Netherton 157 B3
Nether Westcote 68 F5
Nether Worton 32 C1
Nettlebed 224 D2
New Botley 122 E1
Newbridge 156 E8
New Headington 124 C1
New Hinksey 141 D6
Newington 183 E6
Newland 118 D8
New Marston 123 F4
Newnham Murren 221 E6
New Osney 261 A2
Newton Purcell 39 B2
Newtown
  Henley-on-Thames 254 F8
  Wallingford 221 E1
Noke 110 C7
Norham Manor 261 C4
North Aston 48 B6
Northbrook 62 E1
Northcourt 160 A1
Northend 207 E6
North Hinksey Village 140 E8
North Leigh 105 B7
Northmoor 138 C2
North Moreton 220 A2
North Newington 15 B4
North Stoke 221 D1
North Weston 146 F8
Nuffield 223 D3
Nuneham Courtenay 161 A2
Nuney Green 251 E3

O
Oakley 168 B5
Oddington 94 E2
Old Boars Hill 159 D8
Old Town 24 A7
Old Warren 246 E6
Old Woodstock 91 A7
Osney 123 A1
Over Kiddington 60 A1
Over Norton 42 E5
Overthorpe 17 D6
Over Worton 46 D7
Oxford 261 C1

P
Pangbourne 256 C6
Park Corner 224 C6
Park Town 123 D4
Parsonage Green 247 E4
Path Hill 251 A1
Peachcroft 160 C2
Peppard Common 252 F8
Piddington 97 E7
Piddington Cow Leys 82 D3
Pishill 225 D8
Pishill Bank 207 B1
Pishill Bottom 207 A1
Playhatch 260 A5
Play Heath 259 F5
Poffley End 104 C6
Portways 207 B8
Postcombe 166 F5
Potter's Hill 86 C2
Poundon 67 E7
Purley on Thames 257 B6
Pusey 175 B6
Pyrton 186 B4

R
Rack End 137 E3
Radcot 152 F4
Radford 59 F5
Radley 160 E3
Radnage 189 D8
Ramsden 88 A3
Ramsden Heath 87 F4
Ratley 2 A4
Reading 259 A4
Remenham 244 F3
Risinghurst 125 A3
Roke 204 B7
Rokemarsh 204 A6

Rose Hill 142 A4
Rotherfield Greys 243 D1
Rotherfield Peppard 253 A8
Rousham 62 B4
Rout's Green 169 D2
Rowstock 217 B7
Ruscote 16 A7

S
Salford 41 F5
Sandford-on-Thames 161 B7
Sandford St Martin 46 C2
Sandhills 125 B4
Sarsden 55 F3
Sarsden Halt 55 D6
Satwell 242 E4
Scotland End 30 A7
Sevenhampton 190 B2
Shabbington 128 D3
Shalstone 25 E6
Shellingford 193 F7
Shenington 6 E2
Shepherd's Green 243 A3
Shillingford 203 B6
Shilton 115 B5
Shiplake 254 F2
Shiplake Row 254 C2
Shippon 159 C1
Shipton-on-Cherwell 92 B6
Shipton-under-
  Wychwood 85 E8
Shirburn 186 D4
Shores Green 118 F8
Shorthampton 72 B5
Shotteswell 8 D7
Shrivenham 209 B7
Shutford 14 B6
Sibford Ferris 19 A7
Sibford Gower 19 A8
Signet 100 C1
Slade End 202 F1
Somerton 48 F6
Sonning 260 E4
Sonning Common 252 E5
Sonning Eye 260 C5
Souldern 35 E4
Southcoombe 43 D3
Southend
  Garsington 162 E8
  Henley-on-Thames 226 C8
South Hinksey 141 C5
South Leigh 119 C6
Southmoor 156 D1
South Moreton 219 F5
South Newington 31 E2
Southrop
  Hook Norton 30 B6
  Lechlade-on-Thames 131 A3
South Stoke 239 C4
South Weston 166 E1
Sparsholt 212 E4
Spelsbury 72 F8
Sprig's Alley 168 F1
Stadhampton 163 D2
Standlake 137 D4
Stanford in the Vale 194 F7
Stanton Harcourt 138 A8
Stanton St John 125 E7
Steeple Aston 62 A7
Steeple Barton 61 D7
Steventon 198 E4
Stitchens Green 248 F3
Stoke Lyne 51 B5
Stokenchurch 188 E5
Stoke Row 241 F4
Stoke Talmage 165 F3
Stonesfield 89 D7
Stonor 225 F6
Stratton Audley 52 C1
Streatley 249 A7
Studley Green 189 E3
Sulham 256 E2
Summertown 123 C7
Sunningwell 159 E7
Sunnymead 123 B8
Sutton 120 B1
Sutton Courtenay 200 B8
Sutton Green 120 B2
Sutton Wick 179 C2
Swalcliffe 19 E7
Swerford 30 E3
Swerford Heath 31 C4
Swinbrook 101 E5
Swinford 121 B5
Sydenham 167 D8

T
Tackley 77 C5
Tadmarton 20 C8
Taston 58 B1
Taynton 100 A8
Temple Cowley 142 C6
Tetsworth 166 A8
Thame 148 C7
The City 189 D6
The Colony 18 F7
The Green
  Ludgershall 98 C8
  North Aston 48 A6
The Hollows 28 A4
The Moors 118 A5
The Platt 163 A7
The Square 59 A6

Thrupp Faringdon 153 A2
  Kidlington 92 C4
Tiddington 145 F7
Tidmarsh 256 C2
Tilehurst 257 E1
Tokers Green 258 D8
Toot Baldon 162 B6
Touchbridge 247 E3
Towersey 148 E7
Townend 215 F5
Town End 189 C8
Townsend
  Grove 196 D2
  Wantage 214 A4
  Wheatley 127 B2
Town's End 258 A8
Trench Green 258 A8
Tubney 157 F2
Turville park 207 F3
Turweston 24 C8
Twyford 23 B5

U
Uffington 211 D7
Upper Arncott 96 E7
Upper Heyford 62 E8
Upper Inglesham 170 B6
Upper Maidensgrove 225 A7
Upper Rissington 68 B4
Upperton 185 A1
Upper Wardington 10 F8
Upper Wargrave 255 F2
Upper Wolvercote 122 F8
Upton
  Burford 100 C5
  Didcot 218 C2

W
Walcot 72 F4
Wales 23 F5
Wallingford 221 C6
Walton Manor 261 A4
Wantage 214 E3
Warborough 203 B8
Wardington 5 E2
Wargrave 255 D1
Warkworth 17 D5
Warmington 3 A4
Warpsgrove 164 F1
Watchfield 191 F1
Water Eaton 109 D5
Waterend 189 C5
Waterperry 127 B1
Waterstock 145 D8
Watlington 186 C2
Weald 134 D1
Well Place 240 F7
Wendlebury 80 A4
West Adderbury 22 E3
Westbury 25 B4
West Challow 213 C6
Westcot 212 D3
Westcott Barton 60 D8
Westend 57 B1
West End
  Cholsey 220 F1
  Stanton Harcourt 138 C5
West Ginge 216 A2
West Hagbourne 218 D4
Westhall Hill 100 D6
West Hanney 196 F6
West Hendred 216 C6
West Ilsley 235 B1
West Lockinge 215 C4
Weston-on-the-Green 79 B2
Westridge Green 248 B4
Westwell 99 E1
Wheatfield 166 B3
Wheatley 144 A8
Whitchurch Hill 250 E2
Whitchurch-on-
  Thames 256 C7
Whitehall 241 D3
Whiteoak Green 87 F1
Wick Green 196 E2
Widford 101 B4
Wigginton 31 A7
Wigginton Heath 20 B3
Wildmoor 159 F1
Williamscot 10 C8
Winderton 12 B6
Winterbrook 221 C5
Witney 118 C7
Wolvercote 122 E8
Woodcote 250 E7
Woodeaton 110 B4
Woodfields 65 D4
Woodgreen 104 D2
Woodstock 91 B5
Woolstone 211 B4
Wootton
  Abingdon 159 A6
  Woodstock 75 F5
Wootton Village 159 B8
Worminghall 127 E6
Wormleighton 1 B8
Worsham 102 B2
Worton 107 E3
Wroxton 15 A8
Wytham 122 B6

Y
Yarnton 108 A6
Yelford 136 B6

264 Abb – Ban

A

Abberbury Ave OX4..... 142 A4
Abberbury Rd OX4......141 F4
Abbey Brook OX11.....200 E3
Abbey Cl OX14........179 F7
Abbey Ctr OX14....... 180 A7
Abbey Pl
  Eynsham OX29...........120 E7
  Oxford OX1 .... 261 A1
Abbey Rd
  Banbury OX16 ....16 A7
  Oxford OX2 .... 123 A1
Watchfield SN6 ....191 F2
Witney OX28 .... 117 F7
Abbey St OX29.........120 E7
Abbey Wlk OX1........ 123 A1
Abbey Woods Cl OX10 ..182 C5
Abbot Ridge HP18 .... 129 D5
Abbots Cl RG8.........250 F8
Abbotsleigh Gdns RG4.. 259 D4
Abbots Mead OX10 .....239 A8
Abbotsmead Pl RG4....259 A2
Abbots Wlk GL7 .... 150 D4
Abbots Wood OX3 ......142 E8
Abbott Cl OX11........218 E7
Abbott Rd
  Abingdon OX14 ....179 F8
  Didcot OX11...........218 E7
Abbot Wlk HP18 ...... 129 D5
Abelwood Rd OX29 .....90 A1
Aberaman RG4..........258 F6
Abingdon Bsns Pk OX14.179 C7
Abingdon Cl OX14.....129 F1
Abingdon Dr RG4 ......259 C6
Abingdon Hosp OX14...179 C7
Abingdon La OX29 .....117 A3
Abingdon Mus* OX14...179 F7
Abingdon Rd
  Carterton OX18 ....115 E3
  Clifton Hampden OX14 .181 D4
  Culham OX14 ....180 C3
  Cumnor OX2 ....139 E4
  Didcot OX11...........201 B1
  Dorchester OX10.......182 C3
  Drayton OX14 ....179 B2
  Kennington OX1.......141 D4
  Oxford OX1 .... 141 D6
  Rowstock OX11........217 B7
  Standlake OX29 .... 137 C3
  Steventon OX13.......199 A5
  Sutton Courtenay OX14..180 B2
  Tubney OX13 ....157 E2
Abingdon Sch OX14....179 E7
Abingdon Science Pk
  OX14................180 B7
Abingdon Terr OX11....218 C8
Abingdon & Witney Coll
  OX14................159 E1
Abingdon & Witney Coll
  Witney Campus OX28..118 A8
Ablett Cl OX4..........142 A8
Abrahams Rd RG9 .....244 C3
Acacia Ave OX4........142 E1
Acacia Cl OX18 ....115 E1
Acacia Gdns OX13 .....156 E1
Acacia RG9 ....244 D2
Acacia Wlk
  Banbury OX16 ....9 B1
  Bicester OX26 ....65 E5
Acer Cl OX18 ....114 D7
Ackerman Rd OX7 ......42 F3
Acland Cl OX3.........124 C1
Acorn Cl OX26.........65 C5
Acorn Way OX16.........9 F1
Acre Ct OX3..........142 F7
Acre Ditch OX15........19 A8
Acre End St OX29......120 E7
Acremead Rd OX33....143 F8
Adam Ct RG9..........244 E2
Adderbury Ct OX17 .....23 A4
Adderbury Pk OX17.....22 F3
Addiscombe Chase
  RG31................257 B3
Addison Cres OX4 .....141 F6
Addison Dr OX4 ....142 C3
Addison Rd
  Banbury OX16 ....16 C3
  Reading RG1 ....259 A1
Adeane Rd OX44.......184 C7
Adelaide St OX2 ....261 A4
Adkin Way OX12 ....214 D6
Adwell Sq RG9 ....244 D2
Agenvins Ho OX1......261 A2
Agnes Ct OX4.........142 C6
Akeman Ave OX25 .....81 A4
Akeman Cl OX5........78 A5
Akeman St OX29........90 A6
Alan Bullock Cl OX4 ...123 E1
Albert Rd
  Henley-on-T RG9 .....244 E1
  Reading RG4 ....258 F4
Albert St
  Banbury OX16 ....16 D5
  Oxford OX2 ....261 A3

Albion Pl
  Bampton OX18.........134 E3
  Chipping Norton OX7......42 F3
  Oxford OX1 ....261 B1
Albion St OX7 ....42 E3
Albury Cl RG30 ....258 C1
Albury View OX9 ......146 A6
Alchester Rd OX26......80 A7
Alchester Terr 3 OX26...65 F1
Aldbarton Dr OX3.....124 E4
Aldbourne Cl OX26 .....65 D2
Aldeburgh Cl RG4.....259 C8
Alden Cres OX3.......124 F4
Aldenham Cl RG4.....259 C6
Alder Dr OX25.........81 C4
Aldergate Rd OX26.....65 C2
Alderley Cl
  Carterton OX18 ....115 D1
  Sonning RG5 ....260 F1
Aldrich Rd OX2........123 B8
Aldridge Cl OX10......204 A4
Aldsworth Ct OX28....117 E8
Aldworth Ave OX12....214 F6
Alec Issigonis Way OX4..142 D5
Alesworth Gr OX3.....124 B5
Alexander Cl
  Abingdon OX14 ....160 A3
  Longworth OX13 ....218 C2
Alexandra Rd OX2.....122 F1
Alexandra Sq OX7 ......42 D1
Alfreds Pl OX12........197 C7
Alfred St 3 OX12.......214 D4
Alfredston Pl OX12....214 E4
Alfred St OX1..........261 B2
Alfred Terraces OX7....42 E2
Alfriston Pl OX16........9 A1
Alice Smith Sq OX4....142 C2
Alison Clay Ho OX3....124 C2
Alister Taylor Ave OX10..204 C2
Allder Cl OX14........159 F2
Allectus Ave OX25......81 D4
Allens La OX25........48 E1
Allens Orch OX17.......5 F6
Alley The OX7.........73 B4
All Hallows Rd RG4....259 D3
Allin Cl OX4..........142 E3
Allin's La OX12........216 D7
Allison Gdns RG8.....257 C5
Allison Ho RG9 ....254 E8
Allnatt Ave OX10......221 C8
Allnut Cl OX44........179 F2
All Saints CE Prim Sch
  Didcot OX11...........201 A2
  Sutton Courtenay OX14..199 F6
All Saints Cl OX13.....178 C6
All Saints Ct OX11 ....200 E2
All Saints La OX14.....180 B1
All Saints Rd OX3.....124 C2
All Soul's Coll OX1....261 C2
Alma Gn RG9 ....242 A4
Alma Pl OX4..........141 F8
Almhouses OX28.......104 C1
Almond Ave OX5.......108 E6
Almond Dr RG4........259 C6
Almond Rd OX26.......65 E3
Almshouses
  Bourton SN6 ....209 A2
  Goring Heath RG8 .....251 B3
  Lyford OX12..........176 C1
Almshouses The OX5....92 F2
Almshouses HP18.......127 E5
Alpha Ave OX44.......143 C1
Alphin Brook OX11....200 E3
Alston Wlk RG4........259 D2
Altus St OX25..........63 A8
Alvescot Rd OX18 .....115 D2
Alvis Gate OX16........15 F8
Ambassador Ave OX4...142 E4
Ambassador St 1 OX26...65 F1
Amberley Ct OX16.......9 A1
Ambleside Dr OX3 .....124 B4
Ambrose Rise OX33 ...144 C8
Ambury Rd RG8........247 E4
Amersham Rd RG4.....259 D2
Amey Cres OX13 ......159 B6
Ammanford RG4.......258 F5
Amory Cl OX4.........142 D3
Amos Ct OX16..........16 D5
Ampney Orch OX18....134 F3
Amwell Pl OX10........220 F1
Amyce Cl OX14........160 B2
Ancastle Gn RG9......244 D2
Ancholme Cl OX11.....200 F2
Anchor La OX11........220 A4
Ancil Ave OX26.........66 D2
Andersey Way OX14...179 F4
Anderson Cl HP14.....188 E4
Andersons Ct OX5.....108 D8
Andover Cl
  Bicester OX26..........66 A4
  Reading RG1 ....257 D1
Andover La OX18 ......115 D3
Andover Rd OX10......204 D3
Andrew Rd OX10.......203 B1
Andrews Ave NN13......36 E6
Andromeda Cl OX4....142 F1
Anemone Cl OX4......161 E8
Angelica Cl OX4.......142 F1
Angle Field Rd RG4....259 D3
Anglesey Ct HP14.....188 E5
Angus Cl OX16..........16 A8

Anna Pavlova Cl OX14...179 D7
Anne Greenwood Cl
  OX4.................142 A4
Annesley Cl OX5........93 A8
Annesley Rd OX4......142 A4
Ansell Way OX7.........70 B1
Anson Ave OX18.......115 E1
Anson Cl
  Marcham OX13 ....178 D6
  Wheatley OX33 ....144 C8
Anson Rd OX10........204 D3
Anson Way OX26.......66 A3
Anthony Hill Rd OX10..204 C1
Anvil Cl SN7...........194 E7
Anvil La OX12.........214 A1
Anvil Paddock OX12...214 A1
Anxey Way HP17......130 F6
A P Ellis Rd GL54......68 B3
Apley Way OX28......117 E8
Appleby Cl OX16........5 C8
Apple Cl RG31.........257 B4
Appleford Dr OX14....160 B2
Appleford Rd OX14....180 B1
Appleton CE Prim Sch
  OX13................158 A8
Appleton Rd
  Cumnor OX2 ....139 D4
  Longworth OX13 .....156 D3
Appletree Cl
  Sandford-on-T OX4....161 F8
  Sonning Common RG4..252 E6
Appletree Ind Est OX17 ..5 F6
Approach The OX26.....65 D3
Apsley Rd OX2........123 A8
Arbury Banks OX17.....5 F5
Arbury Cl OX16.........16 E2
Arcade The
  7 Wallingford OX10...221 D7
  Goring RG8 ....249 C6
Archery Rd OX17.......11 A1
Archway Rd 1 RG4....259 A2
Arden Cl OX15.........15 D8
Ardington La OX12,OX13..197 E2
Ardler Rd RG4.........259 C2
Ardley Rd
  Ardley OX27...........50 C4
  Bucknell OX27........50 E2
  Middleton Stoney OX25..64 A4
  Somerton OX25........48 F6
Argentan Cl OX14.....179 D4
Argosy Cl OX44.......184 E6
Argosy Rd
  Benson OX10.........204 D3
  Carterton OX18 ......115 F2
Argyle St OX4.........141 F6
Aristotle La OX2.......123 A4
Arkel Cl OX18..........101 A6
Arkell Ave OX18.......115 D2
Arkell Ct OX18........115 D2
Arkwright Rd OX26.....66 A3
Arlington Cl OX18....115 E2
Arlington Dr OX3.....123 F4
Armour Hill RG31.....257 D1
Armour Rd RG31......257 D1
Armour Wlk RG31.....257 D1
Armstrong Rd OX4....142 B1
Arncott Rd OX25.......97 D7
Arncott Wood Rd OX25..96 E6
Arndale Beck OX14....201 A2
Arnold Rd OX4........141 F6
Arnold's Way OX2.....140 D7
Arnold's Yd HP18.....129 D6
Arran Gr OX16.........16 C6
Arrow Cl OX17.........11 A1
Arthray Rd OX2.......140 D8
Arthur Evans Cl OX13..159 A6
Arthur Garrard Cl OX2..261 A4
Arthur St OX2.........123 A1
Arundel Cl
  Carterton OX18 ......115 C2
  Kings Sutton OX17.....23 F5
Arundel Pl OX16........15 F5
Arun Mews OX14.......201 A1
Ascott Hill CV36........18 A1
Ascott Rd OX7.........85 D8
Ascott-under-Wychwood Sta
  OX7.................71 C2
Ashburn Pl OX11......200 F3
Ashburton La OX15.....30 B6
Ashbury Hill SN6......228 B6
Ashbury with Compton
  Beauchamp CE Prim Sch
  SN6.................228 A7
Ashby Ct OX16.........16 D5
Ashby Rd OX26........65 D2
Ash Cl
  Faringdon SN7.......172 E3
  Kidlington OX5.......108 E7
  Watlington OX49 .....186 A2
Ashcombe Cl OX28....118 A8
Ash Copse RG4.......259 F7
Ashcroft Cl
  Chadlington OX7......57 B1
  Oxford OX2 ....122 B1
  Wallingford OX10 ....221 B8
Ash Ct RG4...........259 B3
Ashdene Rd OX26.....65 D2
Ashdown House* RG17..245 E4
Ashdown Park* RG17...245 E8

Ashdown Way RG9......242 A1
Ashenden Cl OX14.....159 F1
Ashfield Rd OX18......115 E1
Ashfields Cl OX12.....197 C7
Ashfields La OX12.....197 C7
Ashford Ave RG4......252 E5
Ashgate OX14.........179 E4
Ash Gr
  Chesterton OX26......79 F7
  Oxford OX3 ....124 D4
Ashhurst Ct OX33.....144 F7
Ash La OX25...........81 D4
Ashlee Wlk RG8.......250 F8
Ashley Hill Pl RG10...255 F7
Ashlong Rd OX3.......124 A5
Ashmead Rd OX16......8 F1
Ashmolean Mus* OX1..261 B3
Ashmole Pl OX4.......142 F3
Ashmole Rd OX14.....179 E4
Ashridge OX39........168 B6
Ashton Rd OX18.......135 D3
Ashdown Way OX12...214 D8
Ashurst Way OX4......142 A3
Ashville Way OX4.....142 F3
Aspen Cl OX26.........65 E5
Aspen Sq OX4.........142 E1
Asquith Rd OX4.......142 A3
Astley Ave OX5........108 F6
Astley Rd OX9.........130 B1
Aston Cl
  Aylesbury OX16.......179 F7
  Banbury OX16 ....16 E2
  Pangbourne RG8 .....256 D5
  Wallingford OX10 ....221 C7
Aston & Cote CE Prim Sch
  OX18................135 E3
Aston Gdns OX49.....167 D3
Aston Hill OX49.......187 E7
Aston Ho 3 OX16......16 E6
Aston Park OX49......167 D2
Aston Rd
  Bampton OX18........134 F3
  Ducklington,Church End
  OX29................118 B3
  Ducklington OX29 ....118 A2
  Standlake OX29 ......137 A3
Aston Rowant CE Sch
  OX49................167 E3
Aston Rowant Nature
  Reserve* HP14......187 E5
Aston St
  Oxford OX2 ....123 A5

B

Bakehouse La OX17......8 D8
Baker Ave OX10.......204 D2
Baker Cl
  Benson OX10.........204 D2
  Bicester OX27.........65 F7
  Oxford OX3 ....124 F2
Baker Rd OX14.........179 C6
Baker's Ct OX29.......90 B1
Bakers La
  Brightwell-cum-S OX10..202 F2
  East Hagbourne OX11...218 F6
  Oxford OX4 ....141 F4
  South Newington OX15..31 F7
  Swalcliffe OX15.......19 F8
Tadmarton OX15 ....20 C8
Baker's Piece Ho OX39..167 F4
Baker's Piece OX28....167 F4
Bakers Piece OX28....104 B2
Bakers Sq SN7........193 A4
Baker St OX11........237 F8
Bakery La
  Clanfield OX18.......152 F8
  Letcombe Regis OX12..214 A1
Baldon La OX44.......161 F3
Baldons Cl RG8.......250 F8
Balfour Cotts OX14....182 A5
Balfour Rd OX4........142 E3
Balfour's Field RG8....241 D3
Balham's La RG9......225 F8
Ballard Chase OX14....160 A3
Ballard Cl OX7.........85 D8
Ballards Cl OX7........85 D8
Balliol Cl OX5..........77 C6
Balliol Coll OX1.......261 B3
Balliol Ct OX2.........123 A4
Balliol Dr OX11........219 B8
Balliol Rd
  Bicester OX26.........65 F3
  Reading RG4 ....258 D3
Bal La OX5............77 B5
Balmoral Ave
  Banbury OX16 ....15 F4
  Banbury OX16 ....16 A4
Balmoral Rd OX11.....219 A8
Balmoral Way OX11.....9 D4
Balmore Dr RG4.......259 B3
Balmore Ho RG4......259 B3
Balmore Pk RG4......259 B3
Baltic Wharf OX1......261 C1
Bampton CE Prim Sch
  OX18................134 F4
Bampton Rd
  Aston OX18...........135 D2
  Clanfield OX18.......133 F1
  Curbridge OX18,OX29..116 F2
Banbury Bsns Pk OX17..23 D3
Banbury Cross Ret Pk
  OX16................16 A6
Banbury Cl 1 OX14...179 F7
Banbury Gdns RG4....259 C3

Aylesbury & Thame Airport
  HP17................130 E7
Aynho Ct OX17.........35 D7
Aynho Pk OX17........35 C7
Aynho Fishing Venue*
  OX17.................34 E6
Aynho Rd OX17.........23 C3
Ayres Yd OX10........221 C8
Ayrshire Cl OX16........9 A1
Aysgarth Rd OX5......108 B6
Azalea Ave OX5.......108 E6
Azalea Wlk OX16.......9 B1
Azor's Ct OX4.........142 A4

Banbury Hill OX7 . . . . 73 C5
Banbury La
 Banbury OX17 . . . . 17 D8
 Kings Sutton OX17 . . . . 23 E6
 Middleton Cheney OX17 . . 11 C3
Banbury Mus & Tooleys
 Boatyard* OX16 . . . . 16 D6
Banbury Rd
 Adderbury OX17 . . . . 23 A6
 Aynho OX47 . . . . 35 B8
 Bicester OX26 . . . . 65 C4
 Bloxham OX15 . . . . 21 E6
 Chacombe OX17 . . . . 10 D4
 Chipping Norton OX7 . . . . 42 F4
 Chipping Warden OX17 . . . 5 F6
 Cutteslowe OX2 . . . . 109 A1
 Deddington OX15 . . . . 33 F5
 Kidlington OX5 . . . . 92 D1
 North Newington OX15 . . . 15 C3
 Over Norton OX7 . . . . 43 D6
 Oxford OX2 . . . . 123 B6
 Shipton-on-C OX5 . . . . 92 B5
 Shutford OX15 . . . . 14 B5
 Swerford OX7 . . . . 30 D1
 Tackley OX5 . . . . 76 E4
 Warmington OX17 . . . . 3 A2
 Woodstock OX20 . . . . 91 D7
Banbury Road Crossing
 OX7 . . . . 42 F3
Banbury Road Rdbt OX2 109 A1
Banbury Sch OX16 . . . . 16 B3
Banbury Sta OX16 . . . . 16 E5
Bandet Way OX9 . . . . 148 B6
Banesberie Cl OX16 . . . . 9 A1
Banjo Rd OX4 . . . . 142 C5
Bank Cotts OX33 . . . . 125 E4
Banks Furlong OX26 . . . . . . 79 F8
Bankside
 Banbury OX16 . . . . 16 F3
 Kidlington OX5 . . . . 92 C2
 Long Hanborough OX29 . . 90 F1
 Oxford OX3 . . . . 124 E3
 West Hendred OX12 . . . . . 216 B6
Bannister Cl OX4 . . . . 141 E7
Bannister Rd OX9 . . . . 148 C7
Barbara's Mdw RG31 . . . . . 257 B2
Barberry Pl OX26 . . . . 65 E4
Barbrook Cl RG31 . . . . 257 D3
Barbury Dr OX12 . . . . 214 D8
Barclose Ave RG4 . . . . 259 C3
Barcombe Cl OX16 . . . . 8 F1
Barcote La SN7 . . . . 174 A6
Bardolph's Cl RG4 . . . . 258 D8
Bardwell Cl OX2 . . . . 148 C7
Bardwell Rd OX2 . . . . 123 C4
Bardwell Sch OX26 . . . . 66 A4
Bardwell Terr OX26 . . . . 65 F2
Barefoot Cl RG31 . . . . 257 B1
Barfleur Cl OX14 . . . . 160 B3
Barford Rd
 Bloxham OX15 . . . . 21 E2
 South Newington OX15 . . . 32 A6
Bargus Cl OX13 . . . . 199 A4
Barksdale Ave NN13 . . . . . . 36 E6
Barkus Way HP14 . . . . 188 F5
Barley Cl
 Bloxham OX15 . . . . 21 E5
 Lewknor OX49 . . . . 187 A8
 Sibford Gower OX15 . . . . . . 19 A8
 Wallingford OX10 . . . . 221 C6
Barleycott La OX1 . . . . 141 C4
Barley Croft OX15 . . . . 21 E5
Barleyfields OX11 . . . . 218 C8
Barleyfield Way OX28 . . . . 104 E1
Barley Hill Prim Sch
 OX9 . . . . 130 A1
Barlow Cl
 Milcombe OX15 . . . . 21 A2
 Wheatley OX33 . . . . 143 F8
Barnacre OX4 . . . . 186 B1
Barnard Cl RG4 . . . . 259 C6
Barnard Way OX12 . . . . 214 F6
Barnfield OX12 . . . . 175 F1
Barnfield Cl OX27 . . . . 65 F6
Barn La RG9 . . . . 244 C4
Barns Cl OX33 . . . . 126 B1
Barns Hay OX3 . . . . 123 F6
Barns Ho OX4 . . . . 142 A4
Barns La OX18 . . . . 100 E4
Barn's Rd OX4 . . . . 142 D4
Baroma Way RG9 . . . . 244 E2
Baronshurst Dr OX44 . . . . . 184 D6
Baronsmead RG9 . . . . 244 D2
Baron Way RG9 . . . . 242 A2
Barracks La
 Oxford OX4 . . . . 142 B7
 Oxford OX4 . . . . 142 D6
Barracks The OX44 . . . . 164 D8
Barrett Cl RG1 . . . . 258 F1
Barrett's Cl OX29 . . . . 89 C7
Barrett St OX2 . . . . 123 A1
Barrett's Way OX14 . . . . . . 199 F6

Barrington Ave SN6 . . . . . . 191 F1
Barrington Cl
 Berinsfield OX10 . . . . 182 C6
 Oxford OX3 . . . . 124 C2
 Witney OX28 . . . . 117 E7
Barrington Ct NN13 . . . . . . 24 A5
Barrington Rd SN6 . . . . 209 D8
Barrow Hill OX14 . . . . 160 C2
Barrow La OX11 . . . . 217 E8
Barrow Pk (Cvn Site)
 OX11 . . . . 217 E8
Barrow Rd
 Abingdon OX13 . . . . 179 B8
 Harwell OX11 . . . . 217 E8
Barry Ave OX26 . . . . 65 D3
Bartholomew Ave OX5 . . . 108 B5
Bartholomew Cl
 Ducklington OX29 . . . . 118 B4
 Eynsham OX29 . . . . 120 D8
Bartholomew Rd OX4 . . . . 142 C4
Bartholomew Sch OX29 . . 120 D8
Bartholomew Tipping Way
 HP14 . . . . 188 F5
Bartlemas Cl OX4 . . . . 142 A4
Bartlemas Rd OX4 . . . . 142 A8
Bartlett Cl
 Wallingford OX10 . . . . 221 C5
 Witney OX28 . . . . 118 A8
Barton Cl OX17 . . . . 23 F6
Barton La
 Abingdon OX14 . . . . 180 B7
 Oxford OX3 . . . . 124 D4
Barton Rd
 Long Compton CV36 . . . . . 27 C7
 Oxford OX3 . . . . 124 E4
Barton Village Rd OX3 . . . 124 E5
Bartsia Rd OX26 . . . . 65 E4
Barwell OX12 . . . . 214 D5
Basildon Park* RG8 . . . . . . 249 D1
Basil Hill Rd OX11 . . . . 200 D3
Baskerville La RG9 . . . . 255 A3
Baskerville Rd RG4 . . . . . . 252 E5
Basmore La RG9 . . . . 255 B4
Bassett Ave OX26 . . . . 65 F3
Bassett Rd
 Letcombe Bassett OX12 . . 231 F7
 Oxford OX3 . . . . 124 F4
Basset Way OX5 . . . . 108 F8
Batchelors Row OX15 . . . . . 33 B4
Bateman St OX3 . . . . 124 D2
Bates Collection of Musical
 Instruments* OX1 . . . . . . 261 B1
Bates La OX27 . . . . 35 D3
Bath Ct OX14 . . . . 179 F7
Bath Pl OX1 . . . . 261 C2
Bath Rd
 Banbury OX16 . . . . 16 C6
 Sonning RG4 . . . . 260 E2
Bath St
 Abingdon OX14 . . . . 179 F8
 Abingdon OX14 . . . . 179 F7
 Oxford OX4 . . . . 123 F1
Batt CE Prim Sch The
 OX28 . . . . 118 A8
Batten Pl OX4 . . . . 142 A1
Batting Cl HP14 . . . . 189 F8
Battle Cl OX26 . . . . 66 A3
Battle Rd
 Benson OX10 . . . . 204 D2
 Goring RG8 . . . . 249 F7
Baulking La SN7 . . . . 194 C2
Baxters Barns GL7 . . . . 131 A4
Bayard's Hill Prim Sch
 OX3 . . . . 124 F4
Baydon Rd SN8 . . . . 245 D1
Baydon St Nicholas CE Prim
 Sch SN8 . . . . 245 E1
Bayliss Rd RG10 . . . . 255 D1
Bayliss Yd OX7 . . . . 73 B3
Bayswater Farm OX3 . . . . . 124 F4
Bayswater Farm Rd OX3 . . 124 A4
Bayswater Rd OX3 . . . . 124 F4
Bay Tree Cl OX4 . . . . 142 A4
Bayworth La OX1 . . . . 159 F8
Bayworth Pk OX1 . . . . 159 F7
Beachborough Sch NN13 . . 25 A4
Beaconsfield Rd OX16 . . . . 16 D7
Beacon View OX49 . . . . 187 B8
Beadnell Cl OX16 . . . . 16 D2
Beagle Cl OX14 . . . . 160 C2
Beagles Cl OX5 . . . . 109 A7
Beale Park Wildlife Pk*
 RG8 . . . . 249 F1
Beam Paddock OX18 . . . . . 135 A3
Beanacre Rd OX15 . . . . 30 B6
Bear Furlong OX17 . . . . 18 E4
Beanhill Cl OX29 . . . . 118 A5
Beanhill Rd OX29 . . . . 118 A5
Beansheaf Terr OX10 . . . . . 221 D7
Bear Close Flats OX20 . . . . 91 B6
Bear Cl OX20 . . . . 91 B6
Bear Ct OX18 . . . . 100 E5
Beargarden Rd OX16 . . . . . . 16 D2
Bear La
 North Moreton OX11 . . . . . 220 A7
 Oxford OX1 . . . . 261 C2
 Stadhampton OX44 . . . . . . 163 C1
 Wallingford OX10 . . . . 221 D7
Bears Hedge OX4 . . . . 142 A4
Beatrice Dr OX16 . . . . 16 A5
Beauchamp La OX4 . . . . . . 142 B4
Beauchamp Pl OX4 . . . . . . 142 B4
Beaufort Cl
 Bicester OX26 . . . . 66 A3
 Didcot OX11 . . . . 219 B8
Beaulieu Cl OX16 . . . . 16 F7
Beaulieu Ct OX13 . . . . 159 F5

Beaulieu Mews OX14 . . . . . 201 A3
Beaumaris Cl OX16 . . . . 15 F7
Beaumont Bldgs OX1 . . . . . 261 A3
Beaumont Bsns Ctr OX16 . . 9 C1
Beaumont Cl OX11 . . . . 214 A2
Beaumont Dr OX1 . . . . 141 E1
Beaumont Ind Est
 Banbury,Hardwick OX16 . . . 9 C1
 Banbury,Ruscote OX16 . . . 16 B8
Beaumont La OX1 . . . . 261 B3
Beaumont Pl OX1 . . . . 261 B3
Beaumont Rd
 Banbury OX16 . . . . 9 C1
 Oxford OX3 . . . . 124 F3
Beaumont St OX1 . . . . 261 B3
Bec Cl OX3 . . . . 214 B5
Beckdale Cl OX26 . . . . 65 B3
Becket St OX1 . . . . 261 A2
Becket Ave SN6 . . . . 209 D7
Beckett Dr SN6 . . . . 209 D7
Beckett Ho OX12 . . . . 214 E4
Becketts Cl OX29 . . . . 90 B1
Beckley CE Prim Sch
 OX3 . . . . 111 A3
Beckley Cl RG8 . . . . 250 F8
Beckley Ct OX3 . . . . 111 B2
Becquerel Ave OX11 . . . . . . 217 A2
Bec Tithe RG8 . . . . 250 F8
Bedford Cl OX16 . . . . 15 F8
Bedford St OX4 . . . . 141 F6
Bedwells Heath OX1 . . . . . 140 D1
Beech Cl
 Faringdon SN7 . . . . 172 E3
 Stokenchurch HP14 . . . . . 188 F3
 Watlington OX49 . . . . 186 A2
 Wootton OX13 . . . . 159 A7
Beech Cres OX5 . . . . 108 F6
Beechcroft OX10 . . . . 182 D1
Beech Croft Rd OX2 . . . . . . 123 B6
Beech Ct RG4 . . . . 259 B3
Beeches The
 Deddington OX15 . . . . 33 F4
 Goring RG8 . . . . 249 B5
 Oxford OX3 . . . . 124 E4
 Reading RG31 . . . . 257 D3
 Shenington OX15 . . . . 6 F2
Beechey Ave OX3 . . . . 123 F4
Beechfield Cres OX16 . . . . . 16 D3
Beechgate OX28 . . . . 118 A6
Beech Gr OX18 . . . . 100 F6
Beech Rd RG9 . . . . 244 D2
Beeching Cl OX11 . . . . 218 C2
Beeching Way OX33 . . . . . . 143 F8
Beech La
 Carterton OX18 . . . . 115 F5
 Woodcote RG8 . . . . 250 D8
 Woodcote RG8 . . . . 250 E8
Beech Lodge OX3 . . . . 124 C3
Beech Pl OX3 . . . . 124 B3
Beech Rd
 Chinnor OX39 . . . . 168 C6
 Eynsham OX29 . . . . 120 E8
 Oxford OX3 . . . . 124 C3
 Oxford,Headington OX3 . . 124 C3
 Purley on T RG8 . . . . 257 B5
 Shillingford OX10 . . . . 203 B4
 Thame OX9 . . . . 147 D8
 Tokers Green RG4 . . . . 258 D7
 Wheatley OX33 . . . . 144 B7
Beech Rise OX4 . . . . 142 E2
Beechwood Cl RG8 . . . . . . 250 D6
Beechwood Ho OX3 . . . . . . 124 E4
Beechwood OX4 . . . . 142 A5
Beef La OX1 . . . . 261 B2
Beehive Cl OX10 . . . . 220 F1
Beesley Rd OX16 . . . . 16 A6
Beeson Ct RG8 . . . . 250 F8
Beeswax Cres OX5 . . . . 92 A1
Begbroke La
 Begbroke OX5 . . . . 92 A1
 Kidlington OX5 . . . . 92 C1
Begbroke Science Pk
 OX5 . . . . 92 B2
Beggarsbush Hill OX10 . . 204 D1
Beggar's La OX13 . . . . 156 C5
Behoes La RG8 . . . . 240 D1
Belbroughton Rd OX2 . . . 123 C5
Belcher Ct OX10 . . . . 182 D2
Belfast Ct OX18 . . . . 133 F8
Belfast Rd OX10 . . . . 182 D2
Belfast Sq OX10 . . . . 133 F8
Belgrave Cres OX16 . . . . . . 16 B6
Belgrove Cl OX5 . . . . 108 D8
Bellamy Cl OX13 . . . . 156 E1
Bell Cl
 Cassington OX29 . . . . 107 D2
 Grove OX12 . . . . 196 E1
 Thame OX9 . . . . 129 E1
Bell Ct RG8 . . . . 259 B6
Belleisle RG8 . . . . 257 B5
Bellinger Way OX5 . . . . 108 F8
Belle Terr OX18 . . . . 115 D1
Belle Vue Rd RG9 . . . . 254 D8
Bell Hill OX15 . . . . 30 B7
Bellingham La SN6 . . . . . . 190 A1
Bellingham Wlk RG4 . . . . . 259 A5
Bell La
 Aldworth RG8 . . . . 247 F4
 Bampton OX18 . . . . 134 E3
 Bicester OX26 . . . . 65 E2
 Brightwell-cum-S OX10 . . 202 E2
 Cassington OX29 . . . . 107 D2
 Henley-on-T RG9 . . . . 244 E1
 Lechlade-on-T GL7 . . . . 150 C3
 Thame OX9 . . . . 129 E1
 Wheatley OX33 . . . . 144 B8
Bell Lodge 8 OX26 . . . . . . 65 E2

Ben's La OX15 . . . . 30 B7
Bell St
 Henley-on-T RG9 . . . . 244 E2
 Hornton OX15 . . . . 7 C6
Bell Street Mews RG9 . . . . 244 E2
Belmont Mews OX9 . . . . . . 147 F8
Belmont OX12 . . . . 214 D5
Belsyre Ct OX2 . . . . 261 A4
Belvedere Rd OX4 . . . . 142 A7
Benares Gr RG9 . . . . 242 A4
Benbow Cl OX14 . . . . 160 B2
Benhams La RG9 . . . . 226 D2
Benmead Rd OX5 . . . . 92 E1
Bennett Cl OX17 . . . . 10 E4
Bennett Cres OX4 . . . . 142 D5
Bennett End Rd HP14 . . . . 189 D7
Bennett Rd SN7 . . . . 172 F3
Benouville Cl OX44 . . . . . . 142 E6
Bensgrove Cl RG8 . . . . 250 F8
Benson CE Prim Jun Sch
 OX10 . . . . 203 E4
Benson CE Prim Sch
 OX10 . . . . 203 F5
Benson La
 Benson OX10 . . . . 204 A2
 Crowmarsh Gifford OX10 . . 221 F8
Benson Rd
 Abingdon OX14 . . . . 159 E2
 Oxford OX3 . . . . 142 D8
Bentley Cl OX16 . . . . 15 F8
Benton Dr OX39 . . . . 168 D7
Benwells OX39 . . . . 168 C6
Bere Court Rd RG8 . . . . 256 B4
Berens Rd SN6 . . . . 209 D8
Bergamont Pl 8 OX4 . . . . 142 E1
Bergen Ave OX14 . . . . 179 D4
Berinscourt Ho OX10 . . . . . 182 B5
Berinsfield Com Prim Sch
 OX10 . . . . 182 C5
Berinsfield Rdbt OX10 . . . 182 B4
Berins Hill OX10 . . . . 241 A6
Berkeley Cl OX16 . . . . 15 E7
Berkeley Rd
 Boars Hill OX1 . . . . 140 E1
 Oxford OX4 . . . . 130 A1
Berkshire Rd RG9 . . . . 254 D8
Bernard Cl OX5 . . . . 108 C5
Berner's Way OX7 . . . . 173 A3
Bernewode Cl HP18 . . . . . . 129 C7
Bernwood Butterfly Trail*
 . . . . 112 C3
Bernwood Forest* OX33 . 112 F2
Bernwood Rd
 Bicester OX26 . . . . 65 F2
 Oxford OX3 . . . . 124 E4
Berrick Rd OX44 . . . . 184 D5
Berry Cl OX4 . . . . 142 F3
Berry Croft OX14 . . . . 159 E1
Berrycroft SN6 . . . . 228 A7
Berryfield Way OX18 . . . . . 115 E5
Berryfield Rd OX12 . . . . 22 F2
Berry La
 Blewbury OX11 . . . . 219 A1
 East Hanney OX12 . . . . 197 B6
Berrylands Rd RG4 . . . . 259 B3
Berrymere Rd OX13 . . . . . . 159 A7
Berrymoor Rd OX16 . . . . 16 B5
Bertie Pl OX1 . . . . 141 D5
Bertie Rd OX2 . . . . 139 F5
Besbury La OX7 . . . . 42 E6
Bessels Lea Rd OX11 . . . . . 219 A1
Bessels Way OX11 . . . . 219 A1
Bessleigh Rd OX13 . . . . 158 F8
Bessels Leigh Sch OX13 . . 158 C2
Bessel's Way OX11 . . . . 237 B8
Bessemer Cl OX26 . . . . 66 A2
Betony Way OX26 . . . . 65 E4
Betterton Cotts OX12 . . . . 215 F2
Bettina Cres OX16 . . . . 9 A1
Betty La OX1 . . . . 141 C3
Between Towns Rd OX4 . . 142 C5
Beverley Cl
 Abingdon OX14 . . . . 159 E1
 Chalgrove OX44 . . . . 184 E6
Beverley Cres OX18 . . . . . . 115 E4
Beverley Gdns
 Bicester OX26 . . . . 66 A4
 Wargrave RG10 . . . . 255 E1
Beverley Rd RG31 . . . . 257 C1
Beverly Cl OX10 . . . . 204 D3
Bevington Rd OX2 . . . . 261 B4
Bhandari Cl OX4 . . . . 142 B6
Bibury Cl OX28 . . . . 117 D8
Bicester Com Coll OX26 . . 65 D2
Bicester Ho OX26 . . . . 65 E1
Bicester North Sta OX26 . . 65 F3
Bicester Rd
 Bucknell OX27 . . . . 64 F7
 Enstone OX7 . . . . 58 F6
 Kidlington OX5 . . . . 108 F7
 Launton OX26 . . . . 66 C2
 Long Crendon HP18 . . . . . 129 C6
 Ludgershall HP18 . . . . 98 C8
 Marsh Gibbon OX27 . . . . . . 67 E3
 Middleton Stoney OX25 . . . 64 B3
 Stratton Audley OX27 . . . . . 66 C8
Bicester Town Sta OX26 . . . 80 F8
Bicester Village Ret Pk
 OX26 . . . . 80 E8
Bickerton Rd OX3 . . . . 124 C2
Biddel Springs SN6 . . . . . . 190 B6
Biddlesden Rd NN13 . . . . . . 25 A5
Bigmore La HP14 . . . . 189 C1
Bignell View OX26 . . . . 79 F8
Bignolds Cl OX17 . . . . 4 D8
Bigwood Cvn Pk OX14 . . . 160 E6

Billings Cl HP14 . . . . 188 F5
Billwell HP18 . . . . 129 C6
Bingley Gr RG5 . . . . 260 F1
Binning Cl OX14 . . . . 199 B8
Binsey La OX2 . . . . 122 E2
Binswood Ave OX3 . . . . 124 E2
Birch Cl RG4 . . . . 252 F4
Birch Dr OX18 . . . . 114 C7
Birchen Cl RG8 . . . . 250 F8
Birches The RG8 . . . . 249 B6
Birchfield Cl OX14 . . . . 142 E2
Birch Gr OX28 . . . . 104 E2
Birch Rd
 Ambrosden OX25 . . . . 81 C3
 Garsington OX44 . . . . 143 D2
Birchwood
 Banbury OX16 . . . . 16 D3
 Carterton OX18 . . . . 115 E2
Birchwood Cl RG4 . . . . 259 C6
Birchwood Dr OX5 . . . . 92 B6
Bird Cl OX16 . . . . 16 B6
Birdlip Cl OX28 . . . . 103 D1
Birds La OX15 . . . . 13 A6
Bird Wood Cl RG4 . . . . 253 A3
Birmingham Yd OX10 . . . . 203 F4
Biscoe Ct OX33 . . . . 144 C8
Bishop Carpenter CE Prim
 Sch OX15 . . . . 15 B4
Bishop Kirk Pl OX2 . . . . 123 A3
Bishop Loveday CE Prim Sch
 OX15 . . . . 16 B3
Bishops Cl OX15 . . . . 32 E6
Bishops Mdw OX29 . . . . . . 88 D8
Bishops Orch OX11 . . . . . . 218 F7
Bishopstone CE Prim Sch
 SN6 . . . . 227 D4
Bishop's Wood OX44 . . . . . 144 C3
Bishopswood Sch RG4 . . . 252 F5
Bisley Cl OX26 . . . . 66 A3
Bitham Rd OX12 . . . . 233 C7
Bitterell OX29 . . . . 120 F7
Bix Comm RG9 . . . . 243 D8
Bix Hill RG9 . . . . 243 E7
Blackberry La OX44 . . . . 88 A8
Blackbird Assarts La
 OX29 . . . . 88 B1
Blackbird Leys Rd
 Oxford OX4 . . . . 142 D2
 Oxford OX4 . . . . 142 E2
Black Bourton Rd
 Carterton OX18 . . . . 115 E1
 Clanfield OX18 . . . . 133 E1
Blackbull La OX5 . . . . 95 C5
Blackburn Wlk OX26 . . . . . . 66 A5
Black Croft OX11 . . . . 214 D6
Blackditch OX29 . . . . 138 A8
Blackfriars Rd OX1 . . . . 261 B1
Blackhall Rd OX1 . . . . 261 B3
Blackhorse La OX13 . . . . . . 158 F3
Black Lands Rd OX10 . . . . . 203 A4
Blacklands OX12 . . . . 212 E4
Blacklands Way OX14 . . . . 179 C7
Blacklocks Hill OX17 . . . . . . 17 B8
Blackmore Cl OX9 . . . . 141 E2
Blackmore La RG4 . . . . 253 B6
Blacknall Rd OX14 . . . . 179 E5
Blacksmiths Cl OX4 . . . . . . 142 E6
Blacksmiths Hill OX17 . . . . 35 C7
Blacksmiths La OX5 . . . . 95 A4
Blacksmiths Mdw 11
 OX4 . . . . 142 E7
Blackstock Cl OX3 . . . . 142 E7
Blackstone Rd OX10 . . . . . 203 D1
Blackthorn Ave OX18 . . . . . 115 E5
Blackthorn Cl
 Blackthorn OX25 . . . . 82 A3
 Oxford OX3 . . . . 124 E4
 Reading RG31 . . . . 257 B1
Blackthorn Rd OX26 . . . . . . 66 E1
Blackwater Cl RG4 . . . . 259 E4
Blackwater Way OX14 . . . 201 A3
Blackwood Pl OX15 . . . . 22 F8
Blackworth Ind Est SN6 . . 190 F7
Bladon CE Prim Sch OX20 . 91 B2
Bladon Cl OX2 . . . . 122 F8
Bladon Rd OX20 . . . . 91 D4
Blaenant RG4 . . . . 258 F5
Blaenavon RG4 . . . . 258 F5
Blagrave Cl OX11 . . . . 200 E1
Blagrave Farm La RG4 . . . . 258 D5
Blagrave La RG4 . . . . 258 D4
Blake CE Prim Sch The
 OX28 . . . . 118 C2
Blakehope Burn OX11 . . . . 200 F3
Blake Rd OX26 . . . . 118 D7
Blakes Ave OX28 . . . . 118 D7
Blake's Field OX11 . . . . 200 E4
Blake Rd RG10 . . . . 255 E6
Blake Way OX9 . . . . 130 A1
Blandford Alley SN6 . . . . . 190 A5
Blandford Ave OX2 . . . . 123 B7
Blandford Cl OX10 . . . . 91 A6
Blandford Rd OX5 . . . . 92 D2
Blandy Ave OX13 . . . . 156 E1
Blandy Rd RG9 . . . . 254 C7
Blankstone Cl OX29 . . . . . . 120 D7
Blay Cl OX4 . . . . 142 E3
Bleache Pl OX4 . . . . 142 E4
Bledington Prim Sch OX7 . 54 D2
Bledlow Rd HP27 . . . . 169 E8
Bledlow Ridge Rd HP14 . . 169 C8
Bledlow Ridge Sch HP14 . 189 F8
Blencowe Cl OX27 . . . . 65 F6

Blenheim Cl
Didcot OX11 . . . . .200 E1
Upper Rissington GL54 . . . .68 B4
Blenheim NN13 . . . . .36 B7
Blenheim Ct
2 Kidlington OX5 . . . . . .108 F8
Carterton OX18 . . . . .115 D3
Oxford OX2 . . . . .123 A8
Blenheim Dr
Bicester OX26 . . . . .65 C3
Launton OX26 . . . . .66 E2
Oxford OX2 . . . . .123 A7
Witney OX28 . . . . .117 E7
Wolvercote OX2 . . . . .122 F8
Blenheim Gdns OX12 . . .196 C1
Blenheim Hill OX11 . . . .217 F7
Blenheim La
Freeland OX29 . . . . .106 A6
Wheatley OX33 . . . . .144 A8
Blenheim Orch OX12 . . .197 B6
Blenheim Palace * OX20 . .91 A5
Blenheim Pl OX10 . . . .204 D2
Blenheim Rd
Banbury OX16 . . . . .16 E2
Horspath OX33 . . . . .143 C7
Kidlington OX5 . . . . .108 F8
Little Milton OX44 . . . . . .164 A6
Reading RG4 . . . . .259 A3
Shirburn OX49 . . . . .186 D4
Blenheim Rise OX17 . . . .23 F6
Blenheim Terr
Bletchingdon OX5 . . . . .93 A8
Chipping Norton OX7 . . . .42 E2
Blenheim Way
Horspath OX33 . . . . .143 C7
Kingston Bagpuize OX13 . .156 D1
Bleriot Rd GL54 . . . . .68 A4
**Blessed George Napier RC
Sch & Sports Coll** OX16 . .16 C3
**Bletchingdon Parochial CE
Prim Sch** OX5 . . . . .93 A8
Bletchingdon Rd
Bletchingdon OX5 . . . . .78 A3
Hampton Poyle OX5 . . . . . .93 A4
Islip OX5 . . . . .93 E2
Blewbury CE Prim Sch
OX11 . . . . .218 F1
Blewbury Hill OX11 . . . .237 B8
Blewbury Rd OX11 . . . .219 B3
Blewitt Cr OX4 . . . . .142 B2
Bissett Terr **3** SN7 . . .172 F3
Bliss Ho OX7 . . . . .42 E1
Bliss Mill OX7 . . . . .42 C2
Blomfield Pl OX2 . . . . .261 A4
Blossom Gr RG5 . . . . .260 E1
Blossoms Glade OX14 . . .160 E6
Blossom Way RG4 . . . .258 F3
Blounts Court Rd RG4,
RG9 . . . . .253 B6
Blowings The OX9 . . . . . .106 A7
Blowingstone Hill OX12 . .212 A2
Bloxham CE Prim Sch
OX15 . . . . .21 C4
Bloxham Grove Rd OX15 . .22 B6
Bloxham Rd
Banbury OX16 . . . . .16 B3
Barford St M OX15 . . . . . .32 F7
Milcombe OX15 . . . . .21 B2
Bloxham Sch OX15 . . . . . .21 E5
Bloxham Village Mus *
OX15 . . . . .21 A4
Bluebell Cl **1** OX26 . . . .65 E3
Bluebell Ct **4** OX4 . . . .142 F1
Bluebell Ride OX14 . . . .160 E7
Bluebell Way OX18 . . . .115 F4
Blue Boar St OX1 . . . . .261 B2
Blue Row OX7 . . . . .42 E5
Blythe Pl OX26 . . . . .65 B3
Boarstall Duck Decoy *
HP18 . . . . .97 A3
Boathouse Reach RG9 . .244 E1
Bobby Fryer Cl OX4 . . . .142 E4
Bockett's Cnr OX18 . . . .102 A7
Boddington La OX29 . . .105 C8
Boddington Rd OX17 . . . .1 D1
Bodleian Liby * OX1 . . . .261 C2
Bodleian (New Library) *
OX1 . . . . .261 C3
Bodley Pl OX2 . . . . .123 B8
Bodley Rd OX4 . . . . .142 C3
Boham's Houses OX11 . .218 F1
Boham's Rd OX11 . . . . . .236 D6
Bolney La RG9 . . . . .255 A5
Bolney Rd RG9 . . . . .255 B5
Bolney Trevor Dr RG9 . . .255 A4
Bolsover Cl OX29 . . . . . .90 A1
Bolton Rd OX16 . . . . .16 C6
Bolton's La OX29 . . . . . .90 C3
Bonar Rd OX3 . . . . .124 E1
Bonds End La OX15 . . . . . .19 A8
Bones La RG9 . . . . .254 A3
Bonham Pl OX18 . . . . .115 D4
Bonnersfield HP18 . . . .129 C7
Bonn Sq OX1 . . . . .261 B2
Book End OX29 . . . . .103 C1
Booth Rd OX16 . . . . .9 C2
Boot St OX8 . . . . .89 C7
Bo-Peep Cvn Pk OX17 . .23 C2
Boreford Rd OX14 . . . .160 B2
Boroma Way RG4 . . . . . .244 E2
Borough Ave OX10 . . . .221 C7
Borough Ct NN13 . . . . . .24 A5
Borough Rd NN13 . . . . . .24 A5
Borough Wlk OX14 . . . .159 E1
Borrowmead Rd OX3 . . . .124 B5

Bosley Cres OX10 . . . . .221 D7
Bosley's Orch
Didcot OX11 . . . . .200 E1
Grove OX12 . . . . .196 E1
Bosley Way OX10 . . . .221 A8
Bostock Rd OX14 . . . . . .179 E7
Boston Rd
Bicester OX26 . . . . .66 A4
Henley-on-T RG9 . . . . .254 E8
Boswell Rd OX4 . . . . .142 D4
Bothy The RG10 . . . . .255 D2
Botley Intc OX2 . . . . .122 D2
Botley Prim Sch OX2 . . .122 D1
Botley Rd OX2 . . . . .122 F1
Botley Works OX2 . . . . . .122 D1
Bottle Square La HP14 . .189 D6
Bottom La RG8 . . . . .241 A4
Bottom Rd HP14 . . . . . .189 E7
Boucher Cl OX14 . . . . .193 B1
Boughton's Mill **6** OX10 221 D7
Boulevard The OX5 . . . . . .92 B2
Boulter Dr OX14 . . . . .160 A3
Boulter St OX4 . . . . .123 F1
Boults Cl OX3 . . . . .123 F5
Boults La OX3 . . . . .123 F5
Boundary Brook Rd OX4 142 A6
Boundary Cl OX20 . . . . . .91 C6
Boundary La OX4 . . . . . .258 E3
Boundary Rd NN13 . . . . . .24 A6
Bourlon Wood OX14 . . .159 D1
Bourne Cl
Bicester OX26 . . . . .65 D1
Cutteslowe OX2 . . . . .109 B1
Bourne La OX15 . . . . .30 A8
Bourne Rd RG8 . . . . .256 E5
Bourne St OX15 . . . . .30 A8
Bourne The
Eastleach Martin GL7 . . .131 A7
Hook Norton OX15 . . . . . . .30 A7
Bourton Cl
Clanfield OX18 . . . . .133 F1
Witney OX28 . . . . .117 E8
Bourton Cotts OX18 . . .134 E3
Bovewell OX27 . . . . .35 E3
Bovingdon Rd OX18 . . .115 F3
Bovington's Yd OX18 . . .115 D3
Bowbank Cl OX3 . . . . .156 C3
Bowbank OX3 . . . . .156 C3
Bower End OX44 . . . . . .184 C7
Bower Gn SN6 . . . . .191 F2
Bowerman Cl OX5 . . . . . .108 D8
Bowers La HP14 . . . . . .189 D7
Bowell Cl RG31 . . . . .257 C2
Bowgrave Copse OX14 . . .160 C1
Bowley Ho OX20 . . . . .91 B6
Bowling Ct RG9 . . . . .244 D3
Bowling Gn HP14 . . . . . .188 D5
Bowling Green Cl OX18 . .134 F4
Bowling Green Farmhouse
RG8 . . . . .257 B5
Bowling Green La RG8 . . .257 B5
Bowmen's Lea OX17 . . . .35 C7
Bowmont Sq OX26 . . . . . .65 B2
Bowmont Water OX11 . . .200 F2
Bowness Ave
Didcot OX11 . . . . .218 D7
Oxford OX3 . . . . .124 A4
Bow Rd SN7 . . . . .174 E1
Bowyer Rd OX14 . . . . . .179 F8
Boxhedge Rd OX16 . . . . . .16 B6
Boxhedge Rd W OX16 . . . .16 B6
Boxhedge Sq **5** OX16 . . .16 B6
Boxhedge Terr **7** OX16 . .16 B6
Boxhill Rd OX14 . . . . . .179 F8
Boxhill Wlk OX14 . . . . . .179 F8
Box Tree La OX9 . . . . .166 F4
Boxwell Cl OX14 . . . . .160 B2
Bracegirdle Rd OX3 . . . .124 E1
Bracken Cl
Carterton OX18 . . . . .115 D4
Reading RG31 . . . . .257 C1
Brackley Rd
Croughton NN13 . . . . .36 D8
Shalstone MK18 . . . . .25 C5
Westbury NN13 . . . . .25 A5
Brackstone Cl RG4 . . . .259 C2
Bradburys The OX27 . . . .66 D8
Braddons Furlong HP18 . . .129 C6
Bradfield Ct OX14 . . . . . .199 D7
Bradford Ct OX15 . . . . . .21 D4
Brading Way RG8 . . . . . .257 D5
Bradlands OX3 . . . . .123 E7
Bradley Arc OX14 . . . . . .15 F6
Bradley Rd RG9 . . . . .224 A5
Bradley's St RG8 . . . . . .241 B4
Bradmore Rd OX2 . . . . . .123 C4
Bradshaw Cl OX25 . . . . . .62 A8
Bradstock's Way OX14 . .196 F6
Bradwell Rd RG31 . . . .257 C3
Brae Hill HP18 . . . . .98 A1
Braemar Ct OX14 . . . . . .115 D5
Braithwaite Cl OX16 . . .16 C6
Brake Hill OX4 . . . . .143 A1
Bramber Cl OX16 . . . . . .15 E7
Bramber Mews RG4 . . .259 E4
Bramble Bank OX28 . . . .104 D2
Bramble La OX18 . . . . . .115 F5
Bramblings RG4 . . . . .258 E6
Bramblings The OX26 . . .16 A1
Brambling Way OX4 . . . .142 D2
Bramley Cl OX12 . . . . .197 B6
Bramley Cres RG4 . . . . . .252 E5
Bramley Hts OX25 . . . . . .23 F8
Brampton Chase RG9 . . .255 A4
Brampton Cl OX14 . . . . . .159 E1
Brampton Dr OX18 . . . .115 E2
Brampton Rd OX3 . . . . . .124 F4
Bramshaw Rd RG30 . . .258 A1

Bramwell Pl OX4 . . . . .141 F8
Branagh Ct RG30 . . . . .258 B1
Brandon Cl OX5 . . . . .108 D8
Brantwood Ct OX16 . . . . . .16 B4
Brantwood Rise OX16 . . . .16 B4
Brasenose Coll OX1 . . . .261 C2
Brasenose Driftway OX4 142 E6
Brasenose Dr OX5 . . . . . .92 F1
Brasenose La OX1 . . . . . .261 C2
Brasenose Rd OX11 . . . .200 D1
Brasenose Villas OX7 . . . .42 E2
Brashfield Rd OX26 . . . .65 E4
Brassey Cl OX7 . . . . .42 F3
Brassey Ho OX7 . . . . .42 E1
Braybrooke Cl OX7 . . . . . .58 F5
Braybrooke Gdns RG10 . .255 D1
Braybrooke Rd RG10 . . .255 D1
Braze La OX10 . . . . .204 A6
Braziers La OX10 . . . . . .240 E5
Breedons Hill RG8 . . . . . .256 C5
Brenda Cl OX16 . . . . .16 B4
Brendon Cl
Didcot OX11 . . . . .200 C2
Reading RG30 . . . . .257 E1
Brent Ave OX11 . . . . .200 F4
Brentford Cl OX10 . . . . . .220 E1
Brereton Dr OX12 . . . . . .196 D1
Bretch Hill OX16 . . . . .15 F6
Brett Cl OX9 . . . . .148 B8
Brewer Cl OX13 . . . . .199 A4
Brewers Ct **1** OX14 . . .179 F6
Brewer St OX1 . . . . .261 B1
Brewery La OX15 . . . . .29 F7
Brewery Row GL56 . . . . . .26 F1
Brewery St SN6 . . . . .190 A5
Briaily HP14 . . . . .189 C2
Briants Ave RG4 . . . . .259 C2
Briant's Ave RG4 . . . . .259 C2
Briar Cl
Banbury OX16 . . . . .16 D2
Kidlington OX5 . . . . .92 C2
Reading RG4 . . . . .259 A5
Briar End OX5 . . . . .92 C2
Briars Ct RG8 . . . . .256 E5
Briarswood CI HP14 . . . .188 E5
Briar Thicket OX20 . . . . . .91 C6
Briar Way OX4 . . . . .142 F3
Briary Rd GL7 . . . . .150 D6
Brice Rd OX25 . . . . .63 C8
Brick Alley **6** OX14 . . .179 F6
Brick Hill OX5 . . . . .30 B6
Brickle La OX15 . . . . .21 E5
Bricks Row OX15 . . . . .19 F8
Brides La HP14 . . . . .189 C4
Bridal Terr **1** OX12 . . .214 D5
Bridens Way HP17 . . . .130 F6
Bridewell Cl OX29 . . . . . .105 B7
Bridge Cl
Didcot OX11 . . . . .219 A8
Lechlade-on-T GL7 . . . . . .150 E3
Bridge Farm Cl OX12 . . .214 E7
Bridge Hill OX15 . . . . .30 B7
Bridge House Cvn Pk
OX14 . . . . .181 D3
Bridge Rd HP18 . . . . .127 F2
Bridges Cl OX14 . . . . .175 C5
Bridge St
Abingdon OX14 . . . . .179 F6
Bampton OX18 . . . . .134 E3
Banbury OX16 . . . . .16 D6
Islip OX5 . . . . .109 F8
Oxford OX2 . . . . .123 A1
Reading RG4 . . . . .259 A2
Witney OX28 . . . . .104 B1
Bridgewater Cl RG30 . . .258 C1
Bridge End OX16 . . . . .16 E3
Bridle Path
Chorney Bassett OX12 . . .175 F2
Woodcote RG8 . . . . .250 E8
Bridle Rd RG8 . . . . .250 E3
Bridus Mead OX11 . . . . . .219 B1
Bridus Way OX11 . . . . . .219 A1
Brierley Pl RG31 . . . . .257 C4
Brigadoon OX16 . . . . .15 F4
Brigham Rd OX12 . . . . . .196 C1
**Brightwell-cum-Sotwell CE
Prim Sch** OX10 . . . . .202 E2
Brightwell St OX10 . . . .202 E2
Brill CE Comb Sch HP18 . .98 B1
Brill Cl RG4 . . . . .259 A4
Brill Rd
Horton-cum-S OX33 . . . . . .112 C6
Ludgershall HP18 . . . . .98 B7
Brindley Cl OX2 . . . . .123 A4
Brinds Cl RG4 . . . . .253 A5
Brinkburn Gr OX16 . . . . . .16 F8
Brinkinfield Rd OX44 . . .184 D7
Bristol Rd
Bicester OX26 . . . . .66 A4
Upper Rissington GL54 . .68 B5
Bristow Ct RG4 . . . . .259 B2
Britannia Ct OX18 . . . . . .115 E4
Britannia Hts **8** OX16 . .16 D5
Britannia Rd OX16 . . . . . .16 D5
Britannia Wharf **8** OX16 16 D5
British Telecom Mus *
OX1 . . . . .261 B1
Britnell Ct HP14 . . . . .188 E5
Britwell Rd
Didcot OX11 . . . . .200 E1
Ewelme OX10 . . . . .204 F4
Watlington OX49 . . . . .186 A1
Brixton Hill OX10 . . . . . .223 A4
Brize Norton Airfield
OX18 . . . . .116 A1
Brize Norton Prim Sch
OX18 . . . . .116 C3

Brize Norton Rd
Carterton OX18 . . . . .115 E2
Minster Lovell OX29 . . . .102 E2
Brizewood OX18 . . . . .115 D4
Broadbrook La OX12 . . .212 F4
Broad Cl
Barford St M OX15 . . . . . .32 E5
Kidlington OX5 . . . . .108 D8
Oxford OX2 . . . . .122 B1
Broad End OX15 . . . . .16 E1
Broad Field Rd OX5 . . . .108 B7
Broadfields OX4 . . . . .142 D2
Broad Gap OX15 . . . . .16 E1
Broadhead Pl OX3 . . . . . .124 B5
Broadhurst Gdns OX4 . .142 A1
Broadmarsh Cl OX12 . . .214 D8
Broad Marsh La OX29 . . .106 A6
Broadmoor La RG5 . . . . . .260 E4
Broad Oak OX3 . . . . .142 E8
Broadshires Way OX18 . .115 F3
Broad St
3 Banbury OX16 . . . . .16 D5
Abingdon OX14 . . . . .179 F7
Bampton OX18 . . . . .134 E3
Long Compton CV36 . . . . . .27 F6
Oxford OX1 . . . . .261 B2
Uffington SN7 . . . . .211 C7
Broadwaters Ave OX9 . .147 F7
Broadway Cl
Harwell OX11 . . . . .217 E6
Witney OX28 . . . . .103 D1
Broadway
Didcot OX11 . . . . .218 E8
Harwell OX11 . . . . .217 E6
Broadway The
Charlton-on-O OX5 . . . . . .95 A4
Kidlington OX5 . . . . .108 F6
Broad Way SN7 . . . . .211 C5
Broadwell Ct OX26 . . . . . .65 D2
Brocklesby Rd OX4 . . . .142 A2
Brocks Way RG9 . . . . .255 A4
Brode Cl OX14 . . . . .160 B2
Brogden Cl OX2 . . . . .160 F7
Brome Pl OX3 . . . . .124 E4
Bromeswell Cl OX25 . . . .62 E6
Bromsgrove SN7 . . . . .172 F3
Brook Cl HP18 . . . . .98 C8
Brook Cottage Gdn * OX15 . .6 F2
Brooke Rd OX16 . . . . .16 A3
Brookfield Cl
Milton-u-W OX7 . . . . .70 A1
Wallingford OX10 . . . . . .221 C5
Brookfield Cres OX3 . . .124 A5
Brookfield Rise OX12 . . . .20 D7
Brookfields Specl Sch
RG31 . . . . .257 C3
Brookhampton Cl OX44 . .163 C1
Brook Hill OX20 . . . . .91 B6
Brook La
Ickford HP18 . . . . .128 A3
Kings Sutton OX17 . . . . . .23 F5
Stonesfield OX29 . . . . . .196 A4
Thame OX9 . . . . .129 E1
West Hagbourne OX11 . .218 C5
Brook Lea **3** RG4 . . . . . .259 C1
Brookline Wlk **3** OX4 . .142 E1
Brooklyn Dr RG4 . . . . . .259 B6
Brookmead Dr OX10 . . .221 C6
Brook Rd
Benson OX10 . . . . .204 A4
Great Tew OX7 . . . . .45 D7
Brooksby Rd RG31 . . . .257 D2
Brookside
Abingdon OX14 . . . . .159 F1
Cholsey OX10 . . . . .220 F1
Brookside Cl OX29 . . . . .145 F7
Brookside Ct
Bicester OX26 . . . . .65 E2
Woodstock OX20 . . . . . .91 A6
Brookside
Cuddesdon OX44 . . . . . .144 A2
East Hanney OX12 . . . . . .197 A6
Brookside Est OX44 . . .184 C7
Brookside
Great Tew OX7 . . . . .45 D7
Harwell OX11 . . . . .217 E7
Hook Norton OX15 . . . . . .30 A7
Oxford OX3 . . . . .124 C2
Brookside Prim Sch OX26 65 D2
Brookside
Thame OX9 . . . . .129 F1
Watlington OX49 . . . . .186 B2
Brookside Way OX15 . . . .21 C4
Brooks Row OX29 . . . . . .87 A4
Brooks Taylor Ct OX1 . . .261 B1
Brook St
Benson OX10 . . . . .204 A4
Kingston Blount OX39 . .167 F4
Oxford OX1 . . . . .141 C7
Sutton Courtenay OX14 . . .200 A8
Watlington OX49 . . . . .186 B1
Brook View OX29 . . . . . .143 A2
Brook Way OX29 . . . . .90 A1
Broome Way OX16 . . . . . .16 F7
Broomfield Rd RG30 . . .258 A1
Broughton Castle * OX15 . .15 B1
Broughton Cl RG30 . . . .258 C1
Broughton OX16 . . . . .15 E3
Broughtons Cl OX3 . . . .123 F5
Browning Dr OX26 . . . . . .65 C4
Browning Rd OX16 . . . . . .16 E3
Browns Cl OX2 . . . . .140 A8
Brown's La
Charlbury OX7 . . . . .73 B4
Woodstock OX20 . . . . . .91 A6
Bruern Rd OX7 . . . . .56 A4
Brumcombe La OX1,OX13 159 F8
Brunel Cres OX12 . . . . . .196 D1

Brunel Dr RG5 . . . . .260 F1
Brunel Rd OX11 . . . . .218 C8
Brunstock Beck OX11 . . .200 F3
Brunswick Pl OX16 . . . .116 E6
Bryan Ho OX26 . . . . .65 B1
Bryant Pl RG8 . . . . .257 B5
Bryan Way OX12 . . . . . .214 F6
Brymbo Cotts OX15 . . . .30 D8
Bryony Cl OX4 . . . . .143 A2
Bryony Gdns OX18 . . . .115 F5
Bryony Rd OX26 . . . . .65 C5
Bryworth La GL7 . . . . .150 A6
Buchanan Rd OX25 . . . .96 E7
Buchan Rd OX26 . . . . . .65 C4
Buckingham Cl OX11 . . .219 B8
Buckingham Cres OX26 . .65 F3
Buckingham Ct NN13 . . . .24 A6
Buckingham Dr RG4 . . . .259 B5
Buckingham Gate RG4 . .259 B4
Buckingham Pl OX18 . . . .115 C5
Buckingham Rd
Bicester OX26 . . . . .65 F4
Brackley NN13 . . . . .24 A6
Westbury NN13 . . . . .25 B5
Buckingham Road Ind Est
NN13 . . . . .24 A6
Buckingham St **1** OX16 . .141 C7
Buckland CE Prim Sch
SN7 . . . . .174 E8
Buckland Ct OX5 . . . . .108 F7
Buckland Mews **3** OX14 179 D7
Buckland Rd
Bampton OX18 . . . . .154 C7
Buckland SN7 . . . . .174 E8
Charney Bassett OX12 . . .175 E2
Buckler Pl OX4 . . . . .142 A1
Buckler Rd OX2 . . . . .123 B8
Bucklers Bury Rd OX14 . .160 B3
Buckles Cl **1** OX14 . . . .179 D7
Bucknell Ave RG8 . . . . . .256 E5
Bucknell Rd OX26 . . . . . .65 D5
Buckner's Cl OX10 . . . .203 F4
Buckside RG4 . . . . .259 A2
Budds Cl OX20 . . . . .91 D7
Bugloss Wlk OX26 . . . . . .65 D4
Bulan Rd OX3 . . . . .142 E8
Bull Baulk
Middleton Cheney OX17 . .11 A1
Middleton Cheney OX17 . .17 F8
Bulldog Cl OX10 . . . . .204 B2
Bull Hill OX7 . . . . .72 B8
Bullingdon Ave OX10 . . .182 C5
Bullingdon Rd OX4 . . . .141 F7
Bull La OX18 . . . . .135 E2
Bullmarsh Cl OX25 . . . . . .64 A4
Bull Mdw The RG8 . . . . . .248 F6
Bullockspits La OX13 . . .176 C8
Bull Ring OX15 . . . . .33 F4
Bulls Cl GL7 . . . . .132 B5
Bull St
Ickford HP18 . . . . .128 A3
Kings Sutton OX17 . . . . . .23 F5
Bullsmead OX13 . . . . . .159 E5
Bullstake Cl OX2 . . . . .122 F1
Bull St OX18 . . . . .135 E2
Bulrush Rd OX4 . . . . .142 F1
Bulwarks La OX1 . . . . .261 B2
Bunce's La RG8 . . . . .251 B2
Bungalow Cl OX3 . . . . . .111 C2
Bunkers Hill OX5 . . . . .77 A1
Buntings The OX26 . . . . . .81 A8
Bunyan Rd OX26 . . . . .65 C4
Burbush Rd OX4 . . . . .142 E5
Burchester Ave OX3 . . .124 E4
Burchester Pl OX16 . . . .16 F7
Burcombe Way RG4 . . .259 B4
Burcot La OX10 . . . . .182 D4
Burcot St OX14 . . . . .181 F5
Burdell Ave OX3 . . . . .125 A4
Burditch Bank OX20 . . . .75 F5
Burdock Cl OX26 . . . . .65 B1
Bure La OX11 . . . . .201 A2
Bure Pl OX26 . . . . .65 C2
Burford Com Hospl
OX18 . . . . .100 D5
Burford Lodge OX4 . . . .141 C7
Burford Prim Sch OX18 . .100 E5
Burford Rd
Black Bourton OX18 . . .133 F6
Brize Norton OX18 . . . . . .116 A5
Carterton OX18 . . . . .115 E2
Carterton OX18 . . . . .115 C7
Chipping Norton OX7 . . . .42 F2
Filkins GL7 . . . . .132 C6
Minster Lovell OX29 . . . .102 C2
Witney OX29 . . . . .103 D2
Burford Sch (Annexe)
OX18 . . . . .100 E5
Burford Sch & Com Coll
OX18 . . . . .100 D4
Burford St GL7 . . . . .150 C4
Burgess Cl OX14 . . . . . .179 A1
Burgess Field OX2 . . . .123 A5
Burgess Mead OX2 . . . .123 A5
Burleigh Mews RG4 . . .259 C6
Burlington Cres OX3 . . .125 A3
Burlington Gdns OX16 . .16 A6
Burnham Rise RG4 . . . .259 C2
Burnhams The HP18 . . .128 D2
Burns Cl HP18 . . . . .129 D7
Burns Cres OX16 . . . . .16 A5
Burns Rd OX16 . . . . .16 A5
Burnt Cl OX44 . . . . .161 A7
Burr Cl OX20 . . . . .91 D7
Burrows Cl OX3 . . . . .124 D3
Burrows Hill OX10 . . . .204 F3

Burr St OX11 . . . . .217 E7
Bursill Cl OX3 . . . . 125 A3
Burswin Rd OX18 . . . . . . 115 D5
Burton OX14 . . . . 179 D6
Burton Pl OX4 . . . . 142 E6
Burtons Bank OX7 . . . . . .48 B5
Burt's La OX18 . . . . 129 D6
Burwell Cl OX28 . . . . 117 E7
Burwell Ct OX28 . . . . 117 F7
Burwell Dr OX28 . . . . 117 F7
Burwell Mdw OX28 . . . . . 117 F6
Bury Court La OX17 . . . . . .8 D8
Bury Croft Rd OX15 . . . . . 30 B6
Burycroft The OX14 . . . . 180 A3
Buryhook Cnr OX33 . . . . 126 C2
Bury La RG20 . . . . 235 A2
Bury Mead OX29 . . . . . . 138 A8
Bury St OX14 . . . . 179 F7
Buryway La CV36 . . . . 27 F7
Busby Cl
  Freeland OX29 . . . . 106 A6
  Stonesfield OX29 . . . . . . .89 D7
Busby's Cl OX18 . . . . 152 E8
Buscot Dr OX14 . . . . 160 B2
Buscot Ho * SN7 . . . . 171 C6
Busgrove La RG9 . . . . . . 242 A4
Bushey Dr OX18 . . . . 152 E7
Bushey Leys Cl OX3 . . . . 124 E5
Bushey Row OX14 . . . . . . 134 F3
Bush Furlong OX14 . . . . . 201 B2
Bushnell Cl OX3 . . . . 124 F3
Bush The HP17 . . . . 130 F5
Bushy Cl OX2 . . . . 122 B1
Butchers Ct OX28 . . . . . . 118 A8
Butcher's Hill OX7 . . . . . . .45 C7
Butcher's Row OX16 . . . . . .16 D6
Butler Cl
  Bloxham OX15 . . . . .21 E6
  Horspath OX33 . . . . 143 D6
  Oxford OX2 . . . . 123 B4
Butler Ho OX4 . . . . 142 B3
Butlers Cl OX36 . . . . .28 A6
Butlers Dr OX18 . . . . 115 E2
Butler's Field GL7 . . . . . . 150 C5
Butlers La CV36 . . . . 27 F5
Butlers Orch RG4 . . . . . . 252 D3
Butlers Pond RG8 . . . . . . 250 D2
Butlers Rd CV36 . . . . .28 C5
Butlers Yd RG2 . . . . 260 B4
Butterbur Gdns OX26 . . . . .65 E5
Buttercup Sq 10 OX4 . . . . 142 F1
Butterly Rd HP14 . . . . . . 188 F4
Butter Market OX7 . . . . . 147 F8
Buttermilk La OX29 . . . . . .86 F1
Butterwort Pl 1 OX4 . . . . 142 F2
Butterwyke Pl OX1 . . . . . 261 B1
Butts Cl OX17 . . . . .35 C7
Butts Hill Rd RG5 . . . . . . 260 E1
Butts La OX3 . . . . 123 F7
Butts Rd
  Faringdon SN7 . . . . 172 F2
  Horspath OX33 . . . . 143 C6
Butts The
  Aynho OX17 . . . . .35 D7
  Long Compton CV36 . . . . .27 F6
  Merton OX25 . . . . .95 D8
  Steventon OX13 . . . . 137 D3
Butts Way OX49 . . . . 167 C1
Buxton Ave OX14 . . . . . . 258 F4
Buzzards Cl OX17 . . . . .9 D5
Byefield Rd OX17 . . . . .5 F7
Byeway The OX16 . . . . . . .16 F7
Bygones Mus * OX17 . . . . . .1 D1
Byres The HP17 . . . . 130 F6
Byron Cl OX14 . . . . 179 C5
Byron Rd OX16 . . . . .16 A3
Byron Way OX26 . . . . .65 C3

C

Cadel's Row 6 SN7 . . . . . 172 F3
Cadogan Pk OX20 . . . . . . .91 B6
Cadogan Pl RG4 . . . . 259 B3
Cadwell La OX44,OX49 . . 184 E4
Caernarvon Way OX16 . . . .15 F6
Caesars Gate NN13 . . . . . .24 A6
Calais Dene OX18 . . . . . . 134 F4
Calais La OX29 . . . . 136 E6
Calcot Cl OX3 . . . . 124 E1
Calcroft La
  Clanfield OX18 . . . . 133 C2
  Langford GL7 . . . . 132 E3
Caldecott Ct OX14 . . . . . . 179 D6
Caldecott Prim Sch
  OX14 . . . . 179 D5
Caldecott Rd OX14 . . . . . 179 E6
Calder Cl OX16 . . . . .16 F7
Calder Way OX14 . . . . . . 201 B2
Caldicott Cl OX10 . . . . . . 203 B6
Caleta Cl RG4 . . . . 259 D2
Calthorpe Rd OX16 . . . . . .16 C5
Calthorpe St OX16 . . . . . .16 C5
Calves Cl OX5 . . . . 108 D8
Cambridge Terr OX1 . . . . 261 B1
Cam Cl OX11 . . . . 200 F1
Camden Cl GL56 . . . . .26 F5
Camel Cross OX12 . . . . . . 214 C5
Camellias The OX14 . . . . 179 C5
Cameron Ave OX14 . . . . . 160 C1
Cameron Cl 10 OX16 . . . . .16 D5
Cameron Cl OX26 . . . . . . .65 E2
Campbell Rd OX4 . . . . . . 142 A5
Campbells Cl OX20 . . . . . .91 C6
Campden Cl OX28 . . . . . . 103 E1
Camp Ind Est OX9 . . . . . . 146 B4
Campion Cl
  18 Sandford-on-T OX4 . . 142 F1

Campion Cl *continued*
Carterton OX18 . . . . 115 E1
Campion Hall Dr OX11 . . .219 B7
Campion Pl OX26 . . . . . . .65 D4
Campion Rd OX14 . . . . . . 180 B8
Campion Way OX28 . . . . . 104 D2
Camp La OX17 . . . . .2 D4
Camp Rd OX25 . . . . .63 C8
Canada Cl OX16 . . . . .16 D7
Canada La SN7 . . . . 172 E4
Canal Ct OX12 . . . . 214 C7
Canal Ho 4 OX12 . . . . . . 214 D5
Canal La OX15 . . . . .16 F1
Canal Rd OX5 . . . . .92 C4
Canal St
  Banbury OX16 . . . . .16 D5
  Oxford OX2 . . . . 261 A3
Canal Way OX12 . . . . 214 A5
Canal Yd OX5 . . . . .92 C4
Candy Way OX13 . . . . . . 159 B6
Cane La OX12 . . . . 214 D8
Canning Cres OX1 . . . . . . 141 E5
Cannons Field OX3 . . . . . 123 F6
Canon Hill's Gdns SN6 . . 209 C6
Canons Dr GL7 . . . . 150 E3
Canterbury Cl OX16 . . . . . .17 A7
Canterbury Rd OX2 . . . . . 123 B4
Capel Cl OX2 . . . . 123 B8
Caps La OX10 . . . . 221 B2
Captains Mill OX28 . . . . . 104 B2
Cardiff Mews RG1 . . . . . . 258 F1
Cardiff Rd RG1 . . . . 258 F1
Cardigan St
  Oxford OX2 . . . . 261 A3
  Oxford OX2 . . . . 261 A4
Cardinal Cl
  Oxford OX4 . . . . 142 B3
  Reading RG4 . . . . 259 B2
Cardwell Cres OX3 . . . . . 124 B2
Carey Ave RG4 . . . . 257 B4
Carey Cl OX2 . . . . 108 F1
Cariad Ct RG8 . . . . 249 B7
Carisbrooke Cl RG4 . . . . . 259 C6
Carlesgill Pl RG9 . . . . . . 254 E7
Carling Rd RG4 . . . . 252 E6
Carlisle Rd RG31 . . . . . . 257 E3
Carlton Cl OX12 . . . . 196 C1
Carlton Rd
  Cutteslowe OX2 . . . . . . 109 B1
  Reading RG4 . . . . 258 E5
Caroline Cl OX20 . . . . .91 B6
Caroline St OX4 . . . . 123 E1
Carpenter Cl OX4 . . . . . . 142 C2
Carr Ave OX18 . . . . 115 C2
Carrdus Sch The OX17 . . . .17 C8
Carse Cl OX14 . . . . 160 B3
Carswell Circ OX25 . . . . . .63 C8
Carswell Com Prim Sch
  OX14 . . . . 179 E7
Carswell Ct 2 OX14 . . . . . 179 F7
Carswell La SN7 . . . . 154 A1
Carter Cl OX3 . . . . 124 F2
Carter Cres SN7 . . . . 172 E1
Carters Cl OX18 . . . . 115 D2
Carters La HP18 . . . . 129 B7
Carterton Com Coll
  OX18 . . . . 115 D3
Carterton Prim Sch
  OX18 . . . . 115 C1
Carterton Rd OX18 . . . . . 116 B3
Carterton South Ind Est
  OX18 . . . . 115 C1
Carterton Park Cvn Site
  OX18 . . . . 133 D8
Cartwright Gdns OX17 . . . .35 D7
Cassington Rd
  Eynsham OX29 . . . . 121 A8
  Yarnton OX5 . . . . 108 B4
Castle Cl
  Benson OX10 . . . . 203 F4
  Bicester OX27 . . . . .65 F7
Castle Cres SN7 . . . . 193 E8
Castle Fields OX27 . . . . . . .50 B4
Castle La OX10 . . . . 221 D8
Castle Mews OX1 . . . . . . 261 A2
Castle Mill Ho OX1 . . . . . 123 A3
Castle Mill OX1 . . . . 123 A2
Castle Quay Sh Ctr OX16 . .16 D6
Castle Rd
  Shirburn OX49 . . . . 186 D4
  Wootton OX20 . . . . .75 F5
Castle Sq OX10 . . . . 203 F4
Castle St
  Banbury OX16 . . . . .16 C6
  Deddington OX15 . . . . . . .33 F4
  Marsh Gibbon OX27 . . . . .67 F3
  Oxford OX1 . . . . 261 B2
  Steventon OX13 . . . . . . 198 F3
  Wallingford OX10 . . . . . 221 D8
Castle Wlk OX15 . . . . 200 E2
Caswell La OX18 . . . . 116 F6
Catharine Cl OX14 . . . . . 160 F3
Catherine Cl SN6 . . . . . . 209 C6
Catherine St OX4 . . . . . . 142 A7
Catkins SN7 . . . . 172 E2
Cat La
  Ewelme OX10 . . . . 204 F4
  Stadhampton OX44 . . . . 163 D1
Catmore Cl OX12 . . . . . . 214 D8
Catmore Rd RG20 . . . . . . 234 F1
Catsham La OX7 . . . . .72 C5
Catslip RG9 . . . . 224 F2
Cat St OX12 . . . . 216 D6
Catte St OX1 . . . . 261 B2
Cattle Mkt OX7 . . . . .42 E3
Catwell Cl OX4 . . . . 142 B6
Caudwell Cl
  Drayton OX14 . . . . 179 B1

Caudwell Cl *continued*
Grove OX12 . . . . 196 E1
Causeway
  Banbury OX16 . . . . .16 F6
  Bicester OX26 . . . . .65 E1
  Bishopsdown OX5 . . . . . .93 A8
Causeway The
  East Hanney OX12 . . . . . 197 A6
  Reading RG4 . . . . 259 D1
  Steventon OX13 . . . . . . 198 F4
  Woodstock OX20 . . . . . . .91 A6
Causmans Way RG31 . . . . 257 C2
Cavalier Rd OX9 . . . . 130 A1
Cavell Rd OX4 . . . . 142 A5
Cavendish Dr OX3 . . . . . . 123 E5
Cavendish Pl OX27 . . . . . .52 D1
Cavendish Rd
  Brize Norton OX18 . . . . . 116 B4
  Swerford OX7 . . . . .30 F3
  Watchfield SN6 . . . . 191 C1
  Wootton OX20 . . . . .75 F4
Cavendish Wlk OX9 . . . . . 130 B1
Caversham Hill RG4 . . . . 258 D2
Caversham Park Dr RG4 . 259 C5
Caversham Park Prim Sch
  RG4 . . . . 259 A6
Caversham Park Rd RG4 . 259 C6
Caversham Prim Sch
  RG4 . . . . 259 A3
Caversham Rd RG1 . . . . . 259 A1
Caversham Wharf RG1 . . . 259 A1
Cave St OX4 . . . . 123 F1
Cawley Rd OX17 . . . . .23 B5
Cawsam Gdns RG4 . . . . . 259 C4
Caxton Cl RG30 . . . . 258 C1
Caxton Ct RG9 . . . . 244 E1
Cecil Aldin Dr RG31 . . . . 257 C4
Cecil Sharpe Ct OX3 . . . . 124 C2
Cedar Cl
  Bicester OX26 . . . . .65 F3
  Pangbourne RG8 . . . . . . 256 C4
  Witney OX28 . . . . 104 D2
Cedar Dr
  Bicester OX26 . . . . .65 F3
  Salford OX7 . . . . .41 F5
  Shipton-u-W OX7 . . . . . . .85 D7
  Shotteswell OX17 . . . . . . .8 C7
  Standlake OX29 . . . . . . 137 D3
  Sutton Courtenay OX14 . . 200 A8
  Turweston NN13 . . . . . . .24 B7
  Uffington SN7 . . . . 211 C7
Cedar Mews 6 OX26 . . . . .65 E1
Cedar Rd
  Carterton OX18 . . . . 115 F5
  Faringdon SN7 . . . . 172 E3
  Oxford OX2 . . . . 140 D7
Cedars The
  Benson OX10 . . . . 204 A5
  Reading RG31 . . . . 257 D2
Cedar Villa OX16 . . . . .16 B6
Cedar Wood Cres RG4 . . . 259 B4
Celandine Cl 8 OX26 . . . . .65 C4
Celandine Pl 6 OX4 . . . . . 142 F1
Celsea Pl OX10 . . . . 221 A1
Cemetery Rd
  Abingdon OX14 . . . . 179 D7
  Bicester OX26 . . . . .65 E1
Century Pl OX4 . . . . 143 A2
Centenary Bsns Pk RG9 . . 244 F1
Centremead OX2 . . . . 141 A8
Centre Rise OX33 . . . . . . 143 D6
Centre St OX16 . . . . .16 F7
Century St SN7 . . . . 173 A3
Century Row OX2 . . . . . . 123 B7
Chacombe CE Prim Sch
  OX17 . . . . .10 F4
Chacombe Rd OX17 . . . . . .10 F1
Chadlington CE Prim Sch
  OX7 . . . . .57 C1
Chadlington Rd
  Chadlington OX7 . . . . . . .57 F1
  Oxford OX2 . . . . 123 C5
  Spelsbury OX7 . . . . .72 F8
Chaffinch Rd OX26 . . . . . .66 A1
Chaffinch Wlk OX4 . . . . . 142 F1
Chain Alley OX1 . . . . 261 A2
Chainhill Rd
  Wantage OX12 . . . . 214 F2
  West Ilsley OX12 . . . . . . 233 A7
Chalcraft Cl RG9 . . . . 254 C8
Chalcroft Cl OX29 . . . . . . 118 A5
Chalfont Rd OX2 . . . . 123 B5
Chalford Cl OX7 . . . . .42 F3
Chalford Rd OX9 . . . . 167 A4
Chalgrove Com Prim Sch
  OX44 . . . . 184 D6
Chalgrove Rd OX9 . . . . . . 130 A1
Chalgrove Way RG4 . . . . 259 B6
Chalk Farm Rd HP14 . . . . 188 C5
Chalk Hill
  Aston Tirrold OX11 . . . . . 237 F8
  Hunt's Green RG9 . . . . . 254 C6
Chalkhousegreen La
  RG4 . . . . 259 A8
Chalkhouse Green La
  RG4 . . . . 253 A1
Chalkhouse Green Rd
  RG4 . . . . 252 E2
Challenor Cl OX14 . . . . . . 179 E4
Challow Rd OX12 . . . . . . 214 B5
Chalmore Gdns OX10 . . . 221 D6
Chalvey Cl OX26 . . . . .65 D1
Chalvey Rd OX26 . . . . .65 D1
Chamberlaine Ct OX16 . . . .16 D6
Chamberlain Pl OX5 . . . . . .92 C1
Chambrai Cl OX14 . . . . . . 200 F8
Champion Rd RG4 . . . . . . 259 C1
Champion Way OX44 . . . . 143 A1
Champs Cl OX14 . . . . 160 C2
Chancellor Ct OX4 . . . . . . 142 D4
Chancel Way
  Lechlade-on-T GL7 . . . . . 150 C4
  Marcham OX13 . . . . 178 C7
Chandler Cl OX18 . . . . . . 134 F4
Chandlers Cl
  Abingdon OX14 . . . . 160 C1

Chandlers Cl *continued*
Wantage OX12 . . . . 214 E4
Chandlings Manor Sch
  OX1 . . . . 160 B7
Chapel Cl
  Blackthorn OX25 . . . . . . .82 A3
  Deddington OX15 . . . . . . .34 E4
  Leafield OX29 . . . . .86 E3
  South Stoke RG8 . . . . . . 239 C3
  Wantage OX12 . . . . 214 E5
Chapel Dr OX25 . . . . .81 C3
Chapel End
  Croughton NN13 . . . . . . .36 C8
  Great Rollright OX7 . . . . . .29 A3
Chapel Hill
  Brize Norton OX18 . . . . . 116 B4
  Swerford OX7 . . . . .30 F3
Chapel La
  Adderbury OX17 . . . . .23 A4
  Benson OX10 . . . . 203 F4
  Berrick Salome OX10 . . . 204 B7
  Bledlow Ridge HP14 . . . . 169 E2
  Blewbury OX11 . . . . 237 A8
  Bodicote OX15 . . . . .22 E8
  Chalgrove OX44 . . . . . . 184 D6
  Charney Bassett OX12 . . . 175 F2
  Cropredy OX17 . . . . .4 F2
  Enstone OX7 . . . . .58 F5
  Fernham SN7 . . . . 193 A4
  Great Bourton OX17 . . . . . .9 D5
  Kingham OX7 . . . . .55 A5
  Little Tew OX7 . . . . .45 B5
  Milton OX15 . . . . .22 C3
  Nettlebed RG9 . . . . 224 E2
  North Leigh OX29 . . . . . 105 B7
  Northmoor OX29 . . . . . . 138 C2
  Oxford OX4 . . . . 142 B2
  Poffley End OX29 . . . . . . 104 B5
  Ratley OX15 . . . . .2 A1
  Salford OX7 . . . . .41 F5
  Shipton-u-W OX7 . . . . . . .85 D7
  Standlake OX29 . . . . . . 137 D3
  Stratton Audley OX27 . . . .52 D1
  Warborough OX10 . . . . . 203 B6
Chapel Mews 6 OX26 . . . . .65 E1
Chapel & Pope's Tower*
  OX29 . . . . 138 B8
Chapel Rd
  Ashbury SN6 . . . . 228 A7
  South Leigh OX29 . . . . . 119 B6
  Stanford in the V SN7 . . . 194 E8
Chapel Row
  Cropredy OX17 . . . . .4 F2
  Little Compton GL56 . . . . .26 F1
Chapel Sq
  Deddington OX15 . . . . . . .33 F4
  East Hendred OX12 . . . . 216 D6
Chapel St
  Bicester OX26 . . . . .65 E1
  Bledington OX7 . . . . .54 D2
  Bloxham OX15 . . . . .21 D7
  Hook Norton OX15 . . . . . .30 B7
  Oxford OX4 . . . . 141 F8
  Warmington OX17 . . . . . . .3 A4
  Watlington OX49 . . . . . . 186 B2
Chapel Way
  Childrey OX12 . . . . 213 C4
  Oxford OX2 . . . . 122 D1
Chapelwick Cl SN6 . . . . . 209 B6
Chapmans La OX15 . . . . . .21 D8
Chapmans Piece OX18 . . . 100 E5
Charbridge La OX26 . . . . . .66 C2
Charbridge Way OX26 . . . .66 C2
Charlbury Cl OX5 . . . . .92 D2
Charlbury Mus OX7 . . . . . .73 B4
Charlbury Prim Sch OX7 . .73 C4
Charlbury Rd
  Finstock OX7 . . . . .88 D7
  Oxford OX2 . . . . 123 C5
  Shrivenham SN6 . . . . . . 209 B6
Charlbury Sta OX7 . . . . . . .73 A3
Charles Cl OX16 . . . . .16 D5
Charles Dr OX9 . . . . 130 A1
Charles Evans Way RG4 . . 259 D2
Charles Ho RG9 . . . . 244 E3
Charles Rd
  Carterton OX18 . . . . 133 D8
  Cholsey OX10 . . . . 239 A8
Charles St OX4 . . . . 141 F6
Charlton Gdns OX12 . . . . 214 F5
Charlton-on-Otmoor CE
  Prim Sch OX5 . . . . .95 A4
Charlton Pk OX12 . . . . . . 214 F5
Charlton Prim Sch OX12 . 214 F5
Charlton Rd
  Aynho OX17 . . . . .35 C7
  Wantage OX12 . . . . 214 F5
Charlton Village Rd
  OX12 . . . . 214 F5
Charney Ave OX14 . . . . . 160 C2
Charter Ho OX12 . . . . 214 E4
Charter Mews 8 OX4 . . . . 179 F7
Charterville Cl OX29 . . . . 102 E2
Charter Way OX10 . . . . . 221 D8
Chartwell Dr OX7 . . . . .73 C4
Charvil La Rd4 . . . . 260 F4
Chase Barn OX27 . . . . .37 C8
Chastleton Ho* GL56 . . . . .40 D7
Chatham Rd OX1 . . . . 141 D5
Chatsworth Cl RG4 . . . . . 259 C6
Chatsworth Dr OX16 . . . . . .9 D1
Chatterpie La OX29 . . . . . .89 F5

Chaucer Cl
  Bicester OX26 . . . . .65 C4
  Reading RG4 . . . . 259 A5
Chaucer Ct OX10 . . . . 204 F4
Chaucer's La OX20 . . . . . . .91 A6
Chaundy Rd OX5 . . . . .77 C5
Chaunterell Way OX14 . . . 179 D6
Chawley La OX2 . . . . 140 A6
Chazey Cl RG4 . . . . 258 C8
Chazey Rd RG4 . . . . 258 D3
Cheapside OX18 . . . . 133 E8
Chearsley Rd HP18 . . . . . 129 E7
Cheatle Cl OX18 . . . . 100 E4
Checkendon CE Prim Sch
  RG8 . . . . 241 C3
Checker Wlk OX14 . . . . . . 179 F7
Chedworth Dr OX28 . . . . . 117 E8
Cheers Farm OX14 . . . . . 179 C1
Chelford Way RG4 . . . . . . 258 F4
Chelmscote Row OX17 . . . .30 F8
Chelsea Cl RG30 . . . . 257 F1
Chenderit Sch OX17 . . . . . .11 A1
Cheney Cl OX17 . . . . .10 F1
Cheney Gdns OX17 . . . . . . .10 F1
Cheney La OX3 . . . . 124 A1
Cheney Rd OX16 . . . . .16 F8
Cheney Sch OX3 . . . . 124 A1
Cheney Student Village
  OX3 . . . . 124 A1
Chepstow Gdns OX16 . . . . .15 F5
Chepstow Rd RG31 . . . . . 257 D2
Chequers Cl OX33 . . . . . . 125 D7
Chequers Pl
  Cholsey OX10 . . . . 220 F2
  Oxford OX3 . . . . 124 E3
Cherbury Gn OX12 . . . . . . 214 D8
Cheriton Pl RG4 . . . . 252 F5
Cherry Cl
  Kidlington OX5 . . . . 108 E7
  Reading RG4 . . . . 259 C8
  Sandford-on-T OX4 . . . . 142 F1
  Stratton Audley OX27 . . . .52 D1
  Warborough OX10 . . . . . 203 B6
Cherry Fields OX17 . . . . . . .4 F1
Cherry Orch
  Great Coxwell SN7 . . . . . 192 C8
  Highworth SN6 . . . . 190 A6
Cherry Rd OX16 . . . . .16 A7
Cherrys Cl OX16 . . . . .21 D3
Cherry St OX6 . . . . .52 D1
Cherry Tree Cl
  Grove OX12 . . . . 214 E8
  Kingston Bagpuize OX13 . 176 D8
  Stoke Row RG9 . . . . 242 A5
Cherry Tree Ct
  Harwell OX11 . . . . 217 E7
  Oxford OX2 . . . . 140 D7
Cherry Tree Dr OX13 . . . . 159 C2
Cherry Tree Rd OX39 . . . . 168 C6
Cherry Tree Way OX28 . . . 104 E1
Cherwell Ave OX5 . . . . . . 109 A8
Cherwell Bank OX25 . . . . .62 E6
Cherwell Bsns Ctr OX5 . . . .92 C2
Cherwell Cl
  Abingdon OX14 . . . . 160 B1
  Bicester OX26 . . . . .65 F4
  Didcot OX11 . . . . 200 F4
  Wallingford OX10 . . . . . 221 D7
Cherwell Ct OX5 . . . . .92 D1
Cherwell Dr OX3 . . . . 124 A4
Cherwell Lodge OX2 . . . . 123 C8
Cherwell Rd
  Berinsfield OX10 . . . . . . 182 C6
  Reading RG4 . . . . 259 A6
Cherwell Sch The OX2 . . . 123 C6
Chester St
  Oxford OX4 . . . . 141 F7
  Reading RG4 . . . . 259 A2
Chesterton CE Prim Sch
  OX26 . . . . .79 F8
Chester Way OX16 . . . . . . .16 C5
Chestnut Ave
  Faringdon SN7 . . . . 172 E3
  Oxford OX3 . . . . 124 D4
  Radley OX14 . . . . 160 E4
  Reading RG4 . . . . 259 E4
  Thame OX9 . . . . 147 D8
Chestnut Cl
  Brize Norton OX18 . . . . . 116 C3
  Chesterton OX26 . . . . . . .80 A7
  Launton OX26 . . . . .66 D1
  Middle Assendon RG9 . . 243 F8
  Witney OX28 . . . . 104 A1
Chestnut Cotts RG8 . . . . . 249 A6
Chestnut Dr OX7 . . . . .71 B2
Chestnut End OX26 . . . . . .65 D1
Chestnut Gr RG8 . . . . 257 D5
Chestnut Rd OX2 . . . . 140 D7
Chestnut Rd
  Mollington OX17 . . . . .4 A3
  Oxford OX2 . . . . 140 D7
Chestnuts The
  Abingdon OX14 . . . . 160 C1
  Deddington OX15 . . . . . . .34 E4
  Kirtlington OX5 . . . . .78 A4
  Lower Shiplake RG9 . . . . 255 A3
  Wantage OX12 . . . . 214 F5

Chestnut Tree Cl OX13 . . **159** C1
Chestnut View OX18. . . . **133** C5
Chetwode
Banbury,Overthorpe OX17. . **17** C6
Banbury OX16 . . . . **16** A8
Chetwyn Mead OX18 . . . **134** F3
Cheviot Way OX16 . . . . **8** F1
Cheyne La OX18 . . . . **134** E3
Cheyney Wlk OX14 . . . . . **159** A8
Chibnall Cl OX44 . . . . **184** D6
Chichester Cl OX26 . . . . . . **65** E2
Chichester Pl OX18 . . . . . **116** C3
Chichester Wlk OX16 . . . . . **9** A1
Chiers Dr OX14 . . . . **179** C1
Chilbridge Rd OX29 . . . . . **120** C7
Childrey Way
Abingdon OX14 . . . . **160** B2
East Challow OX12 . . . . . . **213** F4
Chilford Barns OX7 . . . . . . **55** E5
Chilgrove Dr OX25 . . . . **49** E1
Chillbrook OX11 . . . . **217** E6
Chillingworth Cres OX3 . . **142** E8
Chillingworth Ct OX3 . . . **142** E8
Chilson Hill OX7 . . . . **72** A2
Chilswell La
Boars Hill OX1 . . . . **140** F3
Sunningwell OX1 . . . . **141** A2
Chilswell Rd OX1 . . . . **141** C7
Chiltern App OX26 . . . . **65** E3
Chiltern Bank RG9 . . . . . . **252** E7
Chiltern Cl OX44 . . . . **184** E6
Henley-on-T RG9 . . . . **254** B8
Chiltern Cres OX10 . . . . . **221** B8
Chiltern Ct RG4 . . . . **259** B6
Chiltern Edge Com Sch
RG4 . . . . **252** E4
Chiltern Gdns OX49 . . . . . **186** C1
Chiltern Gr OX7 . . . . **148** A7
Chiltern Hts RG4 . . . . **259** C4
Chiltern Nursery Nurse
Training Coll RG4 . . . . . **259** B3
Chiltern Rd
Reading RG4 . . . . **259** C4
Rotherfield Peppard RG9 . . **252** E7
Chiltern Ridge HP14 . . . . **188** C4
Chiltern Sculpture Trail★
HP14 . . . . **187** D4
Chilterns End Cl RG9 . . . **254** C8
Chilterns The OX1 . . . . . . **261** B2
Chiltern View
Little Milton OX44 . . . . **164** A7
Purley on T RG8 . . . . **257** D5
Tetsworth OX9 . . . . **166** B8
Chiltern Wlk RG8 . . . . . . **256** D5
Chilton Cl OX14 . . . . **160** B1
Chilton Cty Prim Sch
OX11 . . . . **235** C8
Chilton Rd
Long Crendon HP18 . . . . . **129** C7
Upton OX11 . . . . **218** B2
Chilworth Rd OX44 . . . . . **145** D3
Chinalls Cl MK18 . . . . **39** D6
Chinnock Brook OX11 . . **200** F3
Chinnor Hill OX39 . . . . . . **168** E4
Chinnor Hill Nature
Reserve★ OX39 . . . . . . **168** F5
Chinnor Rd
Aston Rowant OX9 . . . . . . **167** D2
Bledlow Ridge HP14 . . . . . **169** C3
Chinnor,Crowell Hill OX39 . **168** H4
Chinnor,Crowell OX39 . . . . **168** E4
Thame OX9 . . . . **148** C5
Towersey OX9 . . . . **148** E6
Chinnor Sta★ OX39 . . . . . **168** D5
Chipmunk Rd OX10 . . . . . **204** D3
Chipperfield Park Rd
OX15 . . . . **21** F6
Chipping Norton Hospl
OX7 . . . . **42** E3
Chipping Norton Mus★
OX7 . . . . **42** E3
Chipping Norton Rd
Chadlington OX7 . . . . **57** A3
Hook Norton OX15. . . . . . . **30** A7
Over Norton OX7 . . . . **42** F2
Chipping Warden Sch
OX17 . . . . **5** F7
Choicehill Rd OX7 . . . . **42** E6
Cholesbury Grange OX3. **124** A4
Cholsey and Wallingford
Rly★ OX10 . . . . **220** F3
Cholsey Cl OX4 . . . . **142** C4
Cholsey Prim Sch OX10 . **220** F2
Cholsey Sta OX10 . . . . . . **220** E1
Cholswell Ct OX13 . . . . . . **159** C3
Cholswell Rd OX13 . . . . . **159** C2
Chorefields OX5 . . . . **92** D1
Choswell Spring OX4 . . . **142** E1
Chowns Cl OX9 . . . . **148** A7
Christ Church Cath★
OX1 . . . . **261** C1
Christ Church Cath Sch
OX1 . . . . **261** B1
Christ Church Coll OX1 . **261** B2
Christchurch Ct OX16 . . . . **16** D6
Christ Church Old Bldgs
OX1 . . . . **261** A2
Christopher Rawlins CE Prim
Sch OX27 . . . . **23** A4
Church Ave
Henley-on-T RG9 . . . . **244** E2

Church Ave *continued*
Kings Sutton OX17. . . . . . . **23** F5
Church Cl
Adderbury OX7 . . . . **23** A3
Ascot-u-W OX7 . . . . **71** C2
Benson OX10. . . . . **203** F4
Black Bourton OX18 . . . . . **133** F5
Charlbury OX7 . . . . **73** B3
Cuddesdon OX44 . . . . **144** C3
East Hagbourne OX11 . . . . **218** F5
Farmoor OX2 . . . . **121** C2
Fringford OX27 . . . . **52** D7
Great Bourton OX17 . . . . . . **9** D8
Islip OX5 . . . . **93** F1
Longcot SN7 . . . . **192** C2
Merton OX25 . . . . **95** D8
Rotherfield Greys RG9. . . . **243** C1
South Hinksey OX1 . . . . . . **141** B5
Stanton St John OX33 . . . . **125** C7
Wardington OX17 . . . . **5** E1
Weston-on-t-G OX25 . . . . . **79** A1
Church Cotts OX44 . . . . . **161** E3
Church Cowley Rd OX4 . **142** B5
Church Cowley St James CE
Prim Sch OX4 . . . . **142** C4
Church End
Blewbury OX11 . . . . **219** A1
Croughton NN13 . . . . **36** D8
Drayton St L OX10. . . . . . . **183** B6
Great Rollright OX7 . . . . . . **29** B3
South Leigh OX29 . . . . **119** C6
Standlake OX29 . . . . **137** D3
Church Farm Ct OX29 . . **137** D4
Churchfield La OX10 . . . . **203** E4
Churchfield RG8 . . . . **223** D3
Churchfields OX29 . . . . **89** C7
Church Furlong OX15 . . . . **20** C8
Church Gn
Long Crendon HP18. . . . . **129** D7
Stanford in the V SN7 . . . . **194** E8
Witney OX28 . . . . **118** B7
Church Hill
Chilton OX11 . . . . **235** D8
Great Haseley OX44 . . . . . **164** E8
Little Milton OX44 . . . . **163** F6
Church Hill Rd OX44 . . . . **142** B4
Church Hill
Stonor RG9 . . . . **225** D8
Tackley OX5. . . . . **77** B5
Warmington OX17 . . . . **3** A4
Churchill Cl
Didcot OX11 . . . . **200** C1
Woodstock OX20 . . . . **91** B6
Churchill Cres
Sonning Common RG4. . . . **253** A6
Thame OX9 . . . . **148** B8
Churchill Dr OX3 . . . . **124** C1
Churchill Gate OX20 . . . . . **91** C5
Churchill Hospl The OX3 **142** C8
Churchill Pl OX42 . . . . . . **122** F8
Churchill Rd
Bicester OX26 . . . . **65** F3
Chipping Norton OX7. . . . . . **42** D1
Didcot OX11. . . . . **200** C1
Kidlington OX5. . . . . **108** E8
Kidlington OX5 . . . . **55** A5
Bicester OX26 . . . . **65** E1
Churchill Way OX29 . . . . **106** B8
Church La
Adderbury OX17 . . . . **23** A3
Ashbury SN6 . . . . **228** A7
Aston Rowant OX9 . . . . . . **167** D3
Banbury OX16 . . . . **16** D6
Bicester OX25 . . . . **65** E1
Bishopstone SN6 . . . . **227** C4
Bledington OX7 . . . . **54** D2
Bledlow Ridge HP14. . . . . **189** F8
Bledlow Ridge,Radnage
HP14. . . . . **189** D8
Brightwell-cum-S OX10 . . **202** E3
Burford OX18. . . . . **100** E5
Cassington OX29 . . . . **107** C2
Chacombe OX17 . . . . **10** E4
Chalgrove OX44. . . . . **184** D6
Charlbury OX7 . . . . **73** B3
Charlton-on-O OX5 . . . . . . **95** A4
Chinnor OX39 . . . . **168** D6
Chipping Norton OX7. . . . . . **42** E3
Claydon OX17 . . . . **1** D1
Coleshill SN6 . . . . **191** B8
Cropredy OX17 . . . . **4** F2
Croughton NN13 . . . . **36** D8
Drayton OX14 . . . . **179** C1
Drayton St L OX10. . . . . . . **183** B5
Dry Sandford OX13 . . . . . **158** F5
Ewelme RG9 . . . . **206** B1
Fernham SN7 . . . . **193** A4
Fringford OX27 . . . . **52** D7
Fulbrook OX18 . . . . **100** F4
Hailey OX29. . . . . **104** A6
Horley OX15 . . . . **8** A6
Hanwell OX17 . . . . **8** F3
Harwell OX11 . . . . **217** E7
Hornton OX15 . . . . **7** C6
Horton-cum-S OX33. . . . . **112** A5
Islip OX5 . . . . **93** F1
Kirtlington OX5 . . . . **78** A4
Langford GL7 . . . . **132** D1
Longworth OX13 . . . . **156** B3
Lower Heyford OX25 . . . . . . **62** D6
Ludgershall HP18 . . . . **98** C7
Marston OX3 . . . . **123** F6
Middle Barton OX7 . . . . . . **46** B1
Middleton Cheney OX17 . . . **10** F1
Milcombe OX15 . . . . **21** A2
Mixbury NN13 . . . . **38** E8
Mollington OX17 . . . . **4** A2
North Stoke OX10 . . . . . . **221** D1
Pyrton OX49 . . . . **186** B4

Church La *continued*
Reading RG4 . . . . **259** F7
Rotherfield Peppard RG9 . . **253** A8
Shilton OX18 . . . . **115** B5
Shiplake RG9 . . . . **254** F1
Shottesnell OX17 . . . . **8** D7
Shutford OX15 . . . . **14** B5
South Moreton OX11 . . . . **219** F5
Spelsbury OX7 . . . . **72** F8
Steventon OX13 . . . . **198** E3
Towersey OX9 . . . . **148** E7
Wallingford OX10 . . . . **221** D7
Wendlebury OX26 . . . . **80** A4
Weston-on-t-G OX25 . . . . . **79** A2
Witney OX28 . . . . **118** C8
Wolvercote OX2 . . . . **122** F8
Yarnton OX5 . . . . **108** B4
Churchlea OX17 . . . . **4** A3
Church Mdw OX7 . . . . **70** A1
Church Mere Rd OX14 . . **180** B1
Church Mews RG8 . . . . . **257** D5
Church Mill Cl OX29 . . . . **137** C4
Church Pas OX16 . . . . **16** C6
Church Path
Stanford in the V SN7 . . . . **194** E7
Stokenchurch HP14 . . . . . **188** D5
Church Pl GL56 . . . . **54** A8
Church Rd
Appleton OX13. . . . . **158** A8
Ardley OX27. . . . . **50** C3
Benson OX10. . . . . **203** F4
Blewbury OX11 . . . . **237** A8
Brackley NN13. . . . . **24** A7
Chadlington OX7 . . . . **57** C1
Chinnor OX39 . . . . **168** D6
Cholsey OX10 . . . . **220** E2
Great Milton OX44. . . . . . . **145** B2
Hinton Waldrist SN7 . . . . . **155** F2
Horspath OX33 . . . . **143** C6
Ickford HP18 . . . . **127** F3
Lewknor OX49 . . . . **187** B8
Long Hanborough OX29. . . **106** C7
Lower Odington GL56 . . . . . **54** A8
Milton-u-W OX7 . . . . **70** A2
North Leigh OX29 . . . . **105** B8
Pangbourne RG8 . . . . **256** C6
Radley OX14 . . . . **160** E3
Reading RG4 . . . . **258** F2
Sandford-on-T OX4 . . . . . **161** A8
Thame OX9 . . . . **129** E1
Weston-on-t-G OX25 . . . . . **79** A2
Wheatley OX33 . . . . **144** B8
Church Rise OX7 . . . . **88** C6
Church Row
Bourton SN6 . . . . **209** A2
Childrey OX12 . . . . **213** C4
Curbridge OX29 . . . . **117** E6
Hinton Parva SN4 . . . . . . **227** A3
Langford GL7 . . . . **132** D2
Church Sq OX5 . . . . **93** F1
Church St
Appleford OX14 . . . . **200** F8
Ardington OX12. . . . . **215** E5
Bampton OX18 . . . . **134** E3
Barford St M OX15 . . . . **32** E6
Bladon OX20 . . . . **91** B2
Bledington OX7 . . . . **54** C2
Bloxham OX15 . . . . **21** D4
Bodicote OX15 . . . . **22** E8
Charlbury OX7 . . . . **73** B3
Chipping Norton OX7. . . . . . **42** E3
Deddington OX15 . . . . **33** F4
Didcot OX11. . . . . **218** F8
Ducklington OX29 . . . . . . **118** B4
East Hendred OX12 . . . . . **216** D6
Eynsham OX29. . . . . **120** E7
Faringdon SN7 . . . . **172** F4
Fifield OX7 . . . . **69** B2
Henley-on-T RG9 . . . . **244** D1
Idbury OX7 . . . . **69** B4
Kidlington OX5 . . . . **92** F2
Kingham OX7 . . . . **55** A4
Marcham OX13 . . . . **178** C6
Marsh Gibbon OX27 . . . . . . **67** F3
Reading RG4 . . . . **259** A2
Shellingford SN7 . . . . **193** F8
Shipton-u-W OX7 . . . . **85** D8
Somerton OX25 . . . . **48** F6
Stokenchurch HP14 . . . . . **188** D5
Stonesfield OX8 . . . . **89** C7
Sutton Courtenay OX14 . . **180** A1
Upton OX11 . . . . **218** C2
Wantage OX12. . . . . **214** D4
Wargrave RG10 . . . . **255** C2
Watlington OX49 . . . . **186** B2
West Hanney OX12 . . . . . **196** E6
Wootton OX20 . . . . **75** F4
Wroxton OX15 . . . . **15** B8
Church Terr
Bicester OX26 . . . . **65** E1
Hatford SN7 . . . . **174** D2
Church View
Ascott-u-W OX7 . . . . **71** C2
Bampton OX18 . . . . **134** E3
Banbury OX16 . . . . **16** B4
Berrick NN13 . . . . **24** A7
Carterton OX18 . . . . **115** E2
Charlton-on-O OX5 . . . . . . **95** A5
Church View Cotts SN7. . **192** C2
Church View Rd
Freeland OX29 . . . . **106** A6
Grove OX12 . . . . **196** E1
Highworth SN6 . . . . **190** A6
Church View Rd OX28 . . **117** F7
Church Way OX4 . . . . **142** F5

Churchward Cl OX12 . . . . **196** D2
Churchward OX11. . . . . . . **200** E4
Church Way
Oxford,Dean Court OX2. . . **122** D1
Oxford,Iffley OX4. . . . . **141** F4
Sparsholt OX12 . . . . **212** E4
Churchway RG20. . . . . . . **235** B1
Church Wlk
Ambrosden OX25. . . . . **81** C3
Banbury OX16 . . . . **16** C5
Bishopstone SN6 . . . . **227** C4
Combe OX29 . . . . **90** A4
Faringdon SN7 . . . . **173** A4
Oxford OX2 . . . . **123** B4
Shipton-u-W OX7. . . . . **70** D1
Shrivenham SN6 . . . . **209** C7
Upper Heyford OX25 . . . . . . **62** F8
Chure The OX5 . . . . **95** A4
Churnet Cl OX14 . . . . **201** B2
Cinnaminta Rd OX3 . . . . **142** E8
Cinnamon Cl OX44 . . . . . **184** C7
Circourt Rd OX12 . . . . **195** F3
Circular Rd OX25,OX26. . . **80** E5
Circus St OX4 . . . . **141** E8
City Rd HP14 . . . . **189** D6
Clack's La OX10 . . . . **222** C8
Clairmore Gdns RG31 . . . **257** C5
Clanfield CE Prim Sch
OX18 . . . . **152** F8
Clanfield Cres RG31. . . . . **257** C2
Clanfield Rd OX18 . . . . . . **133** E2
Clapcot Way OX10 . . . . . . **221** C8
Clapton Rd OX15 . . . . **16** C8
Clarence Pl OX11 . . . . **218** E7
Clarence Rd RG9 . . . . **244** D2
Clarendon Cl OX14. . . . . . **180** B8
Clarendon Dr OX9 . . . . . . **130** A1
Clare Terr OX18 . . . . **115** D1
Clarke's Ct OX16. . . . . **16** C6
Clarks La CV36 . . . . **28** A5
Clark's Row OX1 . . . . **261** B1
Clarkston Rd OX18 . . . . . . **115** D1
Clay Bank OX15. . . . . **30** A7
Clay Cl RG31 . . . . **257** B1
Claydon Ct RG4 . . . . **259** A2
Claydon Rd OX17 . . . . **4** F4
Clayfields SN6 . . . . **209** A3
Clay Hill Cl OX7 . . . . **58** E6
Clay La OX10 . . . . **204** C2
Claymond Rd OX3 . . . . . . **124** F4
Claypit La SN7 . . . . **211** A7
Claypits La SN6. . . . . **209** C7
Clays Cl OX3 . . . . **124** A5
Clays Orch OX14 . . . . **134** E3
Cleavers OX39. . . . . **168** B6
Cleavers Sq OX4 . . . . **142** E1
Cleave The OX11. . . . . **217** E7
Cleeve Ct RG8 . . . . **249** B7
Cleeve Park Cotts RG8 . . **249** D8
Cleeve Rd RG8 . . . . **249** B7
Cleeves Ave OX7. . . . . **42** F4
Cleeves Cnr OX7. . . . . **42** E5
Clematis Pl OX4 . . . . **142** F2
Clements Cl OX12. . . . . . . **214** F6
Clements Green OX11. . . . **219** F5
Clements La OX27 . . . . **67** F2
Clements Rd RG31 . . . . . . **257** B1
Clements Rd RG9 . . . . **244** C3
Clerkenwell Cotts HP17 . . **130** F5
Clevedon Ct OX5. . . . . **108** F8
Clevedon Rd RG31 . . . . . . **257** B3
Cleveland Cl OX5 . . . . **109** A7
Cleveland Dr OX4 . . . . **142** C5
Clevelands OX14. . . . . **160** A1
Cleveley Rd OX7 . . . . **58** F5
Clevemede RG8. . . . . **249** C7
Cleycourt Rd SN6. . . . . . . **209** A6
Clifden Rd HP18 . . . . **127** E5
Clifford Pl OX2 . . . . **122** D8
Clifton Dr OX14 . . . . **179** F8
Clifton Hampden CE Prim
Sch OX14 . . . . **181** D4
Clifton Park Rd RG4 . . . . **259** A3
Clifton Rd OX15 . . . . **24** E8
Clifton Rise RG10 . . . . **255** E1
Clinton Cl OX4. . . . . **141** F3
Clive Rd OX4 . . . . **142** D5
Clock Ho The OX18. . . . . . **115** E2
Clock Tower Ct SN7. . . . . . **172** E2
Cloisters The
Wantage OX12. . . . . **214** D5
Oxford OX1 . . . . **141** C7
Ewelme OX10 . . . . **204** F3
Reading RG4 . . . . **259** A3
Clonmel Cl RG4. . . . . **259** D2
Closes The OX5 . . . . **92** E1
Close The
Ardington OX12. . . . . **215** E5
Aston Tirrold OX11 . . . . . . **237** F8
Benson OX10. . . . . **203** F5
Chipping Warden OX17 . . . . **5** F7
Great Bourton OX17 . . . . . . **9** D7
Henley-on-T RG9 . . . . **254** D8
Lechlade-on-T GL7. . . . . . **150** C5
Salford OX7 . . . . **42** A5
Stanton Harcourt OX29 . . . **138** A8
Stoke Lyne OX27 . . . . **51** B5
Woodcote RG8. . . . . **250** F8
Clover Cl OX2 . . . . **140** B6
Clover Pl
Eynsham OX29. . . . . **120** C7
Oxford OX4 . . . . **142** F2
Coach House Ct RG8. . . . **256** E5
Coach House Mews ●
RG4 . . . . **259** C2
Coach La SN7 . . . . **173** A4
Coach Way OX10. . . . . . . **203** F4
Coalport Way RG30. . . . . **257** E1

Coates La RG9. . . . . **206** C2
Cobden Cres OX1 . . . . **141** C7
Cobden Ctr The OX11 . . . **200** E4
Cochrane Rd OX10. . . . . . **204** D1
Cockcroft Rd OX11. . . . . . **218** E7
Cockington Gn OX16. . . . . **16** E7
Cockpit Cl OX20 . . . . **91** B6
Cockshoot Cl OX29 . . . . . . **89** C7
Cocks La OX33. . . . . **125** D7
Cockwell La SN7. . . . . . . **192** D6
Cogges Hill Rd OX28. . . . **118** C7
Cogges Manor Farm Mus★
OX28 . . . . **118** C8
Coghill OX5 . . . . **93** A8
Coker Cl OX26. . . . . **65** E3
Cokethorpe Sch OX29. . . **118** E1
Colborne Rd OX11 . . . . . . **218** B8
Coldharbour Cl RG9 . . . . **254** C8
Coldharbour Rd OX12. . . **234** A7
Coldicutt St RG4. . . . . **259** C1
Cole Cl OX11 . . . . **200** F3
Colegrave Rd OX15 . . . . . . **21** E5
Colegrove Down OX2 . . . . **140** A6
Colemans Hill OX3. . . . . . **124** E3
Coleridge Cl
● Bicester OX26 . . . . **65** C4
Oxford OX4 . . . . **142** D5
Coleridge Dr OX14. . . . . . **179** D5
Colerne Rd OX18 . . . . **115** C3
Colesbourne Rd OX15. . . **21** D3
Coleshill Dr SN7. . . . . **172** E2
Cole's La OX44 . . . . **184** C7
Colcutt Cl OX33 . . . . **143** C7
College Cl
Cholsey OX10 . . . . **220** F1
Holton OX33 . . . . **126** C1
College Cotts OX25 . . . . . . **95** C8
College Farm
Benson OX10. . . . . **203** F4
College Farm OX7 . . . . **57** B1
College Farm Cotts
OX13 . . . . **177** D4
College Farm La SN6 . . . **228** A6
College Fields OX17 . . . . . . **35** C7
College Flats OX4. . . . . . . **142** B2
College La
Long Compton CV36 . . . . . **28** A4
Oxford OX4 . . . . **142** B2
College Sq OX33. . . . . **156** B3
College The
Marsh Gibbon OX27. . . . . . **67** F3
Swinbrook OX18 . . . . **101** F3
College Way OX33 . . . . . . **143** B6
Collets Cotts OX44 . . . . . . **145** C2
Collett OX11. . . . . **200** E4
Collett Way OX12 . . . . **196** D1
Colley Wood OX1 . . . . **141** D2
Collice St OX5. . . . . **109** F8
Collier's La SN7 . . . . **173** A4
Colliers La RG9. . . . . **252** F8
Collingwood Cl OX14 . . . **159** F1
Collingwood Rd OX11 . . . **218** D8
Collinsmith Dr OX12 . . . . **196** C1
Collinsons Row OX7 . . . . . **73** B3
Collins St OX4 . . . . **141** F8
Collinwood Cl OX3 . . . . . . **124** F5
Collinwood Rd OX3 . . . . . **124** F3
Collyer Rd HP14 . . . . **188** E4
Colmore La RG9 . . . . **252** E8
Colne Cl
Bicester OX26 . . . . **65** D1
Grove OX12 . . . . **196** D1
Colne Dr
Berinsfield OX10 . . . . **182** D6
Didcot OX14. . . . . **201** A3
Coln Rd OX11. . . . . **217** B3
Colonnade The RG31. . . . **257** C2
Colony The OX15. . . . . **18** F7
Colterne Cl OX3 . . . . **124** A5
Coltman Ave HP18 . . . . . . **129** C6
Colton Rd SN6. . . . . **209** B6
Colstock Leyes OX26 . . . . . **65** D4
Coltsfoot Sq OX4 . . . . **142** F1
Columbia Way OX12 . . . . **214** B8
Columbine Gdns OX4 . . . **143** A1
Colvile Cl OX18 . . . . **134** F4
Colville Wlk OX16. . . . . **16** E7
Colwell Dr
Abingdon OX14 . . . . **179** D7
Oxford OX3 . . . . **125** A4
Witney OX28 . . . . **117** F6
Colwell Rd OX10 . . . . **182** C5
Colyton Way RG4 . . . . **259** D5
Combe CE Prim Sch OX29 **90** A4
Combe Gate OX29 . . . . **90** A4
Combe Rd
Oxford OX2 . . . . **123** A2
Stonesfield OX8 . . . . **89** D7
Combe Sta OX29 . . . . **90** B3
Combewell OX44 . . . . **143** C2
Comfrey Rd OX4. . . . . **142** F3
Common Cl
North Leigh OX29 . . . . **105** B6
Shrivenham SN6 . . . . **209** C7
Common La OX7 . . . . **42** C2
Common Rd
Beckley OX3 . . . . **110** F2
North Leigh OX29 . . . . **105** B8
Common The HP14. . . . . . **188** E5
Compass Cl ● OX4 . . . . . **142** C4
Complins Cl OX2 . . . . **123** A6
Compton Ct OX5. . . . . **27** F7
Compton District Prim Sch
The CV36 . . . . **27** F6
Compton Dr OX14 . . . . . . **160** B2
Compton Terr ● OX10 . . **221** C2

Compton Way OX28 . . . . . . 104 C1
Condor Cl RG31 . . . . 257 C3
Conduit Hill Rise OX10 . . . . 147 E7
Conduit House* OX2 . . . . . 140 F7
Conduit Rd OX14 . . . . 179 C7
Conifer Cl OX2 . . . . 140 C8
Conifer Dr
  Bicester OX26 . . . . 65 E5
  Reading RG31 . . . . 257 B2
Conifer Rise OX16 . . . . 9 B1
Conigre OX39 . . . . 168 B6
Conisboro Ave RG4 . . . . . . 258 E5
Conisboro Way RG4 . . . . . 258 E5
Coniston Ave OX3 . . . . 124 A4
Coniston Dr RG30 . . . . . . 257 F2
Connaught Ho RG9 . . . . . . 244 E3
Connolly Dr OX14 . . . . 115 D4
Constable's Croft OX25 . . . 96 E7
Constitution Hill OX10 . . . 221 E4
Convent The OX7 . . . . 68 D6
Conway Dr OX11 . . . . 201 A5
Conway Rd OX13 . . . . 159 D2
Conyger Cl OX5 . . . . 93 E1
Conygree Terr OX7 . . . . 42 F3
Cook La OX10 . . . . 221 E1
Cook Row OX7 . . . . 71 C2
Cook's Hill OX15 . . . . 14 B5
Cooks La OX7 . . . . 41 F5
Coolidge Cl OX3 . . . . 124 D1
Coombe Cotts RG8 . . . . . 248 F6
Coombe Hill Cres OX9 . . . 147 E8
Coombe Rd RG20 . . . . . . 247 A3
Coombes Cl OX7 . . . . 85 D8
Coombe The RG8 . . . . . . 248 F6
Cooper Cl OX7 . . . . 42 F3
Cooper Pl OX3 . . . . 124 F3
Cooper Rd RG9 . . . . 244 D3
Cooper Sch The OX26 . . . . 65 F4
Cooper's Court Rd HP14 188 D5
Coopers Gate OX16 . . . . . 16 C7
Coopers Cl OX26 . . . . 65 F5
Coopers La
  Abingdon OX14 . . . . . . 179 E6
  Wantage OX12 . . . . . . 214 F5
Coopers Piece OX10 . . . . 221 C8
Copcot Pl OX33 . . . . 125 D7
Cope Cl OX2 . . . . 140 D8
Copenhagen Dr OX14 . . . 159 D1
Cope Rd OX16 . . . . 16 C6
Copperage Rd
  Chilton OX12 . . . . 234 A2
  West Ilsley OX12 . . . . . 233 F1
Copperfield Cl OX12 . . . . 214 D6
Copperfields RG4 . . . . . . 258 F3
Coppice Cl OX16 . . . . 16 E4
Coppice The HP14 . . . . . . 188 E5
Coppock Cl OX3 . . . . 124 E2
Copse Ave RG4 . . . . 259 E3
Copse Cl RG31 . . . . 257 D3
Copse La OX3 . . . . 124 A2
Copse Mead RG5 . . . . . . 260 F1
Copse The
  Abingdon OX14 . . . . . . 160 C1
  Wargrave RG10 . . . . . . 255 E3
Copson La OX44 . . . . 163 C2
Copthorne Rd OX5 . . . . . 108 E7
Corbett Rd OX18 . . . . . . 115 C1
Cordrey Gn OX4 . . . . 141 F4
Corfe Mews RG4 . . . . . . 259 E4
Coriander Way ⑨ OX4 142 F1
Corn Avill Cl OX14 . . . . . 160 C2
Corn Bar OX28 . . . . 117 F8
Corncrake Way OX26 . . . . 66 A1
Corndell Gdns OX28 . . . . 118 A8
Corneville Rd OX14 . . . . . 179 B2
Cornfield Cl OX28 . . . . . . 117 E7
Cornhill La OX12 . . . . . . 213 E5
Cornish Rd OX7 . . . . 42 D1
Cornmarket ① SN7 . . . . . 172 F4
Cornmarket St OX1 . . . . . 261 B2
Cornmarket OX9 . . . . . . 147 F8
Corn St OX28 . . . . 118 A8
Cornwall Cl RG31 . . . . . . 257 B4
Cornwallis Cl OX4 . . . . . . 142 A5
Cornwallis Rd OX4 . . . . . 142 A5
Cornwell OX7 . . . . 41 C3
Coromandel OX14 . . . . . 179 D4
Coronation Cotts OX18 . 152 E8
Coronation La OX17 . . . . . 8 D7
Corpus Christi Coll OX1 261 C2
Corunna Cres OX4 . . . . . 142 E6
Cosford Gdns OX26 . . . . . 66 A4
Cosin Cl OX4 . . . . 142 A8
Costar Cl OX44 . . . . 142 D3
Cote Rd OX18 . . . . 135 F3
Cothill House Sch OX13 . 158 F4
Cothill Rd OX13 . . . . 158 F4
Cotman Cl OX14 . . . . 179 E5
Cotmore Cl OX9 . . . . 148 B7
Cotmore Field OX9 . . . . . 148 B7
Cotmore Gdns OX9 . . . . . 148 B7
Cot's Gn OX5 . . . . 92 D1
Cotshill Gdns OX7 . . . . . . 42 F3
Cotswold Cl
  Minster Lovell OX29 . . . 102 E2
  Sibford Ferris OX15 . . . . 19 B7
Cotswold Cnr OX7 . . . . . . 29 A3
Cotswold Crescent Bglws
  OX7 . . . . 42 E1
Cotswold Cres
  Chipping Norton OX7 . . . 42 E1
  Marston OX3 . . . . 123 F5
Cotswold Dene OX29 . . . 137 A5
Cotswold Mdw OX28 . . . 117 D7
Cotswold Pk OX11 . . . . . 200 C2
Cotswold Rd OX7 . . . . . . 140 B6

Cotswolds View Camping
  and Cvn Site OX7 . . . . . 73 C6
Cotswold Terr OX7 . . . . . . 42 E1
Cotswold View OX7 . . . . . 73 B4
Cotswold Way
  Carterton OX18 . . . . . . 115 D4
  Reading RG31 . . . . . . 257 C2
Cotswold Wildlife Park &
  Gardens* OX18 . . . . . 114 C5
Cotswold Woollen Weavers
  Mus* GL7 . . . . 132 B5
Cottage Rd SN7 . . . . 194 D8
Cottages The
  Burford OX18 . . . . 114 A5
  Long Crendon HP18 . . . 129 C6
Cottesmore La OX10 . . . . 204 D5
Cottesmore Rd OX4 . . . . 142 A3
Cotton Grass Cl OX4 . . . . 142 E1
Couching St OX49 . . . . . . 186 B1
Coulings Cl OX12 . . . . . . 216 D7
Council Cotts RG4 . . . . . 252 B5
Council Hos
  Binfield Heath RG9 . . . . 254 B2
  Bloxham OX15 . . . . 21 D3
  Great Tew OX7 . . . . 45 C7
  Spelsbury OX7 . . . . 72 F8
Council Hos The
  Barford St M OX15 . . . . . 32 F5
  Charlbury OX7 . . . . 73 B3
  Hanwell OX17 . . . . 8 E2
  Nettlebed RG9 . . . . . . 224 E2
Council Houses The OX17 10 F8
County Rd NN13 . . . . 24 A6
County Trad Est OX4 . . . . 142 F4
County View OX15 . . . . . . 34 D4
Coupland Rd OX13 . . . . . 159 A6
Court Cl OX5 . . . . 108 D8
Court Close Rd OX4 . . . . 148 E7
Court Cl
  Shipton-u-W OX7 . . . . . 85 D7
  Warmington OX17 . . . . . 3 A4
Court Dr OX10 . . . . 203 B5
Courtenay Cl OX14 . . . . . 200 A7
Courtenay Dr RG4 . . . . . 259 B7
Courtenay Rd OX12 . . . . 214 E5
Court Farm Barns OX5 . . . 77 B6
Court Farm Rd OX4 . . . . . 141 F3
Courtfield Rd OX33 . . . . . 125 D7
Court Gdns RG8 . . . . . . 249 C7
Court Hill Rd
  Letcombe Bassett OX14 . 232 C7
  Letcombe Regis OX12 . . 214 A1
Courthouse* HP18 . . . . . 129 E7
Courtiers Gn OX14 . . . . . 181 D4
Courtington La OX15 . . . . 21 D5
Courtland Rd OX4 . . . . . . 142 A4
Courtlands Rd OX7 . . . . . . 85 D8
Court Place Gdns OX4 . . . 141 F3
Court Rd RG12 . . . . 214 A2
Courts Gdns OX28 . . . . . 118 D8
Court The OX14 . . . . 179 F6
Courtyard The
  Banbury OX17 . . . . 17 D5
  Crawley OX29 . . . . 103 D5
  Tadmarton OX15 . . . . . . 21 A6
Covent Cl OX14 . . . . 160 B3
Coverley Rd OX3 . . . . . . 142 D7
Covert The OX20 . . . . 91 C5
Cowdery Pl SN7 . . . . 194 E7
Cow La
  Denchworth OX12,SN7 . . 195 E4
  Didcot OX14 . . . . 200 F2
  Grove OX12 . . . . 196 A1
  Harwell OX11 . . . . 217 F8
  Kennington OX1 . . . . . . 141 E1
  Longworth OX13 . . . . . 156 C3
  Moulsford OX10 . . . . . . 238 F3
  Reading RG1 . . . . 258 E1
  Steeple Aston OX25 . . . . 62 B8
  Sutton Courtenay OX11 . 199 F2
Cowleaze OX39 . . . . 168 B6
Cowleaze Cl SN6 . . . . . . 209 D5
Cowleaze Cnr OX15 . . . . 134 C2
Cowley Junc OX4 . . . . . . 142 E4
Cowley Pl OX4 . . . . 141 E8
Cowley Rd
  Oxford,Littlemore OX4 . . 142 B2
  Oxford OX4 . . . . 142 A7
Cowper Cl ② OX26 . . . . . 65 C4
Coxfield Cl HP14 . . . . . . 188 F5
Cox La OX7 . . . . 42 B2
Coxmoor Cl OX7 . . . . 54 F4
Cox's Alley OX3 . . . . 124 F4
Cox's Ground OX2 . . . . . 123 A5
Cox's La
  Crowmarsh Gifford
    OX10 . . . . 222 A6
  Enstone OX7 . . . . 58 F4
  Stoke Row RG9 . . . . . . 242 A5
Cox's Rd SN6 . . . . 209 B6
Cromer Rd RG31 . . . . . . 257 C1
Coxwell Gdns SN7 . . . . . 172 E3
Coxwell Hall Mews SN7 172 E1
Coxwell Lodge Dr SN7 . . 172 E1
Coxwell Rd SN7 . . . . 172 F2
Coxwell St SN7 . . . . 172 F3
Cozens La OX7 . . . . 54 F4
Crabtree Cnr OX10 . . . . . 240 D7
Crabtree La OX14 . . . . . . 179 B2
Crabtree Pl OX14 . . . . . . 160 B2
Crabtree Rd
  Haddenham HP17 . . . . . 130 F5
  Oxford OX2 . . . . 140 D8
Crafts End OX11 . . . . 235 E8
Cranberry Rd OX28 . . . . . 117 C7
Cranbourne Gdns RG30 258 A2
Cranbrook Ct OX18 . . . . . 118 A6

Cranbrook Dr OX1 . . . . . 160 E7
Crane Furlong SN6 . . . . . 190 A7
Cranesbill Dr OX26 . . . . . . 65 D5
Cranesbill Way ⑧ OX4 . . 142 E1
Cranford House Sch
  RG10 . . . . 238 F5
Cranham St OX2 . . . . . . 261 A4
Cranham Terr OX2 . . . . . 261 A4
Cranleigh Cl OX16 . . . . . . 16 A4
Cranley Rd OX3 . . . . 124 F4
Cranmer Cl RG31 . . . . . . 257 B3
Cranmer Rd OX4 . . . . . . 142 E6
Cranston Cl ① OX4 . . . . . 142 B3
Cranwell Ave OX18 . . . . . 115 E3
Craster Ct OX16 . . . . 16 D3
Cratlands Cl OX44 . . . . . 163 C2
Craufurd Rd OX4 . . . . . . 142 E6
Craven Comm SN7 . . . . . 211 D7
Craven Way OX11 . . . . . . 218 E7
Crawborough Rd OX7 . . . . 73 C4
Crawborough Terr OX7 . . . 73 C4
Crawley Villas OX7 . . . . . . 73 C4
Crawley Mill Ind Est
  OX29 . . . . 103 D4
Crawley Rd OX28 . . . . . . 104 A2
Crawshay Dr RG4 . . . . . . 259 B7
Cray Ct OX11 . . . . 200 F4
Craysleaze RG4 . . . . 252 D3
Crazies Hill CE Prim Sch
  RG10 . . . . 255 F6
CR Bates Ind Est HP14 . . 188 E5
Creampot Cl OX17 . . . . . . 5 A2
Creampot Cres OX17 . . . . 4 F2
Creampot La OX17 . . . . . 4 F2
Crecy Wlk OX20 . . . . 91 C5
Cremyll Rd RG1 . . . . 258 F1
Crendon Ct ③ RG4 . . . . . 259 A2
Crescent Cl OX4 . . . . . . 142 D6
Crescent Ct OX4 . . . . . . 142 D6
Crescent Rd
  Oxford OX4 . . . . 142 D6
  Reading RG1 . . . . 257 D1
Crescent The
  Adderbury OX17 . . . . . . 23 A5
  Bicester OX26 . . . . 65 D3
  Carterton OX18 . . . . . . 133 C8
  East Hagbourne OX11 . . 218 F6
  Long Wittenham OX14 . . 201 D8
  Lower Shiplake RG9 . . . 255 B4
  Oxford OX2 . . . . 123 A3
  Sandford-on-T OX4 . . . . 161 C8
  Steeple Aston OX25 . . . . 62 B7
  Witney OX29 . . . . 104 C2
Crescent Way OX10 . . . . 220 F1
Cress Hill Pl OX3 . . . . . . 124 F4
Crest The
  Bledlow Ridge HP14 . . . 189 F8
  Reading RG4 . . . . 259 C5
Cricket Ground HP14 . . . 188 D5
Cricket Rd OX4 . . . . 142 B6
Cricklade Rd SN6 . . . . . . 190 A5
Crick Rd OX2 . . . . 123 C4
Cripley Pl OX2 . . . . 123 A1
Cripley Rd OX2 . . . . 123 A1
Crispin Cl RG4 . . . . 258 D5
Crispin Pl OX10 . . . . 221 C7
Crisp Rd RG9 . . . . 244 C3
Croasdell Cl OX14 . . . . . 179 E4
Crocker End RG9 . . . . . . 224 F2
Crockwell Cl OX26 . . . . . . 65 E2
Crockwell St CV36 . . . . . . 27 F7
Croft Ave OX5 . . . . 108 F8
Croft Cl
  Marston OX3 . . . . 123 F4
  Thame OX9 . . . . 95 D8
  Thame OX9 . . . . 148 A7
Croft Cotts OX15 . . . . . . 181 E5
Croft Ct OX9 . . . . 148 A7
Croft End OX12 . . . . 214 A2
Croft La
  Adderbury OX17 . . . . . . 23 A4
  Brighthampton OX29 . . . 137 B2
Croft Rd
  Goring RG8 . . . . 249 C5
  Marston OX3 . . . . 123 F4
  Thame OX9 . . . . 148 A7
  Wallingford OX10 . . . . . 221 C7
Croft's La OX15 . . . . 30 A6
Crofts The OX28 . . . . 118 A7
Croft Terr ⑯ OX10 . . . . . 221 D7
Croft The
  Aston Tirrold OX11 . . . . 219 F1
  Didcot OX11 . . . . 218 F8
  East Hagbourne OX11 . . 218 F5
  Haddenham HP17 . . . . . 130 F5
  Harwell OX11 . . . . 217 E8
  Nuneham Courtenay OX44 162 A4
  Oxford OX3 . . . . 124 C3
  West Hanney OX12 . . . . 196 F6
Croft Villas ② OX10 . . . . 221 C7
Croft Way RG8 . . . . 250 F8
Cromer Rd RG31 . . . . . . 257 C1
Cromwell Ave OX16 . . . . 130 A1
Cromwell Cl
  Chalgrove OX44 . . . . . 184 C6
  Faringdon SN7 . . . . . . 173 A3
  Henley-on-T RG9 . . . . . 254 E8
  Marston OX3 . . . . 123 F5
Cromwell Cl OX16 . . . . . . 16 B7
Cromwell Dr OX11 . . . . . 219 A7
Cromwell Pk OX7 . . . . . . 42 F4
Cromwell Rd
  Banbury OX16 . . . . 16 A6
  Henley-on-T RG9 . . . . . 254 E8
  Reading RG4 . . . . 259 B2
Cromwell St OX1 . . . . . . 261 B1
Cromwell Way OX5 . . . . . 109 A7

Cronshaw Cl OX11 . . . . . 200 E2
Crookdale Beck OX14 . . . 201 A3
Crook's Terr OX12. . . . . . 214 D5
Croom Cotts OX11 . . . . . 217 A7
Cropredy CE Prim Sch
  OX17 . . . . 4 F1
Cross Ave OX10 . . . . 204 D2
Cross Cl OX10 . . . . 204 E2
Cross Hill Rd OX17 . . . . . . 22 F4
Cross Keys Rd RG8 . . . . 239 C4
Crosslands Dr OX14 . . . . 159 E1
Crosslands OX17 . . . . 52 D6
Cross Leys OX7 . . . . 42 E2
Cross Rd OX10 . . . . 220 F2
Cross's La OX7 . . . . 56 E1
Cross St OX4 . . . . 141 F8
Cross The OX29 . . . . 89 C7
Cross Tree La GL7 . . . . . . 132 B5
Crossville Cres OX11 . . . 200 D2
Crossway OX7 . . . . 60 F8
Crossways The OX27 . . . . 50 C4
Crotch Cres OX3 . . . . . . 124 A4
Crouch Hill Rd OX16 . . . . 16 A6
Crouch St OX16 . . . . 16 C5
Croughton All Saints' CE
  Prim Sch NN13 . . . . . . 36 D8
Croughton Elementary Sch
  NN13 . . . . 36 F7
Croughton Rd OX17 . . . . . 35 D7
Crowberry Rd OX4 . . . . . 142 F2
Crowell Rd
  Chinnor OX39 . . . . 168 B5
  Oxford OX4 . . . . 142 C4
Crow La
  Great Bourton OX17 . . . . 9 D7
  Wootton OX20 . . . . 75 C7
Crowmarsh Gifford CE Sch
  OX10 . . . . 222 B6
Crowmarsh Hill OX10 . . . 222 B6
Crowmarsh Rd OX27 . . . . 64 F6
Crown La
  Benson OX10 . . . . 203 F4
  Dorchester OX10 . . . . . 182 D1
  South Moreton OX11 . . . 220 A5
Crown Mdw OX12 . . . . . 197 C2
Crown Mews ⑧ OX14 . . 179 E7
Crown Rd
  Kidlington OX5 . . . . . . 108 D8
  Wheatley OX33 . . . . . . 144 B8
Crown Sq
  Benson OX10 . . . . 204 A4
  Wheatley OX33 . . . . . . 144 B8
Crown St OX4 . . . . 141 F8
Crown Wlk OX26 . . . . 65 E4
Crowsley Rd RG9 . . . . . . 255 A3
Crowsley Way RG4 . . . . . 252 B5
Croxford Gdns OX16 . . . . 108 E6
Crozier Cl OX2 . . . . 140 D8
Crumps Butts OX26 . . . . . 65 F4
Crutch Furlong OX10 . . . 182 C6
Cuckamus La OX29 . . . . 105 B6
Cuckoo Cl OX27 . . . . 65 F6
Cuckoo La OX29 . . . . . . 106 A3
Cuddesdon Cl RG8 . . . . . 250 F8
Cuddesdon Rd OX33 . . . 143 E5
Cuddesdon Way OX4 . . . 142 F2
Cues La SN6 . . . . 227 C4
Culham Cl OX14 . . . . . . 160 A1
Culham No 1 Site OX14 . 181 A3
Culham Parochial CE Sch
  OX14 . . . . 180 B3
Culham Sta OX14 . . . . . 180 F3
Cullen Cl OX11 . . . . 218 E8
Cullerne Rd OX4 . . . . . . 142 E4
Cullerns The SN6 . . . . . . 190 A6
Cullum Ho OX33 . . . . . . 144 C8
Cullum Rd OX33 . . . . . . 144 C7
Culworth Rd OX17 . . . . . . 5 E6
Cumberford Cl OX15 . . . . 21 D3
Cumberford Hill OX15 . . . 21 D4
Cumberland Rd OX4 . . . . 142 B7
Cumberlege Cl OX3 . . . . 123 F7
Cummings Cl OX3 . . . . . 124 E2
Cumnor CE Prim Sch
  OX2 . . . . 139 E5
Cumnor Hill OX2. . . . . . . 140 B7
Cumnor Rd
  Cumnor OX2 . . . . 139 C8
  Wootton,Boars Hill OX1 . 159 A8
Cumnor Rise Rd OX2 . . . 140 C6
Cunliffe Cl OX2 . . . . 123 C6
Cup & Saucer OX17 . . . . . 4 F2
Curbridge Rd
  Ducklington OX29 . . . . 118 A4
  Witney OX28 . . . . 117 E7
Curie Ave OX11 . . . . 217 A3
Cursus The GL7 . . . . 150 C5
Curson Ave OX14 . . . . . . 180 B7
Curtis Rd
  Kidlington OX5 . . . . 92 E1
  Shrivenham SN6 . . . . . 209 A6
Curtiss Cl OX26 . . . . 66 A5
Curtyn Cl OX14 . . . . 179 D8
Curzon Gate Ct HP14 . . . 188 E5
Cuthwine Pl ⑤ OX12 . . . 150 C5
Cutteslowe Prim Sch
  OX2 . . . . 109 C1
Cuttle Brook Gdns OX9 . . 129 E1
Cutham Rd OX49 . . . . . . 186 A2
Cwmcarn RG4 . . . . 258 F6
Cygnet Cl OX9 . . . . 166 B8
Cygnet Ct OX14 . . . . 179 E6
Cypress Gdns OX26 . . . . . 65 F5
Cyprus Terr OX2 . . . . . . 122 F8

D

Dacey Dr OX25 . . . . 63 B8
Dacre Ave RG4 . . . . 259 E6
Daedings The OX15 . . . . . 33 E4
Dagdale Dr OX11 . . . . . . 200 F3
Daimler Ave OX14 . . . . . 115 A5
Dairyground The OX15 . . . 14 A5
Dairy Mdw OX13 . . . . . . 177 C5
Daisy Bank OX14 . . . . . . 180 B8
Daisy Hill OX25 . . . . 47 D5
Dale Cl
  Brackley NN13 . . . . 24 A7
  Oxford OX1 . . . . 261 A1
Dale Pl OX5 . . . . 92 E1
Dale The OX3 . . . . 125 A4
Dale Wlk OX29 . . . . 118 A5
Dalton Ave OX11 . . . . . . 217 A2
Damer Gdns RG9 . . . . . . 254 E8
Damson Trees SN6 . . . . . 209 A6
Dancers Hill OX7 . . . . 73 C3
Danesmoor OX16 . . . . . . 16 B8
Danes Rd OX26 . . . . 65 C2
Danvers Cl OX15 . . . . 15 C2
Danvers Rd
  Broughton OX15 . . . . . . 15 C2
  Oxford OX4 . . . . 142 A3
Darcey Lode OX14 . . . . . 201 B2
Darell Rd RG4 . . . . 258 F3
Darent Pl OX14 . . . . 201 A2
Dark La
  Great Coxwell SN7 . . . . 192 C6
  Reading RG31 . . . . . . 257 B2
  Sunningwell OX13 . . . . 159 E5
  Wargrave RG10 . . . . . . 255 D2
  Witney OX28 . . . . 104 A1
  Wroxton OX15 . . . . 15 A8
Darnell Wlk OX26 . . . . . . 65 F5
Darrell Way OX14 . . . . . . 159 F1
Dart Dr OX11 . . . . 200 E3
Dart Rd OX13 . . . . 159 B5
Dashwood Ave OX5 . . . . 108 B5
Dashwood Ct OX49 . . . . 186 B1
Dashwood Mews OX5 . . . . 77 F4
Dashwood Prim Sch
  OX16 . . . . 16 D5
Dashwood Rd
  Banbury OX16 . . . . 16 F7
  Oxford OX16 . . . . 142 A3
Dashwood Rise OX25 . . . . 47 D6
Dashwood Terr ① OX16 . 16 F7
Datchet Gn OX10 . . . . . . 202 F2
Daubeny Rd OX4 . . . . . . 141 F6
Daubigny Mead OX18 . . . 116 C4
Davenant Cl OX2 . . . . . . 109 A1
Davenant Rd OX2 . . . . . 123 A5
Davenport Pl OX49 . . . . . 186 B1
Davenport Rd OX28 . . . . 103 F1
Daventry Rd
  Banbury OX16 . . . . 16 F7
  Banbury OX16 . . . . 9 F1
David Nicholls Cl OX4 . . . 142 B2
David Walter Cl OX2 . . . . 109 B1
Davis Cl OX18 . . . . 115 C2
Davis Gdns OX27 . . . . 65 F7
Dawls Cl OX7 . . . . 71 B1
Dawson St ① OX4 . . . . . 141 E8
Days Ground SN6 . . . . . . 209 C7
Day's La OX10 . . . . 221 B8
Deaconfield RG8 . . . . . . 239 C3
Deacon Way
  Banbury OX16 . . . . 16 B5
  Reading RG30 . . . . . . 258 A2
Deadman's La RG8 . . . . . 251 C4
Dean Cl OX16 . . . . 16 E8
Dean Court Rd OX2 . . . . 140 B7
Deanes Cl OX13 . . . . 198 F4
Deanfield Ave RG9 . . . . . 244 D1
Deanfield Rd
  Henley-on-T RG9 . . . . . 244 D1
  Oxford OX2 . . . . 122 B1
Deans Ct OX26 . . . . 65 F1
Dean Wood Cl RG8 . . . . . 240 E1
Deanery Ct OX14 . . . . . . 159 E2
Deaufort Cl OX5 . . . . . . 108 F8
Deddington Castle
  Earthworks* OX15 . . . . . 34 A4
Deddington CE Prim Sch
  OX15 . . . . 33 F4
Deddington Hill OX15 . . . . 33 F6
Deene Cl OX17 . . . . 23 B4
Deer Park Rd OX18 . . . . 117 D7
Deers Cl OX15 . . . . 22 E8
Deers Farm OX15 . . . . . . 22 E7
Deer's La RG8 . . . . 241 C2
Deer Wlk OX4 . . . . 142 F1
Defiant Cl OX26 . . . . 66 A3
De Havilland Rd GL54 . . . . 68 B5
Delamare Way OX2 . . . . 140 B8
Delagre Dr OX16 . . . . 16 F7
Delbush Ave OX3 . . . . . . 125 A4
Dell Rd RG31 . . . . 257 C2
Dell The OX14 . . . . 188 F3
Delly Cl OX29 . . . . 104 A4
Delly Hill OX29 . . . . 104 A4
De Montfort Rd RG1 . . . . 259 A1

Denbeigh Pl RG1 . . . . 258 F1
Denbigh Cl OX16 . . . . 15 F4
Denbigh Rd OX9 . . . . 130 A1
Denby Way RG30 . . . . 257 F1
Denchfield Rd OX16 . . . . . 16 D2
Denchworth Rd
  Grove OX12 . . . . 196 D2
  Wantage OX12 . . . . 214 C6
Denefield Sch RG81 . . . . . . 257 B3
Dene Hollow OX11 . . . . . . 235 E8
Dene Rd OX3 . . . . 142 D8
Dene Rise OX28 . . . . 117 F8
Denman's La OX2 . . . . 139 E5
Denmark St OX4 . . . . 141 F7
Denton Cl
  Abingdon OX14 . . . . 180 B8
  Oxford OX2 . . . . 140 A8
Denton Hill OX44 . . . . 144 B2
Denton La OX44 . . . . 143 F1
Dents Cl OX3 . . . . 124 A5
Derby Rd RG4 . . . . 259 B3
Derwent Ave
  Didcot OX14 . . . . 201 A1
  Oxford OX3 . . . . 124 A4
  Reading RG31 . . . . 257 E2
Derwent Cl OX13 . . . . 159 C2
Derwent Rd OX26 . . . . 65 B3
Desborough Cres OX4 . . . 142 A3
Desmesne Furze OX3 . . . . 124 C1
Des Roches Sq OX28 . . . . 118 B7
Devereux Pl OX4 . . . . 142 A3
Devil's Hill RG9 . . . . 253 D6
De Vitre Pl OX12 . . . . 214 D8
Devon Cl OX10 . . . . 204 D3
Devon Dr RG4 . . . . 259 C4
Devon Pl OX18 . . . . 115 F2
Devonshire Gdns RG31 . . 257 B3
Devon Way OX16 . . . . 16 A8
Dexter Cl OX16 . . . . 16 D4
Diamond Cl OX2 . . . . 123 B6
Diamond Pl OX2 . . . . 123 B6
Dibleys OX11 . . . . 237 A8
Dickens Cl
  Bicester OX26 . . . . 65 C3
  Reading RG4 . . . . 259 D2
Dickenson Ct OX7 . . . . 42 F3
Dickredge The OX25 . . . . . 62 B8
Didcot Girls' Sch OX11 . . 200 D1
Didcot Hospl OX11 . . . . . . 218 C8
Didcot Parkway Sta
  OX11 . . . . 200 F2
Didcot Railway Ctr (Mus)*
  OX11 . . . . 200 E2
Didcot Rd
  Brightwell-cum-S OX10 . . 202 D3
  Didcot OX11 . . . . 218 A8
  Long Wittenham OX14 . . . 201 D8
Dido Rd OX11 . . . . 217 A1
Digberry La RG9 . . . . 224 C5
Digby Cl OX9 . . . . 130 B1
Digging La
  Fyfield OX13 . . . . 157 C1
  Fyfield OX13 . . . . 157 C2
Dillon Ct OX15 . . . . 22 E8
Dirac Pl OX11 . . . . 219 A8
Diston's La OX7 . . . . 42 E3
Ditchend Cotts OX44 . . . . 164 A5
Ditchley Rd OX7 . . . . 73 E5
Dittander Cl OX26 . . . . 65 D4
Divinity Rd OX4 . . . . 142 A8
Dixon's Row OX12 . . . . . . 214 E8
Dobson's La RG9 . . . . 226 C1
Dobson's La RG9 . . . . 244 C8
Dodd Dr GL54 . . . . 68 B4
Dodgson Rd OX4 . . . . 142 C4
Dodson Ct OX14 . . . . 179 F8
Doe Lea OX11 . . . . 200 F3
Dog Cl OX17 . . . . 22 F3
Dog Kennel La SN7 . . . . . . 193 F7
Dog Kennel La OX7 . . . . . . 85 C7
Dog La
  Childrey OX12 . . . . 213 C3
  Rotherfield Peppard RG9 . 253 B8
Doily Cl OX15 . . . . 30 A7
Dollicott HP17 . . . . 130 F6
Dolphin La OX18 . . . . 100 F6
Don Boscoe Cl OX4 . . . . . 142 D6
Don Cl OX14 . . . . 201 A3
Donegal Cl RG4 . . . . 259 C3
Donkin Hill RG4 . . . . 259 C3
Donnington Bridge Rd
  OX4 . . . . 141 F6
Donnington Cl OX28 . . . . . 117 D7
Donnington Lodge OX4 . . 141 F6
Donnington Pl OX12 . . . . . 214 D6
Dora Carr Cl OX3 . . . . 142 B7
Dorcas Rd OX16 . . . . 17 A6
Dorchester Abbey Mus*
  OX10 . . . . 182 D1
Dorchester Cl OX3 . . . . . . 124 F1
Dorchester Cres OX14 . . . 160 A1
Dorchester Ct
  ⬛ Kidlington OX5 . . . . . . 108 F8
  Oxford OX4 . . . . 123 B6
Dorchester Gr OX16 . . . . . 15 F4
Dorchester Pl OX7 . . . . . . 147 F8
Dorchester Rd OX10 . . . . . 182 F4
Dorchester St Birinus CE Sch
  OX10 . . . . 182 D1
Doris Field Cl OX3 . . . . 124 A3
Dormer Rd OX9 . . . . 148 B6
Dormers The SN6 . . . . 190 B6
Dorn Cl OX7 . . . . 60 F8
Dorn View OX20 . . . . 76 A4

Dorothy Hodgkin Rd
  OX1 . . . . 261 C3
Douglas Downes Cl OX3 . 124 E2
Douglas Rd RG4 . . . . 259 D2
Dovecot Cl OX15 . . . . 21 A2
Dovecote Cl
  Haddenham HP17 . . . . . . 130 F6
  Milcombe OX15 . . . . 21 A2
Dovecote OX17 . . . . 130 F6
Dove Ct
  ⬛ Bicester OX26 . . . . 65 E1
  Carterton OX18 . . . . 115 E4
Dovedale Cl RG4 . . . . 258 F3
Dove Gn OX26 . . . . 65 B3
Dovehouse Cl OX29 . . . . . 120 F8
Dove House Cl OX12 . . . . . 122 F8
Dove La RG9 . . . . 252 D8
Doveleat OX39 . . . . 168 D7
Dover Ave OX16 . . . . 15 F6
Dovetrees OX18 . . . . 115 E3
Down End OX15 . . . . 30 B7
Downhill La OX29 . . . . 104 B4
Downlands SN7 . . . . 192 D2
Downs Cl OX11 . . . . 217 E6
Downside OX11 . . . . 217 C1
Downside End OX3 . . . . . . 125 A3
Downside Rd OX3 . . . . 125 A3
Downsmead SN8 . . . . 245 D1
Downs Rd
  Aldworth RG20 . . . . 247 A4
  Curbridge OX29 . . . . 117 B7
  Didcot OX11 . . . . 218 D7
  Standlake OX29 . . . . 137 B6
  Witney OX29 . . . . 103 B1
Downs The OX29 . . . . 137 C5
Downs View
  Aston Tirrold OX11 . . . . . 237 F8
  Highworth SN6 . . . . 190 A6
Downsview Rd OX12 . . . . . 214 B7
Downs Way OX11 . . . . 234 F8
Downsway Prim Sch
  RG31 . . . . 257 C3
Downs Way RG31 . . . . 257 C2
Dow St OX25 . . . . 63 C8
Doyley Rd
  Oxford OX2 . . . . 141 A8
  Wallingford OX10 . . . . . . 203 C1
Dragonhill Rd SN7 . . . . . . 211 B2
Dragon Sch OX2 . . . . 123 C4
Drake Ave OX11 . . . . 218 D8
Drakes Dr HP18 . . . . 129 E5
Drakes Farm HP18 . . . . . . 129 E5
Draycott Rd
  Kingston Bagpuize OX13 . 156 D1
  Longworth OX13 . . . . 156 D1
Draymans Croft ⬛ OX26 . 65 E2
Draymans Wlk ⬛ OX14 . . 179 E6
Dray's La RG9 . . . . 253 A8
Drayton Cty Prim Sch
  OX14 . . . . 179 B2
Drayton East Way OX14 . . 199 D8
Drayton Mill OX14 . . . . . . 199 D7
Drayton Rd
  Abingdon OX14 . . . . 179 D5
  Berinsfield OX10 . . . . 182 E3
  Dorchester OX10 . . . . 182 D2
  Drayton OX14 . . . . 179 D1
  Sutton Courtenay OX14 . . 199 F8
Drayton Sch OX16 . . . . 15 E8
Dresden Way RG30 . . . . . . 257 F1
Drewett Cl OX2 . . . . 122 E8
Drewitts Cnr OX11 . . . . . . 217 E7
Drift Acre OX15 . . . . 20 D7
Drift Ctr OX4 . . . . 142 F6
Drinkwater Cl OX25 . . . . . 97 D7
Drivers La GL56 . . . . 27 A1
Drive The OX7 . . . . 58 A5
Drove Acre Rd OX4 . . . . . . 142 A7
Drovers La RG9 . . . . 226 C8
Droveside OX10 . . . . 220 F1
Drove Way OX12 . . . . 212 B4
Dr Radcliffe's CE Prim Sch
  OX29 . . . . 48 B1
Dr South's CE Prim Sch
  OX5 . . . . 93 E1
Druce Way OX4 . . . . 142 F3
Druids Wlk
  Chinnor OX39 . . . . 168 C6
  Didcot OX11 . . . . 200 E2
Dryden Ave OX26 . . . . 65 B3
Dry La OX29 . . . . 103 D3
Drylands Rd OX29 . . . . 102 E2
Dry Sandford Prim Sch
  OX13 . . . . 158 F6
Drysdale Cl OX14 . . . . 160 E2
Duchess Cl RG8 . . . . 256 D7
Duck End La OX29 . . . . . . 120 C1
Duck La HP18 . . . . 98 C8
Ducklington CE Prim Sch
  OX29 . . . . 118 B3
Ducklington La OX28 . . . . 117 F7
Duck Sq OX39 . . . . 168 C6
Dudgeon Dr OX4 . . . . 142 B2
Dudley Cl RG31 . . . . 257 E1
Dudley Ct OX2 . . . . 123 A7
Dudley Gdns OX4 . . . . 123 F1
Dudley La RG9 . . . . 226 F7
Dudley Mews RG31 . . . . . 257 E1
Duffield Cl OX14 . . . . 160 B2
Duffield Pl OX13 . . . . 178 C7
Duffield Rd RG5 . . . . 260 F1
Duke of York Ave OX4 . . . 199 D3
Dukes Cl OX11 . . . . 128 C2
Dukes Rd OX5 . . . . 108 F8
Duke St
  Banbury OX16 . . . . 16 E6
  Henley-on-T RG9 . . . . . . 244 E2

Duke St continued
  Oxford OX2 . . . . 122 F1
Dulas Cl OX11 . . . . 200 F2
Dumas Cl OX26 . . . . 65 C2
Dumbarton Way RG4 . . . . 259 E5
Dunbar Dr OX9 . . . . 130 A1
Duncan Cl OX29 . . . . 120 D8
Duncan Gdns RG8 . . . . . . 257 C4
Dundas Cl OX14 . . . . 180 B8
Dundas Ct SN7 . . . . 172 E3
Dunkin's Cl OX26 . . . . 65 E2
Dunlin Ct
  ⬛ Bicester OX26 . . . . 65 F1
  Banbury OX16 . . . . 16 E3
Dunluce Gdns RG8 . . . . . . 256 E5
Dunmore Jun & Inf Schs
  OX14 . . . . 159 F1
Dunmore Rd OX14 . . . . . . 159 E2
Dunnock Cl OX26 . . . . 66 A1
Dunnock Way
  Sandford-on-T OX4 . . . . . 142 F1
  Wargrave RG10 . . . . 255 E3
Dunsden Cl OX11 . . . . 200 D1
Dunsomer Hill OX11 . . . . . 220 A7
Dunstan Ave OX7 . . . . 42 E2
Dunstan Rd OX3 . . . . 124 C4
Dunstead La OX2 . . . . 122 B6
Dunster Cl RG4 . . . . 259 C6
Dunthrop Rd OX7 . . . . 44 A4
Durant Way RG31 . . . . 257 D3
Durham La OX29 . . . . 107 C1
Durham Mews OX16 . . . . . 9 A1
Duxford Cl
  Bicester OX26 . . . . 66 B4
  Carterton OX18 . . . . 115 E3
Dyers Hill OX7 . . . . 73 B4
Dyer Straits OX11 . . . . 234 F8
Dyngham Pl OX3 . . . . 124 D1
Dysonswood La RG4 . . . . . 258 E8

E

Eady Rd OX25 . . . . 63 B8
Eagle Ind Est OX28 . . . . . . 118 A8
Eagle La SN6 . . . . 191 F1
Eagles Close Almshouses ⬛
  OX12 . . . . 214 D4
Eagles SN7 . . . . 172 F3
Eagle Sq SN7 . . . . 192 F7
Earlsfield Cl RG4 . . . . 259 E4
Earl's La OX15 . . . . 33 F4
Earlstone Cl OX16 . . . . 16 E8
Earl St OX2 . . . . 122 F1
Early Rd OX28 . . . . 104 D2
Easington Gdns OX16 . . . 16 C4
Easington Rd OX16 . . . . . . 16 C4
Eason Dr OX14 . . . . 160 C1
East Allcourt GL7 . . . . 150 C4
East Ave OX4 . . . . 142 A8
Eastbrook Cl OX6 . . . . 97 E7
Eastbury Ct ⬛ OX12 . . . . 214 D5
Eastchurch OX4 . . . . 141 F3
East Cl OX16 . . . . 16 F7
East End
  Combe OX29 . . . . 90 D3
  Hook Norton OX15 . . . . . 30 B7
Easterfield OX12 . . . . 196 E1
Eastern Ave OX4 . . . . 142 B3
Eastern By-Pass Rd OX3,
  OX4 . . . . 142 E5
Eastern Ho OX4 . . . . 142 B3
Eastern Terr OX15 . . . . . . 22 E8
Eastfield OX4 . . . . 237 A8
East Field Cl OX3 . . . . 142 E7
Eastfield Ct ⬛ SN7 . . . . . 172 F4
Eastfield La
  Whitchurch-on-T RG8 . . 256 D7
  Woodcote RG8 . . . . 250 E6
Eastfield Pl OX4 . . . . 142 F6
Eastfield Rd OX8,OX28 . . 104 B3
Eastgate OX15 . . . . 7 C7
East Hawthorn Rd OX25 . 81 D4
Eastmanton La OX12 . . . . 212 F1
East Oxford Prim Sch
  OX4 . . . . 141 F8
East St Helen St OX14 . . . 179 F6
East St
  Banbury OX16 . . . . 16 E7
  Bicester OX26 . . . . 65 D3
  Bodicote OX15 . . . . 22 E8
  Didcot OX11 . . . . 219 A8
  Fritwell OX27 . . . . 49 F7
  Long Compton CV36 . . . . 27 F6
  Oxford OX2 . . . . 123 A1
  Thame OX9 . . . . 148 A8
East View OX25 . . . . 82 A3
East View Cl RG10 . . . . . . 255 C2
East View OX5 . . . . 77 F3
East View Rd RG10 . . . . . . 255 E2
Eastview Terr SN6 . . . . 190 A6
East Way OX14 . . . . 199 B8
Eastway Mobile Home Pk
  OX14 . . . . 199 B8
Eastwood Rd
  Stokenchurch HP14 . . . . . 188 F3
  Witney OX29 . . . . 103 C1
Eaton Cl SN7 . . . . 172 E2
Eaton Ct OX3 . . . . 123 C8
Eaton Rd OX13 . . . . 139 B2
Ebbes La OX12 . . . . 197 B7
Eccles Cl RG4 . . . . 259 C2
Eden Croft OX14 . . . . 160 A2
Edencroft SN6 . . . . 190 B7
Eden Cl OX14 . . . . 201 A1
Eden Dr OX3 . . . . 124 B4

Edenhall Cl RG31 . . . . 257 D3
Eden Rd OX3 . . . . 124 A4
Eden Way OX26 . . . . 65 B2
Edgar Milward Cl RG30 . . 258 A1
Edgecombe Rd OX3 . . . . . 124 F4
Edgehill Cty Pk* OX17 . . 2 D5
Edgehill OX9 . . . . 129 F2
Edgeway Rd OX3 . . . . 123 F3
Edgeworth Dr OX18 . . . . . 115 C2
Edinburgh Cl OX16 . . . . . . 15 E7
Edinburgh Dr
  Didcot OX11 . . . . 200 F1
  Kidlington OX5 . . . . 109 A8
Edinburgh Way OX16 . . . . 15 E6
Edington Pl OX12 . . . . 196 D1
Edington Rd OX28 . . . . . . 117 D8
Edington Sq OX28 . . . . . . 117 D8
Edith Cl OX1 . . . . 141 D1
Edith Moorhouse Prim Sch
  OX18 . . . . 115 D2
Edmonds Ct OX11 . . . . . . 218 D8
Edmund Halley Rd OX4 . . 142 B1
Edmund Rd OX4 . . . . 142 C5
Edmunds Rd OX16 . . . . . . 15 F5
Edward Feild Prim Sch
  OX5 . . . . 108 F7
Edward Rd OX1 . . . . 141 E2
Edward St
  Abingdon OX14 . . . . 179 D7
  Banbury OX16 . . . . 16 F6
Edward Stone Rise OX7 . . 42 D1
Edwin Ct OX2 . . . . 122 F1
Edwin Rd OX11 . . . . 218 D7
Egerton Cl NN13 . . . . 24 A7
Egerton Rd
  Oxford OX4 . . . . 142 A4
  Wallingford OX10 . . . . . . 221 C7
Egle St OX25 . . . . 63 A8
Eighteenth St OX11 . . . . . 217 A3
Eighth Ave OX3 . . . . 142 F8
Eighth St OX11 . . . . 217 B3
Elbourne OX11 . . . . 218 C8
Elder Cl RG31 . . . . 257 C1
Elderdene OX39 . . . . 168 D8
Elderfield Cres OX11 . . . . 235 D8
Elderfield Rd OX27 . . . . . . 65 F7
Elder Way OX4 . . . . 142 E1
Eldridge Cl OX14 . . . . 159 F2
Eleanor Cl OX4 . . . . 142 B4
Electric Ave OX2 . . . . 141 A8
Eleventh St OX11 . . . . 217 B2
Eliot Cl RG4 . . . . 259 A4
Elizabeth Ave OX14 . . . . . 160 C2
Elizabeth Cl RG9 . . . . 254 A8
Elizabeth Rd RG10 . . . . . . 255 E2
Elizabeth Dr OX12 . . . . . . 214 D6
Elizabeth Jennings Way
  OX2 . . . . 123 A6
Elizabeth Rd
  Henley-on-T RG9 . . . . . . 254 B8
  Stokenchurch HP14 . . . . . 188 F4
Elizabeth Rise OX16 . . . . . 16 B4
Ellesmere Cl RG4 . . . . 259 B3
Ellesmere Rd OX4 . . . . 142 A4
Elliots Way RG4 . . . . 259 B2
Ellison Dr OX15 . . . . 8 F1
Ell's La OX15 . . . . 21 C7
Elm Bridge Rdbt OX10 . . 203 D4
Elm Cl
  Ambrosden OX25 . . . . . . 81 C4
  Bicester OX26 . . . . 65 E4
  Carterton OX18 . . . . 115 F4
  Kidlington OX5 . . . . 108 E8
  Tetsworth OX9 . . . . 166 B8
  Wheatley OX33 . . . . 144 C7
  Witney OX28 . . . . 117 E8
Elm Cres OX7 . . . . 73 C4
Elmcroft RG8 . . . . 249 C5
Elm Ct
  Henley-on-T RG9 . . . . . . 254 D7
  Sonning Common RG4 . . 252 F4
Elm Dr
  Chinnor OX39 . . . . 168 C5
  Garsington OX44 . . . . 143 D2
Elm Farm Cl OX12 . . . . . . 214 D7
Elm Gr
  Brize Norton OX18 . . . . . 116 C5
  Kidlington OX5 . . . . 108 F6
  Milton-u-W OX7 . . . . 70 B1
Elmhurst Rd RG8 . . . . 249 C7
Elmhurst Way OX18 . . . . . 115 E5
Elm La OX25 . . . . 81 C4
Elmleigh Ct RG4 . . . . 259 C3
Elm Pl OX29 . . . . 120 C8
Elm Rd
  Faringdon SN7 . . . . 172 E3
  North Moreton OX11 . . . . 220 A8
  Tokers Green RG4 . . . . . . 258 D7
Elmscote Rd OX16 . . . . . . 16 D2
Elms Dr OX3 . . . . 124 A5
Elms Par OX2 . . . . 122 E1
Elms Rd
  Cassington OX29 . . . . . . 107 C2
  Thame OX9 . . . . 147 F8
Elms The
  Highworth SN6 . . . . 190 A5
  Langford GL7 . . . . 132 D1
Elmstone Dr RG31 . . . . . . 257 C1
Elms Way RG9 . . . . 224 D3
Elmthorpe Rd OX2 . . . . . . 122 E8
Elm Tree Cl OX4 . . . . 142 B3
Elm Tree Farm OX25 . . . . 82 A4

Elm Trees HP18 . . . . 129 B7
Elm Tree Wlk OX13 . . . . . 159 C1
Elsfield Rd OX3 . . . . 123 F6
Elsfield Way OX2 . . . . 109 B1
Elsley Rd RG31 . . . . 257 E3
Elstow Ave RG4 . . . . 259 C6
Elstree Cl RG31 . . . . 257 D2
Elswith Cl OX12 . . . . 214 D8
Eltham Ave RG4 . . . . 259 E5
Elton Cl OX3 . . . . 125 B4
Elton Cres OX33 . . . . 144 C7
Elton Rd OX16 . . . . 16 E2
Elvendon La RG8 . . . . 250 C7
Elvendon Rd RG8 . . . . 249 D7
Elwes Cl OX14 . . . . 180 B8
Elwes Rd OX13 . . . . 178 D6
Ely Cl
  Abingdon OX14 . . . . 179 C6
  Carterton OX18 . . . . 115 E3
Elyham RG8 . . . . 257 B5
Emden Ho OX3 . . . . 124 D4
Emma La RG10 . . . . 255 E2
Emmanuel Christian Sch
  OX4 . . . . 142 B2
Emmens Cl RG8 . . . . 241 D3
Emmens La RG8 . . . . 241 D3
Emmer Green Ct RG4 . . . 259 C5
Emmer Green Prim Sch
  RG4 . . . . 259 B6
Emperor Gdns OX4 . . . . . 142 E1
Empstead Ct RG9 . . . . 244 D2
Emey Cl OX14 . . . . 160 C2
English La RG9 . . . . 223 E1
Enstone Airfield Complex
  (Ind Est) OX7 . . . . 59 D8
Enstone Prim Sch OX7 . . . 58 F5
Enstone Rd
  Charlbury OX7 . . . . 73 B4
  Little Tew OX7 . . . . 45 A5
  Middle Barton OX7 . . . . . 60 E8
EP Collier Prim Sch RG1 . 259 A1
Epwell Rd OX15 . . . . 13 E6
Erica Cl
  Banbury OX16 . . . . 9 A1
  Oxford OX4 . . . . 142 F3
Eric Ave RG4 . . . . 259 A6
Ermont Way OX16 . . . . . . 16 F8
Ernest Rd OX11 . . . . 218 E8
Ermicote Cl OX25 . . . . 81 E4
Essex Rd OX9 . . . . 148 B7
Essex St OX4 . . . . 142 A7
Essex Way RG4 . . . . 253 A3
Ester Carling La RG9 . . . . 252 D8
Estover Way OX39 . . . . . . 168 B6
Ethelhelm Cl OX14 . . . . . . 160 C3
Ethelred Ct OX3 . . . . 124 C4
Eton Cl OX28 . . . . 118 D7
European Sch of Culham The
  (Schola Europaea)
  OX14 . . . . 180 C4
Evans Cl OX18 . . . . 120 D8
Evans Ct OX15 . . . . 108 F8
Evans La OX15 . . . . 108 F8
Evans Rd OX29 . . . . 120 E8
Evans Yd ⬛ OX26 . . . . . . 65 E2
Evelin Rd OX14 . . . . 159 E1
Evelyn Cl OX2 . . . . 140 B8
Evenley Rd NN13 . . . . 24 D1
Evenlode OX16 . . . . 16 B7
Evenlode Cl
  Bicester OX26 . . . . 65 C1
  Charlbury OX7 . . . . 73 B4
  Grove OX12 . . . . 196 D1
  North Leigh OX29 . . . . . . 105 B6
Evenlode Cres OX5 . . . . . 92 A2
Evenlode Ct OX28 . . . . . . 118 B8
Evenlode Dr
  Berinsfield OX10 . . . . 182 C6
  Didcot OX11 . . . . 200 F1
  Long Hanborough OX29 . 90 A1
Evenlode Ho OX26 . . . . . . 65 D2
Evenlode Pk OX14 . . . . . . 160 B1
Evenlode Twr OX4 . . . . . . 142 E2
Everard Cl OX3 . . . . 124 D1
Eversley Cl OX7 . . . . 57 B1
Evesham Rd RG4 . . . . 259 B5
Ewart Cl OX26 . . . . 65 D3
Ewelme CE Prim Sch
  OX10 . . . . 204 E2
Ewert Pl OX2 . . . . 123 B6
Ewin Cl OX3 . . . . 123 F5
Ewin Ct OX3 . . . . 123 F5
Exbourne Rd OX14 . . . . . . 179 D7
Exe Cl OX11 . . . . 200 F2
Exeter Coll OX11 . . . . 261 B2
Exeter Ct
  ⬛ Kidlington OX5 . . . . . . 108 F7
  Didcot OX11 . . . . 219 B8
Exeter Rd OX5 . . . . 92 E1
Eynsham Cl OX16 . . . . 115 E3
Eynsham Com Prim Sch
  OX29 . . . . 120 F8
Eynsham Rd OX29 . . . . . . 105 D5
Eynsham Rd
  Cassington OX29 . . . . . . 107 C2
  Farmoor OX2 . . . . 121 C1
  Oxford OX2 . . . . 140 B8
  Sutton OX29 . . . . 120 A2
Eyot Pl OX4 . . . . 141 E7
Eyres Cl OX10 . . . . 204 D4
Eyre's La OX10 . . . . 204 E5
Eyston Way OX14 . . . . 179 C7

F

Faber Cl OX4 . . . . 142 C2
Fairacres OX14 . . . . 179 C7

Fairacres Rd
Didcot OX11 . . . . .218 E8
Oxford OX4 . . . . .141 F6
Fair Cl OX26 . . . . .65 F4
Fairfax Ave OX3 . . . . . . .123 E4
Fairfax Cl
Banbury OX16 . . . . .16 A5
Reading RG4 . . . . .259 B3
Thame OX9 . . . . .148 A8
Fairfax Ctr OX5 . . . . .108 F6
Fairfax Gate OX33 . . . . .144 C8
Fairfax Rd
Chalgrove OX44 . . . . .184 D6
Kidlington OX5 . . . . .108 F6
Oxford OX4 . . . . .142 E6
Fairfield OX10 . . . . .220 F1
Fairfield Cl OX12 . . . . . . .214 D8
Fairfield Dr OX28 . . . . . . .117 F7
Fairfield Pl OX14 . . . . . . .179 F8
Fairfield Rd RG8 . . . . . . .249 D7
Fairfield OX29 . . . . .136 F8
Fairford Rd RG31 . . . . . .257 C2
Fairford Way OX26 . . . . . .66 A4
Fairhaven Rd OX27 . . . . . .65 F7
Fairlawn End OX2 . . . . . .122 F8
Fairlawn Flats OX2 . . . . .122 F8
Fairlawn Wharf OX14 . . .179 F6
Fairlie Rd OX4 . . . . .142 B3
Fairmile Ct RG9 . . . . .244 D3
Fair Mile RG9 . . . . .244 C4
Fairspear Rd OX29 . . . . . .86 E3
Fairthorne Way SN6 . . . .209 B6
Fair View OX3 . . . . .142 D7
Fairview Rd OX16 . . . . . . .16 C4
Fairview Trad Est RG9 . .254 F8
Fairway The OX16 . . . . . .16 A6
Falcon Cl
Banbury OX16 . . . . .16 A4
Carterton OX18 . . . . .115 C3
Oxford OX4 . . . . .142 D2
Falcon Mead OX26 . . . . . .81 A8
Falcon Villas OX7 . . . . . . .73 C5
Falkland Ho **4** OX18 . . .115 E2
Falkland Rd RG4 . . . . . . .259 B2
Falkner's Cl OX17 . . . . . . .23 A4
Fallowfield **5** RG4 . . . . .259 B4
Fallowfield Cres OX28 . . .104 D1
Fallowfields OX26 . . . . . . .65 F2
Fallowfields Ct **3** OX26 . .65 F2
Fallow Way OX16 . . . . . . .16 E2
Falstaff Cl OX29 . . . . .120 E8
Fane Cl OX26 . . . . .65 D4
Fane Dr OX10 . . . . .182 D6
Fane Ho **2** OX26 . . . . .65 E2
Fane Rd OX3 . . . . .123 E5
Fanshawe Pl OX4 . . . . . . .142 E5
Fanshawe Rd OX9 . . . . . .148 B8
Faraday Ave OX11 . . . . . .217 B2
Farbury End OX7 . . . . .29 B3
Faringdon Com Coll SN7 .172 E1
Faringdon Inf Sch SN7 . .172 F4
Faringdon Rd
Abingdon,Gozzard's Ford
OX13 . . . . .159 A2
Abingdon OX14 . . . . .179 D8
Cumnor OX2 . . . . .139 E2
Kingston Bagpuize OX13 . .156 E1
Shrivenham SN6 . . . . .209 C7
Stanford in the V SN7 . . . .194 D7
Watchfield SN6 . . . . .191 E1
West Challow OX12 . . . . . .213 E6
Farleigh Mews RG4 . . . . .259 E5
Farleigh Rd SN6 . . . . .209 A6
Farley Cl OX29 . . . . .89 C8
Farman Cres GL54 . . . . . .68 A4
Farm Cl
Aston OX18 . . . . .135 E2
Chalgrove OX44 . . . . .184 E6
Ickford HP18 . . . . .127 F3
Kidlington OX5 . . . . .92 F2
Farm Close La OX33 . . . .144 B8
Farm Close Rd OX33 . . . .144 B8
Farm Cl
Purley on T RG8 . . . . .257 C5
Sandford-on-T OX4 . . . . . .142 F1
Sonning Common RG4 . . . .252 E5
Farm Ct SN6 . . . . .227 D4
Farm End
Grove OX14 . . . . .214 D8
Woodstock OX20 . . . . .91 A7
Farmer Pl OX3 . . . . .123 F4
Farmers Cl OX28 . . . . . . .104 B2
Farmfield Rd OX16 . . . . . .16 D3
Farmhouse Cl OX29 . . . . .138 A8
Farmhouse Mdw OX28 . . .117 E7
Farmhouse Mews OX49 . .186 B2
Farmiloe Cl RG8 . . . . .257 C4
Farmington Dr OX28 . . . .117 E8
Farm La OX29 . . . . .103 D5
Farm Mill La OX28 . . . . . .118 B7
Farmoor Ct OX2 . . . . .121 C2
Farm Piece SN7 . . . . .194 D7
Farm Pl OX39 . . . . .149 E1
Farm Rd
Abingdon OX14 . . . . .159 F2
Brackley NN13 . . . . .24 A6
Churchill OX7 . . . . .55 C8
Goring RG8 . . . . .249 C6
Henley-on-T RG9 . . . . .254 F8
Farmstead Cl OX12 . . . . .196 D1
Farm Way OX16 . . . . .16 F3
Farnborough Hall* OX17 . . .3 E7
Farndon Rd OX2 . . . . .123 B4
Farnham Ct OX5 . . . . .108 F8
Farnham Dr RG4 . . . . . . .259 E4
Farriers Cl OX27 . . . . .52 C6
Farrier's Mead OX25 . . . . .80 A4

Farriers Mews OX14 . . . .180 A7
Farriers Rd OX7 . . . . .60 E8
Farthings The OX15 . . . . .178 C7
Faulder Ave OX18 . . . . . . .115 D3
Faulkner St OX1 . . . . .261 B1
Fawkner Way SN7 . . . . . .194 D7
Fawler La OX7 . . . . .88 D7
Fawler Rd
Charlbury OX7 . . . . .73 C2
Uffington OX12,SN7 . . . . . .211 E6
Fawley Bottom La RG9 . .226 B1
Fawley Cl OX18 . . . . .134 C8
Fawley Court House & Mus*
RG9 . . . . .244 F5
Featherbed La
Bishopstone SN6 . . . . .227 E6
East Hendred SN6 . . . . . . .216 F8
Milton Hill OX13 . . . . .199 A1
Mixbury NN13 . . . . .38 D5
Feathers Yd **2** OX10 . . . .221 D7
Feilden Cl OX3 . . . . .118 B4
Feilden Gr OX3 . . . . .124 A3
Fells Cl HP18 . . . . .129 D6
Feltwell Cl OX18 . . . . .115 E3
Fencott Rd OX5 . . . . .95 A4
Fenlock Cl OX29 . . . . .90 F1
Fenlock Rd OX29 . . . . .90 F1
Fennel Way OX14 . . . . . . .180 C8
Fenny Compton Rd OX17 . . .1 D1
Fenway OX25 . . . . .48 A1
Ferguson Pl OX14 . . . . . . .180 C8
Fergusson Rd OX16 . . . . . .16 E7
Fermi Ave OX11 . . . . .217 B1
Fernbrook Rd RG4 . . . . . .258 E5
Ferndale Cl
Reading RG31 . . . . .257 E3
Stokenchurch HP14 . . . . . .188 E4
Ferndale Prep Sch SN7 . .172 F3
Ferndale Rd OX4 . . . . . . .142 E6
Ferndale St SN7 . . . . .173 A4
Ferne Cl RG8 . . . . .249 C7
Fern Glen RG31 . . . . .257 C1
Ferngrove **9** SN7 . . . . . .172 F3
Fernham Gate SN7 . . . . .172 E1
Fernham Rd
Faringdon SN7 . . . . .172 E1
Little Coxwell SN7 . . . . . . .192 E8
Longcot SN7 . . . . .192 D2
Shellingford SN7 . . . . .193 D6
Fernhill Cl
Kidlington OX5 . . . . .108 D8
Milcombe OX15 . . . . .21 A2
Tiddington OX9 . . . . .146 A6
Fernhill Rd OX5 . . . . .108 A8
Fern La OX18 . . . . .115 F5
Ferny Cl OX14 . . . . .160 E3
Ferriston OX16 . . . . .9 A1
Ferry Ct OX14 . . . . .179 E7
Ferry Hinksey Rd OX2 . . .123 A1
Ferry La
Goring RG8 . . . . .249 B6
Moulsford OX10 . . . . .239 A4
South Stoke OX10,RG8 . . . .239 B4
Wargrave RG10 . . . . .255 C2
Ferry Mills OX2 . . . . .141 A8
Ferry Pool Rd OX2 . . . . . .123 C6
Ferry Rd
Marston OX3 . . . . .123 F3
South Stoke RG8 . . . . .239 B4
Ferry Way OX10 . . . . .239 B8
Ferry Wlk OX14 . . . . .179 F6
Fettiplace Cl OX13 . . . . . .158 A7
Fettiplace OX7 . . . . .70 B1
Fettiplace Rd
Marcham OX13 . . . . .178 D6
Witney OX28 . . . . .124 E5
Fettit Pl OX12 . . . . .214 F6
Fewcott Rd OX27 . . . . .49 F7
Fiddlers Hill OX15 . . . . . . .85 E6
Fidlers Wlk RG10 . . . . . . .255 E2
Field Ave OX14 . . . . .142 F2
Field Cl
Ickford HP18 . . . . .128 A3
Kidlington OX5 . . . . .108 F8
Kingston Bagpuize OX13 . .156 E1
Stonesfield OX29 . . . . .89 C8
Yarnton OX5 . . . . .108 B6
Field Ct OX25 . . . . .47 C5
Fielden Cl OX10 . . . . .204 D2
Field End
Long Crendon HP18 . . . . . .129 F5
Wargrave RG10 . . . . .255 F2
Field Farm Bsns Ctr OX6 .67 A5
Field Gdns
East Challow OX12 . . . . . . .213 F5
Steventon OX13 . . . . .199 A5
Field Ho OX2 . . . . .140 C8
Field House Dr OX2 . . . . .123 A8
Field La OX44 . . . . .144 B3
Fieldmere Cl OX28 . . . . . .117 F8
Field Rd
Kingham OX7 . . . . .54 F3
Murcott OX5 . . . . .96 A5
Fieldside
Abingdon OX14 . . . . .159 D1
East Hagbourne OX11 . . . .219 A5
Long Wittenham OX14 . . . .201 C8
Upton OX11 . . . . .218 C2
Field St OX26 . . . . .65 E2
Field The OX13 . . . . .158 F6
Field View RG4 . . . . .259 B3
Fiennes Rd
Banbury OX16 . . . . .16 A5

Fiennes Rd *continued*
Oxford OX4 . . . . .142 A3
Fifield Farm Barns OX10 .204 C5
Fifteenth St OX11 . . . . . . .217 A2
Fifth Ave NN13 . . . . .36 E7
Fifth St E NN13 . . . . .36 E7
Fifth St NN13 . . . . .36 E7
Filkins Rd GL7 . . . . .132 C2
Finch Cl OX3 . . . . .124 C1
Finchdale Cl OX18 . . . . . .115 D3
Finches La SN8 . . . . .245 E1
Finches The SN8 . . . . .245 C2
Finchley La OX26 . . . . .65 D1
Finham Brook OX11 . . . . .200 F3
Finlay Ho OX3 . . . . .244 E3
Finmere CE Prim Sch
MK18 . . . . .39 C7
Finmore Cl **3** OX4 . . . . . .179 E8
Finmore Rd OX2 . . . . .140 D8
Finsbury Pl OX7 . . . . .42 E3
Finstock CE Prim Sch
OX7 . . . . .88 C5
Finstock Sta OX7 . . . . .88 D7
Fir Cl OX10 . . . . .240 D7
Fircroft
Banbury OX16 . . . . .16 D4
Bicester OX26 . . . . .65 F5
Fircroft Cl RG31 . . . . .257 C1
Firebrass Hill OX10 . . . . .204 F5
Firs Cl OX7 . . . . .54 D2
Firs Mdw OX4 . . . . .161 E8
First Ave
Didcot OX11 . . . . .200 D2
Oxford OX3 . . . . .142 F8
Firs The
Oxford OX2 . . . . .123 B8
Wroxton OX15 . . . . .15 A8
First St
Croughton NN13 . . . . .36 F6
Harwell OX11 . . . . .217 C2
First Turn OX2 . . . . .122 F8
Fir Tree Ave OX10 . . . . . .221 B8
Firtree Cl OX16 . . . . .9 A1
Fir Tree Cl OX13 . . . . .156 E1
Fir Tree Cotts RG20 . . . . .235 A2
Fir Tree Jun Sch OX10 . . .221 B8
Fir Tree Paddock RG20 . .235 A2
Fir Trees OX14 . . . . .160 E7
Fisher Cl
Banbury OX16 . . . . .16 F8
Drayton OX14 . . . . .179 A1
Fishermans Wharf OX14 .179 F6
Fisher Row OX1 . . . . .261 A2
Fishers Cl OX29 . . . . .104 A6
Fishers Cotts RG4 . . . . . .259 C6
Fisher's La OX7 . . . . .73 B3
Fish Ponds OX9 . . . . .129 E1
Fitchett Yd OX14 . . . . . . .179 E7
Fitzcount Way OX10 . . . . .203 D1
Fitzharris Ind Est OX14 . .179 F8
Fitzharry's Rd OX14 . . . . .179 F8
Fitzharrys Sch OX14 . . . .159 F1
Fitzherbert Cl OX4 . . . . . .141 F4
Five Acre RG31 . . . . .257 B1
Five Acres OX5 . . . . .95 A4
Five Acres Prim Sch
OX5 . . . . .81 D4
Five Mile Dr OX2 . . . . . . .109 A1
Fiveways Cl SN8 . . . . .245 E1
Flambards **1** RG4 . . . . . .259 C2
Flatford Pl OX5 . . . . .92 C2
Flavius Gate NN13 . . . . . . .24 A7
Flaxfield Rd OX4 . . . . .142 F2
Fleet Way OX11 . . . . .219 A8
Fleetwood Way OX9 . . . . .129 F2
Fleming Cl
Bicester OX26 . . . . .65 C4
Middle Barton OX7 . . . . . . .60 F8
Fleming Dr OX7 . . . . .60 E8
Flemings Rd OX20 . . . . . . .91 C6
Fleming Way OX44 . . . . . .184 C7
Fletcher Cl
Faringdon SN7 . . . . .173 A3
Yarnton OX5 . . . . .108 B5
Fletcher Rd OX4 . . . . .142 E6
Flexney Pl OX3 . . . . .124 D1
Flexneys Paddock OX29 . .138 A8
Flint Hollow OX39 . . . . . . .168 B6
Flint St HP17 . . . . .130 F5
Floral Cl OX12 . . . . .214 E8
Florence Cl OX5 . . . . .108 F4
Florence Park Rd OX4 . . .142 B5
Florey's Cl OX29 . . . . .104 A8
Flower's Hill RG8 . . . . . . .256 C4
Floyd's Row OX1 . . . . . . .261 B1
Fludger Cl OX10 . . . . .221 C7
Fluellen Pl OX26 . . . . .65 D5
Fogwell Rd OX2 . . . . .122 B1
Foliat Cl OX12 . . . . .214 E5
Foliat Dr OX12 . . . . .214 E5
Follets Cl OX5 . . . . .108 B5
Folly Bridge Ct OX1 . . . . .261 B1
Folly Cres
Highworth SN6 . . . . .190 A7
Watchfield SN6 . . . . .191 E1
Folly Ct OX15 . . . . .19 C7
Folly Dr SN6 . . . . .190 A7
Folly Gn OX15 . . . . .19 C7
Folly Orchard Rd RG8 . . .240 E1
Folly View Cres SN7 . . . .172 E2
Folly View Rd SN7 . . . . . .172 E2
Folly Way SN6 . . . . .190 A7

Ford La
Drayton St L OX10 . . . . . . .183 B6
Frilford OX13 . . . . .178 A7
Ford's Cl HP14 . . . . .189 F8
Fords Cl OX33 . . . . .143 C6
Fordy La OX12 . . . . .216 D6
Forest Cl
Launton OX26 . . . . .66 D2
Milton-u-W OX7 . . . . .70 B1
Foresters
Beacon's Bottom HP14 . . .189 C5
Chinnor OX39 . . . . .168 B6
Foresters Tower OX3 . . . .124 E1
Forest Hill RG30 . . . . . . .257 F2
Forest Rd
Charlbury OX7 . . . . .73 A4
Oxford OX3 . . . . .124 F3
Forest Side OX10 . . . . . . .222 D3
Forestry Hos OX49 . . . . . .207 A7
Forest Side OX1 . . . . .141 D2
Forge Cl
Benson OX10 . . . . .203 F4
Horton-cum-S OX33 . . . . .112 B5
Marsh Gibbon OX27 . . . . . .67 F3
Merton OX25 . . . . .95 C6
Reading RG4 . . . . .259 C2
Forge La OX17 . . . . .42 E7
Forge Pl OX27 . . . . .49 F7
Forget-me-not Way **1**
OX4 . . . . .142 F1
Forgeway OX16 . . . . .9 A1
Forrest Cl SN6 . . . . .209 A6
Forster La OX2 . . . . .139 E4
Forsythia Cl OX26 . . . . . . .65 E5
Forsythia Wlk OX16 . . . . . .9 A1
Fortescue Dr OX26 . . . . . .80 A7
Forties The OX44 . . . . . . .145 A2
Fortnam Cl OX3 . . . . .124 B3
Forty Cross OX11 . . . . . . .237 A8
Forty Gn HP27 . . . . .149 F3
Forty The
Bishopstone SN6 . . . . .227 D5
Cholsey OX10 . . . . .220 F2
Foscote Private Hospl
OX16 . . . . .16 D4
Foscote Rise OX16 . . . . . .16 E4
Fosseway Ct GL7 . . . . . . .150 C5
Fosseway The OX18 . . . . .116 C3
Foster Rd OX3 . . . . .159 F3
Fothergill Pl OX9 . . . . . . .147 F8
Foudry Ct OX4 . . . . .201 A2
Foundry St OX16 . . . . .16 C6
Fountain Cl OX14 . . . . . . .179 F8
Fourteenth St OX11 . . . . .217 B3
Fourth Ave
Croughton NN13 . . . . .36 E6
Oxford OX3 . . . . .142 F8
Fourth St
Croughton NN13 . . . . .36 E6
Harwell OX11 . . . . .217 B3
Fowler Rd OX16 . . . . .16 E7
Fowlers Farm Rd HP14 . .188 E4
Fowler's Rd OX7 . . . . .55 A4
Foxborough Rd OX14 . . . .160 E2
Foxburrow Cl OX29 . . . . . .120 A1
Foxburrow La OX29 . . . . . .103 F4
Fox Cl
Bampton OX18 . . . . .134 F3
Chipping Norton OX7 . . . . . .42 F2
Garsington OX44 . . . . .143 D2
Hailey OX29 . . . . .104 A4
Foxcombe Ct OX14 . . . . . .179 C8
Foxcombe La OX1 . . . . . . .141 A1
Foxcombe Rd
Boars Hill OX1 . . . . .140 F1
Sunningwell OX1 . . . . .141 A2
Fox Cover OX39 . . . . .168 C6
Fox Cres OX1 . . . . .141 E5
Foxcroft Dr OX18 . . . . . . .115 D3
Foxden Way OX17 . . . . .9 D7
Foxdown Cl OX5 . . . . .92 E1
Foxfield OX7 . . . . .42 F2
Fox Furlong OX4 . . . . .142 A1
Foxglove Cl
7 Sandford-on-T OX4 . . .142 E1
Bicester OX26 . . . . .65 D5
Foxglove La OX11 . . . . . . .218 D8
Foxglove Rd OX5 . . . . . . .108 B8
Foxhall Manor Pk OX1 . . .200 D2
Foxhall Rd OX11 . . . . .200 D1
Foxhill Cl RG4 . . . . .260 A5
Foxhill La
Reading RG4 . . . . .259 E6
Souldern OX27 . . . . .35 E3
Foxholes Nature Reserve*
OX7 . . . . .69 E5
Fox La
Bicester OX26 . . . . .65 D1
Middle Barton OX7 . . . . . . .60 E8
Wootton OX1 . . . . .159 D7
Foxton Cl OX2 . . . . .108 F1
Foxtowns Gn OX5 . . . . . . .78 A5
Foxwell Dr OX3 . . . . .124 C5
Foxwood Cl OX1 . . . . .135 E3
Foxwood La OX16 . . . . . . .114 C6
Framlands Cl OX12 . . . . . .214 B5
Framlingham Dr RG4 . . . .259 E5
Frampton Cl RG5 . . . . . . .260 E1
Frances Rd OX7 . . . . .42 E3
Francis Little Dr OX14 . . .179 D6
Frank Cook Ct OX5 . . . . . .92 F1
Franklin Cl
Chalgrove OX44 . . . . .184 D6
Kidlington OX5 . . . . .92 F1

Franklin Rd OX3 . . . . .124 B3
Franklyn Cl OX14 . . . . . . .159 F2
Frank's La OX13 . . . . .198 F4
Frank Wise Specl Sch
OX16 . . . . .16 B5
Fraser Ave RG4 . . . . .259 C6
Fraser Cl OX16 . . . . .16 E6
Fraser Gdns OX10 . . . . . .221 C6
Frax Cl OX13 . . . . .156 F1
Frederick Rd OX4 . . . . . . .142 D4
Freeborn Cl OX5 . . . . .92 F2
Freehold St OX25 . . . . . . .62 D6
Freeland CE Prim Sch
OX29 . . . . .106 A7
Freelands Cotts OX33 . . .125 D7
Freelands Rd OX4 . . . . . .141 F5
Freeman Rd OX11 . . . . . .200 C1
Freemans Cl OX15 . . . . . . .22 E8
Frenchay Rd OX2 . . . . . . .123 A5
French Cl OX28 . . . . .117 F7
French Laurence Way
OX44 . . . . .184 D6
Frensham Cl OX16 . . . . . . .9 A1
Frethern Cl OX18 . . . . . . .100 E4
Frewin Ct OX1 . . . . .261 B2
Friars Cl SN6 . . . . .209 A6
Friar's Ct OX18 . . . . .152 F6
Friars' Entry OX1 . . . . . . .261 B2
Friars Furlong HP18 . . . . .129 B7
Friars Wharf OX1 . . . . . . .261 B1
Friday La OX33 . . . . .144 B8
Friday St RG9 . . . . .244 E2
Friends' Cl OX29 . . . . .89 C7
Frieze Way OX5 . . . . .108 F4
Frilford Rd OX13 . . . . .178 C6
Frilsham St OX14 . . . . . . .179 A1
Fringford CE Prim Sch
OX27 . . . . .52 C6
Frith The OX11 . . . . .201 B2
Fritwell CE Prim Sch
OX27 . . . . .49 F7
Fritwell Rd OX27 . . . . .50 B4
Frog La
Bloxham OX15 . . . . .21 D4
Milton-u-W OX7 . . . . .70 B1
Frogmore La
Long Crendon HP18 . . . . . .129 C5
Stanford in the V SN7 . . . .194 E8
Frome Rd OX11 . . . . .217 C1
Frouds Cl OX12 . . . . .213 C4
Fruitlands OX29 . . . . .120 D8
Fry Ct RG4 . . . . .259 B3
Frys Hill OX4 . . . . .142 E1
Fuchsia Wlk OX16 . . . . .9 B1
Fulbrook Cres RG31 . . . . .257 D3
Fullers Field OX44 . . . . . .145 C2
Fullers Rd OX11 . . . . .219 E1
Fullwell Cl OX14 . . . . .159 E3
Fulmar Ct OX26 . . . . .66 B4
Fulmar Pl OX12 . . . . .196 D1
Fulwell Rd
Finmere MK18 . . . . .39 C7
Westbury NN13 . . . . .25 A4
Furlong Row OX18 . . . . . .152 E8
Furlongs The OX9 . . . . . .147 C6
Furlong The OX29 . . . . . . .137 B6
Fyfield Cl OX12 . . . . .214 F4
Fyfield Rd OX2 . . . . .123 C4

G

Gadge Cl OX9 . . . . .129 E1
Gainsborough Cres RG9 . .254 E1
Gainsborough Gn OX14 . .179 E5
Gainsborough Hill RG9 . . .254 D5
Gainsborough Rd RG9 . . .254 C4
Gaisford Rd OX4 . . . . .142 C4
Gales Ct GL7 . . . . .150 C4
Galingale Ct OX4 . . . . . . .142 C4
Galley Field OX14 . . . . . . .180 B8
Gallowstree Rd RG9 . . . . .252 E2
Galpin Cl OX4 . . . . .142 A5
Galsworthy Dr RG4 . . . . .259 E5
Gangsdown Hill RG9 . . . .223 E4
Gap The OX13 . . . . .178 D6
Gap Way RG8 . . . . .250 E8
Garage Yd OX7 . . . . .70 A5
Garden City OX9 . . . . .148 B7
Garden Cl
Banbury OX16 . . . . .16 C7
Didcot OX11 . . . . .218 C7
Gardens The
Langford GL7 . . . . .132 D2
South Stoke RG8 . . . . .239 C3
Garde Rd RG4 . . . . .260 E3
Gardiner Cl
Abingdon OX14 . . . . .180 C8
Wheatley OX33 . . . . .144 B8
Gardiner St OX3 . . . . .124 E3
Garford Cl OX14 . . . . .160 B2
Garford Rd OX2 . . . . .123 C4
Garner Cl OX18 . . . . .115 C5
Garner Ct OX26 . . . . .66 B4
Garsington CE Prim Sch
OX44 . . . . .143 E2
Garsington Rd OX4 . . . . . .142 E4
Garsons La OX44 . . . . . . .240 E6
Garston Cl OX12 . . . . .214 E5

Garston Ct OX18 . . . . .116 B5
Garston La OX12 . . . . .214 E5
Garth Rd OX11 . . . . .200 E1
Garth The
　Oxford OX2 . . . . 140 D8
　Yarnton OX5 . . . . .108 B6
Garton End RG8 . . . . 250 D6
Gas Alley OX9 . . . . 148 A8
Gascoigne Way OX15 . . . . . .21 E2
Gaskells End RG4 . . . . 258 D8
Gas La OX7 . . . . .85 D8
Gassons Mead OX18 . . . . 133 C5
Gassons Rd GL7 . . . . 150 C5
Gassons The GL7 . . . . .132 B5
Gassons Way GL7 . . . . 150 C4
Gate Farnham SN7 . . . . 172 E1
Gatehampton Rd RG8 . . . 249 C5
Gateley OX33 . . . . .143 D6
Gateway Prim Sch OX18 .115 E2
Gathorne Rd OX3 . . . . 124 D2
Gatteridge St OX16 . . . . .16 D5
Gauntlets Cl OX15 . . . . .21 E5
Gaveston Gdns OX15 . . . . . 33 E4
Gaveston Rd OX11 . . . . . . .217 E7
Gavray Dr OX26 . . . . .66 B1
Gaydon Cl OX18 . . . . .115 A3
Gaydon Wlk OX26 . . . . .66 A4
Gayhurst Cl RG4 . . . . 259 D6
Gelt Burn OX14 . . . . 201 B2
Gentian Cl OX26 . . . . .65 D5
Gentian Rd OX4 . . . . 142 F2
Geoffrey Barbour Rd
　OX14 . . . . .179 F8
Geoffreyson Rd RG4 . . . . 258 E5
Geoffrey Tuttle Dr OX10 . 204 C2
George Moore Cl OX4 . . . 142 A6
George Morland Ho ❽
　OX14 . . . . .179 F6
George Rd HP14 . . . . .188 E5
George St
　Banbury OX16 . . . . .16 D5
　Bicester OX26 . . . . .65 D3
　Oxford OX1 . . . . .261 B2
　Reading RG1,RG4 . . . . . . 259 B1
George Street Mews
　OX1 . . . . 261 A2
Gerard Pl OX4 . . . . 142 C5
Germander Way OX26 . . . . .65 D5
Gibbs Cres OX2 . . . . 261 A1
Gibbs Rd OX16 . . . . .16 E7
Gibson Cl OX14 . . . . 160 A3
Gibson Dr OX25 . . . . .63 C7
Gidley Way OX33 . . . . .143 D7
Giernalls Rd OX29 . . . . 104 A6
Giffard Way HP18 . . . . 129 C7
Gifford Cl RG4 . . . . .259 E5
Giles Cl OX4 . . . . .142 B2
Giles Ct OX18 . . . . .113 C5
Giles Rd OX4 . . . . 142 C2
Gilkes Yd OX16 . . . . .16 B5
Gillett Cl OX16 . . . . .16 B5
Gillett Rd OX16 . . . . .16 B5
Gillians Way OX4 . . . . 142 B6
Gillotts Cl RG9 . . . . 254 B8
Gillott's Hill RG9 . . . . 254 C7
Gillott's La RG9 . . . . 254 C7
Gillott's Sch RG9 . . . . 254 A7
Ginge Cl OX14 . . . . .160 B2
Gipsy La
　Great Coxwell SN7 . . . . . 192 C8
　Grove OX12 . . . . .214 F8
　Oxford OX3 . . . . .124 B1
　Reading RG30 . . . . 257 E1
Girdlestone Cl OX3 . . . . 124 D1
Girdlestone Rd OX3 . . . . 124 D1
Glades The OX26 . . . . .66 D2
Glade The RG8 . . . . 257 C4
Gladstone Ct OX3 . . . . 124 E3
Gladstone Rd OX3 . . . . . . 124 E3
Glamis Pl OX14 . . . . .15 F6
Glanville Gdns OX16 . . . . .16 B6
Glanville Rd OX4 . . . . 142 B7
Glean Cotts OX28 . . . . . . 104 D1
Glebe Cl
　Ambrosden OX25 . . . . .81 D4
　Moulsford OX10 . . . . . . 238 F5
Glebe Cotts
　Postcombe OX9 . . . . 166 F4
　South Stoke RG8 . . . . . . 239 C3
Glebe Ct OX25 . . . . .47 D5
Glebe Dr NN13 . . . . .24 A7
Glebe Gdns
　Grove OX12 . . . . .196 E1
　Sonning RG4 . . . . 260 E3
Glebe House Dr MK18 . . .25 E6
Glebelands
　Bampton OX18 . . . . 134 A4
　Oxford OX13 . . . . 142 D7
Glebe La RG4 . . . . 260 E3
Glebe Pl SN6 . . . . 190 A6
Glebe Rd
　Cumnor OX2 . . . . .139 E5
　Didcot OX11 . . . . .218 E7
　Purley on T RG8 . . . . 257 B5
　Stanford in the V SN7 . . 194 D7
Glebe Ride RG8 . . . . 249 B6
Glebe St OX4 . . . . .123 F1
Glebe The
　Aldworth RG8 . . . . 247 F3
　Aynho OX17 . . . . .35 D7
　Cumnor OX2 . . . . .139 E5
　Highmoor Cross RG9 . . . 242 E5
　Hook Norton OX15 . . . . . . .30 B8
　Lewknor OX49 . . . . .187 B8

Glebe The continued
　Standlake OX29 . . . . 137 C4
　West Challow OX12 . . . . . 213 D5
　Wheatley OX33 . . . . .144 B8
Glen Cl OX27 . . . . .52 D1
Glenham Rd OX9 . . . . .148 B8
Glenmore Bsns Ctr OX29 103 C1
Glenmore Rd OX18 . . . . . . 115 D4
Glenhampda RG4 . . . . 258 F6
Gliffard Ho ❻ RG4 . . . . . . 259 E5
Glimbers Gr OX39 . . . . 168 C5
Glissard Way OX18 . . . . . . 114 C6
Glory Farm Prim Sch
　OX26 . . . . .66 A4
Gloucester Court Mews
　OX28 . . . . .104 B1
Gloucester Gn OX1 . . . . . 261 B2
Gloucester La OX1 . . . . . 261 A2
Gloucester Mews ❹
　SN7 . . . . .172 F4
Gloucester Pl OX28 . . . . .104 B1
Gloucester St
　Faringdon SN7 . . . . .172 F4
　Oxford OX1 . . . . .261 B2
Glover Mews OX9 . . . . .91 B6
Glovers Cl
　Chipping Norton OX7 . . . .42 E2
　Woodstock OX20 . . . . . . .91 C6
Glovers La OX17 . . . . .10 F1
Glyme Cl
　Abingdon OX14 . . . . 160 B1
　Woodstock OX20 . . . . . . .91 B7
Glyme Dr OX10 . . . . 182 D6
Glyme Way OX29 . . . . .106 B8
Glympton Rd OX20 . . . . .75 E6
Glyn Ave OX11 . . . . .218 D8
Glyncastle RG4 . . . . 258 F5
Glyndebourne Gdns OX16 . .9 A1
Glyn Rd OX10 . . . . 203 D1
Glynswood OX39 . . . . 168 C6
Gobles Ct OX26 . . . . .65 F1
Goddards La OX7 . . . . .42 E3
Godfrey Cl
　❸ Abingdon OX14 . . . . . .179 E6
　Oxford OX3 . . . . .124 E1
Godfreys Cl
　Brill HP18 . . . . .98 B1
　Grove OX12 . . . . .196 F1
Godstow Cl RG5 . . . . 260 E1
Godstow Rd OX2 . . . . 122 D8
Godwyn Cl OX14 . . . . .179 E8
Goffe Cl OX9 . . . . .148 A8
Goggs The OX49 . . . . 186 A1
Golafre Rd OX14 . . . . .179 E5
Goldbury Cotts OX12 . . . .216 B4
Goldcrest Way OX26 . . . . . .81 A8
Golden Cross OX1 . . . . . . 261 B2
Golden Hills OX39 . . . . . . 168 D6
Golden La OX7 . . . . .42 A5
Golden Rd OX4 . . . . 142 A7
Golden Villa Cl OX16 . . . . . .16 A6
Golder's Cl HP18 . . . . .127 F3
Goldfinch Cl OX4 . . . . .142 F1
Goldfinch La OX10 . . . . 221 A2
Goldsmith Cl ❸ OX26 . . . . .65 C4
Goldsmith's La OX10 . . . . 221 D7
Goldsmith's Terr ❼
　OX10 . . . . 221 D7
Gold St OX44 . . . . .145 B3
Goodall Cl RG9 . . . . 244 D1
Goodlake Ave ❷ SN7 . . . . .172 F3
Goodliffe Gdns RG31 . . . 257 C4
Goodrich Cl RG4 . . . . 259 E5
Goodrington Cl OX16 . . . . .16 B6
Goodsons Ind Mews OX9 147 F8
Goodson Wlk OX3 . . . . . . .123 F3
Goor La SN8 . . . . .245 C4
Goosacres OX14 . . . . 160 E2
Goose Gn OX15 . . . . .33 F3
Goose Green Cl OX2 . . . . 122 E8
Goose La OX15 . . . . .22 D8
Goose Wlk OX15 . . . . .21 D4
Goosey La SN7 . . . . 195 A4
Gordon Cl OX3 . . . . .123 F5
Gordon Dr OX14 . . . . 160 C1
Gordon Pl RG30 . . . . 258 C1
Gordon Rd OX25 . . . . .63 C8
Gordon St OX1 . . . . .141 D6
Gordon Way OX28 . . . . . . 118 A7
Gordon Woodward Way
　OX1 . . . . 141 D5
Goring CE Prim Sch
　RG8 . . . . 249 C7
Goring Lodge ❼ OX1 . . 141 C7
Goring Rd RG8 . . . . 250 E8
Goring & Streatley Sta
　RG8 . . . . 249 C6
Gorselands RG4 . . . . 259 A6
Gorse Leas OX3 . . . . 124 B5
Gorton Playne OX7 . . . . . . .70 D1
Gorwell OX49 . . . . .186 A2
Gosbrook Ho ❹ RG4 . . . . 259 C1
Gosbrook Rd RG4 . . . . 259 B2
Gosford Cl OX5 . . . . .108 F6
Gosford Hill Ct OX5 . . . . .108 F6
Gosford Hill Sch OX5 . . .108 F7
Goslyn Cl OX3 . . . . 124 D1
Gossway Fields OX5 . . . . . .78 A3
Gott Cl OX27 . . . . .66 A6
Goulders Cotts RG10 . . . 255 E1
Gouldland Gdns OX3 . . . 124 B5
Goulds Villas OX16 . . . . . . .16 A5
Grafton Ho OX18 . . . . 168 C7
Grafton Lodge ❼ OX16 . .16 D5
Grafton Orch OX33 . . . . . 168 D7
Graham Cl OX11 . . . . 237 A8
Grahame Ave RG8 . . . . . . 256 D5

Graham Rd OX26 . . . . .65 D3
Grainge Cl NN13 . . . . .25 A5
Grammar School Hill OX7 73 B3
Gramp's Hill OX12 . . . . . . .231 E6
Grandison Ho RG9 . . . . . . 244 E3
Grandpont Pl OX1 . . . . . . .261 B1
Grange Ave RG9 . . . . 253 A8
Grange Beck OX14 . . . . . . 201 A3
Grange Cl
　Goring RG8 . . . . .249 B6
　Highworth SN6 . . . . 190 A5
Grange Farm Rd OX14 . . . .11 D2
Grange Farm Rd HP14 . . .189 B7
Grange La OX15 . . . . .19 D7
Grange Mews OX26 . . . . . .66 C2
Grange Mill Ct OX29 . . . . 120 D7
Grange Pk OX25 . . . . .48 A1
Grange Rd
　Banbury OX16 . . . . .16 D2
　Henley-on-T RG9 . . . . . . 244 E1
　Oxford OX4 . . . . .142 B2
Grangers Pl OX28 . . . . . . .104 B1
Grange Sch The OX16 . . . .16 D2
Grange The
　Kingham OX7 . . . . .55 A4
　Reading RG4 . . . . 258 D6
Grantham Ho OX2 . . . . . . 261 A4
Grants Mews ❷ OX4 . . . . 141 F8
Granville Ct OX3 . . . . 124 A1
Granville Way OX26 . . . . . . .66 B2
Grasmere Ave RG30 . . . . . 257 F2
Grass Hill RG4 . . . . 258 E3
Grates The OX4 . . . . 142 C4
Gravel Cl OX10 . . . . 203 F4
Gravel Hill Cres RG9 . . . . 252 F6
Gravel Hill
　Henley-on-T RG9 . . . . . . 244 D2
　Reading RG4 . . . . 258 F6
　Sonning Common RG9 . . 252 F6
Gravel La
　Drayton OX14 . . . . .179 B1
　Warborough OX10 . . . . . . 203 B7
Gravel Pits La OX5 . . . . . . 108 B6
Gravel Rd RG4,RG9 . . . . . .253 F1
Gravel Wlk
　Drayton St L OX10 . . . . . .183 B5
　Faringdon SN7 . . . . .172 F3
Graveney Dr RG4 . . . . 258 E3
Gravenhill Rd N OX26 . . . . .81 A7
Graveney Dr RG4 . . . . 258 E3
Grayling Ct ❾ RG1 . . . . . . 259 A1
Grays Cl OX44 . . . . .184 C7
Grays Rd OX3 . . . . 124 B2
Great Barn* SN7 . . . . .172 B1
Great Clarendon St OX2 . 261 A3
Great Close Rd OX5 . . . . . 108 C5
Great Haseley Ind Est
　OX44 . . . . .145 C1
Great Mead
　Didcot OX11 . . . . 219 A6
　Oxford OX1 . . . . .261 A2
Great Milton CE Prim Sch
　OX44 . . . . .145 C3
Great Rissington Prim Sch
　GL54 . . . . .83 A7
Great Rollright CE Prim Sch
　OX7 . . . . .29 B3
Great Tew Cty Prim Sch
　OX7 . . . . .45 D7
Great Western Dr OX11 . . 200 E2
Grebe Cl
　Abingdon OX14 . . . . .179 F5
　Sandford-on-T OX4 . . . . .142 E1
Grebe Rd
　Banbury OX16 . . . . .16 E3
　Bicester OX26 . . . . .65 F1
Grebe Sq GL54 . . . . .68 B4
Greenacres OX14 . . . . 179 B2
Greenacres Dr OX12 . . . . 214 C4
Greenacres La OX18 . . . . 135 D3
Green Cl
　Benson OX10 . . . . .204 A5
　Bicester OX26 . . . . .65 F2
　Didcot OX11 . . . . .218 F6
　Steventon OX13 . . . . 198 F5
　Wallingford OX10 . . . . . . 221 C7
Green Cnr OX28 . . . . 104 C2
Green Coll OX2 . . . . .261 A4
Green Dean Hill RG4 . . . . 252 C1
Green End Rd HP14 . . . . . .189 E5
Green Farm OX17 . . . . .23 A4
Greenway
　Haddenham HP17 . . . . . . .130 F5
　Lower Heyford OX25 . . . . .63 A4
Greenways RG8 . . . . 256 D5
Greenway OX9 . . . . .129 F1
Greenway The OX12 . . . . 216 B6
Greenwich La OX29 . . . . . . .87 B3
Greenwood Dr OX26 . . . . . .65 B3
Greenwood Mdw OX39 . .168 D6
Gregory Est OX29 . . . . . . 185 C3
Grenoble Rd
　Oxford OX4 . . . . .143 A1
　Sandford-on-T OX4 . . . . .142 D1
Grenville Way OX9 . . . . . . 130 B1
Gresham Way RG30 . . . . . 258 A2
Greygoose La GL56 . . . . . . .41 B6
Greyhound La OX29 . . . . . 129 F1
Greyhound Wlk OX9 . . . . .147 F8
Greys Cl OX16 . . . . .15 F6
Greys Court* RG9 . . . . . . 243 C3
Greystoke Rd RG4 . . . . . . 259 C4
Greystones Ct
　Alvescot OX18 . . . . 133 C5
　Kidlington OX5 . . . . .92 D1
Griffin Cl OX17 . . . . .23 A5

Green La
　North Leigh OX29 . . . . . . 105 A7
　Oxford OX2 . . . . .140 A8
　Pangbourne RG8 . . . . . . 256 C5
　Sonning Common RG4 . . 252 F5
　South Newington OX15 . . .31 F7
　Stokenchurch HP14 . . . . 188 C5
　Sunningwell OX13 . . . . . 160 A6
　Swalcliffe OX15 . . . . .14 A1
　Uffington SN7 . . . . .211 C7
　Upper Arncott OX25 . . . . .96 E7
　Warborough OX10 . . . . . . 203 B7
　Woodcote RG8 . . . . .250 F7
　Woodstock OX20 . . . . . . .91 B7
　Wootton OX13 . . . . 159 A5
Greenleas Ave RG4 . . . . . 259 B7
Greenmere OX10 . . . . 202 E3
Greenmere Prim Sch
　OX11 . . . . .218 F8
Greenmore RG8 . . . . 250 F8
Green N The OX10 . . . . . . 203 C8
Green Pl OX1 . . . . 141 D6
Green Rd
　Didcot OX11 . . . . .218 F7
　Kidlington OX5 . . . . .108 E8
　Oxford OX3 . . . . .124 F3
Green Ridges OX3 . . . . . . 125 A4
Greens Garth OX15 . . . . . . .21 F5
Greens Keep HP17 . . . . . . 130 F6
Green S Rd OX29 . . . . .120 E8
Green S The OX10 . . . . . . 203 C8
Green St OX4 . . . . 142 A7
Greensward The OX17 . . . . .5 E1
Green The
　Adderbury OX17 . . . . .23 A4
　Alvescot OX18 . . . . 133 C5
　Ascott-u-W OX7 . . . . .71 C2
　Aston Rowant OX49 . . . . . 167 D3
　Barford St M OX15 . . . . . . .32 E6
　Baydon SN8 . . . . 245 E1
　Bladon OX20 . . . . .91 B2
　Bledington OX7 . . . . .54 D2
　Cassington OX29 . . . . . . .107 C2
　Chalgrove OX44 . . . . 184 D6
　Charlbury OX7 . . . . .73 C4
　Charney Bassett OX12 . . 176 A2
　Chesterton OX26 . . . . .79 F7
　Chilton OX11 . . . . .235 E8
　Chipping Norton OX7 . . . .42 E2
　Clanfield OX18 . . . . .152 E8
　Cuddesdon OX44 . . . . . . 144 B8
　Culham OX14 . . . . 180 A3
　Drayton OX14 . . . . .179 B1
　East Hanney OX12 . . . . . .197 B7
　Fawler OX7 . . . . .88 E6
　Fernham SN7 . . . . 193 A4
　Fifield OX7 . . . . .69 C2
　Freeland OX29 . . . . .106 B5
　Fringford OX27 . . . . .52 C6
　Great Bourton OX17 . . . . . .9 D8
　Great Milton OX44 . . . . . 145 B3
　Great Rollright OX7 . . . . . .29 A3
　Great Tew OX7 . . . . .45 D7
　Highworth SN6 . . . . 190 A5
　Hook Norton OX15 . . . . . . .30 B7
　Hornton OX15 . . . . .7 C6
　Horspath OX33 . . . . 143 C5
　Horton-cum-S OX33 . . . . 112 A5
　Launton OX26 . . . . .66 E2
　Lyford OX12 . . . . 176 C1
　Middle Assendon RG9 . . 243 F8
　Milcombe OX15 . . . . .20 F2
　North Leigh OX29 . . . . . . .89 D2
　Salford OX7 . . . . .42 A5
　Shrivenham SN6 . . . . 209 A6
　Shutford OX15 . . . . .14 B5
　Stadhampton OX44 . . . . .163 D2
　Standlake OX29 . . . . .137 D3
　Stanton Harcourt OX29 . . 138 A8
　Steventon OX13 . . . . 199 A5
　Stoke Lyne OX27 . . . . .51 B5
　Sutton Courtenay OX14 . . 180 A1
　Swalcliffe OX15 . . . . .19 F8
　Tackley OX5 . . . . .77 B5
　Turweston NN13 . . . . .24 D8
　Uffington SN7 . . . . .211 D7
　Upper Heyford OX25 . . . . .62 F8
　West Hanney OX12 . . . . . .196 E5
Greenway

Griffin Rd OX9 . . . . 148 C8
Griffith Rd OX16 . . . . .9 C1
Griffiths Cl OX29 . . . . 138 C3
Griffiths Gdns OX27 . . . . . .66 A7
Grimbly Pl OX2 . . . . .123 B8
Grimmer Way RG8 . . . . . . 250 F8
Grimsbury Dr OX16 . . . . . . .16 F7
Grimsbury Gn OX16 . . . . . .16 E8
Grimsbury Green OX16 . . .16 E8
Grimsbury Sq OX16 . . . . . .16 E7
Grindon La OX10 . . . . 205 B1
Grosvenor Pl OX12 . . . . . . 214 B5
Grosvenor Rd
　❼ Banbury OX16 . . . . . . .16 D5
　Oxford OX2 . . . . .140 E6
　Reading RG4 . . . . 259 C4
Grove CE Sch OX12 . . . . . 196 E2
Grove Cotts
　Brightwell-cum-S OX10 . 202 D2
　Little Coxwell SN7 . . . . . 192 E7
　Reading RG4 . . . . 259 A5
Grove Ct
　Deddington OX15 . . . . . . .33 F4
　Oxford OX4 . . . . .142 A5
Grove Farm The OX14 . . . 199 C1
Grove Hill
　Highworth SN6 . . . . 190 A7
　Reading RG4 . . . . 259 A4
　Woodstock OX20 . . . . . . .91 A6
Grove La OX49 . . . . .205 A6
Grovelands Ctr OX12 . . . . 196 D1
Grovelands OX5 . . . . 108 D8
Grovelands Rd OX3 . . . . . 125 A2
Grove La OX7 . . . . .72 E8
Grove Mews RG4 . . . . 259 B5
Grove Park Dr
　Ardington OX12 . . . . 215 C7
　Grove OX12 . . . . .197 B1
Grove Rd
　Bladon OX20 . . . . .91 C3
　Grove OX12 . . . . .214 E7
　Harwell OX11 . . . . 217 D8
　Henley-on-T RG9 . . . . . . 244 E1
　Sonning Common RG4 . . 252 F5
　South Stoke RG8 . . . . . . 239 E2
Groves Ind Est OX7 . . . . . .70 B1
Grove St
　Banbury OX16 . . . . .16 D5
　Oxford OX2 . . . . .123 B7
　Wantage OX12 . . . . 214 D5
Grove Terr OX11 . . . . 218 D4
Grove The
　Abingdon OX14 . . . . 160 B2
　Bourton SN6 . . . . 209 A3
　Deddington OX15 . . . . . . .33 F4
Grundy Cl OX14 . . . . .180 B8
Grundy Cres OX1 . . . . .141 E1
Grunsell Cl OX3 . . . . 124 C5
Guardian Ct ❽ OX16 . . . . .16 C6
Guelder Rd OX4 . . . . 142 D1
Guernsey Way OX16 . . . . . . .9 A1
Guildenford OX18 . . . . . . 100 E5
Guildford Ct ❼ OX5 . . . . 108 F8
Guild Ho The OX12 . . . . . 214 E4
Gulley Row OX25 . . . . .95 D8
Gullicote La OX17 . . . . .8 E3
Gulliver's Cl OX15 . . . . .8 B4
Gurden Pl OX3 . . . . 124 E4
Gurney Cl RG4 . . . . 258 D5
Gurney Dr RG4 . . . . 258 D5
Gwilym Ct ❺ OX10 . . . . . 221 C7
Gwyneth Rd OX4 . . . . 142 A2
Gwynne Cl RG31 . . . . 257 D3

H

Hackers La OX7 . . . . .55 E4
Hack La CV36 . . . . .25 E8
Haddenham Bsns Pk
　HP17 . . . . .130 F7
Haddenham & Thame
　Parkway Sta HP17 . . . . . .130 E6
Hadden Hill OX11 . . . . 201 D1
Haddow Rd OX14 . . . . 180 C8
Hadleigh Rise RG4 . . . . . . 259 E5
Hadley Rd OX4 . . . . 124 A4
Hadrian's Gate NN13 . . . . .24 A7
Hafod OX4 . . . . 258 F6
Hagbourne CE Prim Sch
　OX11 . . . . .218 F5
Hagbourne Cl RG8 . . . . . . 250 F8
Hagbourne Rd
　Aston Tirrold OX11 . . . . . 219 A8
　East Hagbourne OX11 . . 219 D2
Hailey Ave OX7 . . . . .42 E1
Hailey CE Prim Sch
　OX29 . . . . .104 A6
Hailey Cres OX7 . . . . .42 E1
Hailey Croft OX39 . . . . . . .168 B6
Hailey Rd
　Oxford OX4 . . . . .142 C2
　Reading RG4 . . . . 258 E5
Hale Rd OX10 . . . . 202 D2
Halfpenny La OX10 . . . . . . 238 E5
Halifax Rd OX26 . . . . .81 A3
Hall Cl OX49 . . . . .186 B4
Hall Cl The OX25 . . . . .48 B6
Hallett Cl OX12 . . . . .214 B5
Halliday Hill OX3 . . . . 124 B5

Halls Cl
Drayton OX14 . . . . 179 C1
Oxford OX2 . . . . 140 B7
Halls La OX12 . . . . 197 B7
Hallsmead Ct 8 RG1 . . . . 259 A1
Halse Water OX14 . . . . . . 201 A2
Halton Rd OX18. . . . . 115 F2
Hambidge La GL7. . . . . . . 150 C5
Hambleden Dr OX10 . . . . . 221 B8
Hamble Dr OX14. . . . . 160 B1
Hamble Rd OX14. . . . . 201 A1
Hambleside OX26 . . . . 65 B2
Hamcroft OX12 . . . . 214 C5
Hamels La OX1 . . . . 140 F1
Hamel The OX1. . . . . 261 A2
Hamfield OX12 . . . . 214 C4
Hamilton Ave RG9 . . . . 244 E1
Hamilton Cl
Banbury OX16 . . . . 16 E7
Bicester OX26 . . . . 65 E3
Hamilton Rd
Oxford OX2 . . . . 123 B7
Thame OX9 . . . . 130 A1
Wargrave RG10. . . . . 255 E2
Ham La OX18. . . . . 135 E1
Hamlet The RG4 . . . . 252 B5
Hamlyn Cl OX12 . . . . 214 A2
Hammer La OX10 . . . . 183 A1
Hammett Pl OX18. . . . . . . 115 D1
Hammond's End RG8 . . . . 241 B4
Hampden Ave OX9. . . . . . . 147 F7
Hampden Cl
Banbury OX16 . . . . 15 F5
Bicester OX26 . . . . 66 A3
Chalgrove OX44. . . . . 184 D6
Faringdon SN7. . . . . 173 A3
Hampden Dr OX5 . . . . 108 F6
Hampden Rd
Oxford OX4 . . . . 142 C4
Reading RG4 . . . . 259 B2
Wantage OX12. . . . . 214 E5
Hampden Way OX10 . . . . . 204 F4
Hampdon Villas OX27 . . . . . 67 F7
Hampstead Hill RG9 . . . . . 260 C8
Hampton Dr OX17 . . . . 23 F6
Ham Rd OX12. . . . . 214 C4
Hamstyles OX49 . . . . 205 E7
Hanborough Bsns Pk
OX29 . . . . 90 E1
Hanborough Cl OX29. . . . . 120 E8
Hanborough Manor CE Sch
OX29 . . . . 90 C1
Hanborough Rd OX29. . . . 120 E8
Hanborough Sta OX29 . . . . 90 E1
Handlo Pl OX3. . . . . 124 F4
Hanney Rd
Kingston Bagpuize OX13 . . 176 D7
Steventon OX13. . . . . 198 C6
Hannis Rd OX7 . . . . 42 D1
Hanover Cl OX7. . . . . 73 C3
Hanover Ct
9 Wallingford OX10. . . . . 221 C7
Didcot OX11. . . . . 218 E7
Reading RG4 . . . . 259 C6
Hanover Gdns
Bicester OX26 . . . . 65 E1
Wargrave RG10. . . . . 255 F3
Hans Ave OX12 . . . . 214 E5
Hanson Rd OX14. . . . . 159 F3
Hanwell Ct OX17. . . . . 8 F4
Hanwell Fields Com Sch
OX16 . . . . 9 B1
Hanwood Cl RG5 . . . . 260 C1
Harberton Mead
Marston OX3 . . . . 123 F3
Oxford OX3 . . . . 124 A3
Harbord Rd OX2 . . . . 109 B2
Harborne Rd OX5. . . . . 77 C5
Harcourt Arboretum &
Garden★ OX44 . . . . 161 E1
Harcourt Cl RG9. . . . . 244 C1
Harcourt Gn OX12 . . . . . . 214 F6
Harcourt Hill OX2. . . . . . . 140 E6
Harcourt Ho 5 OX26 . . . . . 65 E2
Harcourt Rd OX12 . . . . . . 214 E5
Harcourt Terr OX3 . . . . . . 124 B2
Harcourt Way
Abingdon OX14 . . . . 159 F1
Wantage OX12. . . . . 214 E5
Harding Cl SN7. . . . . 173 A3
Harding Rd OX14 . . . . 179 D8
Hardings OX44. . . . . 184 D6
Hardings Cl OX4 . . . . 142 B3
Hardings Strings OX11 . . . 218 E7
Hardwell Cl OX12 . . . . 196 D1
Hardwick Ave OX5 . . . . . . 108 E7
Hardwick Bsns Pk OX16. . . . 9 E2
Hardwick Pk OX16 . . . . 8 F1
Hardwick Prim Sch OX16. . 16 A8
Hardwick Rd
Hethe OX27 . . . . 52 A7
Whitchurch-on-T RG8 . . . . 256 D7
Hardy Cl RG4. . . . . 259 C2
Harebell Rd OX4. . . . . 142 F2
Harebell Way OX26 . . . . . . 65 D4
Harecourt OX12. . . . . 214 F4
Harefields OX2 . . . . 109 B1
Hare Warren Ct RG4 . . . . . 259 B4
Harewood Rd OX16 . . . . 16 E2
Harlech Ave RG4. . . . . 259 D6
Harlech Cl OX16 . . . . 15 F5
Harlequin Way OX16 . . . . 9 B1
Harley Rd
Oxford OX2 . . . . 122 F1
Reading RG4 . . . . 259 B2
Harlington Ave OX12. . . . . 196 E1
Harlow Way OX3. . . . . 123 F7
Harmon Cl OX27. . . . . 66 A6
Harolde Cl OX3. . . . . 124 D4
Harold Hicks Pl OX4 . . . . . 141 F6
Harolds Cl OX29 . . . . 87 A3
Harold White Cl OX3. . . . . 124 F2
Harper Cl OX25. . . . . 96 D7
Harpes Rd OX2 . . . . 123 B8
Harpsden Rd RG9. . . . . 254 E8
Harpsden Way RG9 . . . . . . 254 E7
Harpsichord Pl OX4. . . . . . 123 F1
Harrier Pk OX11 . . . . 200 D3
Harriers Ground Com Prim
Sch OX16 . . . . 16 C4
Harriers View OX16 . . . . 16 C4
Harrier Way OX26. . . . . 66 A4
Harris Gdns GL54 . . . . 68 B4
Harrison Pl OX9 . . . . 129 F1
Harrison's La OX20 . . . . 91 A6
Harris Rd OX25 . . . . 63 C7
Harris's La OX13. . . . . 156 C2
Harrisville OX25 . . . . 62 B8
Harroell
Long Crendon HP18. . . . . . 129 D5
Long Crendon HP18. . . . . . 129 D6
Harrogate Rd RG4 . . . . 258 E4
Harrowby Ct OX16 . . . . 16 D2
Harrowby Rd OX16. . . . . 16 D2
Harrow Rd OX4. . . . . 142 F3
Hart Ave SN7. . . . . 172 F3
Hart Cl
Abingdon OX14 . . . . 180 C8
Banbury OX16 . . . . 9 C1
Hartley Cl OX10. . . . . 203 B6
Hartleys Barns OX7 . . . . 85 D7
Hart Moor Cl HP14. . . . . . . 188 E4
Hart Pl OX26 . . . . 66 A4
Harts Cl OX5 . . . . 108 D8
Hartslock Bridleway
Whitchurch Hill RG8 . . . . . 250 B1
Whitchurch-on-T RG8 . . . . 256 B8
Hartslock Ct RG8 . . . . 256 B6
Hartslock View RG8. . . . . . 249 E2
Hartslock Way RG31 . . . . . 257 C2
Hart St
11 Wallingford OX10. . . . . 221 D7
Henley-on-T RG9 . . . . 244 E2
Oxford OX2 . . . . 261 A3
Hart-synnot Ho OX2 . . . . . 261 A4
Harvest Cres OX18. . . . . . . 115 F5
Harvest Pl RG10 . . . . 255 E1
Harvest Way OX28 . . . . 104 E2
Harveys Nurseries Pk Cvn
Site RG4. . . . . 259 C4
Harwell Cl OX14 . . . . 160 A1
Harwell Int Bsns Ctr
OX11 . . . . 217 A1
Harwell Prim Sch OX11 . 217 D7
Harwell Rd OX14. . . . . 199 F6
Harwood Rd OX11 . . . . 218 F5
Haseley Rd OX44 . . . . 163 F6
Haslemere Gdns OX2 . . . 109 A2
Haslemere Tramway Est
OX16 . . . . 16 E5
Haslemere Way OX16 . . . . . 16 E5
Hastings Cl OX16 . . . . 15 F6
Hastings Dr OX18 . . . . 115 F2
Hastings Hill OX7. . . . . 55 E5
Hastings Rd OX16. . . . . 15 F7
Hastoe Grange OX3 . . . . . 124 A4
Hatch Cl OX5 . . . . 77 F4
Hatch End Ind Est OX25 . . . 48 B2
Hatch End OX5 . . . . 77 F4
Hatchet Hill SN4. . . . . 227 A2
Hatch Gate La RG10. . . . . . 255 F7
Hatching La OX29. . . . . 87 A4
Hatch Way OX5. . . . . 77 F4
Hatfield Pits La OX29 . . . 104 C7
Hathaways OX33. . . . . 144 B8
Hatwell Row OX18 . . . . 115 E2
Havelock Rd OX4 . . . . 142 C5
Haven Cl OX10. . . . . 202 D8
Haven Vale OX12. . . . . 214 E5
Havers Ave OX14 . . . . 199 D2
Hawke La OX15 . . . . 21 D4
Hawker Sq GL54 . . . . 68 B4
Hawkins Ho 5 OX18. . . . . 115 E2
Hawkins St 1 OX4. . . . . . . 141 F7
Hawkins Way OX13 . . . . . . 159 B6
Hawk's La OX15 . . . . 19 C8
Hawksmead OX26. . . . . 81 A8
Hawksmoor Rd OX2. . . . . . 109 B1
Hawkswell Gdns OX2 . . . . 123 C7
Hawkswell Ho OX2. . . . . . . 123 C7
Hawksworth Cl OX12. . . . . 196 D1
Hawksworth OX11 . . . . 200 D4
Haw La
Aldworth RG8 . . . . 247 E1
Bledlow Ridge HP14 . . . . . . 189 F8
Hawlings Row OX4. . . . . . . 143 A1
Hawthorn Ave
Oxford OX3 . . . . 124 D3
Thame OX9 . . . . 147 E8
Hawthorn Cl
Oxford OX2 . . . . 140 D8
Wallingford OX10 . . . . 221 C7
Hawthorn Cres OX12. . . . . 214 E8
Hawthorn Dr
Burford OX18. . . . . 114 C7
Stoke Row RG9 . . . . 242 A1
Hawthorne Ave OX13 . . . . 159 C2
Hawthorne Rd RG4 . . . . . . 259 E4
Hawthornes RG31. . . . . . . 257 B3
Hawthorn Gr OX18. . . . . . . 115 D1
Hawthorn Rd
Eynsham OX29. . . . . 120 E8
Faringdon SN7. . . . . 172 E3
Hawthorns The OX16. . . . . . 16 D3
Hawthorn Way
Kidlington OX5. . . . . 108 E7
Hawthorn Way *continued*
Sonning RG4 . . . . 260 E3
Hawthorn Wlk 2 OX26. . . . . 65 F4
Hayden La RG9 . . . . 224 A3
Haydon Rd OX11. . . . . 200 E1
Hayes Ave OX13 . . . . 176 D8
Hayes Cl OX3. . . . . 123 F3
Hayes The OX1 . . . . 261 B2
Hayfield Rd OX2 . . . . 123 B5
Hayford Ho OX18 . . . . 115 F5
Haynes Rd OX3 . . . . 123 E5
Hayward Dr OX18. . . . . . . 115 D1
Hayward Rd OX2. . . . . 109 B2
Haywards Cl
Henley-on-T RG9 . . . . 244 C1
Wantage OX12. . . . . 214 E5
Haywards Rd OX14. . . . . . . 199 B7
Hazel Ave OX9. . . . . 147 E8
Hazel Cl
Abingdon OX14 . . . . 159 E1
Witney OX28 . . . . 104 E2
Hazel Cres OX5. . . . . 108 F6
Hazeldene Cl OX29 . . . . . . 105 B6
Hazeldene Gdns OX16. . . . . 16 D3
Hazeldene GL7 . . . . 150 D5
Hazel End OX44. . . . . 143 D2
Hazel Gdns RG4 . . . . 252 F5
Hazel Gr
Bicester OX26 . . . . 65 F4
Stoke Row RG9 . . . . 242 B2
Wallingford OX10 . . . . 221 C7
Hazells La GL7. . . . . 132 B5
Hazell's La SN6. . . . . 209 C6
Hazelmoor La RG4. . . . . . . 252 D4
Hazelnut Path OX14. . . . . 160 E7
Hazel Rd
Oxford OX2 . . . . 122 C1
Purley on T RG8. . . . . 257 C4
Hazelrig Cl OX9 . . . . 148 A8
Hazelton Cl OX9 . . . . 147 E8
Hazel Wlk OX5 . . . . 108 F6
Hazelwood Cl RG31. . . . . . 257 C1
Headington Jun Sch
OX3 . . . . 124 C2
Headington Rdbt OX3. . . . 124 F3
Headington Rd OX3. . . . . . 124 A2
Headington Sch OX3. . . . . 124 B2
Headley Ho OX3 . . . . 124 A4
Headley Way OX3. . . . . 124 B3
Healey Cl OX14 . . . . 179 E6
Hean Cl OX14. . . . . 160 B2
Hearns La RG4 . . . . 252 C5
Hearthway OX16 . . . . 9 B1
Heath Cl
Milcombe OX15 . . . . 20 F2
Oxford OX3 . . . . 142 D8
Heathcote Ave OX16 . . . . . . 16 E2
Heathcote Pl OX14. . . . . . 160 C1
Heath Ct OX15. . . . . 30 B7
Heath Dr RG9 . . . . 254 A1
Heather Cl
Carterton OX18 . . . . 115 E4
Sonning Common RG4. . . . 253 A5
Heather Pl OX3. . . . . 123 F4
Heather Rd
Bicester OX26 . . . . 65 E5
Milton OX14. . . . . 199 D6
Heathfield Ave RG9 . . . . . . 254 B2
Heathfield Cl RG9. . . . . . . 254 B2
Heath La OX20. . . . . 91 B1
Heath The OX7 . . . . 70 A2
Hedge End OX20. . . . . 91 C6
Hedge Hill Rd OX12. . . . . . 213 F5
Hedgemead Ave OX14. . . . 160 C2
Hedgerley OX39 . . . . 168 B6
Hedges Cl OX3 . . . . 124 E3
Hedges The OX15. . . . . 14 B8
Heigham Ct SN7. . . . . 194 D7
Helen Rd OX2 . . . . 122 F1
Helen's Way OX10 . . . . 203 F4
Hellebourine Cl OX4 . . . . . 142 F1
Helwys Pl OX5. . . . . 92 D2
Hemdean Hill RG4 . . . . 259 A3
Hemdean House Sch
RG4 . . . . 259 A3
Hemdean Rd RG4. . . . . 259 A3
Hemdean Rise RG4 . . . . . . 259 A3
Hemingway Dr OX26 . . . . . . 65 C2
Hemplands
Great Rollright OX7. . . . . 29 A3
Poffley End OX29. . . . . 104 C6
Hempton Rd OX15 . . . . 33 E4
Henderson Ho OX10 . . . . . 221 B7
Hendon Pl OX26 . . . . 66 A4
Hendred Ho OX4. . . . . 142 B6
Hendreds CE Sch The
OX12 . . . . 216 D6
Hendred St OX4 . . . . 142 B6
Hendred Way OX14 . . . . . . 160 B1
Henfield View OX10 . . . . . . 203 B8
Hengest Gate OX11 . . . . . . 217 E7
Hengrove Cl OX3 . . . . 124 D5
Henley Ave OX4 . . . . 142 A5
Henley Coll (Deanfield
Bldgs) The RG9. . . . . 244 D1
Henley Coll (Rotherfield
Bldgs) The RG9. . . . . 244 C1
Henley Dr SN6. . . . . 190 A7
Henley Gdns 9 OX26 . . . . . 65 E2
Henley-on-Thames Sta
RG9 . . . . 244 E1
Henley Rd
Reading RG4 . . . . 259 D3
Sandford-on-T OX4 . . . . . . 161 B8
Shillingford,Bridge End
OX10. . . . . 202 F7
Shillingford OX10. . . . . 203 A6
Shiplake RG9. . . . . 260 C8
Henleys La OX14. . . . . 179 B1
Henley St OX4 . . . . 141 F7
Hennef Way OX16. . . . . 16 E8
Henor Mill Cl OX14 . . . . . . 160 B2
Henrietta Rd OX9. . . . . . . 130 A1
Henry Box Cl OX28. . . . . . 118 A7
Henry Box Sch The
OX28 . . . . 118 A7
Henry Rd OX2 . . . . 122 F1
Henry Taunt Cl OX3 . . . . . 124 E5
Hensington Cl OX20. . . . . . . 91 C6
Hensington Rd OX20. . . . . . 91 B6
Hensington Wlk OX20. . . . . 91 C6
Henwood Cotts OX1 . . . . . 139 F1
Henwood Dr OX1 . . . . 140 A1
Herald Way OX26 . . . . 66 A4
Herbert Cl OX4 . . . . 142 B7
Hereford Way OX16 . . . . 9 A1
Heritage La OX7 . . . . 71 B2
Herman Cl OX14. . . . . 180 B8
Hermitage Rd OX14. . . . . . 179 E6
Hernes Cl OX2. . . . . 123 B8
Hernes Cres OX2 . . . . 123 B8
Hernes Rd OX2 . . . . 123 B8
Heron Cl OX18. . . . . 115 C3
Heron Ct
Abingdon OX14 . . . . 179 F4
Bicester OX26 . . . . 66 B1
Heron Dr OX26 . . . . 66 B1
Heron Island RG4. . . . . . . 259 C1
Heron Rd OX10 . . . . 204 D3
Heron Shaw RG8 . . . . 249 C7
Herons Pl OX2. . . . . 123 B8
Heron's Wlk OX14 . . . . 159 F1
Heron Way OX16. . . . . 16 A4
Herringcote OX10. . . . . 182 D2
Herschel Cres OX4. . . . . . . 142 C3
Herschel Ct OX4. . . . . 142 C3
Hertford Cl
Bicester OX26 . . . . 65 F3
Reading RG4 . . . . 259 D6
Hertford Coll OX1. . . . . 261 C2
Hertford Ct 8 OX5 . . . . . . 108 F8
Hertford St OX4 . . . . 142 A7
Hethe Rd
Cottisford NN13. . . . . 38 A3
Hardwick OX27 . . . . 51 D8
Hewett Ave RG4 . . . . 258 D4
Hewett Cl RG4. . . . . 258 D4
Hewgate Ct RG9 . . . . 244 E1
Hewitts Cl OX29 . . . . 87 A3
Hey Croft OX29 . . . . 120 E7
Heydons Terr OX17. . . . . 3 E8
Heyford Cl OX29 . . . . 137 C5
Heyford Hill La OX4. . . . . . 141 F2
Heyford Hill Rdbt OX4 . . . 141 F2
Heyford Ho 7 OX16 . . . . . . 16 E6
Heyford Mead OX5. . . . . 92 D1
Heyford Pk OX25. . . . . 63 C8
Heyford Rd
Kirtlington OX5 . . . . 78 A5
Middleton Stoney OX25. . . . . 64 A4
Steeple Aston OX25. . . . . 62 B7
Heyford Sta OX25. . . . . 62 C6
Hicks Cl OX29 . . . . 104 A6
Hid's Copse Rd OX2 . . . . . 140 B7
Higgs Cl OX11 . . . . 219 A6
High Acres OX16. . . . . 16 E4
Highbridge Cl RG4. . . . . . . 259 E5
Highclere Gdns
Banbury OX16 . . . . 15 E6
Wantage OX12. . . . . 214 D6
Highcliffe Cl RG5 . . . . 260 F1
High Cross Way OX3 . . . . . 124 E5
Highdown Ave RG4 . . . . . . 259 A6
Highdown Hill Rd RG4 . . . 259 A6
Highdown Sch & Sixth Form
Ctr RG4. . . . . 259 A5
Highfield Ave OX3 . . . . . . 124 C1
Highfield Cl OX9. . . . . 147 C8
Highfield HP18 . . . . 129 C7
Highfield Pk RG10 . . . . 255 F3
Highfield Rd RG31 . . . . 257 C4
High Furlong OX16 . . . . 16 B8
High House Cl OX18 . . . . . 152 E8
High Land Cl HP18. . . . . 98 A1
Highlands OX16. . . . . 9 A1
Highlands La RG9. . . . . 254 A8
Highlands OX15. . . . . 21 A6
Highlands Sch The RG31 257 D1
High Mdw
Reading RG4 . . . . 258 D3
Sibford Gower OX15 . . . . 13 A1
Highmoor Rd RG4 . . . . 258 F3
High Rd
Brightwell-cum-S OX10 . . . 202 E3
Brightwell-cum-S,Slade End
OX10. . . . . 203 A2
High Road Cotts OX10 . . . 202 D3
High St
Abingdon OX14 . . . . 179 F7
Adderbury OX17 . . . . 23 A4
Ardington OX12. . . . . 215 E5
Ascott-u-W OX7. . . . . 71 C2
Ashbury SN6 . . . . 228 A7
Aston OX18 . . . . 135 D3
Bampton OX18. . . . . 134 F3
Barford St M OX15 . . . . 32 F5
Beckley OX3. . . . . 111 A3
Benson OX10. . . . . 203 F4
Bishopstone SN6. . . . . 227 D4
Bloxham OX15 . . . . 21 E5
Bodicote OX15. . . . . 22 D8
Burford OX18. . . . . 100 E5
Chalgrove OX44. . . . . 184 C7
Charlton-on-O OX5 . . . . 95 A4
Childrey OX12 . . . . 213 C4
Chinnor OX39 . . . . 168 D7
High St *continued*
Chipping Norton OX7. . . . . . . 42 E3
Clifton Hampden OX14 . . . 181 C3
Cropredy OX17 . . . . 4 F2
Croughton NN13 . . . . 36 C8
Cuddesdon OX44. . . . . 144 B2
Culham OX14. . . . . 180 B3
Cumnor OX2 . . . . 139 D5
Deddington OX15. . . . . 33 F4
Didcot OX11. . . . . 218 F8
Dorchester OX10. . . . . 182 D1
Drayton OX14 . . . . 179 B1
Drayton St L OX10. . . . . 183 B5
East Hendred OX12. . . . . . . 216 E6
Ewelme OX10 . . . . 204 E4
Eynsham OX29. . . . . 120 E7
Fernham SN7. . . . . 193 A4
Fifield OX7. . . . . 69 B2
Finstock OX7 . . . . 88 B5
Goring RG8 . . . . 249 A6
Great Rollright OX7. . . . . 29 A3
Haddenham HP17 . . . . 130 F6
Harwell OX11 . . . . 217 E7
Highworth SN6 . . . . 190 A5
Hinton Waldrist SN7 . . . . . . 155 F2
Hook Norton OX15. . . . . 30 B7
Islip OX5 . . . . 93 F1
Kidlington OX5. . . . . 92 E1
Kingston Blount OX9 . . . . . 167 F3
Lechlade-on-T GL7. . . . . . . 150 C4
Lewknor OX49 . . . . 187 B8
Little Milton OX44 . . . . 163 F6
Long Crendon HP18. . . . . . 129 D6
Long Wittenham OX14. . . . 201 D8
Ludgershall HP18 . . . . 98 B8
Lyneham OX7. . . . . 70 D5
Middleton Cheney OX17 . . . . 17 F8
Milton OX14. . . . . 199 D5
Milton-u-W OX7. . . . . 70 A1
Nettlebed RG9. . . . . 224 D2
North Moreton OX11. . . . . . 220 A7
Oxford OX1 . . . . 261 C2
Pangbourne RG8 . . . . 256 C5
Ramsden OX7 . . . . 88 A3
Ratley OX15. . . . . 2 A3
Shipton-u-W OX18. . . . . 85 D8
Shrivenham SN6 . . . . 209 C6
Shutford OX15. . . . . 14 A5
Sonning RG4 . . . . 260 D4
Souldern OX27. . . . . 35 E3
South Moreton OX11. . . . . . 219 F5
South Newington OX15 . . . . . 31 F7
Standlake OX29. . . . . 137 D3
Stanford in the V SN7 . . . . . 194 E7
Steventon OX13. . . . . 199 A4
Stonesfield OX29. . . . . 89 C7
Streatley RG8 . . . . 249 C6
Sutton Courtenay OX14. . . . 200 A8
Tetsworth OX9. . . . . 166 B8
Thame OX9 . . . . 129 E1
Uffington SN7 . . . . 211 D7
Upper Heyford OX25 . . . . 48 F1
Upton OX11. . . . . 218 C2
Wallingford OX10 . . . . 221 D7
Wargrave RG10. . . . . 255 D2
Watchfield SN6 . . . . 191 D1
Watlington OX49 . . . . 186 B2
Wheatley OX33 . . . . 144 B8
Whitchurch-on-T RG8 . . . . . 256 C7
Witney OX28 . . . . 118 B8
Woodstock OX20. . . . . 91 B6
Hightown Gdns OX16 . . . . . 16 D3
Hightown Leyes OX16. . . . . . 16 D3
Hightown Rd OX16. . . . . 16 D4
High View OX12. . . . . 214 A4
Highworth Pl OX28 . . . . . . 118 A7
Highworth Rd
Faringdon SN7. . . . . 172 E2
Shrivenham SN6 . . . . 209 A7
Highworth Warneford Sch
SN6 . . . . 190 A4
Highworth Way RG31 . . . . 257 B2
Hikers Way HP18 . . . . 129 F4
Hillary Dr OX11 . . . . 218 E7
Hillary Way OX33 . . . . 144 C7
Hill Bottom Cl RG8 . . . . . 250 E3
Hill Cl
Charlbury OX7 . . . . 73 C3
Chipping Norton OX7. . . . . . . 42 E1
East Challow OX12 . . . . . . 214 A4
Hillcraft Rd OX33 . . . . 125 D7
Hill Cres OX7. . . . . 88 C5
Hillcrest La RG9 . . . . 252 F7
Hill Ct OX18 . . . . 115 D4
Hill Farm Ct OX39 . . . . . . 168 D6
Hill Farm La OX25 . . . . 47 D6
Hill Gdns RG8 . . . . 249 A6
Hill Ho OX25. . . . . 62 A8
Hilliard Ho OX14. . . . . 179 E5
Hilliat Fields OX14 . . . . 179 B1
Hilliers Cl OX14. . . . . 200 A8
Hill Lands RG10. . . . . 255 D2
Hill Lawn Ct OX7 . . . . 42 E3
Hill Piece OX11 . . . . 235 E7
Hill Prim Sch The RG4 . . 259 C5
Hill Rd
Chinnor OX39 . . . . 168 D5
Lewknor OX49 . . . . 187 A7
Lewknor OX49 . . . . 187 C6
Watchfield SN6 . . . . 191 D1
Watlington OX49 . . . . 206 E8
Hill Rise
Great Rollright OX7. . . . . 29 A3
Horspath OX33 . . . . 143 D6
Woodstock OX20. . . . . 91 A8

Hillsborough Cl **5** OX4...142 B3
Hillsborough Rd OX4...142 B4
Hillside Cl
  Banbury OX16...16 E3
  Upper Arncott OX25...96 E7
Hillside Cotts OX14...202 A6
Hillside
  Harwell OX11...217 B3
  Oxford OX2...140 B6
Hillside Rd OX7...46 E1
Hillside RG8...256 D8
Hill The
  Aynho OX17...35 C7
  Bourton SN6...209 A3
  Burford OX18...100 E4
  Burford,Westwell OX18...99 F1
  Garsington OX44...143 E1
Hilltop Cl OX4...142 B8
Hilltop Gdns OX5...93 F1
Hill Top La OX39...168 F4
Hilltop HP18...129 D5
Hill Top Rd OX4...142 B8
Hilltop Rd RG4...258 D5
Hill View OX18...115 D4
Hillview Cl RG31...257 E2
Hill View Cres OX16...16 A7
Hill View OX12...212 B4
Hill View La OX1...159 A8
Hill View OX3...125 A4
Hill View Prim Sch OX16...16 A7
Hillview Rd
  Abingdon OX14...159 F2
  Oxford OX2...123 A1
Hill View SN7...211 C7
Hillwerke OX39...168 C6
Hillyard Barns OX44...200 A8
Hilton Rd OX16...16 B6
Hinksey Bsns Ctr OX2...122 D1
Hinksey Hill OX1...141 C3
Hinksey Hill OX1...141 B3
Hinshelwood Rd OX1...261 C3
Hinton Hill SN4...227 A3
Hinton Rd OX13...156 B3
Hinton Springs SN4...227 B3
Hirstwood RG30...257 E1
Hiskins OX12...214 B5
Hitching Ct OX14...179 C7
Hitchman Dr OX7...42 E2
Hithercroft Ct OX10...221 B6
Hithercroft Ind Est OX10...221 B7
Hithercroft Rd
  Cholsey OX10,OX11...220 D5
  Wallingford OX10...221 C7
Hive Mews **3** OX14...179 F6
Hixet Wood OX7...73 B3
Hobbs Cl OX14...180 B8
Hobbs End RG9...254 B8
Hobby Ct OX4...142 F1
Hobbyhorse La OX14...200 B7
Hobson Rd OX2...123 B7
Hocker Bench SN6...227 D4
Hocketts Cl RG8...250 F8
Hockmore St OX4...142 C4
Hodge Ct OX1...141 C1
Hodgson Cl OX27...49 F7
Hogarth Pl OX14...179 E5
Hogg End
  Bloxham OX15...21 E4
  Chipping Warden OX17...5 F6
Holborn Hill OX12...231 D7
Holcombe La OX10...183 D6
Holford Rd OX28...117 F7
Holkam Cl RG30...257 C7
Holland Cl OX39...168 D7
Holland Pl OX3...142 E8
Holland Rd OX14...160 A2
Hollandridge La OX49,
  RG9...207 D4
Holland Rise OX17...23 F4
Holley Cres OX3...124 E3
Holliers Cl
  Sydenham OX39...167 D8
  Thame OX9...147 F8
Holliers Cres OX7...60 F8
Hollies Ct The **9** OX16...16 D5
Hollington HP18...129 B7
Hollis Cl OX28...118 D7
Holloway Hill OX15...12 A2
Holloway La
  Northend RG9...207 F5
  Winderton OX15...12 A1
Holloway Rd The SN7...192 B8
Holloway Rd
  Wheatley OX33...144 B8
  Witney OX28...118 A8
Holloway The
  Harwell OX11...217 B6
  Mollington OX17...4 A3
Hollow Furlong OX29...107 C2
Hollow Rd The SN7...172 B1
Hollow Way
  Aynho OX17...35 C7
  Childrey OX12...213 C3
  Oxford OX4...142 D6
  Upton OX11...218 C1
Hollybush Rd
  Carterton OX18...115 D2
  Hook Norton OX15...30 B8
Hollybush Row OX1...261 A2
Holly Cl
  Bicester OX26...65 F5
  Highmoor Cross RG9...242 E5
  Kidlington OX5...108 E7
Holly Ct OX4...142 E3

Hollyhocks OX11...217 B7
Holmemoor Dr RG4...260 E2
Holme Park Farm La
  RG4...260 C2
Holmlea Rd RG8...249 C5
Holm Sq OX26...65 E5
Holm Way OX26...65 E5
Holt The
  Abingdon OX14...179 F8
  Mollington OX17...3 F3
  Purley on T RG8...257 D4
Holt Weer Cl OX2...108 F2
Holyoake Rd OX3...124 D3
Holyrood Cl RG4...259 B8
Holy Trinity RC Sch OX7...42 F3
Holywell Bsns Cntr OX2...141 A8
Holywell Cl OX14...160 C2
Holywell St OX1...261 C3
Home Cl
  Carterton OX18...115 D2
  Kidlington OX5...92 E1
  Shabbington HP18...128 D3
  Wolvercote OX2...122 D8
  Wootton OX13...159 B7
Home Croft RG31...257 B1
Home Farm OX17...23 B4
Home Farm Barns OX18...133 B6
Home Farm Cl
  Ambrosden OX25...81 C3
  East Hendred OX12...216 D7
  Shipton-u-W OX7...85 D7
Home Farm Cotts
  Leafield OX29...102 F8
  Rousham OX25...62 A4
Home Farm OX10...221 F7
Home Farm Ct OX17...23 B4
Home Farm Dr OX15...6 D8
Homelands Way RG8...244 D1
Homeleaze Rd SN6...209 E8
Homestall Cl OX2...108 A1
Homestead Cres OX25...63 A8
Homestead Rd OX16...16 E2
Homestead The
  Binfield Heath RG9...254 B1
  Bladon OX20...91 C3
  Kidlington OX5...108 D8
  Thame OX9...129 E1
Hone Ct OX7...73 B3
Honeybottom La OX13...159 B5
Honeyham Cl OX18...116 C3
Honey La OX10...221 C6
Honey Meadow Cl RG4...259 E2
Honeysuckle Cl OX26...65 F5
Honeysuckle Gr OX4...143 A2
Honor Cl OX5...108 F8
Hookend La RG8...251 D8
Horley Path Rd OX15...8 B1
Hornbeam Cl
  Banbury OX16...16 B5
  Purley on T RG8...257 C5
Hornbeam Dr OX4...143 A2
Hornbeam Rd OX26...65 F5
Horne OX27...66 A7
Horn Hill OX15...32 F6
Horn Hill Rd OX17...22 F3
Horn La
  Chastleton GL56...40 A4
  East Hendred OX12...216 D5
Hornsea Cl RG30...257 E1
Hornton Hollow OX15...21 D4
Horse Close Cotts OX44...164 D8
Horse Cl The RG4...259 C4
Horsecroft SN7...194 E7
Horse Fair
  Banbury OX16...16 C6
  Chipping Norton OX7...42 E3
  Deddington OX15...33 F4
Horseman Cl OX3...124 A5
Horsemere La OX29...105 C7
Horsepath Park Cvn Site
  OX33...143 D6
Horsepond Rd RG4...252 B5
Horse Shoe La OX7...72 B8
Horseshoe La OX10...75 F4
Horseshoe Pk RG8...256 D5
Horseshoe Rd
  Bledlow Ridge HP14...189 C8
  Pangbourne RG8...256 D5
Horseshoes Cl OX13...158 A7
Horseshoes La OX10...203 F4
Horseshoes Pl OX9...148 A7
Horspath CE Prim Sch
  OX33...143 C7
Horspath Driftway OX3...143 B5
Horspath Rd Ind Est OX4...142 F6
Horspath Rd OX4...142 E6
Horton Ave OX9...148 A7
Horton Cl OX9...148 A7
Horton General Hospl
  OX16...16 D4
Horton La OX15...21 A2

Horton View OX16...16 C3
Horwood OX3...124 C3
Hosker Cl OX3...125 A3
Hound Cl OX14...160 C2
Howard Ave OX12...196 E1
Howard Cornish Rd
  OX13...178 D7
Howard Rd OX16...16 F6
Howard St OX4...142 A6
Howbery Farm OX10...221 F7
Howe Cl OX3...144 A8
Howe Rd OX49...206 C8
Howes La OX26...65 B7
Howgate Dr RG8...249 C7
Howland Rd OX9...148 B7
Hoyle Cl OX28...104 A3
Hubble Cl OX3...124 E5
Huckleberry Cl RG8...257 C4
Hudleston Ave OX10...204 C2
Hudson Cl OX15...33 F4
Hudson St
  Bicester OX26...65 D3
  Deddington OX15...33 F4
Hugh Allen Cres OX3...123 F3
Hughes Cl OX7...73 C2
Hughes Cres SN7...192 C3
Hughes Ho OX4...141 F8
Hugh Price Ho OX4...142 B7
Humber Cl
  Didcot OX14...201 A1
  Wantage OX12...214 E5
Humber St OX15...21 E4
Humber Wlk OX16...15 F8
Humfrey Rd OX3...124 F4
Humphries Cl OX18...115 E3
Hunder Ct OX1...141 D2
Hundley Way OX7...73 C4
Hundred Acres Cl OX3...142 F7
Hungerford Rd OX13...199 B1
Hunsdon Rd OX4...142 A4
Hunt Cl OX26...65 E2
Hunt Ct HP14...188 F4
Hunter Cl
  Abingdon OX14...160 B3
  Oxford OX4...142 E6
Huntercombe End La
  RG9...224 B4
Hunters Chase RG4...258 F5
Hunters Cl OX12...196 C1
Hunters Field SN7...194 E7
Hunters Piece SN6...209 A2
Hunters Point OX39...168 C6
Hunt Rd OX9...148 B7
Hunts Cl OX18...100 E4
Hunt's Cl OX8...89 C7
Hurdeswell OX29...90 A1
Hurdlers Gn OX49...186 A2
Hurst Cl OX10...221 C6
Hurst La
  Freeland OX29...106 A4
  Oxford OX2...140 B6
Hurst Rise Rd OX2...140 C8
Hurst St OX4...141 F7
Huscarle Way RG31...257 C4
Hutchcombe Farm Cl
  OX2...140 C7
Hutchcomb Rd OX2...140 C8
Huxley Cl
  Bicester OX26...65 C3
  Wootton OX13...159 B6
Hyacinth Wlk OX4...161 E8
Hyde Copse OX13...178 D7
Hyde Pl OX15...21 C3
Hyde Rd
  Abingdon OX14...179 D5
  Oxford OX2...123 A7
Hyde Rd OX12...196 A5
Hydes The RG31...257 C4
Hyde The OX14...179 D5
Hydrangea Wlk OX16...9 B1
Hythe Bridge St OX1...261 A2

I

Ian Mikardo Way RG4...259 D2
Ibstone Ave RG4...259 E5
Ibstone Rd HP14...188 E3
Ickford Comb Sch HP18...128 A3
Ickford Rd
  Shabbington HP18...128 D2
  Tiddington OX9...145 F8
  Worminghall HP18...127 E6
Ickleton Rd OX12...214 B4
Icknield Cl
  Chinnor OX39...168 A4
  Didcot OX11...200 C1
Icknield Com Coll OX49...186 B2
Icknield Cotts RG8...249 B6
Icknield La OX12...214 E4
Icknield Line Steam Rly*
  OX39...168 C7
Icknield Pl RG8...249 B8
Icknield Rd RG8...249 D8
Icknield Way
  Bishopstone SN6...227 C4
  Bishopstone SN6...227 D4
Idbury Cl OX28...117 D7
Idstone Hill SN6...228 A4
Idstone Rd SN6...228 A6
Iffley Mead Sch OX4...141 F5
Iffley Rd OX4...141 F7
Iffley Turn OX4...142 A5
Ilchester Mews RG4...259 E6
Ilex Cl RG4...252 F4
Ilges La OX10...221 A2
Ilkley Rd RG4...258 E3
Illingworth Ave RG4...259 E6

Ilsley Cl RG4...252 F5
Ilsley Rd OX3...124 E4
Imperial Ct RG9...244 E1
Independent Bsns Pk
  HP14...188 C5
Ingham La OX49...186 B1
Ingle Cl OX3...124 B4
Inglewood Cl RG4...252 F6
Ingrebourne Way OX11...200 F3
Inkerman Cl OX14...159 D1
Innsworth Rd OX18...115 E3
Inott Furze OX3...142 D7
Insall Rd OX7...42 E4
Inst Of Virology &
  Experimental Microbiology
  OX1...261 C3
Ireton Cl OX44...184 D6
Ireton Ct OX9...129 F1
Iron Down Hill OX15,OX7...32 C3
Ironside Dr SN6...191 D1
Ironstone Hollow OX15...30 C8
Ironstones OX16...16 A8
Ishree Cotts RG9...242 A5
Isis Ave OX26...65 B2
Isis Bsns Ctr OX4...142 F6
Isis CE Mid Sch OX4...141 E6
Isis Cl
  Abingdon OX14...160 B1
  Long Hanborough OX29...106 B8
Isis Ct RG1...259 B1
Islip Rd
  Bletchingdon OX5...93 A7
  Oxford OX2...123 B8
Islip Sta OX5...93 F1
Itchen Cl OX14...201 A3
Ivatt Wlk OX16...16 E8
Ivybank RG31...257 C1
Ivy Cl OX4...142 D5
Ivydene Rd RG30...258 C1
Ivy La
  Mollington OX17...4 A3
  Oxford OX3...124 C4
  Shutford OX15...14 B5

J

Jack Argent Cl **16** OX4...142 F1
Jackdaw La OX4...141 E7
Jackies La OX33...144 C7
Jackman Cl OX14...180 A7
Jackson Cl OX18...115 D2
Jackson Cole Ho OX1...261 A2
Jackson Dr OX1...141 D2
Jackson Rd
  Bledington OX7...54 D2
  Cutteslowe OX2...109 B1
Jacksons La RG4...258 C5
Jack Straw's La OX3...124 A3
Jacobs Cl OX28...104 B1
Jacobs Yd OX7...60 F8
James Cl OX18...152 E8
James St OX4...141 F8
James Wolfe Rd OX4...142 E7
Janaway OX4...142 A1
Jane Morbey Rd OX9...148 A7
Jane Seaman Ct OX4...143 A1
Japonica Cl OX26...65 F5
Japonica Wlk OX16...9 B1
Jarn Way OX1...140 D1
Jarvis' La OX26...66 B2
Jasmine Cl OX4...142 F3
Jasmine Pl OX26...65 F5
Jasmine Way OX18...115 E5
Jasmine Wlk OX16...9 B1
Javelin Way OX10...204 D3
Jay Cl OX26...81 A8
Jaynes Ct OX14...16 D2
Jefferson Cl RG4...259 C7
Jeffersons Piece OX7...73 C4
Jenner Way OX9...148 A7
Jeff's Terr OX7...73 B4
Jemmetts Cl OX10...182 D1
Jennings La OX11...217 E7
Jenyns Ct OX14...179 C6
Jericho St OX2...261 A4
Jerome Way OX5...92 B6
Jersey Dr OX16...9 A1
Jersey Rd OX4...142 A3
Jerusalem Cl OX7...60 F8
Jespers Hill SN7...173 A3
Jesse's La HP18...129 C6
Jessops Cl
  Marston OX3...123 C5
  Oxford OX3...124 A5
Jesus Coll OX1...261 B2
Jethro Tull Gdns OX10...221 E7
Jetty The OX17...5 E1
Jeune Hall **1** OX4...141 F8
Jeune St OX4...141 F8
Joan Lawrence Pl OX3...124 E1
John Allen Ctr OX4...142 C5
John Blandy Prim Sch
  OX13...156 E1
John Buchan Rd OX3...124 B5
John Garne Way OX3...124 A3
John Hampden Prim Sch
  OX9...148 A7
John Henry Newman CE
  Prim Sch The OX4...142 B2
John Kallie Ho OX4...142 B6
John Lopes Rd OX29...120 E7
John Mason Rd OX14...180 A8
John Mason Sch OX14...179 E8
John Morris Rd OX14...179 E6
John Piers La OX1...141 C5
John Radcliffe Hospl
  OX3...124 B4

John Smith Dr OX4...142 D4
John Snow Pl OX3...124 E3
John Towle Cl OX1...141 D5
John Watson Sch OX33...126 B1
Jordan Cl
  Didcot OX14...201 A2
  Reading RG4...259 E5
Jordan Hill OX2...109 A2
Jordans OX7...88 A3
Josca's Prep Sch OX13...178 A7
Josey Cl RG4...252 F6
Jourdain Rd OX4...142 F3
Jowett Wlk OX1...261 C3
Joyce's Rd SN7...194 D8
Jubilee Cl OX12...215 E5
Jubilee Cotts OX12...215 E5
Jubilee Gdns OX9...147 D8
Jubilee La OX7...85 A8
Jubilee Rd HP14...188 F3
Jubilee Terr OX1...261 B1
Jubilee Way
  Didcot OX11...219 A8
  Witney OX28...104 E1
Judds Cl OX18...115 D8
Judges Cl OX5...108 D8
Judges Rd RG9...241 E4
Jugglers Cl OX16...16 E8
Junction Rd
  Banbury OX16...16 E6
  Churchill OX7...55 E4
  Oxford OX4...142 D6
Juniper Cl OX16...9 B1
Juniper Ct
  4 Abingdon OX14...179 D7
  8 Banbury OX16...16 D5
Juniper Dr OX4...142 F2
Juniper Gdns OX26...65 E5
Juniper Way RG31...257 D2
Juxon St OX2...261 A4

K

Kames Cl OX4...142 B5
Karenza HP14...188 E5
Kassam Stad (Oxford Utd FC)
  OX4...142 D1
Katchside OX14...199 F6
Katherine's Wlk GL7...150 D4
Keats Cl **4** OX4...65 C4
Keats Rd OX16...16 A4
Keble Cl GL7...150 D5
Keble Coll OX1...261 B4
Keble Rd
  Bicester OX26...65 F3
  Oxford OX1...261 B4
Kedleston Rise OX16...16 E2
Keene Cl OX4...161 B8
Keens Cl OX7...58 F5
Keens La OX39...168 D6
Keeys Ct OX27...50 C4
Kelburne Rd OX4...142 B4
Kelham Hall Dr OX33...144 B7
Kelly's Rd OX33...143 F8
Kelmscott Cl RG4...258 F3
Kelmscott Manor* GL7...151 E2
Kelso Mews RG4...259 E6
Kelvedon Way RG4...259 D3
Kempson Cres OX4...142 A2
Kemps Rd OX17...23 A5
Kempster Cl OX14...180 B8
Kendal Ave RG4...259 E5
Kendall Cres OX2...109 B1
Kendal Piece OX7...73 C4
Kenhill Rd OX15...6 E2
Kenilworth Ave OX4...142 B7
Kenilworth Ct OX4...142 B7
Kenilworth Rd OX2...139 E4
Kenilworth Way OX16...115 F5
Kenley Ave OX18...115 E3
Kennedy Cl OX4...142 E7
Kennedy Cres OX10...220 F1
Kennedy Dr RG8...256 E5
Kennedy Ho OX16...16 B6
Kennedy Rd OX26...65 C1
Kennel La
  Chipping Norton OX7...42 B2
  Steventon OX13...199 A5
Kennet Cl
  Berinsfield OX10...182 C4
  Bicester OX26...65 D1
  Grove OX12...196 D1
Kennet Rd
  Abingdon OX14...160 B1
  Harwell OX11...217 C1
Kennett Pl **3** OX11...219 A8
Kennett Rd OX3...124 D2
Kennetts Hos OX15...21 D4
Kennington Rdbt OX1...141 D3
Kennington Rd
  Kennington OX1...141 D4
  Kennington OX1...141 E4
  Kennington OX1...160 E6
Kennylands Rd RG4...253 A3
Kensington Cl
  Abingdon OX14...179 E4
  Kings Sutton OX17...23 F6
Kent Cl
  Abingdon OX14...180 B8
  Oxford OX4...142 E3
Kenton's La RG10...255 D7
Kentwood Cl
  Cholsey OX10...220 F1

Kentwood Cl *continued*
  Reading RG30 . . . . .257 E1
Kentwood Hill RG31. . . . . . .257 E1
Kenville Rd OX1 . . . . .141 D2
Kernham Dr RG31. . . . . .257 C4
Kerry Cl OX16 . . . . .9 A1
Kersington Cres OX4. . . . . .142 D3
Kerwood Cl OX20 . . . . .91 C7
Keston Cl RG4 . . . . .259 C2
Kestrel Cl OX18 . . . . .115 D3
Kestrel Cres OX14 . . . . .160 A1
Kestrels The OX12 . . . . .196 D2
Kestrel Way OX26 . . . . .81 A7
Ketchmere Cl HP18 . . . . . . .129 C6
Kew Win OX14. . . . . .201 A2
Keydale Rd OX33 . . . . .143 F8
Keyser Rd OX15. . . . . .22 E8
Keyte's Ct OX17 . . . . .23 B4
Kibble Cl OX11 . . . . .219 A8
Kiddington Dr OX7. . . . . .74 D7
Kiddington Rd OX7 . . . . .60 E8
Kidlington Ctr The OX5. . . . . .92 E1
Kidlington Rd OX5 . . . . .93 E1
Kidmore End CE Prim Sch
  RG4 . . . . .252 D3
Kidmore End Rd RG4 . . . . . .259 D7
Kidmore La RG4 . . . . .252 E4
Kidmore Rd RG4. . . . . .258 F5
Kilbale Cres OX16. . . . . .16 D4
Kildare Gdns RG4. . . . . .259 C3
Kilkenny La OX18 . . . . .115 E6
Kiln Cl
  Aston OX18 . . . . .135 D3
  Sandford-on-T OX4 . . . . . .161 C8
Kiln La
  Garsington OX44. . . . . . . .143 C2
  Oxford OX3 . . . . .124 F2
  Shiplake Row RG9 . . . . . . .254 C2
  Wheatley OX33 . . . . .144 A8
Kiln Rd RG4 . . . . .259 D8
Kiln Terr SN7 . . . . .173 B3
Kimbells Cl HP18 . . . . .128 D2
Kimber Cl OX33. . . . . .144 B8
Kimberley Villas **12** OX16 .16 D5
Kimber Rd OX14 . . . . .179 C7
Kimbers Cl OX12. . . . . .196 A4
Kinecroft OX10 . . . . .221 D7
Kineton Rd OX1 . . . . .141 C7
King Alfred Dr OX11 . . . . . . .200 F1
King Alfred's Com & Sports
  Coll (East Site) OX12 . . . .214 F4
King Alfred's Com & Sports
  Coll OX12. . . . . .214 D4
King Alfred's Com & Sports
  Coll (West Site) OX12. . . .214 B4
King Edward St OX1 . . . . . . .261 C2
Kingfisher Cl OX14. . . . . . . .179 F5
Kingfisher Dr
  Banbury OX16 . . . . .16 E4
  Witney OX28 . . . . .118 A6
Kingfisher Gn OX4 . . . . .142 F1
Kingfishers OX12 . . . . .214 E4
Kingfisher Specl Sch
  OX14 . . . . .180 B8
Kingfisher Way OX26. . . . . . .81 A8
Kingham Dr OX18. . . . . .115 D2
Kingham Hill Sch OX7 . . . . . .41 B1
Kingham Prim Sch OX7 . . . . .55 A5
Kingham Rd OX7 . . . . .55 E5
Kingham Sta OX7 . . . . .54 F2
King James Way RG9 . . . . . .254 C8
Kings Ave
  Bicester OX26 . . . . .65 D1
  Highworth SN6 . . . . .190 A5
  Marcham OX13 . . . . .178 D7
Kings Cl SN6 . . . . .228 A7
Kingsclere Rd OX26. . . . . . . .65 D2
Kings Cl
  Henley-on-T RG9 . . . . . . .244 D2
  Letcombe Regis OX12 . . . .214 A2
King's Cl OX1. . . . . .141 A2
Kings Cl HP18 . . . . .127 D5
Kings Common Cl RG9 . . . . .254 B1
King's Cross Rd OX2 . . . . . . .123 B7
King's Cross Rd OX18 . . . . . .115 E3
King's End OX26 . . . . .65 C1
Kingsey Rd
  Thame OX9 . . . . .148 B8
  Towersey OX9 . . . . .130 D1
Kings Farm La RG9 . . . . .253 E6
Kingsfield Cres OX28. . . . . . .104 C1
Kingsgate OX4. . . . . .142 D4
King's Head La OX5. . . . . .93 F1
King's Head Mews OX7 . . . . .42 E3
Kingsholme Cl OX11 . . . . . . .218 F5
Kings La
  Filkins GL7 . . . . .132 D4
  Harwell OX11 . . . . .217 E7
King's La SN7 . . . . .192 C3
Kingsley Rd **6** OX26 . . . . . . .65 C4
Kingsmead GL7 . . . . .150 C5
Kings Meadow Ind Est
  OX2 . . . . .140 F8
Kings Meadow Prim Sch
  OX26 . . . . .65 B3
King's Mill La OX3 . . . . .123 F2
King's Orch OX10 . . . . .182 D6
King's Rd OX15. . . . . .21 B5
King's Rd RG9 . . . . .244 D2
Kings Rd RG9. . . . . .244 E2
King's Rd
  Reading RG4 . . . . .259 C2
  Thame OX9 . . . . .148 A8
Kings Row HP14 . . . . .188 E5
King's Sch The OX29 . . . . . . .104 D3
Kings Stile OX17. . . . . .10 F1
Kings Sutton Sta OX17. . . . . .23 A4

Kingston Bsns Pk OX13 . .176 F8
Kingston Cl OX14 . . . . .179 F8
Kingston Ct OX2. . . . . .261 A4
Kingstone Bagpuize House *
  OX13 . . . . .176 E8
Kingston Hill OX39 . . . . .188 B8
Kingston Hts OX29 . . . . .105 B7
Kingston Rd OX2 . . . . .123 B4
King St OX2 . . . . .261 A4
Kingsway OX16 . . . . .16 B5
Kingsway Cotts OX18 . . . . . .135 D2
Kingsway Dr OX5 . . . . .109 A8
Kingsway RG4 . . . . .259 E6
Kings Wlk RG9 . . . . .244 D2
Kingswood La HP18 . . . . .98 F6
King Wlk OX11 . . . . .200 E2
Kinson Rd RG30 . . . . .258 A1
Kipling Cl OX26 . . . . .65 C4
Kirby Cl
  Middle Barton OX7 . . . . . . .60 F8
  South Moreton OX11 . . . . .219 F5
Kirby Pl OX4 . . . . .142 D5
Kirby Rd GL54 . . . . .68 B3
Kirk Cl
  Cutteslowe OX2 . . . . .109 A1
  Kennington OX1. . . . . .160 E8
Kirkfell Cl RG31 . . . . .257 C2
Kirkham Cl RG4 . . . . .259 E6
Kirtlington CE Prim Sch
  OX5 . . . . .78 A4
Kirtlington Rd OX25. . . . . . . .63 A7
Kit La RG8. . . . . .241 D6
Knapp Cl OX14 . . . . .179 D8
Knappe Cl RG9 . . . . .254 C8
Knapton's Croft OX25 . . . . . .62 D6
Knighton Cl RG4 . . . . .259 A3
Knighton Hill SN6 . . . . .210 E1
Knightsbridge La OX49 . .186 B5
Knights Ho OX3 . . . . .124 F2
Knights Rd OX4. . . . . .142 E2
Knights Way RG4 . . . . .259 B5
Knoll Cl OX12. . . . . .231 E7
Knolles Dr SN7 . . . . .194 D7
Knolles Rd OX4 . . . . .142 C5
Knoll The RG31 . . . . .257 B2
Knollys Cl OX14 . . . . .160 A3
Knott Oaks OX29 . . . . .89 F5
Knowlands SN6 . . . . .190 A7
Knowle Cl RG4 . . . . .258 D4
Knowle La OX25. . . . . .79 B1
Knowsley Rd RG31 . . . . .257 C3
Kybald St OX1 . . . . .261 C2
Kynaston Rd OX11 . . . . .218 F8
Kysbie Cl OX14 . . . . .159 F3

L

Laburnum Ave OX13 . . .159 C1
Laburnum Cl
  Ambrosden OX25. . . . . . . .81 C3
  Carterton OX18 . . . . .115 F4
Laburnum Cres OX5 . . . . . . .108 E6
Laburnum Gr
  Banbury OX16 . . . . .16 D2
  Didcot OX11. . . . . .218 F8
Laburnum Rd OX2 . . . . .140 D7
Lacemakers
  Chinnor OX39 . . . . .168 C6
  Long Crendon HP18. . . . . .129 C7
Lacey Dr OX9. . . . . .148 B7
Lackmore Gdns RG8 . . . . . . .250 F8
Ladburn La OX18 . . . . .115 A6
Ladder Hill OX33. . . . . .144 A7
Ladenham Rd OX4 . . . . .142 E3
Ladman Villas SN7 . . . . .173 F7
Ladycroft Cvn Pk OX11. .219 A1
Lady Gr OX14 . . . . .201 B4
Ladygrove Paddock
  OX14 . . . . .179 D6
Ladygrove Park Prim Sch
  OX11 . . . . .200 F2
Ladygrove Rd OX14 . . . . . . .159 F1
Lady Jane Ct RG4. . . . . .259 B3
Lady Margaret Hall Coll
  OX2 . . . . .123 D4
Lady Pl OX14 . . . . .200 A8
Ladywell Cl OX29 . . . . .105 E4
Lady Wlk SN7 . . . . .211 C7
Laggots Cl SN7 . . . . .155 F2
Lains Ct OX12 . . . . .214 D7
Lakefield Rd OX4 . . . . .142 B1
Lake Rd
  East Hagbourne OX11. . . . .218 E5
  Shrivenham SN6 . . . . .209 D7
Lakeside OX2. . . . . .122 C2
Lakeside Ind Est OX29 . . .137 F7
Lakeside OX28 . . . . .118 A6
Lakesmere Cl OX5 . . . . .92 C2
Lake St OX1. . . . . .141 D6
Lake View NN13. . . . . .38 A3
Lake Wlk OX17 . . . . .23 B4
Lamarsh Rd OX2 . . . . .122 C1
Lambe Ave OX14. . . . . .199 C3
Lambert Wlk OX9. . . . . .177 B1
Lamb La OX20 . . . . .91 B2
Lambourough Hill OX13 .159 B6
Lambourne Cres OX26 . . . . . .66 F5
Lambourn Rd RG4 . . . . .252 E5
Lambourne Way OX17. . . . . .23 B4
Lambourn Rd OX4 . . . . .142 A3
Lambrick Way OX14. . . . . . .179 E4
Lambridge La RG9. . . . . .244 C3
Lambridge Wood Rd
  RG9 . . . . .244 B4
Lambs Cl OX5. . . . . .92 E2
Lamb's Cres OX16. . . . . .16 E4

Lamb's La OX20 . . . . .75 F4
Lambton Ct OX44 . . . . .64 A7
Lambwath Stream OX11. .200 F3
Lammas Cl OX14. . . . . .159 F1
Lamorna Cres RG31. . . . . . . .257 C1
Lampitts Gn OX15. . . . . .15 A8
Lancaster Cl OX10 . . . . .204 D3
Lancaster Cl OX26 . . . . .66 A4
Lancaster Dr GL54 . . . . .68 B4
Lancaster Pl OX18 . . . . .115 E1
Lanchester Dr OX16. . . . . . . .15 F8
Lancott La OX29 . . . . .137 B4
Lancut Rd OX28 . . . . .103 E1
Landells OX18 . . . . .134 E4
Landscape Cl OX25 . . . . .79 A5
Landscape Rd OX25. . . . . . . .79 A5
Landseer Wlk OX25 . . . . . . .179 E5
Lane Cl
  Horley OX15 . . . . .8 B4
  Oxford OX3 . . . . .124 F4
Lane End OX10 . . . . .222 A7
Lanes End OX26 . . . . .66 E2
Lane The OX18. . . . . .134 F3
Lane The
  Ashbury SN6 . . . . .228 A7
  Chastleton GL56. . . . . .40 D7
  Chilton OX11. . . . . .235 E8
  Cuddesdon OX44. . . . . . . .144 B2
  Fritwell OX27. . . . . .49 F7
  Great Tew OX7 . . . . .45 C7
  Hempton OX15 . . . . .33 B4
  Hinton Parva SN4 . . . . . . .227 A4
  Lower Heyford OX25. . . . . .62 D6
  Uffington SN7 . . . . .211 C7
Langdale Ct OX28. . . . . .118 B8
Langdale Gate OX28 . . . . . . .118 B8
Langdale Rd OX9 . . . . .148 A8
Langdenhills Bsns Pk OX5 . . .92 B2
Langford Cl RG4 . . . . .259 C5
Langford Gdns OX26 . . . . . . .65 E2
Langford La
  Kidlington OX5. . . . . .92 A2
  Wendlebury OX25 . . . . .80 D5
Langford Locks OX5 . . . . . . .92 C2
Langford Village Com Sch
  OX26 . . . . .81 A8
Langhams Way RG10 . . . . . .255 E2
Langley Cl OX3 . . . . .124 D2
Langley La OX13 . . . . .152 D5
Langley Rd
  Abingdon OX14 . . . . .159 F2
  Chalgrove OX44 . . . . .184 C6
Langley's La OX29 . . . . .137 C1
Langston Ct OX7 . . . . .55 E5
Langston Priory Workshops
  OX7 . . . . .55 E5
Langton Ave OX25 . . . . .81 D4
Langtree Sch RG8 . . . . .240 F1
Lanham Way OX4 . . . . .142 B2
Lansdown Cl OX16. . . . . .16 B3
Lansdowne Rd OX13 . . . . . . .159 A6
Lansdown Rd SN7 . . . . .173 A3
Lapsley Dr OX16 . . . . .9 C2
Lapwing Cl OX26 . . . . .81 A8
Lapwing La OX10 . . . . .221 A1
Larch Cl
  Bicester OX26 . . . . .65 E4
  Kingston Bagpuize OX13 . .156 E1
  Oxford OX2 . . . . .140 D8
Larch Ct RG4. . . . . .259 B3
Larch End OX44. . . . . .143 D2
Larches The
  Carterton OX18 . . . . .115 D2
  Oxford OX3 . . . . .125 A3
Lardon Cotts RG8. . . . . .249 A6
Larissa Cl RG31. . . . . .257 E1
Larkdown OX12. . . . . .214 F4
Larkfield OX10 . . . . .221 A1
Larkfields OX3. . . . . .124 E2
Lark Hill
  Ardington OX12. . . . . .215 A2
  Oxford OX2 . . . . .123 A6
Larkhill Pl OX14 . . . . .159 D1
Larkhill Rd OX14 . . . . .179 E8
Larkins La OX3 . . . . .124 D4
Larkmead Sch OX14 . . . . . . .179 C8
Larkrise Prim Sch OX4 . .142 A6
Larksfield Cl OX18. . . . . .133 C8
Larkspur Gr OX26 . . . . .65 E4
Larkspur Sq OX26. . . . . .65 E4
Larkswood Cl RG31 . . . . . . .257 D3
Larsen Rd OX25. . . . . .63 D8
Lashbrook Mead RG9 . . . . . .255 B4
Lashbrook Rd RG9 . . . . .255 B4
Lashford La OX13 . . . . .158 F7
Lashlake Rd OX9 . . . . .129 F1
Latchford La OX44 . . . . .162 F8
Lathbury Rd OX2. . . . . .123 B5
Latimer Grange OX3 . . . . . . .124 C2
Latimer Rd
  Carterton OX18 . . . . .115 C2
  Oxford OX3 . . . . .124 C2
Latton Cl
  Chilton OX11. . . . . .235 E8
  Kingston Bagpuize OX13 . .156 D1
Laud's Cl RG9 . . . . .244 C1
Laughton Hill OX4 . . . . .89 C7
Launceston Ave RG4 . . . . . . .259 E6
Laundry Cotts GL56. . . . . . . .40 C2
Laundry La OX18 . . . . .135 D3
Launton Bsns Ctr OX26. . .66 A2
Launton CE Prim Sch
  OX26 . . . . .66 A2
Launton Rd
  Bicester OX26 . . . . .66 A3
  Stratton Audley OX27 . . . . .66 D8

Laurel Cl
  Banbury OX16 . . . . .16 D2
  Carterton OX18 . . . . .115 D3
  Chalgrove OX44 . . . . .184 D7
Laurel Cres OX12 . . . . .214 E8
Laurel Ct OX4 . . . . .142 A8
Laurel Dr OX13 . . . . .156 E1
Laurel Farm Cl OX3 . . . . . . .124 C4
Laurels The
  Fringford OX27. . . . . .52 C6
  Great Coxwell SN7. . . . . . .192 C8
  Pangbourne RG8 . . . . .256 D5
  Sonning RG5 . . . . .260 E1
  Stadhampton OX44 . . . . . .163 C2
  Tetsworth OX9 . . . . .166 B8
Laurence Allison Mews
  RG4 . . . . .258 E2
Lavender Cl OX16. . . . . .9 B1
Lavender Pl
  Bampton OX18. . . . . .134 F3
  Carterton OX18 . . . . .115 C2
Lavender Sq OX18 . . . . .134 F3
Lavender View OX28 . . . . . . .104 D2
Lawns The HP18 . . . . .98 B1
Lawrence Cl OX12 . . . . .213 C4
Lawrence Fields OX25 . . . . . .62 B8
Lawrence La OX18 . . . . .100 E5
Lawrence Leys OX15. . . . . . . .21 E5
Lawrence Rd OX4 . . . . .142 C5
Lawrence Way OX26. . . . . . . .65 C2
Lawson Dr RG4 . . . . .258 E5
Lawson La OX11 . . . . .235 E8
Lawson Rd RG9. . . . . .254 F7
Lawton Ave OX18 . . . . .115 D2
Laxton Way OX16 . . . . .8 F1
Lay Ave OX10 . . . . .182 C6
Laytom Rise RG31 . . . . .257 C3
Leabrook Cl OX16. . . . . .16 C2
Leach Rd
  Berinsfield OX10 . . . . .182 D5
  Bicester OX26 . . . . .65 C2
Leafield CE Prim Sch
  OX29 . . . . .86 F3
Leafield Rd
  Crawley OX29 . . . . .103 E5
  Oxford OX4 . . . . .142 C6
  Shipton-u-W OX29 . . . . . .102 A6
Leafield Tech Ctr OX29 . . . . .86 C3
Lea Cl OX14 . . . . .200 F2
Lea La HP18 . . . . .129 F4
Leamington Dr SN7 . . . . . . .172 E2
Lea Rd RG4. . . . . .252 F4
Leaver Rd RG9. . . . . .244 C1
Lechlade Rd
  Buscot SN7 . . . . .171 C7
  Faringdon SN7 . . . . .172 C5
  Highworth SN6 . . . . .190 A7
  Langford GL7. . . . . .132 D2
Lechlade-on-T GL7,SN7 . . . .150 E2
Leckford Pl OX2 . . . . .261 A4
Leckford Rd OX2 . . . . .261 A4
Ledbury Cl RG30. . . . . .258 C1
Ledgers Cl OX4 . . . . .142 C3
Ledwell Rd OX7 . . . . .46 B2
Lee Ave OX14 . . . . .180 B8
Lee Cl
  Charlbury OX7 . . . . .73 C3
  Kidlington OX5. . . . . .92 D7
Lee Ct OX9 . . . . .147 F8
Lee Rd HP27. . . . . .169 F6
Lees Hts OX7 . . . . .73 C3
Lees The SN7 . . . . .172 F3
Le Hall Pl OX17 . . . . .22 F3
Leicester Cl RG9 . . . . .244 D3
Leiden Rd OX3 . . . . .142 E8
Leigh Cl OX29 . . . . .105 B5
Leigh Croft OX13. . . . . .159 A7
Leigh Gr OX16 . . . . .16 C5
Lely Ct OX14. . . . . .179 E5
Lennox Gdns OX16. . . . . .16 A4
Lenthall OX5 . . . . .93 A7
Lenthall Rd
  Abingdon OX14 . . . . .179 F8
  Oxford OX4. . . . . .141 F3
Lenton Rd OX16 . . . . .16 D2
Leoline Jenkins Ho OX4. .142 B2
Leon Cl OX4 . . . . .141 F8
Leopold St OX4 . . . . .142 A7
Lerwick Croft OX26 . . . . .66 A4
Lester Cl OX17 . . . . .23 A6
Lester Way OX10. . . . . .221 B7
Letcombe Ave OX14. . . . . . .179 F8
Letcombe Hill OX12. . . . . . .214 A4
Letcombe Ct OX12 . . . . .214 E4
Letcombe Wlk OX12 . . . . . . .196 D1
Letts Alley OX49 . . . . .186 B2
Level The OX15 . . . . .6 E2
Leverkus Ho OX39 . . . . .168 C6
Leverndale Ct OX18. . . . . . . .115 D2
Levery Cl OX14 . . . . .180 C8
Lewell Ave OX3 . . . . .124 C2
Lewin Cl **1** OX4 . . . . .142 C4
Lewington Cl OX44. . . . . . . .164 B8
Lewis Cl OX3 . . . . .125 A2
Lewis Rd OX7 . . . . .42 E2
Lewknor CE Prim Sch
  OX49 . . . . .187 B8
Lewknor Cl OX49 . . . . .187 B8
Leyburne Gdns OX39. . . . . . .168 C7
Leyland Cl OX16 . . . . .16 D3
Leys App OX7 . . . . .42 E2
Leys Cl OX15 . . . . .15 A8
Leys Ho OX16. . . . . .16 D2
Leyshon Rd OX33 . . . . .144 C7
Leys Rd OX2 . . . . .139 C5

Laurel Cl
  Chalgrove OX44. . . . . .184 D7
Laurel Cres OX12 . . . . .214 E8
Leys The
  Adderbury OX17 . . . . .22 F3
  Chipping Norton OX7. . . . . .42 D2
  Lyneham OX7 . . . . .70 E5
  Salford OX7 . . . . .41 F5
Leys View GL7 . . . . .132 E1
Leys Villas OX28 . . . . .118 A7
Ley The OX20 . . . . .91 C6
Library Ave OX11 . . . . .217 B2
Liddell Rd OX4 . . . . .142 C4
Lidderdale Rd GL54. . . . . . . .68 B3
Liddiard Cl
  Kennington OX1. . . . . .160 E8
  Wantage OX12. . . . . .214 D6
Liddiard's Row **7** SN7 . .172 F3
Liddon Rd OX4 . . . . .184 D6
Lido Rd OX11. . . . . .234 F8
Lidsey Rd OX16 . . . . .16 A5
Lilac Cl RG8 . . . . .257 C5
Lilacs Pl OX49 . . . . .186 B1
Lily Cl OX26 . . . . .65 D5
Limborough Rd OX12 . . . . .214 D5
Lime Ave
  Banbury OX16 . . . . .16 E4
  Stoke Row RG9 . . . . .242 A1
Lime Cres OX26. . . . . .65 F5
Lime Gr
  Chinnor OX39 . . . . .168 D6
  Kingston Bagpuize OX13 . .156 D1
Lime Kiln Rd OX5. . . . . .77 C5
Lime Rd OX2 . . . . .140 D7
Limes The
  Crowmarsh Gifford OX10 . .221 F7
  Dorchester OX10. . . . . . . .182 D2
  Stratton Audley OX27 . . . . .52 D1
Lime Tree Cl OX18 . . . . .115 D3
Limetree Cl OX12 . . . . .196 D1
Lime Tree Rd RG8 . . . . .249 B6
Limetrees OX11. . . . . .217 E1
Lime Wlk
  Oxford OX3 . . . . .124 C2
  Witney OX28 . . . . .104 E1
Limmings La OX9 . . . . .148 A6
Linacre Cl OX11 . . . . .219 B8
Linacre Coll OX1 . . . . .261 C3
Linacre Ct OX4 . . . . .124 F2
Lince La OX5 . . . . .77 E2
Linch Farm OX2 . . . . .122 A4
Linch Hill L Pk* OX29 . . .138 B5
Lincoln Cl
  Banbury OX16 . . . . .16 B6
  Bicester OX26 . . . . .66 A4
  Standlake OX29 . . . . .137 D4
  Upper Rissington GL54 . . . .69 D8
Lincoln Coll OX1 . . . . .261 B2
Lincoln Gdns OX11. . . . . . . .219 B8
Lincoln Pk NN13 . . . . .24 A5
Lincoln Pl OX9 . . . . .147 F8
Lincoln Rd OX1 . . . . .141 D5
Lincombe La OX1. . . . . .159 E7
Lincraft Cl OX5. . . . . .108 C7
Linden Cotts RG8 . . . . .250 E2
Linden Cres OX14 . . . . .196 F1
Linden Ct OX3 . . . . .124 D3
Linden Gate OX11 . . . . .217 E2
Linden Rd OX26 . . . . .65 F2
Lindsay Dr OX14 . . . . .160 B2
Linkside Ave OX2 . . . . .108 F2
Links Rd OX1 . . . . .160 E8
Link The
  Banbury OX16 . . . . .16 A6
  Marston OX3 . . . . .123 D4
  Oxford OX3 . . . . .123 D3
Linkwood Rd OX29. . . . . . . .103 C1
Linnet Cl
  Clifton Hampden OX14 . . .182 B4
  Oxford OX4 . . . . .142 D2
Linton Rd OX2 . . . . .123 C5
Lion Brewery The OX1. . . . . .261 A2
Lion Mdw RG9 . . . . .224 D2
Lipscombe Pl OX18 . . . . . . .115 D4
Lister Cl RG8 . . . . .257 C5
Litchfield Cl OX7 . . . . .58 F5
Lithgow Rd GL54. . . . . .68 B3
Little Acreage OX3. . . . . .123 F6
Little Baldon Farm Cotts
  OX44 . . . . .162 B5
Little Blenheim OX5 . . . . . . .108 B5
Little Bowden La RG8 . . . . . .256 A4
Little Brewery St OX4. . . . . .123 F1
Little Bridge Rd OX15. . . . . . .21 E5
Little Bury OX4 . . . . .143 A2
Little Clarendon St OX1 . . . .261 B3
Little Croft Rd RG8 . . . . .249 C5
Little Ct OX12 . . . . .214 D7
Littlefields OX4 . . . . .142 D3
Littlegate St OX1 . . . . .261 B1
Little Glebe RG4 . . . . .260 E3
Little Gn OX15 . . . . .21 E5
Little Ground OX15 . . . . .22 C5
Littlehay Rd OX4 . . . . .142 A3
Little Howe Cl OX14 . . . . . . .160 E3
Little La SN6 . . . . .209 B6
Little
  Aynho OX17 . . . . .35 C7
  Bledington OX7 . . . . .54 D2
  Horley OX15 . . . . .8 B4
  Milton OX44 . . . . .163 C5
Little Langlands OX11. . . . . .218 F7
Little Milton CE Prim Sch
  OX44 . . . . .163 F6
Littlemore Rdbt OX4 . . . . . .142 B3

Littlemore Rd OX4 . . . . 142 C4
Little Paddock OX27 . . . . . .52 C7
Littlestead Cl RG4 . . . . .259 E5
Little Wittenham Nature
Reserve* OX14 . . . . 202 C6
Little Wittenham Rd
OX14 . . . . .201 F8
Little Wood HP14 . . . . 188 E5
Littleworth Bsns Ctr
OX33 . . . . .143 F7
Littleworth Hill OX12 . . . . 214 C5
Littleworth Ind Est OX33 .143 F7
Littleworth Pk OX33 . . . . .143 F8
Littleworth Rd
Benson OX10 . . . . .203 F4
Wheatley OX33 . . . . .144 A8
Livingstone Cl OX5 . . . . . . .108 B7
Lobelia Rd OX4 . . . . .142 F2
Lock Cres OX5 . . . . .108 E6
Lockheart Cres OX4 . . . . . 142 D4
Lockheed Cl OX14 . . . . .16 C8
Lockinge Cl OX11 . . . . .218 E7
Locks La OX12 . . . . 214 C4
Lockstile Mead RG8 . . . . . .249 C6
Lockstile Way RG8 . . . . . . .249 C6
Lockway OX14 . . . . .199 A8
Locombe Hill GL7 . . . . .131 B8
Lodden Ave OX10 . . . . .182 C5
Loddon Cl
Abingdon OX14 . . . . .160 B1
Bicester OX26 . . . . .65 D1
Loddon Dr
Didcot OX14 . . . . .201 B1
Wargrave RG10 . . . . .255 B1
Loder Rd OX11 . . . . .217 E7
Lodersfield GL7 . . . . .150 C4
Lodge Cl
Banbury OX16 . . . . .16 D4
Bicester OX26 . . . . .65 E5
Marston OX3 . . . . .123 F7
Lodge Hill OX14 . . . . .160 B4
Lodge Hill Intc OX14 . . . .160 B5
Lodge Rd OX29 . . . . .90 F1
Lodge Terr OX7 . . . . .42 F3
Logic La OX1 . . . . .261 C2
Lombard St
5 Abingdon OX14 . . . . . . .179 F7
Eynsham OX29 . . . . .120 E7
Lombard Way OX16 . . . . . . .17 A7
Lomond Ave RG4 . . . . .259 E5
London Cl OX3 . . . . .124 C2
London La OX7 . . . . .71 C2
London Pl OX4 . . . . .123 F1
London Rd
Bicester OX26 . . . . .80 B8
Blewbury OX11 . . . . .236 E8
Chipping Norton OX7 . . . . . .43 B3
Milton Common OX9 . . . . .146 B3
Oxford OX3 . . . . .124 D3
Sonning RG4 . . . . .260 C1
Tiddington OX9,OX44 . . . .145 E5
Wheatley OX33 . . . . .144 D7
London St SN7 . . . . .173 B4
London Yd **1** OX16 . . . . . .16 C6
Long Alley Almshouses **10**
OX14 . . . . .179 F6
Long Barn OX14 . . . . .200 A8
Long Barrow OX17 . . . . .5 F7
Long Cl
Oxford,Dean Court OX2 . . .122 B1
Oxford,New Headington
OX3 . . . . .142 G8
Longcot & Fernham CE Prim
Sch SN7 . . . . .192 C2
Longcot Rd
Longcot SN7 . . . . .192 B1
Shrivenham SN6 . . . . .209 D6
Long Crendon Ind Est
HP18 . . . . .129 E5
Long Crendon Rd HP18 . .128 D3
Long Crendon Sch HP18 129 C7
Longelandes Cl OX16 . . . . .16 A8
Longelandes Way OX16 . .16 B8
Longfellow Cl **1** OX26 . . . .65 C3
Longfellow Dr OX14 . . . . .179 C5
Longfellow Rd OX16 . . . . .16 B4
Longfields OX26 . . . . .65 F2
Longfields Cl OX26 . . . . . . .65 F2
Longfields OX13 . . . . .178 D7
Longfields Prim Sch OX26 65 F2
Long Ford Cl OX1 . . . . .141 C7
Longford Way OX14 . . . . . .200 F2
Long Furlong HP17 . . . . . . .130 F6
Long Furlong Prim Sch
OX14 . . . . .160 A3
Long Furlong Rd OX13 . . .159 D4
Long Ground OX4 . . . . .142 E1
Longhurst Cl RG4 . . . . .259 C3
Longlands Rd OX4 . . . . . . .142 E3
Long Lane Prim Sch
RG31 . . . . .257 B3
Long La
Oxford OX4 . . . . .142 C3
Reading RG31 . . . . .257 B3
Longleat Cl OX16 . . . . .16 E2
Longleat Dr RG31 . . . . .257 B3
Long Mdw RG8 . . . . .249 B5
Longmead OX14 . . . . .159 E1
Longmore Ave GL54 . . . . . .68 B3
Longore Ct OX29 . . . . .89 D8
Longore OX29 . . . . .89 C8
Long Tdole RG8 . . . . .251 A5
Long Tow OX13 . . . . .159 D2
Long Wall HP17 . . . . .130 F5
Longwall OX4 . . . . .142 B3

Longwall St OX1 . . . . .261 C2
Long Wittenham CE Prim
Sch OX14 . . . . .201 D8
Long Wittenham Rd
OX11 . . . . .219 F8
Longworth Cl OX16 . . . . . . .16 E7
Longworth Prim Sch
OX13 . . . . .156 C3
Longworth Rd
Charney Bassett OX12 . . . .176 A3
Oxford OX2 . . . . .261 A4
Lonsdale Cl OX7 . . . . .29 A3
Lonsdale Rd OX2 . . . . .123 B7
Lord Cl OX18 . . . . .115 D3
Lord Grandison Way OX16. .9 C2
Lords Piece Rd OX7 . . . . . . .42 D1
Lord William's Lower Sch
OX9 . . . . .148 B8
Lord William's Sch OX9 . .147 D8
Lostock Pl OX11 . . . . .200 F2
Lovatt Cl OX18 . . . . .115 D5
Lovegrove's La RG8 . . . . . .241 C4
Lovelace Cl OX14 . . . . .160 A3
Lovelace Dr OX5 . . . . .109 A8
Lovelace Rd OX2 . . . . .109 A1
Lovelace Sq OX2 . . . . .109 A1
Love La OX49 . . . . .186 B2
Lovell Cl
Ducklington OX29 . . . . . . .118 B4
Henley-on-T RG9 . . . . .254 C8
Minster Lovell OX29 . . . . . .102 E2
Loverock Rd RG30 . . . . . . .258 D1
Lowell Pl OX28 . . . . .118 A8
Lower Armour Rd RG31 . .257 D1
Lower Cherwell St OX16 . .16 D5
Lower Church St HP14 . . .188 E5
Lower Cres OX15 . . . . .22 E8
Lower Comm SN7 . . . . .221 D8
Lower Cres OX29 . . . . .102 E3
Lower Elmstone Dr
RG31 . . . . .257 C1
Lower End Cotts CV47 . . . . .2 F8
Lower End
Great Milton OX44 . . . . . . .145 B3
Piddington OX25 . . . . .97 E8
Salford OX7 . . . . .41 F4
Shutford OX15 . . . . .14 B5
Lower Farm Barns OX27 . .65 A8
Lower Farm Cl HP18 . . . . .128 D3
Lower Farm La
Mollington OX17 . . . . .3 F3
Sandford-on-T OX4 . . . . . .161 B6
Lower Hades Rd OX5 . . . . . .77 B6
Lower Henley Rd RG4 . . . .259 D3
Lower Heyford Rd OX25 . . .63 B5
Lower High St OX18 . . . . . .100 E5
Lower Icknield Way
OX39 . . . . .168 D8
Lower Radley Cvn Pk
OX14 . . . . .160 F2
Lower Rd
Blackthorn OX25 . . . . .82 A4
Chilton OX11 . . . . .235 D8
Chinnor OX39 . . . . .168 C7
Long Hanborough OX29. . . .90 F1
Postcombe OX9 . . . . .166 F4
Lower St
Barford St M OX15 . . . . .32 E6
Islip OX5 . . . . .93 F1
Lower Wharf OX10 . . . . . . .221 D7
Lower Whitley Rd OX2 . . .139 C8
Lower Rd
Lower Shiplake RG9 . . . . . .255 B4
Stokenchurch HP14 . . . . . .188 C5
Lowfield Ct RG4 . . . . .259 C5
Lowfield Gn RG4 . . . . .259 E4
Lowfield Rd RG4 . . . . .259 D5
Loyd Cl OX14 . . . . .160 A3
Loyd Rd OX11 . . . . .218 D6
Lucas Pl OX4 . . . . .141 F5
Lucca Dr OX14 . . . . .179 D4
Lucerne Ave OX26 . . . . .65 D4
Lucerne Dr OX44 . . . . .163 C2
Lucerne Rd OX2 . . . . .123 C8
Lucey Cl RG31 . . . . .257 B3
Lucky La OX16 . . . . .16 D5
Ludford Gdns OX15 . . . . . .21 D3
Ludgershall Rd OX25 . . . . . .97 E7
Ludlow Dr
Banbury OX16 . . . . .15 F8
Thame OX9 . . . . .148 A8
Ludsden Gr OX9 . . . . .148 A8
Luker Ave RG9 . . . . .244 D3
Lumberd Rd OX14 . . . . . . .160 B2
Lune Cl OX14 . . . . .201 A1
Lupton Rd
Thame OX9 . . . . .148 A6
Wallingford OX10 . . . . .221 B7
Luscombe Cl RG4 . . . . .259 D2
Luther Ct OX1 . . . . .261 B1
Lych Gate La OX44 . . . . . . .145 B2
Lycroft Cl RG8 . . . . .249 C7
Lydalls Cl OX11 . . . . .200 D1
Lydalls Rd OX11 . . . . .200 E1
Lydia Cl OX3 . . . . .124 F4
Lydsee Gate OX12 . . . . . . .214 B5
Lyefield Ct RG4 . . . . .259 B6
Lye Valley OX3 . . . . .142 D7
Lyford Cl OX14 . . . . .179 B2
Lyford Way OX14 . . . . .160 B2
Lymbrook Cl OX29 . . . . . . .119 C5
Lyme Gr RG31 . . . . .257 D1
Lymington Gate RG4 . . . . .258 E5
Lynch The OX12 . . . . .216 D5
Lyndene Rd OX11 . . . . .200 D2
Lyndhurst Rd
Goring RG8 . . . . .249 C6
Reading RG30 . . . . .258 A1

Lyndworth Cl OX3 . . . . . . .124 F4
Lyndworth Mews OX3 . . . .124 E3
Lyneham Cl
Carterton OX18 . . . . .115 E3
Witney OX28 . . . . .103 E1
Lyneham Rd
Bicester OX26 . . . . .66 B3
Milton-u-W OX7 . . . . .70 B3
Lyne Rd OX5 . . . . .92 D1
Lynges Cl OX14 . . . . .160 B2
Lynmouth Ct RG1 . . . . . . .259 B1
Lynmouth Rd
Didcot OX11 . . . . .218 E8
Reading RG1 . . . . .259 A1
Lynn Cl OX3 . . . . .123 F4
Lynn Cl OX14 . . . . .160 A1
Lysander OX26 . . . . .66 A4
Lytham End RG31 . . . . .257 B3
Lytton Rd OX4 . . . . .142 B5

M

Mabel Prichard Sch OX4 .142 B2
Maberley Cl OX14 . . . . . . .179 C6
Mably Gr OX12 . . . . .214 D6
Mably Way OX12 . . . . .214 D7
Macaulay Cl RG26 . . . . .65 C3
McCrae's Wlk RG10 . . . . . .255 D2
Macdonald Cl OX11 . . . . . .200 D1
McKay Trad Est OX26 . . . . .80 F8
McKee Sq OX10 . . . . .204 D2
McKeever Pl **1** OX16 . . . . . .16 E6
Mackenzie Ave OX14 . . . . .199 D3
Mackenzie Cl **5** OX26 . . . . .65 C3
Mackley Cl OX15 . . . . .33 E4
Mackney La OX10 . . . . .202 E1
McMullan Cl OX10 . . . . . . .221 C8
Macray Rd OX29 . . . . .118 B4
Maddle Rd RG17 . . . . .229 C1
Madley Brook Com Prim Sch
OX28 . . . . .104 B2
Mafeking Row OX49 . . . . .186 E4
Magdalen Cl OX26 . . . . .65 F3
Magdalen Coll OX1 . . . . . .123 E1
Magdalen Coll Sch OX4 . .141 E8
Magdalen Pl OX18 . . . . . . .115 D2
Magdalen Rd OX4 . . . . . . .141 F7
Magdalen St OX1 . . . . .261 B2
Magnette Cl OX14 . . . . . . .179 F7
Magnolia Cl OX5 . . . . .108 F8
Magnolias The
Banbury OX16 . . . . .9 B1
Bicester OX26 . . . . .65 F5
Magnolia Way OX18 . . . . .115 E4
Magpie Alley OX7 . . . . .85 D8
Magpie La OX1 . . . . .261 C2
Maharajah's Well* RG9 . .244 E3
Maidcroft Rd OX4 . . . . . . .142 C5
Maiden's Cl SN6 . . . . .191 D1
Maidley Cl OX28 . . . . .104 C2
Main Ave OX4 . . . . .161 C8
Main Pk OX18 . . . . .133 D8
Main Rd
Appleford OX14 . . . . .200 F7
Broughton OX15 . . . . .15 C1
Curbridge OX29 . . . . .117 C6
East Hagbourne OX11 . . . .218 E5
Fyfield OX13 . . . . .157 C2
Long Hanborough OX29. . . .90 F1
Middleton Cheney OX17 . . .17 F8
Stanton Harcourt OX29 . . .138 B8
Tadmarton OX15 . . . . .20 C8
Main St
Adlestrop GL56 . . . . .40 C3
Bledington OX7 . . . . .54 D2
Charney Bassett OX12 . . . .175 F2
Chilton OX11 . . . . .235 D8
Clanfield OX18 . . . . .152 E7
Claydon OX17 . . . . .1 D1
Duns Tew OX25 . . . . .47 D5
East Hanney OX12 . . . . . . .197 B6
Fawler OX7 . . . . .88 E7
Fringford OX27 . . . . .52 D7
Grove OX12 . . . . .214 E8
Hanwell OX17 . . . . .8 F5
Hethe OX6 . . . . .52 A8
Letcombe Regis OX12 . . . .214 A2
Long Compton CV36 . . . . . .27 F6
Mollington OX17 . . . . .4 A4
North Newington OX15 . . . . .15 A4
Over Norton OX7 . . . . .42 F5
Poundon OX27 . . . . .67 C7
Shalstone MK18 . . . . .25 E6
Sibford Ferris OX15 . . . . . . .19 B7
Sibford Gower OX15 . . . . . .19 A8
Tadmarton OX15 . . . . .20 D8
Turweston NN13 . . . . .24 C8
Westbury NN13 . . . . .25 A4
West Hagbourne OX11 . . . .218 C4
West Hanney OX12 . . . . . . .196 E6
West Ilsley RG20 . . . . .235 A2
Wroxton OX15 . . . . .15 A8
Maisonettes The RG8 . . . .249 D8
Majors Rd SN6 . . . . .191 D2
Makins Rd RG9 . . . . .254 B8
Malet Cl HP14 . . . . .188 F5
Malford Rd OX3 . . . . .124 F3
Mallard Cl OX4 . . . . .142 D2
Mallard Cl OX18 . . . . .115 F3
Mallards Way
Bicester OX26 . . . . .66 A1
Bicester OX26 . . . . .80 E8

Mallard Way OX12 . . . . . . .196 D1
Mallins La SN7 . . . . .192 D3
Mallinson Ct OX2 . . . . .123 A1
Mallory Ave RG4 . . . . .259 D6
Mall The SN6 . . . . .209 E7
Maltfield Rd OX3 . . . . .124 B5
Malthouse La OX44 . . . . . . .66 B3
Malthouse Cl SN6 . . . . .228 A7
Malthouse La
Bodicote OX15 . . . . .22 D8
Dorchester OX10 . . . . .182 D1
Long Compton CV36 . . . . . .27 F6
Shutford OX15 . . . . .14 B5
Malthouse Paddock SN7 .174 E8
Malthouses The SN6 . . . . .228 B7
Malthouse Wlk **4** OX16. . .16 D6
Maltings Ct OX15 . . . . .21 D4
Maltings The
Carterton OX18 . . . . .115 F5
West Ilsley RG20 . . . . .235 B1
Malsters OX29 . . . . .89 C7
Malvern Cl
Banbury OX16 . . . . .16 D2
Didcot OX11 . . . . .200 C2
Malyns Cl OX39 . . . . .168 C7
Malyns Way RG31 . . . . .257 B4
Managua Cl RG4 . . . . .259 E2
Manchester Coll OX1 . . . . .261 C3
Manchester Terr **2** OX26 . .65 F3
Mandarin Pl OX12 . . . . . . .196 D1
Mandeville Cl OX14 . . . . . .160 A2
Mandhill Cl OX12 . . . . .214 E8
Mandlebrote Dr OX4 . . . . .142 B1
Manning Cl OX15 . . . . .21 E2
Mannings Cl OX15 . . . . .19 B7
Mann Way RG4 . . . . .150 E3
Manor Cl
Appleford OX14 . . . . .200 F8
Aston OX18 . . . . .135 E2
Cassington OX29 . . . . .107 C2
Chilton OX11 . . . . .217 E1
Drayton OX14 . . . . .179 B1
Enstone OX7 . . . . .58 F5
Great Bourton OX17 . . . . . . .9 D8
Shrivenham SN6 . . . . .209 B7
West Hagbourne OX11 . . . .218 C4
Manor Cotts OX29 . . . . . . .138 B7
Manor Court Yd OX33 . . . .127 B2
Manor Cres
Didcot OX11 . . . . .200 D1
Standlake OX29 . . . . .137 D3
Stanford in the V SN7 . . . .194 E7
Manor Ct
Abingdon OX14 . . . . .179 E6
Carterton OX18 . . . . .115 D2
Chadlington OX7 . . . . .57 C1
Wootton OX20 . . . . .75 F4
Manor Dr OX3 . . . . .143 C6
Manor Farm Cl
Fernham SN7 . . . . .193 A4
Kingham OX7 . . . . .54 F5
Merton OX25 . . . . .95 D8
Manor Farm Cotts
Garford OX13 . . . . .177 D5
Wendlebury OX25 . . . . .80 A3
Manor Farm Ct OX14 . . . .180 A2
Manor Farm La RG8 . . . . .256 C2
Manor Farm Rd
Dorchester OX10 . . . . .182 D1
Horspath OX33 . . . . .143 C6
Manor Fields OX12 . . . . . .214 A2
Manor Gdns GL7 . . . . .150 C4
Manor Gn
Harwell OX11 . . . . .217 E7
Stanford in the V SN7 . . . .194 E7
Manor La
Clanfield OX18 . . . . .152 E8
Shrivenham SN6 . . . . .209 B6
West Hendred OX12 . . . . . .216 B5
Manor Orch OX15 . . . . .8 B4
Manor Pk
Claydon OX17 . . . . .1 D1
Oxford OX3 . . . . .124 C3
Manor Pl OX1 . . . . .123 E2
Manor Prep Sch The
OX13 . . . . .159 C1
Manor Rd
Adderbury OX17 . . . . .22 E3
Banbury OX16 . . . . .16 F8
Bladon OX20 . . . . .91 B2
Brize Norton OX18 . . . . . . .116 B4
Carterton OX18 . . . . .115 D5
Chinnor OX9 . . . . .149 A6
Didcot OX11 . . . . .200 D1
Ducklington OX29 . . . . . . .118 A4
Fringford OX27 . . . . .52 D7
Goring RG8 . . . . .249 B5
Great Bourton OX17 . . . . . . .9 D8
Henley-on-T RG9 . . . . .244 E1
Oxford OX1 . . . . .123 E2
Sandford St Martin OX7 . . .46 C1
South Hinksey OX1 . . . . . .141 B5
Towersey OX9 . . . . .148 F7
Wantage OX12 . . . . .232 C5
Whitchurch-on-T RG8 . . . .256 C7
Witney OX28 . . . . .118 C7
Woodstock OX20 . . . . .91 A7
Manor Sch OX11 . . . . .200 D1
Manorsfield Rd OX26 . . . . .65 E2

Manor View
Bampton OX18. . . . . .134 E4
Bucknell OX27 . . . . .64 F8
Manor Way OX5 . . . . .92 F2
Manor Wood Gate RG9 . . .255 A4
Manor Yd OX27 . . . . .52 D7
Mansell Cl OX29 . . . . .106 D6
Mansell Pl OX18 . . . . .115 D1
Mansfield Coll OX1 . . . . . .261 C3
Mansfield Gdns OX15 . . . .219 B8
Mansfield Rd OX1 . . . . . . .261 C3
Mansion Hill OX17 . . . . . . .17 F8
Mansmoor Rd OX5 . . . . . . .94 F7
Manston Cl OX26 . . . . .66 B3
Manzel Rd OX27 . . . . .66 A6
Manzil Way OX4 . . . . .142 A8
Maple Ave OX5 . . . . .108 F7
Maple Cl
Bodicote OX15 . . . . .16 E1
Oxford OX2 . . . . .140 D8
Sonning Common RG4 . . . .253 A4
Maple Cotts SN7 . . . . .172 E3
Maple Ct
Goring RG8 . . . . .249 B6
Kidlington OX5 . . . . .108 F7
Mapledene RG4 . . . . .258 E3
Mapledurham Dr RG8 . . . .257 E6
Mapledurham Ho* RG8 . .257 E6
Mapledurham View
RG31 . . . . .257 D6
Mapledurham Watermill*
RG4 . . . . .257 D6
Maple Gr RG5 . . . . .260 E1
Maple Ho RG4 . . . . .259 E3
Maple Rd
Bicester OX26 . . . . .65 F2
Faringdon SN7 . . . . .172 E3
Thame OX9 . . . . .147 D8
Maples The
Carterton OX18 . . . . .115 D1
Grove OX12 . . . . .196 D2
Maple Way OX7 . . . . .71 B2
Maplewell Ho OX29 . . . . . .89 D7
Maplewell OX29 . . . . .89 C7
Mapledurham CE Prim Sch
OX13 . . . . .178 D6
Marcham Rd
Abingdon OX14 . . . . .179 C6
Drayton OX14 . . . . .179 A6
Marcham OX13 . . . . .178 F6
March Rd OX17 . . . . .3 D3
Marchwood Ave RG4. . . . .259 C8
Marcourt Rd HP14 . . . . . . .188 F3
Marcy Rd RG4 . . . . .258 E5
Margaret Cl
Banbury OX16 . . . . .16 A5
Bicester OX26 . . . . .65 D4
Margaret Rd
Adderbury OX17 . . . . .23 B5
Oxford OX3 . . . . .124 C2
Maria Cres OX12 . . . . .214 E5
Marie Cl OX27 . . . . .67 F7
Marigold Cl **12** OX4 . . . . . .142 F1
Marigold Wlk OX26 . . . . . . .65 E5
Marina View OX14 . . . . . . .179 F4
Marines Dr SN7 . . . . .172 E3
Mariot Ct **8** OX10 . . . . . . .221 D7
Marjoram Cl OX4 . . . . .143 A2
Market End Way OX26 . . . .65 D3
Market Pl
3 Wallingford OX10 . . . . .221 D7
Abingdon OX14 . . . . .179 F7
Market Place Mews RG9 .244 D3
Market Pl
Banbury OX16 . . . . .16 D6
Chipping Norton OX7 . . . . . .42 E3
Deddington OX15 . . . . .33 F4
Didcot OX11 . . . . .200 F1
Faringdon SN7 . . . . .172 F4
Henley-on-T RG9 . . . . .244 D2
Highworth SN6 . . . . .190 A5
Lechlade-on-T GL7 . . . . . . .150 C4
Wantage OX12 . . . . .214 D4
Woodstock OX20 . . . . .91 A6
Market Sq
Bampton OX18. . . . . .134 E3
Bicester OX26 . . . . .65 F1
Lower Heyford OX25 . . . . . .62 D6
Witney OX28 . . . . .118 B8
Market St
Charlbury OX7 . . . . .73 B4
Chipping Norton OX7 . . . . . .42 E3
Oxford OX1 . . . . .261 B2
Woodstock OX20 . . . . .91 B6
Market The OX1 . . . . .261 B2
Mark Rd OX3 . . . . .124 E2
Marlborough Ave OX5 . . . . .92 D2
Marlborough CE Sch The
OX20 . . . . .91 D6
Marlborough Cl
Long Hanborough OX29. . .106 B8
Oxford OX4 . . . . .90 A1
Marlborough Ct OX2 . . . . .122 F1
Marlborough Dr OX9 . . . . .107 C1
Marlborough Gdns SN7 . .172 F2
Marlborough La
Kings Sutton OX17 . . . . . . .23 F6
Oxford OX2 . . . . .92 D2
Marlborough Cres
Long Hanborough OX29. . .106 B8
Oxford OX2 . . . . .90 A1
Marlborough Dr OX9 . . . . .107 C1
Marlborough Gdns SN7 . .172 F2
Marlborough La
Stanford in the V SN7 . . . .194 E7
Witney OX28 . . . . .118 A8
Marlborough Pl
2 Banbury OX16 . . . . .16 D5

Marlborough Pl continued
Charlbury OX7 . . . . .73 B3
Eynsham OX29 . . . . .120 E8
Faringdon SN7 . . . . .172 E2
Marlborough Rd
Banbury OX16 . . . . .16 D5
Chipping Norton OX7 . . . . .42 F4
Oxford OX1 . . . . .141 C7
Marlborough St SN7 . . . .172 F3
Marley Ind Est OX16 . . . . .16 D8
Marley La OX44 . . . . . . .184 C7
Marley Way OX16 . . . . . .16 D7
Marling Cl RG31 . . . . . .257 C2
Marlow Cl OX10 . . . . . .221 B8
Marlow Ct RG4 . . . . . . .259 D3
Marlowe Cl OX16 . . . . . .15 F6
Marlow Rd
Henley-on-T RG9 . . . . . .244 E3
Stokenchurch HP14 . . . . .188 F3
Marnyon Ho RG9 . . . . . .244 E3
Marns Hey OX12 . . . . . .214 C5
Marriott Cl
Cutteslowe OX2 . . . . . . .109 B1
Wootton OX20 . . . . .76 A4
Marriott's Cl HP17 . . . . .130 F6
Marriott's La HP17 . . . . .130 F6
Marriott's Way HP17 . . . .130 F6
Marsack St RG4 . . . . . .259 C2
Marshall Cl
Chipping Norton OX7 . . . . .42 E1
Purley on T RG8 . . . . . . .257 D4
Marshall Cres OX7 . . . . . .46 E1
Marshall Rd OX4 . . . . . .142 D6
Marshalls Cl OX15 . . . . . . .6 E2
Marsh Baldon CE Prim Sch
OX44 . . . . .162 A4
Marsh Cl OX5 . . . . .108 C5
Marsh Ct OX14 . . . . . . .179 F8
Marsh End OX29 . . . . . .147 B1
Marsh Gibbon CE Inf Sch
OX27 . . . . .67 F3
Marsh La
Clanfield OX18 . . . . .152 F8
Crowmarsh Gifford OX10 . .222 A8
East Challow OX12 . . . . . .213 F7
Fyfield OX13 . . . . .157 B4
Marston OX3 . . . . .124 A5
Marshland Sq RG4 . . . . .259 B5
Marsh Pl RG8 . . . . .256 D5
Marsh Rd
Oxford OX4 . . . . .142 C6
Shabbington HP18 . . . . . .128 D3
Marsh Way SN7 . . . . . . .211 A5
Marston Ferry Ct RG4 . . .123 C6
Marston Ferry Rd OX2 . . .123 D6
Marston Rd
Marston OX3,OX4 . . . . . .123 F1
Thame OX9 . . . . .130 A1
Marston St OX4 . . . . . . .141 F8
Marten Gate OX16 . . . . . .16 E3
Marten Pl RG31 . . . . . . .257 C3
Martens La OX13 . . . . . .156 C2
Martens Rd SN6 . . . . . . .209 B6
Martin Cl OX26 . . . . .80 F8
Martin Ct OX12 . . . . . . .123 B7
Martin's La OX10 . . . . . .182 D2
Martyn's Way OX10 . . . . .204 F4
Maryfield OX12 . . . . . . .214 E4
Marygreen OX12 . . . . . .214 D8
Marylands Gn OX44 . . . . .162 D2
Marymead OX14 . . . . . . .220 F2
Mary Towerton Sch The
HP14 . . . . .189 D3
Mary Whipple Ct OX12 . .214 C4
Mascall Ave OX3 . . . . . .142 E7
Mascord Cl OX16 . . . . . . .16 A5
Mascord Rd OX16 . . . . . .16 A5
Masefield Cl OX26 . . . . . .65 C3
Masefield Cres OX14 . . . .179 C5
Masefield Rd OX16 . . . . . .16 A4
Masey Cl OX3 . . . . .124 D1
Masons Ct OX12 . . . . . .215 E6
Masons Rd OX3 . . . . . . .124 E1
Mather Rd OX3 . . . . . . .124 F4
Mathews Way OX13 . . . . .159 B6
Matlock Rd RG4 . . . . . . .258 E4
Matson Dr RG9 . . . . . . .244 F4
Matthew Arnold Sch
OX2 . . . . .140 C7
Mattock Cl OX3 . . . . . . .124 D1
Mattock Way OX14 . . . . .160 B3
Maud Cl OX26 . . . . .65 C4
Maud Hale Cotts 11
OX14 . . . . .179 F6
Maud Ho OX12 . . . . . . .214 F5
Maule Cl OX15 . . . . .21 E2
Maunds The OX15 . . . . . .33 F4
Mavor Cl OX20 . . . . .91 A7
Mawkes Cl SN7 . . . . . . .194 D7
Mawle Ct 1 OX16 . . . . . .16 D5
Mawles La OX7 . . . . .85 D8
Maxwell Ave OX11 . . . . .217 B3
Maycroft 4 OX26 . . . . . .65 F4
Mayfair Rd OX4 . . . . . . .142 B4
Mayfield Ave OX12 . . . . .196 F1
Mayfield Cl
Carterton OX18 . . . . . . .115 D1
Chalgrove OX44 . . . . . . .184 D6
Mayfield Dr RG4 . . . . . . .259 D3
Mayfield Rd
Banbury OX16 . . . . .16 D2
Farmoor OX2 . . . . .121 B2
Oxford OX2 . . . . .123 B7
Mayott's Rd 1 OX14 . . . .179 E7
May's Cl OX27 . . . . .49 F7
May Tree Cl OX16 . . . . . .65 E3
Meaden Hill OX3 . . . . . . .124 B5

Mead La
Longcot SN7 . . . . .192 D2
Lower Basildon RG8 . . . . .249 F1
Meadowbank Cl
Ascott-u-W OX7 . . . . .71 B2
Long Crendon HP18 . . . . .129 C7
Meadow Bank SN7 . . . . .172 F3
Meadow Cl
Farmoor OX2 . . . . .121 B3
Goring RG8 . . . . .249 C6
Grove OX12 . . . . .196 E1
Moulsford OX10 . . . . . . .238 F4
Shipton-u-W OX7 . . . . . . .70 D1
Meadow End OX18 . . . . .100 E6
Meadow La
Crowmarsh Gifford
OX10 . . . . .222 A6
Fulbrook OX18 . . . . .100 F6
Long Crendon HP18 . . . . .129 C7
Oxford OX4 . . . . .141 E7
Oxford OX4 . . . . .141 F5
Pangbourne RG8 . . . . . . .256 D5
Shipton-u-W OX7 . . . . . . .70 D1
Meadow Pl OX7 . . . . . . .55 D5
Meadow Prospect OX22 . .122 D8
Meadow Rd
Chinnor OX39 . . . . .168 D6
Henley-on-T RG9 . . . . . .244 E1
Reading RG1 . . . . .258 F1
Watchfield SN6 . . . . .191 E2
Meadowside OX14 . . . . .179 E6
Meadowside Ct 1 OX14 . .179 E6
Meadowside RG8 . . . . . .256 D5
Meadowside RG31 . . . . .257 B1
Meadows The OX49 . . . . .186 B2
Meadow View
Adderbury OX17 . . . . .23 A4
Banbury OX16 . . . . .16 E4
Kidlington OX5 . . . . .92 E2
Long Crendon HP18 . . . . .129 C4
Oxford OX2 . . . . .123 C8
Meadow View Rd OX1 . .160 F8
Meadow Way
Carterton OX18 . . . . . . .115 F5
Didcot OX11 . . . . .218 C7
Faringdon SN7 . . . . .172 F2
Kingham OX7 . . . . .54 F3
Thame OX9 . . . . .129 F1
Yarnton OX5 . . . . .108 C5
Meadow Wlk OX20 . . . . . .91 C6
Mead Platt HP14 . . . . . . .188 D5
Mead Rd
Barford St M OX15 . . . . . .32 F7
Yarnton OX5 . . . . .108 C4
Meads Cl OX14 . . . . . . .179 B2
Meadside OX10 . . . . . . .202 E8
Meads The OX12 . . . . . .196 E7
Mead The OX17 . . . . .3 F3
Mead Way OX5 . . . . . . .108 B4
Meashill Way OX11 . . . . .234 F8
Medcroft Rd OX5 . . . . . . .77 B6
Medill Cl OX8 . . . . .250 E8
Medina Cl OX14 . . . . . . .201 B1
Medina Gdns OX26 . . . . .65 B2
Medlar Rd SN6 . . . . . . .209 C7
Medlicott Dr OX14 . . . . . .179 C6
Medlock Gr OX11 . . . . . .200 F3
Medway Cl OX13 . . . . . .159 C3
Medway Ct OX12 . . . . . .197 B6
Medway Gr 5 OX11 . . . . .219 A8
Medway Rd OX13 . . . . . .159 C3
Meer The OX10 . . . . . . .204 A5
Melbourne Cl OX16 . . . . . .16 E3
Melford Gn RG4 . . . . . . .259 E6
Melrose Ct OX16 . . . . .8 F1
Melton Dr OX11 . . . . . . .200 E1
Melville Cl OX26 . . . . . . .65 B2
Membury Way OX12 . . . . .214 D8
Memorial Ave RG9 . . . . . .254 E2
Mendip Hts OX11 . . . . . .200 C2
Menmarsh Rd HP18 . . . . .127 E6
Menpes Rd RG31 . . . . . .257 C4
Mercury Cl OX13 . . . . . .134 F3
Mercury Ct OX13 . . . . . .134 F3
Mercury Rd OX4 . . . . . . .143 A2
Meredith Cl OX26 . . . . . .65 C3
Mere Dyke Rd OX13 . . . . .198 F5
Mere La MK18 . . . . .39 E6
Mereland Rd OX11 . . . . . .218 E7
Mere Rd
Finmere MK18 . . . . .39 D6
Wolvercote OX2 . . . . . . .122 F8
Merewood Ave OX3 . . . . .125 A4
Merganser Dr OX26 . . . . .81 B8
Meriden Ct OX11 . . . . . .221 C7
Merlin Cl
Benson OX10 . . . . .204 D2
Carterton OX18 . . . . . . .115 D3
Merlin Rd
Abingdon OX13 . . . . .159 B2
Oxford OX4 . . . . .142 E2
Merlin Way OX26 . . . . . . .81 B8
Merritt Rd OX11 . . . . . . .200 C1
Merrivale's La OX15 . . . . .21 E4
Merrivale Sq OX2 . . . . . .123 A4
Merrymouth Rd OX7 . . . . .69 A2
Mersey Way OX13 . . . . . .201 A3
Merthyr Vale RG4 . . . . . .259 A6
Merton Cl
Didcot OX11 . . . . .219 B8
Eynsham OX29 . . . . .120 D7
Merton Coll OX1 . . . . . . .261 C2
Merton Ct OX1 . . . . . . .123 A4
Merton Gr OX1 . . . . . . .261 C2

Merton Rd OX25 . . . . . . .81 C3
Merton St
Banbury OX16 . . . . .16 E6
Oxford OX1 . . . . .261 C2
Merton Way OX5 . . . . . .108 B5
Merton Wlk OX26 . . . . . . .65 F3
Metcalfe Cl
Abingdon OX14 . . . . . . .179 E4
Drayton OX15 . . . . .15 D8
Meteor Cl OX26 . . . . .66 A3
Mewburn Rd OX16 . . . . . .16 B5
Mews The
Baydon SN8 . . . . .245 B5
Highworth SN6 . . . . .190 A6
Sonning RG4 . . . . .260 D4
Warborough OX10 . . . . . .203 B5
Watchfield SN6 . . . . .191 D1
Meyseys Rd OX3 . . . . . . .142 E7
Michaelmas Cl OX12 . . . . .10 F1
Michaels Chase RG4 . . . .259 C3
Micklands Prim Sch
RG4 . . . . .259 D4
Micklands Rd RG4 . . . . . .259 E4
Mickle Way OX33 . . . . . .125 E4
Middi Haines Ct SN6 . . . .190 A6
Middle Aston La OX25 . . . .48 A4
Middle Aston Rd OX25 . . . .48 A4
Middle Barton Sch OX7 . . . .61 A6
Middle Barton Sch OX7 . . . .47 D5
Middle Furlong OX14 . . . .201 B2
Middle Hill OX15 . . . . . . .30 B7
Middle La
Balscote OX15 . . . . .14 C8
Shutteswell OX17 . . . . . . .8 D8
Middle Orch OX7 . . . . . . .54 D2
Middle Rd
Burford OX18 . . . . .99 B6
Stanton St John OX33 . . .125 D7
Middle Row
Chipping Norton OX7 . . . . .42 E3
Great Rollright OX7 . . . . . .29 A3
Middle Springs RG8 . . . . .249 C8
Middleton Cheney Com Prim
Sch OX17 . . . . .17 F8
Middleton Cl OX16 . . . . . .17 A2
Middleton Pk OX25 . . . . . .63 E3
Middleton Rd
Banbury OX16 . . . . .16 F7
Bucknell OX27 . . . . .64 F8
Chacombe OX17 . . . . . . .10 E4
Middleton Stoney Rd
OX25 . . . . .65 C1
Middleway Bottom OX12 . .213 C2
Middle Way
Chinnor OX39 . . . . .168 B6
Islip OX5 . . . . .93 F1
Oxford OX2 . . . . .123 B7
Midget Cl OX14 . . . . . . .179 D5
Midsummer Mdw RG4 . . . .258 F6
Midway OX17 . . . . .11 A1
Midwinter Ave OX14 . . . . .199 C3
Miles Dr OX12 . . . . .214 D8
Milestone Cl OX10 . . . . . .260 F6
Milestone Cl HP14 . . . . . .188 C5
Milestone Rd OX18 . . . . . .115 D1
Milestone View Ct RG4 . .259 E4
Mileway Gdns OX3 . . . . . .124 C1
Milking La OX28,OX29 . . . .104 A3
Millaway La SN7 . . . . . . .195 C5
Millbank OX2 . . . . .141 A8
Millbrook Cl
Blewbury OX11 . . . . .219 A1
Wallingford OX10 . . . . . . .221 C7
Millbrook Sch OX12 . . . . .196 D1
Millbrook Sq OX12 . . . . . .196 E1
Millbuck Ind Est OX28 . . . .118 B6
Mill Cl
Chadlington OX7 . . . . .57 A1
Charlton-on-O OX5 . . . . . .95 A5
Deddington OX15 . . . . . . .33 E4
Middle Assendon RG9 . . .243 F8
Milldown Ave RG8 . . . . . .249 C7
Milldown Rd RG8 . . . . . . .249 C7
Mill End OX5 . . . . .93 A1
Miller Ho OX16 . . . . .16 A6
Miller Rd
Banbury OX16 . . . . .16 A6
Wheatley OX33 . . . . .144 C7
Miller's Acre 1 OX2 . . . .109 B1
Millers Cl
Chalgrove OX44 . . . . . . .184 C7
Goring RG8 . . . . .249 B7
Millers Ct OX4 . . . . .142 A8
Millers La OX15 . . . . .7 C7
Millers Mews OX28 . . . . .118 A8
Millers Turn OX39 . . . . . .168 B6
Millets Farm Cotts OX13 . . .177 D5
Millfield Ave OX27 . . . . . . .67 F3
Millfield Cl OX27 . . . . .67 F3
Milford Rd RG1 . . . . .258 F1
Mill Gn
Bampton OX18 . . . . .134 E2
Reading RG4 . . . . .259 C1
Mill La
Adderbury OX17 . . . . .23 A3
Alvescot OX18 . . . . .133 C6
Ascott-u-W OX7 . . . . .71 D2
Benson OX10 . . . . .203 F4
Black Bourton OX18 . . . . .133 F5
Brackley NN13 . . . . .24 A6
Chalgrove OX44 . . . . . . .184 C6
Chinnor OX39 . . . . .168 B7
Chipping Warden OX17 . . . .5 F6

Mill La continued
Clanfield OX18 . . . . .152 D8
Croughton NN13 . . . . .36 C7
Drayton OX15 . . . . .15 D8
East Challow OX12 . . . . . .213 E7
East Hendred OX12 . . . . .216 D6
Great Bourton OX17 . . . . . .9 F7
Great Haseley OX44 . . . . .164 D8
Grove OX12 . . . . .214 F8
Haddenham OX9 . . . . . . .130 B3
Henley-on-T RG9 . . . . . .254 F8
Horton-cum-S OX33 . . . . .112 A6
Kidmore End RG4 . . . . . .252 C1
Kings Sutton OX17 . . . . . .23 F4
Kirtlington OX5 . . . . .77 F4
Lechlade-on-T GL7 . . . . . .150 F4
Lower Heyford OX25 . . . . .62 D6
Lower Shiplake RG9 . . . . .255 A2
Marston OX3 . . . . .123 E8
Marston OX3 . . . . .123 F7
Middle Barton OX7 . . . . . .60 E8
Milton OX14 . . . . .199 C6
Mill Lane Sch OX39 . . . . .168 B7
Mill La
Oxford OX4 . . . . .141 F4
Sandford St Martin OX7 . . . .46 B1
Shenington OX15 . . . . . . .6 E2
South Moreton OX11 . . . . .220 A5
Stokenchurch HP14 . . . . .188 C5
Sutton Courtenay OX14 . . .199 F7
Upper Arncott OX25 . . . . .96 F7
Upper Heyford OX25 . . . . .48 F1
Wallingford OX10 . . . . . . .221 D7
Westbury NN13 . . . . .25 A4
West Hendred OX12 . . . . .216 C6
Weston-on-t-G OX25 . . . . .79 A2
Wootton OX20 . . . . .75 F4
Millmoor Cres OX29 . . . . .120 E8
Mill Orch OX12 . . . . .197 A6
Mill Paddock
7 Abingdon OX14 . . . . . . .179 F6
Letcombe Regis OX12 . . . .214 A2
Mill Rd
Abingdon OX14 . . . . . . .179 C5
Goring RG8 . . . . .249 C7
Lower Shiplake RG9 . . . . .255 B3
Marcham OX13 . . . . .178 D5
Nettlebed RG9 . . . . .224 E3
Reading RG4 . . . . .259 C1
Stokenchurch HP14 . . . . .188 C5
Stratton Audley OX6 . . . . .52 E1
Wolvercote OX2 . . . . . . .122 D8
Mill St Mews OX29 . . . . .120 E7
Mills La OX15 . . . . .15 A8
Mill St
Eynsham OX29 . . . . .120 E8
Islip OX5 . . . . .109 E8
Kidlington OX5 . . . . .92 F1
Oxford OX2 . . . . .123 A1
Millstream Ct OX2 . . . . . .123 A1
Mill St
Stanton St John OX33 . . .125 E8
Steventon OX13 . . . . . . .198 F3
Wantage OX12 . . . . .214 D5
Witney OX28 . . . . .104 A1
Mill The OX7 . . . . .42 C2
Millview OX49 . . . . .185 D3
Mill View OX49 . . . . .185 D3
Millway Cl OX2 . . . . .122 F8
Millway La OX13 . . . . . . .157 F6
Millwood End OX29 . . . . . .90 A1
Millwood Farm Barns
OX29 . . . . .90 A1
Millwood Vale OX29 . . . . .90 A1
Millwright Cl 3 OX16 . . . .16 B6
Milne Pl OX3 . . . . .124 B5
Milton Bsns & Tech Ctr
OX13 . . . . .199 A2
Milton CE Prim Sch
OX14 . . . . .199 C2
Milton Cl
4 Bicester OX26 . . . . . . .65 C3
Henley-on-T RG9 . . . . . .244 D2
Milton Cres OX33 . . . . . .125 F4
Milton Hill OX13 . . . . . . .199 B2
Milton Intc OX14 . . . . . . .199 A5
Milton La OX13 . . . . .199 A5
Milton Manor Dr OX4 . . . . .163 F6
Milton Manor House*
OX14 . . . . .199 C5
Milton Park Est OX14 . . . . .199 F1
Milton Rd
Bloxham OX15 . . . . .21 C5
Didcot OX11 . . . . .200 B3
Milton OX17 . . . . .22 C2
Oxford OX4 . . . . .142 B6
Shipton-u-W OX7 . . . . . . .70 D1
Sutton Courtenay OX14 . . .199 F6
Milton St OX16 . . . . .16 C5
Milvery Way OX4 . . . . . . .142 B3
Minchery Farm Cotts
OX4 . . . . .142 C1
Minchery Rd OX4 . . . . . . .142 C1
Minchins Cl OX14 . . . . . .180 C8
Minnow La OX18 . . . . . . .99 B6
Minster Ind Pk OX29 . . . . .103 B1
Minster Lovell Hall &
Dovecote* OX29 . . . . . . .103 A3
Minster Rd
Brize Norton OX18 . . . . . .116 D6
Oxford OX4 . . . . .142 A8
Minster Riding OX12 . . . . .214 E4
Minster The OX30 . . . . . .257 F1
Mint The 1 OX16 . . . . . . .221 D7
Minty Cl OX13 . . . . .115 C1
Mirfield Rd OX28 . . . . . . .117 E8
Mistletoe Gn OX4 . . . . . .142 E1

Mitchell Cl
Thame OX9 . . . . .147 E8
Wootton OX13 . . . . .159 A7
Mitford Cotts OX18 . . . . . .99 E1
Moat Cl OX18 . . . . .116 B3
Moat La OX27 . . . . .67 F2
Moat's Cres OX9 . . . . . . .148 A8
Moberly Cl OX4 . . . . .141 F8
Model Cotts OX18 . . . . . .133 F4
Moir Ct OX12 . . . . .214 D5
Mold Cres OX16 . . . . . . .16 A6
Mole Pl
17 Sandford-on-T OX4 . . . .142 E1
Oxford OX4 . . . . .143 A1
Mollington La OX17 . . . . . .3 B4
Mollington Rd
Claydon OX17 . . . . .4 D8
Shotteswell OX17 . . . . . . .8 D8
Molyneux Dr OX15 . . . . . .22 E8
Molyns Ho RG9 . . . . .244 E3
Monarchs Ct OX14 . . . . . .203 F4
Monard Terr 2 OX4 . . . . .141 F7
Monique Ct OX4 . . . . .9 A1
Monkey Ct 2 RG4 . . . . . .259 C1
Monks Cl
Carterton OX18 . . . . . . .115 D5
Dorchester OX10 . . . . . . .182 E1
Oxford OX4 . . . . .142 D2
West Hanney OX12 . . . . . .196 F6
Monks Dene Bsns Ctr
OX2 . . . . .42 E3
Monks Lode OX11 . . . . . .200 F3
Monks Mead OX10 . . . . . .202 E2
Monks Wlk GL7 . . . . .150 B4
Monmouth Ct 5 RG1 . . . .259 A1
Monmouth Rd OX1 . . . . . .141 D5
Monnhan Way OX18 . . . . .115 F4
Mons Way OX14 . . . . . . .159 D1
Montabaur Rd NN13 . . . . . .24 A7
Montague St RG4 . . . . . .259 C1
Montagu Rd OX2 . . . . . . .140 D8
Montgomery Rd OX27 . . . . .66 A7
Montpelier Dr RG4 . . . . . .259 D5
Montrose Way OX9 . . . . . .148 A8
Monument Ind Pk OX44 . .184 F7
Monument St OX16 . . . . . .16 C5
Moody Rd OX3 . . . . .123 F3
Moorbank OX4 . . . . .142 E2
Moorbrook OX11 . . . . . . .200 A1
Moorend La
Thame OX9 . . . . .129 F1
Thame OX9 . . . . .130 A2
Moorfield Cl OX16 . . . . . .16 E6
Moorgate GL7 . . . . .150 B4
Moorhen Wlk OX4 . . . . . .142 E1
Moorland Ave OX28 . . . . .104 C1
Moorland Rd OX18 . . . . . .117 F8
Moorlands The
Benson OX10 . . . . .204 A4
Kidlington OX5 . . . . .92 E2
Moor La OX15 . . . . .31 F7
Moor Pond Cl OX26 . . . . .65 F2
Moors Cl OX29 . . . . .118 A5
Moors Dr The OX17 . . . . . .17 F8
Moors The
Kidlington OX5 . . . . .92 D2
Pangbourne RG8 . . . . . . .256 D5
Morecambe Ave RG4 . . . . .258 E5
Moreton Ave OX10 . . . . . .221 B7
Moreton La
Newbridge OX29 . . . . . . .156 F7
Thame OX9 . . . . .147 E8
Moreton Rd
Aston Tirrold OX11 . . . . . .219 F2
Oxford OX2 . . . . .123 B6
Morgan Cl OX16 . . . . . . .15 F8
Morlais RG4 . . . . .259 A5
Morland Cl OX33 . . . . . . .144 B8
Morland Rd OX13 . . . . . . .178 D6
Morlands The OX12 . . . . .197 B7
Morrell Ave OX4 . . . . . . .142 A8
Morrell Cl OX5 . . . . .108 D8
Morrell Cres OX4 . . . . . . .142 A2
Morrells Cl OX11 . . . . . . .200 D1
Morris Cres OX4 . . . . . . .142 B6
Morris Dr OX16 . . . . .15 F8
Morris Ho OX4 . . . . .142 C4
Morse Rd OX11 . . . . .218 E8
Mortimer Dr OX3 . . . . . . .123 F4
Mortimer Rd OX4 . . . . . . .141 F3
Morton Ave OX5 . . . . .108 E7
Morton Cl
Abingdon OX14 . . . . . . .180 C8
Kidlington OX5 . . . . .108 E8
Morton King Cl HP18 . . . . .128 D3
Mosquito La OX4 . . . . . . .204 D2
Moss Cl RG4 . . . . .259 C3
Motte The OX14 . . . . . . .179 F7
Moulsford Prep Sch
OX10 . . . . .239 A6
Mountfield OX28 . . . . . . .249 C7
Mountfield Rd OX13 . . . . .117 A7
Mount Owen Rd OX18 . . . .135 A3
Mount Pleasant SN6 . . . . .227 D4
Mount Pleasant Cotts
OX12 . . . . .216 D6
Mount Pleasant
Lechlade-on-T GL7 . . . . . .150 C4
Shipton-u-W OX7 . . . . . . .85 E7
Wardington OX17 . . . . . . .5 E1
Mount Pl OX2 . . . . .261 A3

Mount St OX2 . . . . 123 A2
Mount The
  Reading RG4 . . . . 258 F3
  Tetsworth OX9 . . . . 166 B8
Mount View Ct RG9 . . . . 244 D2
Mount View RG9 . . . . . . 244 D2
Mousey La 6 OX10 . . . . 221 D7
Mowbray Dr RG30 . . . . . 258 A1
Mowbray Rd OX11 . . . . . 218 E6
Mowforth Cl RG8 . . . . . . 240 E1
Mulberries The OX12 . . . 197 A6
Mulberry Bush Sch
  OX1 . . . . 137 C2
Mulberry Ct OX2 . . . . 123 A8
Mulberry Dr
  Bicester OX26 . . . . 65 E5
  Wheatley OX33 . . . . 144 B8
Mulcaster Ave OX5 . . . . 108 F8
Mullard Way OX14 . . . . . 179 E7
Mullein Rd OX26 . . . . 65 E5
Mullens Terr RG4 . . . . . . 258 D8
Mumbery Hill RG10 . . . . 255 E1
Murcott Rd OX25 . . . . 96 D6
Murdock Cl OX15 . . . . 33 E4
Murdock Rd OX26 . . . . . . 66 A2
Murray Ct OX2 . . . . 123 C4
Murren Croft OX10 . . . . . 221 E7
Murren The OX10 . . . . . . 221 D6
Museum Rd OX1 . . . . 261 B3
Musgrave Rd OX39 . . . . 168 D7
Musgrave Wlk HP14 . . . 188 F5
Mus Of Modern Art*
  OX1 . . . . 261 B2
Mus Of Oxford* OX1 . . . 261 B2
Musson Cl 3 OX14 . . . . 179 E6
Mustard La RG4 . . . . 260 E2
Myrtle Cl
  Long Hanborough OX29 . . . 90 B1
  Reading RG31 . . . . 257 C3

N

Naldertown OX12 . . . . . . 214 C5
Napier Ct OX14 . . . . 180 B7
Napier Rd OX4 . . . . 142 D5
Nappins Cl HP18 . . . . . . 129 D5
Naseby Cl OX9 . . . . 130 B1
Nash Ct OX4 . . . . 142 D4
Nash Dr OX14 . . . . 179 C6
Nash La OX29 . . . . 106 A7
National Herb Ctr The*
  OX17 . . . . 3 A3
Navigation Way OX2 . . . 123 A5
Neals La RG4 . . . . 242 A2
Neal's La RG4 . . . . 242 A2
Neave Mews 9 OX14 . . . 179 F6
Neithrop Ave OX16 . . . . . 16 B7
Neithrop Cl OX16 . . . . . . 16 B7
Nell Hill SN6 . . . . 227 D4
Nelson Cl OX10 . . . . 221 C8
Nelson Rd RG4 . . . . 259 C2
Nelson St
  Oxford OX2 . . . . 261 A3
  Thame OX9 . . . . 147 F8
Nene Gr OX14 . . . . 201 B2
Nene Rd OX13 . . . . 159 C2
Netheravon Cl OX18 . . . 115 E2
Nether Cl NN13 . . . . 24 A7
Nethercote La OX49 . . . 167 A1
Nethercote Rd OX5 . . . . . 77 C6
Nethercote Mdw CV36 . . . 27 F7
Nether Durnford Cl OX13 . 142 F7
Netherton La OX13 . . . . 157 C6
Netherton Rd OX13 . . . . 157 E6
Netherwoods Rd OX3 . . . 124 F2
Netherworton Rd OX15 . . . 32 E5
Netley Cl RG4 . . . . 259 E6
Netting St OX15 . . . . 30 A7
Nettlebed Com Sch RG9 . 224 D2
Nettlebed Mead OX4 . . . 142 E1
Nettleton Dr OX25 . . . . . 63 C7
Neunkirchen Way OX26 . . 81 A7
Neville Way SN7 . . . . . . 194 E7
Nevis Rd RG31 . . . . 257 D3
Newalls Rise RG10 . . . . 255 E2
Newbery Cl RG31 . . . . . . 257 D1
New Bldgs
  Uffington SN7 . . . . 211 D8
  Whitchurch Hill RG8 . . . . 250 D2
Newbold Cl OX16 . . . . . . 16 E4
Newbury Rd
  East Hendred OX12 . . . . . 216 E5
  Rowstock OX11 . . . . 217 B6
Newbury St OX12 . . . . . 214 D4
New Close La OX28 . . . . 117 F5
New College La OX1 . . . 261 C2
New College Sq OX5 . . . . 48 F1
Newcombe Ct OX2 . . . . . 123 A4
New Coll Sch OX1 . . . . . 261 C3
Newcombe Ct OX3 . . . . . 21 A1
Newcombe Ct OX2 . . . . . 123 A4
New Cross Rd OX3 . . . . . 124 E3
Newells Cl OX44 . . . . . . 163 C1
Newell's La RG4 . . . . 258 B2
Newfield Rd RG4 . . . . . . 252 F6
Newgate Rd OX5 . . . . 95 E5
New High St OX3 . . . . . . 124 C2
New Hill RG8 . . . . 257 C5
New Hinksey CE Prim Sch
  OX1 . . . . 141 C6
New Hope Terr 2 RG1 . . 259 A1
New House Yd OX7 . . . . . 42 A5
Newington OX44 . . . . . . 163 C1
New Inn Hall St OX1 . . . 261 B2

New Inn Rd OX3 . . . . . . 111 A2
Newland Cl OX29 . . . . . . 120 E7
Newland Mill OX28 . . . . 104 C1
Newland Pl OX16 . . . . 16 D5
Newland Rd OX16 . . . . . . 16 D5
Newlands Ave
  Didcot OX11 . . . . 218 E7
  Reading RG4 . . . . 259 B3
Newlands Dr OX12 . . . . . 196 C1
Newlands La RG9 . . . . . 242 B5
Newland St OX29 . . . . . . 120 E8
Newland Terr OX9 . . . . . 147 F8
Newlin Cl OX4 . . . . 141 F3
New Look Mobile Home Pk
  OX18 . . . . 115 E1
Newman Ct
  Oxford OX4 . . . . 123 F1
  Witney OX29 . . . . 103 C1
Newman La OX14 . . . . . . 179 B2
Newman Rd OX4 . . . . . . 142 B3
Newmans Cl OX11 . . . . . 218 C3
New Marston Prim Sch
  OX3 . . . . 124 A5
Newmill La OX28 . . . . . . 103 F2
Newnham Gn OX10 . . . . 221 F7
Newnhamhill Bottom
  RG9 . . . . 242 B5
New Pl OX17 . . . . 4 F2
New Pond La OX5 . . . . . . 95 A5
Newport Cl OX5 . . . . . . 108 D7
Newport Rd RG1 . . . . . . 259 A1
Newport Terr 1 OX26 . . . 65 F1
New Rd
  Adderbury OX17 . . . . 22 F3
  Bampton OX18 . . . . 134 F4
  Banbury OX16 . . . . 16 C5
  Bledington OX7 . . . . 54 D2
  Bletchingdon OX5 . . . . 93 B8
  Charney Bassett OX12 . . . 175 F2
  Childrey OX12 . . . . 213 B6
  East Hagbourne OX11 . . . 219 A6
  Glympton OX20 . . . . 75 D8
  Great Tew OX7 . . . . 45 D7
  Hailey OX29 . . . . 104 A6
  Kingham OX7 . . . . 54 F4
  Long Hanborough OX29 . . . 90 B1
  Lower Shiplake RG9 . . . . 255 A3
  Marcham OX13 . . . . 178 C6
  Milcombe OX15 . . . . 21 A1
  Oxford OX1 . . . . 261 B2
  Ratley OX15 . . . . 2 A4
  Shotteswell OX17 . . . . 8 C8
  Shrivenham SN6 . . . . 209 E3
  Stokenchurch HP14 . . . . 188 F4
  Sutton OX29 . . . . 120 A1
  Wallingford OX10 . . . . . . 221 D7
  Warborough OX10 . . . . . 203 B6
  Watlington OX49 . . . . . . 186 B1
  Woodstock OX20 . . . . 91 B6
New Row
  Ambrosden OX25 . . . . 81 C3
  Bucknell OX27 . . . . 64 F8
Newscut La OX17 . . . . 4 F2
New St
  Abingdon OX14 . . . . 179 F7
  Bicester OX26 . . . . 65 E3
  Chipping Norton OX7 . . . . 42 E3
  Deddington OX15 . . . . 33 F3
  Henley-on-T RG9 . . . . . . 244 E2
Newtec Pl OX4 . . . . 141 F7
New Theatre* OX1 . . . . . 261 B2
Newton Ave RG4 . . . . . . 259 D5
Newton Rd OX1 . . . . 141 C7
Newton Way OX10 . . . . . 204 A5
New Town GL56 . . . . 26 F8
New Town Cotts SN6 . . . . 227 D4
Newtown Gdns RG9 . . . . 254 E8
Newtown OX10 . . . . 240 C7
New Town La SN6 . . . . . . 227 D4
Newtown Rd RG9 . . . . . . 254 F8
New Yatt Bsns Ctr OX29 . 104 F7
New Yatt La OX29 . . . . . 104 D7
New Yatt Rd OX28,OX29 . 104 E4
Niagara Rd RG9 . . . . 254 E8
Nicholas Ave OX3 . . . . . 123 F4
Nicholas Rd OX3 . . . . . . 254 B8
Nichol Ct 8 SN7 . . . . . . 172 F3
Nicholson Rd OX3 . . . . . 123 F3
Nigel Ct NN13 . . . . 24 A5
Nightingale Ave OX4 . . . 142 E1
Nightingale La SN3 . . . . 208 A5
Nightingale Pl OX26 . . . . 81 A8
Nine Acres Cl OX7 . . . . . 73 B4
Nine Acres La OX7 . . . . . 73 B4
Nineteenth St OX11 . . . . 217 A1
Ninety Cut Hill OX18 . . . 102 A4
Ninth Ave OX3,OX4 . . . . 142 F7
Ninth St OX11 . . . . 217 B2
Nire Rd RG4 . . . . 259 E2
Nixon Rd OX4 . . . . 141 F5
Nizewell Head OX25 . . . . 62 B8
Nobles Rd RG9 . . . . 254 F8
Nobles Cl
  Grove OX12 . . . . 196 D1
  Oxford OX2 . . . . 140 A8
Nobles La OX2 . . . . 140 A8
Noral Way OX16 . . . . 9 D2
Nor Brook Cl OX14 . . . . . 160 C2
Norcot Rd RG30 . . . . . . 258 A1
Norfolk Cl OX14 . . . . 160 C1
Norfolk St OX1 . . . . 261 B1
Norham End OX2 . . . . . . 123 C4
Norham Gdns OX2 . . . . . 261 C4
Norham Rd OX2 . . . . 123 C4
Norman Ave
  Abingdon OX14 . . . . 160 A1
  Henley-on-T RG9 . . . . . 244 E1

Normandy Cres OX4 . . . 142 E5
Norman Pl RG1 . . . . 259 B1
Norman Rd RG4 . . . . . . 259 C2
Norman Smith Rd 14
  OX4 . . . . 142 F1
Normanstead RG9 . . . . . 244 D1
Norman Way OX10 . . . . 221 C7
Norreys Ave OX1 . . . . . . 141 D6
Norreys Cl OX11 . . . . . . 218 D7
Norreys Rd
  Cumnor OX2 . . . . 139 F5
  Didcot OX11 . . . . 218 D8
Norries Dr OX10 . . . . . . 203 D1
Norris Cl
  Abingdon OX14 . . . . 160 B2
  Adderbury OX17 . . . . 22 F2
Norris Rd OX25 . . . . 96 E8
Northampton Rd OX1 . . . 141 D5
North Aston Rd OX25 . . . 47 D6
North Ave OX14 . . . . 160 A2
North Bar Pl OX16 . . . . . 16 C6
North Bar St OX16 . . . . . 16 C6
Northbourne CE Prim Sch
  OX11 . . . . 218 E7
Northbourne Rd OX11 . . 218 F8
Northbrook No 1 OX4 . . 142 E2
Northbrook Rd RG4 . . . . 259 D6
North Bush Furlong
  OX14 . . . . 201 B1
North Cl OX9 . . . . 145 F7
Northcot La OX16 . . . . . . 16 B7
Northcourt La OX14 . . . . 160 A1
Northcourt Rd OX14 . . . . 159 F1
Northcourt Wlk OX14 . . . 180 A8
North Croft OX11 . . . . . . 218 F5
North Culham St OX14 . . 181 A5
North Dr
  Grove OX12 . . . . 196 E2
  Harwell OX11 . . . . 217 C4
Northern By-Pass Rd
  Cutteslowe OX2 . . . . 108 E1
  Oxford OX3 . . . . 124 C5
Northfield Ave RG9 . . . . 255 A4
Northfield Cl OX4 . . . . . . 142 C2
Northfield Cotts OX2 . . . 122 A8
Northfield Ct RG9 . . . . . 244 D3
Northfield End RG9 . . . . 244 D3
Northfield Rd
  Abingdon OX14 . . . . 160 A3
  Lower Shiplake RG9 . . . . 255 B4
  Oxford OX3 . . . . 124 E4
  Reading RG1 . . . . 259 A1
Northfield Sch OX4 . . . . 142 D1
Northford Cl SN6 . . . . . . 209 C8
Northford Ind Est SN6 . . 209 C8
North Gn OX12 . . . . 196 F7
North Hill HP18 . . . . 98 A1
North Hinksey CE Prim Sch
  OX2 . . . . 140 E8
North Hinksey La OX2 . . 140 E8
North Hinksey Village
  OX2 . . . . 140 F7
North Kidlington Prim Sch
  OX5 . . . . 92 D1
North La OX25 . . . . 79 A2
North Leigh Bsns Pk
  OX29 . . . . 105 C7
North Leigh CE Sch
  OX29 . . . . 105 B6
North Leigh Roman Villa*
  OX29 . . . . 89 D3
North Lodge OX2 . . . . . 122 D1
North Manor Estate The
  OX44 . . . . 143 E2
Northmead La OX12 . . . 196 A7
North Mill Rd HP27 . . . . 149 F5
Northmoor Pk OX29 . . . . 138 C2
Northmoor Pl OX2 . . . . . 123 C5
Northmoor Rd OX2 . . . . 123 C5
Northolt Rd OX18 . . . . . . 115 D3
North Parade Ave OX2 . . 123 C4
North Pl OX3 . . . . 124 B3
North Quay OX14 . . . . . 179 F4
North Rd
  Didcot OX11 . . . . 200 D2
  Moulsford OX10 . . . . . . 238 F4
North Side OX25 . . . . 48 A1
North St
  Aston OX18 . . . . 135 E3
  Banbury OX16 . . . . 16 E7
  Bicester OX26 . . . . 65 E2
  Fritwell OX27 . . . . 49 E7
  Islip OX5 . . . . 93 F1
  Marcham OX13 . . . . 178 C6
  Middle Barton OX7 . . . . . 60 F8
  Oxford OX2 . . . . 123 A1
  Reading RG1 . . . . 259 B2
  Thame OX9 . . . . 129 F1
  Watchfield SN6 . . . . 191 D1
Northumberland Ct 4
  OX16 . . . . 16 E6
Northview Prim Sch
  SN6 . . . . 190 A4
North Way
  Cutteslowe OX2 . . . . 108 F1
  Oxford OX3 . . . . 124 E4
  Steventon OX13 . . . . . . 198 F5
Northwood Cres OX18 . . 115 E4
Northwood Rd OX29 . . . 103 C1
Norton Cl OX3 . . . . 124 D2
Norton Green Ct OX7 . . . 42 E2
Norton Pk OX7 . . . . 42 E2
Norton Terr OX29 . . . . . 102 D8
Norton Way OX15 . . . . . . 21 E4
Norwood Ave OX13 . . . . 156 E1
Nosworthy Way OX10 . . 221 C8
Nottwood La RG9 . . . . . 242 A5
Nourse Cl OX3 . . . . 110 B5

Nowell Rd OX4 . . . . 142 A3
Nuffield Cl
  Bicester OX26 . . . . 65 F3
  Didcot OX11 . . . . 219 A8
Nuffield Coll OX1 . . . . . . 261 A2
Nuffield Dr OX16 . . . . 16 A8
Nuffield Hill RG9 . . . . . . 223 C4
Nuffield Ind Est OX4 . . . 142 C2
Nuffield La OX10 . . . . . . 222 E6
Nuffield Orthopaedic Ctr
  OX3 . . . . 124 D1
Nuffield Rd OX3 . . . . . . 124 F1
Nuffield Way OX14 . . . . 179 C7
Nuneham Sq OX14 . . . . 179 F8
Nunhide La RG8 . . . . . . 256 F1
Nunnery Cl OX4 . . . . . . 142 D2
Nunney Brook OX11 . . . 200 F3
Nun's Acre RG8 . . . . . . 249 B7
Nurseries Rd OX5 . . . . . 108 D8
Nursery Cl
  Lower Shiplake RG9 . . . 255 A4
  Oxford OX3 . . . . 124 C1
Nursery Gdns RG8 . . . . 257 B5
Nursery La OX16 . . . . 16 C7
Nursery Rd OX29 . . . . . 105 C7
Nursery The OX14 . . . . . 200 A8
Nursery View SN7 . . . . . 173 B3
Nuthatch Cl 1 OX4 . . . . 142 E1
Nut Hatch Cotts RG8 . . 241 D3
Nuthatch Way OX26 . . . . 65 F1
Nyatt Rd OX14 . . . . 180 C8
Nye Bevan Cl OX4 . . . . 142 A8

O

Oak Ave OX14 . . . . 160 E6
Oak Cl OX26 . . . . 65 F4
Oak Cotts OX10 . . . . . . 239 D6
Oakdale Cl 3 OX10 . . . . 221 C7
Oakdene RG8 . . . . 250 F7
Oakdown Cl RG8 . . . . . . 250 E3
Oak Dr OX5 . . . . 92 F1
Oak End Way OX39 . . . . 168 D6
Oakes La OX2 . . . . 121 C2
Oakey Cl OX18 . . . . 133 C5
Oak Farm Cl OX9 . . . . . 166 B7
Oakfield Ind Est OX29 . . 120 D6
Oakfield Pl OX28 . . . . . . 118 B7
Oakfield Rd OX18 . . . . . 115 D1
Oakham Cl RG31 . . . . . . 257 D2
Oakham Rd GL56 . . . . . . 27 B1
Oak La OX25 . . . . 81 D4
Oakland Cl OX29 . . . . . . 105 F7
Oakland Rd OX16 . . . . . . 16 D2
Oaklands OX2 . . . . 121 B3
Oak La SN7 . . . . 194 F6
Oakley Cl OX10 . . . . 222 F5
Oakley Ho OX13 . . . . . . 158 C2
Oakley La OX39 . . . . . . 168 B6
Oakley Rd
  Chinnor OX39 . . . . 168 C6
  Horton-cum-S OX33 . . . . 112 C5
  Reading RG4 . . . . 258 F4
Oakmead OX28 . . . . 104 D2
Oak Rd SN6 . . . . 191 C1
Oaks Meade OX18 . . . . . 115 F4
Oaksmere OX13 . . . . . . 158 A6
Oaks Rd RG9 . . . . 255 A4
Oaks The OX18 . . . . 115 E4
Oakthorpe Pl OX2 . . . . . 123 B6
Oakthorpe Rd OX2 . . . . 123 B6
Oak Tree Copse RG31 . . 257 E3
Oak Tree Wlk RG8 . . . . . 257 E5
Oak View OX18 . . . . 114 C7
Oasis Pk OX29 . . . . 120 D6
Oathurst Est OX18 . . . . 134 F3
Oatland Rd OX11 . . . . . . 218 E8
Oatlands Cl OX10 . . . . . 203 B7
Oatlands Rd OX2 . . . . . . 122 F1
Observatory Cl OX10 . . . 204 A4
Observatory St OX2 . . . . 261 A4
Ock Dr OX10 . . . . 221 D8
Ockham Ct OX2 . . . . . . 123 C4
Ockley Brook OX14 . . . . 201 A2
Ock Mews 5 OX14 . . . . 179 E7
Ock Mill Cl OX14 . . . . . . 179 D6
Ock St OX14 . . . . 179 D6
O'Connors Rd OX29 . . . 102 E2
Octavian Way NN13 . . . . 24 A7
Oddley La HP27 . . . . . . 149 D8
Odiham Ave RG4 . . . . . . 259 E5
Odiham Cl OX18 . . . . . . 115 F3
Offas Cl OX10 . . . . 204 A5
Ogbourne Cl OX12 . . . . 214 B5
Old Arncott Rd OX26 . . . . 81 C3
Old Bakery The OX1 . . . 261 A2
Old Barn Cl
  Benson OX10 . . . . 204 A4
  Reading RG4 . . . . 259 A6
Old Barn Ground OX3 . . 142 F7
Old Bath Rd
  Sonning RG4 . . . . 260 D1
  Sonning RG4 . . . . 260 E2
Old Bix Rd RG9 . . . . 243 F7
Old Blackalls Dr OX10 . . 221 A3
Old Bldgs 15 OX10 . . . . 221 D7
Old Boars Hill
  Boars Hill OX1 . . . . 140 D1
  Wootton OX1 . . . . 159 C8
Old Bourne OX11 . . . . . 200 F3
Old Bridge Rd OX15 . . . . 21 E4
Old Burford Rd OX7 . . . . 54 D1
Old Chapel Cl OX5 . . . . . 92 E1
Old Coach Rd OX13 . . . . 157 F2

Old Coach Yard The
  OX28 . . . . 104 B1
Old Copse Gdns RG4 . . 252 F6
Old Council Hos The
  Horley OX15 . . . . 8 B4
  South Newington OX15 . . 31 F7
Old Croft Cl OX39 . . . . . 167 F4
Old Dashwood Hill HP14 . 189 F7
Olean Cl RG21 . . . . 257 D1
Old Farm Cl
  Abingdon OX14 . . . . . . 180 C8
  Worminghall HP18 . . . . . 127 D5
Old Farm Cres RG31 . . . 257 C2
Old Field OX44 . . . . 164 A7
Old Forge Cl OX7 . . . . . . 54 D2
Old Forge Rd OX7 . . . . . . 29 A3
Old Forge The RG8 . . . . 249 A6
Old George Yd OX18 . . . 100 E5
Old Glebe OX15 . . . . 20 C8
Old Gn The OX33 . . . . . 112 A5
Old Greyfriars St OX1 . . 261 B1
Old Grimsbury Rd OX16 . 16 E7
Old High St OX3 . . . . . . 124 D3
Old Kiln* RG9 . . . . 224 E2
Old Kiln Rd RG9 . . . . . . 224 E2
Old London Rd
  Benson OX10 . . . . 204 A4
  Chipping Norton OX7 . . . . 56 C7
  Tiddington OX9 . . . . 145 F4
  Wheatley OX33 . . . . 144 D8
Old Luxters Farm Brewery*
  RG9 . . . . 226 C8
Old Maltings The OX9 . . 129 E1
Old Manor Ct OX12 . . . . 214 A2
Old Marston Rd OX3 . . . 123 F4
Old Mill Cl OX12 . . . . . . 196 E1
Old Mill The
  8 Wantage OX12 . . . . . . 214 D4
  Pangbourne RG8 . . . . . . 256 D6
Old Moor Cl OX10 . . . . . 221 C7
Old Moor OX14 . . . . 199 D5
Old Nursery View OX1 . . 141 D3
Old Orchard OX39 . . . . . 149 E2
Old Parr Cl OX16 . . . . 16 D5
Old Parr Rd OX16 . . . . . . 16 D4
Old Place Yd OX26 . . . . . 65 E1
Old Plough Wlk OX15 . . . 33 A4
Old Pound The OX13 . . . 159 B6
Old Rd
  East Hendred OX12 . . . . 216 E6
  Great Tew OX7 . . . . 45 D7
  Littleworth OX33 . . . . . . 143 E8
  Oxford OX3 . . . . 124 E1
  Ratley OX15 . . . . 2 A4
Old Reading Rd OX10 . . 221 F5
Old Rectory Ct OX25 . . . . 80 A4
Old Rectory Mews OX28 . 118 A7
Old Rectory OX25 . . . . . . 48 F1
Old Sawmills Rd SN7 . . 172 F2
Old School Cl
  Stokenchurch HP14 . . . . 188 E4
  OX5 . . . . 65 F7
Old School End OX15 . . . 30 A7
Old School Ho The OX7 . . 70 B2
Old School La OX12 . . . 213 F5
Old School Pl
  Banbury OX16 . . . . 16 E6
  Wallington OX45 . . . . . . 186 B1
Old School The OX3 . . . 142 C6
Old Stables The OX3 . . . 124 C4
Old Stables Yd OX12 . . . 214 A1
Old Station Yd 6 OX14 . 179 F7
Old Town NN13 . . . . 24 A2
Old Vicarage La SN3 . . . 208 A3
Old Wallingford Way
  OX14 . . . . 200 B8
Old Warehouse Flats The
  OX28 . . . . 104 C1
Old Well Ct RG4 . . . . . . 260 D4
Old Wharf Rd SN7 . . . . . 210 C8
Old Windmill Way HP18 . 129 C7
Old Witney Rd OX29 . . . 120 C8
Oliver Rd OX4 . . . . 142 E5
Olson Cotts HP14 . . . . . 188 F4
Omega Pl RG1 . . . . 200 E3
One End La OX10 . . . . . 203 F4
Onley Ct 8 OX41 . . . . . 141 C7
Onslow Dr OX9 . . . . 130 B1
Onslow Gdns RG4 . . . . 259 C3
Oracle Parkway RG5 . . . 260 A1
Orange Cl SN6 . . . . 190 A6
Oratory Prep Sch The
  RG8 . . . . 250 A8
Oratory Sch The RG8 . . 251 A8
Orchard Ave RG4 . . . . . 252 E5
Orchard Cl
  Abingdon OX14 . . . . . . 160 A1
  Banbury OX16 . . . . 16 E6
  Buckland SN7 . . . . 174 E8
  Cassington OX29 . . . . . . 107 C2
  Chalgrove OX44 . . . . . . 184 D7
  Charney Bassett OX12 . . 175 F2
  Combe OX29 . . . . 90 A4
  Didcot OX11 . . . . 200 C1
  East Hanney OX12 . . . . 197 B6
  East Hendred OX12 . . . . 216 D7
  Eynsham OX29 . . . . 120 F8
  Henley-on-T RG9 . . . . . 244 E1
  Lechlade-on-T GL7 . . . . 150 C4
  Reading RG31 . . . . 257 C3
  Salford OX7 . . . . 41 F5
  Shiplake RG9 . . . . 254 E2
  Thame OX9 . . . . 148 A8
  Upton OX11 . . . . 218 C2
  Wallingford OX10 . . . . . 221 D6
  Warborough OX10 . . . . 203 A6
  Wheatley OX33 . . . . 144 B7
Orchard Coombe RG8 . . 250 D3

Orchard Cotts OX7 . . . . .57 B1
Orchard Ct OX4 . . . . .142 B4
Orchard Field RG4 . . . . . . .252 C5
Orchard Field La OX20 . . .91 D3
Orchard Fields Com Sch
  OX16 . . . . .16 A6
Orchard Furlong OX12 . .213 C4
Orchard Gdns OX12 . . . .213 D5
Orchard Gr OX12 . . . . . . .213 C4
Orchard Ground OX7 . . . .69 C2
Orchard Gr RG4 . . . . .259 E4
Orchard Haven OX10 . . .202 D8
Orchard Hill SN7 . . . . . . .172 E3
Orchard La
  Boars Hill OX1 . . . . .140 C1
  East Hendred OX12 . . .216 D6
  Upper Heyford OX25 . .62 F8
Orchard Meadow Fst Sch
  OX4 . . . . .142 E2
Orchard Pl
  Upper Heyford OX25 . .62 F8
  Westbury NN13 . . . . . . .25 A4
Orchard Rd
  Ardley OX27 . . . . .50 B4
  Buckland SN7 . . . . .174 E8
  Hook Norton OX15 . . . .30 B8
  Oxford OX2 . . . . .140 A8
Orchard Rise
  Burford OX18 . . . . .100 E4
  Chesterton OX26 . . . . . .79 F8
Orchard Row OX18 . . . . . .100 F6
Orchard The
  Appleton OX13 . . . . . . .158 A8
  Ascott-u-W OX7 . . . . . . .71 B1
  Brighthampton OX29 . .137 A4
  East Challow OX12 . . . .214 A5
  Horton-cum-S OX33 . . .112 C6
  Merton OX25 . . . . .95 D8
Orchard View OX17 . . . . . 4 F2
Orchard Way
  Banbury OX16 . . . . .16 B6
  Bicester OX26 . . . . .65 C3
  Chinnor OX39 . . . . .168 C6
  Harwell OX11 . . . . .217 D7
  Kidlington OX5 . . . . . . .108 F8
  Kingham OX7 . . . . .54 F4
  Marcham OX13 . . . . . . .178 D6
  Middle Barton OX7 . . . .46 E1
  Oxford OX4 . . . . .142 C3
  Wantage OX12 . . . . .214 E4
  Witney OX28 . . . . .118 A8
Orchard Wlk OX49 . . . . .186 C2
Orchid Cl OX26 . . . . .65 E5
Orchids The OX11 . . . . . .235 D7
Orchid Way OX18 . . . . . .115 E4
Ordnance Rd OX11 . . . . .200 D2
Oregon Ave RG31 . . . . .257 D3
Oriel Coll OX1 . . . . .261 C2
Oriel Ct OX11 . . . . .219 B8
Oriel Sq OX1 . . . . .261 C2
Oriel St OX1 . . . . .261 C2
Oriel Way OX26 . . . . .65 F3
Orkney Pl OX28 . . . . . . .117 F8
Ormerod Sch OX3 . . . . . .125 A3
Ormond Rd
  Thame OX9 . . . . .130 A1
  Wantage OX12 . . . . .214 E4
Orpine Cl OX26 . . . . .65 D5
Orpwood Way OX14 . . . .179 C6
Orwell Cl RG4 . . . . .258 F4
Orwell Dr OX14 . . . . . . .201 A1
Osberton Rd OX2 . . . . . .123 A7
Osborne Cl
  Bicester OX26 . . . . .65 C3
  Kidlington OX5 . . . . . . .108 D7
  Wolvercote OX2 . . . . . .122 F8
Osiers The OX10 . . . . . . .183 B5
Osier Rd OX4 . . . . .124 C3
Osney Cl OX15 . . . . .30 B7
Osney La
  Oxford OX1 . . . . .123 A1
  Oxford OX1 . . . . .261 A2
Osney Mead Ind Est OX2 141 A8
Osney Mead OX2 . . . . . .141 A8
Osney Mews OX2 . . . . . .123 A1
Osprey Cl OX26 . . . . .66 E4
Osterley Dr RG4 . . . . . . .259 E6
Osterley Gr OX16 . . . . . . .16 B4
Oswestry Rd OX1 . . . . . .141 D5
Otmoor La
  Beckley OX3 . . . . .111 B4
  Charlton-on-O OX5 . . . .95 A4
Otmoor View OX25 . . . . .95 C8
Otters Reach OX1 . . . . . .141 E1
Ottery Way OX14 . . . . . .201 A2
Otwell Cl OX14 . . . . .160 B2
Our Lady of Lourdes RC Prim
  Sch OX28 . . . . .117 E7
Our Lady's Convent Jun &
  Senior Sch OX14 . . . . .180 A8
Our Lady's RC Prim Sch
  OX4 . . . . .142 D5
Ouse Cl OX11 . . . . .200 F3
Ouseley Ct OX3 . . . . .123 F4
Outram Rd OX4 . . . . .142 B5
Oval The
  Bicester OX26 . . . . .65 D3
  Didcot OX11 . . . . .200 C2
  Oxford OX4 . . . . .142 A4
Overbrooke Gdns OX4 . .143 A2
Overdale Cl OX10 . . . . . .65 D5
Overdown Rd RG31 . . . .257 D3
Overlanders End RG31 . .257 E3
Overmead OX14 . . . . . . .179 E4
Over Norton Rd OX7 . . . .42 F4
Overstrand Cl OX26 . . . .66 A4

Overthorpe Prep Sch
  OX17 . . . . .17 C8
Overthorpe Rd OX16 . . . .17 A4
Overton Dr OX9 . . . . .130 B1
Owlington Cl OX2 . . . . . .122 C1
Ox Cl OX14 . . . . .180 A8
Oxen Piece OX44 . . . . . .145 C2
Oxeye Ct OX4 . . . . .161 E8
Oxford Airport OX5 . . . . .92 A4
Oxford Brookes Univ
  OX3 . . . . .124 B2
Oxford Brookes Univ, Sch of
  Occupational Therapy
  OX3 . . . . .124 C2
Oxford Bsns Ctr The
  OX1 . . . . .261 A1
Oxford Bsns Pk OX2 . . . .109 A2
Oxford Bsns Pk N OX4 . .142 D5
Oxford Bsns Pk S OX4 . .142 D4
Oxford Bus Mus Trust*
  OX29 . . . . .90 E1
Oxford & Cherwell College
  (Banbury Campus) OX16 16 B5
Oxford & Cherwell Coll
  OX9 . . . . .129 E1
Oxford Cl OX5 . . . . .77 F4
Oxford Com Sch OX4 . . .142 B7
Oxford Cres OX11 . . . . .218 E8
Oxford Ct OX25 . . . . .79 A2
Oxford High Sch For Girls
  OX2 . . . . .123 C6
Oxford Hill OX28,OX29 118 D8
Oxford Ice Rink* OX1 . . .261 A1
Oxford La OX12 . . . . . . .196 E2
Oxford Motor Pk OX5 . . .92 B2
Oxford Rd
  Abingdon OX1,OX13,
  OX14 . . . . .160 B5
  Adderbury OX17 . . . . . . .23 A3
  Benson OX10 . . . . .203 E4
  Bicester OX25,OX26 . . .80 D8
  Bletchingdon OX5 . . . . .93 A7
  Bodicote OX15 . . . . .16 D6
  Burford OX18 . . . . .100 E4
  Clifton Hampden OX14,
  OX44 . . . . .181 E6
  Cumnor OX2 . . . . .139 F5
  Cutteslowe OX2 . . . . . .109 A3
  Dorchester OX10 . . . . .182 D2
  Duns Tew OX25 . . . . . . .47 F5
  Enstone OX7 . . . . .58 F5
  Eynsham OX29 . . . . . . .120 F7
  Farmoor OX2,OX29 . . .121 A4
  Frilford OX13 . . . . .178 A7
  Garsington OX44 . . . . .143 C2
  Hampton Poyle OX5 . . . .93 B3
  Horspath OX33 . . . . . . .143 B6
  Kidlington OX5 . . . . . . .108 F7
  Kingston Bagpuize OX13 156 F1
  Kirtlington OX5 . . . . . . .77 F5
  Marston OX3 . . . . .123 F5
  Marston OX3 . . . . .123 F6
  Middleton Stoney OX25 .64 A3
  Oxford,Littlemore OX4 .142 B3
  Oxford,Temple Cowley
  OX4 . . . . .142 C5
  Reading RG8,RG30,RG31 .257 D4
  South Hinksey OX1 . . . .141 B2
  Stokenchurch HP14 . . .188 C5
  Thame OX9 . . . . .147 D8
  Tiddington OX9 . . . . . .145 E6
  Woodcote RG8 . . . . . . .240 E1
  Woodstock OX20 . . . . . .91 C5
Oxford Retail Pk OX4 . .142 E4
Oxford Science Pk The
  OX4 . . . . .142 C1
Oxfordshire Hospital Sch
  OX3 . . . . .124 D1
Oxfordshire Mus The*
  OX20 . . . . .91 A6
Oxford Spires Bsns Pk
  OX5 . . . . .92 B3
Oxford Sq SN6 . . . . .191 C1
Oxford Sta OX2 . . . . .123 A1
Oxford Story (Mus) The*
  OX1 . . . . .261 B2
Oxford St
  Reading RG4 . . . . .259 A2
  Woodstock OX20 . . . . . .91 B6
Oxford Union The* OX1 .261 B2
Oxford Univ Botanic Gdns*
  OX1 . . . . .261 C2
Oxford University Press*
  OX2 . . . . .261 A3
Oxford Univ Inst Of
  Experimental Psychology
  OX1 . . . . .261 C3
Oxford Univ Mus of Natural
  History The* OX1 . . . .261 B3
Oxhey Hill OX17 . . . . .4 D3
Oxhey Rise OX15 . . . . . . .31 B7
Oxlease OX28 . . . . .118 C8
Oxlip Leyes OX26 . . . . . .65 D4
Oxon Pl SN6 . . . . .227 D4
Oxpens Rd OX1 . . . . .261 A1

P

Pack And Prime La RG9 .244 C2
Packhorse La OX13 . . . .178 D6
Pack La OX7 . . . . .61 B7
Paddick Cl RG4 . . . . .260 E3
Paddock Cl
  Benson OX10 . . . . .204 A4
  Chalgrove OX44 . . . . . .184 D7
  Wantage OX12 . . . . .214 F6
Paddock Farm La OX15 . .22 D8

Paddock Mews OX13 . . . .156 D1
Paddock Rd
  Ardley OX27 . . . . .50 B4
  Reading RG4 . . . . .259 D1
  Wallingford OX10 . . . .221 D7
Paddocks The
  Aston OX18 . . . . .135 E2
  Bampton OX18 . . . . . . .134 E1
  Deddington OX15 . . . . . .33 E4
  East Hanney OX12 . . . .197 B6
  Mollington OX17 . . . . . . .3 F3
  Souldern OX27 . . . . .35 E3
  Yarnton OX5 . . . . .108 B5
Paddock The
  Chilton OX11 . . . . .235 D8
  Highworth SN6 . . . . . . .190 A5
  Kennington OX1 . . . . . .160 E8
  Kingston Bagpuize OX13 156 D1
  Somerton OX25 . . . . . . .48 F5
Paddox Cl OX2 . . . . .123 A8
Paddox The OX2 . . . . . . .123 A8
Page Furlong OX10 . . . .182 D2
Pages La OX15 . . . . .7 C6
Pages Orch RG4 . . . . . . .252 E5
Paget Rd OX4 . . . . .142 E6
Pagisters Rd OX14 . . . .160 C2
Paines Hill OX25 . . . . . .62 B8
Painswick Cl OX28 . . . .103 E1
Painters Cl OX15 . . . . . .21 D4
Palladian St OX4 . . . . . .142 B6
Palmer Ave OX25 . . . . . .96 F8
Palmer Pl OX14 . . . . . . .179 E5
Palmer Rd OX3 . . . . .144 C4
Palmers Cl OX11 . . . . . .214 F5
Pampas Cl OX18 . . . . . . .115 E4
Pangbourne Coll RG8 . .256 A4
Pangbourne Hill RG8 . .256 C5
Pangbourne Mews RG8 .256 D6
Pangbourne Pl RG8 . . . .256 D6
Pangbourne Prim Sch
  RG8 . . . . .256 E5
Pangbourne Sta RG8 . . .256 C6
Pangbourne St RG30 . .258 B1
Panters Rd OX10 . . . . . .221 A1
Paper Mill Cotts OX10 . .99 D6
Paper Mill La OX11 . . . .220 A5
Papist Way OX10 . . . . . .239 B8
Parade The
  Kidlington OX5 . . . . . . .108 F6
  Oxford OX3 . . . . .124 D3
Paradise La OX15 . . . . . .21 A2
Paradise Mews RG9 . . . .244 D2
Paradise Rd RG9 . . . . . . .244 C1
Paradise Sq OX1 . . . . . . .261 A1
Paradise St OX1 . . . . . . .261 A2
Paradise Terr OX7 . . . . . .42 D1
Park 34 OX11 . . . . .200 E3
Park Ave
  Highworth SN6 . . . . . . .190 A5
  Shrivenham SN6 . . . . . .209 D7
Park Cl
  Avon Dassett CV47 . . . . .2 F8
  Banbury OX16 . . . . .16 C6
  Bladon OX20 . . . . .91 B3
  Cutteslowe OX2 . . . . . .109 B2
  Didcot OX11 . . . . .218 D8
  Hanwell OX17 . . . . .8 F4
  Hook Norton OX15 . . . .30 B6
  Kirtlington OX5 . . . . . . .77 F5
  Middleton Stoney OX25 .64 A4
  North Leigh OX29 . . . .105 C6
  Sonning Common RG4 . .253 A6
  Yarnton OX5 . . . . .108 B4
Park Cres OX14 . . . . . . .179 E7
Park Ct OX9 . . . . .148 A8
Park End OX15 . . . . .16 E1
Park End Cl OX15 . . . . . .16 E1
Park End NN13 . . . . .36 D8
Park End Pl OX1 . . . . . . .261 A2
Park End St OX1 . . . . . . .261 A2
Park End Works NN13 . .36 D7
Parkers Cl SN7 . . . . .173 A3
Parkers Hill OX9 . . . . . .166 B8
Parker St OX4 . . . . .141 F6
Park Farm Cl OX25 . . . . .81 C3
Park Farm Cotts OX25 . .63 E5
Parkhill Dr RG31 . . . . . .257 D2
Park Hill
  Hook Norton OX15 . . . .30 B7
  Wheatley OX33 . . . . . . .126 B1
Park Hospl For Children
  OX3 . . . . .124 C1
Park La
  Appleton OX13 . . . . . . .158 A7
  Ardington OX12 . . . . . .215 D3
  Bladon OX20 . . . . .91 B2
  Checkendon RG4 . . . . . .251 E6
  Kingston Blount OX39 .167 F3
  Long Hanborough OX29 .90 D1
Parkland Pl OX26 . . . . . .80 A5
Parklands
  Banbury OX16 . . . . .16 B7
  Farmoor OX2 . . . . .121 E2
  Freeland OX29 . . . . . . .105 F7
  Oxford OX3 . . . . .123 F5
Park La
  North Newington OX15 . .15 C4
  Stanford in the V SN7 . .195 B6
  Stokenchurch HP14 . . .188 E6
  Stonor RG9 . . . . .225 D6
  Swalcliffe OX15 . . . . . . .21 A5
  Woodstock OX20 . . . . . .91 B6
Park Rd
  Abingdon OX14 . . . . . . .179 E7
  Banbury OX16 . . . . .16 B8
  Chipping Norton OX7 . . .42 F4

Park Rd continued
  Combe OX29 . . . . .90 B1
  Didcot OX11 . . . . .218 D8
  Ducklington OX29 . . . .118 A4
  Faringdon SN7 . . . . . . .172 F2
  Henley-on-T RG9 . . . . .244 E1
  Hook Norton OX15 . . . .30 B7
  North Leigh OX29 . . . .105 B8
  Witney OX28 . . . . .103 F1
Park Rise OX25 . . . . .81 C3
Parkside
  Checkendon RG4 . . . . . .241 D3
  Cuddesdon OX44 . . . . .144 C3
  Henley-on-T RG9 . . . . .244 C2
Park Side OX13 . . . . .178 C6
Parkside
  North Leigh OX29 . . . .105 C6
  Witney OX28 . . . . .118 B6
Parks Rd OX1 . . . . .261 B3
Park St
  Bladon OX20 . . . . .91 B2
  Charlbury OX7 . . . . .73 B3
  Thame OX9 . . . . .148 A7
  Woodstock OX20 . . . . . .91 A6
Park Terr
  East Challow OX12 . . . .214 A5
  Thame OX9 . . . . .148 A7
Park The
  Cumnor OX2 . . . . .139 E4
  East Challow OX12 . . . .214 A5
  Harwell OX11 . . . . .217 E6
Park Town OX2 . . . . .123 C4
Park View
  Crowmarsh Gifford
  OX10 . . . . .222 A6
  Sydenham OX39 . . . . . .148 F1
  Wantage OX12 . . . . .214 E5
Park Wall La RG8 . . . . . .249 D1
Parkway Ct OX4 . . . . . . .142 D4
Parkway Dr RG4 . . . . . . .260 E3
Park Way OX3 . . . . .123 F7
Park Wlk OX28 . . . . .118 B6
Parliament Rd OX9 . . . .129 F1
Parma Ho OX4 . . . . .123 B7
Parrs Rd HP14 . . . . .188 E4
Parry Cl OX3 . . . . .123 F3
Parslow Ho OX49 . . . . . .186 C1
Parsonage Cl OX12 . . . .215 A6
Parsonage Ct SN6 . . . . .190 A6
Parson's La OX10 . . . . . .143 A4
Parsons Mead OX14 . . . .159 E2
Parsons Pl OX4 . . . . .142 A8
Parson's St OX17 . . . . . .23 A4
Parson's St OX16 . . . . . .16 D6
Partridge Chase OX26 . .81 A8
Partridge Cl OX12 . . . .214 E4
Partridge Ct OX17 . . . . .22 F3
Partridge Pl OX5 . . . . . .92 C1
Partridge Wlk OX4 . . . .143 A1
Pascali Pl OX16 . . . . .9 A1
Passey Cres OX10 . . . . .204 A4
Patemore La OX49,RG9 .206 E2
Paternoster La OX10 . .220 F1
Patrick Haugh Rd OX5 . .96 F7
Patrick Rd OX4 . . . . .259 B2
Patricks Orch SN7 . . . .211 D7
Pattison Pl OX4 . . . . . . .160 A8
Pauling Rd OX3 . . . . .124 E1
Pauls Way OX49 . . . . . .186 B2
Paxmans Pl OX16 . . . . . .16 C4
Paynes End OX27 . . . . . .65 F6
Peachcroft Sh Ctr OX14 .160 B2
Peacock Ho [8] OX12 . . .214 D4
Peacock Rd OX3 . . . . . . .123 F3
Peaks La OX29 . . . . .86 E7
Pearce Ct OX9 . . . . .147 F8
Pearce Dr OX7 . . . . .42 E2
Pearces Mdw RG9 . . . . .224 D3
Pearce's Orch RG9 . . . .244 D3
Pearson Rd RG4 . . . . . . .260 D3
Peartree Cl [1] OX4 . . . .142 F1
Pear Tree Cotts RG9 . . .243 D1
Pear Tree Farm Ind Units
  OX27 . . . . .67 E2
Peartree Interchange
  OX2 . . . . .108 E2
Peascroft HP18 . . . . . . .129 D6
Peat Moors OX3 . . . . . . .142 D8
Pebble Ct OX18 . . . . . . .101 D5
Pebble Hill OX44 . . . . . .162 B8
Pebble La NN13 . . . . .24 A7
Peeble Dr OX11 . . . . . . .219 A8
Peeble Hlll Mobile Home Pk
  OX14 . . . . .160 E6
Peel Cl
  Ducklington OX29 . . . .118 B4
  Reading RG4 . . . . .259 D2
Peel Pl
  Carterton OX18 . . . . . .115 E2
  Oxford OX1 . . . . .141 D5
Peep-O-Day La OX14 . .179 F3
Peers Cl OX4 . . . . .142 C2
Pegasus Ct [5] OX1 . . . .141 C7
Pegasus Rd OX4 . . . . . . .142 F2
Pegswell La OX44 . . . . .145 B2
Pelham Rd OX9 . . . . .130 B1
Pelican Pl OX29 . . . . . . .120 E8
Pembroke Coll OX1 . . . .261 B1
Pembroke Ct [1] OX4 . . .141 F8
Pembroke Ho [6] RG4 . .259 C1
Pembroke La OX14 . . . .199 D5
Pembroke Pl
  Bampton OX18 . . . . . . .134 F2

Pembroke Pl continued
  Reading RG4 . . . . .259 C3
Pembroke Sq OX1 . . . . .261 B1
Pembroke St OX1 . . . . . .261 B2
Pembroke Way OX26 . . . .65 F3
Pemscott Cl OX18 . . . . .133 C5
Pendennis Ave RG4 . . . .259 E6
Pendles Paddock HP14 .188 F2
Pendon Mus* OX14 . . . .201 C8
Penfield OX7 . . . . .42 E5
Penfold Ct OX3 . . . . .124 B5
Pen La OX13,OX14 . . . .159 F5
Penley Cl OX39 . . . . . . .168 B6
Penn Cl
  Abingdon OX14 . . . . . . .160 C2
  Reading RG4 . . . . .259 A6
Pennington Pl OX9 . . . .130 B1
Penn The OX7 . . . . .42 E5
Pennycress Rd OX4 . . . .143 A2
Pennyfarthing Pl OX1 .261 B2
Pennyhooks La SN6 . . . .209 B8
Pennypiece RG8 . . . . . . .249 C4
Pennyroyal RG4 . . . . . . .250 F5
Pennywell Dr OX2 . . . . .109 B1
Penpont Water OX14 . .201 A2
Penrhyn Cl OX16 . . . . . .15 E7
Penrose Cl OX16 . . . . . . .16 A5
Penrose Dr OX16 . . . . . .16 A6
Pensclose OX28 . . . . . . .104 C1
Pensfield OX10 . . . . .178 D6
Penson's Gdns OX4 . . . .123 E1
Penstones Ct SN7 . . . . .194 E7
Pentagon The OX14 . . .180 B7
Pen Way OX16 . . . . .9 C1
Peppard CE Prim Sch
  RG9 . . . . .253 A8
Peppard Hill RG9 . . . . . .252 F8
Peppard La RG9 . . . . . . .254 E7
Peppard Rd RG4 . . . . . .253 B3
Pepper Alley
  [2] Banbury OX16 . . . . . .16 D6
  Deddington OX15 . . . . . .34 E4
Peppercorn Ave OX3 . .142 E8
Percy St OX4 . . . . .141 F6
Peregrine Rd OX4 . . . . .142 D2
Peregrine Way
  Bicester OX26 . . . . .81 A8
  Grove OX12 . . . . .196 D1
Perian Cl RG9 . . . . .254 C8
Perimeter Rd OX11 . . . .217 C1
Periwinkle Pl [3] OX4 . .142 F2
Perkins Cl OX15 . . . . . . .7 C7
Perkins OX 141 D2
Perpetual Park Dr RG9 .254 F8
Perrinsfield GL7 . . . . . .150 D6
Perrin St OX3 . . . . .124 D3
Perrott Cl OX29 . . . . . .105 A7
Perry's Rd SN7 . . . . .194 D8
Perseverance Hill RG9 .254 A5
Peterley Rd OX4 . . . . . .142 F6
Peter's Way OX4 . . . . . .142 C3
Pether Rd OX3 . . . . .124 E1
Pethers Piece OX18 . . .100 D5
Petre Pl OX4 . . . . .92 F1
Pettiwell OX44 . . . . . . .142 B8
Pevensey Ave RG4 . . . .259 E5
Pheasant Wlk OX4 . . . .142 A1
Phelps Pl OX4 . . . . .123 F1
Phelps The OX5 . . . . . . .108 D8
Philcote St OX15 . . . . . .33 F4
Phillimore Rd RG4 . . . .259 D5
Phipps Rd OX4 . . . . .142 D4
Phoebe Ct OX2 . . . . . . .142 A6
Phyllis Court Dr RG9 . .244 E3
Pickenfield OX9 . . . . . . .148 B7
Pickering Rd OX12 . . . .214 E5
Pickett Ave OX3 . . . . . .142 E7
Picklers Hill OX14 . . . .160 A2
Picton Way OX4 . . . . . . .259 B4
Piddington Rd HP18 . . .98 A8
Pieces The OX18 . . . . . .134 F3
Pierce's Hill RG31 . . . . .257 C1
Piers Row OX5 . . . . .33 E4
Pigeon Farm Rd HP14 .188 E5
Pigeon House La OX29 .106 C6
Pigeonhouse La OX5 . . . .95 F3
Piggott's Rd [1] RG4 . .259 C1
Piggy La OX26 . . . . .65 E1
Pikeshaw Way RG31 . . .257 C2
Pike Terr OX1 . . . . .261 B1
Pilcher Ct OX4 . . . . .123 F1
Pilgrims Cl SN6 . . . . . . .191 F2
Pill La GL56 . . . . .26 F1
Pimpernel Cl OX4 . . . . .143 A2
Pinchester Cl OX18 . . . .27 A1
Pinchgate La OX5 . . . . . .93 D7
Pine Cl
  Bicester OX26 . . . . .65 F5
  Garsington OX44 . . . . .143 C2
  Oxford OX4 . . . . .142 F3
Pinecroft OX18 . . . . . . .115 D2
Pine Rise OX26 . . . . . . .104 D2
Pines The SN7 . . . . .172 E3
Pinetree Ct RG4 . . . . . .259 A5
Pinewood Cl [1] OX18 . .115 E2
Pinewood Dr RG4 . . . . .258 E6
Pinewood Sch SN6 . . . .209 A2
Pine Woods Rd OX13 . .156 B2
Pingle Dr OX26 . . . . . . .80 E8
Pinhill Rd OX16 . . . . . . .16 B7
Pinkhill La OX29 . . . . . .120 E6
Pinnocks Way OX2 . . . .140 B8
Pinsley Rd OX29 . . . . . .106 B8
Pioneer Rd
  Bicester OX26 . . . . .81 B6

Pioneer Rd *continued*
Faringdon SN7...............172 F2
Pipe Line OX16............16 D7
Pipers Croft OX16..........16 A4
Piper St OX3..............124 D2
Pipit Cl OX4..............142 E1
Pipits Croft OX26..........81 A8
Pipkin Way OX4...........142 A6
Pipley Furlong OX4........142 B2
Pitch The HP14...........189 D3
Pitmaston Cl OX16...........8 F1
Pitreavie Ave OX18.......115 E4
Pitters Piece HP18.......129 B7
Pitt Rivers Mus * OX1....261 B3
Pitts La OX7...............46 B3
Pitts Rd OX3..............124 E3
Pixey Pl OX2..............122 F8
Pixton Cl OX11............218 D8
Plain Rd The OX15..........14 B5
Plain La OX18.............115 E4
Plane Tree Way OX20........91 C6
Plantation Rd
Chilton OX11................234 F8
Oxford OX2.................261 A4
Plantation The OX17.........4 F1
Plater Coll OX3............124 A2
Plater Dr OX2.............123 A4
Playfield Rd OX1..........168 E7
Playford Ct OX9...........147 F8
Playhatch Rd RG4..........260 B5
Playing Cl The OX7.........73 B4
Playing Field Rd NN13......25 A4
Pleck La OX39.............167 F4
Plot Rd OX15...............14 B6
Plough Cl
Warborough OX10...........203 B6
Wolvercote OX2.............122 F8
Plough Cnr OX39...........148 F1
Plough La RG9.............254 E1
Ploughley Cl
Ardley OX27..................50 C4
Kidlington OX5..............108 D8
Ploughley Rd
Ambrosden OX25..............81 D3
Upper Arncott OX25...........96 E8
Plover Dr OX4.............142 E1
Plowden Rd OX49...........167 E3
Plowden Way RG9...........254 E1
Plumbe Ct OX12............214 D6
Plum La OX7...............85 D7
Pluto Rd OX11.............234 F8
Plym Dr OX14..............201 A2
Pochard Pl 8 OX4..........142 F1
Pococks Cl OX18...........134 F1
Poffley End La OX29.......104 B5
Polecat End La OX33.......125 F4
Pollocks La OX10..........221 E1
Polstead Rd OX2...........123 B4
Polsted Rd RG31...........257 D1
Pond Cl
Oxford OX3.................125 A3
West Ilsley OX12...........233 E1
Pond End Rd RG4...........253 A6
Pond Hill OX8..............89 C7
Ponds La OX3..............123 F6
Pony Rd OX4...............142 F6
Pool Cl GL56...............26 F1
Pool Close Cotts GL56......26 F1
Pooles La OX7..............73 B3
Poolside Cl OX16...........16 B5
Popes Acre HP17...........130 F5
Pope's Piece OX28.........103 F1
Poplar Cl
Banbury OX16................16 E2
Garsington OX44............143 C2
Kidlington OX5..............108 F7
Poplar Farm Cl OX7.........70 A1
Poplar Farm Rd OX44.......184 D2
Poplar Gr OX1.............160 E8
Poplar Rd OX2.............122 C1
Poplars Rd OX17...........110 F4
Poplars The OX26...........66 D1
Poppylands OX26............65 D4
Portal Dr N OX25...........63 C8
Portal Dr S OX25...........63 C7
Portal Dr OX25.............63 C8
Port Hill RG9.............224 B2
Port Hill Rd OX10.........203 F5
Port Hill OX7..............42 F3
Portland Rd
Milcombe OX15...............21 A2
Oxford OX2.................123 B7
Portman Rd OX16...........258 C1
Portmeirion Gdns RG30.....257 F1
Portway
Aynho OX17..................35 D7
Banbury OX16................16 A8
Port Way OX25.............62 F3
Portway Cres NN13..........36 E7
Portway NN13...............36 E7
Port Way OX10.............221 F4
Portway OX11..............218 C2
Portway Dr NN13............36 D7
Portway SN7...............172 F3
Portway Gdns OX17..........35 D7
Port Way
Ipsden OX10................240 A8
Kirtlington OX5..............78 A7
Portway Mews OX12.........214 D4
Portway OX12..............214 D4
Port Way OX12.............215 A5
Post Office La
6 Wantage OX12............214 A1
Letcombe Regis OX12........214 A1
Potenger Way OX14.........179 D6

Potkiln La RG8............250 E7
Potters La OX10...........205 A1
Pottery Fields RG9........224 E2
Pottery Piece OX4.........142 E1
Pottery Rd RG30...........257 F1
Pottle Cl OX2.............122 B1
Pott's Cl OX44............145 B3
Poultney Pl OX18..........115 D3
Poulton Pl OX4............142 F3
Pound Bank OX7.............46 B3
Pound Cl
Ducklington OX29...........118 B4
Kirtlington OX5..............77 F4
Pound Cotts OX29..........108 B5
Pound Cotts RG8...........249 A6
Pound Croft OX12..........214 D8
Pound Ct OX15..............33 F4
Pound Field Cl OX3........124 E5
Pound Hill OX7.............73 A4
Pound La
Cassington OX29.............107 C2
Cholsey OX10................220 F2
Clanfield OX18..............133 E1
Sibford Gower OX15..........13 A2
Sonning RG4................260 E2
Stanton St John OX33........125 D8
Upton OX11.................218 C2
Pound Piece SN6...........228 A7
Pound The
Bloxham OX15................21 E5
Cholsey OX10................220 F2
North Newington OX15........15 B4
Wantage OX12................215 A5
Pound Way OX4.............142 C4
Powell Cl OX33............125 F4
Powys Gr OX16.............15 F7
Preachers La OX1..........261 B1
Preece Ct OX18............115 E1
Prescott Ave OX16..........15 F6
Prescott Cl OX16...........16 A6
Prestidge Pl OX5..........108 F8
Preston Rd OX4............179 E4
Prestwich Pl OX2..........122 F1
Prestwick Burn OX11.......200 F3
Prew Cotts OX7............29 A3
Price Cl OX16..............65 F3
Prichard Rd OX3...........124 A3
Priest Cl RG9.............224 D3
Priest End OX9............129 E2
Priest Hill La OX29.......103 F5
Priest Hill RG4...........259 A3
Primrose Cl
Purley on T RG8.............257 C5
Witney OX28.................104 E1
Primrose Dr OX26...........65 E4
Primrose La OX18..........134 E2
Primrose Pl 20 OX4........142 F1
Primsdown Ind Est OX7......42 C3
Prince Christian Victor
Berkshire Memorial Homes
OX12.......................214 D2
Prince Gr OX14............160 A3
Princes Ride OX20..........91 C6
Princess Gdns OX12........214 C8
Princes St OX4............141 F8
Princethorpe Dr OX16.......16 F7
Prince William Dr RG31....257 C1
Prior's Forge OX2.........109 B1
Prior's La SN7............155 F3
Priors Wlk GL7............150 E3
Priory Ave RG4............259 E6
Priory Bank Cotts OX44....145 C2
Priory Cl
Bicester OX26................65 F1
Horton-cum-S OX33..........112 B5
Priory Copse RG9..........252 F6
Priory Ct
4 Bicester OX26...........65 E1
Cuttleslowe OX2............109 B1
Reading RG4.................259 A3
Priory Farm Cotts OX27.....67 E2
Priory Gn SN6.............190 B6
Priory Green SN6..........190 A6
Priory La
Bicester OX26................65 E1
Burford OX18...............100 E5
Lyneham OX7.................70 D5
Marcham OX13...............178 D6
Priory Mead SN7...........192 D2
Priory Mews 10 OX10.......221 D7
Priory Orch OX12..........214 C5
Priory Rd
Bicester OX26................65 F1
Lyneham OX7.................70 D5
Oxford OX4.................142 C2
Wantage OX12...............214 D4
Priory Vale Rd OX16........16 F7
Pritchard Cl OX10.........182 C6
Promenade Rd RG4..........259 A2
Prospect Cl OX29...........89 C7
Prospect Pk OX33..........143 C7
Prospect Pl OX49..........186 B2
Prospect Rd
Banbury OX16................16 D5
Upton OX11.................218 C2
Prospect St RG4...........259 B2
Prunus Cl OX4.............142 F3
Puck La OX28..............104 B1
Puddleduck La SN7.........192 B8
Puddle La OX44............192 C2
Pudsey Cl OX14............179 E4
Pugsden La OX13...........199 A4
Pulker Cl OX4.............142 C4
Pullens Field OX3.........124 A2
Pullens La OX3............124 A2
Pulling Cl SN7............172 F3
Pulpit Hill SN7...........213 A4
Puma Cl OX10..............204 D2

Pumbro OX29................89 C7
Purcell Rd OX3............123 F3
Purfield Dr RG10..........255 E2
Purland Cl OX4............142 C6
Purley CE Inf Sch RG8.....257 C5
Purley La RG8.............257 C5
Purley Rise RG8...........257 A5
Purley Village RG8........257 C5
Purley Way RG8............256 E5
Purrants La OX29...........86 E1
Purslane OX14.............180 B8
Purslane Dr OX26...........65 D4
Purslane Rd OX26...........65 D5
Pusey La OX1..............261 B3
Pusey St OX1..............261 B3
Putman Cl OX4.............148 B8
Putman Pl RG4.............244 E1
Pye St SN7................173 A3
Pykes Cl OX14.............160 B2
Pym Wlk OX9...............129 F1
Pyrton La OX49............186 A2
Pytenry Cl OX14...........160 B3
Pytt's La OX18............100 E5

Q

Quadrangle The
Bicester OX26................65 E1
Wolvercote OX2..............122 F8
Woodstock OX20...............91 C7
Quadrant The OX4..........180 B7
Quaker La OX10............203 B8
Quantock Ave RG4..........259 D5
Quantock View OX11........200 C2
Quarhill Cl OX7............42 E5
Quarry Cl
Bloxham OX15................21 C4
Enstone OX7.................59 A5
Long Crendon HP18..........129 C7
Quarry End OX5............108 B8
Quarry Ground
Fifield OX7..................69 B2
Idbury OX7...................69 A5
Quarry High St OX3........124 E3
Quarry Hollow OX3.........124 E2
Quarry La
Charlbury OX7................73 C4
Lower Shiplake RG9..........255 A4
Quarry Rd
Chadlington OX7..............57 B2
Oxford OX3.................124 E2
Sunningwell OX13...........159 F7
Witney OX28.................104 A2
Quarry School Pl OX3......124 E2
Quarry The OX13...........159 F7
Quartermain Cl OX4........142 A6
Quartermain Rd OX44.......184 C7
Quebec Rd OX13............254 E8
Queen Annes Gate RG4......259 C5
Queen Anne's Sch RG4......259 B3
Queen Cl RG9..............244 E1
Queen Eleanor Ct OX29....106 B8
Queen Elizabeth Cl 8
OX11.......................219 A8
Queen Elizabeth Ho OX1....261 B3
Queen Emma's Dyke
OX28.......................117 F8
Queenford Farm OX10.......182 E2
Queens Ave
Bicester OX26................65 E2
Highworth SN6..............190 A6
Kidlington OX5..............109 A8
Queen's Ave OX10..........203 B1
Queensborough Dr RG4......258 E5
Queens Cl OX10............182 D1
Queen's Cl OX29...........120 E7
Queens Cl
Oxford OX2.................140 B8
Thame OX9..................129 F2
Queens Coll OX1...........261 C2
Queen's Cres
Clanfield OX18.............152 E8
Oxford OX2.................140 B8
Queens Ct OX26.............65 E2
Queen's Dyke Com Prim Sch
OX28.......................117 F7
Queens La OX29............120 E7
Queen's La OX1............261 C2
Queen's Rd
Banbury OX16................16 B6
Carterton OX18.............115 E1
Reading RG4,OX10...........220 F1
Queen's Rd
Reading RG4................259 C1
Thame OX9..................148 B8
Queen St OX15..............21 D4
Queen St
Abingdon OX14..............179 F7
Bampton OX18...............134 F3
Dorchester OX10............182 D1
Eynsham OX29...............120 E7
Henley-on-T RG9............244 E1
Hook Norton OX15............30 B7
Middleton Cheney OX17.......17 F8
Oxford OX1.................261 B2
Reading RG4................259 A3
Queensway
Banbury OX16................16 B4
Didcot OX11.................218 E7
Hook Norton OX15...........219 F8
Oxford OX29................259 D6
Queensway Sch OX16..........16 A4
Quercus Ct OX2............123 B6
Quickset Cl OX7............72 F8
Quintan Ave OX25...........81 D4

R

Race Farm Cotts OX13......176 E8
Race Farm La OX13.........176 F8
Rack End OX29.............137 E3
Radbone Hill OX7...........42 F6
Radcliffe Infmy The OX2...261 A4
Radcliffe Rd OX4..........141 F5
Radcliffe Science Liby
OX1.......................261 B3
Radcliffe Sq OX1..........261 C2
Radcot Cl RG5.............260 E1
Radcot Rd SN7.............172 F6
Radford Cl OX4............141 F3
Radley CE Prim Sch
OX14.......................160 D4
Radley Coll OX14..........160 D4
Radley Ct OX14............160 B8
Radley Ho OX4.............123 C6
Radley Rd OX14............160 C1
Radley Road Ind Est
OX14.......................160 D4
Radley Sta OX14...........160 F2
Radnage CE Inf Sch
HP14.......................189 D6
Radnage Common Rd
HP14.......................189 D5
Radnage La HP14...........169 C2
Radnor Cl RG9.............244 E2
Radnor Rd OX10............221 B8
RAF Benson Com Prim Sch
OX10.......................204 D2
Raghouse La OX2............49 F5
Raglan Gdns OX4...........259 C4
Ragley Mews RG4...........259 D6
Ragnall's La OX33.........111 F7
Rahere Rd OX4.............142 C4
Railway Cotts SN7.........195 A2
Railway La OX4............142 B2
Railway Cotts RG8.........249 C6
Railway Terr GL7..........150 D5
Railway View RG8..........256 D6
Rainbow Way OX14..........160 B3
Raincliffe Cl OX17........35 C7
Ralegh Cees OX4...........117 D7
Raleigh Park Rd OX2.......140 E7
Ramilles Ho 3 OX18.......115 E2
Rampion Cl OX4............124 E3
Ramsey Rd OX3.............124 E3
Ramsons Way OX14.........180 C8
Randall Rd GL54...........68 B3
Randolph Rd RG1...........259 A1
Randolph St 7 OX4.........141 F8
Range Rd OX28,OX29........117 C8
Rannal Dr OX39............168 C6
Rastel Ho 2 OX16...........16 E6
Rattlecombe Rd OX15........6 D2
Raven Cl OX27..............66 A7
Ravencroft OX26............81 A7
Raven Rd HP14.............188 F4
Ravensbourne Dr RG5.......260 E1
Ravenscroft Rd RG9........244 D2
Ravensmead
Banbury OX16................16 A4
Chinnor OX39...............168 D6
Rawdon Way SN7............173 A2
Rawlings Gr OX14..........179 D8
Rawlins Cl OX17...........23 A5
Rawlinson Cl OX7...........57 B1
Rawlinson Rd OX2..........123 B5
Rawson Cl OX2.............108 F1
Rawthey Ave OX11..........200 F4
Ray Ct OX14...............201 A2
Raymond Rd OX26...........65 C4
Raymund Rd OX3............123 F5
Raynham Cl OX18...........115 E4
Ray Rd OX25...............65 C5
Rayson Ho OX3.............124 B4
Ray View OX5..............94 F4
Reade Ave OX14............180 B8
Reade Cl OX7..............70 B1
Reade's La RG4............252 D4
Reading Blue Coat Sch
RG4.......................260 C3
Reading Ct 2 OX26..........65 E2
Reading Rd
Aldworth RG8...............248 A2
Cholsey OX10...............239 A7
Goring RG8.................249 E6
Harwell OX11...............217 D6
Henley-on-T RG9............254 F8
Pangbourne RG8.............256 D5
Streatley RG8..............249 A6
Wallingford OX10...........221 C4
Wallingford,Winterbrook
OX10.......................221 C4
West Hendred OX12..........216 B7
Woodcote RG8...............240 F1
Reading Ret Pk RG30........258 B1
Recreation Rd
Wargrave RG10..............255 E2
Woodstock OX20..............91 C6
Rectory Cl
Marsh Gibbon OX27..........67 F3
Warmington OX17............3 A4
Wendlebury OX25............80 A4
Rectory Cres OX7..........60 E8
Rectory Ct OX49..........187 B8
Rectory Farm Cl OX10......196 F7
Rectory Gdns OX15.........15 D8
Rectory Hill RG9..........206 A1
Rectory La
Aston Tirrold OX11.........237 F8
Bix RG9...................243 D7
Fringford OX27..............52 C6
Kingston Bagpuize OX13....176 F8
Letcombe Bassett OX12.....231 E7

Rectory La *continued*
Longworth OX13.............156 B3
Middleton Cheney OX17.......10 F1
Rectory Lane Trad Est
OX13.......................176 F8
Rectory La
South Weston OX9...........166 E1
Woodstock OX20..............91 A6
Rectory Mdw OX39..........168 D7
Rectory Rd
Great Haseley OX44.........164 E8
Hook Norton OX15............30 B8
Oxford OX4.................141 F8
Reading RG4................259 A2
Streatley RG8..............248 C7
Redberry Cl RG4...........259 D5
Red Bridge Hollow OX1....141 C4
Red Copse La
Boars Hill OX1.............140 F2
Sunningwell OX1............141 A2
Red Cross Rd RG8..........249 C6
Redcot Cl OX3.............124 E1
Red Hill RG9..............253 F5
Red House Dr RG4..........253 A5
Red House Rd OX15..........22 E8
Red La OX49,RG9...........206 D2
Redland Rd OX3............124 B5
Redlands Cl SN6...........190 A4
Redlands Row GL56..........27 A1
Red La RG8................240 C3
Red Lion Dr HP14..........188 D5
Red Lion Mews SN6.........190 A6
Red Lion Sq OX1...........261 B2
Red Lion St
Cropredy OX17................4 F2
Kings Sutton OX17...........23 F5
Redmayes OX18............135 E2
Redmoor Cl OX4............142 C2
Redmoor Ct OX26............65 C3
Red Poll Cl OX16...........16 A8
Redwood Cl
Kingston Bagpuize OX13....156 E1
Oxford OX4.................143 A2
Redwood Way RG31..........257 D3
Reed Cl OX28..............104 E2
Reedmace Cl OX4...........143 A2
Reedmace Rd OX26...........65 E4
Reeds Cl OX12.............214 C5
Reema Hos The SN6.........190 B1
Regal Ct 8 OX26............65 F1
Regal Way SN7.............172 F3
Regency Hts RG4...........258 E4
Regent Gdns OX11..........219 B8
Regent Mall 5 OX12.......214 D4
Regent Mews SN7...........172 F4
Regents Park Coll OX1.....261 B3
Regents Riverside 7
RG1.......................259 A1
Regent St OX4.............141 F8
Regis Pl OX12.............214 A2
Reid Pl OX25..............63 B7
Reliance Way OX4..........142 B7
Remenham La RG9...........244 F3
Remenham Row RG9..........244 F2
Remus Gate NN13............24 A1
Rene Rd OX4...............141 F5
Renault Ho OX4............141 F6
Rest Harrow 2 OX14.......142 F2
Restharrow Mead OX26.......65 C4
Retford Cl RG5............260 F1
Retreat Gdns OX10.........221 E7
Retreat La HP14...........169 D2
Rewley Abbey Ct OX1.......261 A2
Rewley Rd OX1.............261 A2
Reynard Ct 3 OX26..........65 E2
Reynolds Cl OX7............70 D1
Reynolds Way
Abingdon OX14..............179 E5
East Challow OX12..........213 F5
Rhigos RG4................258 F6
Rhine Cl RG4..............259 D2
Rhodes Ho OX1.............261 C3
Richard Gray Ct OX1.......261 A4
Richard Nevill Ct 2 RG4..259 C2
Richards La OX2............123 A7
Richardson Ct OX4.........123 F1
Richards Way OX3..........124 F2
Richens Dr OX18...........115 C2
Richfield Ave RG1.........258 F1
Richman Gdns OX16..........15 F8
Richmond Rd OX11..........218 F7
Richmond Rd
Oxford OX1.................261 A3
Reading RG4................258 E4
Richmond St OX17..........23 F5
Rickyard Cl OX1...........261 A3
Rickyard The
Ardington OX12.............215 D5
Chalgrove OX44.............184 C6
Riddell Pl OX2............109 A1
Riders Way OX39...........168 C6
Ride The OX13.............158 B5
Ridge Cl OX16..............16 D4
Ridgefield Rd OX4.........142 A7
Ridge Hall Cl RG4.........258 E3
Ridgemont Cl OX2..........123 A7
Ridgemont Rd RG31.........257 B2
Ridge The
Lower Basildon RG8.........249 F1
Tackley OX5.................77 C6
Ridgeway OX1..............140 D1
Ridgeway CE Prim Sch The
OX12.......................213 B3
Ridgeway Cl RG9...........223 D3

Ridgeway Ct OX12 ...... 214 D7
Ridge Way HP18 .... 129 F5
Ridgeway Rd
  Didcot OX11............218 F7
  Oxford OX3 ....124 F3
Ridgeway The
  Bloxham OX15...........21 E4
  Chilton OX12 ....234 C7
  Nettlebed RG9.........224 D2
  Reading RG4 ....259 B3
  Wantage OX12.........232 D5
Ridgeway RG10...........255 E2
Ridgeway (YH) The*
  OX12 ....232 C6
Riding La OX29 ....103 C7
Ridings Bglws OX29.....86 E3
Ridings The
  Banbury OX16 ....16 F7
  Kidlington OX5........92 C1
  Leafield OX29..........86 E2
  Oxford OX3 ....142 F8
  Reading RG4 ....259 C8
  Stonesfield OX29.......89 C8
Ridley Rd OX4 ....142 E6
Riely Cl OX29 ....90 C1
Riley Cl OX14 ....179 D6
Riley Dr OX16...........15 F8
Riley Ho OX4 ....142 C4
Rimes Cl OX13.........156 F1
Rimmer Cl OX3.........123 F5
Ring The OX17..........10 E4
Ringwood Rd
  Oxford OX3 ....125 A3
  Reading RG30 ....258 A1
Ripley Ave OX29 ....102 E2
Ripley Rd RG30 ....258 A1
Ripon Coll OX44 ....144 B3
Rippington Ct OX14....179 B2
Rippington Dr OX3.....123 F4
Rise The
  Adderbury OX17 ....23 A4
  Islip OX5 ....93 F1
  Kingston Blount OX39 .167 F4
  Reading RG4 ....259 B4
Rising Hill OX25.........48 E1
Rissington Cl RG31....257 E3
Rissington Dr OX28 ...117 E8
Rivacres RG8 ....250 E3
River Cl OX14..........179 E5
River Gdns RG8.........257 D5
Rivermead Rd OX4.....141 F3
River Rd RG4 ....258 D3
River & Rowing Mus*
  RG9 ....244 F1
Riverside OX16 ....16 E5
Riverside Ct
  2 Reading RG4 ....259 A2
  Oxford OX1 ....141 C7
Riverside Cvn Pk OX29 .138 E6
Riverside Gdns OX28...104 B1
Riverside Rd OX2......122 F1
River View OX11........141 E1
Riverview Rd RG8.......256 C5
River View
  Sandford-on-T OX4 ...161 A7
  Shillingford OX10.....203 B4
River View Terr OX14 .179 F6
Rivington Glebe GL56 ...27 A1
Rivy Cl OX14...........180 C8
Road Eighteen OX11...217 B1
Road Eight OX11.......217 A1
Road Eleven OX11......217 A1
Road Fifteen OX11.....217 A1
Road Five OX11........217 B1
Road Four OX11........217 B1
Road Nine OX11........217 A1
Road One OX11.........217 A1
Roadside Cotts SN7....171 E6
Road Six OX11..........217 B1
Road Thirteen OX11....217 B1
Road Twelve OX11......217 A1
Road Two OX11.........217 A1
Robert Palmer Cotts The
  RG4 ....260 D3
Robert Piggott CE Inf Sch
  RG10 ....255 E1
Robert Piggott Jun Sch
  RG10 ....255 E2
Robert Robinson Ave
  OX4 ....142 C1
Roberts Cl OX3 ....125 A4
Robert Sparrow Gdns
  OX10 ....222 A6
Robin Hill OX29.........90 A4
Robin Pl OX4 ....142 E1
Robins Cl
  Barford St M OX15 .....32 F6
  Great Rollright OX7....29 B3
Robinson Cl
  Blewbury OX11 ....237 A8
  Carterton OX18 ....115 D3
Robins Platt OX39.....168 B6
Robins Way OX26........81 A7
Robinswood OX16 ....16 A4
Robsart Pl OX2 ....139 E4
Rochester Ave RG5 ....260 E1
Rochester Way OX17....73 C3
Rochester Way OX17...23 B5
Rochford Gdns OX26....66 A4
Rockbourne Gdns RG30 .258 A1
Rock Hill OX7 ....42 F3
Rockhill Farm Ct OX7...42 F3
Rockley Cotts OX2.....139 E1
Rock Rd OX18 ....115 D3
Rock The OX15 ....32 F6

Rocky Banks OX18......115 F6
Rocky La RG9 ....243 B4
Roding Way OX14......201 A2
Rodney Pl OX13 ....156 C3
Rodway Rd RG30 ....257 F1
Roebuck Ct OX11 ......219 A8
Roebuck Rise RG31 ...257 D3
Roentgen Ave OX11 ...217 A2
Rofford La OX44 ....164 B3
Roger Bacon La OX1...261 B1
Roger Dudman Way OX1,
  OX2 ....123 A2
Rogers St OX2 ....123 B7
Rokeby Dr RG4 ....258 D8
Rolfe Pl OX3 ....124 A3
Rollright Stones* OX7...28 B2
Rolls Ct OX12...........214 D5
Roman Cl OX11 ....200 D2
Roman Rd OX33 ....144 C7
Roman Way
  Beckley OX3...........111 B3
  Bicester OX26 ....65 E2
  Brackley NN13.........24 A7
  Lechlade-on-T GL7....150 D5
  Oxford OX4 ....142 E6
  Wantage OX12.........214 C6
Roman Wlk SN6 ....191 E2
Romany Cl OX11 ....258 A1
Romany La OX30.......258 A1
Romney Rd OX16 ....8 F1
Romsey Rd RG30 ......258 A1
Romulus Way NN13....24 A6
Rookery Cl
  Abingdon OX13 ....159 B1
  Bodicote OX15..........22 E8
Rookery Ho OX44 .....143 E1
Rookery The OX5........92 D1
Rookery Way OX26......65 D3
Rooks La OX9 ....147 F8
Roosevelt Dr OX3.....124 C1
Roosevelt Rd OX29....106 B8
Roper Rd OX25 ....63 C8
Rope Way OX15 ....30 B6
Rope Wlk OX14 ....16 D6
Rosamund Dr OX20 .....91 A7
Rosamund Rd OX2......122 E8
Rose and Crown OX9 ...89 C7
Rose Ave OX14 ....159 F3
Rosebank OX15 ....21 E5
Roseway Cres OX12 ...214 D8
Rosebery Rd OX4......258 D7
Rose Cl
  Bucknell OX27..........64 F7
  Carterton OX18 ....115 D2
Rose Cnr HP14 ....188 E5
Rose Cott OX17..........8 F4
Rose Ct 2 OX4 ....142 B3
Rosedale Ave OX16 .....9 A1
Rosehill Ho RG4 ......259 C4
Rose Hill OX4 ....142 B4
Rosehill Pk RG4 ......259 C4
Rose Hill Prim Sch OX4 .142 A3
Rose La OX1 ....261 C2
Rosemary Ct OX4......141 F7
Rosemary La OX18 ....134 E3
Rosemead Ave RG31 ..257 B3
Rose Pl OX1............261 B1
Roses La OX7 ....41 F5
Rose Terr OX12 ....196 A4
Rosina Wlk OX16 ....9 A1
Ross Ct OX1 ....141 E1
Rossendale Rd RG4 ...259 D3
Ross Rd 3 RG1........259 A1
Rotha Field Rd OX27 ..109 A1
Rotherfield Rd RG9 ...254 E7
Rotherfield Way RG4 ..259 B4
Rother Garth OX14....201 A3
Rother Rd OX16 ....8 F1
Rothwell Gdns RG5 ...260 F1
Rothwells Cl OX10 ....221 A2
Rothwell Wlk RG4 ....259 D2
Rotten Row OX10 .....182 D1
Round Close Rd
  Adderbury OX17 ......22 F3
  Hook Norton OX15.....30 A7
Roundham Cl OX5......92 D1
Roundhead Dr OX9 ...129 F2
Roundhill Ct HP17 ....130 E8
Roundhills Mead SN6 .190 B7
Roundtown OX17 ....35 C7
Roundway The OX3 ...124 F3
Rouses La GL7..........132 B5
Rousham Park House &
  Gardens* OX25 ....62 B5
Rousham Rd OX5.......77 C7
Routh Rd OX3 ....124 F4
Routs Gn OX14 ....169 D2
Roves Farm* SN6 .....208 B6
Roves La SN6..........208 B7
Rowallan Cl RG4 ......259 D6
Rowan Cl
  Carterton OX18 ....115 D3
  Kidlington OX5........108 E7
  Sonning Common RG4...252 F7
Rowan Gr OX4 ....143 A1
Rowan Rd OX26 ....65 E3
Rowans The OX10......220 E1
Rowel Dr OX5 ....108 E8
Rowell Way OX7 ....42 F3
Rowland Cl
  Wallingford OX10 ....203 C1
  Wolvercote OX2.......122 D8
Rowland Hill Ct OX1 ..261 A2
Rowland Rd OX11 .....221 A1
Rowlands Ho OX3......125 A3
Row La RG4 ....259 E7
Rowles Cl OX1..........141 E1

Rowles Paddock RG20 ..235 A2
Rowney Pl OX4 ....142 A4
Row The
  Bletchingdon OX5 ....93 A8
  Glympton OX20 ....75 D8
  Hinton Waldrist SN7 ...155 F2
  Lechlade-on-T GL7....150 F7
  Lyneham OX7.........70 D5
  Mollington OX17 ....3 F3
  Stanton Harcourt OX29 ...138 A8
Roxburgh Dr OX11 ....200 D3
Royal Berkshire Ct OX11 .218 F7
Royal Mans RG9 ....244 E1
Royal Military Coll of
  Science SN6 ....209 E7
Ruck Keene Ct OX26....65 C2
Rufus Isaacs Rd RG4...259 B2
Rugge Furlong OX14 ..201 B1
Rumbolds Cl OX10 ....203 F5
Rumsey's La OX11 ....237 A8
Rupert Cl
  Chalgrove OX44.......184 D6
  Oxford OX4 ....142 E6
Rupert Rd
  Chalgrove OX44.......184 E6
  Oxford OX4 ....142 E6
Rupert's La RG9 ......244 E3
Rupert Way RG9 ......130 A1
Ruscote Arc OX16......16 B8
Ruscote Ave OX16......16 B8
Ruscote Sq OX16........16 B8
Rushall Rd OX9 ....130 A1
Rushbeds Wood Nature
  Reserve* HP18 ....98 D4
Rush Common Sch OX14 .160 B1
Rushmead Copse OX14 .160 C2
Ruskin Ave OX16......179 E5
Ruskin Cl OX11 ....219 A8
Ruskin Coll
  Oxford,Headington OX3.124 C4
  Oxford OX1 ....261 A3
Ruskin Rd OX16........16 C3
Ruskin Wlk OX26.......65 F3
Russell Ct OX2.........123 B4
Russell Jackson Cl OX10 .182 C6
Russell Rd RG4 ....258 D7
Russell St OX2.........123 A1
Russet Ave OX17 ....37 A8
Russet Cl RG4 ....252 E5
Russet Glade RG4.....259 C7
Russet Rd OX27.........50 C6
Russett Ave OX18 ....115 F5
Rutherford Ave OX11...217 B3
Rutherford Ct OX14 ...160 A1
Rutherway OX2 ....123 A3
Rycote La OX9 ....108 A6
Rutters Cl OX5 ....108 D8
Rycote La OX9 ....146 C5
Rydal Ave RG30 ......257 F2
Ryder Cl OX4 ....108 B6
Rydes Cl OX15..........22 E8
Rydes The OX15 ....22 E8
Rye Cl OX16............22 E8
Ryecote Chapel* OX9...146 D6
Ryecroft Cl
  Sonning RG5 ....260 E1
  Wargrave RG10 ....255 E2
Rye Grass OX20.........91 C6
Rye St Antony Sch OX3 .124 B3
Rymans Cres OX11....219 A6
Rymers La OX4 ....142 B5

S

Sackler Liby The OX1 ...261 B3
Sackville St OX4........8 E4
Sacred Heart RC Prim Sch
  RG9 ....244 D1
Sadlers Croft OX44....143 E1
Sadlers Ct OX14 ......160 B3
Sadlers The RG31.....257 B1
Sadler Wlk OX1........261 A2
Saffron Cl OX26........65 D5
Saffron Ct OX14 ......180 B8
Sage Rd RG31.........257 C3
Sage Wlk 7 OX4 .....142 F1
St Alban's Ct 5 OX10...221 D7
St Aldate's Sch 261 B1
St Aloysius RC Prim Sch
  OX2 ....123 B4
St Amand Dr OX14 ...160 C3
St Amand's RC Prim Sch
  OX12 ....216 E5
St Andrew's CE Prim Sch
  Chinnor OX39 ....168 C5
  Didcot OX11..........218 F8
  Henley-on-T RG9 .....254 D8
  Oxford OX3 ....124 C4
St Andrew's Rd
  Reading RG4 ....258 F4
St Andrew's Sch OX14 ...201 A7
St Andrews Sq OX20 ...91 A7
St Anne's Cl OX3 ......65 F4
St Anne's Coll OX1 ...261 A4
St Anne's Coll RG9 ...244 D1
St Annes RC Prim Sch
  RG4 ....259 B2
St Anne's Rd
  Banbury OX16 ....16 D3

St Anne's Rd *continued*
  Oxford OX3 ....124 D2
  Reading RG4 ....259 A2
St Anthony's Wlk OX26...66 A3
St Antonys Coll OX2 ...16 A4
St Barnabas CE Prim Sch
  OX2 ....261 A3
St Barnabas Rd RG4 ..259 A6
St Barnabas St OX2...261 A3
St Benets Way RG4 ...259 C7
St Bernard's Rd OX2 ..261 A4
St Birinus Ct GL7 ....150 C5
St Birinus Sch OX11 ...218 F7
St Catherine's Coll OX1 .123 E2
St Catherines Ho OX4 ..123 E1
St Christopher's CE Prim Sch
  OX4 ....142 C6
St Christopher's CE Sch
  GL7 ....132 C1
St Cristopher Cotts 4
  SN7 ....172 F3
St Cross Bldg OX1 ...261 C3
St Cross Coll (Annexe)
  OX1 ....261 B3
St Cross Coll OX1 ....261 B3
St Cross Rd OX1......261 B3
St David's Cl RG4 ....258 F5
St David's Ct NN13.....24 A8
St Denys Cl SN7 .....194 E7
St Ebbe's CE Fst Sch
  OX1 ....141 C7
St Ebbes St OX1 ......261 B2
St Edburg's CE Sch 65 C2
St Edburg's Prim Sch
  OX26 ....65 E1
St Edith's Way OX26....65 E1
St Edmund Hall OX1 ..261 C2
St Edmund's La 4 OX4 .179 F6
St Edmund's RC Prim Sch
  OX4 ....180 A8
St Edward's Ave OX2..123 A7
St Edwards Ct OX2....123 B6
St Edwards Sch
  Oxford OX2 ....123 A7
  Oxford OX2 ....123 B6
SS Philip & James Prim Sch
  OX2 ....261 A4
St Francis CE Prim Sch
  OX4 ....142 E6
St Francis Cl OX14 ....142 E7
St Francis Rd HP14 ...189 D3
St Frideswides CE OX11 .218 E8
St George's Cl OX10 ..220 F1
St George's Cres OX16...16 C4
St Georges Gate OX1 ..261 B2
St George's Pl OX1 ...261 B2
St George's Rd SN7 ...154 D1
St Georges Rd OX10 ..221 C8
St Giles OX1 ....93 A8
St Giles Cl OX25 ....80 A4
St Giles' OX1..........261 B3
St Gregory the Great RC Sec
  OX14 ....179 F6
St Helen's Ave OX10 ..203 F3
St Helen's Cres OX10 .204 A3
St Helen's Ct OX14 ...179 F6
St Helen's Mews 5
  OX14 ....179 F6
St Helen's Mill 12 OX14 ...179 F6
St Helen's Pas OX1 ...261 C2
St Helen's Wharf OX14 .179 F6
St Hilda's Cl OX26.....65 F4
St Hilda's Coll OX1 ...219 B7
St Hilda's Coll OX14 ..141 E8
St Hughs Cl OX16......16 C3
St Hugh's Cl
  Bicester OX26 ....65 F4
  Stokenchurch HP14 ...188 F4
St Hugh's Coll OX2 ...123 B4
St Hugh's Pl HP14 ....188 F4
St Hughs Rise OX11 ..219 B7
St Hugh's Sch SN7 ...174 B8
St Ives La OX11 ......214 E8
St Ives Rd OX11 ......214 E8
St James CE Sch OX12...197 A6
St James Cl RG8......256 C6
St James Cl OX29 .....89 C7
St James Rd OX4 .....160 E3
St James Terr OX14 ..160 E2
St James St OX12 ....197 B6
St James OX1..........261 A4
St John Fisher RC Prim Sch
  OX4 ....142 D3
St John's Cl
  Didcot OX11..........219 A8
  Fyfield OX13 ....157 C2
  Upper Heyford OX25 ...48 E6
St John's Cl OX14.....261 B3
St John's Ct
  2 Banbury OX16 ......16 D5
  Oxford OX1 ....196 E1
St Johns Dr
  Carterton OX18 ......115 E3
  Kidlington OX5........92 F1
St John's Gn 18 OX10 ...221 D7
St John's Ho 2 OX16 ...16 C5
St John's Priory Sch OX11 221 C2
St John's RC Prim Sch
  OX16 ....16 E3
St John's Rd
  Abingdon OX14 ......180 A8

Rid – St N 281

St Johns Rd OX5........77 C6
St John's Rd OX10 ....221 C7
St John's Row OX10 ..201 C8
St Johns OX12 ....212 F4
St John's St
  Bicester OX26 ....65 E2
  Lechlade-on-T GL7....150 D4
  Oxford OX1 ....261 B3
St John's Terr 7 OX10 .221 C7
St John St OX1 ....261 B3
St John's Way OX15 ...33 B4
St John the Evangelist CE
  Prim Sch OX16 ......115 F4
St Joseph's RC Prim Sch
  OX16 ....15 F6
St Joseph's RC Sch
  Carterton OX18 ......115 D2
  Oxford OX3 ....124 A4
St Josephs OX29 ......147 E8
St Katherine's Rd RG9 .254 D7
St Kenelm's CE Sch
  OX29 ....102 E2
St Kenelm's Cl OX29 ..102 E2
St Laurence CE Prim Sch
  OX10 ....203 B7
St Lawrence CE Prim Sch
  GL7 ....150 D3
St Lawrence La OX10 ..203 B8
St Lawrence Ho OX10 .203 B8
St Lawrence Rd
  Lechlade-on-T GL7....150 D4
  South Hinksey OX1 ...141 B5
St Leonard's CE Prim Sch
  OX16 ....16 E6
St Leonards Cl OX16 ...16 E6
St Leonards Cl OX49 ..186 B2
St Leonards Ct OX7....54 C2
St Leonard's Cl OX10 .221 D6
St Leonard's La OX10 .221 D7
St Leonard's Rd OX3..124 D3
St Leonard's Sq 10 OX10 221 D7
St Lucian's La OX11 ..221 D6
St Lukes Ct RG4 .....259 A6
St Luke's Rd OX4 ....142 D5
St Lukes Way RG4 ...259 B5
St Margaret's Rd OX2.123 B4
St Mark's Rd
  Henley-on-T RG9 .....244 E1
  Henley-on-T RG9 .....254 D8
St Martins RC Prim Sch
  RG4 ....259 E6
St Martin's Rd OX4 ...142 A3
St Martin's St OX10 ..221 D7
St Mary and John CE Prim
  Sch OX4 ....142 A7
St Mary's Ave RG8 ...257 D5
St Mary's CE Inf Sch
  OX28 ....118 B7
St Mary's CE Prim Sch
  Banbury OX16 ....16 C6
  Chipping Norton OX7...42 E2
St Mary's Cl
  2 Banbury OX16 ......16 C6
  Bicester OX26 ....65 D1
  Chalgrove OX44.......184 D6
  Henley-on-T RG9 .....254 A8
  Kidlington OX5........92 E2
  Oxford OX14 ....142 B2
  Wheatley OX33 ......144 B8
St Mary's Ct OX18 ...134 E2
St Mary's Gn OX18 ...159 A7
St Mary's Gn OX29 ...159 F1
St Mary's Ho OX33....144 B8
St Mary's La OX7 ......30 E3
St Marys Mead OX28 .118 B7
St Mary's RC Prim Sch
  OX26 ....65 E2
St Mary's Rd
  Adderbury OX17 ......22 F2
  East Hendred OX12 ...216 E6
  Oxford OX4 ....141 F7
St Mary's Sch
  Henley-on-T RG9 .....254 E8
  Wantage OX12........214 D4
St Mary's St OX10 ....221 D7
St Mary's Way OX12 ..214 D4
St Mary's Wlk OX27....50 C3
St Michael's Ave
  Abingdon OX14 ......179 E7
  Highworth SN6 ....190 A5
St Michaels CE Prim Sch
  OX3 ....123 F2
St Michael's CE Prim Sch
  OX13 ....198 F4
St Michael's Cl OX27...52 D8
St Michael's Cl OX7....85 D8
St Michael's La OX15 .107 F8
St Michael's St OX1 ..261 B2
St Michaels OX12......214 D4
St Michael's Way OX13 .198 F4
St Nicholas CE Inf Sch
  OX10 ....203 D7
St Nicholas CE Prim Sch
  OX13 ....213 F4
St Nicholas Pk (Cvn Pk)
  OX3 ....123 F7
St Nicholas Prim Sch
  OX13 ....123 F5
St Nicholas Rd
  Oxford OX4 ....142 C4
  Tackley OX5...........77 C6
  Wallingford OX10 ....221 C8
St Nicolas CE Prim Sch
  OX14 ....179 F8

St Omer Rd OX4 . . . . 142 C5
St Paul's Cres OX2 . . . . . . 140 D8
St Peter's Ave RG4 . . . . . 258 E3
St Peter's CE Inf Sch
  OX18 . . . . 133 C5
St Peter's CE Prim Sch
  OX29 . . . . 107 C2
St Peter's Cl OX29 . . . . . . 107 D2
St Peter's Cl OX15 . . . . 31 F7
St Peter's Cl
  Stoke Lyne OX27 . . . . 51 B5
  Wootton OX13 . . . . 159 B6
St Peter's Coll OX1 . . . . . . 261 B2
St Peter's Cres OX26 . . . . . 65 F4
St Peter's Gate NN13 . . . . . 24 A7
St Peter's Hill RG4 . . . . . . 258 F3
St Peter's Pl ▲ OX10 . . . . 221 D7
St Peter's Rd
  Abingdon OX14 . . . . 160 C1
  Brackley NN13 . . . . 24 A8
  Didcot OX11 . . . . 218 E8
  Wolvercote OX2 . . . . 122 F8
St Peter's St OX10 . . . . . . 221 D7
St Ruald's ▲▲ OX10 . . . . . 221 D7
St Rumbold's Rd OX10 . . . 221 D7
St Stephens Cl ▲ RG4 . . . 259 A2
St Swithun's CE Prim Sch
  OX1 . . . . 160 E8
St Swithun's Rd OX14 . . . 160 E8
St Thomas More RC Prim
  Sch OX5 . . . . 108 E7
St Thomas' Cl SN7 . . . . . . 155 F2
St Thomas Cl OX15 . . . . 33 F3
St Thomas' St OX1 . . . . . . 261 A2
Salegate La OX4 . . . . 142 D5
Salesian Gdns OX4 . . . . . . 142 D6
Salesian Ho OX4 . . . . 142 D6
Salford Rd OX3 . . . . 124 F3
Salisbury Cres OX2 . . . . . 123 B8
Sallow Cl OX26 . . . . 65 F5
Salmon Cl OX15 . . . . 21 F6
Salop Cl SN6 . . . . 209 B6
Salter Cl OX1 . . . . 141 C7
Salters Cl HP18 . . . . 98 C8
Salters La HP18 . . . . 98 C8
Salt La OX5 . . . . 166 E2
Salvia Cl OX16 . . . . 9 B1
Samian Way OX10 . . . . . . 202 D8
Samor Way OX11 . . . . 218 D8
Samphire Rd OX4 . . . . 142 F2
Samuelson Ct ▲▲ OX16 . . . 16 D5
Sandcroft Rd RG4 . . . . . . 258 E6
Sandell Cl OX16 . . . . 16 B5
Sanderling Cl OX26 . . . . . . 81 A8
Sanderling WIk OX16 . . . . 16 E3
Sandfield Rd OX3 . . . . 124 B3
Sandfine Rd OX15 . . . . 15 B2
Sandford Cl
  Abingdon OX14 . . . . 160 B2
  Woodcote RG8 . . . . 250 F8
Sandford Dr RG5 . . . . 260 F1
Sandford Gn OX16 . . . . 15 F7
Sandford La OX1 . . . . 160 E4
Sandford Mount OX7 . . . . . 73 C3
Sandford Park OX7 . . . . . . 73 C3
Sandford Rd OX4 . . . . 142 A1
Sandford Rise OX7 . . . . 73 C3
Sandford St Martin Rd
  OX7 . . . . 46 C1
Sandgate Ave RG30 . . . . . 257 F2
Sandhill Rd OX5 . . . . 108 A8
Sandhills Com Prim Sch
  OX3 . . . . 125 B4
Sand Hill SN6 . . . . 209 A7
Sand La OX3 . . . . 111 A2
Sandleigh Rd OX13 . . . . . . 159 A7
Sandpiper Cl OX26 . . . . 81 A8
Sandpit Hill MK18 . . . . 39 F6
Sandpit La RG4 . . . . 259 F8
Sandringham Rd
  Didcot OX11 . . . . 219 B8
  Kings Sutton OX17 . . . . 23 F5
Sands Cl
  Bletchingdon OX5 . . . . 93 A8
  Cumnor OX2 . . . . 139 E5
Sands La OX15 . . . . 31 F7
Sands Rd OX11 . . . . 219 F6
Sands The
  Benson OX10 . . . . 204 C6
  Milton-u-W OX7 . . . . 70 B1
Sands Way OX10 . . . . 203 F5
Sand View SN7 . . . . 172 F2
Sandy La
  Boars Hill OX1 . . . . 140 C2
  Cholsey OX10 . . . . 220 E1
  Hatford SN7 . . . . 174 C4
  Kingston Bagpuize OX13 . . 156 E1
  Long Crendon HP18 . . . . . . 129 B6
Sandy Lane Ct GL54 . . . . . . 68 A4
Sandy Lane Est OX9 . . . . 145 F7
Sandy La
  Oxford OX4 . . . . 142 E3
  Shrivenham SN6 . . . . 209 B6
  Tiddington OX9 . . . . 145 F5
  Upper Rissington GL54 . . . . 68 A4
Sandy La W OX4 . . . . 142 D3
Sandy La OX5 . . . . 108 D7
Sarajac Ave OX12 . . . . . . 213 F4
Sarsden Cl OX7 . . . . 57 B1
Sarum Cl OX18 . . . . 115 F3
Satin La OX15 . . . . 33 F3
Satwell Cl RG9 . . . . 243 A3
Saunders Cl OX49 . . . . . . 186 B2
Saunders Ct RG8 . . . . 257 B5
Saunders Rd OX4 . . . . 142 B6

Saunders Wood Copse
  HP14 . . . . 188 F4
Savile Rd OX1 . . . . 261 C3
Savile Way OX12 . . . . 196 D1
Saw Cl OX4 . . . . 184 C7
Sawpit Rd OX4 . . . . 142 E3
Sawpits La GL56 . . . . 40 A1
Saxel Cl OX18 . . . . 135 E3
Saxifrage Sq ▲ OX4 . . . . 142 E1
Saxon Cl OX10 . . . . 221 C7
Saxon Ct
  Benson OX10 . . . . 203 F4
  Bicester OX26 . . . . 65 F1
Saxon Orch SN6 . . . . 191 D2
Saxon Pl
  Pangbourne RG8 . . . . 256 D6
  Wantage OX12 . . . . 214 B5
Saxons Cl GL7 . . . . 132 B5
Saxons Heath OX14 . . . . . 201 D7
Saxons Way OX11 . . . . 219 A7
Saxon Way
  Oxford OX3 . . . . 124 B4
  Witney OX28 . . . . 118 A7
Saxton Rd OX14 . . . . 179 E5
Sayer Milward Terr ▲▲
  OX10 . . . . 221 D7
Sayers Orch OX11 . . . . . . 200 D1
Scafell Cl RG31 . . . . 257 B2
Scampton Cl OX26 . . . . 66 B3
Schilling St OX25 . . . . 63 A8
Sch of Geography OX1 . . 261 C3
Schofield Ave OX28 . . . . . 104 A1
Schofield Gdns OX28 . . . 104 A3
Schofields Way OX15 . . . . 21 E5
Scholar Cl SN6 . . . . 191 F2
Scholar Pl OX2 . . . . 140 C7
Scholars Acre OX18 . . . . . 115 D4
Scholars Cl RG4 . . . . 258 F2
Scholar's Mews OX2 . . . . 123 B6
Schongau Cl OX14 . . . . . . 179 D4
School Cl
  Ickford HP18 . . . . 128 A3
  Long Compton CV36 . . . . . . 27 F6
  Longworth OX13 . . . . 156 C3
  Steventon OX13 . . . . 198 F4
School Cotts RG9 . . . . 243 C2
School Ct OX2 . . . . 261 A3
School End
  Aymho OX17 . . . . 35 C7
  Chetwode MK18 . . . . 53 D8
Schooler's La GL56 . . . . . . 40 C3
School Hill
  Minster Lovell OX29 . . . . . 102 F3
  Mollington OX17 . . . . 3 F3
  Wargrave RG10 . . . . 255 D1
School La
  Appleford OX14 . . . . 200 F8
  Aston Rowant OX9 . . . . . . 167 E3
  Banbury OX16 . . . . 16 C6
  Black Bourton OX18 . . . . . 133 F5
  Chilson OX7 . . . . 71 F3
  Coleshill SN6 . . . . 191 B8
  Great Bourton OX17 . . . . 9 D7
  Grove OX12 . . . . 196 E1
  Harwell OX11 . . . . 217 E7
  Kingston Bagpuize OX13 . . 156 F1
  Middleton Stoney OX25 . . . . 66 A4
  Milton Heights OX14 . . . . . 199 C3
  Milton OX14 . . . . 199 D5
  Minster Lovell OX29 . . . . . 102 E3
  North Newington OX15 . . . . 15 C4
  Reading,Emmer Green
    RG4 . . . . 259 B6
  Reading RG4 . . . . 259 A2
  Shabbington HP18 . . . . 128 D3
  Stadhampton OX44 . . . . . . 163 C2
  Stoke Lyne OX27 . . . . 51 B5
  Stoke Row RG9 . . . . 241 F4
  Upper Heyford OX6 . . . . 62 F8
  Wargrave RG10 . . . . 255 D2
  Warmington OX17 . . . . 3 A4
School of St Helen & St
  Katherine OX14 . . . . 179 D8
School Paddock OX27 . . . . 64 F8
School Pl OX1 . . . . 141 D6
School Rd
  Ardington OX12 . . . . 215 D5
  Finstock OX7 . . . . 88 C5
  Kidlington OX5 . . . . 92 E1
  West Hanney OX12 . . . . . . 196 F6
School Row OX16 . . . . 16 F6
School View OX16 . . . . 16 F6
School Yd OX44 . . . . 163 C2
Scotland End OX15 . . . . . . 30 A7
Scotsgrove Cotts OX9 . . . 130 A3
Scotsgrove Hill OX9 . . . . . 130 A3
Scott Cl
  Bicester OX26 . . . . 65 C3
  Kidlington OX5 . . . . 108 D8
  Reading RG4 . . . . 259 A5
Scott Rd OX2 . . . . 123 B8
Scotts Cnr NN13 . . . . 25 C1
Scotts La OX27 . . . . 67 E2
Scours La RG30 . . . . 258 B1
Scrutton Cl OX3 . . . . 124 E3
Seacourt Rd OX2 . . . . 122 C1
Sealham Rd OX29 . . . . . . 118 B4
Second Ave OX11 . . . . 200 D2
Second St
  Croughton NN13 . . . . 36 E6
  Harwell OX11 . . . . 217 C3
Sedgefield Cl RG4 . . . . . . 252 F6
Sedgemoor Dr OX9 . . . . . 130 A1
Sedgewell Rd RG4 . . . . . . 252 F6
Seelscheid Way OX26 . . . . 81 A7
Seesen Way OX12 . . . . . . 214 E4
Sefton Pl OX15 . . . . 22 E7

Sefton Rd OX3 . . . . 124 E3
Segrave Cl RG10 . . . . 260 E2
Segsbury Ct OX12 . . . . . . 214 B5
Segsbury Rd OX12 . . . . . . 214 B5
Selborne Gdns RG30 . . . . 258 A1
Sellwood Dr OX18 . . . . . . 115 E3
Sellwood Rd OX14 . . . . . . 159 F1
Selwyn Cres OX14 . . . . . . 160 E2
Send Rd RG4 . . . . 259 C1
Sermon Cl OX3 . . . . 124 F2
Setler Ho ▲ OX16 . . . . 16 E6
Setts The SN7 . . . . 172 E2
Seven Acres
  Long Crendon HP18 . . . . . 129 B7
  Thame OX9 . . . . 148 A8
Sevenfields SN6 . . . . 190 A7
Seventeenth St OX11 . . . . 217 A2
Seventh Ave OX3 . . . . 142 F8
Severalls Cl OX10 . . . . . . 203 D1
Severalls Cotts OX10 . . . . 203 B3
Severn Cl OX26 . . . . 65 B3
Severn Cres ▲ OX11 . . . . 219 A8
Severn Rd
  Abingdon OX13 . . . . 159 D2
  Harwell OX11 . . . . 217 B1
Sewell Cl OX14 . . . . 160 C1
Sewell's La OX39 . . . . 167 E8
Shackleton Cl OX26 . . . . . . 66 A4
Shades The OX16 . . . . 16 C5
Shadwell Rd OX10 . . . . . . 182 C5
Shaftesbury Rd OX3 . . . . 124 E5
Shakenoak OX29 . . . . 105 C6
Shakespeare Cl RG4 . . . . 259 D5
Shakespeare Dr OX26 . . . . 65 C3
Shakespeare Rd OX29 . . . 120 D8
Shannon Cl OX12 . . . . 196 F1
Shannon Rd
  ▲ Didcot OX11 . . . . 219 A8
  Bicester OX26 . . . . 65 B2
Sharland Cl OX12 . . . . 214 E8
Sharman Beer Ct OX9 . . . 147 E8
Sharpes Cotts OX26 . . . . . 66 E2
Shaw Cl OX26 . . . . 65 B4
Shaw's Copse OX14 . . . . . 160 F2
Sheards La SN7 . . . . 194 E7
Shearings The OX15 . . . . . 30 A7
Shearwater Dr OX26 . . . . . 81 B8
Sheen Cl OX27 . . . . 49 E4
Sheep St
  Bicester OX26 . . . . 65 E2
  Burford OX18 . . . . 100 E5
  Charlbury OX7 . . . . 73 B3
Sheepstead Rd OX13 . . . . 178 C8
Sheep St SN6 . . . . 190 A5
Sheepwash La OX13 . . . . . 199 A4
Sheepway Ct OX4 . . . . 142 A4
Sheepways La RG4 . . . . . . 258 B8
Sheep Wlk RG4 . . . . 259 B4
Sheerstock HP17 . . . . 130 C4
Sheldonian Theatre *
  OX1 . . . . 261 C2
Sheldon Rd HP18 . . . . 128 A3
Sheldons Piece OX49 . . . . 186 A2
Sheldon Way OX4 . . . . 142 C3
Shelford Pl OX3 . . . . 124 D1
Shelley Cl
  ▲ Bicester OX26 . . . . 65 C3
  Abingdon OX14 . . . . 160 A1
  Banbury OX16 . . . . 16 A3
  Oxford OX3 . . . . 124 F2
Shelley Rd OX4 . . . . 142 B6
Shellingford CE Prim Sch
  SN7 . . . . 193 F7
Shenington CE Prim Sch
  OX15 . . . . 6 C2
Shenington Kart Club *
  OX15 . . . . 6 C2
Shepard Way OX7 . . . . 42 F3
Shepherd Gdns OX4 . . . . 179 C6
Shepherds Cl
  Grove OX12 . . . . 196 D2
  Sibford Gower OX15 . . . . . . 19 B8
  Weston-on-t-G OX25 . . . . . . 79 A2
Shepherds Hill
  Sandford-on-T OX4 . . . . . . 142 F1
  Sonning RG4 . . . . 260 C1
  Steeple Aston OX25 . . . . . . 48 A1
Shepherds La RG4 . . . . . . 258 D6
Sheraton Dr RG31 . . . . . . 257 B1
Sherborne St GL7 . . . . . . 150 C4
Sherbourne Rd OX28 . . . . 117 D8
Sheridan Ave RG4 . . . . . . 258 F4
Sheriff's Dr OX2 . . . . 122 F8
Sherwood Ave OX14 . . . . 160 B8
Sherwood Cl OX26 . . . . 66 D2
Sherwood Gdns RG9 . . . . 254 C8
Sherwood Pl RG8 . . . . 257 B4
Sherwood Rd OX11 . . . . . 218 D8
Sherwood Rise RG8 . . . . . 257 B5
Shifford La OX29 . . . . 137 C2
Shilbrook Manor OX18 . . 133 F4
Shilbrook Ave OX18 . . . . . 115 D5
Shildeane Dr OX18 . . . . . . 115 D4
Shilson La OX7 . . . . 73 B3
Shilton Rd
  Burford OX18 . . . . 100 F3
  Carterton OX18 . . . . 115 D4
Shinmoor Cl OX11 . . . . . . 201 B2
Shiplake Bottom RG9 . . . . 252 F6
Shiplake CE Sch RG9 . . . . 254 E2
Shiplake Coll RG9 . . . . . . 254 F1
Shiplake Sta RG9 . . . . 255 B4
Shipston Rd CV36 . . . . 27 F7
Ship St OX1 . . . . 261 B2
Shipton Cl RG31 . . . . 257 C2
Shipton Rd
  Ascott-u-W OX7 . . . . 71 B1
  Shipton-u-W OX7 . . . . 70 B1

Shipton continued
  Woodstock OX20 . . . . 91 D6
Shipton Sta OX7 . . . . 70 E2
Shirburn Rd OX49 . . . . . . 186 C2
Shirburn St OX49 . . . . . . 186 C2
Shire Lake Cl OX1 . . . . . . 261 B1
Shires Bsns Pk The NN13 . 24 A6
Shires Rd NN13 . . . . 24 A6
Shirley Pl OX2 . . . . 261 A4
Shirvell's Hill RG8 . . . . . . 250 E7
Shoe La
  East Hagbourne OX11 . . . . 218 F5
  Oxford OX1 . . . . 261 B2
Shooter's Hill RG8 . . . . . . 256 C6
Shorte Cl OX3 . . . . 142 E7
Short Furlong OX11 . . . . . 201 B2
Shortlands Hill OX10 . . . . 238 D4
Short St
  ▲ Reading RG4 . . . . 259 B2
  Pangbourne RG8 . . . . 256 D5
  Watchfield SN6 . . . . 191 D1
Short The RG8 . . . . 257 D5
Shotover Ctry Pk * OX3 . . 125 B1
Shotover Kilns OX3 . . . . . 124 F1
Shotover Trad Est OX3 . . . 124 F1
Shotover SN7 . . . . 211 C6
Shrewsbury Rd OX18 . . . . 134 E3
Shrieves Cl OX14 . . . . 160 C2
Shrivenham CE Sch SN6 . 209 B7
Shrivenham Hundred Bsns
  Pk SN6 . . . . 191 D2
Shrivenham Rd
  Highworth SN6 . . . . 190 B3
  Longcot SN7 . . . . 192 C2
Shrubbery The GL7 . . . . . 150 C4
Shute Ave SN6 . . . . 209 D8
Shutford Rd
  North Newington OX15 . . . . 15 B4
  Tadmarton OX15 . . . . 20 E8
Sibford Gower Prim Sch
  OX15 . . . . 19 A8
Sibford Rd
  Hook Norton OX15 . . . . . . 30 B8
  Shutford OX15 . . . . 13 E3
Sibford Sch OX15 . . . . 19 B7
Sibthorp Rd OX1 . . . . 261 C3
Sideleigh Rd OX15 . . . . . . 22 E8
Sidings Ind Est The NN13 . 24 A8
Sidings Rd OX7 . . . . 55 E5
Sidings The OX10 . . . . . . 221 C7
Signet End OX18 . . . . 100 E3
Signet Rd OX18 . . . . 100 E3
Silkdale Cl OX4 . . . . 142 D5
Silver Birches OX33 . . . . . 125 E7
Silverdale Rd RG10 . . . . . 255 E1
Silver La OX12 . . . . 213 D6
Silvermead HP18 . . . . 127 D5
Silver Rd OX4 . . . . 142 A7
Silver St W OX17 . . . . 10 E4
Silver St
  Bourton SN6 . . . . 209 A2
  Chacombe OX17 . . . . 10 E4
  Fernham SN7 . . . . 193 A4
  Tetsworth OX9 . . . . 166 B8
  Wroxton OX15 . . . . 15 B8
Silverthorne Dr RG4 . . . . 258 E6
Simms Cl OX33 . . . . 125 D7
Simmonds Wlk OX12 . . . . 214 D6
Simmons Rd RG9 . . . . 244 D3
Simmons Way OX9 . . . . . . 129 F1
Simon Ho OX3 . . . . 124 D3
Simons Cl RG31 . . . . 257 C4
Simon's Cl OX33 . . . . 144 A8
Simons La OX7 . . . . 85 D7
Simon's Way MK18 . . . . . . 25 E7
Simpsons Way OX1 . . . . . 160 E8
Sinclair Ave OX16 . . . . 16 A7
Sinclair Dr OX16 . . . . 66 B1
Singers Cl RG9 . . . . 254 E8
Singers La RG9 . . . . 244 E1
Singletree OX4 . . . . 142 B4
Sinnels Field OX7 . . . . 85 E8
Sinnet Ct OX4 . . . . 142 A8
Sinodun Cl OX14 . . . . 201 D7
Sinodun Rd
  Didcot OX11 . . . . 218 F7
  Wallingford OX10 . . . . 203 C1
Sinodun Row OX14 . . . . . 200 F7
Sinodun View OX10 . . . . . 203 B8
Sint Niklaas Cl OX14 . . . . 179 D4
Sires Hill
  Long Wittenham OX11,
    OX14 . . . . 201 E5
  North Moreton OX11 . . . . . 202 C4
Sir Georges La OX17 . . . . . 23 A4
Sir Henry Jake Cl OX16 . . . 9 C2
Sir Mortimer's Terr
  OX14 . . . . 199 D6
Sir William Dunn Sch of
  Pathology OX1 . . . . 261 C4
Siskin Rd
  Bicester OX26 . . . . 66 A1
  Upper Rissington GL54 . . . . 68 A5
Sixpenny La OX44 . . . . . . 184 E6
Sixteenth St OX11 . . . . . . 217 B3
Sixth St
  Croughton NN13 . . . . 36 E7
  Harwell OX11 . . . . 217 B3
Skarries View RG4 . . . . . . 258 D8
Skelton Ct OX4 . . . . 123 F1
Skene Cl OX3 . . . . 124 C1
Skerritt Way RG8 . . . . 257 D4
Skilton Rd RG31 . . . . 257 C1
Skimmingdish La
  Bicester,Caversfield OX27 . . 65 F6
Skinner Rd OX26 . . . . 66 D2
Skippett La OX7 . . . . 88 A4

Skippon Way OX3 . . . . . . 129 F2
Skittle Alley OX17 . . . . 35 C7
Skylark Pl OX4 . . . . 142 D2
Slade Cl OX3 . . . . 124 D1
Slade End OX10 . . . . 202 F2
Slade End Rdbt OX10 . . . 203 A2
Slade Farm Cotts OX5 . . . 63 B1
Slade Hill NN13 . . . . 24 D1
Slade Rd
  Cholsey OX10 . . . . 221 A2
  Didcot OX11 . . . . 200 C1
  Stokenchurch HP14 . . . . . 188 E4
Slade The
  Charlbury OX7 . . . . 73 C4
  Oxford OX3 . . . . 142 E8
Slatters Ct OX29 . . . . 90 A1
Slave Hill HP17 . . . . 130 F5
Slaymaker Cl OX3 . . . . . . 124 F2
Sloane Cl RG8 . . . . 249 C6
Slopes The RG4 . . . . 259 D2
Small Ho OX15 . . . . 19 C7
Smith Barry Cir GL54 . . . . 68 B4
Smith Barry Cres GL54 . . . 68 B4
Smith Barry Rd GL54 . . . . 68 B4
Smith Cl RG4 . . . . 252 F5
Smiths Cl OX29 . . . . 123 E7
Smiths Cvn Site OX15 . . . . 21 F3
Smiths Farm La OX11 . . . 200 D1
Smith's Hill OX12 . . . . 231 F5
Smiths Rickyard OX12 . . . 216 D7
Smiths Wharf ▲ OX12 . . . 214 D5
Snakehill La OX15 . . . . 33 B4
Snipe Rd GL54 . . . . 68 A4
Snowdon Mede OX3 . . . . . 124 A4
Snowshill Dr OX28 . . . . . . 117 D8
Snows La OX33 . . . . 125 D8
Snowswick La SN7 . . . . . . 170 E5
Snuff La OX17 . . . . 8 C8
Snuggs La OX12 . . . . 197 B7
Soane End RG4 . . . . 259 A7
Soden Pl OX13 . . . . 156 D1
Soden Rd OX25 . . . . 63 D8
Soldier Ct OX2 . . . . 108 F2
Somerton Rd
  Ardley OX27 . . . . 50 B4
  North Aston OX25 . . . . 48 B7
  Upper Heyford OX25 . . . . . 48 F1
Somerville Coll OX2 . . . . 261 A3
Somerville Ct OX17 . . . . . . 23 D3
Somerville OX11 . . . . 219 B8
Somerville Dr OX26 . . . . . . 65 F4
Songers Cl OX2 . . . . 140 B8
Sonning CE Prim Sch
  RG4 . . . . 260 D3
Sonning Common Prim Sch
  RG4 . . . . 252 F5
Sonning Gate RG10 . . . . . 260 C2
Sonning La RG4 . . . . 260 D3
Sonning Mdws RG4 . . . . . 260 C1
Soot La OX17 . . . . 3 A4
Sopwith Rd GL54 . . . . 68 A5
Sorrel Mead OX26 . . . . 65 D4
Sorrel Rd OX4 . . . . 143 A2
Sotwell St OX10 . . . . 202 F2
Southampton St
  ▲ Faringdon SN7 . . . . 172 F4
  Faringdon SN7 . . . . 172 F3
Southam Rd
  Banbury,Little Bourton
    OX17 . . . . 9 D3
  Banbury OX16 . . . . 16 C7
  Mollington OX17 . . . . 4 A3
South Ave
  Abingdon OX14 . . . . 159 F2
  Henley-on-T RG9 . . . . 254 E8
  Kidlington OX5 . . . . 108 F6
South Bank
  South Stoke RG8 . . . . 239 C3
  Turweston NN13 . . . . 24 C7
South Bar St OX16 . . . . 16 C5
South Bridge Row OX1 . . 261 B1
Southby OX18 . . . . 134 F4
Southby Cl OX13 . . . . 158 A8
South Cl OX5 . . . . 108 F5
Southcroft OX3 . . . . 123 F6
Southdale Rd OX2 . . . . . . 123 B8
Southdown St SN7 . . . . . . 194 E7
Southdown Rd RG4 . . . . . 259 B5
South Dr
  Harwell OX11 . . . . 217 C3
  Sonning RG4 . . . . 260 A3
Southend OX10 . . . . 78 A3
Southend Cotts OX5 . . . . . 78 A3
Southend OX44 . . . . 162 E8
South End
  Great Rollright OX7 . . . . . . 29 A3
  Haddenham HP17 . . . . 130 F5
Southern By-pass Rd
  Kennington OX1 . . . . 141 D4
  Oxford,Botley OX2 . . . . 140 D4
Southerndene Cl RG31 . . 257 C2
Southern Rd OX9 . . . . 147 E8
Southfield Dr OX14 . . . . . 199 F7
Southfield Jun Sch SN6 . . 190 F5
Southfield La OX7 . . . . 42 A8
Southfield Pk OX4 . . . . . . 142 A8
Southfield Rd OX4 . . . . . . 142 A8
South Gate Ct GL54 . . . . . . 68 A5
South Gn OX5 . . . . 78 A4
South Hills HP18 . . . . 98 A1
Southlands OX18 . . . . 135 E2
Southlawn OX28 . . . . 117 F7
South Lodge The ▲ OX28 . 119 F7
South Mdw OX15 . . . . 8 E4
Southmead Ind Pk OX11 . 200 D4
South Mere OX10 . . . . 78 A3
Southmoor Pl OX2 . . . . . . 123 B4
Southmoor Rd OX2 . . . . . 123 A4

Southmoor Way OX14...179 E8
South Moreton Sch
  OX11 ....219 F5
South Newington Rd
  Barford St M OX15 ....32 C6
  Bloxham OX15 ....21 B1
South Parks Ave OX11 ...218 D7
South Park Ct 5 OX4 ....141 F8
South Parks Rd OX1 .....261 C3
South Par OX2 ....123 B7
South Quay OX14 ....179 F4
Southrop CE Prim Sch
  GL7. ....131 A4
Southrop Rd OX15 ....30 B6
South Row OX11. ....235 D7
South Side OX25. ....62 A8
South St
  Banbury OX16 ....16 E7
  Blewbury OX11 ....237 A8
  Caulcott OX25 ....63 B5
  Letcombe Regis OX12 ...214 A1
  Middle Barton OX7 ....60 F8
South Stoke Prim Sch
  RG8. ....239 B4
South Stoke Rd RG8 ...240 B2
South St
  Oxford OX2 ....141 A8
  Reading RG4 ....259 B2
  Watchfield SN6 ....191 D1
South View OX10 ....221 C7
South View Ave RG4 ....259 C2
South View OX17. ....9 D7
South View Pk RG4 ......259 C2
South View Cres OX14 ...145 F7
Southwold 3 OX26 ....65 F4
Southwold CE Prim Sch
  OX26 ....65 E5
Southwood Rd OX29 .....103 C1
Sovereign Cl OX11 ....219 A8
Sovereign Pl OX10 ....221 C7
Spa Cl SN6 ....190 B7
Span Hill RG4 ....260 B7
Sparacarte La OX29 .....108 D8
Sparrow Way OX4 ....142 F1
Sparsey Pl OX2 ....109 B1
Sparsholt St OX12 ....212 F4
Spears The OX5. ....108 B6
Speedwell Croft OX26. ....65 E5
Speedwell St OX1 ....261 B1
Spencer Ave OX5 ....108 B5
Spencer Cres OX4 ....142 B8
Spencer Ct 14 OX16. ....16 D5
Spencers Cl SN7. ....194 D7
Spendlove Ctr The OX7 ...73 B4
Spenlove Cl OX14. ....159 F2
Spenser Cl OX26. ....65 C3
Spey Rd OX13 ....159 C3
Speyside Cl OX18 ....115 D5
Spiceball Country Pk*
  ....16 E7
Spiceball Park Rd OX16 ...16 D6
Spier's La OX27. ....67 F2
Spinage Cl SN7. ....173 A3
Spindleberry Cl OX4 .....142 E2
Spindlers OX5 ....92 F2
Spindleside 1 OX26. ......65 F4
Spinney Bank OX17 ....23 F5
Spinney Cl RG4. ....259 B7
Spinney Field OX4. ....142 E1
Spinneys Cl OX14. ....160 F3
Spinneys The OX7. ....58 F5
Spinney The
  Abingdon OX14 ....159 D1
  East Hendred OX12. .....216 D6
  Launton OX26 ....66 D2
  Lechlade-on-T GL7. ......150 C4
Spitfire Cl
  Benson OX10. ....204 B2
  Bicester OX26 ....66 A3
Spooner Cl OX3 ....124 E3
Sprigs Holly La HP14.....189 B8
Spring Cl OX28 ....118 A7
Spring Copse OX1 ....141 C3
Springdale 6 OX10. ......221 C7
Spring Farm Mews RG8 .239 C1
Springfield Ave OX16 ....16 C3
Springfield Cl
  Shrivenham SN6 ....209 B6
  Watlington OX49 ....186 C1
Springfield Dr OX14. ....179 E8
Springfield Gdns OX5 ...168 C7
Springfield OX17. ....2 E4
Springfield Hollow HP14 .188 E5
Springfield Mews RG4 ...259 B4
Springfield Oval OX3 ....103 F2
Springfield Pk OX28 .....103 F1
Springfield Rd
  Bicester OX27 ....67 F7
  Kidlington OX5. ....108 F8
  Oxford OX2 ....140 C8
  Stokenchurch HP14. ....188 F4
  Wantage OX12. ....214 F4
Springfield Sch
  Witney OX28 ....103 F1
  Witney,Woodstock Gn OX28. ..104 D2
Spring Gdns
  Abingdon OX14 ....179 D7
  Lechlade-on-T GL7. ......150 C4
Spring Hill OX13 ....176 C8
Springhill Rd OX5. ....107 F8
Springhill Rd RG8 ....249 C8
Spring La
  Aston Tirrold OX11 ......237 E8
  Great Bourton OX17 ....9 D5
  Horspath OX33 ....143 C7
  Idbury OX7 ....69 B4

Spring La continued
  Oxford,Headington Quarry
  OX3. ....124 F2
  Oxford OX4 ....142 D2
  Playhatch RG4 ....260 B5
  Watlington OX49 ....186 C1
Spring Meadows Bsns Ctr
  RG10 ....255 F5
Spring Path OX9 ....147 E8
Spring Pl OX7 ....42 E2
Spring Rd OX14. ....179 D7
Spring St OX7 ....42 E3
Springs The OX28 ....118 A7
Spring Terr 2 OX14. ....179 D7
Springwell Hill OX5. .....78 A1
Springwell Ho 8 OX16. ...16 D5
Spring Wlk RG10 ....255 D1
Springwood La RG9 .....253 A2
Spruce Dr OX4 ....65 F5
Spruce Gdns OX4. ....161 E8
Spruce Rd OX4. ....108 E7
Spur The RG10. ....255 E3
Square Firs OX29 ....90 A5
Square The
  2 Oxford OX4. ....142 C4
  5 Abingdon OX14. ......179 F7
  Aston OX18 ....135 E3
  Aynho OX17 ....35 C7
  Brightwell-cum-S OX10 ..202 D2
  Churchill OX7. ....55 E5
  Ducklington OX29 ....118 B4
  Eynsham OX29 ....120 E7
  Great Tew OX7 ....48 D7
  Kings Sutton OX17. ....23 F5
  Long Crendon HP18. .....129 C6
  Longworth OX13 ....156 B3
  Milton-u-W OX7. ....70 B1
  Oxford,Botley OX2. ......122 D1
  Pangbourne RG8 ....256 D6
  Swalcliffe OX15 ....19 F8
Squires Cl OX18 ....116 C3
Squires Ho 5 OX12. .....214 D5
Squires Rd SN6. ....191 D1
Squire's Wlk OX10. ......221 D6
Squitchey La OX2. ....123 A8
Stable Cl
  Finmere MK18 ....39 C7
  Oxford OX1 ....261 A2
Stable Cotts GL56. ....40 C2
Stable Rd OX26. ....65 E3
Stables The GL7. ....158 E3
Staddlestone Cl RG31. ..257 C2
Stadhampton Prim Sch
  OX44 ....163 C2
Stadhampton Rd
  Drayton St L OX10. ......183 B6
  Little Milton OX44 ....163 F5
Stadium Ind Est RG30. ..258 B1
Stadium Way RG30. ......258 B1
Staffordshire Cl RG30. ..257 C1
Stainer Pl OX3. ....123 F4
Stainfield Rd OX3. ....124 B5
Stainswick La SN6 ....209 C4
Stallpits Rd SN6 ....209 A7
Stanbridge Cl OX16. .....16 A5
Standlake CE Prim Sch
  OX29 ....137 D3
Standlake Rd
  Ducklington OX29 ....118 C3
  Hardwick OX29 ....118 E2
  Northmoor OX29 ....138 A2
Standon Ct OX3 ....124 C2
Stanford Dr OX14. ....179 F8
Stanford in the Vale CE Prim
  Sch SN7 ....194 E7
Stanford Rd SN7. ....173 A3
Stanier Pl OX16. ....16 A8
Staniland Ct OX14 ....179 F8
Stanley Cl
  Oxford OX2 ....140 D8
  Yarnton OX5 ....108 B7
Stanley Rd OX4 ....141 F7
Stanmore Cres OX18. ....115 E3
Stansfield Pl OX3. ....124 E1
Stansfield Cl OX3 ....124 F1
Stanton Cl OX18 ....117 E8
Stanton Cotts OX15 .....125 D7
Stanton Harcourt CE Prim
  Sch OX29 ....138 B8
Stanton Harcourt Ind Est
  OX29 ....138 C6
Stanton Harcourt Rd
  South Leigh OX29 ....119 D5
  Witney,Cogges OX28 .....118 C8
  Witney OX29. ....118 D7
Stanton Rd
  Forest Hill OX33 ....125 E4
  Oxford OX2. ....140 E6
Stanville Rd OX2. ....140 B7
Stanway Cl OX3 ....103 D1
Stanway Rd OX3 ....125 A3
Stanwell Cl OX17 ....11 A1
Stanwell Dr OX17 ....11 A1
Stanwell La OX17. ....9 D8
Stanwell Lea OX17. ......11 A2
Stapleton Rd OX3 ....124 C2
Starina Croft OX17. ....9 A1
Star La SN6 ....191 C1
Starnham Rd OX3. ....118 A4
Star Rd RG4 ....259 C2
Starwort Path 4 OX4 ...142 F2
Station App
  Bicester OX26 ....65 F1
  Kidlington OX5. ....92 C2
Station Field Ind Est OX5 .92 C2
Station La OX28 ....118 B6
Station Rd
  Alvescot OX18 ....133 E5

Station Rd continued
  Ardley OX27. ....50 C3
  Ashbury SN6 ....228 A7
  Aynho OX17 ....35 B6
  Bampton OX18 ....134 E6
  Blackthorn OX25 ....82 A4
  Bletchingdon OX5 ....93 A8
  Brize Norton OX18. ......116 C3
  Chinnor OX39 ....168 C6
  Chipping Norton OX7. .....42 D2
  Cholsey OX10. ....220 F1
  Cropredy OX17 ....4 F1
  Culham OX14. ....180 F3
  Didcot OX11. ....200 F1
  Eynsham OX29. ....120 E7
  Faringdon SN7. ....172 F3
  Goring RG8 ....249 C6
  Grove OX12 ....214 E8
  Haddenham HP17 ....130 E5
  Henley-on-T RG9 ....244 E1
  Highworth SN6 ....190 A6
  Hook Norton OX15. ....30 C8
Station Rd Ind Est OX10. 221 C7
Station Rd
  Kingham OX7. ....54 F3
  Launton OX26 ....66 E3
  Lechlade-on-T GL7. ......150 D5
  Lower Heyford OX25. .....62 D6
  Lower Shiplake RG9 .....255 A4
  Marsh Gibbon OX27 ......67 F3
  Pangbourne RG8 ....256 C6
  Shipton-u-W OX7. ....70 E1
  Shrivenham SN6 ....209 A6
  South Leigh OX29 ....119 C5
  Uffington SN7 ....211 E8
  Upton OX11 ....218 C2
  Wallingford OX10 ....221 C8
  Wargrave RG10. ....255 C1
  Wheatley OX33 ....144 B8
Station Yard Ind Est
  Adderbury OX17 ....23 B2
  Chipping Norton OX7. .....42 D2
Station Yd
  Steventon OX13. ....199 A4
  Thame OX9 ....148 A7
Staunton Rd OX3 ....124 B3
Staverton Rd OX2. ....123 B5
Steady's La OX29 ....138 B7
Steeple Cl OX14 ....179 E5
Steepness Hill OX15 ......32 F4
Steep Rise OX3 ....124 C5
Stenton Cl OX14. ....179 E5
Stephen Ct OX4. ....31 B5
Stephen Freeman Com Prim
  Sch OX11 ....200 C2
Stephen Rd OX3 ....124 C3
Stephenson Ho OX1 .....261 B1
Steppingstone La SN6 ...209 A4
Sterling Cl OX12 ....196 D2
Sterling Cl
  Bicester OX26 ....66 A3
  Kidlington OX5. ....108 E8
Sterling Rd OX5 ....108 E8
Sterling Road App OX5 ...92 C1
Stert Rd OX39 ....167 E4
Stert St OX14 ....179 F7
Stevens Cl OX3 ....123 B4
Stevens La RG9. ....252 D8
Stevenson Cl OX26. ....65 C3
Stevenson Dr OX14 ......179 D8
Steventon Rd
  Drayton OX14. ....199 B7
  East Hanney OX12,OX13 .197 E7
Stewart St OX1 ....141 C6
Stile Rd OX3. ....124 D3
Stileway Rd
  Chilton OX11. ....234 F8
  East Hendred OX12. .....216 F3
Stimpsons Cl OX2. ....140 A8
Stirling Cl
  Carterton OX18 ....115 C3
  Reading RG4 ....259 D6
  Wantage OX12. ....214 E5
Stirling Cl OX16 ....115 F6
Stirlings Rd 4 OX12. ....214 D4
Stockey End OX14. ....160 C2
Stockham Pk OX12 ......214 C5
Stockham Prim Sch
  OX12. ....214 C5
Stockham Way OX12 ....214 C5
Stockleys Rd OX3. ....124 A5
Stockmore St OX4. ......141 F8
Stocks La OX13. ....198 F4
Stocks The OX7. ....57 B1
Stocks Tree Cl OX5. .....108 B5
Stockwell HP17. ....188 E5
Stoke Lyne Rd OX27. .....52 D1
Stokenchurch Prim Sch
  HP14 ....188 E5
Stoke Row CE Prim Sch
  RG9 ....241 F4
Stoke Row CE Sch RG9 .241 F4
Stoke Row Rd RG9. ......252 E8
Stokes View RG8. ....256 C5
Stonebridge Rd OX13 ...198 F5
Stoneburge Cres OX26. ..65 E3
Stonebury Cl OX12. .....214 E5
Stonecl Cl OX29. ....122 B1
Stonecrop Leyes OX4. ....65 E5
Stone Ct
  1 Banbury OX16 ....16 D5
  Great Rollright OX7. ....29 A3
Stonefield Cl SN6 ....209 C6
Stonefield Dr SN6 ....190 A4
Stonegables OX18 ....118 A6
Stone Hill OX15. ....21 D4

Stonehill La
  Abingdon OX14 ....179 D3
  Kingston Bagpuize OX13. .176 D8
Stonehill Wlk OX14 .....179 D4
Stone House Cl OX13 ...156 E1
Stoneleigh Cl OX7. ....57 B1
Stoneleigh Dr OX18. .....115 D5
Stone Mdw OX2 ....123 A5
Stone Quarry La OX4 ....142 A4
Stonesfield La OX7 ....73 C2
Stonesfield Rd OX29 ......90 A5
Stonesfield Riding OX29 ..74 D2
Stonesfield Sch OX29 .....89 C7
Stone St
  Oxford OX4 ....142 A8
  Reading RG30 ....258 B1
Stoney La OX9,OX49 .....185 E8
Stonhouse Cres OX14 ...160 E2
Stonor Cl OX11 ....200 E1
Stonor Gn OX49 ....186 B1
Stonor Ho* RG9. ....226 A7
Stonor Pl OX3 ....124 C2
Stort Cl OX11. ....200 F3
Stoutsfield Cl OX5. ......108 A5
Stow Ave OX28 ....117 D8
Stowford Ct OX3. ....124 F5
Stowford Rd OX3. ....124 F4
Stowhill OX12 ....213 C3
Stowood Cl OX3. ....124 E4
Stow Rd
  Bledington OX7. ....54 C2
  Chipping Norton OX7. .....69 B2
Strachay Cl RG8 ....256 C2
Strafford Way OX9 ......148 A8
Strafford La OX20 ....76 B2
Strafford Rd
  Drayton OX15. ....15 E8
  Shenington OX15. ....6 F7
Strafford St OX4. ....141 F7
Strathmore Cl OX18. ....115 D5
Stratton Audley Manor
  ....52 D1
Stratton Audley Rd
  Fringford OX27. ....52 D5
  Stoke Lyne OX27. ....51 B5
Stratton Way OX14. .....179 F7
Strawberry Hill OX15. ....21 E5
Strawberry Path OX4 ...142 F2
Strawberry Terr OX15. ...21 E5
Stream Rd OX11 ....218 C2
Streatley CE Sch RG8. ..248 F6
Streatley Hill RG8. ....248 F6
Streatley Lodge 6 OX1. .141 C7
Street The
  Crowmarsh Gifford OX10 .221 F7
  Ipsden OX10. ....240 C7
  Moulsford OX10. ....239 A6
  North Stoke OX10 ....221 E1
  South Stoke RG8 ....239 B2
  Stoke Lyne OX27. ....51 B5
  Tidmarsh RG8 ....256 D2
Stroud Cl OX16 ....16 E8
Stuart Cl RG4. ....259 B5
Stuart Way OX9 ....130 A1
Stubble Cl OX2 ....140 A8
Stubbs Ave OX3 ....142 E7
Stuchfield Cl OX25. ....79 F4
Studdridge Ct HP14. ....188 C6
Stud Farm Cl OX17. ....9 B7
Sturges Cl OX3 ....124 D5
Sturt Cl OX7. ....73 C2
Sturt Rd OX7. ....73 C3
Styles Cl OX27. ....67 E2
Styles The OX11 ....217 D7
Sudbury Ct SN7 ....173 A4
Sudbury La OX13 ....156 C3
Suffolk Cl OX27. ....67 F2
Suffolk Ho OX10 ....204 E4
Suffolk Way OX14. ......179 D6
Sugarswell La OX15. ....6 B6
Sugworth Cres OX14. ...160 E6
Sugworth La OX14. ......160 D6
Sulham La RG8 ....256 E3
Summerfield OX1. ....141 D6
Summerfield OX2. ....123 B7
Summerfield Rise RG8. .249 D7
Summer Fields OX15. ...160 B3
Summerhill Rd OX2. .....123 B7
Summer Ley OX15. ....32 F6
Summers Cl OX17 ....23 A5
Summerside OX7. ....174 F8
Summerside SN7 ....174 E8
Summerton Pl OX7. ......42 F3
Summertown Ct OX2. ...123 A7
Summertown La OX29 ..197 B6
Summertown Ho OX2. ..123 A8
Sunderland Dr OX26. .....66 A4
Sunderland Ave OX2 ....109 A1
Sunningwell CE Prim Sch
  OX13 ....159 C6
Sunningwell Rd
  Oxford OX1 ....141 D6
  Sunningwell OX13 ....159 E4
Sunny Bank OX7. ....29 A3
Sunnymeade Ct 2 OX2. .109 B1
Sunny Rise OX3. ....143 D6
Sunnyside
  Benson OX10. ....203 F5
  Oxford OX4 ....142 D6

Sunnyside continued
  Wheatley OX33 ....144 C8
Sun Rising Hill OX15. ......6 C8
Surley Row RG4 ....259 A5
Sussex Dr OX16. ....15 F8
Sutherland Beck OX11. .200 E3
Sutton Cl OX14 ....179 F7
Sutton Courtenay La
  OX14 ....199 F5
Sutton La OX29 ....120 B1
Sutton Rd
  Milton OX14. ....199 E6
  Oxford OX3 ....124 B5
Sutton Wick La OX14 ...179 C2
Suzan Cres OX12 ....214 E5
Swain Ct OX28. ....118 A6
Swalcliffe Barn* OX15. ...19 F8
Swalcliffe Lea OX15. ......14 B1
Swalcliffe Park Sch OX15 .19 F8
Swale Dr OX14. ....200 A2
Swale Dr OX14 ....201 A2
Swallow Cl
  15 Sandford-on-T OX4 ...142 F1
  Bicester OX26 ....81 A8
Swan Cl
  Blackthorn OX25 ....82 A3
  Grove OX12 ....196 D1
  Lechlade-on-T GL7. ......150 C4
  Middleton Cheney OX17 ..17 F8
Swan Close Rd OX16. ....16 D5
Swan Ct
  Oxford OX1 ....261 A2
  Witney OX28 ....118 A8
Swan Gdns OX9 ....166 B8
Swanhall La OX29. ......104 B5
Swan Ind Est OX16. ....16 D5
Swan La
  Burford OX18. ....100 E5
  Faringdon SN7. ....172 F4
  Great Bourton OX17 ....9 D8
  Long Hanborough OX29 ..90 B1
Swanlands Ho OX29 .....120 E7
Swan Lane OX18 ....100 E5
Swansea Rd RG1 ....259 A1
Swansea Terr RG31 .....257 D1
Swansfield
  Bicester OX26 ....81 A7
  Lechlade-on-T GL7. ......150 D6
Swan St OX29 ....120 E7
Swanston Field RG8 .....256 D7
Swan St OX3 ....123 A1
Swan Wlk OX9 ....147 F8
Swarbourne Cl OX11. ...200 F2
Sweeps La OX18 ....100 E5
Sweet Briar OX13 ....178 C6
Sweet Green Cl OX3. ....125 B4
Sweetmans Rd OX2 .....140 E7
Swerford Rd OX15. ....30 B5
Swift Cl
  19 Sandford-on-T OX4 ...142 F1
  Bicester OX26 ....65 C5
  Oxford OX4 ....143 A1
Swift Way OX10. ....204 D3
Swinbourne Rd OX4 ....142 B2
Swinbrook Cl RG31 .....257 D3
Swinbrook Rd OX28 ....118 B7
Swinbrook Rd
  Carterton OX18 ....115 D5
  Shipton-u-W OX7. ....85 E6
Swinburne Rd
  Abingdon OX14 ....180 A8
  Oxford OX4 ....141 F6
Swindon Rd SN6. ....190 A5
Swindon St SN6 ....190 A5
Swingburn Pl OX28 .....118 A8
Swin La OX18. ....101 E5
Swinnerton Ho RG9. ....244 E1
Swinstead Ct OX44 .....184 D6
Sworford La OX33 ....144 F5
Sycamore Cl
  Abingdon OX13 ....159 C1
  Long Crendon HP18. .....129 C6
  Sibford Gower OX15 ......19 A8
  Watlington OX49 ....186 A2
  Witney OX28 ....104 C2
Sycamore Cres OX14. ...160 E7
Sycamore Ct RG8. ....256 C6
Sycamore Dr
  Banbury OX16 ....16 D2
  Carterton OX18 ....115 D3
  Thame OX9 ....147 D8
Sycamore Gdns OX26 ....65 F4
Sycamore Pl OX18 ......114 D7
Sycamore Rd
  Ambrosden OX25. ....81 C4
  Launton OX26 ....66 D2
  Oxford OX2 ....140 C8
Sycamores The OX5. ....124 E4
Sycamore Terr OX15 .....21 D4
Sycamore Wlk OX12 ....196 D1
Sydenham Cl OX17. ....23 B4
Sydenham Gr OX39 .....167 E8
Sylvester Cl OX12 ....100 E5
Sympson Cl 5 OX14 ....179 E6
Synderford Cl OX11. ....201 A2
Syringa Wlk OX16. ....9 B1

Tackley CE Prim Sch OX5 .77 C6
Tackley Pl OX2 ....123 B4
Tackley Sta OX5. ....77 C6
Tacks La HP17. ....130 F6
Tadmarton Park OX15. ...21 A6

Tadmarton Rd OX15...........21 B5
Taggs Gate OX3 ....124 F5
Tait Dr OX25..............63 B7
Talbot Cl
  Banbury OX16 ....15 F8
  Reading RG4 ....259 D2
Talbot Fields OX18......135 A3
Talbot Rd OX2 ....109 A2
Talbot Way RG31.......257 C3
Talisman Bsns Ctr The
  OX26 ....80 F8
Talisman Rd OX26 ....80 F8
Tamar Cres OX26 ....65 B3
Tamarisk Gdns OX26....65 E5
Tamar Way OX14.......201 A2
Tamesis Pl RG4.........259 B1
Tangmere Ave OX18..115 E4
Tangmere Cl OX26 ......66 B4
Tanners Ct OX7 ....73 B3
Tanners La
  Adderbury OX17 ....22 F3
  Burford OX18...........100 D4
  Eynsham OX29.........120 F7
  Tokers Green RG4.....258 F8
Tannery Cl OX18.......100 E5
Tannery Yd OX18.......100 F5
Taphouse Ave OX28 ..104 B2
Tarragon Dr OX4.......142 F1
Tarrant Ave OX28 .....104 D2
Tarret Burn OX11 .....200 F2
Taston Rd OX7 ....73 A8
Tatham Rd OX14.......159 F1
Tatlings Rd OX13 .....198 F5
Taverner Pl OX3 ....123 F4
Tavistock Ave OX11 ..218 D7
Tavy Cl OX11...........200 F3
Tawney St OX4 ....142 A8
Tay Gdns OX26........65 C3
Taylor Cl OX26.........65 E4
Taylor Inst Main Liby
  OX1 ....261 B3
Tays Gateway OX15....33 F4
Tchure The OX15 ......33 F4
Teal Cl
  Banbury OX16...........16 E3
  Grove OX12...........196 D1
  Sandford-on-T OX4 ..142 F1
Teale Cl OX25...........96 E7
Teasel Way OX18......115 F5
Teescroft OX14.........201 A3
Telford Cres RG5......260 F1
Telford Rd OX26........66 B3
Templar Ho OX4.......142 C5
Templar Rd OX2.......109 B1
Templars Dr OX16 ....144 A8
Templars Sq 5 OX4 ..142 C4
Temple Cloisters OX4..142 D6
Temple Mill Rd OX15...19 A8
Temple Rd OX4.......142 C6
Temple St
  Brill HP18 ....98 B1
  Oxford OX4 ....141 E8
Templeton Coll OX1...141 D3
Templeton Ho RG9....254 F7
Tenby Ave RG4........259 D5
Tenlands OX17..........17 F8
Tennis The OX29 .....107 D2
Tennyson Cl OX16 .....16 A3
Tennyson Dr OX14 ..179 C5
Tenpenny OX10 ......202 D8
Tenth St OX11.........217 B3
Tern Wlk OX4..........142 E1
Terrace The OX7........70 A1
Terrett Ave OX3........125 B4
Terrington Cl OX14 ..160 A2
Tessa Rd RG1.........258 F1
Tetbury Dr OX28......103 D1
Tetsworth Prim Sch OX9.166 B8
Tewer The OX8..........89 C7
Tew La OX20............9 F5
TF Smith Bldgs OX28 ..118 C8
Thackley End OX2 ....123 B5
Thame La
  Clifton Hampden OX14 ..181 B5
  Culham OX14...........180 D4
Thame Park Rd OX9...147 F4
Thame Pk Bsns Ctr OX9. 148 A7
Thame Rd
  Blackthorn OX25........82 A3
  Chinnor OX39 ....168 B8
  Great Haseley OX44..164 E8
  Great Milton OX44....145 C2
  Haddenham HP17......130 D5
  Little Milton OX44 ....146 A7
  Long Crendon HP18,OX9.129 D4
  Piddington OX25,HP18 ..97 D6
  Sydenham OX39......148 F1
  Towersey OX9........148 E7
  Warborough OX10....203 B8
Thames Ave
  Bicester OX26..........65 B3
  Pangbourne RG8......256 D6
  Reading RG1..........259 A1
Thames Bank RG8....249 B7
Thames Ct
  4 Didcot OX11........219 A8
  Abingdon OX14......180 A7
  Eynsham OX29........120 E7
  Goring RG8............249 B6
  Oxford OX1............124 A2
Thames Dr RG10......260 F7
Thames Gdns OX7....73 B4
Thames Ho RG9......244 E3
Thameside RG9......244 E2

Thameside Mansion
  OX10 ....221 E8
Thameside Park Cvn Pk
  OX29 ....138 E5
Thameside Prim Sch
  Abingdon OX14......179 F6
  Reading RG4..........259 B2
Thameside Reach OX10. 239 A4
Thames Mead OX10 ..221 E7
Thames Pk OX10......221 E7
Thames Rd
  Goring RG8............249 B6
  Harwell OX11........217 A3
Thames Reach RG8 ..257 D5
Thames Side 6 RG1 ..259 A1
Thames Side Prom RG4. 259 A2
Thames St
  Abingdon OX14......179 F6
  Charlbury OX7........73 B4
  Eynsham OX29........120 E7
  Lechlade-on-T GL7....150 C3
  Oxford OX1............261 B1
  Sonning RG4..........260 D4
  Wallingford OX10....221 D7
Thames Valley Bsns Pk
  RG8 ....260 A1
Thames View OX14..180 A7
Thames View Ind Pk
  OX14 ....180 A7
Thames View Rd OX4..141 F3
Thatchers Cl OX15......13 A5
Thelwell Ho OX4......142 B7
Thenford Rd OX17 ....11 D1
Theobald Dr RG31 ..257 D4
Thesiger Rd OX4......179 F8
Thetford Mews RG4..259 D6
Third Acre Rise OX2..140 B8
Third St
  Croughton NN13 ......36 E6
  Harwell OX11........217 B2
Thirlmere Ave RG30..257 F1
Thirteenth St OX11 ..217 A2
Thistlecroft Cl OX14 ..160 B2
Thistle Down OX4 ....161 E8
Thistledown RG31 ....257 C1
Thistle Dr OX4........143 A2
Thomas Mews OX4 ..123 F1
Thomas Reade Prim Sch
  OX14 ....180 B8
Thompson Dr OX27 ....65 F7
Thomson Ave OX11 ..217 B3
Thomson Terr OX4 ..142 A2
Thornbury Rd OX29..120 D7
Thornbury Rise OX26. 15 F5
Thorncliffe Rd OX2 ..123 B6
Thorne
  Henley-on-T RG9.....254 B7
  Kidlington OX5........92 C1
Thorney Leys Ind Pk
  OX28 ....117 F6
Thorney Leys OX28 ..117 E6
Thornhill OX17........10 F4
Thornhill Cl OX12....214 D5
Thornhill Wlk OX14 ..159 E1
Thorningdown OX11 ..235 D8
Thorpe Cl OX16 ......16 F6
Thorpe Dr OX16......16 F6
Thorpe La OX16......16 F6
Thorpe Mead OX16..16 F5
Thorpe Pl OX16......16 F5
Thorpe Rd
  Chacombe OX17......10 E4
  Wardington OX17......10 F8
Thorpes Field OX18..133 C5
Thorpe St OX11........219 E1
Thorpe Way OX16......16 F5
Three Corners Rd OX4.143 A2
Three Fields Rd OX3..147 A8
Three Gables La RG8.249 A7
Three Pigeons OX12..214 E4
Three Poplar Mobile Home
  Pk OX14................201 C7
Threshers Ct OX18.....115 F5
Thrift Cl OX7..........142 F2
Thrupp La OX14......201 A6
Thrupp Turn SN7 ....172 F8
Thurne View OX11 ..201 A1
Thurston Cl 4 OX14..179 E6
Tichborne OX4........194 E7
Ticknell Piece Rd OX7. 73 C4
Tidmarsh La
  Oxford OX1............261 A2
  Tidmarsh RG8........256 B2
Tidmarsh Rd RG8....256 C4
Tidmarsh St RG30..258 B1
Tidmore La RG8......240 F1
Tidworth Row OX18..152 E8
Tigel Mews RG30......257 C1
Tilbury Cl RG4........259 C3
Tilbury La OX2........122 C1
Tilebarn Cl RG9......244 C1
Tilebarn La RG9......254 B8
Tilehouse Cl OX3......124 E3
Tilehurst Sta RG31..257 E3
Tilgarsley Rd OX29..120 D8
Tilling Cl RG31........257 B2
Tilsley Rd OX7........42 D1
Timbers La RG9......223 D2
Timber Way OX39....168 C6
Timber Yard Cotts OX7.74 C8
Timms Rd OX16........16 B8
Timothy Way 2 OX4..142 F2
Timsbury Ct OX13....199 A4
Tinkerbush La OX12..214 D6
Tinkers La OX7..........3 F3
Tirrold Way OX12....214 F5
Titchener Cl OX26....65 D4
Tite La OX15............30 B7

Tithe Ct OX16 ....16 A5
Tithe La OX15 ....34 D5
Tithings The OX15 ....19 F8
Titup Hall Dr OX3....124 E1
Tiverton Cl RG5 ....260 E1
Tokers Green La RG4. 258 D7
Tollbrook Cnr OX5 ....78 D1
Tollgate Ho 4 OX5 ..239 A4
Tollgate Rd OX13 ....180 B3
Tollington Ct SN7 ..172 E1
Tolsey Mus* OX18 ..100 E5
Tom Brown's School Mus*
  SN7 ....211 C7
Tomkin's Almshouses 4
  OX14 ....179 E7
Tompkins La OX27 ....67 E2
Toot Hill Butts OX3..124 F3
Top Station Rd OX11..24 A8
Top Station Road Ind Est
  NN13 ....24 A8
Torridge Dr OX14 ....201 A2
Tothill OX7..............70 D1
Tower Cl
  Abingdon OX14 ......179 D6
  Marcham OX13 ......178 D6
  Reading RG4..........259 C8
Tower Cres OX1......261 B2
Tower Ct OX26........115 E2
Tower Ctr The OX18..115 E4
Tower Est OX44......185 A4
Tower Gdns OX1......200 C2
Tower Hill Com Prim Sch
  OX28 ....104 A1
Tower Hill OX28 ......117 F8
Tower Rd OX10......182 D6
Towersey Dr OX9 ....148 B7
Towersey Rd
  Thame OX9............148 B8
  Thame OX9............148 C8
Tower View SN7 ....172 F2
Town Cl
  Abingdon OX14 ......179 D6
  Sutton Courtenay OX14.200 A7
Town End Rd
  Bledlow Ridge HP14 ..189 C8
  Faringdon SN7......172 F2
Town Farm Cl
  Lewknor OX49........187 B8
  Thame OX9............147 D8
Town Furlong
  Appleton OX13........158 A8
  Bodicote OX15........22 D8
  Oxford OX2............140 B6
Town Furze OX4......142 D7
Town Gn The OX5......92 F1
Town Hill OX4..........2 A3
Townlands Com Hospl
  RG9 ....244 D2
Town Pond La OX13.. 176 D8
Townsend
  Abingdon OX14 ......179 F5
  Harwell,Chilton OX11 ..16 B6
  Barford St M OX15 ..32 F5
Towns End OX29......104 A6
Townsend La
  Marsh Gibbon OX27 ..67 E2
  Middleton Cheney OX17.11 F6
  Oxford OX27..........67 E2
Townsend Rd
  Aldworth RG8........247 E3
  Shrivenham SN6 ....209 A6
  Streatley RG8........249 A7
Townsend Sq OX4 ..141 F6
Townside OX17........133 A8
Town Well Rd OX7 ..49 E7
Toy La OX7............42 C2
Toynbee Cl OX1......140 D8
Trafford Rd
  Oxford OX3............124 C3
  Reading RG1..........258 E1
Traitor's Ford La OX15. 18 D4
Tramhill HP18..........98 B2
Tramway Ind Est The
  OX16 ....16 E5
Tramway Rd OX16....16 E5
Treadwells SN7......194 E7
Treble House Terr OX11.237 A8
Tredegar Rd RG4....259 A6
Tree Close Bay OX4..142 A4
Treeground Pl OX5..108 E8
Tree La OX4............142 A4
Trefoil Dr OX26........22 E8
Trefoil Pl OX4..........143 A2
Trefoil Way OX18....115 F5
Treforgan RG4........258 F5
Trelawney Dr RG31..257 B1
Trenchard Ave OX14. 199 C3
Trenchard Circ OX25..49 D1
Trenchard Pl OX14 ..159 E1
Trenchard Rd OX14..201 A2
Trent Cres OX26......65 B3
Trenthams Ct RG8 ..257 B5
Trent Rd OX11........201 A2
Trevor Pl OX4..........142 B5
Trill Mill Ct OX1......261 B1
Trinder Rd OX12......214 E4
Tring Rd RG31........257 C2
Trinity CE Prim Sch RG9. 244 D1
Trinity Cl
  Abingdon OX14 ......160 B2
  Banbury OX16........15 E7
  Bicester OX26........65 F3
Trinity Coll OX1......261 B3
Trinity Ct OX16......124 F2
Trinity St OX1........261 B1

Trinity Way OX17 ....23 D3
Tristram Rd OX29 ....118 B4
Troika Cl OX16........9 A1
Trot's La OX7..........85 D7
Trout Hollow HP27 ..169 E8
Troy Cl OX3............142 E7
Troy La OX5............77 F3
Truelocks Way OX12..214 F6
Trumper Gr OX27 ....65 F7
Trust Cnr RG9........254 E8
Tubb Cl OX26..........65 C2
Tubbs La OX15......214 D8
Tubbs Cl OX26........80 A7
Tubbs Yd OX26........80 A7
Tucker Rd OX4......142 E3
Tuckers La SN4......227 A3
Tuckers Rd SN7......173 A3
Tuck's La OX13......156 B4
Tudor Cl
  8 Wallingford OX10..221 C7
  Banbury OX16........16 D2
  Oxford OX4............141 F4
Tudor Ct OX4........140 A8
Tudor Hall Sch OX16..22 A8
Tudor Wlk OX11 ....217 B7
Tuer The
  Chadlington OX7......57 A2
  Eynsham OX29......120 E7
Tullis Cl OX14........199 F7
Tulwick Ct OX12......214 D7
Tulwick La OX12......197 A2
Tumbledown Hill OX2. 139 D6
Tumbling Bay Ct OX2.123 A1
Tuns La RG9............244 E2
Turberville Cl OX14..179 E6
Turley La OX29......104 A8
Turl St OX1............261 B2
Turnagain La OX1....179 F6
Turn Again La OX1..261 B1
Turnberry Cl OX26....66 B4
Turner Cl OX14......142 D6
Turner Ct OX5........108 F7
Turner Dr OX26......142 D6
Turners Cl OX14......160 F2
Turner's Gn OX49....205 D7
Turner's Green La
  Britwell Salome OX49..205 D8
  Cuxham OX49........185 C2
Turnfields OX18......128 A3
Turnpike Rd
  Bicester OX27........66 A6
  Highworth SN6......190 A6
  Oxford OX2............140 B6
Turnstone Gr OX26 ..81 A8
Turret Ho OX3........124 C3
Turweston Manor NN13. 24 C8
Tuscan Ct RG30......257 E1
Tweed Cres OX26 ....65 B3
Tweed Dr OX11......200 F4
Twelve Acre Dr OX14.160 C2
Twentieth St OX11 ..217 A3
Twin Oaks RG4......259 B6
Two Rivers Ind Est OX28.118 B6
Two Tree Hill RG9....254 B8
Twyford Ave OX17....23 A6
Twyford Gdns OX17..23 A6
Twyford Gr OX17......23 A6
Twyford Mill Ind Est
  OX17 ....23 A2
Twyford Rd OX17 ....23 C7
Tyburn Glen OX11....200 F2
Ty-Craig OX26........65 F2
Tyler Cl RG4..........258 E5
Tylorstown RG4......258 F5
Tymawr RG4..........258 F5
Tyndale Pl OX33......144 C8
Tyndale Rd OX4......141 E8
Tyne Ave OX11......200 F2
Tyne Rd OX13........159 C2
Tyne Sq 8 OX11......219 A8
Tyrell Cl SN7..........194 D8
Tyrrells Cl OX11......217 D6
Tyrrell's Way OX14..179 E6
Tyte End OX7..........29 B3
Tythings The OX17....10 F2

U

Uffington Castle* SN7....211 B1
Uffington CE Prim Sch
  SN7 ....211 C7
Uffington Gorse Nature
  Reserve* SN7........211 E8
Uffington Trad Est SN7. 193 E1
Uffington White Horse*
  SN7 ....211 D1
Ulfgar Rd OX2........122 F8
Ullswater Dr RG31..257 D3
Ulster Cl RG4........259 D5
Underhill Cir OX3....124 F3
Underhill OX10......239 A4
Unicorn St OX15......6 B5
Union Sq OX10........75 F4
Union St
  Banbury OX16........16 B6
  Oxford OX4............141 E8
  Woodstock OX20....117 B6
Union Way OX28....117 F8
Unity Cl RG4..........259 B5
Unity Ct OX4..........259 B5
Univ Coll Oxford (Annexe)
  OX2 ....123 A3
University Coll OX1..261 C2
Univ Of Oxford Mathematical
  Inst OX1................261 B3
Untons Pl SN7........173 A3

Upavon Way OX18 ....115 C3
Upland Park Rd OX2..123 A8
Upland Rise OX17......9 D5
Uplands Rd RG4......258 E5
Upper Barr 3 OX4 ..142 C4
Upper Brook Hill OX20.91 B6
Upper Campsfield Rd
  OX20 ....91 E5
Upper Common La SN7.211 D7
Upper Crale SN7......194 D8
Upper Cres OX29 ....102 E2
Upper Cross La OX11.218 F5
Upper End
  Fulbrook OX18........100 F7
  Shipton-u-W OX7......85 D6
Upper Fisher Row OX1..261 A2
Upper Gn SN7........194 E8
Upper High St OX7 ..147 F8
Upper Icknield Way
  HP27 ....169 E7
Upper Rd OX1........141 E2
Upper Red Cross Rd
  RG8 ....249 C6
Upper Rissington Bsns Pk
  GL54 ....68 B3
Upper Warren Ave RG4.258 D3
Upperway Furlong OX14.201 B2
Upper Windsor St OX16.16 D4
Upper Woodcote Rd
  RG4 ....258 D4
Uppingham Dr RG5..260 F1
Uppingham Gdns RG4..259 D6
Upthorpe Dr OX12..214 E6
Upton Cl
  Abingdon OX14 ......160 A1
  Henley-on-T RG9 ....244 E1
  Oxford OX4............142 C2
Upton Ct OX16........16 C5
Upton House* OX15 ..6 D8
Upway Rd OX3......124 B5
Upwood Dr OX18 ....115 E4
Urquhart La OX10....241 A7
Ushercombe View OX15.80 B8
Usher Dr OX16........8 F1
Usk Way OX14........201 B3
Uxmore Rd RG8......241 E4

V

Vale Ave OX12........196 E1
Vale Cres RG30......257 E1
Vale & Downland Mus*
  OX12 ....214 D4
Valence Cres OX28..103 E1
Valentia Rd OX3......124 C2
Valentia Rd RG4......124 C2
Valentine Cres RG4. 259 C4
Vale Rd
  Harwell OX11........217 B3
  Witney OX28..........117 E8
Valetta Way OX10..204 D3
Valley Cl
  Brackley NN13..........24 A8
  Goring RG8............249 C6
  Reading RG4..........259 A4
Valley Cotts RG9....243 F8
Valley Cres NN13 ....24 A8
Valley Rd
  Banbury OX16........16 A4
  Brackley NN13..........39 D6
  Finmere MK18..........39 D6
  Henley-on-T RG9....254 B8
  Horspath OX33......143 E6
Valley Rise SN6......194 E8
Valley View
  Great Bourton OX17 ..9 D8
  Lower Heyford OX25 ..62 E6
Vanalloys Bsns Pk RG9. 242 A4
Vanbrugh Cl OX20....91 A7
Van-Dieman's Rd OX4.142 C3
Van Dieman's Rd OX9.147 F7
Van Diemans SN7....194 D8
Van Diemens OX39 ..168 C7
Vane Rd OX9..........148 B8
Vastern Rd RG1......259 A1
Vauxhall Way OX11..200 D3
Venables Cl OX2......261 A4
Venetia Cl OX4......259 C7
Venneit Cl OX1......123 A2
Venners Water OX11..261 A4
Ventfield Cl OX33....112 A5
Ventnor Rd RG31....257 D1
Venwell Cl OX7........58 F5
Verbena Way 2 RG4. 142 E1
Verinia Ct OX20........91 C6
Verlam Gr OX14......201 B2
Vermont Dr OX20 ....91 A7
Vernon Ave OX2......140 E6
Vernon Ho OX7........42 C2
Vervain Cl OX26......65 C5
Vestry Cl OX14......196 D2
Vetch Pl OX4..........142 F2
Vicarage Cl
  Aston OX18............135 D2
  Chalgrove OX44......184 D7
  Grove OX12............196 E1
  Oxford OX1............142 B2
Vicarage Ct
  5 Banbury OX16......16 D5
  Oxford OX4............141 E2
Vicarage Flats OX17....4 F2
Vicarage Gdns OX17....4 F2
Vicarage La
  Highworth SN6......190 A6

Vicarage La *continued*
Long Compton CV36 . . . . 27 F6
Oxford OX1 . . . . 141 C6
Piddington OX25 . . . . 97 E6
Shrivenham SN6 . . . . 209 C6
Vicarage Rd
Didcot OX11. . . . . 218 F8
Henley-on-T RG9 . . . . 254 E8
Kidlington OX5. . . . . 92 F1
Oxford OX1 . . . . 141 D6
Steventon OX13. . . . . 198 E4
Vicarage Wood Way
RG31 . . . . 257 B1
Vicars Row 2 OX12. . . . . 214 D4
Vickers Rd GL54 . . . . 68 B5
Vicks Cl OX18. . . . . 100 E5
Victoria Cotts OX18 . . . . . . 134 E3
Victoria Ct
Bicester OX26 . . . . 65 F1
Henley-on-T RG9 . . . . 244 E1
Oxford,Headington OX3. . . . 124 B2
Oxford OX1 . . . . 261 B2
Victoria Gate OX2. . . . . 123 B8
Victoria Hospl OX9 . . . . . 148 A8
Victoria Mead OX9. . . . . . 148 A7
Victoria Pl
Banbury OX16 . . . . 16 E6
Chipping Norton OX7. . . . . . . 42 E3
Victoria Rd
Abingdon OX14 . . . . 179 D7
Bicester OX26 . . . . 65 F2
Oxford OX2 . . . . 123 B8
Reading RG4 . . . . 259 A3
Reading,Tilehurst RG31. . . 257 D1
Wargrave RG10. . . . . 255 E2
Victoria Terr OX15 . . . . 33 F4
Victor St OX2. . . . . 261 A3
Viking Dr OX11 . . . . 219 A7
Viking Terr OX10. . . . . 204 D3
Village Farm Ct OX25 . . . . . 79 A2
Village Rd OX17 . . . . 3 A4
Villeboys Cl OX14. . . . . . . 180 C8
Villiers Ct OX4. . . . . 142 B4
Villiers La OX4. . . . . 142 B4
Villiers Rd OX26 . . . . 65 D2
Vine Cotts
5 Bicester OX26 . . . . 65 E1
Cuddesdon OX44. . . . . 144 B2
Viner Cl OX28 . . . . 104 C2
Vinery The RG10. . . . . 255 D2
Vines The 2 OX14 . . . . . . 179 F7
Vine The HP18. . . . . 128 D3
Vineyard OX14. . . . . 179 F7
Vineyard Cl OX16 . . . . 16 C7
Vinters Ho RG31 . . . . 257 D1
Violet Way OX4 . . . . 161 E8
Virginia Gdns HP14 . . . . . . 189 F8
Virginia Way OX14 . . . . . . 179 D4
Viscount Ind Est
Bampton OX18. . . . . 134 D8
Brize Norton OX18. . . . . . . 116 D1
Vivienne Ct OX3 . . . . 124 D1
Volunteer Way SN7 . . . . . 173 A2
Vorda Rd SN6 . . . . 190 A7

W

Wadard's Mdw OX28. . . . 118 D8
Wadham Cl OX26 . . . . 65 F3
Wadham Coll OX1 . . . . . . 261 C3
Waine Rush View OX28. . . 118 B8
Wainwrights HP18 . . . . 129 D6
Waites Cl OX18 . . . . 135 E2
Wales St OX17. . . . . 23 F5
Waleys Pl 3 RG4 . . . . 259 C2
Walford Rd OX15 . . . . 19 B7
Walker Cl RG8. . . . . 240 E1
Walker's Cl OX18 . . . . 101 F3
Walkers Cl OX29 . . . . 106 B6
Walkers Dr OX9. . . . . 148 B7
Walker's Ht OX7 . . . . 88 C5
Walk The OX5 . . . . 93 F1
Wallace Cl OX14. . . . . 179 E5
Wallbrook Ct OX2. . . . . . . 122 D1
Walled Gdns OX14 . . . . 160 E3
Walled Gdns The OX26 . . . . 65 E2
Walled Gdn The RG10 . . . 255 D2
Waller Ct RG4 . . . . 259 B2
Waller Dr OX16 . . . . 16 A3
Wallingford Com Hospl
OX10 . . . . 221 C6
Wallingford Mus★ OX10. 221 D8
Wallingford Rd
Cholsey OX10 . . . . 221 B3
Crowmarsh Gifford OX10 . . 221 F2
Goring RG8 . . . . 249 C8
North Moreton OX11. . . . . . 202 A1
South Stoke OX10,RG8 . . . 239 C5
Streatley RG8 . . . . 249 A7
Warborough OX10. . . . . 203 B5
Wallingford Sch OX10. . . 221 D8
Wallingford St OX12 . . . . 214 E4
Walls The SN7 . . . . 194 E7
Wally Cnr OX10. . . . . 182 E4
Walmer Rd RG5. . . . . 260 F1
Walnut Cl
Bicester OX26 . . . . 65 F5
Deddington OX15. . . . . 34 E4
Long Crendon HP18. . . . . . . 129 C7
Sonning Common RG4 . . . . 252 E5
Witney OX28 . . . . 117 F8
Wootton OX20 . . . . 75 F4
Walnut Ct SN7. . . . . 172 F3
Walnut Gdns OX17. . . . . 1 D1
Walnut Rise OX25. . . . . 48 F6
Walnut Row OX18. . . . . . . 100 E6
Walnut Tree Ct RG8 . . . . . 249 C6
Walnut Trees Hill SN6 . . . . 228 B7
Walpole Cl 7 OX26. . . . . . . 65 C4
Walsingham Cl OX15. . . . . . . 21 C4
Walter Bigg Way OX10 . . 221 C8
Walterbush Rd OX7 . . . . 42 E1
Walter's Row OX4 . . . . 123 F1
Waltham Ct RG8 . . . . 249 C8
Waltham Gdns OX16 . . . . . . 17 A6
Walton Ave
Adderbury OX17 . . . . 23 B5
Henley-on-T RG9 . . . . 254 E8
Walton Cl OX15. . . . . 22 E8
Walton Cres OX1 . . . . 261 A3
Walton La OX1 . . . . 261 A3
Walton Manor Ct OX2. . . 261 A4
Walton St OX1,OX2. . . . . . 261 A3
Walton Well Rd OX2 . . . . 123 A3
Wanbourne La RG9 . . . . . 224 D2
Wandhope Way RG31 . . . . 257 C2
Wandle Beck OX11. . . . . . . 200 F3
Wansbeck Dr OX26 . . . . 65 B3
Wansbeck Wood OX14 . . 201 A3
Wantage CE Inf Sch
OX12 . . . . 214 D4
Wantage CE Prim Sch
OX12 . . . . 214 D3
Wantage Hospl OX12. . . . . 214 E5
Wantage Rd
Didcot OX11. . . . . 218 C8
Harwell OX11 . . . . 217 D6
Rowstock OX11 . . . . 217 A7
Streatley RG8 . . . . 248 F8
Wallingford OX10 . . . . 203 B1
Wapping HP18. . . . . 129 D6
Warbler Wlk OX4 . . . . 142 E1
Warborough Rd
Letcombe Bassett OX12 . . 232 A7
Warborough OX10. . . . . 203 B6
Warbreck Dr RG31 . . . . 257 B3
Warburg Cres OX4. . . . . . . 142 F3
Warburg Nature Reserve★
RG9 . . . . 225 B5
Wardington Rd OX17. . . . . . 10 D6
Wardle Ave RG31 . . . . 257 D1
Ward Rd NN13. . . . . 24 A5
Wards Cres OX15 . . . . 22 E7
Ward's La OX7. . . . . 88 C5
Wards Rd OX7 . . . . 42 F3
Ware Leys Cl OX27. . . . . 67 E3
Ware Rd SN7 . . . . 194 C7
Wargrave Hill RG10. . . . . . 255 D2
Wargrave Rd
Henley-on-T,Newton
RG9. . . . . 255 B8
Henley-on-T,Remenham
RG9. . . . . 244 F1
Wargrave Sta RG10 . . . . . 255 C1
Warkworth Cl OX16. . . . . . . 15 F8
Warkworth Rd OX17 . . . . . . 17 E7
Warley Rise RG31. . . . . . . 257 C3
Warmans Cl OX12. . . . . . . 214 B5
War Memorial Pl RG9. . . . 254 E7
Warnborough Rd OX2. . . . 123 B4
Warneford Hospl OX3,
OX4 . . . . 124 B1
Warneford La OX3,OX4 . . . 124 B1
Warneford Rd OX4. . . . . . 142 A8
Warner Cres OX11 . . . . . . 218 D7
Warping House Cotts
OX7 . . . . 42 C2
Warren Barn Farm OX44 . 163 E7
Warren Ct RG4 . . . . 258 F2
Warren Hill OX44 . . . . 163 C1
Warren Ho RG4. . . . . 258 F2
Warren House Ct RG4. . . . 258 F2
Warren Rd RG5. . . . . 260 D1
Warren Row Rd RG10 . . . . 255 F7
Warren The
Abingdon OX14 . . . . 180 B8
Hinton Waldrist SN7 . . . . . 156 A2
Reading RG4 . . . . 258 D3
Warren View OX44 . . . . . . 163 F7
Warriner Sch The OX15 . . . 21 F6
Warwick Cl
Abingdon OX14 . . . . 180 A8
Carterton OX18 . . . . 115 C3
Stanford in the V SN7 . . . . 194 E7
Warwick Ct OX26 . . . . 66 A4
Warwick Rd
Banbury OX16 . . . . 16 C6
Banbury,Ruscote OX16 . . . . . 16 A7
Hanwell OX16 . . . . 8 E3
Warwick St OX4 . . . . 141 F7
Wasbrough Ave OX12 . . . . 214 C6
Washford Glen OX14. . . . . 201 A2
Washington Rd RG4. . . . . . 259 B2
Washington Terr OX7 . . . . . 60 F8
Wastie's Orch OX29. . . . . . . 90 B1
Watchfield Prim Sch
SN6 . . . . 191 D1
Watcombe Manor Ind Est
OX49 . . . . 186 B1
Watcombe Rd OX49. . . . . . 186 B1
Watercress Cl OX15. . . . . . . 22 E8
Water Eaton La OX5 . . . . . 109 A7
Water Eaton Rd OX2 . . . . 123 C8
Water End Rd
Beacon's Bottom HP14 . . . 189 D3
Bledlow Ridge HP14 . . . . . 189 C5
Waterford Rd OX28 . . . . . . 104 D1
Waterfowl Sanctuary &
Children's Farm★ OX15. . 20 A1
Water La
Adderbury OX17 . . . . 23 A3
Ardley OX27. . . . . 50 A3
Bloxham OX15. . . . . 21 E5
Brackley NN13. . . . . 24 A7
Drayton St L OX10. . . . . 183 B5
Water La *continued*
Little Tew OX7 . . . . 45 A6
Steeple Aston OX25. . . . . 62 A8
Waterloo Cl OX10. . . . . . . 239 A7
Waterloo Dr OX16 . . . . 16 E6
Waterman Pl RG1. . . . . 259 A1
Waterman's Rd RG9 . . . . . 254 F8
Watermans Reach 2
OX1 . . . . 141 C7
Waterman's Way RG10 . . 255 C1
Watermead OX5 . . . . 109 A8
Watermill Way OX3 . . . . . . 125 A4
Waterperry Ct 8 OX16. . . . 16 E6
Waterperry Gdns★ OX33 . 127 B1
Waterperry Rd HP18 . . . . . 127 D5
Waterperry OX33 . . . . 127 B1
Waterside Cotts RG4. . . . . 260 B4
Waterside Dr RG8 . . . . 257 D5
Waterside Villas OX14 . . . . 181 F4
Waterslade Pens HP17 . . . 130 E6
Waters La OX17. . . . . 11 B1
Water St OX25 . . . . 48 F6
Watery La
Brackley NN13. . . . . 24 A7
Clifton Hampden OX14 . . . 181 D4
Hook Norton OX15. . . . . 30 A7
Sparsholt OX12 . . . . 212 F4
Wates Way OX16. . . . . 16 E8
Watling La OX10. . . . . 182 D1
Watlington Hill★ OX49 . . . 206 E8
Watlington Ind Est OX49 186 A2
Watlington Rd
Benson OX10. . . . . 203 F4
Garsington OX44 . . . . 162 D7
Lewknor OX49. . . . . 187 A7
Oxford OX4,OX44. . . . . 143 B2
Shirburn OX49 . . . . 186 E6
Watlington St RG9 . . . . 224 E2
Watson Cres OX13 . . . . . . 159 A7
Watsons Cl OX18 . . . . 115 E1
Watt's La OX11 . . . . 237 A8
Watts Way OX5 . . . . 92 E1
Waveney Cl
Bicester OX26 . . . . 65 B2
Didcot OX14. . . . . 201 A1
Waverley Ave OX5 . . . . 109 A8
Wavers Ground OX18 . . . . 115 F3
Waxes Cl OX14 . . . . 160 C2
Wayfaring Cl OX4. . . . . 161 E8
Wayfarings OX26 . . . . 65 E5
Wayland Cres OX11 . . . . . . 217 C1
Wayland Rd OX12. . . . . . . 196 D1
Wayland's Smithy Long
Barrow★ SN6 . . . . 228 E7
Waynflete Rd OX3 . . . . . . 125 A4
Wayside Gn RG8. . . . . 240 E1
Wayside Ho 4 OX26 . . . . . . 65 E3
Wealden Way RG30 . . . . . . 257 E1
Weald Rise RG30 . . . . 257 F2
Weald St OX18. . . . . 134 E2
Wear Rd OX26 . . . . 65 B2
Weaver Croft OX14. . . . . . 201 A3
Weavers Cl OX28 . . . . 118 A7
Weavers Cotts CV36. . . . . . . 27 F5
Weavers Ct OX18 . . . . 115 F5
Webb Cl OX16 . . . . 16 E7
Webb Cres OX7. . . . . 42 D2
Webbs Cl OX7 . . . . 57 B1
Webb's Cl OX2. . . . . 122 D8
Webb's Way OX5. . . . . 92 F1
Webster Cl OX9. . . . . 129 F1
Websters Cl OX29. . . . . 106 A6
Wedgewood Way RG30. . . 257 F1
Wedgwood Rd OX26 . . . . . . 66 A3
Weedon Cl OX10. . . . . 239 A8
Weedon Ct OX10. . . . . 221 C8
Weeping Cross OX15. . . . . . 22 E8
Weighbridge Row RG1. . . . 258 F1
Weir La OX25. . . . . 82 A5
Weirs La OX1. . . . . 141 D5
Welch Way OX28. . . . . 118 A8
Weldon Rd OX3. . . . . 123 F3
Weldon Way OX9 . . . . 148 A8
Welford Gdns OX14 . . . . . 160 A2
Welland Ave OX14 . . . . 201 B2
Welland Cl
Abingdon OX13 . . . . 159 C2
Reading RG31 . . . . 257 C1
Welland Croft OX26. . . . . . . 65 B3
Well Bank OX15 . . . . 30 B7
Weller Cl OX10 . . . . 204 A8
Wellesbourne Cl OX14 . . . 180 B8
Wellesley Cl OX16 . . . . 16 E6
Well Hill OX7. . . . . 88 C5
Wellington Ave OX16. . . . . . 16 E6
Wellington Cl OX26 . . . . 66 A3
Wellington Cotts OX7 . . . . . 73 B2
Wellington Pl OX1 . . . . 261 B3
Wellington Rd GL54 . . . . 68 B4
Wellington Sq
Oxford OX1 . . . . 261 B3
Watchfield SN6 . . . . 191 D1
Wellington St
Oxford OX2 . . . . 261 A3
Thame OX9 . . . . 148 A8
Well La
Curbridge OX29. . . . . 117 C6
Shenington OX15. . . . . 6 F2
Stonesfield OX29. . . . . 89 C7
Wellplace Zoo★ OX10. . . . 240 F7
Wellshead La OX11 . . . . . . 217 E6
Wellsprings OX10. . . . . 202 E2
Well St OX12 . . . . 215 E5
Well View RG9. . . . . 241 F5
Wenlock Cl OX11 . . . . 200 C2
Wenman Rd
Thame OX9 . . . . 148 A6
Witney OX28 . . . . 117 E8
Wenrisc Dr OX29 . . . . 102 E2
Wensum Cres OX26 . . . . 65 B3
Wensum Dr OX14 . . . . 201 A2
Wentworth Rd
Oxford OX2 . . . . 123 B8
Thame OX9 . . . . 148 A8
Wesley Cl
Bicester OX26 . . . . 65 C4
Oxford OX4 . . . . 142 E3
Wesley Dr OX16. . . . . 16 B4
Wesley La 6 OX26. . . . . 65 E2
Wesley Pl OX17. . . . . 10 E4
Wesley Wlk OX28 . . . . 118 B8
Wessex Cl SN7. . . . . 173 A3
Wessex Ind Est OX28. . . . . 118 B6
Wessex Rd
Benson OX10. . . . . 204 D2
Didcot OX11. . . . . 218 F8
Wessex Way
Bicester OX26 . . . . 65 F1
Grove OX12 . . . . 214 D8
Highworth SN6 . . . . 190 B7
Westacott Rd OX26 . . . . 81 A6
West Allcourt GL7 . . . . . . 150 C4
West Ave OX14 . . . . 160 A2
West Bar St OX16. . . . . 16 C5
Westbeech Ct OX16 . . . . 16 C5
Westbourne Ct OX15 . . . . . . 21 E3
Westbrook SN7. . . . . 172 F3
Westbrook Gn OX11. . . . . . 236 F8
Westbrook OX12. . . . . 196 E2
Westbrook Rd RG30. . . . . 258 C1
Westbrook St OX11 . . . . . . 236 F8
Westbury Court Bsns Ctr
OX27 . . . . 67 C4
Westbury Cres OX4 . . . . . . 142 B4
Westbury La RG8 . . . . 257 A6
Westbury Terr OX27. . . . . . . 67 E2
West Chiltern RG8 . . . . 250 E8
Westcote Cl OX28. . . . . 117 D7
Westcot La OX12. . . . . 212 E5
West Cotts OX27. . . . . 52 D1
West Croft OX10. . . . . 182 C5
West Ct
Banbury OX16 . . . . 16 E6
Sonning RG4 . . . . 260 E2
Westdene Cres RG4. . . . . . 258 E4
West Dr
Harwell OX11 . . . . 217 A3
Sonning RG4 . . . . 260 D1
West Edge OX27 . . . . 67 E2
West End
Brightwell-cum-S OX10 . . . 202 D2
Chipping Norton OX7. . . . . . . 42 E2
Cholsey OX10 . . . . 220 E1
West End Cl OX26. . . . . 66 D1
West End
Combe OX29 . . . . 90 A4
Hornton OX15 . . . . 7 C6
West End Ind Est OX28. . . 104 B1
West End OX7 . . . . 54 F4
West End La
Bishopstone SN6. . . . . 227 C4
Merton OX25 . . . . 95 D8
West End
Launton OX26 . . . . 66 D1
Shilton OX18 . . . . 115 A5
Witney OX28 . . . . 104 B2
Wootton OX20 . . . . 75 F4
Western Ave
7 Didcot OX11. . . . . 219 A8
Henley-on-T RG9 . . . . 254 E8
Sonning RG5 . . . . 260 E1
Western By-Pass Rd
Cutteslowe OX2. . . . . 108 E1
Wytham OX2 . . . . 122 C5
Western Cl RG9. . . . . 254 E8
Western Cres OX16 . . . . 16 E4
Western Oaks RG31. . . . . . 257 E2
Western Rd
Henley-on-T RG9 . . . . 254 E8
Oxford OX1 . . . . 141 C7
Westfield Cl
Benson OX10. . . . . 204 A4
Grove OX12. . . . . 214 D7
Oxford OX4 . . . . 142 B6
Westfield Cres RG9 . . . . . . 255 B3
Westfield OX11 . . . . 217 D7
Westfield Rd
Benson OX10. . . . . 204 A4
Cholsey OX10 . . . . 238 D6
Long Wittenham OX14. . . . 201 D8
Reading RG4 . . . . 259 B2
Wheatley OX33 . . . . 126 A1
Witney OX28 . . . . 104 B2
Westfields OX14 . . . . 179 D7
Westfield Way OX12. . . . . . 215 A6
Westgate Sh Ctr OX1 . . . . 261 B2
Westgate OX7 . . . . 85 D8
West Gr OX2. . . . . 123 B8
West Hawthorn Rd OX25 . . 81 D4
West Hill OX12. . . . . 214 C4
Westholme Ct OX26. . . . . . . 65 F1
West Ilsley Ho RG20. . . . . . 235 B1
West Kidlington Prim Sch
OX5 . . . . 108 E7
West La RG9. . . . . 244 D2
Westland Rd SN7 . . . . 172 E2
Westlands Ave OX25 . . . . . . 79 A2
Westlands Dr OX3 . . . . 124 B5
Westland Way OX20. . . . . . . 91 A7
Westleigh Dr RG4. . . . . 252 F4
Westminster Cl NN13 . . . . . . 24 A7
Westminster Cres NN13 . . . 24 A7
Westminster Inst of Ed
(Harcourt Hill Campus)
OX2 . . . . 140 D6
Westminster Way
Banbury OX16 . . . . 16 F6
Oxford OX2 . . . . 140 E8
Westonbirt Dr RG4. . . . . . . 258 E3
Weston Bldgs OX1 . . . . 261 B2
Weston Bsns Pk OX5. . . . . . 78 F5
Weston Cotts SN7 . . . . . . 170 D8
Weston Ct CV36 . . . . 28 A6
Weston La OX9 . . . . 146 F8
Weston Old Bsns Pk OX25 79 A5
Weston Rd
Bletchingdon OX5 . . . . 93 A8
Lewknor OX49. . . . . 187 A8
West Oxford Com Prim Sch
OX2 . . . . 123 A1
West Oxon Ind Pk OX18 . . 115 F3
West Quay OX14 . . . . 179 F4
Westridge Ave RG8 . . . . . 257 C5
Westrop SN6 . . . . 190 A6
Westrup Cl OX3. . . . . 123 F3
West St Helen St OX14. . . 179 F6
West St
Banbury OX16 . . . . 16 E7
Bicester OX26 . . . . 65 D3
Childrey OX12 . . . . 213 B3
Chipping Norton OX7. . . . . . . 42 E2
Henley-on-T RG9 . . . . 244 D2
Kingham OX7. . . . . 54 F5
Oxford OX2 . . . . 123 A1
Shutford OX15. . . . . 14 A5
Sparsholt OX12 . . . . 212 F4
West View
Oxford OX4 . . . . 142 A4
Somerton OX25. . . . . 49 A6
Westwater Way OX14 . . . . 201 B2
Westway RG8. . . . . 249 C8
West Way
Lechlade-on-T GL7. . . . . . . 150 C5
Oxford OX2 . . . . 122 D1
West Witney Prim Sch
OX28 . . . . 117 E8
West Wood Farm Inf Sch
RG31 . . . . 257 C3
West Wood Farm Jun Sch
RG31 . . . . 257 C3
Westwood Glen RG31 . . . 257 C1
Westwood Rd
Reading RG31 . . . . 257 D1
Witney OX29 . . . . 103 C1
Westwood Row RG31 . . . 257 C2
Wetherby Cl RG4 . . . . 259 C6
Weycroft OX14. . . . . 201 A3
Weyland Rd OX3. . . . . 124 E2
Wey Rd OX10 . . . . 182 D5
W & G Ind Est OX12. . . . . . 213 E6
Whales La OX27 . . . . 67 E2
Wharf Cl OX14. . . . . 179 F6
Wharfe La RG9 . . . . 244 E2
Wharf La
Lechlade-on-T GL7. . . . . . . 150 D4
Somerton OX25. . . . . 48 F6
Souldern OX27. . . . . 35 B4
Wharf Rd OX10 . . . . 203 A6
Wharf The
7 Wantage OX12. . . . . . . 214 D5
Pangbourne RG8 . . . . 256 C6
Wharton Rd OX3. . . . . 124 D3
Whatleys Orch SN6 . . . . . 227 C4
Wheatcroft Cl OX14. . . . . . 160 A2
Wheatfields OX11. . . . . . . 218 C7
Wheatley Bsns Ctr OX33 144 C8
Wheatley Campus (Brookes
Univ)
Holton OX33 . . . . 126 C1
Wheatley OX33 . . . . 144 C8
Wheatley CE Prim Sch
OX33 . . . . 144 A8
Wheatley Cl OX16. . . . . 16 E2
Wheatley Park Sch OX33 126 B2
Wheatley Rd
Forest Hill OX33 . . . . 125 F4
Garsington OX44. . . . . 143 E3
Islip OX5 . . . . 109 F8
Wheeler Ct RG31 . . . . 257 E1
Wheelers End OX39. . . . . . 168 C6
Wheeler's Rise NN13. . . . . . 36 C8
Wheel Wright Ct SN7 . . . . . 174 F8
Whimbrel Cl OX26 . . . . 66 A1
Whimbrel Way OX16 . . . . . . 16 E3
Whirlwind Way OX10. . . . . 204 D3
Whitamore Row RG9. . . . . 254 E8
Whitby Ct RG4. . . . . 259 D6
Whitby Gn RG4 . . . . 259 D6
Whitchurch Prim Sch
RG8 . . . . 256 E7
Whitchurch Rd RG8. . . . . 256 D6
White Barn OX1 . . . . 140 C2
Whitecross OX13 . . . . 159 D4
Whitecross Rd HP17 . . . . . 130 F5
Whitehall Cl OX29 . . . . . . 102 D2
Whitehall La RG8 . . . . 241 D3
White Hart Cl
Benson OX10. . . . . 203 F4
Ludgershall HP18 . . . . 98 B7
White Hart OX3. . . . . 123 F6
White Hart Wlk 1 SN7 . . 172 F3
White Hill
Burford OX18. . . . . 101 B3
Henley-on-T RG9 . . . . 244 F2
Hinton Parva SN4 . . . . 227 A2
Hunt's Green RG9 . . . . 254 A5
White Hill La OX1. . . . . . . 140 A1
Whitehills Gn RG8 . . . . . . 249 C6
Whitehorns Farm Rd
OX12 . . . . 215 A5

Whitehorns Way OX14 . . 179 A1
White Horse Bsns Pk
  SN7 . . . . 194 C7
White Horse Cres OX12 . 214 C8
White Horse Ho OX12 . . . 214 D7
White Horse Mews OX18 100 E4
White Horse SN7 . . . . . . 211 D7
White Hos MK18 . . . . 39 D6
Whitehouse Cl OX13 . . . 159 C1
Whitehouse La OX7 . . . . . 42 E3
White House Rd OX10 . . 239 F8
Whitehouse Rd
  Oxford OX1 . . . . 141 C7
  Woodcote RG8 . . . . 250 E8
White La RG9 . . . . 243 E8
White Leys Cl OX11 . . . . 200 F1
White Lion Wlk **1** OX16 . .16 D6
Whitelock Rd OX14 . . . . 159 F1
White Lodge Cl RG31 . . 257 B3
White Post Rd OX15 . . . . .16 E1
White Rd
  East Hendred OX12 . . . . 216 F7
  Oxford OX4 . . . . 142 E6
Whites Forge OX13 . . . . 158 A7
White Shoot OX11 . . . . . 237 A5
White's La OX14 . . . . . . 160 D3
Whitethorn Way **2** OX14 . .142 E2
White Way OX5 . . . . 108 E8
Whiteway OX17 . . . . .3 F3
Whitings La OX29 . . . . . . 104 B7
Whitley Cres OX26 . . . . . .66 A3
Whitley Dr OX25 . . . . .63 C8
Whitley Rd OX10 . . . . . . 221 B7
Whitson Pl OX4 . . . . 142 A7
Whittall St OX17 . . . . .23 F5
Whittington Pl OX18 . . . 115 D1
Whittle Rd OX9 . . . . 148 B8
Whittons Cl OX15 . . . . . . .30 B8
Whitworth Pl OX2 . . . . . 123 A2
Wick Cl
  Abingdon OX14 . . . . . . 160 C2
  Oxford OX3 . . . . 124 E4
Wick Farm Pk OX3 . . . . 124 E5
Wick Gn OX12 . . . . 196 D2
Wick Hall OX14 . . . . 180 D8
Wicks Cl OX18 . . . . 152 E8
Widmore La RG4 . . . . . . 253 A6
Widnell La OX25 . . . . .97 C7
Wigan's La HP14 . . . . . . 169 C5
Wigginton Rd OX15 . . . . .31 D7
Wigmore La RG30 . . . . . 258 C1
Wigod Way OX10 . . . . . . 203 C1
Wilberforce St OX3 . . . . 124 D2
Wilcher Cl OX11 . . . . .218 F6
Wilcote Cl OX3 . . . . .88 B3
Wilcote Rd OX3 . . . . 124 F4
Wilcote Riding OX7 . . . . . .88 D5
Wilcote View OX29 . . . . 105 C6
Wilcox Rd OX7 . . . . .42 E4
Wilder Ave RG8 . . . . 256 E5
Wilding Rd OX10 . . . . . . 203 C1
Wildmere Cl OX16 . . . . . . .16 E8
Wildmere Ind Est OX16 . .16 F8
Wildmere Rd OX16 . . . . . . .7 F1
Wildmoor Gate OX14 . . 159 E1
Wilkins Ho OX7 . . . . .42 E1
Wilkins Rd OX4 . . . . 142 E6
Willes Cl SN7 . . . . .172 F3
William Bliss Ave OX7 . . .42 E2
William Cl OX16 . . . . .15 F7
William Fletcher Prim Sch
  OX5 . . . . 108 A5
William Kimber Cres
  OX3 . . . . 124 E3
William Morris Sch OX16 .15 F7
William Orchard Cl OX4 124 C4
Williamscot Hill OX17 . . .10 A5
Williams Mews OX28 . . . 118 A7
William Smith Cl OX7 . . . .55 E4
William Way OX44 . . . . . 142 E4
William St OX3 . . . . 123 F3
Willis Ct OX7 . . . . .70 D1
Willoughby Rd OX16 . . . .16 D2
Willow Bank Jun & Inf Sch
  RG5 . . . . 260 F1
Willow Brook OX14 . . . . 179 D2
Willowbrook OX29 . . . . .137 F8
Willow Cl
  Garsington OX44 . . . . . 143 D2
  Watlington OX49 . . . . . 186 A2
  Yarnton OX5 . . . . 108 B6
Willow Court La OX10 . . .238 F5
Willow Dr
  Bicester OX26 . . . . .65 E4
  Carterton OX18 . . . . . . 115 F4
Willow End
  Ambrosden OX25 . . . . . .81 C4
  Little Compton GL56 . . . .27 E4
Willow Gdns RG31 . . . . .257 B2
Willow La
  Milton OX14 . . . . 199 D5
  Wantage OX12 . . . . 214 D3
  Wargrave RG10 . . . . . . 255 C4
Willow Mead OX44 . . . . 184 D6
Willow Rd
  Ambrosden OX25 . . . . . .81 C4
  Banbury OX16 . . . . .16 D2
  Brackley NN13 . . . . .24 A6
  Chinnor OX39 . . . . 168 C6
  Thame OX9 . . . . 129 F1
Willows Ct RG8 . . . . 256 C6
Willows Edge OX29 . . . . 120 D8
Willows Gate OX27 . . . . . .52 D1
Willowside RG5 . . . . 260 F1
Willows The
  Grove OX12 . . . . 214 D7
  Highworth SN6 . . . . . . 190 B5
  Reading RG4 . . . . 259 A2
  Witney OX28 . . . . 104 C1
  Wootton OX1 . . . . 159 A7
Willow Tree Cl OX13 . . . 159 C1
Willow Way
  Begbroke OX5 . . . . .92 A1
  Kennington OX14 . . . . . 160 E7
  Oxford OX4 . . . . 142 E2
Willow Wlk OX12 . . . . . . 214 D6
Wills Rd OX11 . . . . 200 C1
Wilmot Cl OX28 . . . . 117 F6
Wilmots OX4 . . . . 162 A6
Wilmot Way OX12 . . . . . 214 F6
Wilsdon Way OX5 . . . . . . .92 D1
Wilsham Rd OX14 . . . . . 179 F5
Wilson Ave RG9 . . . . . . 254 E8
Wilsons Cl OX14 . . . . . . 201 C8
Wilson Way OX27 . . . . . . .65 F7
Wilwyne Cl RG4 . . . . . . 259 C4
Wimblestraw Rd OX10 . . 182 C5
Wimborn Cl OX15 . . . . . . .33 E4
Wimborne Ave OX16 . . . .16 B6
Wimbourne Gdns RG30 . 258 A1
Winaway OX11 . . . . 217 D6
Winchelsea Cl OX16 . . . . .8 F1
Winchester Cl OX16 . . . . .16 F7
Winchester Rd OX22 . . . 123 B4
Winchester Way OX12 . . 214 C5
Wincroft Rd RG4 . . . . . . 258 E5
Windale Ave OX4 . . . . . . 142 E1
Windale Com Prim Sch
  OX4 . . . . 142 E1
Windale Ho **3** OX4 . . . . 142 E2
Windle Gdns OX4 . . . . . . .65 C2
Windmill Ave OX26 . . . . . .65 E4
Windmill Cl
  Banbury OX16 . . . . .16 D4
  Deddington OX15 . . . . . .33 E4
  North Leigh OX29 . . . . 105 B6
  Towersey OX9 . . . . 148 E2
Windmill Hts OX29 . . . . 105 B6
Windmill La OX33 . . . . . 143 F7
Windmill Pl OX12 . . . . . 214 D7
Windmill Prim Sch The
  OX3 . . . . 124 D2
Windmill Rd
  Haddenham HP17 . . . . 130 F6
  North Leigh OX29 . . . . 105 B6
  Oxford OX3 . . . . 124 D2
  Thame OX9 . . . . 147 F7
  Towersey OX9 . . . . 148 E3
Windmill St
  Brill HP18 . . . . .98 A1
  Deddington OX15 . . . . . .33 E4
Windows Ct OX33 . . . . . 144 C7
Windrush OX16 . . . . .16 B8
Windrush Cl
  Bicester OX26 . . . . .65 D1
  Burford OX18 . . . . 100 E4
  Grove OX12 . . . . 196 D1
  Witney OX28 . . . . .117 E8
Windrush Ct
  Abingdon OX14 . . . . . . 179 C7
  Burford OX18 . . . . 100 E4
Windrush Ind Pk OX29 . . 103 C1
Windrush Mews OX11 . . 201 A3
Windrush Park Rd OX29 . 103 C1
Windrush Pl OX29 . . . . . 138 B2
Windrush Rd OX10 . . . . 182 C4
Windrush Twr OX4 . . . . . 142 E2
Windrush Valley Rd
  OX28 . . . . 103 C1
Windrush Valley Sch OX7 .71 C2
Windrush Way
  Abingdon OX14 . . . . . . 160 B1
  Standlake OX29 . . . . . . 137 C5
Windsor Cl
  Carterton OX18 . . . . . . 115 C2
  Didcot OX11 . . . . 219 A8
  Kings Sutton OX17 . . . . .23 F6
Windsor Cotts OX18 . . . 134 E3
Windsor Cres
  East Hagbourne OX11 . . .218 F6
  Marston OX3 . . . . 123 E5
Windsor Dr OX10 . . . . . . 221 C7
Windsor Ho RG9 . . . . . . 254 E8
Windsor St
  Abingdon OX14 . . . . . . 179 C7
  Oxford OX3 . . . . 124 D2
Windsor Terr **15** OX16 . . .16 D5
Windy Ridge SN7 . . . . . 173 A3
Wingate Cl OX4 . . . . 142 E3
Wingfield Cl OX10 . . . . . 204 E3
Wingfield Ct OX4 . . . . . . 123 F1
Winnyards The OX2 . . . . 139 E4

Winslet Pl RG30 . . . . . . 258 B1
Winsmore La **2** OX14 . . 179 F6
Winston Cl OX5 . . . . 108 E7
Winston Dr OX17 . . . . .8 F1
Winston Way RG8 . . . . . 257 B5
Winterberry Way RG4 . . 258 E6
Winterborne Rd OX14 . . 179 D7
Winterbourne Cl OX26 . . .65 D2
Winterbrook La OX10 . . 221 C5
Winterbrook OX10 . . . . . 221 D5
Wintergreen La OX10 . . 221 C5
Winter La OX14 . . . . .196 F7
Winter's Field OX10 . . . .221 F7
Winters Way OX15 . . . . . . .21 D4
Wintringham Way RG8 . 257 D5
Wise Ave OX5 . . . . .92 D1
Wise Cl OX15 . . . . .92 B1
Wise Cres OX27 . . . . .52 C6
Wise Ct **3** OX26 . . . . . . .65 E3
Wisterias The OX16 . . . . . .9 B1
Witan Pk OX18 . . . . 118 B6
Witan Way
  Wantage OX12 . . . . 214 D6
  Witney OX28 . . . . 118 B8
Witheridge Cross OX29 . 104 B5
Withers Ct OX7 . . . . .42 E3
Withers Way OX7 . . . . . . .42 E2
Withington Ct OX14 . . . .179 F7
Withington Rd OX26 . . . .65 F2
Withycombe Dr OX16 . . . .15 F6
Witney Com Prim Sch
  OX28 . . . . 104 B3
Witney & District Mus*
  OX28 . . . . 104 B1
Witney Hill OX29 . . . . . . 103 E4
Witney La OX29 . . . . .86 F3
Witney Rd
  Brize Norton OX18 . . . . 116 D5
  Crawley OX29 . . . . 103 F3
  Ducklington OX29 . . . . 118 A5
  Eynsham OX29 . . . . . . 120 D8
  Finstock OX7 . . . . .88 E4
  Leafield OX29 . . . . .87 A1
  Long Hanborough OX29 . .90 A1
  Standlake OX29 . . . . . . 137 A4
Witney St OX18 . . . . 100 E5
Wittenham Cl
  Wallingford OX10 . . . . . 203 D1
  Woodcote RG8 . . . . 250 F8
Wittenham La OX10 . . . . 202 D8
Woburn Cl
  Banbury OX16 . . . . .16 F7
  Reading RG4 . . . . 258 E4
Wolage Dr OX12 . . . . . . 214 D7
Wolfson Coll OX2 . . . . . 123 C5
Wolseley Cl OX16 . . . . . . .16 A8
Wolsely Ho OX4 . . . . . . 142 C4
Wolsey Cl OX20 . . . . .91 F3
Wolsey Rd
  Cutteslowe OX2 . . . . . . 109 B1
  Reading RG4 . . . . 259 A2
Wolvercote Gn OX2 . . . . 122 F8
Wolvercote Prim Sch
  OX2 . . . . 122 F8
Wolvercote Rdbt OX2 . . 108 F1
Woodberry Cl RG4 . . . . 259 A5
Woodbine Pl OX1 . . . . . . 261 A2
Woodbridge Cl OX18 . . . 135 E2
Woodcote Prim Sch RG8 240 F1
Woodcote Rd
  Bicester OX27 . . . . .66 A7
  Reading RG4 . . . . 258 E4
  South Stoke RG8 . . . . . 239 E4
Woodcote Way
  Abingdon OX14 . . . . . . 179 B4
  Reading RG4 . . . . 258 D5
Woodcroft OX1 . . . . 141 A5
Wood Dewatton Manor Sch
  OX3 . . . . 110 A5
Wood End OX16 . . . . .16 E3
Wood Farm Prim Sch
  OX3 . . . . 124 E1
Wood Farm Rd OX3 . . . . 124 E1
Woodfield OX4 . . . . 162 A6
Woodfield Cotts RG8 . . . 249 A6
Woodfield OX4 . . . . .73 C3
Woodfield Rd OX26 . . . . .65 E3
Woodford Cl
  Enstone OX7 . . . . .58 F5
  Reading RG4 . . . . 258 E4
Woodford Mill OX28 . . . 104 A1
Woodgate Cl OX12 . . . . 196 D1
Wood Gn OX28 . . . . 104 C1
Woodgreen Ave OX16 . . .16 A5
Wood Green Sch OX28 . 104 D1
Woodgreen OX28 . . . . . 104 C1
Woodhall Dr OX16 . . . . . .16 E3
Woodhill Dr OX12 . . . . . 214 D8
Woodhill La OX12 . . . . . 214 A7
Woodhouse Way OX4 . . 142 A4
Wood La
  Hailey OX29 . . . . 104 A7
  Kidmore End RG4 . . . . 252 C4
  Leafield OX29 . . . . .87 E1
Woodland Pk Cvn Site The
  OX14 . . . . 160 E7
Woodland Rise OX29 . . . .89 C7

Woodlands
  Banbury OX16 . . . . .16 B5
  Carterton OX18 . . . . . . 115 F4
Woodlands Cl
  Milton-u-W OX7 . . . . . . .70 B1
  Oxford OX3 . . . . 124 B3
Woodlands Ct OX28 . . . 104 C2
Woodlands OX29 . . . . . . 106 A7
Woodlands Gr RG4 . . . . 259 E4
Woodlands Rd OX5 . . . . 109 A8
Woodlands Rd
  Didcot OX11 . . . . 218 C8
  Oxford OX3 . . . . 124 B3
  Shiplake RG9 . . . . 254 E4
  Sonning Common RG4 . . 252 F6
  Witney OX28 . . . . 104 C1
Woodlands OX29 . . . . . . 137 D3
Woodlands The OX6 . . . . .79 F7
Woodland Wlk OX1 . . . . 140 F1
Wood Lane Cl RG4 . . . . 252 F5
Wood La
  Sonning Common RG4 . . 252 F5
  Whiteoak Green OX29 . . 103 F8
  Woodcote RG8 . . . . 250 D8
Woodley Cl OX14 . . . . . . 159 F3
Woodman Ct OX4 . . . . . 123 F1
Woodman Villas OX3 . . . 124 C2
Woodpecker Cl OX26 . . . .66 A1
Woodpecker Gn **1** OX4 142 F1
Woodperry Rd OX3 . . . . .111 B2
Woodpiece Rd OX25 . . . .96 E7
Woodrow Ct RG4 . . . . . . 258 F2
Woodruff Cl
  Bicester OX26 . . . . .65 D5
  Oxford OX4 . . . . 142 F2
Woodrush Gdns OX18 . . 115 F4
Wood's Farm Rd OX12 . . 216 D8
Woodside Dr OX18 . . . . 114 C6
Woodside La RG4 . . . . . 252 C5
Woodside OX29 . . . . 105 C6
Woods Rd RG4 . . . . 259 E4
Woodstock CE Prim Sch
  OX20 . . . . .91 C6
Woodstock Close Flats
  OX2 . . . . 123 A8
Woodstock Cl OX2 . . . . . 123 A8
Woodstock Ct OX2 . . . . 123 A7
Woodstock Rd OX7 . . . . . .73 C2
Woodstock Rd E OX5 . . . .91 F1
Woodstock Rd
  Kidlington OX20 . . . . . . .91 F3
  Oxford OX2 . . . . 123 B5
  Stonesfield OX8 . . . . . . .89 D7
Woodstock Rd W OX20 . . .91 F1
Woodstock Rd
  Witney OX28 . . . . 104 D2
  Wolvercote OX2 . . . . . . 108 D4
Wood St OX10 . . . . 221 D7
Woodview Rd RG8 . . . . . 256 D5
Woodville OX39 . . . . 168 C5
Woodway Rd
  Blewbury OX11 . . . . . . 237 A7
  Middle Barton OX7 . . . . .60 E8
  Sibford Ferris OX15 . . . . .19 A7
Woolgate Sh Ctr OX28 . .118 B8
Woolstone Rd
  Uffington SN7 . . . . 211 C7
  Woolstone SN7 . . . . . . 211 B5
Wootten Dr OX4 . . . . . . 142 A4
Wootton Bsns Pk OX13 . .158 F7
Wootton-by-Woodstock CE
  Prim Sch OX20 . . . . . . .75 F4
Wootton End OX29 . . . . . .89 D8
Wootton Rd
  Abingdon OX13,OX14 . . 159 E2
  Abingdon OX14 . . . . . . 179 E8
  Kingston Bagpuize OX13 . 156 D1
Worcester Coll OX1 . . . . 261 A3
Worcester Dr OX11 . . . . 219 B8
Worcester Pl
  Oxford OX1 . . . . 261 A3
  Oxford OX1 . . . . 123 A1
Worcester Rd OX7 . . . . . . .42 B2
Worcester Road Ind Est
  OX7 . . . . .42 C3
Worcester St OX1 . . . . . 261 A2
Wordsworth Cl
  6 Bicester OX26 . . . . . .65 C4
  Stanford in the V SN7 . . 194 D8
Wordsworth Ct RG4 . . . 259 C7
Wordsworth Rd OX14 . . 179 D5
Workhouse La OX15 . . . . .21 D5
Work House Yd OX20 . . . .75 F4
Wormald Rd OX10 . . . . . 221 C6
Worminghall Rd HP18 . . 127 F4
Wormsley Cres HP14 . . 188 C4
Wornal Pk HP18 . . . . . . 127 C8
Worsham Turn OX29 . . . 102 B5
Wortham Rd OX11 . . . . . 200 D2
Worthington Way OX12 . 214 D6
Worton Rd OX7 . . . . .46 E1
Wotton End HP18 . . . . . . .98 C7
Wren Cl OX33 . . . . 144 B8
Wrenfield Dr RG4 . . . . . 258 F5
Wren Rd OX2 . . . . 109 C1

Wren Way OX26 . . . . .80 F8
Wretchwick Way OX26 . . .81 A8
Wright Cl GL54 . . . . .68 A5
Wright Rd GL54 . . . . .68 A5
Wrightson Cl OX33 . . . . 143 C6
Wroslyn Rd OX29 . . . . . 106 A7
Wroslyn Road Ind Est
  OX29 . . . . 106 A7
Wroxton CE Prim Sch
  OX15 . . . . .15 A8
Wroxton Coll OX15 . . . . . .15 B8
Wroxton Ct OX15 . . . . . . .15 B8
Wroxton Ho OX15 . . . . . . .15 B8
Wyatt Rd OX2 . . . . 109 B1
Wychcotes RG4 . . . . . . 258 F3
Wychwood CE Prim Sch
  OX7 . . . . .70 C1
Wychwood Cl
  Benson OX10 . . . . 204 A4
  Carterton OX18 . . . . . . 115 D5
  Charlbury OX7 . . . . .73 C4
  Milton-u-W OX7 . . . . . . .85 A8
  Sonning Common RG4 . . 252 F5
  Witney OX28 . . . . .117 E8
Wychwood Dr OX7 . . . . . .70 A1
Wychwood Gdns OX16 . . .16 A4
Wychwood La OX3 . . . . 125 A2
Wychwood Paddocks OX7 .73 B4
Wychwood Sch OX2 . . . 123 C4
Wychwood View OX29 . . 102 E2
Wycombe Rd HP14 . . . . 189 D3
Wycombe Way OX18 . . . 115 E2
Wye Cl OX26 . . . . .65 B3
Wyfold Ct RG9 . . . . 242 A1
Wyfold La RG4,RG9 . . . . 252 C8
Wykeham Cres OX4 . . . 142 B4
Wykeham Gate HP17 . . . 130 F5
Wykeham Pk OX9 . . . . . 148 A8
Wykeham Rise OX39 . . . 168 D6
Wykeham Way HP17 . . . 130 F6
Wykham Gdns OX16 . . . .16 B3
Wykham La
  Banbury OX16 . . . . .16 B1
  Broughton OX15 . . . . . . .15 E1
Wykham Pl OX16 . . . . . . .16 B3
Wylie Cl OX3 . . . . 124 D1
Wynbush Rd OX4 . . . . . 142 A3
Wynchway Ho OX15 . . . . .33 F4
Wyndale OX4 RG9 . . . . . 244 E1
Wyndham Cres RG5 . . . 260 D1
Wyndham Gdns OX10 . . 221 D6
Wyndham Way OX2 . . . . 123 A8
Wyndyke Furlong OX14 . 179 C8
Wyre Ct RG31 . . . . 257 C3
Wysdom Way OX18 . . . . 100 F4
Wytham Cl OX29 . . . . . . 120 E8
Wytham St OX1 . . . . 141 D5
Wytham View OX29 . . . . 120 E8

Y

Yare Cl OX14 . . . . 201 B2
Yarnell's Hill OX2 . . . . . 140 D7
Yarnell's Rd OX2 . . . . . . 140 E8
Yarnton Cl RG4 . . . . 259 C6
Yarnton Ct OX5 . . . . 108 E8
Yarnton La OX5 . . . . 108 D6
Yarnton Rd
  Cassington OX29 . . . . . 107 D3
  Kidlington OX5 . . . . 108 E8
Yarrow Cl OX4 . . . . 142 E1
Yatesbury Rd OX18 . . . . 115 E4
Yealm Cl OX11 . . . . 200 F4
Yeates Cl OX9 . . . . 129 F1
Yeats Cl OX4 . . . . 142 E6
Yeftly Dr OX4 . . . . 142 A1
Yeld Hall Rd OX14 . . . . 160 B2
Yeomans CI NN13 . . . . . .24 A8
Yew Cl
  Bicester OX26 . . . . .65 E5
  Oxford OX4 . . . . 143 A2
Yew Tree Cl OX9 . . . . . . 166 B8
Yew Tree Ct RG8 . . . . . . 249 C6
Yewtree Mews OX14 . . . 179 F7
Yew Tree Mews OX29 . . .118 B4
Yew Tree Rise OX29 . . . . .36 D8
Yolsum Cl HP17 . . . . . . 130 E6
York Ave OX3 . . . . 124 E1
York Cl OX26 . . . . .66 A3
York Pl OX4 . . . . 123 E1
York Rd
  Carterton OX18 . . . . . . 115 E4
  Henley-on-T RG9 . . . . . 244 D2
  Oxford OX3 . . . . 124 E2
  Reading RG1 . . . . 259 A1
  West Hagbourne OX11 . . 218 C4
Youens Dr OX9 . . . . 148 A8
Youghal Cl SN6 . . . . 209 B6
Ypres Way OX14 . . . . . . 159 D1
Yule Ct **1** OX16 . . . . .16 B6

Z

Zedcor Bsns Pk OX28 . . . 104 B1

Any feature in this atlas can be given a unique reference to help you find the same feature on other Ordnance Survey maps of the area, or to help someone else locate you if they do not have a Street Atlas.

The grid squares in this atlas match the Ordnance Survey National Grid and are at 500 metre intervals. The small figures at the bottom and sides of every other grid line are the National Grid kilometre values (**00** to **99** km) and are repeated across the country every 100 km (see left).

To give a unique National Grid reference you need to locate where in the country you are. The country is divided into 100 km squares with each square given a unique two-letter reference. Use the administrative map to determine in which 100 km square a particular page of this atlas falls.

The bold letters and numbers between each grid line (**A** to **F**, **1** to **8**) are for use within a specific Street Atlas only, and when used with the page number, are a convenient way of referencing these grid squares.

Example   The railway bridge over *DARLEY GREEN RD* in grid square *B1*

Step 1: Identify the two-letter reference, in this example the page is in **SP**

Step 2: Identify the 1 km square in which the railway bridge falls. Use the figures in the southwest corner of this square: Eastings **17**, Northings **74**. This gives a unique reference: **SP 17 74**, accurate to 1 km.

Step 3: To give a more precise reference accurate to 100 m you need to estimate how many tenths along and how many tenths up this 1 km square the feature is (to help with this the 1 km square is divided into four 500 m squares). This makes the bridge about **8** tenths along and about **1** tenth up from the southwest corner.

This gives a unique reference: **SP 178 741**, accurate to 100 m.

Eastings (read from left to right along the bottom) come before Northings (read from bottom to top). If you have trouble remembering say to yourself "Along the hall, THEN up the stairs"!

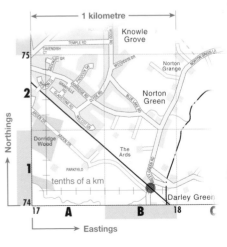

PHILIP'S MAPS

the Gold Standard for serious driving

- ◆ Philip's street atlases cover every county in England and Wales, plus much of Scotland
- ◆ All our atlases use the same style of mapping, with the same colours and symbols, so you can move with confidence from one atlas to the next
- ◆ Widely used by the emergency services, transport companies and local authorities
- ◆ Created from the most up-to-date and detailed information available from Ordnance Survey
- ◆ Based on the National Grid

BEST BUY • BEST BUY • Auto EXPRESS • BEST BUY • BEST BUY

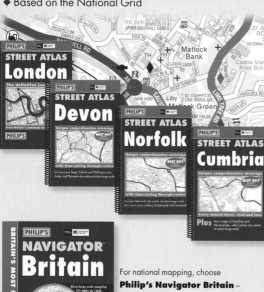

For national mapping, choose **Philip's Navigator Britain** – the most detailed road atlas available of England, Wales and Scotland. Hailed by Auto Express as 'the ultimate road atlas', this is the only one-volume atlas to show every road and lane in Britain.

Street atlases currently available

England

Bedfordshire	
Berkshire	**All England and Wales coverage**
Birmingham and West Midlands	
Bristol and Bath	Suffolk
Buckinghamshire	Surrey
Cambridgeshire	East Sussex
Cheshire	West Sussex
Cornwall	Tyne and Wear
Cumbria	Warwickshire
Derbyshire	Birmingham and West Midlands
Devon	Wiltshire and Swindon
Dorset	Worcestershire
County Durham and Teesside	East Yorkshire Northern Lincolnshire
Essex	North Yorkshire
North Essex	South Yorkshire
South Essex	West Yorkshire
Gloucestershire	**Wales**
North Hampshire	Anglesey, Conwy and Gwynedd
South Hampshire	
Herefordshire Monmouthshire	Cardiff, Swansea and The Valleys
Hertfordshire	Carmarthenshire, Pembrokeshire and Swansea
Isle of Wight	
Kent	
East Kent	Ceredigion and South Gwynedd
West Kent	
Lancashire	Denbighshire, Flintshire, Wrexham
Leicestershire and Rutland	
	Herefordshire Monmouthshire
Lincolnshire	
London	Powys
Greater Manchester	**Scotland**
Merseyside	Aberdeenshire
Norfolk	Ayrshire
Northamptonshire	Edinburgh and East Central Scotland
Northumberland	
Nottinghamshire	Fife and Tayside
Oxfordshire	Glasgow and West Central Scotland
Shropshire	Inverness and Moray
Somerset	Lanarkshire
Staffordshire	

How to order

Philip's maps and atlases are available from bookshops, motorway services and petrol stations. You can order direct from the publisher by phoning **01903 828503** or online at **www.philips-maps.co.uk**
For bulk orders only, phone 020 7644 6940